MEDIEVAL ST ANDREWS

St Andrews Studies in Scottish History

Series Editor
Professor Roger Mason (Institute of Scottish Historical Research, University of St Andrews)

Editorial Board
Dr David Allan (Institute of Scottish Historical Research, University of St Andrews)
Professor Dauvit Broun (University of Glasgow)
Professor Michael Brown (Institute of Scottish Historical Research, University of St Andrews)
Dr Catriona MacDonald (University of Glasgow)

Sponsored by the Institute of Scottish Historical Research at the University of St Andrews, St Andrews Studies in Scottish History provides an important forum for the publication of research on any aspect of Scottish history, from the early Middle Ages to the present day, focusing on the historical experience of Scots at home and abroad, and Scotland's place in wider British, European and global contexts. Both monographs and essay collections are welcomed.

Proposal forms can be obtained from the Institute of Scottish Historical Research website: http://www.st-andrews.ac.uk/ishr/studies.htm. They should be sent in the first instance to the chair of the editorial board at the address below.

Professor Roger Mason
Institute of Scottish Historical Research
St Andrews University
St Andrews
Fife KY16 9AL
UK

Previous volumes in the series are listed at the back of this book

MEDIEVAL ST ANDREWS

Church, Cult, City

Edited by
Michael Brown and Katie Stevenson

THE BOYDELL PRESS

© Contributors 2017

All Rights Reserved. Except as permitted under current legislation no part of this work may be photocopied, stored in a retrieval system, published, performed in public, adapted, broadcast, transmitted, recorded or reproduced in any form or by any means, without the prior permission of the copyright owner

First published 2017
The Boydell Press, Woodbridge
Paperback edition 2021

ISBN 978 1 78327 168 9 hardback
ISBN 978 1 78327 597 7 paperback

The Boydell Press is an imprint of Boydell & Brewer Ltd
PO Box 9, Woodbridge, Suffolk IP12 3DF, UK
and of Boydell & Brewer Inc.
668 Mount Hope Ave, Rochester, NY 14620–2731, USA
website: www.boydellandbrewer.com

A catalogue record for this book is available
from the British Library

The publisher has no responsibility for the continued existence or accuracy of URLs for external or third-party internet websites referred to in this book, and does not guarantee that any content on such websites is, or will remain, accurate or appropriate

The publishers acknowledge the generous financial support of the Marc Fitch Fund in the production of this volume.

Contents

List of Illustrations, Charts and Tables	ix
Contributors	xiii
Abbreviations	xv

1. 'Ancient Magnificence': St Andrews in the Middle Ages: An Introduction   1
   Michael H. Brown and Katie Stevenson

2. From *Cinrigh Monai* to *Civitas Sancti Andree*: A Star is Born   20
   Simon Taylor

3. The Idea of St Andrews as the Second Rome Made Manifest   35
   Ian Campbell

4. The Medieval Ecclesiastical Architecture of St Andrews as a Channel for the Introduction of New Ideas   51
   Richard Fawcett

5. When the Miracles Ceased: Shrine and Cult Management at St Andrews and Scottish Cathedrals in the Later Middle Ages   84
   Tom Turpie

6. Religion, Ritual and the Rhythm of the Year in Later Medieval St Andrews   99
   David Ditchburn

7. Living in the Late Medieval Town of St Andrews   117
   Elizabeth Ewan

8. The Burgh of St Andrews and its Inhabitants before the Wars of Independence   141
   Matthew Hammond

9. The Archaeology of Medieval St Andrews   173
   Derek W. Hall with Catherine Smith

10. Prelates, Citizens and Landed Folk: St Andrews as a Centre of Lordship in the Late Middle Ages   205
    Michael H. Brown

11. Augmenting Rentals: The Expansion of Church Property in St
   Andrews, c. 1400–1560   223
   Bess Rhodes

12. The Prehistory of the University of St Andrews   237
   Norman H. Reid

13. University, City and Society   268
   Roger A. Mason

14. The Medieval Maces of the University of St Andrews   298
   Julian Luxford

15. Heresy, Inquisition and Late Medieval St Andrews   331
   Katie Stevenson

Appendix 1   The St Andrews Foundation Account   345
Simon Taylor

Appendix 2   The Augustinian's Account   369
Simon Taylor

Appendix 3   The Boar's Raik   380
Simon Taylor

Appendix 4   University of St Andrews Library, UYSL 110/6/4   384
Matthew Hammond

Index   388

Illustrations, Charts and Tables

Illustrations

1. 'Ancient Magnificence': St Andrews in the Middle Ages: An Introduction, *Michael H. Brown and Katie Stevenson*
1.1 John Geddy, S. Andre sive Andreapolis Scotiae Universitas Metropolitana, c.1580. National Library of Scotland MS 20996. (Reproduced by permission of the National Library of Scotland) — 2
1.2 St Andrews in the Viking Age. (Reproduced with the permission of Dr Alex Woolf, University of St Andrews) — 11

2. From *Cinrigh Monai* to *Civitas Sancti Andree*: A Star is Born, *Simon Taylor*
2.1 Long Cist Cemetery. The Hallow Hill Excavation, St Andrews. (© Edwina Proudfoot. Licensor www.scran.ac.uk) — 21
2.2 The Sarcophagus, St Andrews Cathedral. (Crown Copyright reproduced courtesy of Historic Environment Scotland) — 26

3. The Idea of St Andrews as the Second Rome Made Manifest, *Ian Campbell*
3.1 Plan of St Andrews Cathedral. (© Historic Environment Scotland) — 36
3.2 Pre-burghal Kinrimund from N. P. Brooks and G. Whittington, 'Planning and Growth in the Medieval Scottish Burgh: The Example of St Andrews', *Transactions of the Institute of British Geographers* 2 (1977), pp. 278–95, figure 6. (©1977 Royal Geographical Society) — 41
3.3 Conjectural Plan of the Development of the Burgh of St Andrews from N. P. Brooks and G. Whittington, 'Planning and Growth in the Medieval Scottish Burgh: The Example of St Andrews', *Transactions of the Institute of British Geographers* 2 (1977), pp. 278–95, figure 5. (© 1977 Royal Geographical Society) — 45

4. The Medieval Ecclesiastical Architecture of St Andrews as a Channel for the Introduction of New Ideas, *Richard Fawcett*
4.1 St Rule's Church, viewed from the north-west. (Reproduced with the permission of Richard Fawcett) — 52

4.2 St Andrews Cathedral, the internal face of the east gable. (Reproduced with the permission of Richard Fawcett) — 56
4.3 Holy Trinity Parish Church by James Gordon of Rothiemay, *Andreopolis*, 1642. — 62
4.4 St Salvator's Collegiate Chapel, viewed from the south-east. (Reproduced with the permission of Richard Fawcett) — 64
4.5 The North Chapel of the Dominican Church, viewed from the north-west. (Reproduced with the permission of Richard Fawcett) — 71
4.6 A corbel with the *Arma Christi* thought to be from the chapel of St Mary's College. (Reproduced with the permission of Richard Fawcett) — 74
4.7 St Leonard's College Chapel, viewed from the south-east. (Reproduced with the permission of Richard Fawcett) — 76
4.8 St Andrews Castle, the range to the east of the gatehouse tower thought to have contained the chapel, by John Slezer in *Theatrum Scotiae*, London, 1693. — 80

5. When the Miracles Ceased: Shrine and Cult Management at St Andrews and Scottish Cathedrals in the Later Middle Ages, *Tom Turpie*
5.1 Pilgrim badge from St Andrews, c.1450–1500, found in Sluis. Museum Catharijneconven, inventory number RMCC m33. (Image published with the permission of the Museum Catharijneconvent, Utrecht/foto Ruben de Heer) — 86

7. Living in the Late Medieval Town of St Andrews, *Elizabeth Ewan*
7.1 Image of the Crucifixion from the Minute Book of the Hammermen of St Andrews, 1553–1792. (Courtesy of University of St Andrews Library, msDA890.S1H2) — 136

8. The Burgh of St Andrews and its Inhabitants before the Wars of Independence, *Matthew Hammond*
8.1 King Máel Coluim grants liberties and customs to the burgesses of St Andrews, 1153×62. Charter of Malcolm IV, University of St Andrews Library, B65/23/1c. (Crown Copyright) — 142

9. The Archaeology of Medieval St Andrews, *Derek W. Hall with Catherine Smith*
9.1 Map of St Andrews showing archaeological area boundaries. After Munro 1997. (© SUAT Ltd) — 174
9.2 St Nicholas Farm excavation. General view of excavation of leper hospital bakehouse. (© SUAT Ltd) — 182
9.3 Deep garden soil, Alexandra Place. General view of medieval stone-built corn dryer below deep garden soil (1991). (© SUAT Ltd) — 187

9.4	Logies Lane pot. Virtually complete cooking vessel from excavations in Logies Lane in 1991. (© SUAT Ltd)	190
9.5	Kirkhill cists. General view of excavation of Early Christian long cists on Kirkhill in 1980 looking north. (© SDD, Urban Archaeology Unit)	198

12. The Prehistory of the University of St Andrews, *Norman H. Reid*

12.1	The surviving papal bull of 28 August 1413. (Courtesy of University of St Andrews Library, UYUY100)	240
12.2	The priory cloister book presses. (Courtesy of University of St Andrews Library)	249
12.3	The priory's ownership inscription on the Augustine *Opera*. (Courtesy of University of St Andrews Library, msBR65.A9)	250
12.4	The 'armariolo' inscription on the binding fragment in Franz Lambert's *Exegeseos Francisci Lamberti Avenionensis, in sanctam diui Ioannis Apocalypsim, libri VII* (Basel, 1539). (Courtesy of University of St Andrews Library, Typ SwB.B39BL)	251

13. University, City and Society, *Roger A. Mason*

13.1	Image of the seal matrix of the university, 1414×18, reversed. (Courtesy of University of St Andrews Library, UYUY103)	274

14. The Medieval Maces of the University of St Andrews, *Julian Luxford*

14.1	The St Andrews maces, with the Arts faculty mace on the left, the St Salvator's College mace in the centre and the Canon Law faculty mace on the right.	299
14.2	The head of the Arts faculty mace.	310
14.3	The head of the Canon Law faculty mace.	311
14.4	The engraved images of saints on the Arts faculty mace. Clockwise, from top left: SS Andrew, Ninian, Margaret, the Virgin Mary and Christchild, SS John the Baptist, Michael. (Reproduced by permission of the University of St Andrews)	316
14.5	The engraved images of saints on the Canon Law faculty mace. Clockwise, from top left: SS Andrew, Peter, the Holy Trinity, SS John the Baptist, Kentigern and the Virgin Mary and Christchild. (Reproduced by permission of the University of St Andrews)	321
14.6	The head of St Salvator's College mace.	323
14.7	Inscription of the pendant formerly attached by a chain to the St Salvator's College mace.	324
14.8	Figure of apocalyptic Christ within the head of the St Salvator's College mace.	325

Appendix 4. University of St Andrews Library, UYSL 110/6/4, *Matthew Hammond*

Appendix 4.1   Charter of sale of land on Market Street to Adam Purrock, citizen, version 1. (Image courtesy of University of St Andrews Library, UYSL 110/6/4) 385

Appendix 4.2   Charter of sale of land on Market Street to Adam Purrock, citizen, version 2. (Image courtesy of University of St Andrews Library, UYSL 110/6/4) 386

Charts

8. The Burgh of St Andrews and its Inhabitants before the Wars of Independence, *Matthew Hammond*
8.1   Conjectural family tree: descendants of Mainard the Fleming. 159
8.2   Conjectural family tree: descendants of Lambin. 164
8.3   Conjectural family tree: descendants of Gilla Muire mac Martáin. 166

Tables

12. The Prehistory of the University of St Andrews, *Norman H. Reid*
12.1   Bishops' documents, c.1140–1300. 255

13. University, City and Society, *Roger A. Mason*
13.1   Graduation and Incorporation Data 1413–1573, by decade. 282
13.2   BA graduation by college 1483–1573. 292

The editors, contributors and publishers are grateful to all the institutions and persons listed for permission to reproduce the materials in which they hold copyright. Every effort has been made to trace the copyright holders; apologies are offered for any omission, and the publishers will be pleased to add any necessary acknowledgement in subsequent editions.

Contributors

Michael H. Brown is Professor of Medieval Scottish History at the University of St Andrews.

Ian Campbell is Professor of Architectural History and Theory at Edinburgh College of Art, University of Edinburgh.

David Ditchburn is Associate Professor of Medieval History at Trinity College Dublin.

Elizabeth Ewan is University Research Chair and Professor of History and Scottish Studies at the University of Guelph.

Richard Fawcett OBE is an emeritus professor in the School of Art History at the University of St Andrews. Most of his career was in the Inspectorate of Ancient Monuments of Historic Scotland.

Derek W. Hall is an archaeologist and ceramic specialist, formerly working for the Scottish Urban Archaeological Trust Ltd and Historic Scotland as Inspector of Monuments. He is an associate of the Centre for Environmental History and Policy at the University of Stirling.

Matthew Hammond is a Research Associate at the University of Glasgow and a former Lecturer in Scottish History at the University of Edinburgh.

Julian Luxford is Reader in Art History at the University of St Andrews.

Roger A. Mason is Professor of Scottish History at the University of St Andrews.

Norman H. Reid is Honorary Research Fellow in the School of History at the University of St Andrews.

Bess Rhodes is a postdoctoral researcher and tutor at the University of St Andrews.

Catherine Smith is an archaeozoologist, currently working for Alder Archaeology.

Katie Stevenson is Keeper of Scottish History and Archaeology at National Museums Scotland and Senior Lecturer in Late Mediaeval History at the University of St Andrews.

Simon Taylor is a lecturer in Scottish onomastics at the University of Glasgow.

Tom Turpie gained his PhD from the University of Edinburgh in 2011. He is a freelance researcher and a tutor at the University of Stirling.

Abbreviations

AA	The Augustinian's Account
ACR	Aberdeen, City Archive, Ms Council Register
Arb. Lib.	*Liber S. Thome de Aberbrothoc*, ed. C. Innes and P. Chalmers, 2 vols (Edinburgh, 1848–56).
Ash, 'The Administration'	M. Ash, 'The Administration of the Diocese of St Andrews, 1202–1328' (unpublished PhD Thesis, University of Newcastle-upon-Tyne, 1972).
AU	*Annals of Ulster (Annals of Ulster (to 1131)*, ed. S. Mac Airt and G. Mac Niocaill (Dublin, 1983)
BA	*Breviarium Aberdonense* (Edinburgh, 1510)
Balm. Lib.	*Liber S. Marie de Balmorinach*, ed. W. B. D. D. Turnbull, Abbotsford Club (Edinburgh, 1841).
BL	British Library
Brooks and Whittington	N. P. Brooks and G. Whittington, 'Planning and Growth in the Medieval Scottish Burgh: the Example of St Andrews', *Transactions of the Institute of British Geographers* n. s. 2 (1977), pp. 278–95.
Camb. Reg.	*Registrum Monasterii S. Marie de Cambuskenneth*, ed. William Fraser (Grampian Club, Edinburgh, 1872).
Cant, *St Salvator*	R. Cant, *The College of St Salvator* (Edinburgh and London, 1950).
Cant, *University*	R. Cant, *The University of St Andrews: A Short History* (Edinburgh, 1946).
CDS	*Calendar of Documents relating to Scotland*, ed. J. Bain, 5 vols (Edinburgh, 1881–88).
Chrs David	*The Charters of David I: The Written Acts of David I King of Scots, 1124–53 and of his Son Henry Earl of Northumberland, 1139–52*, ed. G. W. S. Barrow (Woodbridge, 1999).
Copiale	*Copiale Prioratus Sanctiandree*, ed. J. H. Baxter (St Andrews, 1930).

CPL	*Calendar of Entries in the Papal Registers relating to Great Britain and Ireland: Papal Letters*, ed. W. H. Bliss, 20 vols (London, 1893–).
CSSR	*Calendar of Scottish Supplications to Rome*, ed. E. R. Lindsay, A. I. Cameron et al., 5 vols (Edinburgh, 1934–).
DES	*Discovery and Excavation in Scotland*
Dunf. Reg.	*Registrum de Dunfermelyn*, ed. C. Innes (Bannatyne Club, Edinburgh, 1842).
Dunlop, *Kennedy*	A. I. Dunlop, *The Life and Times of James Kennedy, Bishop of St Andrews* (St Andrews Univ. Pubns, 46), (1950).
Early Records	*Early Records of the University of St Andrews*, ed. J. M. Anderson, Scottish History Society (Edinburgh, 1926).
ER	*Exchequer Rolls of Scotland, 1264–1600*, ed. John Stuart et al., 23 vols (Edinburgh, 1878–1909).
EUL	Edinburgh University Library
FAA	Foundation Account A
FAB	Foundation Account B
FO	*Félire Óengusso Céli Dé: The Martyrology of Oengus the Culdee*, ed. Whitley Stokes, Henry Bradshaw Society 29 (London 1905; reprinted Dublin 1984)
Glas. Reg.	*Registrum Episcopatus Glasguensis*, ed. C. Innes, 2 vols (Bannatyne and Maitland Clubs, 1843).
Higgitt, *St Andrews*	*Medieval Art and Architecture in the Diocese of St Andrews*, ed. John Higgitt (British Archaeological Association Conference Transactions, XIV) (Leeds, 1994).
Instrumenta Publica	*Instrumenta Publica sive Processus super Fidelitatibus et Homagiis Scotorum Domino Regi Angliae Factis 1291–96*, ed. Thomas Thomson (Bannatyne Club, 1834).
Lind. Cart.	*The Chartulary of Lindores Abbey*, ed. J. Dowden (Edinburgh, 1903).
McRoberts, *St Andrews*	D. McRoberts, ed., *The Medieval Church of St Andrews* (Glasgow, 1976).
Newb. Reg.	*Registrum Sancte Marie de Neubotle*, ed. Cosmo Innes (Edinburgh, 1849).
NLS	National Library of Scotland
NRS	National Records of Scotland
n. s.	new series
PL	*Patrologia Latina*, ed. J. P. Migne, 221 vols (Paris 1844–64)

PNF, i	S. Taylor with G. Márkus, *The Place-Names of Fife, Volume One: West Fife between Leven and Forth* (Donington, 2006).
PNF, ii	S. Taylor with G. Márkus, *The Place-Names of Fife, Volume Two: Central Fife between the Rivers Eden and Leven* (Donington, 2008).
PNF, iii	S. Taylor with G. Márkus, *The Place-Names of Fife, Volume Three: St Andrews and the East Neuk* (Donington, 2009).
PNF, iv	S. Taylor with G. Márkus, *The Place-Names of Fife, Volume Four: North Fife between Eden and Tay* (Donington, 2010).
PNF, v	S. Taylor with G. Márkus, *The Place-Names of Fife, Volume Five: Discussion, Glossaries and Edited Texts* (Donington, 2012).
PoMS	People of Medieval Scotland 1093–1314, online database (www.poms.ac.uk)
PSAS	*Proceedings of the Society of Antiquaries of Scotland*
Rains and Hall, *Excavations*	M. J. Rains and D. Hall, *Excavations in St Andrews 1980–89* (Tayside and Fife Archaeological Committee, 1997).
RCAHMS Fife	*Royal Commission on the Ancient and Historical Monuments of Scotland, Inventory of Monuments in Fife, Kinross and Clackmannan* (Edinburgh, 1933).
Reg. KS	*Register of the Minister, Elders and Deacons of the Christian Congregation of St Andrews, Comprising the Proceedings of the Kirk Session …, 1559–1600*, ed. D. H. Fleming, 2 vols (Edinburgh, 1889–90).
Rentale	*Rentale Sancti Andree AD 1538–1546*, ed. R. K. Hannay, Scottish History Society (Edinburgh, 1913).
RMS	*Registrum Magni Sigilli Regum Scotorum*, ed. J. M. Thomson et al., 11 vols (Edinburgh, 1882–1914).
RPS	*Records of the Parliament of Scotland to 1707*, ed. K. M. Brown et al. (St Andrews, 2007–15) (www.rps.ac.uk).
RRS, i	*Regesta Regum Scottorum I, The Acts of Malcolm IV King of Scots 1153–65*, ed. G. W. S. Barrow (Edinburgh, 1960).
RRS, ii	*Regesta Regum Scottorum II, The Acts of William I King of Scots 1165–1214*, ed. G. W. S. Barrow (Edinburgh, 1971).

RRS, iii	*Regesta Regum Scottorum III, The Acts of Alexander II King of Scots 1214– 1249*, ed. Keith Stringer (Edinburgh, forthcoming).
RRS, iv	*Regesta Regum Scottorum IV, The Acts of Alexander III*, ed. Cynthia J. Neville and Grant Simpson (Edinburgh, 2013).
RRS, v	*Regesta Regum Scottorum V, The Acts of Robert I King of Scots 1306–1329*, ed. A. A. M. Duncan (Edinburgh, 1988).
RRS, vi	*Regesta Regum Scottorum VI, The Acts of David II King of Scots 1329 –1371*, ed. B. Webster (Edinburgh 1982).
Scone Lib.	*Liber Ecclesie de Scon*, ed. C. Innes (Bannatyne and Maitland Clubs, Edinburgh, 1843).
Scotichronicon	*Scotichronicon*, ed. D. E. R. Watt et al., 9 vols (Aberdeen and Edinburgh, 1987–98).
SEA	*Scottish Episcopal Acta, i: The Twelfth Century*, ed. Norman Shead, Scottish History Society, Sixth Series 10 (Woodbridge, 2016).
SHR	*Scottish Historical Review* (Edinburgh, 1903–).
St Andrews Acta	*Acta Facultatis Artium Universitatis Sanctiandree, 1413–1588*, ed. A. I. Dunlop, 2 vols, Scottish History Society (Edinburgh, 1964).
St A. Liber	*Liber Cartarum Prioratus Sancti Andree in Scotia*, ed. T. Thomson (Edinburgh, 1841).
StAUL	St Andrews University Library
SUAT	Scottish Urban Archaeological Trust Ltd
TA	*Accounts of the Lord High Treasurer of Scotland*, 12 vols (Edinburgh, 1877–1970).
TFAJ	*Tayside and Fife Archaeological Journal*
Watt, *Graduates*	D. E. R. Watt, *A Biographical Dictionary of Scottish Graduates to AD 1410* (Oxford, 1977).

CHAPTER ONE

'Ancient Magnificence': St Andrews in the Middle Ages: An Introduction

Michael H. Brown and Katie Stevenson

SET along its rocky outcrop between two long sandy beaches, the St Andrews skyline is dominated by its medieval buildings. The towers of the churches of St Salvator, Holy Trinity and St Regulus, the gables of the cathedral and the remains of the castle retain a visual prominence. These buildings are reminders of the status and wealth of St Andrews between the twelfth and sixteenth centuries. In this era St Andrews was a centre of unique significance in Scotland. It could claim to be the ecclesiastical capital of the land. St Andrews was the seat of the leading bishop, and from 1472 the archbishop, of Scotland whose diocese was both the richest in the Scottish church and included the core regions of the kingdom. Its cathedral was by far the largest church (and the largest building) in medieval Scotland and housed relics of the figure increasingly adopted as the nation's patron saint. The long history of scholarship at this site was reflected by the foundation of the first Scottish university in 1413. Though removed from the natural routes between royal residences and the largest burghs, and possessing a rich, but relatively small, hinterland, medieval St Andrews' claims to be a city rested less on size than on the status provided to an urban community which grew under the wing of powerful clerical patrons and benefited from the flow of clergy, pilgrims and students through its streets and dwellings.

However, the ruinous state of the cathedral, the castle and several of the churches has also been a reminder to modern visitors of the violent closing of the era of St Andrews' greatest significance in the second half of the sixteenth century. The destruction, neglect and loss of status caused by the Scottish Reformation had a devastating effect on the fortunes of the town. Even in the earliest depiction of the city, drawn by John Geddy around 1580, St Andrews shows the scars of recent upheaval. The cathedral and the churches of the Black and Grey Friars are shown as roofless and uninhabited.[1] These are scars that were never healed. When he included St Andrews in his Scottish tour in 1773, Dr Johnson described it as 'a city, which only history shews to have once flourished'

---

[1] The map is National Library of Scotland [hereafter NLS], MS 20996. For an image of the map see http://maps.nls.uk/towns/detail.cfm?id=215.

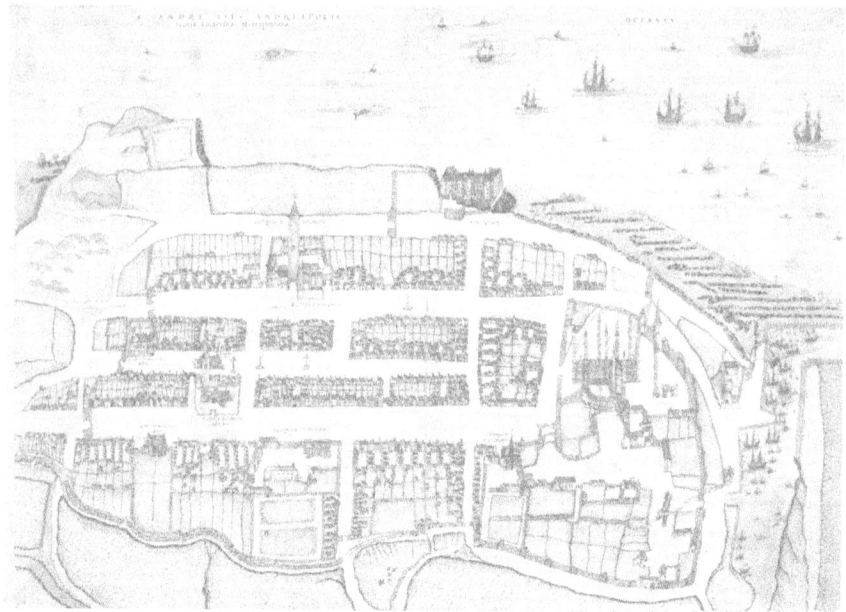

Figure 1.1: John Geddy, S. Andre sive Andreapolis Scotiae Universitas Metropolitana, c.1580. National Library of Scotland MS 20996.

as he 'surveyed the ruins of ancient magnificence'.[2] The ruins and decline struck not only Johnson but also Sir Walter Scott. He reported in 1827 that 'they were chiefly remarkable for their size not their richness in ornament' and that 'they had lately been cleared out', an observation which must surely sink the hearts of archaeologists and architectural historians as they ponder the great loss of material remains that St Andrews has suffered.[3] However, the revival of the town from the late nineteenth century still rested on the surviving medieval remains, both directly and indirectly. The reputation and economy of modern St Andrews relies on the foundations provided by its one surviving medieval ecclesiastical foundation, the university, but as much, if not more, on the fame which developed from the pleasure its burgesses derived from playing their game of golf on the sandy links north-west of the town. Students, golfers and others who visit or live in the small town on the rocky east coast of Scotland can hardly fail to be aware of the relics, not only of St Andrew himself, but also of the special centre which grew up around his name.

The story of St Andrews has long drawn the attention of historians. A strand of antiquarian and historical interest runs from George Martine, secre-

---

[2] S. Johnson and J. Boswell, *A Journey to the Western Islands of Scotland and the Journal of a Tour to the Hebrides*, ed. P. Levi (Harmondsworth, 1984), p. 36.

[3] *The Complete Works of Sir Walter Scott with a Biography*, 7 vols (New York, 1833), vii, p. 513.

tary of the controversial assassinated Archbishop Sharpe of St Andrews, who wrote his history of the see of St Andrews, *Reliquiae divi Andreae*, in 1673.[4] It extends through a second inhabitant, David Hay Fleming, who wrote numerous studies of the town in the late nineteenth and early twentieth centuries, and runs on to the works of the great historian of St Andrews University, Ronald Cant, who published histories of St Salvator's College and of the university.[5] Since 1950 all dimensions of the history of medieval St Andrews have received the attention of scholars. We know much more about the origins and early history of the site,[6] the reform of the church at St Andrews in the twelfth century and the changes associated with it,[7] the cult of the saint,[8]

---

[4] G. Martine, *Reliquiae divi Andreae or the state of the venerable and primitial see of St Andrews ... by a true (though unworthy) sone of the church* (St Andrews, 1797).

[5] D. Hay Fleming, *A Handbook to St Andrews and Neighbourhood* (St Andrews, 1894); D. Hay Fleming, *The Accounts of St Salvator's College, St Andrews, comprising the ordinary revenue and expenditure, the casual and contingent profits, etc., from 1679 to 1689, and details of the revenue in 1691* (Edinburgh, 1922); D. Hay Fleming, *Historical Notes & Extracts Concerning the Links of St Andrews 1552-1893* (St Andrews, 1893); R. G. Cant, *The College of St Salvator: Its Foundation and Development* (Edinburgh, 1950) [hereafter Cant, *St Salvator*]; R. G. Cant, *The University of St Andrews: A Short History* (Edinburgh, 1946) [hereafter Cant, *University*].

[6] M. O. Anderson, 'St Andrews before Alexander I', *The Scottish Tradition*, ed. G. W. S. Barrow (Edinburgh 1974), pp. 1-13; M. O. Anderson, 'The Celtic Church in Kinrimund', *The Medieval Church of St Andrews*, ed. D. McRoberts (Glasgow, 1976) [hereafter McRoberts, *St Andrews*], pp. 1-10; T. O. Clancy, 'Scotland, the "Nennian" Recension of the *Historia Brittonum*, and the *Lebor Bretnach*', *Kings Clerics and Chronicles in Scotland 500-1297*, ed. S. Taylor (Dublin, 2000), pp. 87-107; *The St Andrews Sarcophagus*, ed. S. Foster (Dublin, 1998); J. E. Fraser, 'Rochester, Hexham and Cennrigmonaid: the Movements of St Andrew in Britain, 604-747', *Saints' Cults in the Celtic World*, ed. S. Boardman, J. R. Davies and E. Williamson (Woodbridge, 2009), pp. 1-17; J. Kenworthy, 'A Further Fragment of Early Christian Sculpture from St Mary's on the Rock, St Andrews, Fife', *Proceedings of the Society of Antiquaries of Scotland* [hereafter *PSAS*] 110 (1979-80), pp. 356-63; E. Proudfoot, 'Excavations of a Long Cist Cemetery on Hallow Hill, St Andrews, Fife, 1975-77', *PSAS* 126 (1996), pp. 387-454.

[7] S. Taylor, 'The Coming of the Augustinians to St Andrews and Version B of the St Andrews Foundation Legend', *Kings, Clerics and Chronicles in Scotland 500-1297*, ed. S. Taylor (Dublin, 2000), pp. 115-23; K. Veitch, 'Replanting Paradise: Alexander I and the Reform of the Church in Scotland', *Innes Review* 52 (2001), pp. 136-66; A. A. M. Duncan, 'The Foundation of St Andrews Cathedral Priory, 1140', *Scottish Historical Review* [hereafter *SHR*] 84 (2005), pp. 1-37; M. Dilworth, 'Dependent Priories of St Andrews', *Innes Review* 26 (1975), pp. 56-64; M. Dilworth, 'The Augustinian Chapter of St Andrews', *Innes Review* 25 (1974), pp. 15-30.

[8] M. Ash and D. Broun, 'The Adoption of St Andrew as Patron Saint of Scotland', *Medieval Art and Architecture in the Diocese of St Andrews*, ed. J. Higgitt (Leeds, 1994) [hereafter Higgitt, *St Andrews*], pp. 16-24; D. Broun, 'The Church of St Andrews and its Foundation Legend in the Early Twelfth Century: Recovering the Full Text of Version A of the Foundation Legend', *Kings, Clerics and Chronicles in Scotland, 500-1297*, ed. S. Taylor (Dublin, 2000), pp. 108-14; David Ditchburn, '"Saints at the door don't make miracles"? The Contrasting Fortunes of Scottish Pilgrimage, c.1450-1550', *Sixteenth-Century Scotland: Religion, Politics and Society: Essays in Honour of Michael Lynch*, ed. J. Goodare and A. A. Macdonald (Leiden, 2008), pp. 69-98.

the medieval bishops,[9] the burgh,[10] its organisation and people, and the architecture and material remains of church and city.[11] Though there have been two earlier collections of essays focusing specifically on aspects to do with the church of St Andrews, this volume represents the first attempt to treat the history of St Andrews collectively and coherently. The aim here is to consider St Andrews as a centre with multiple roles and communities, and to examine the nature of these in different periods and with an eye to points of overlap and interaction, in work by scholars who are all either experts in the study of St Andrews itself or in the varied elements which made up the medieval church, cult and city.

At the heart of the history and significance of St Andrews were the relics of the apostle, which by the late eleventh century had given the place its new name. In the twelfth century two accounts were written of the foundation of St Andrews, drawing on earlier material; they are discussed below by Simon Taylor.[12] The longer of these claimed that the relics of the saint – his kneecap, upper arm bone, three fingers and a tooth – were brought to Scotland by the Greek monk Regulus, to save them from the Emperor Constantius II in the 350s. In a dream, an angel advised Regulus to take the relics to 'northern parts', building a shrine for them wherever his ship was wrecked. The real origin of the link between the apostle and the settlement that bears his name continues to be debated, as Simon Taylor shows in his chapter. However, there is good reason to place the formative period of this centre in the eighth century. It was referred to as *Cindrighmonaidh*, the end of the king's muir or headland, meaning either the wider upland between Crail and St Andrews or the craggy headland where

---

[9] M. Ash, 'William Lamberton, Bishop of St Andrews, 1297–1328', *The Scottish Tradition*, ed. G. W. S. Barrow (Edinburgh, 1974), pp. 44–55; M. Ash, 'The Diocese of St Andrews under its "Norman" Bishops', *SHR* 55 (1976), pp. 105–26; M. Ash, 'David Bernham, Bishop of St Andrews, 1239–53', *Innes Review* 25 (1974), pp. 3–14; A. I. Dunlop, *The Life and Times of James Kennedy, Bishop of St Andrews* (St Andrews Univ. Pubns, 46), (St Andrews, 1950) [hereafter Dunlop, *Kennedy*]; M. H. B. Sanderson, *Cardinal of Scotland: David Beaton c.1494–1546* (Edinburgh, 1986).

[10] N. P. Brooks and G. Whittington, 'Planning and Growth in the Medieval Scottish Burgh', *Transactions of the Institute of British Geographers* n. s. 2 (1977) [hereafter Brooks and Whittington], pp. 278–95; M. Hammond, 'The Bishop, the Prior and the Foundation of the Burgh of St Andrews', *Innes Review* 66 (2015), pp. 72–101.

[11] Neil Cameron, 'St Rule's Church, St Andrews, and Early Stone Built Churches in Scotland', *PSAS* 124 (1994), pp. 367–78; M. Thurlby, 'St Andrews Cathedral-Priory and the Beginnings of Gothic Architecture in Northern Britain', Higgitt, *St Andrews*, pp. 47–60; I. Campbell, 'Planning for Pilgrims: St Andrews as the Second Rome', *Innes Review* 64 (2013), pp. 1–22; E. Cambridge, 'The Early Building-History of St Andrews Cathedral, Fife, and its Context in Northern Transitional Architecture', *Antiquaries Journal* 57 (1978), pp. 277–88; J. Hamilton and R. Toolis, 'Further Excavations at the Site of a Medieval Leper Hospital at St Nicholas Farm, St Andrews', *Tayside and Fife Archaeological Journal* [hereafter *TFAJ*] 5 (1999); M. J. Rains and D. Hall, *Excavations in St Andrews 1980–89* (Fife and Tayside Archaeological Committee, 1997) [hereafter Rains and Hall, *Excavations*].

[12] See also S. Taylor with G. Márkus, *The Place-Names of Fife, Volume Three: St Andrews and the East Neuk* (Donnington, 2009) [hereafter *PNF*, iii], pp. 564–615; Broun, 'The Church of St Andrews', pp. 108–14.

the cathedral now stands. The royal association indicated by this name suggests that Cennrígmonaid was already an important location.[13] Rather than brought directly from Greece, it has been argued that Andrew's relics came, much more prosaically, from Hexham in Northumbria, carried not by Regulus but by a refugee English bishop whose patron, St Wilfrid, may have acquired them in Rome.[14] The decision to house the relics in Cennrígmonaid may have been a deliberate attempt to raise its status to 'the most prominent church in southern Pictland'.[15]

This idea of growing status in the mid eighth century is supported by the mention in an Irish annal of the death of an abbot of *Cindrighmonaidh* in the year 747 and by the dating of the St Andrews sarcophagus to slightly later.[16] The sarcophagus, discovered in the cathedral grounds in 1833, is a finely carved stone tomb dating to the latter part of the eighth century and most likely commissioned for a Pictish king, possibly Onuist son of Vurguist, the ruler remembered in the twelfth-century account as the initial patron of the church at the site.[17] However, its presence suggests the continued importance of Cennrígmonaid as a royal, as well as a religious, centre, forming with Scone and Dunkeld what Alex Woolf calls the 'central transit zone' of the tenth- and eleventh-century Scottish kings.[18] This standing as a site known outside Scotland from the tenth century as a place of pilgrimage and ecclesiastical importance may have led to the change of its name to Kilrimund or Cilrígmonaid (church of the king's muir) by the twelfth century. It may also have led to its gradual association with the leading bishop of the Scots.[19] While historians writing after 1400 dated this to Bishop Cellach in the early tenth century, the connection may have developed more gradually and in competition with alternative sites like Abernethy and Dunkeld. In this contest, the association with the apostle may have trumped Abernethy's ties to St Brigid and Dunkeld's to St Columba.[20]

St Andrews' status as a centre of Scotland's religious life with a wider reputation was founded in the centuries from 700. By 1100 the site possessed a great church dedicated to St Andrew, attended by a group of seven clergy.[21] Since

---

[13] *PNF*, iii, pp. 476–9.
[14] J. Fraser, *From Caledonia to Pictland: Scotland to 795* (Edinburgh, 2009), p. 309; Fraser, 'Rochester, Hexham and Cennrigmonaid', p. 17 n. 87; A. Woolf, 'Onuist son of Uurguist: *Tyrannus carnifex* or a David for the Picts?', *Æthelbald and Offa: Two Eighth-Century Kings of Mercia*, ed. D. Hill and M. Worthington (Oxford, 2005), pp. 35–42.
[15] Fraser, 'Rochester, Hexham and Cennrigmonaid', p. 16.
[16] Ibid., pp. 2–3.
[17] D. Broun, 'Pictish Kings 761–839: Integration with Dál Riata or Separate Development?', *St Andrews Sarcophagus*, ed. Foster, pp. 71–83; S. T. Driscoll, 'Political Discourse and the Growth of Christian Ceremonialism: the Place of the St Andrews Sarcophagus', in ibid., pp. 168–78; Fraser, *From Caledonia to Pictland*, p. 318.
[18] A. Woolf, *From Pictland to Alba 789–1070* (Edinburgh, 2007), p. 198.
[19] *PNF*, iii, p. 477.
[20] Woolf, *From Pictland to Alba*, p. 103. We are grateful to Alex Woolf for his ideas on this subject.
[21] *PNF*, iii, p. 608.

the ninth century a community of *céli Dé* (culdees), followers of an ascetic Irish monasticism, had existed, perhaps on the clifftop north of the church.[22] Finally there was a third foundation, a hospital dedicated to the care of pilgrims that was administered by the clergy.[23] However, it was the years around and after 1100 which would see the reshaping of this ecclesiastical centre. The physical form and institutional structures of St Andrews, and the consistent use of that name, were products of the great period of church reform which began in the late eleventh century and reached its peak in the twelfth. Our knowledge of Kilrimund in 1100 is itself derived from the foundation accounts produced by the reformed clergy of the site in the subsequent decades. The existence of such written narratives is indicative of the new era and they represent the confidence and ambition of churchmen drawn from a much wider geographical area and motivated by a movement whose impact on local religious custom extended across Latin Christendom. By tracing the history of the cult of Andrew in Fife, the authors of the foundation accounts sought to provide a usable history of their church as the basis for claiming 'ancient' rights and status for new foundations and the place they inhabited. For example, by stressing degeneracy and decline, especially of the married and hereditary clergy of the church of St Andrew, the authors could justify the transfer of rights and the transformation of custom and personnel. Similarly, by claiming the primacy of their bishop as 'high archbishop' or 'high bishop of the Scots', asserting that rights over a territory covering much of eastern Fife had been given to the clergy of Kilrimund by King Onuist and recording that Alexander I had renewed this grant of a land known as the Boar's Raik (*cursus apri*), the authors of the two accounts aimed to demonstrate the extent and legitimacy of their own religious community.[24]

All the elements of early medieval St Andrews experienced major change in practices and personnel during the twelfth century. In this, as earlier, the kings were major drivers of change. Royal sponsorship clearly lay behind the choice of bishops from English monastic houses after 1100. Turgot, prior of Durham and biographer of Queen Margaret; Eadmer, the friend and biographer of Archbishop Anselm of Canterbury; and Robert, a monk from Nostell in Yorkshire, were all committed to ecclesiastical reform. Alexander I's grant of the Boar's Raik and items from his treasury to the church indicated the support of the royal dynasty for the church of St Andrew.[25] These bishops failed to assert the claims of their church and office to a formal primacy over an *ecclesia Scoticana*. However, as defined diocesan structures developed in the mid twelfth century,

---

[22] It is unclear whether the Culdees had their own small church or 'celebrated their office' in a small corner of the main church (*PNF*, iii, p. 610).

[23] *PNF*, iii, p. 608; Duncan, 'The Foundation', pp. 17–18.

[24] Taylor, 'The Coming of the Augustinians'; Broun, 'The Church of St Andrews'. Opinions vary about whether Alexander's grant was a new one based on a forged precedent or the church had been deprived of lands granted in the eighth century. See Duncan, 'The Foundation', pp. 6–8; Woolf, *From Pictland to Alba*, p. 318.

[25] Veitch, 'Replanting Paradise', pp. 148–51; Ash, 'The Diocese of St Andrews under its "Norman" Bishops'.

Bishop Robert was assigned spiritual authority over a see that included not just the lands north of the Forth and in the lower valley of the Tay which had been in the scope of the bishop of the Scots before 1100, but also incorporated the province of Lothian, south of the Forth.[26] This diocese, stretching through eastern Scotland from Berwick to just south of Aberdeen, encompassed almost all the core regions of the kings and the richest areas of his realm. The lands and earthly rights which were assigned to the bishops were similarly impressive, as Marinell Ash showed. In 1206 they included, along with the Boar's Raik, estates throughout Fife, lands round Loch Leven and in the Ochils, and a network of properties in Angus, Aberdeenshire, Lothian and Wedale in the borders. Ash assessed the value of the bishops' estates and churches at £1,000 per year in the thirteenth century. If correct, this would almost certainly make the bishops of St Andrews the wealthiest figures in Scotland after the king, and the episcopal seat, the *cathedra*, a major centre for economic and political, as well as spiritual, reasons.[27]

Two creations of the mid twelfth century essentially formed the St Andrews of the later medieval period. The first of these was the priory founded in 1140 by Bishop Robert to serve the church which housed the apostle's relics. Unlike other cathedral churches in Scotland, the chapter at St Andrews was not to be a group of individual priests but rather a community of canons, living together after the rule derived from the writings of St Augustine.[28] This rule was designed to combine monastic discipline with pastoral duties and its adoption was probably the choice of Bishop Robert, himself from the order. The plans for such a foundation had been intended to aid the bishop in the reform of his church. However, recent discussions by Archie Duncan and Matthew Hammond have argued that Bishop Robert had to be compelled by King David I to endow the priory from his own possessions, and the history of the priory included in the fifteenth-century *Scotichronicon* speaks of ongoing tensions between the bishop and his chapter like those found elsewhere.[29] The canons guarded their rights against the bishop while he was alive and their claims to elect his successor at his death. The latter prompted a long-running conflict with the members of the old Culdee community.[30] Housed outside the priory in the church of St Mary of the Rock north of the cathedral, as Simon Taylor explains below, the culdees were

---

[26] The date of this extension of St Andrews' episcopal authority over Lothian (previously within the orbit of Durham) is not clear. The earliest reference to the bishops of St Andrews acting in this area is c. 1150. See D. Matthew, 'Durham and the Anglo-Norman World', *Anglo-Norman Durham 1093–1193*, ed. D. Rollason, M. Harvey and M. Prestwich (Woodbridge, 1994), pp. 1–24, at 4 n.12.

[27] M. Ash, 'The Administration of the Diocese of St Andrews, 1202–1328' (unpublished PhD thesis, University of Newcastle-upon-Tyne, 1972), [hereafter Ash, 'The Administration'], pp. 219–20.

[28] C. H. Lawrence, *Medieval Monasticism* (Harlow, 2001), pp. 162–6; M. Dilworth, 'The Augustinian Chapter of St Andrews', *Innes Review* 25 (1974), pp. 15–30.

[29] Duncan, 'The Foundation', pp. 9–28; Hammond, 'The Bishop, the Prior and the Founding of the Burgh', pp. 75–86; *Scotichronicon*, ed. D. E. R. Watt et al., 9 vols (Aberdeen and Edinburgh, 1987–88) [hereafter, *Scotichronicon*], iii, pp. 373–75, 397.

[30] G. W. S. Barrow, *The Kingdom of the Scots*, 2nd edn (Edinburgh, 2003), pp. 187–213.

transformed into a house of secular priests from the 1190s. This group of often well-connected clergy challenged the canons for a role in episcopal elections until the early fourteenth century. These tensions with bishops and other clergy reflect the fact that the foundation of the priory gave the church and shrine of St Andrew a much stronger corporate voice.

This voice was expressed in the composition of the foundation accounts mentioned above and also runs through the fifteenth-century history of the bishops and priors in the *Scotichronicon*. These literary activities also reflect the early and continuing association of the churches of St Andrews with learning, and with the production and ownership of written materials. Within Bishop Robert's foundation charter of 1140 was included the gift of all his books to provide the basis of a library.[31] Norman Reid demonstrates below that something of the expansion of this library and the intellectual activity it fostered can be traced in subsequent centuries. As Reid discusses, in the catalogue of monastic libraries compiled by Franciscan friars from Oxford in the late thirteenth century, St Andrews Cathedral Priory was recorded as possessing some ninety-five texts.[32] Given the religious affiliations of the priory, it is not surprising that a number of these were specifically Augustinian works. Some of these texts are in a manuscript that survives in the library of the University of St Andrews.[33] A second work which can be identified from the catalogue, a theological collection, is now in Germany at the Herzog-August-Bibliothek in Wolfenbüttel.[34] It is one of a number of manuscripts in this collection which were taken from St Andrews in the mid sixteenth century. They were acquired by a German collector, Marcus Wagner, when he visited Scotland in 1553. Wagner was entertained in the priory by the 'royal abbot', James Stewart, bastard son of James V, from whom he acquired at least five manuscripts.[35]

By the far the best known of these is a manuscript of medieval music which has been regarded as 'holding a special position in the history of late-medieval music'.[36] The manuscript was almost certainly produced in Paris in the first half of the thirteenth century and contains crucial evidence of musical developments during the preceding hundred years. These changes were centred on the cathedral of Notre Dame de Paris and the works included in the manuscript show the evolution of choral polyphony, where different voices moved independently,

---

[31] Duncan, 'The Foundation', p. 17.
[32] J. Higgitt, ed., *Corpus of British Medieval Library Catalogues*, xii: *Scottish Libraries* (London, 2006), pp. 236–7.
[33] University of St Andrews Library [hereafter StAUL], MS BR.65.A9.
[34] Wolfenbüttel, Herzog-August-Bibliothek, MS Helmstedt 1108.
[35] *Copiale Prioratus Sanctiandree*, ed. J. H. Baxter (St Andrews, 1930) [hereafter *Copiale*], xxiii–xxix.
[36] Wolfenbüttel, Herzog-August-Bibliothek, MS Helmstedt 628; J. H. Baxter, ed., *An Old St Andrews Music Book* (St Andrews, 1931); M. Everist, 'From Paris to St Andrews: The Origins of W_1', *Journal of the American Musicological Society* 43:1 (1990), pp. 1–42; J. Brown, S. Patterson, and D. Hiley, 'Further Observations on WI', *Journal of the Plainsong and Mediaeval Music Society* 4 (1981), pp. 53–67.

under the influence of Parisian composers like Leoninus and Perotinus. The manuscript also reflects changed practices in musical notation.[37] The decoration of this volume has been linked to that of a Parisian liturgical manuscript which bears the arms of Bishop David Bernham of St Andrews (1239–53) and which contains a list of parish churches in the diocese of St Andrews that the bishop dedicated in the 1240s.[38] Though Bernham clearly possessed this codex, and, it seems likely, the musical work, it has been argued that it was his predecessor, the Frenchman William Malvoisin, bishop from 1202–38, who had acquired these items through his strong connections with Paris.[39] They may have been donated to the priory by one of Bernham's successors. Though perhaps neglected by the 1550s, in the later thirteenth century they would have been objects of prestige which would have reminded the canons and visitors of St Andrews' links to the centres of the western church.[40]

The thirteenth-century catalogue also included works of ancient and ecclesiastical history by Josephus and Eusebius, while preserved in extracts copied from the, now lost, great register of the priory are references to other pieces of historical writing. These include a work described as 'the names of the kings of the Scots and Picts', a genealogy of the kings of England to Henry II and an account of the sequence of priors of St Andrews.[41] There was also a work described as 'The history of the origins of the Scots from Egypt to Spain, briefly in Ireland, from there to Britain'.[42] Among the St Andrews volumes in Wolfenbüttel is a mid-fifteenth-century manuscript containing John de Fordun's *Chronica Gentis Scottorum* (chronicle of the Scottish people), which includes an account of the mythical wanderings of the Scots as well as their later history.[43] This manuscript also includes the text known as *Gesta Annalia*, which is a narrative of events between the 1160s and 1360s.[44] The survival of this manuscript is testament to the importance of medieval St Andrews as a centre of historical writing. A disproportionate number of historical narratives surviving from medieval Scotland have strong associations with St Andrews. In the thirteenth century a now-lost history of Scotland was composed by Richard Vairement, one of the clergy provided from the old culdee house.[45] *Gesta Annalia* also has St

---

[37] E. H. Roesner, 'The Origins of W_1', *Journal of the American Musicological Society* 29:3 (1976), pp. 337–80, 337.

[38] Everist, 'From Paris to St Andrews', pp. 4–5. The manuscript is Paris, Bibliothèque Nationale, MS Latin, 1218.

[39] Ibid., pp. 14–26.

[40] Ibid., pp. 31–2.

[41] T. Thomson, ed., *Liber Cartarum Prioratus Sancti Andree in Scotia* (Edinburgh, 1841) [hereafter *St A. Liber*], xxvi, xxx.

[42] *St A. Liber*, xxvi.

[43] Wolfenbüttel, Codex Helmstedt 538; *Scotichronicon*, ix, p. 200.

[44] D. Broun, 'A New Look at *Gesta Annalia* Attributed to John of Fordun', *Church, Chronicle and Learning in Medieval and Early Renaissance Scotland*, ed. B. E. Crawford (Edinburgh, 1999), pp. 9–30.

[45] Barrow, *Kingdom of the Scots*, pp. 192–3, 198; D. Broun, *Scottish Independence and the Idea of Britain from the Picts to Alexander III* (Woodbridge, 2007), pp. 255–62.

Andrews connections. It has been shown to have been composed in two segments written in about 1285 and 1363.[46] The latter section has been tentatively linked to Thomas Bisset, prior of St Andrews between 1354 and 1363.[47] Two early fifteenth-century chronicles of Scotland have even closer links with the priory. Andrew Wyntoun and Walter Bower were both Augustinians trained at St Andrews. Wyntoun was a canon of St Andrews and became prior of St Serf's, the dependent priory of St Andrews on an island in Loch Leven. His *Original Chronicle of Scotland* was a vernacular history written in the 1410s which incorporated much material relating to Fife and to the church of St Andrews. Copies of it were owned by several Fife families.[48] Walter Bower was educated in the cathedral priory and became abbot of Inchcolm in the Forth. He also used St Andrews material extensively to compose his *Scotichronicon* during the 1440s and included and extended what was clearly a separate text of lives of the bishops and priors of St Andrews in his history.[49] Moreover, his description of the priory as 'the paradise of a cloister at St Andrews', his portraits of the priors he knew and, elsewhere, his account of the celebration of the founding of the university all present Bower as a first-hand witness to the city in the years around 1400.[50]

In the same way as the priory became from 1140 the focus of learning in St Andrews, so the canons were deliberately given the responsibility and opportunity of running the cult of Andrew and tending to the pilgrims who were coming to his shrine. As Taylor shows below, there is evidence to demonstrate that the flow of pilgrims was already sufficient before 1140 to require not just facilities around the shrine but ferries and chapels on the different routes to St Andrews. 'The hospital with its land, possession and rents for the maintenance of pilgrims' was specifically assigned to the new priory at its foundation along with additional funds from the bishops' own revenues.[51] Though, as Tom Turpie discusses herein, it is hard to assess the volume of such traffic over the next 250 years, the prestige and income from being the centre of a major saint's cult were sufficient to merit its support by the priory and other religious institutions. That by 1200 Kilrimund had generally been superseded by St Andrews as the name for the whole location is further testament to the growing centrality of the cult of the apostle and the priory (and bishopric) which bore his name.[52]

[46] Broun, 'A New Look at *Gesta Annalia*'.
[47] S. Boardman, 'Robert II', *Scottish Kingship 1306–1542: Essays in Honour of Norman Macdougall*, ed. M. Brown and R. Tanner (Edinburgh, 2008), pp. 72–108, 95; A. Grant, 'The Death of John Comyn: What was Going On?' *SHR* 86 (2007), pp. 176–224, 189–90.
[48] C. Edington, 'Wyntoun, Andrew', *Oxford Dictionary of National Biography* (Oxford University Press, May 2006) [www.oxforddnb.com/view/article/30164].
[49] *Scotichronicon*, ix, pp. 204–8. There is a third version of this history of the bishops and priors which extends to 1483 included in the manuscript compiled by John Law, principal of St Leonard's College in St Andrews in the mid sixteenth century (J. Durkan, 'St Andrews in the John Law Chronicle', *Innes Review* 25 (1974), pp. 49–62).
[50] *Scotichronicon*, iii, pp. 431–9; viii, pp. 411–13.
[51] Duncan, 'The Foundation', p. 17.
[52] *PNF*, iii, pp. 478, 524–5.

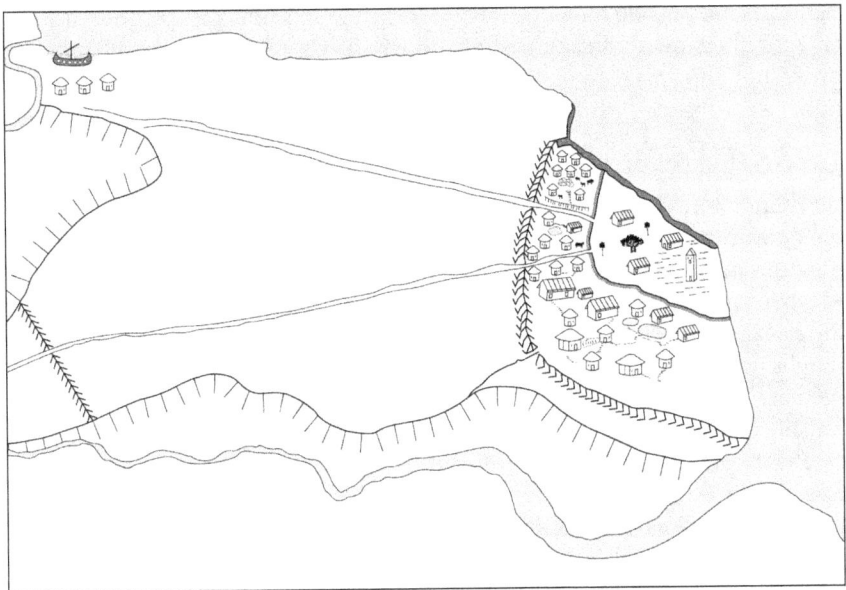

Figure 1.2: St Andrews in the Viking Age.

The name St Andrews was also consistently attached to the second major foundation of the mid twelfth century. Within two decades of the establishment of the Augustinian Priory, Bishop Robert issued a charter which stated that 'we have established a burgh at St Andrews in Scotland'.[53] This was not the earliest record of a wider community around the ecclesiastical centre. In the late tenth century, a Continental saint's life named 'Rigmonaid' as one of two *urbes* in Scotland.[54] An *urbs* in this context is understood as a major church settlement and its form and area are considered by Alex Woolf in figure 1.2. Moreover, as Matthew Hammond outlines here, in the early twelfth century a secular settlement known as the 'Clochin' existed west of the church's lands. However, despite these precursors, Bishop Robert's charter clearly indicates a major change. He was creating a new type of urban community, following models drawn from recently founded northern English boroughs like Newcastle-upon-Tyne, and before that from the arrangements made by Continental lords with their urban subjects.[55] Charters from the 1190s confirmed the rights of the property-owning burgesses of St Andrews to hold a market with a monopoly over an area roughly corresponding to the Boar's Raik in eastern Fife, to enjoy

---

[53] For the full text of this charter see *PNF*, iii, pp. 429–30.
[54] Woolf, *From Pictland to Alba*, p. 103.
[55] R. Bartlett, *The Making of Europe* (London, 1993), pp. 167–96; R. Oram, *Domination and Lordship: Scotland 1070–1230* (Edinburgh, 2011), pp. 265–94.

rights to land outside the burgh and to form a merchants' guild.[56] They already enjoyed their own officials, Bishop Robert naming Mainard the Fleming as provost or chief magistrate. Hammond discusses here the significance of these rights and observes elsewhere that St Andrews was the first Scottish burgh whose founder was not King David I. He has also argued convincingly that the burgh of St Andrews was not part of an integrated plan of development. Instead the foundation was the response of Bishop Robert to the growing ambitions of the new priory over the ecclesiastical centre.[57] Hammond's chapter also shows how the burgh's initial population was probably composed of Flemings like Maynard and English-speakers, but that it integrated with the Scottish landowning class in the hinterland of Fife. This process of integration, paralleled in other burghs north of the Forth, like Perth and Aberdeen, marked off Scotland's high medieval development from that of Wales or Ireland where urban corporations remained assertively English islands surrounded by hostile native populaces.

These two institutions, the priory and the burgh, were founded and developed in a close inter-relationship under the (not always welcome) sponsorship of the bishop. Together, their growth created the medieval centre which can be interpreted today both in terms of physical remains and geographical layout. As Bess Rhodes describes in her chapter, in the east there was a distinct ecclesiastical zone physically dominated by the Augustinian priory. Around this still stand the impressive remains of the precinct wall. Uniquely in Scotland, the wall still has its three gates, the most impressive of which, the Pends, faces the burgh, and thirteen surviving towers. Rather than a physical defence, this wall was built by c.1300 and enlarged in the early sixteenth century as a boundary which displayed jurisdictional rights and spiritual authority.[58] As Richard Fawcett describes, within the wall stood two churches, both begun in the twelfth century. The small church with its high tower dedicated to St Regulus or 'Rule' was probably built in the early twelfth century. It was overshadowed by the construction of the largest and most impressive structure in medieval Scotland, built to reflect the status of the bishop and the shrine of St Andrew. This ambitious cathedral was begun in the 1160s and only finally consecrated in 1318 at a ceremony attended by King Robert Bruce, and, as Fawcett shows, can be placed in the context of the great age of Gothic ecclesiastical design.[59] Also within the precinct, on the site of St Leonard's school, stood the great pilgrim hospital, now only surviving in the much-remodelled chapel.[60] The wall physically marked off the shrine and great church from other centres in St Andrews. The culdee house, whose foundations alone can be seen, lay on the cliffs immediately to the north of the wall. The residence of the bishop was in the castle which lay north-west along the cliffs

---

[56] StAUL, B65/23/2c; B65/23/2 (a) c
[57] Hammond, 'The Bishop, the Prior and the Founding of the Burgh', pp. 86–96.
[58] *Royal Commission on the Ancient and Historical Monuments of Scotland, Inventory of Monuments in Fife, Kinross and Clackmannan* [hereafter *RCAHMS Fife*], pp. 241–3.
[59] D. McRoberts, '"The Glorious House of St Andrew"', *Innes Review* 25 (1974), pp. 95–158; M. Penman, *Robert the Bruce King of the Scots* (New Haven, 2014), pp. 185–6.
[60] See Hall and Smith below.

from the precinct, leaving the bishop symbolically excluded from his cathedral. The castle was, as Michael Brown considers, both a centre of ecclesiastical and temporal authority for the burgh, the tenants of the bishop's lands and for the people of his diocese. The landed rights of both bishop and prior added to St Andrews' significance as a focus of lordship and legal activity via the holding of courts covering both spiritual and earthly matters. The ruined structure of the castle visible today almost wholly dates from after 1390, but a castle residence on this site is mentioned from the late twelfth century onwards.

Though fewer architectural remains survive of the medieval burgh, as Matthew Hammond shows and others have discussed previously, the growth and design of the burgh can be extracted from documentary evidence and from the layout of the modern streets. This suggests the possibility that St Andrews' initial plan followed those of Edinburgh and Stirling, with its main axis focused on the castle of its founder, the bishop. This north–south alignment, on the line of modern Castle Street (then Castlegate), was replaced by a west-to-east axis. Two principal streets developed, North and South Street, which focused on the cathedral, while a third focused on the burgh's market. This new alignment has been taken as proof of the importance of the cult and shrine of Andrew to the economy of the burgh in the later twelfth and early thirteenth centuries.[61] Ian Campbell argues that the layout of the whole site in the twelfth century also had an ideological significance. St Andrews was planned to remind visitors of the shrine of Andrew's brother, Peter, in Rome, in a manner similar to the great pilgrimage centre of Santiago de Compostella in north-western Spain.

The character of St Andrews as the closely intertwined religious centre and urban community which had developed by the late twelfth century is the subject of most of the essays in this volume. In his chapter David Ditchburn assesses the uniqueness of St Andrews within Scotland. He estimates the population of St Andrews as being in the range of 2,500–3,000. This would place the city below the largest Scottish burghs like Edinburgh, and Aberdeen, but probably on a par with, or larger than, Dunfermline or Stirling. However, the population of St Andrews included a significant body of clergy, most of them attached to the priory but also from the bishop's household, the clerks of St Mary's of the Rock, the hospital of St Nicholas south of the city and from the friaries and university founded after 1400. Ditchburn suggests that these amounted to several hundred men, adding to the size of the city and creating a disproportionately male population. Though all medieval burghs held a significant body of clergy, for St Andrews this would have had a greater influence on urban life. Ditchburn illustrates this point by tracing the yearly life of the burgh. He demonstrates how this calendar would have been dominated by the sequence of religious festivals and seasons, probably to a greater extent than elsewhere. This ecclesiastical character would also have been evident in the role of religious houses as property owners in the burgh. Bess Rhodes demonstrates the growing role of churchmen and institutions in the ownership of lands and buildings after 1400.

[61] Brookes and Whittington, pp. 285–88.

Part of this was a product of new foundations occupying space in St Andrews; part came from the assignment of rents to clerical landlords. The role of the bishops as lords of the burgh was more than purely notional. As Michael Brown shows, strong connections existed between the followings of successive bishops and the leading figures of both the burgh and the surrounding locality.

However, it is important not to regard the burgh of St Andrews as simply an offshoot of the ecclesiastical centre from which it had developed. Elizabeth Ewan's chapter is a depiction of St Andrews as a full urban society. Her discussion covers the existence and operation of rights of self-government and identifies the centres of public life in the burgh in the now-vanished tolbooth alongside the market place. The early grant of the right to a merchants' guild indicates that trading possibilities were a consideration in the founding of the burgh. As Ewan shows, mercantile activity was significant in the fifteenth century. The customs payments made from St Andrews in 1474–75 may suggest levels of exports well below other east coast burghs like Dundee, Montrose, Aberdeen, Perth and, of course, Edinburgh. However, they were higher than those of the other Fife burghs and royal centres like Stirling and Linlithgow.[62] Ewan and Hammond both reveal something of the people who lived in the burgh, via records of their occupations and their living conditions. These show the urban community to be defined by its relationship with the bishop and priory, but it was much more than a service settlement. Instead, in their dealings with these lords and neighbours, the burgesses (or citizens) showed a keen sense of their rights and distinct identity, capable of independent interaction with other burghs and serving as a centre of the surrounding district.

The clearest expression of this sense of identity was the construction of the parish church of Holy Trinity in South Street in the 1410s. This moved the place of worship of the inhabitants of the burgh from within the cathedral precincts and gave the burgesses a large civic church as a focal point for their devotions. Bess Rhodes identifies this as part of a significant period of change in the fifteenth century which redrew the map of the burgh and redirected its focus. Along with the parish church, the foundation of the two friaries, the Blackfriars on South Street and the Greyfriars at the west end of Market Street, only occurred in the mid fifteenth century. This was two centuries after mendicant houses were founded in Scotland's major burghs, suggesting that St Andrews, with its great ecclesiastical institutions, was perceived as unsuitable ground for the friars. The reason for their foundation in the fifteenth century should probably be linked to wider changes. One element of this related to the cult at the heart of the town's identity. As Tom Turpie argues, a paradox existed in that as St Andrew became the focus for Scottish communal identity as patron saint, especially in the fifteenth century, there was at the same time a gradual decline in importance of the saint's shrine. While throughout Western Europe pilgrimage as an activity was never more popular, the focus changed to sites linked to the cult of Mary or to the

---

[62] *Exchequer Rolls of Scotland, 1264–1600*, ed. John Stuart et al., 23 vols (Edinburgh, 1878–1909) [hereafter *ER*], viii, pp. 318–19.

Passion.[63] As local interest in St Andrews waned, Turpie detects that the bishops used the opportunity of the devastating fire in the cathedral in 1378 and substantial storm damage in 1410 as a platform for a sustained campaign to refocus attentions on St Andrew. In doing so, however, they emphasised contemporary trends and remodelled the Lady Chapel to give it more prominence in the 1420s.

Such developments suggest that the fifteenth century was, for St Andrews, a final period of major change that altered and added to the character of the church and city before the Reformation. The most lasting of these changes was the university. As Norman Reid proves, scholars had been in residence well before the burgh was founded, and it is clear that an active intellectual population thrived in the town. Reassessing the extant evidence, Reid concludes that there was a significant level of organised education taking place in St Andrews by the eleventh century and that this was more than simply devotional study of canons or culdees within cloisters. Reid suggests instead that the university was a gradual development out of an existing *universitas*, an academically active community that was there from before the foundation of the burgh, perhaps making St Andrews the earliest centre of higher learning in Britain and not just Scotland's first university. Under the leadership of Bishop Henry Wardlaw, a charter of privileges was granted to the masters in early 1412, with the papal bull arriving the following year, formally ratifying the foundation. The bishops ran the university and its medieval inheritance is significant, from the rich collection of incunabula housed in the University Library to the remarkable collection of three fifteenth-century silver maces, explored in depth here by Julian Luxford, as objects held in reverence for their antiquity, but also as evocative reminders of the past, of the vitality of material display in an age where an object could represent the single purpose of the founders, masters and scholars striving to attain enlightenment.

The early university, small though it was, had a considerable impact on St Andrews. The endowment of the institution and especially the foundation of St Salvator's College by Bishop James Kennedy in 1450 altered the physical layout of the burgh. As Bess Rhodes points out, along with the new friaries and Holy Trinity, the construction of St Salvator's chapel established church buildings on all the entries into the burgh from the west. Attracting masters and students may have partly replaced the dwindling flow of pilgrims, a shift illustrated in 1512 when the pilgrims' hospice was transformed into student accommodation for St Leonard's College. In his chapter Roger Mason considers the nature of this in the context of the foundation of two further universities in Scotland in the fifteenth century and wider, revolutionary trends in university learning throughout Europe. What Mason makes clear is that St Andrews was plugged directly into Continental intellectual circles and he observes that the foundation of the university did not hinder, but instead promoted, intellectual exchange beyond Scotland. Katie Stevenson sees this aspect as a key factor in the spread

---

[63] Robert N. Swanson, *Church and Society in Late Medieval England* (Oxford, 1989), pp. 287–90.

of heretical and heterodox thinking and the enthusiasm for its detection, placing St Andrews at the heart of the inquisition in Scotland. She argues that because of the distinctive characteristics of the town, including the range of ecclesiastical institutions and the university, this made St Andrews an obvious focal point for reformist thinkers and for those who wished to counteract the threat. Detection and teaching were significant parts of clerical life in late medieval St Andrews and the foundation of the Dominican and Franciscan houses, whose orders had long-standing roles as teachers and inquisitors, may also reflect heightened concerns about education and orthodoxy.

St Andrews was the chief site of the medieval Scottish church and one of the centres which defined the kingdom. The bishops were finally given archiepiscopal rank in 1472 and made primates of Scotland.[64] Though opposed by other prelates and countered by the elevation of Glasgow in 1492, their status confirmed a claim which had been made since the twelfth century. Further evidence of the pre-eminence of St Andrews had been demonstrated in the formal recognition that the prior of St Andrews was the senior head of a religious house in Scotland. The wealth and standing of its prelates, the international prestige of its cult, the scale and design of its cathedral and, in comparison with other ecclesiastical settlements, the size of its burgh all raised St Andrews above all Scottish counterparts in status and power. However, the elements mentioned above and examined more fully in this volume were not unique but occurred in other settings in ecclesiastical centres across the insular world and other parts of northern Europe. Consideration of some of these can highlight the character and role of St Andrews as well as external models for its development.

An obvious model for early medieval St Andrews can be found in Armagh whose claims to primacy in Ireland rested on its authority over the cult of St Patrick. These claims were asserted in the seventh century, prior to those of Cennrígmonaid over Andrew. Armagh's complex layout, with multiple enclosures and churches, a 'sacred way' leading pilgrims to the shrine and a house of *céli Dé*, suggests a form of Irish ecclesiastical centre which may have influenced the early character of St Andrews.[65] Though, like St Andrews, Armagh also underwent change after 1100 to bring it into greater conformity with the reformed church, new ecclesiastical influences at this time reached Fife from the south rather than the west.[66] An obvious model, and comparator, for this reformed St Andrews was its immediate neighbour to the south, the bishopric

---

[64] L. J. MacFarlane, 'The Primacy of the Scottish Church 1472–1521', *Innes Review* 20 (1969), pp. 111–29.

[65] T. M. Charles-Edwards, *Early Christian Ireland* (Cambridge, 2000), pp. 416–40; K. Hughes, 'The Irish Church, 800–1050', *New History of Ireland*, i: *Prehistoric and Early Ireland*, ed. D. Ó Cróinín (Oxford, 2005), pp. 635–55; R. Stalley, 'Ecclesiastical Architecture before 1169', in ibid., pp. 714–43, 716–21, 725, 733; N. B. Aitchison, *Armagh and the Royal Centres in Early Medieval Ireland: Monuments, Cosmology and the Past* (Woodbridge, 1994).

[66] J. A. Watts, *The Church in Medieval Ireland* (Dublin, 1972), pp. 9–24; M. T. Flanagan, *The Transformation of the Irish Church in the Twelfth Century* (Woodbridge, 2010), pp. 101–2.

of Durham. Durham's significance rested on the shrine of Cuthbert, which conferred status and attracted pilgrims. It underwent reform a generation before St Andrews, when its secular clergy were replaced with a monastic community which served the cathedral. The prior of this house, Turgot, would serve the Scottish royal dynasty and bring reform to St Andrews as its bishop. A monastic cathedral, rebuilt in the new style, with an adjacent episcopal castle, suggests a similar plan to St Andrews.[67] The powers of the prince bishops over their palatinate also suggest some similarity with the regality rights developed by the bishops over their temporalities in Fife.[68] However, Durham did not develop a significant, self-governing urban centre. The settlement below the castle and cathedral did not receive the rights and status accorded to St Andrews.[69] More importantly, the future of the bishop and church of Durham was as a diocese far removed from the centres of royal government, very different to the centrality of the diocese and prelates based in St Andrews.

On the broad level, comparisons for late medieval St Andrews can be identified in every realm or major principality of northern Europe. While clearly different from the episcopal principalities of the Low Countries and the Rhineland, there were many ecclesiastical centres which possessed their own powers of temporal jurisdiction, were physically removed from royal or princely courts and associated with significant, though usually secondary, urban communities. Fewer of these cities developed universities before 1500. Most late medieval universities were founded in centres of princely power, like Prague, Krakow, Heidelberg, Nantes and Copenhagen, or, like in Cologne and Rostock, by urban initiative.[70] As a fifteenth-century episcopal foundation, St Andrews University had few counterparts. One of these, Uppsala in Sweden, provides an interesting comparison. It was situated in the principal see of its kingdom, whose status and location developed in the twelfth century in association with its role as the shrine of a martyred saint, in this case St Erik. The university was founded in 1477 by local clergy led by Archbishop Jakob Ulfsson Örnefot at a time of weakened and disputed authority. Distinct, but not far from, the centres of Swedish kingship at Stockholm and Kalmar, Uppsala's medieval development suggests parallels with that of St Andrews.[71]

---

[67] Matthew, 'Durham in the Anglo-Norman World', pp. 7–16; J. Crook, 'The Architectural Setting of the Cult of St Cuthbert in Durham Cathedral', *Anglo-Norman Durham 1093–1193*, ed. D. Rollason, M. Harvey and M. Prestwich, pp. 235–50; E. C. Fernie, 'The Architectural Influence of Durham Cathedral', in ibid., pp. 269–82; P. Dalton, 'Scottish Influence on Durham 1066–1214', in ibid., pp. 339–52. For the later medieval priory see R. B. Dobson, *Durham Priory 1400–1450* (London, 1973).

[68] C. Liddy, *The Bishopric of Durham in the Late Middle Ages: Lordship, Community and the Cult of Cuthbert* (Woodbridge, 2008).

[69] Margaret Bonney, *Lordship and the Urban Community: Durham and its Overlords 1250–1540* (Cambridge, 1990).

[70] A. B. Cobban, *The Medieval Universities: Their Development and Organisation* (London, 1975), pp. 118–19.

[71] *The Cambridge History of Scandinavia*, i: *Prehistory to 1520*, ed. K. Helle (Cambridge, 2003), pp. 225, 229, 392–3, 534–5, 673–5.

The St Andrews depicted in the Geddy map reflected a history of growing status and scale which spanned the eight centuries from 750 to 1550. The landscape of wide streets and clustered spacious houses, of great ecclesiastical buildings, especially the spires of Holy Trinity, St Salvator's and St Regulus and the huge cathedral which dominated the image, of the archbishop's castle on the cliffs and the surrounding well-populated seascape, depicted different aspects of this glorious history. It also depicted a recent revolution which, in a matter of weeks, had shattered foundations laid down over centuries. In the words of Bess Rhodes, 'in the spring of 1559 St Andrews was still a functioning Catholic city. By the end of the summer the burgh had become a bastion of the Protestant cause.'[72] The preaching of John Knox in Holy Trinity Church between 11 and 14 June marked the beginning of a planned attack on the institutions of Scotland's ecclesiastical capital. This change altered all aspects of the medieval city. The archbishop was forced to flee, leaving his castle occupied by the reformers. The friaries were sacked and partially demolished. The cathedral priory was also attacked and 'put down' and the books and sculptures of the community destroyed. The relics which had formed the centre of devotion at the site for eight centuries were removed or destroyed. The life of the Augustinian house effectively ended. Over the next few years, the possessions and revenues of these houses in and beyond St Andrews were assigned to, or uplifted by, other individuals or bodies. This change was not just an external assault. Its architect, James Stewart, the bastard son of James V, held the office of prior of St Andrews. Moreover, the attacks had support from a sizeable group of St Andrews burgesses, whose motives may, in part, reflect tensions between the urban community and its overlords.[73] For St Andrews, however, the events of 1559 marked the end not just of its pre-Reformation history, but of its history as a major centre of power and spirituality.

Its revived fortunes lay several centuries in the future. The reasons for one part of this revival would have surprised both the reformers and their opponents but were not unknown to them. In 1552, just seven years before he was expelled from his seat, Archbishop John Hamilton received a licence from the provost and community of St Andrews concerning the use of the unfruitful dunes north-west of the burgh by the River Eden. This allowed him to 'plant' rabbits 'within the northe pairt of thair commond Linkis nixt adjacent to the watter of Eddin'. However, he reserved to the community all other right and possession n of the links

> baith in pastoring of their guds, casting and lading of divattis and scherettis to thair uis and profitt, playing at golf, futball, schuting at all gamis, with all uther maner of pastyme as ever thai plais.[74]

---

[72] E. Rhodes, 'The Reformation in the Burgh of St Andrews: Property, Piety and Power' (unpublished PhD thesis, University of St Andrews, 2013), p. 85.

[73] For these events see Rhodes, 'Reformation in St Andrews', pp. 85–116; Jane Dawson, '"The Face of Ane Perfyt Reformed Kyrk": St Andrews and the Early Scottish Reformation', *Humanism and Reform: Essays in Honour of James K. Cameron*, ed. J. Kirk (Oxford, 1991), pp. 413–35.

[74] StAUL, msdep106/1.

While it would be stretching matters to suggest that a dispute over access to the burgesses' playing grounds, or even the impact of the archbishop's rabbits on the rules of golf, might have shaped the history of St Andrews, it cannot be denied that, to much of the world, St Andrews today is less the town, let alone the shrine, than these 'commond Linkis' which were already used for 'playing at golf'.

CHAPTER TWO

From Cinrigh Monai to Civitas Sancti Andree: A Star is Born

Simon Taylor

THIS chapter has as its focus the earliest written material concerning the place now known as St Andrews, from the mid eighth century to the end of the twelfth. Because of the nature both of the sources and the place, this material is overwhelmingly ecclesiastical in context and content. However, the Christian, ecclesiastical story of St Andrews begins already in the pre-documentary, archaeological record. Excavations have revealed early Christian long cist cemeteries both beside St Mary's Collegiate Church on the headland above the harbour (at Kirkheugh) and at Hallow Hill, a low hill bounded on three sides by burns, the Kinness Burn on the north and the Cairnsmill Burn on the west and south-west, just over 2km south-west of the St Andrews cathedral complex.[1] The earliest documentary reference to the place now known as St Andrews comes in 747 when 'the death of Tuathalán abbot of Kinrymont' is recorded in the Annals of Ulster.[2] Already by this time the place must have been of more than local importance, since this reference occurs in a source probably written in Brega (east central Ireland) and is a rare instance of interest shown by these annals in a Pictish religious house.[3] The St Andrews sarcophagus, one of the finest pieces of early medieval sculpture from northern Europe, discovered in 1833 at the heart of the early church precinct, probably dates to only a short

---

[1] At NO493156; see E. Proudfoot et al., 'Excavations at the Long Cist Cemetery on Hallow Hill, St Andrews, Fife, 1975–7', *PSAS* 126 (1996), pp. 387–454. Hallow Hill is probably Eglesnamin, one of the core lands granted to St Andrews Priory by Bishop Robert on the priory's foundation in 1140. For this identification, see Proudfoot et al., ibid., pp. 391–8. For a full discussion of the names Eglesnamin, containing the Pictish church-element *egles*, and Hallow Hill, see *PNF*, iii, pp. 466–7, p. 473.

[2] *Annals of Ulster (to 1131)*, ed. S. Mac Airt and G. Mac Niocaill (Dublin, 1983), p. 202. Also found in the Annals of Tigernach: 'The Annals of Tigernach. Third fragment, A.D. 489–766', ed. W. Stokes, *Revue Celtique* 17 (1896), pp. 119–263, at p. 249. Its appearance in both the Annals of Ulster and the Annals of Tigernach means that it was part of the 'Chronicle of Ireland', for which see T. Charles-Edwards, *The Chronicle of Ireland*, 2 vols (Liverpool, 2006).

[3] It is possible that a Pictish source was informing the Chronicle of Ireland at this time (Nick Evans, pers. comm.); Charles-Edwards, *The Chronicle of Ireland*, i, pp. 9–15.

Figure 2.1: Long Cist Cemetery. The Hallow Hill Excavation, St Andrews.

time after this annal reference and is further proof of the very high status of the place in this period.[4]

There are no secure references to Kinrymont for the ninth century, although the fifteenth-century historians Andrew Wyntoun and Walter Bower, both following an account (now lost) drawn up at an earlier date at St Andrews, name Cellach as the first bishop of St Andrews and state that he held this office from the time of King Giric (878–89).[5] A more secure reference to a Bishop Cellach concerns the year 906, when he presided with Constantine son of Aodh (Cústantin mac Aeda) over an assembly in Scone.[6] It is probably correct to assume that Cellach was based at St Andrews, although, as with other later and better-attested bishops of St Andrews who are styled variously bishop of Alba or bishop of the Scots, his office had national rather than merely local diocesan significance. The death of Mael Dúin in 1055, who, as the donor of the church of Markinch in Fife to the Culdees of Lochleven is styled bishop of St Andrews, is recorded in the Annals of Tigernach in glowing terms.[7] A remarkable letter written by Nicholas of Evesham, prior of Worcester, to Eadmer of Canterbury, who was bishop-elect of St Andrews in 1120, and was caught between the competing claims of the archbishops of Canterbury and York for archiepiscopal authority over the Scottish Church, as well as Alexander I's determination that St Andrews should be the seat of Scotland's own archbishop, argued against York and for Alexander's position: 'Since the leader of St Andrew[s] is called

---

[4] For more see Sally Foster, ed., *The St Andrews Sarcophagus* (Dublin, 1998).
[5] *Scotichronicon*, ii, p. 318; iii, pp. 342, 461–2.
[6] Chronicle of the Kings of Alba; original Latin text M. O. Anderson, *Kings and Kingship in Early Scotland* (first edition, 1973; revised edition, Edinburgh, 1980, which supplies all the references in this chapter; first edition 1973), pp. 249–53 at p. 251; translation B. T. Hudson, '"The Scottish Chronicle"', *SHR* 77 (1998), pp. 129–61.
[7] 'The Annals of Tigernach', p. 397; translation from A. O Anderson, *Early Sources of Scottish History, AD 500 to 1268*, 2 vols (Edinburgh, 1922; reprinted with preface, bibliographical supplement and corrections by M. O. Anderson, Stamford, 1990), i, p. 599; *St A. Liber*, p. 116.

"chief bishop of the Scots", he is indeed "chief" in no other way but that he is over others. And how is he over other bishops if what he is is not an archbishop?'[8] The position of the bishop of St Andrews within the Scottish Church is also succinctly expressed in the mid twelfth-century Augustinian Account (see Appendix 2). Writing of the election of Robert as 'bishop of the Scots' in 1124, the author (almost certainly another Robert, the first prior of the Augustinian house of St Andrews) goes on:

> Indeed from ancient times they have been called the bishops of St Andrew[s], and in both ancient and modern writings they are found called 'High Archbishops' or 'High Bishops of the Scots'. Which is why Bishop Fothad, a man of the greatest authority, caused to be written on the cover of a gospel-book these lines:
> Fothad, who is the High Bishop to the Scots,
> made this cover for an ancestral gospel-book.[9]
> So now in ordinary and common speech they are called *Escop Alban*, that is 'Bishops of Alba'. And they have been called, and are (still) called this on account of their pre-eminence by all the bishops of the Scots, who are called after the places over which they preside.[10]

King Constantine (Cústantín mac Aeda), already mentioned in connection with Bishop Cellach, ruled for much of the first half of the tenth century. In his old age he is said to have resigned the kingship and retired into religion to serve the Lord, handing over the kingdom to Malcolm son of Donald (Mael Coluim mac Domnaill).[11] Though the *Chronicle of the Kings of Alba* does not name the place of retirement, the author of the late eleventh-century *Prophecy of Berchán* leaves us in no doubt that he believed it to be St Andrews, stating that Constantine retired 'to the church on the brow of the wave; in the house of the apostle he will die'.[12] Most explicit of all are the notes on individual kings, probably added to a Scottish regnal list between about 1105 and 1165, which state that Constantine, having reigned forty years, resigned the kingdom and

---

[8] Cambridge, Corpus Christi College, MS 371, pp. 8–9, written in Eadmer's own hand. See also A. O. Anderson, *Scottish Annals from English Chroniclers, 500 to 1286* (London, 1908; reprinted with foreword, bibliographical supplement and corrections by M. O. Anderson, Stamford, 1991), p. 144 n. 2. Nicholas may well have been one of the two Canterbury monks with Eadmer in St Andrews in the summer of 1120 (ibid. p. 144).

[9] This verse is also quoted in *Scotichronicon*, iii, p. 343 and translated into Scots by Wyntoun, both of whom attribute it to Fothad I, bishop of St Andrews in the mid tenth century. However, it might equally well be Fothad II (died 1093).

[10] For a detailed account of the bishops of St Andrews (and of Alba) before Bishop Robert, see M. O. Anderson, 'The Celtic Church in Kinrimund', McRoberts, *St Andrews* [reprint of article which first appeared in *Innes Review* 25 (1974), pp. 67–76], pp. 1–10; and D. E. R. Watt, ed., *Series Episcoporum Ecclesiae Catholicae Occidentalis ab initio usque ad Annum MCXCVIII* Series VI, Britannia Tomus I Ecclesia Scoticana (Stuttgart, 1991), pp. 77–83.

[11] Chronicle of the Kings of Alba (M. O. Anderson, *Kings and Kingship*, 1980, p. 251).

[12] See B. T. Hudson, *Prophecy of Berchán: Irish and Scottish High-Kings in the Early Middle Ages* (Westport, Connecticut and London, 1996) for the most recent edition and translation of this enigmatic and difficult text.

spent his last five years as abbot of the Culdees of St Andrews, and on his death was buried there.[13]

The next mention of Kinrymont is also the first indication that it was a place not only of pilgrimage but of pilgrimage on an international scale. Again the source is an Irish annal entry, this time for 965. This states that 'Aodh son of Maolmithigh (Aed mac Maíl Mithig) died on pilgrimage, that is in Kinrymont'.[14]

The final quarter of the tenth century produces another piece of evidence of Kinrymont's key national, and perhaps also international, status: this is its inclusion in the introduction to the remarkable *Life of Cathróe*. Cathróe was a Scottish cleric born in the early tenth century, who around 940 settled in Flanders. Someone in the Belgian monastic milieu that Cathróe had inhabited wrote his *Life* shortly after his death in the 970s, drawing on contemporary Scottish material.[15] The introduction contains the following passage:

> Several years passed [after the Scottish settlement in Ireland] and they [the Scots] crossed over the sea that is beside them, and occupied the island of *Eu*, which is now called Iona. Not resting there, they passed the neighbouring sea of Britain, and over the river *Rosis*, and settled the district of Ross. They went also to Rymont and Bellethor, situated far apart from each other, and overcame them, to hold them [ever after]. And thus they called the whole land Scotia [which previously had been] called by its own name *Chorischia*.[16]

From Kinrymont to St Andrews

ONE of the great questions regarding early medieval St Andrews is when did the relics believed to be those of St Andrew the Apostle first come to be venerated there? It is quite possible that the exceptionally high profile of the place as a religious centre from the earliest reference in 747 onwards is due to the fact that Andrew's relics were already thought to be there. The St Andrews Foundation Accounts would certainly have us believe that the apostle's bones were brought here during the reign of a king called Ungus, who is probably to be

---

[13] 'Constantine makEdha xl a[nnis] reg[navit] et dimisso regno sponte deo in habitu religionis abbas factus est in keldeorum sancti Andree quinque annis servivit ibi et mortuus est ac sepultus', M. O. Anderson's Regnal List D (*Kings and Kingship*, p. 267). The same or a similar note appears in other mss of group X, for which see ibid. pp. 274–5 (F), 283 (I), pp. 290–1 (N). For Marjorie Anderson's Group X, see ibid. pp. 52 ff. See also A. O. Anderson, *Early Sources* i, p. 447. See also Dauvit Broun, *The Irish Identity of the Kingdom of the Scots in the Twelfth and Thirteenth Centuries* (Woodbridge, 1999), pp. 153–60 for a different view of the king-list development.

[14] A. O. Anderson, *Early Sources* i, p. 472, from *Chronicon Scotorum*.

[15] See A. O. Anderson, *Early Sources* i, p. lxxiii for details of editions and a note on authorship; pp. 431–43 for a long extract (in translation) and summary. For St Cathróe, see D. N. Dumville, 'St Cathróe of Metz and the hagiography of Exoticism', *Studies in Irish Hagiography: Saints and Scholars*, ed. J. Carey, M. Herbert and P. Ó Riain (Dublin, 2001), pp. 172–88.

[16] *Chronicles of the Picts: Chronicles of the Scots*, ed. W. F. Skene (Edinburgh, 1867), p. 108.

identified with Unuist I son of Urguist (Angus son of Fergus), king of the Picts c.729–61. However, there is no absolute proof that there was any Andrew cult at St Andrews before the late eleventh century. Even if the above-mentioned *Prophecy of Berchán*'s reference to the house of the apostle cannot be taken as evidence for the tenth century, it can certainly be taken as evidence that there was an Andrew cult at St Andrews at the time it was written in the 1090s. The *Life of Margaret*, queen of Scots from c.1070 to 1093, written by her confessor Turgot, prior of Durham and later, from 1109 to 1115, bishop of St Andrews, is the earliest of the flurry of texts which testify to the importance of St Andrews as a centre of the cult of St Andrew in the final quarter of the eleventh century. It is also one of the most explicit and revealing. Turgot, in his lengthy account of the good works of his saintly heroine, wrote:

> And because the church of St Andrew is frequented by the religious devotion of visitors from the peoples round about, she had built dwellings upon either shore of the sea which divides Lothian from Scotland, so that pilgrims and poor might turn aside there to rest, after the labour of the journey; and might find there ready everything that necessity might require for the restoration of the body. She appointed attendants for this purpose alone, to have always ready all that was needed for guests, and to wait upon them with great care. She provided for them also ships, to carry them across, both going and returning, without ever demanding any price for the passage from those who were to be taken over.[17]

What Turgot is describing here are the beginnings of the royally endowed ferry service across the Forth at Queensferry.[18] In an earlier passage, Turgot also recounts that 'similarly also she has left signs of her faith and holy devotion in other churches [besides Dunfermline]; for instance the church of St Andrew(s), as may be seen today, preserves a most elegant image of a crucifix, which she herself erected there'.[19]

In the same decade as Margaret's death there is the first explicit evidence from beyond the kingdom of Scotland for the cult of Andrew at St Andrews. In the *Vita Cadoci*, the *Life* of the sixth-century Welsh St Cadoc, written by Lifris of Llancarfan in Glamorgan in the late 1090s, Cadoc travelled 'with three disciples into Scotland and approached the threshold of the aforementioned church

---

[17] This translation is taken from A. O. Anderson, *Early Sources* ii, p. 77, which is based on Turgot's Latin Life of Margaret, *Vita Margaretae Reginae*, published in *Symeonis Dunelmensis Opera et Collectanea*, ed. J. Hodgson Hinde (Surtees Society 51, 1868), p. 247. For a modern translation see Lois L. Huneycutt, *Matilda of Scotland: A Study in Medieval Queenship* (Woodbridge, 2003), pp. 172–3.

[18] For a good account of the pilgrimage routes to St Andrews, see McRoberts, *St Andrews*, pp. 98–9.

[19] Adapted from A. O. Anderson, *Early Sources* ii, p. 65. Two manuscript copies of the *Life of Margaret* are extant: London, British Library [hereafter BL], Cotton Tiberius, D.iii, which was much injured in a fire at the British Museum, and another version copied in the fifteenth century at Dunfermline and surviving as Madrid Biblioteca del Palacio Real, II 2097, fos 26–41v.

of the blessed Andrew'.[20] Lifris himself was well connected within the upper echelons of the insular Church, since he was the son of Herwald, chief bishop in south-east Wales from 1056 to 1104.[21] He would have been aware of the growing importance of St Andrews as an international pilgrimage centre, which is no doubt why he has his saint-hero pay a visit there, and perhaps also the audience of the *Vita* would have expected it.

About the same time, Reginald of Durham in his *Life of St Godric of Finchale* (written in the 1170s) states that Godric as a young man on his travels as a merchant frequently visited 'that famous house of St Andrew the Apostle'. Godric was born c.1069, so this would probably place his visits in the 1090s. Reginald's intention was to emphasise the piety of the young merchant, but incidentally he also provides an early reference not only to St Andrews as a place of pilgrimage with specifically Andrean connections, but also to St Andrews as an international trading centre. The growth of the apostolic cult would no doubt have greatly stimulated trade, which in turn would have helped spread the word about the cult along the trade-routes of northern Europe.

While all these sources (except the *Life of Cathróe*) emphasise Kinrymont's religious importance, there is one later eleventh-century reference that may allude only to its status as a trading centre. This is a line in the Middle Gaelic poem on the legendary birth-tale of the sixth-century kings Aedán mac Gabráin and Brandub mac Echach of Leinster. It dates from the early part of Malcolm III's reign (1058–93) and may well have been written for recitation at his court.[22] It relates how Aedán was born near the Forth, which lay at the heart of Gabrán's kingdom, while Gabrán is away 'uniting kingdoms'. Later in the poem Aedán is addressed as *rí Forthe na fledol* ('king of Forth of the carousal'). These references to the Forth are almost certainly for the benefit of Malcolm, one of whose chief residences was at Dunfermline. In verse 34 Gabrán is addressed by his druid as *rí Monaid in marggaid* ('king of Monad of the market'). This is almost certainly a reference to, even a word-play on, Kinrymont (Cenn Rí(g)monaid), stressing not only its royal status but also its importance as a market-place many decades before the establishment of the burgh there by Bishop Robert, with the support of King David, in the 1140s.[23]

This reference also reminds us of another aspect of the place, which, like its trade, tends to become eclipsed by its religious status: that is its royal connections. These are expressed at the most basic level by the name Kinrymont itself,

---

[20] A. W. Wade-Evans, *Vitae Sanctorum Britanniae et Genealogiae* (Cardiff, 1944), p. 82.
[21] Ibid., xi.
[22] M. A. O'Brien, 'A Middle-Irish Poem on the Birth of Áedán mac Gabráin and Brandub mac Echach', *Eriu* 16 (1952), pp. 157–70. Another translation appears in T. O. Clancy, ed., *The Triumph Tree: Scotland's Earliest Poetry, AD 550–1350* (Edinburgh, 1998), pp. 178–82.
[23] For a recent reassessment of the politics, both local and national, surrounding the founding of the episcopal burgh of St Andews by Bishop Robert, see M. H. Hammond, 'The Bishop, the Prior, and the Founding of the Burgh of St Andrews', *Innes Review* 66:1 (2015), pp. 72–101.

Figure 2.2: The Sarcophagus, St Andrews Cathedral.

the 'end or head of the king's upland or muir', a name which cannot be later than the mid eighth century, and which was presumably a Gaelicisation of a Pictish name, *Penn Ri Monad or the like. The eponymous upland or muir (G *monadh*) is probably the whole upland area between St Andrews (Kilrymont) and Crail, with Kilrymont at the north-west end. The south-east section of the upland above Crail, and stretching towards Dunino, is still known as Kingsmuir, the Scots equivalent of *Ríg monad*.[24]

The St Andrews Sarcophagus also testifies to Pictish royal patronage, perhaps even a royal place of burial.[25] The name of the saint who brought the relics of St Andrew to Kilrymont is Regulus, which is Latin for 'little king'. According to the longer Foundation Account B (FAB) there may have been a royal nunnery at Kilrymont first presided over by Mouren, daughter of Hungus (Unuist) king of the Picts.[26] The shorter Foundation Account (FAA) mentions in passing the fact that at the time of writing (c.1100) there was a king's hall somewhere near the church precinct.

The most extended and eloquent testimony to, as well as advertisement for, the cult of Andrew at St Andrews was written at around the same time as Godric was a regular visitor to the relics. This is the Foundation Account A (FAA) (see

---

[24] The name is discussed by W. J. Watson, *The History of the Celtic Place-Names of Scotland* (Edinburgh and London, 1926; reprinted with an introduction by Simon Taylor, Edinburgh 2004; and, with an extended introduction, Edinburgh, 2011), pp. 396–8; and *PNF*, iii, under Kilrymont and Kingsmuir.

[25] See *The St Andrews Sarcophagus*, ed. S. Foster (Dublin, 1998).

[26] See Appendices 1 and 2.

Appendix 1), written by the local church hierarchy to promote not only the cult of St Andrew at St Andrews, but also the church of St Andrews' claim to be the archiepiscopal seat of the kingdom of the Scots.[27] It underlines just how cosmopolitan St Andrews was (or at least aspired to be) at this time. Having described how Regulus had brought some of the bones of Andrew from the eastern Mediterranean to east Fife, and with the support of Ungus king of the Picts had established a church at Kinrymont, the Account goes on:

> For pilgrims come together to this city, palmers from Jerusalem – Romans, Greeks, Armenians, Teutons, Germans, Saxons, Danes, Gauls, English, Britons; men and women; rich and poor; the healthy and the sick; the lame and the blind; and the weak, brought here on horse and in carts.

For various reasons, not least that of increased production and survival of written sources, the Andrew cult at St Andrews seems to have experienced a surge of popularity and promotion in the late eleventh century. It is extremely unlikely that the cult itself was a creation of this period: such international fame and such sweeping claims could scarcely have been conjured up out of a parvenu tradition at this relatively late date. There is little doubt that the Andrew cult was already long established on the coast of north-east Fife by the time of the first explicit evidence of that cult. Yet the question remains, and may always remain, as to just how long-established it was. A recent article by James Fraser tentatively suggests that a church dedicated to Andrew was founded at Kinrymont by Naiton king of the Picts in the second decade of the eighth century.[28] While admitting to the fragility of such exact dating, Fraser very usefully places the foundation both within the immediate political context of the time, as far as the fragmentary sources allow us to piece this together, and within a wider pattern of binary Petrine and Andrean dedications found elsewhere in early medieval Christendom.[29] An argument based on this dedication pattern still holds good even if the time-frame for the foundation of Kinrymont is advanced by a few decades to the reign of Unust son of Uurguist (732–61). St Andrews tradition itself, as embodied in the two Foundation Accounts, certainly points to this king as the prime mover in the establishment of the church here, and such historical evidence as exists for this is well marshalled by Alex Woolf.[30]

---

[27] For full details see Dauvit Broun, 'The Church of St Andrews and its Foundation Legend in the Early Twelfth Century: Recovering the Full Text of Version A of the Foundation Legend', *Kings, Clerics and Chronicles in Scotland, 500–1297*, ed. Simon Taylor (Dublin, 2000), pp. 108–14.

[28] James E. Fraser, 'Rochester, Hexham and Cennrígmonaid: The Movements of St Andrew in Britain, 604–747', *Saints' Cults in the Celtic World*, ed. S. Boardman, J. R. Davies and E. Williamson (Woodbridge, 2009), pp. 1–17.

[29] The Petrine dedications are to be found in northern Scotland, around Burghead in Moray and Rosemarkie in the Black Isle, Ross & Cromarty. For details, see Fraser, 'Movements', pp. 13–14, 15–16.

[30] Alex Woolf, 'Onuist Son of Uurguist: *tyrannus carnifex* or a David for the Picts?', *Æthelbald and Offa: Two Eighth-Century Kings of Mercia*, ed. D. Hill and M. Worthington, British Archaeological Reports, British Series 383 (Oxford, 2005), pp. 35–42, at p. 39.

If this eighth-century foundation was dedicated to Andrew from the outset, as seems likely, then it is quite possible that relics of the saint were acquired at the same time, as part of the process and ritual of foundation. The important church at Hexham in Northumberland, founded by Bishop Wilfred in 674, was dedicated to Andrew, and possessed certain relics of the apostle. It was also the seat of a bishopric from 678.[31] 150 years ago W. F. Skene proposed that the cult of St Andrew, along with his relics, was brought to Pictland by Acca, bishop of Hexham, when he went into exile in 732.[32] This argument has been endorsed more recently by Alex Woolf, who suggests that Kinrymont may even have been a daughter house of Hexham.[33]

Foundation Accounts

THE remarkable Foundation Accounts were compiled in St Andrews in the first half of the twelfth century and are known variously as the shorter Foundation Account (or Foundation Account A, FAA) and the longer Foundation Account (or Foundation Account B, FAB), which forms a single entity with the Augustinian Account. The earlier of these texts is FAA. Dauvit Broun has identified three twelfth-century manuscripts in which it has survived.[34] Previously only two medieval copies were known to modern scholarship,[35] that in British Library Additional 25014 fos 118vb–119vb, dated to the late twelfth century (N), and that in Paris, Bibliothèque Nationale MS latin 4126 (known as the Poppleton Manuscript) fos 31r–32r (P), written around 1360.[36] The newly identified manuscripts are British Library Arundel MS 36, fos 15vb–16va (pencil), dating to the second half of the twelfth century (A); and British Library Cotton Tiberius MS D iii, fos 93rb–94ra, dating to the end of twelfth century or possibly the beginning of the thirteenth (C).[37]

The foundation text tells the story of how St Andrew's corporeal relics came to be at St Andrews, thereby justifying claims that St Andrews is a second Rome and worthy to be the seat of an archbishopric of all Scotia (that is Scotland north of the Forth).

---

[31] *Bede's Ecclesiastical History of the English People*, ed. and trans. Bertram Colgrave and R. A. B. Mynors (Oxford, 1969), iv, ch. 12.
[32] William F. Skene, 'Notice of the Early Ecclesiastical Settlements at St Andrews', *PSAS* 4 (1862), pp. 300–21 at pp. 312–16.
[33] Woolf, 'Onuist Son of Uurguist', p. 38.
[34] Broun, 'The Church of St Andrews and its Foundation Legend', pp. 109–10.
[35] In *PNF*, iii, p. 412, I wrongly stated that only one such was known (P), including N in the list of those newly identified by Broun.
[36] See M. O. Anderson, *Kings and Kingship*, pp. 235–60.
[37] See Broun, 'The Church of St Andrews and its Foundation Legend', pp. 108–14. There are two manuscript copies of longer or fuller versions of the Life of Margaret. For more see Alice Taylor, 'Historical Writing in Twelfth- and Thirteenth-Century Scotland: The Dunfermline Compilation', *Historical Research* 83 (2010), pp. 228–52, at p. 229 n. 7.

Thereupon he [Regulus] came [from Constantinople, with St Andrew's relics] with an angel attending and guarding his way, [and] he arrived successfully at the top of the king's hill, that is *Rithmonut*. The same hour in which he had encamped there, tired, with his seven companions, a divine light shone around the king [Ungus] of the Picts who was coming with his army [from his victory over the peoples of southern Britain] to a special place which is called *Cartenan*. And they fell on their faces, unable to bear the brightness. And the lame and blind were healed to the number of seven. And one man, blind from birth, received his sight; and then he saw a place filled with a visitation of angels, and at once called out in a loud voice, saying: 'behold, I see a place filled with a visitation of angels!' Finally, according to God's design, the king came with his army to the place which the Lord showed the blind man to whom He had given sight. Regulus, a monk from the city of Constantinople, indeed, met the king at the gate called *Matha*, that is *Mordurus*, with the relics of St Andrew the apostle which he had brought with him thence [from Constantinople] to this place. And citizens and foreigners exchanged greetings, and put up their tents there, where the king's hall now is. King Ungus, indeed, gave this place and this city to Almighty God and to St Andrew the apostle in freedom for ever, that it might be the head and mother of all churches which are in the kingdom of the Scots.[38]

It is not clear from the narrative where *Cartenan* might be: it could be anywhere between the place of the king's victory (perhaps as far afield as Mercia in the English Midlands) and St Andrews.[39] However, given the strong focus on St Andrews itself in the second part of FAA, it is likely to be in the immediate environs. It is just possible that it is an early form of Carron, a small settlement that lay on the old main route from the south-west (the Bishop's Road), within about 3km of St Andrews Cathedral. The 'gate called *Matha* that is *Mordurus*' was probably the main entrance into the church complex or precinct around the cathedral and St Regulus Church (formerly St Andrew's Church). In the final section of FAA, which Dauvit Broun has reinstated as an integral part of the original text, we are told that Regulus and his companions, having been given Kinrymont as the site of their church, to house the relics of St Andrew, lived a monastic life there and 'planted vegetable gardens where there is now the house of Master Samuel and his ancestors and successors' and that they made a mill with their own hands and built everything which belongs honourably and honestly to the monks.[40] Samuel, whose title of 'master' marks him out as a scholar and teacher, was clearly an important figure in the St Andrews (and thus in the Scottish) Church around 1100, and may even have been the Samuel for

---

[38] From an unpublished edition and translation by Dauvit Broun, acknowledged with thanks. The place-name forms are from A, with variant readings from C, N and P where appropriate.

[39] *campum Mercie*, A, C; *merc*, N, P. This could represent either Mercia in the English Midlands or the Merse, an area roughly equivalent to later Berwickshire. Alex Woolf argues that it represents the former, being a reference to a dimly remembered campaign that Unust son of Uurguist led jointly with King Eadberht of Northumbria against Æthelbald of Mercia in 756. Woolf, 'Onuist Son of Uurguist', p. 39.

[40] Broun, 'The Church of St Andrews and its Foundation Legend', pp. 108–14.

whom one of the recensions of the early medieval *Historia Britonum* was written.[41] Apart from Archbishop Giric, Macbethad and Gregory, the three leading clerics at St Andrews (or even in the Scottish Church), Samuel is the only other contemporary figure to be mentioned in FAA, and it is possible that, as a conspicuous man of learning, he was the author of the text.

While FAA, and to a much greater extent FAB, contain a wealth of information about early medieval St Andrews, the completely distorted time-frame and the thoroughly miraculous story-line do not inspire confidence in these texts as being a true record of anything. However, it is a useful exercise to strip away the miracles, the myths and the propaganda, and look at what they can tell us about St Andrews in this early period. The problem with at least some of this information relating to the physical description of the place is not so much whether or not it is true – the assumption is that it is – but the fact that any individual description could be assigned to any century between the eighth and the early twelfth.

From FAA we learn that there was a large gate called something like Matha, which led into the church complex, and that near it, in around 1100, stood the king's hall. We also learn that there was a very precise geography linking the fabulous or semi-fabulous past with the contemporary and mundane world of the late eleventh century, complete with a vegetable garden, a mill and other buildings. In FAB we learn that there were probably still extant in the 1140s twelve stone crosses that defined the church precinct. We also learn that there were at this time, over and above the church of St Andrew and the parish church of the Holy Trinity, seven other churches within the precinct at Kilrymont: St Regulus; St Aneglas (the deacon), where it was believed that three virgins from Collossia, viz Triduana, Potentia and Emeria, were buried; St Michael the Archangel; St Mary; St Damian the elder; St Brigid virgin; and (St) Mouren virgin, who was buried at the east end along with '50 virgins born of royal stock, all dedicated to God, having taken the veil at eleven years of age'. One of several remarkable features of this inventory of churches is the high number of female saints and religious who figure in the early ecclesiastical traditions of St Andrews, and it leads to the speculation that there was an otherwise unrecorded royal nunnery here perhaps as early as the eighth century. Perhaps the double monastery of Coldingham at St Abb's Head, another North Sea headland, founded by Aebbe, a female member of the Northumbrian royal family in the late seventh century, was not the furthest north of such foundations on the east coast of Britain.[42]

---

[41] T. O. Clancy, 'Scotland, the "Nennian" recension of the *Historia Brittonum*, and the *Lebor Bretnach*', *Kings, Clerics and Chronicles in Scotland, 500–1297*, ed. S. Taylor (Dublin, 2000), pp. 87–107, at pp. 89–90, 101.

[42] *Bede's Ecclesiastical History of the English People*, book 4, chs 19, 25.

The Culdees of St Andrews

THERE was also a church of the Culdees (*Céli Dé*) at St Andrews. It is not clear what precise relationship existed between this community and the principal church and monastery of St Andrews in the early medieval period. There was certainly an abbey in existence before 747 AD, but this preceded the existence of the Culdees as a distinct body, since the Culdees do not appear in the Gaelic church until the end of the eighth century.[43] From what we know of Culdee houses elsewhere, they often appear as communities alongside and within existing ecclesiastical structures, and this seems to have been the case in St Andrews, where a monastic community clearly pre-dated the Culdee foundation. It is a moot point as to whether King Constantine became their abbot in 943, as is claimed by a note added to a king-list in the twelfth century, probably at St Andrews.[44] As Anderson pointed out, this note may be anachronistic, since, when it was written 'regular Celtic [*sic*] life at Kinrimund, other than that of the *céli Dé*, had probably been long forgotten'. In other words, had Constantine entered the (non-Culdee) monastery of St Andrews, by the time this note was written the monastery would nonetheless have been described in the twelfth century as the Culdee one, since that was the only one of which people knew. Anderson does suggest, however, that it is likely that the Culdees were established at St Andrews by the middle of the tenth century.[45]

As Bishop Robert's re-organisation of the church of St Andrews began to take effect in the 1130s, the Culdee community, whose monastic, liturgical and pastoral observance by this time were perceived to have fallen somewhat short of the ideals for which the Culdees had come into existence, began to be sidelined, a process greatly accelerated by the establishment by Bishop Robert of an Augustinian house at St Andrews in 1140.[46] In c.1150, David I sought to bring this community into more regular observance by having its members received into the Augustinian discipline of the prior and canons of St Andrews or, if some of the Culdees refused this measure, allowing them to continue in their old ways until their deaths, stipulating that on their deaths their possessions were to be transferred to the Augustinian priory to be used to support regular canons in their places.[47] In spite of this provision, the Culdees continue to appear in the

---

[43] For the emergence and identity of the Culdees in Ireland, see Westley Follett, *Céli Dé in Ireland: Monastic Writing and Identity in the Early Middle Ages* (Woodbridge, 2006). For the roots of the Culdees in Scotland, see T. O. Clancy, 'Iona, Scotland and the Céli Dé', *Scotland in Dark Age Britain*, ed. B. E. Crawford (Aberdeen, 1996), pp. 111–30.

[44] Marjorie Anderson's Group X (Anderson, *Kings and Kingship*, pp. 52, 267).

[45] M. O. Anderson, 'The Celtic Church in Kinrimund', pp. 4–5.

[46] A. A. M. Duncan, 'The Foundation of St Andrews Cathedral Priory, 1140', *SHR* 84 (2005), pp. 1–37.

[47] *The Charters of David I: the Written Acts of David I King of Scots, 1124–53, and of His Son Henry, Earl of Northumberland, 1139–52*, ed. G. W. S. Barrow (Woodbridge 1999), no. 209.

record throughout the thirteenth century, but they do so as members of a secular collegiate church, 'a small college of highly-placed secular clerks closely connected with the bishop and the king', living from the income of the older 'Celtic' foundation.[48] Though they were still being called Culdees in the fourteenth century, they were not in fact a survival of the older order: they were thoroughly modern clerks, a useful counterbalance for bishop and king to the powerful regular canons of the Augustinian priory.[49]

Projecting back from the early thirteenth century, and using the remarkably detailed set of charters and other documents mainly contained in the cartulary of St Andrews Priory from 1140 onwards, a relatively precise inventory can be made of the lands belonging to the Culdees within the parish of the Holy Trinity of St Andrews around 1150. This inventory probably reflects to a large extent their original endowment. In addition to a cluster of lands around Ceres and Kemback, the earliest holdings of the Culdees of St Andrews consisted of Strathtyrum and part of Strathkinness (both west of St Andrews), Kinkell with the associated lands of Kingask, *Pitsporgy, *Pitkenny and Kinglassie (all forming a continuous block of land along the coast to the south-east of St Andrews as far as Boarhills, which would have been part of Kinglassie), and most if not all of Kinaldy, and Cairns with Cameron to the south.[50]

Over the next fifty or so years most of the changes affecting these lands can be charted. The first such change occurred in the second half of the 1150s, when the Culdees exchanged with St Andrews Priory their part of Strathkinness for Lambieletham along with Carngour (Kininnis).[51] This will have extended and consolidated their land-holdings in the eastern part of the parish. In the 1170s Gilla Críst, abbot of the Culdees of St Andrews, farmed out in fee and heritage the associated lands of Kinkell, *Pitsporgy and *Pitkenny to Odo, brother of Bishop Matthew of Aberdeen and steward of the bishop of St Andrews. The rent stipulated for these lands throws light on their husbandry at this time: Odo was to pay the Culdees annually 32 bolls of cheese, 32 bolls of barley and a one-year-old pig, besides the forinsec service due to the king.[52]

The next major change in the Culdees' land-holdings came when they were persuaded to hand over Strathtyrum to St Andrews Priory. This happened in 1198 or 1199 as part of a much wider-ranging agreement between the canons

---

[48] G. W. S. Barrow, *Kingdom of the Scots*, (London, 1973; second edition Edinburgh, 2003), chapter 8 (pp. 187–202, 2nd edn), p. 195.

[49] For a full account of the relations of the Culdees with the collegiate church and the Augustinians, see Barrow, *Kingdom of the Scots* (2003), chapter 8.

[50] See *PNF*, iii, appendix 2; *St A. Liber*, pp. 318–19.

[51] G. W. S. Barrow, ed., *Regesta Regum Scottorum*, i: *The Acts of Malcolm IV King of Scots 1153–65* (Edinburgh, 1960) [hereafter *RRS*, i], no. 173; see *PNF*, iii, under Lambieletham (now Cameron parish), Strathkinness and Balmartin.

[52] G. W. S. Barrow, 'The Early Charters of the Family of Kinninmonth of that Ilk', *The Study of Medieval Records: Essays in Honour of Kathleen Major*, ed. D. A. Bullough and R. L. Storey (Oxford, 1971), pp. 107–31, nos. 2, 3, both dated 1172×78; G. W. S. Barrow, ed., *Regesta Regum Scottorum*, ii: *The Acts of William I King of Scots 1165–1214* (Edinburgh, 1971) [hereafter *RRS*, ii], no. 347.

of St Andrews Priory on the one hand and the Culdees of St Andrews on the other.⁵³ G. W. S. Barrow regards this agreement as a key moment in the transformation process of the Culdees into the above-mentioned college of secular clerks.⁵⁴ Its importance is reflected in its witness list, which included most of the leading men of the kingdom, both secular and ecclesiastical, as well as an impressive group of local worthies. By this agreement the Culdees were to keep all the teinds from the lands, but the canons were to retain the revenue arising from marriage, purification, offerings, baptism and burial of the dead, except for the bodies of the Culdees, who could be buried wherever they wanted. The fullest inventory of the lands of the Culdees of St Andrews is set out in the Terrier (i.e. list of lands) of the Church of St Andrews dating from c.1220.⁵⁵ This Culdee community, later St Mary's Collegiate Church, occupied the church of St Mary of the Rock, also known as Kirkheugh, and it continued as a distinct body with its properties and rights until the Reformation.

St Andrews and Learning

THE evidence for St Andrews as a centre of learning starts to appear around 1100, pre-dating by over 300 years the founding there of the first university in Scotland (for more on this see Norman Reid, Chapter 12, in this volume). The first unequivocal reference to scholarly activity is from the shorter Foundation Account (FAA), which mentions almost in passing the house of Master Samuel within the church precinct. When Eadmer arrived in 'the church of St Andrew' to become bishop-elect in the summer of 1120, he tells us by his own account that he was met by the queen (Sybilla) and was welcomed 'by the scholars and the people'.⁵⁶ In the early thirteenth century (December 2011 × August 1213)⁵⁷ an important agreement was reached between St Andrews Priory and the poor scholars of St Andrews, the latter represented by Master Patrick, who is described as 'the Master of the Schools of the city of St Andrew(s)'.⁵⁸ It is clear from this agreement that the resources of the schools of St Andrews had been under considerable pressure from the ever-expanding priory, but that through the negotiations conducted on the schools' behalf by Master Patrick and Laurence the archdeacon, who as *Fer Léginn* (literally 'man of reading')⁵⁹

---

⁵³ *St A. Liber*, pp. 318–19.
⁵⁴ Barrow, *Kingdom of the Scots* (2003), pp. 196–7.
⁵⁵ For a full edition of which see *PNF*, iii, appendix 2 (pp. 616–22).
⁵⁶ A. O. Anderson, *Scottish Annals from English Chroniclers*, 142; M. O. Anderson, 'The Celtic Church in Kinrimund', p. 8.
⁵⁷ For the dating of this document, see S. Taylor with G. Márkus, *The Place-Names of Fife, Volume Five: Discussion, Glossaries and Edited Texts* (Donington, 2012) [hereafter *PNF*, v], p. 618.
⁵⁸ *St A. Liber*, pp. 316–18. For translation and commentary, see *PNF*, iii, pp. 418–20; see also Addenda and Corrigenda, *PNF*, v, pp. 618–19.
⁵⁹ See *PNF*, v, pp. 618–19, for a brief discussion of this term, with references.

had ultimate responsibility for education at St Andrews, the income on which the scholars depended was protected. This agreement secured the future of St Andrews as an important centre of learning, but it also mentions several places in the St Andrews area with unique information on their rents and produce. Five land-holdings or estates are mentioned as contributing to the needs of the poor scholars, all of which seem to be within the medieval parish of St Andrews. Together these land-holdings are to contribute annually 40 stones of cheese and 70 bolls of dry barley, a huge quantity when one considers that one boll was approximately 12 gallons or 218 litres.

Conclusion

This chapter is about the sanctification and politicisation of a coastal headland, with its beach and burn-mouth, both of which provide the only safe landing-place along an otherwise inhospitable stretch of rocky north-east-facing coastline exposed to the winds and waves of the North Sea. The transformation of this place was already well under way by 747 AD, and is neatly reflected in the evolution of its name, from a secular, topographical one (Kinrymont), through an ecclesiastical reinterpretation of the same (Kilrymont), to a name which proclaims loudly and clearly its association with one of the founding figures of Christianity (St Andrew), befitting what had become by the twelfth century the ecclesiastical centre of Scotland, and which was to remain as such until the Reformation. The dynamic push and pull of the apostolic association and the growing political-ecclesiastical importance of the place are explored as fully as the fragmentary and incomplete sources allow, but, until anything dramatically new comes to light, it cannot be said with any certainty which came first, the relics or the fame.

CHAPTER THREE

The Idea of St Andrews as the Second Rome Made Manifest

Ian Campbell

THERE are two principal versions of the St Andrews foundation legend that try to account for the known presence of the body of St Andrew in Constantinople and the presence of corporeal relics in Fife. They are usually referred to simply as Foundation Account A (FAA) and Foundation Account B (FAB), dated c.1000 and mid twelfth century respectively.[1] In FAA we find the audacious claim that:

> the archiepiscopacy of all Scotia should be exercised from this city where the apostolic see is [and] no bishop ought to be ordained in Scotia without the approval of the elders of this place. For in relation to the first Rome this is the second. This is the preeminent city of refuge. This is the city of cities of Scotia.[2]

This essay revises and extends three of my earlier attempts to explore whether this claim was expressed physically in the forms of the cathedral and of the burgh, both founded in the mid twelfth century.[3] It has been argued that St

---

[1] FAA is best edited by Marjorie O. Anderson in *Kings and Kingship in Early Scotland*, revised edn (Edinburgh, 1980), pp. 258–60, but for important additions see Dauvit Broun, 'The Church of St Andrews and its Foundation Legend in the Early Twelfth Century: Recovering the Full Text of Version A of the Foundation Legend', *Kings, Clerics and Chronicles in Scotland 500–1297*, ed. Simon Taylor (Dublin, 2000), pp. 108–14. FAB is edited and translated in this volume (see **pp. 345–68**) and again, with discussion and notes, in *PNF*, iii, pp. 564–600.

[2] This portion survives in London, British Library, MS Arundel 36 and MS Cotton Tiberius D iii, and is transcribed and translated by Broun in 'The Church of St Andrews', p. 111: 'Ex hac itaque ciuitate esse archiepiscopatus debet tocius Scotiae, ubi apostolica sedes est; nect abasque consilio seniorum istius loci ullus episcopus in Scotia debet ordinari. Hec est enim Roma secunda a prima. Hec est ciuitas refugii precipua. Hec est ciuitas ciuitatum Scotie'. This additional text was printed by Archbishop Ussher in the seventeenth century but he did not give his immediate source: James Ussher, *Britannicarum Ecclesiarum Antiquitates* (Dublin, 1639), p. 651.

[3] I am grateful to the editor of the *Innes Review* for permission to reprint here in revised form Ian Campbell, 'Planning for Pilgrims: St Andrews as the Second Rome', *Innes Review* 64:1 (2013), pp. 1–22. See also I. Campbell, 'St Andrews Cathedral, "the biggest church in Christendom"', *La Festa delle Arti. Scritti in onore di Marcello Fagiolo per cinquant'anni*

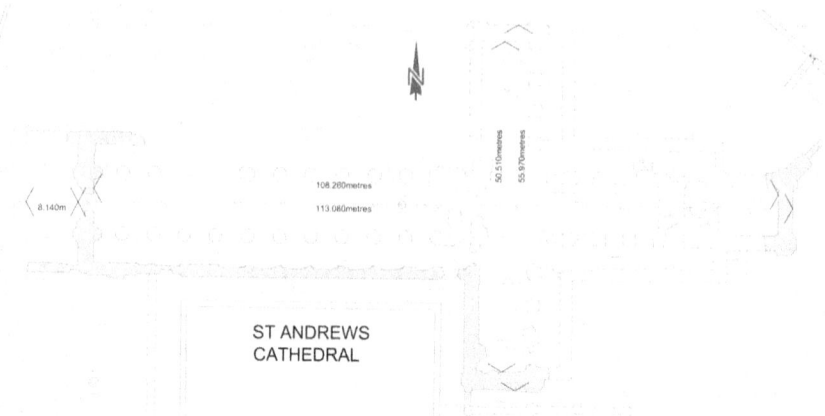

Figure 3.1: Plan of St Andrews Cathedral.

Andrews – as cathedral and burgh – was planned as 'a single grandiose conception'; but even if that were not the case, the arguments for each element can still stand alone.[4] After examining the evidence for first the cathedral and then the burgh, this essay will then consider the parallels (or lack thereof) at Compostela, which made a contemporary and successful bid to gain the status of an apostolic see.

Some believe that the ruins of the church known as St Rule's since the sixteenth century represent a rebuilding of the original church housing the shrine of St Andrew, by Bishop Robert, around the time of his consecration in 1127.[5] If this is so one wonders at its modest size compared with the claims made in FAA, and whether the scale of the present cathedral, formally founded by Bishop Arnold in 1162, more truly reflects the ambitions of Bishop Robert, who died in 1159.[6] It was the largest church in Scotland, with a nave originally fourteen bays long, making the length of the whole cathedral about 121.22m (see figure 3.1).[7] However, after the collapse of the west front around 1272, the nave

---

  di studi, ed. Vincenzo Cazzato, Sebastiano Roberto, Mario Bevilacqua, 2 vols (Rome, 2014), i, pp. 80–5; Ian Campbell, 'Planning for Pilgrims: Parallels between the Burgh of St Andrews, the Vatican Borgo and Compostela', *Artistic Practices and Cultural Transfer in Early Modern Italy. Essays Dedicated to Deborah Howard*, ed. N. Avcioglu and A. Sherman (Aldershot, 2015), pp. 15–27.
[4] Brooks and Whittington, pp. 278–95, at p. 291.
[5] Richard Fawcett argues this case in his *Scottish Cathedrals* (London, 1997), pp. 17–19, but in his *The Architecture of the Scottish Medieval Church, 1100–1560* (New Haven and London, 2011), pp. 13–17, he avoids expressing an opinion.
[6] Eric Cambridge, 'The Early Building-History of St Andrews Cathedral, Fife, and its Context in Northern Transitional Architecture', *Antiquaries Journal* 57 (1977), pp. 277–88 at 280–1, has speculated that perhaps the footings began to be laid in the late 1150s.
[7] On the building of the cathedral besides Cambridge, 'The Early Building-History

was reduced to twelve bays, making the present overall length 113.08m. Even in its sad post-Reformation state, it still impressed John Slezer (d. 1717). Slezer published the first printed collection of views of Scottish towns and antiquities, fifty-seven engravings, with accompanying commentaries, in the *Theatrum Scotiae*, in 1693.[8] The commentaries, originally intended to be in Latin by Sir Robert Sibbald (1641–1722), are in English based on Sibbald's drafts without acknowledgement.[9] In the preface, titled 'To the Reader', is the startling claim that

> the Metropolitan Church of St. *Andrews* was probably the biggest in *Christendom,* being Seven Foot longer and Two Foot broader than that of St. *Peter* at *Rome*; and for the Heighth and Embellishing of its Pillars and Roof, the Beauty of its Stones, and Simetry of its parts, was one of the best of the *Gothick* kind in the World.[10]

It is not – several medieval English cathedrals are longer, and many French cathedrals are higher – but one is left wondering why Slezer should make such a demonstrably false claim. Slezer was a German military engineer, and had presumably seen more impressive buildings on his travels. Nevertheless, Slezer does make very specific comparisons with St Peter's: that it was seven feet longer and two feet wider. If Slezer was referring to the contemporary Scottish foot (30.5287cm), the differences translate to 2.14m longer and 61cm wider.[11] The external length of Old St Peter's, taken from the end wall of the nave to the back of the apse, is estimated to have been 121.45m, while the external width across the nave and aisles was about 63.70m.[12] As we have already said, the original overall length of St Andrews was around 121.22m (figure 3.1). The 23cm difference is small enough to make the correspondence look too close to be the product of chance. On the other hand, the breadth of St Andrews cathedral, even at its widest point across the transepts, is only 55.97m, far less than the 63.70m

---

    of St Andrews Cathedral', see Malcolm Thurlby, 'St Andrews Cathedral-Priory and the Beginnings of Gothic Architecture in Northern Britain', Higgitt, *St Andrews*, pp. 47–60 and Fawcett, *The Architecture of the Scottish Medieval Church*, pp. 60–6.

[8] John Slezer, *Theatrum Scotiae* (London, 1693).
[9] On the text see Keith Cavers, *A Vision of Scotland: The Nation Observed by John Slezer 1671 to 1717* (Edinburgh, 1993), p. 12; on Sibbald, see Charles W. J. Withers, 'Sibbald, Sir Robert (1641–1722)', *Oxford Dictionary of National Biography* (Oxford University Press, May 2006) [www.oxforddnb.com/view/article/25496 (accessed 1 March 2012)].
[10] Slezer, *Theatrum Scotiae*, 'To the Reader' p. (a).
[11] Scottish Archive Network, 'Scottish Weights and Measures: Distance and Area', at www.scan.org.uk/measures/distance.asp (accessed 27 February 2012). R. D. Connor and A. D. C. Simpson, *Weights and Measures in Scotland: A European Perspective*, ed. A. D. Morrison-Low (Edinburgh, 2004), p. 555, give the length of the foot on the official 1663 Edinburgh measure of the ell as 30.55cm, but all measures in the book are rounded up or down to 0.5mm.
[12] Calculated from the plan in Turpin C. Bannister, 'The Constantinian Basilica of Saint Peter at Rome', *Journal of the Society of Architectural Historians* 27 (1968), pp. 3–32, at 12 (fig. 14).

width of Old St Peter's nave, so that this dimension cannot have been modelled on the Vatican Basilica. Instead, we find that the 55.97m of St Andrews is very close to the width of the nave of the Lateran Basilica (55.22m), the cathedral of Rome. Indeed the 59cm difference approximates to two (ancient Roman) feet (2 × 29.6cm). We know that the medieval notion of a copy in architectural terms was far looser than ours, and that the mere use of a shape or a significant dimension was enough to evoke the original.[13] Thus it appears that St Andrews Cathedral was deliberately designed to emulate the two most prestigious churches in Rome by using a combination of their dimensions: the length of St Peter's and the width of St John Lateran.[14] This raises three questions: first, about how Slezer knew the dimensions of the Roman basilicas; second, about how the designers of St Andrews Cathedral knew them; and third, about the intention in emulating St Peter's and the Lateran.

The first question cannot be answered definitively, but Slezer's project was already in progress as early as 1678, and can be seen in the context of James's patronage of all kinds of learning in Scotland, while and after he was resident in Edinburgh, as duke of Albany and York, from 1679 to 1682.[15] It seems possible that the information came from a pre-Reformation source transmitted to Slezer. Sibbald, with his antiquarian interests, would be an obvious channel, but there is nothing in his drafts for the commentary to *Theatrum Scotiae* to suggest he had knowledge.[16] Nor do the various versions of Scottish chronicles and histories, written in the Middle Ages and the Renaissance, which continued to be read in late-seventeenth-century Scotland, make any comparisons with the Roman churches. So the source of Slezer's assertion remains unknown.

The second question is equally impossible to answer definitively, but it would not have been difficult for a Scottish cleric visiting the Holy See some time before the foundation of the new cathedral in 1162 to have acquired the information

---

[13] Richard Krautheimer, 'Introduction to an "Iconography of Mediaeval Architecture"', *Journal of the Warburg and Courtauld Institutes* 5 (1942), pp. 1–33.

[14] Thurlby, 'St Andrews Cathedral-Priory', p. 52, already proposed that St Peter's might be the inspiration for the extreme length, citing the suggestions that the dimensions of Ely Cathedral echo those of S. Paolo fuori le Mura (Eric Fernie, 'Observations on the Norman Plan of Ely Cathedral', *Medieval Art and Architecture at Ely Cathedral*, ed. Nicola Coldstream and Peter Draper (Leeds, 1979), pp. 1–7) and that those at Winchester were taken from St Peter's (Richard Gem, 'The Romanesque Cathedral of Winchester: Patron and Design in the Eleventh Century', *Medieval Art and Architecture at Winchester Cathedral*, ed. T. A. Heslop and V. A. Sekules (Leeds, 1983), pp. 13–19). The third abbey church at Cluny, begun in 1088, which matches Old St Peter's in length, was measured in Roman feet, the use of which had been revived at Montecassino during the abbacy of Desiderius (1066–75); see Anne Baud, *Cluny: un grand chantier médiéval au coeur de l'Europe* (Paris, 2003), pp. 172–3; Kenneth John Conant, *Carolingian and Romanesque Architecture*, 4th edn (Harmondsworth, 1978), p. 199.

[15] Cavers, *A Vision of Scotland*, p. 3; Hugh Ouston, 'York in Edinburgh: James VII and the Patronage of Learning in Scotland, 1679–88', *New Perspectives on the Politics and Culture of Early Modern Scotland*, ed. John Dwyer, Roger A. Mason and Alexander Murdoch (Edinburgh, 1982), pp. 133–55, at p. 136.

[16] Edinburgh, National Library of Scotland [hereafter NLS], Adv. MS 33.3.22.

on the size of the Roman churches. A likely candidate would be William, bishop of Moray, who was sent to Rome soon after Bishop Robert's death, returning in 1160 with legatine powers, to pass on to whomever was elected the new bishop of St Andrews, should it not be himself, as indeed transpired.[17] William could easily have found out the measurements of the Vatican and Lateran basilicas in preparation for the founding of what he hoped would be his new cathedral, just as a twelfth-century Life of St Petronius of Bologna (died c.445) relates that in constructing the monastery of S. Stefano in Bologna, he copied the Church of the Holy Sepulchre, and that he had measured everything accurately with a measuring-rod during a stay in the Holy Land.[18]

The legatine powers were a consolation prize for William, since he was almost certainly visiting Rome to press the case for making St Andrews a metropolitan see in order to resist the claim of the archbishops of York to take control of the Scottish church, which gives us the answer to our third question. Their claim was based on Gregory the Great's instructions to St Augustine of Canterbury in 601 to set up two metropolitan sees in what had been the two major cities of Roman *Britannia*, London and York. The Roman province did not extend beyond Hadrian's Wall, but from the late twelfth century, the archbishops of York interpreted *Britannia* to mean the whole island now known as Great Britain, 'even to the utmost edges of Scotland' (*usque ad extremos Scotiae fines*).[19] The Scottish Church and crown resisted such claims vigorously and one bishop of St Andrews around 1100 was already styling himself archbishop without papal sanction – a claim that David I first pursued in 1125.[20]

Before leaving the cathedral, we should note one feature that remains a mystery, namely the well at the east end of the nave. Wells in churches are relatively rare of course, although there was one (now capped) in the south aisle of the nave of Dunfermline Abbey and St Kentigern's well is still visible in the southeast corner of the crypt of Glasgow Cathedral.[21] It has been suggested that the one at St Andrews was merely a pre-existing well, perhaps associated with the former Pictish royal hall that probably stood in the vicinity, with no sacred significance, which was then capped when the present cathedral was built on the site.[22] However, given its prominent siting on the central axis at the end of the nave, this seems improbable. It has been surprisingly little explored and is a

[17] D. E. R. Watt, *Medieval Church Councils in Scotland* (Edinburgh, 2001), pp. 19–20.
[18] 'Vita auctore anonymo ex Chronico monachorum S. Stephani Bononiæ', *Acta Sanctorum*, October vol. 2, ed. Constantinus Suyskeno, Cornelius Byeo, Jacobus Bueo, Josephus Ghesquiero (Antwerp, 1768), p. 459.
[19] Watt, *Medieval Church Councils*, p. 12.
[20] Dauvit Broun, *Scottish Independence and the Idea of Britain from the Picts to Alexander III* (Edinburgh, 2007), pp. 111–14.
[21] David McRoberts, '"The Glorious House of St Andrew"', McRoberts, *St Andrews*, pp. 63–120, at pp. 78–9. On the Dunfermline well, see *RCAHMS Fife*, p. 113. On the Glasgow well, see J. Russell Walker, '"Holy Wells" in Scotland', *PSAS* 17 (1882–83), pp. 152–210, at p. 182, fig. 10.
[22] Suggestion voiced at the workshop on medieval St Andrews, St John's House, University of St Andrews, 14 January 2014.

prime candidate for excavation to see if any objects deposited in it can shed light on its function and dating.

The Burgh of St Andrews and the Vatican Borgo

TURNING to St Andrews, Bishop Robert founded the new burgh of that name between 1140 and 1153 (with Matthew Hammond making a strong case for 1152), next to a pre-existing settlement.[23] Burial remains, excavated on the headland above the present harbour, suggest a Christian presence back to the fifth century.[24] The earliest reference to an important Pictish royal monastery in the vicinity, called Kinrimund (Cennrígmonaid), is in 747.[25] It grew in prestige, and by the tenth century was the seat of the principal bishop of Scotland. Like other ecclesiastical sites in early medieval North Britain and Ireland (Whithorn and Armagh in particular), there was a lay settlement outside the ecclesiastical precincts (see figure 3.2).[26]

Mainard the Fleming laid out the new burgh, having already performed the same task for Berwick-upon-Tweed.[27] Brooks and Whittington argued that both North Street and South Street in St Andrews follow the line of earlier routes converging on the original site of the shrine of St Andrew, almost certainly on the site of the earlier cathedral, now known as St Rule's (see figure 3.3).[28] Whittington speculates that the two-street burgh of St Andrews, converging on the site where the new cathedral was begun a few years later, suggests

---

[23] Bishop Robert's charter of foundation for the burgh is printed with a translation in *PNF*, iii, p. 430 n.78 (text) and pp. 429–30 (translation). On the foundation see Matthew Hammond, 'The Bishop, the Prior, and the Founding of the Burgh of St Andrews', *Innes Review* 66 (2015), pp. 72–101. For the dating to 1152, see Ibid. pp. 85–6.

[24] Derek W. Hall, 'Pre-burghal St Andrews: Towards an Archaeological Research Design', *TFAJ* 1 (1995), pp. 23–7; Jonathan Wordsworth and Peter R. Clark, 'Kirkhill', Rains and Hall, *Excavations*, pp. 7–18. For further discussion of the archaeology and layout of Kinrimund, see Leslie Alcock, *Kings and Warriors, Craftsmen and Priests in Northern Britain AD 550–850* (Edinburgh, 2003), pp. 225–9.

[25] Under the year 747 the Annals of Tigernach record 'the death of Túathalán, abbot of Cennrígmonaid', ed. Whitley Stokes, *Revue Celtique* 17 (1896), pp. 119–263, at p. 249; see also Marjorie O. Anderson, 'The Celtic Church in Kinrimund', *Innes Review* 25 (1974), pp. 67–76.

[26] Ibid., p. 228.

[27] Hammond, 'The Bishop, the Prior, and the Founding of the Burgh of St Andrews', pp. 73–5; also Brooks and Whittington, p. 290; Richard Oram, *Domination and Lordship in Scotland 1070–1230* (Edinburgh, 2011), pp. 275–6.

[28] Brooks and Whittington, p. 292; Peter Yeoman, *Pilgrimage in Medieval Scotland* (London, 2003), p. 57, fig. 35, has a map of pilgrimage routes to St Andrews through Fife. The date of the remains of St Rule's are still disputed; Neil Cameron, 'St Rule's Church, St Andrews, and Early Stone-Built Churches in Scotland', *PSAS* 124 (1994), pp. 367–78, argued that substantial parts are pre-twelfth century; Fawcett, *Architecture of the Scottish Medieval Church*, pp. 13–17, maintains a more conservative interpretation, seeing all the remains as part of a replacement rather than an enlargement of the previous church, by Bishop Robert (1127–59).

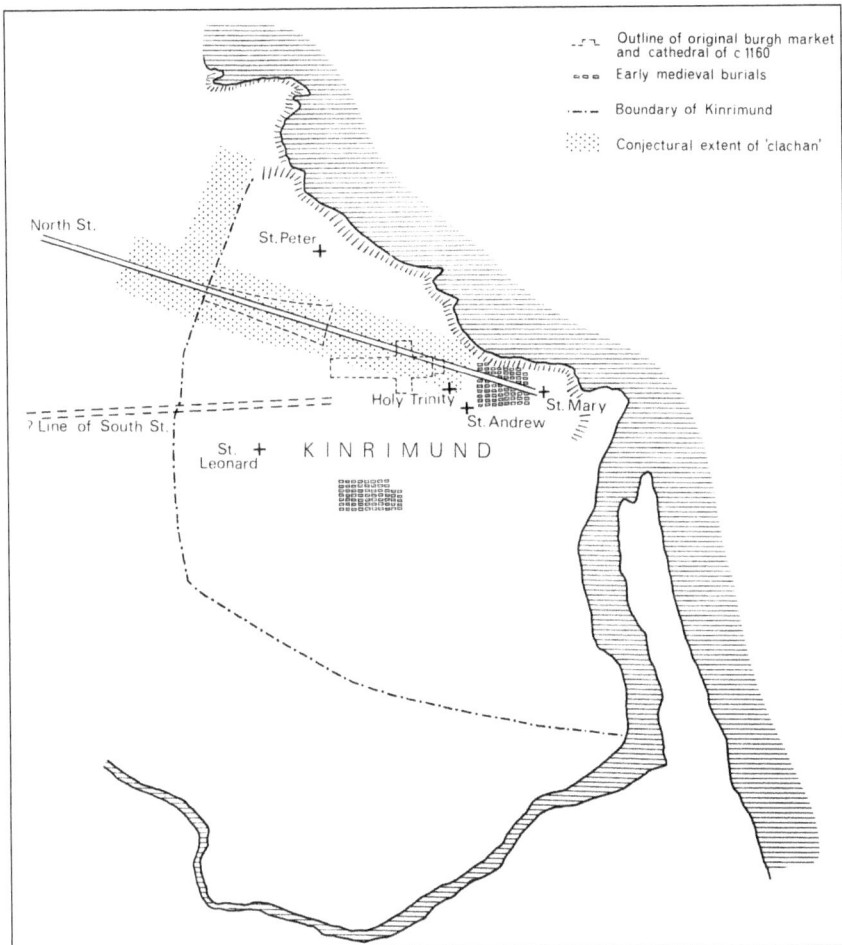

Figure 3.2: Pre-burghal Kinrimund from N. P. Brooks and G. Whittington, 'Planning and Growth in the Medieval Scottish Burgh: The Example of St Andrews', Transactions of the Institute of British Geographers 2 (1977), pp. 278–95, figure 6.

that both elements were planned together as 'a single grandiose conception'.[29] However, the vast majority of burghs were established as single-street plans, although some, like Edinburgh, acquired parallel streets later (in Edinburgh's case the Cowgate), when the burgage plots in the original high street were all filled. Perth, second only in status to Edinburgh, had two principal parallel streets already in the twelfth century, but it is now thought that the High Street dates from the first founding of the burgh by David I before 1127, while South

---

[29] Ibid.; Ronald G. Cant, 'The Building of St Andrews Cathedral', McRoberts, *St Andrews*, pp. 11–32, at p. 12, makes a similar point.

Street was laid out in a major expansion by William the Lion, which evidence would date to 1178×95.[30]

Similarly, the new burgh of St Andrews, as first laid out, was juridically confined to South Street, thereby avoiding potential legal disputes with the owners of existing properties around the east end of North Street, which is thought to have been the nucleus of the pre-burghal settlement.[31] This seems to go against the notion that there was any grandiose conception, but the result of the development of South Street is that from the beginning St Andrews had two major streets, running roughly from west to east, converging towards the cathedral precinct, a plan which recalls the Vatican Borgo.

The works of Enrico Guidoni and Keith Lilley have demonstrated beyond doubt the role of symbolism in the planning of medieval towns in Europe.[32] However, neither has explored the influence of the Vatican Borgo as a model.[33] It has been argued elsewhere that the general similarities between the plan of the twin burghs of Edinburgh and the Canongate and the plan of the Borgo, both long, thin settlements, aligned east–west with a castle at one end and a church-palace complex at the other, may be more than coincidental.[34] However, the resemblance between St Andrews and the Borgo is even more compelling: the former has North and South Streets converging on the cathedral with a market place (now Market Street) in between, while the latter in the Middle Ages consisted of two main streets, the Porticus Sancti Petri and the Borgo Santo Spirito, converging on St Peter's with Piazza Scossacavalli serving as a market place linking the two half way down.

The Vatican Borgo was created after the sack of St Peter's Basilica by the Saracens in 846. The emperor Lothar (817–55) ordered the building of defen-

---

[30] For King William's charter, *RRS*, ii, p. 304, no. 278. A charter of King David I, issued before July 1127, refers to the burgh of Perth. See *The Charters of King David I: The Written Acts of David I King of Scots, 1124–53 and of his Son Henry Earl of Northumberland, 1139–52*, ed. G. W. S. Barrow (Woodbridge, 1999), no. 19. See also Jeremy W. R. Whitehand and Khan Alauddin, 'The Town Plans of Scotland: Some Preliminary Considerations', *Scottish Geographical Magazine* 85 (1969), pp. 109–21, at pp. 111–17; David P. Bowler, *Perth: The Archaeology and Development of a Scottish Burgh* (Perth, 2004), pp. 21, 25–9.

[31] Hall, 'Pre-burghal St Andrews', pp. 25–6.

[32] For example, Enrico Guidoni, *La città europea: formazione e significato dal IV all' XI secolo* (Milan, 1978); Keith D. Lilley, 'Cities of God? Medieval Urban Forms and their Christian Symbolism', *Transactions of the Institute of British Geographers*, n. s. 29 (2004), pp. 296–313; Keith D. Lilley, *City and Cosmos: The Medieval World in Urban Form* (London, 2009).

[33] Giada Lepri, *L'urbanistica di Borgo e Vaticano nel Medioevo* (Rome, 2004), pp. 57–8, discusses the significance of the three gates of the Borgo and points to other towns with three gates, such as Cortona, but does not suggest the latter copies the former.

[34] Ian Campbell, 'James IV and Edinburgh's First Triumphal Arches', *The Architecture of Scottish Cities: Essays in Honour of David Walker*, ed. Deborah Mays (East Linton, 1997), pp. 26–33; Ian Campbell and Margaret Stewart, 'The Evolution of the Medieval and Renaissance City', *Edinburgh: The Making of a Capital City*, ed. Brian Edwards and Paul Jenkins (Edinburgh, 2005), pp. 21–40.

sive walls round St Peter's, which were erected between 848 and 852, during the pontificate of Leo IV (847–55).[35] The walls encircled the basilica and its ancillary buildings and extended in two parallel tracts eastwards towards to the river Tiber.[36] The northern stretch, still largely extant, runs as far as the second-century AD mausoleum of the emperor Hadrian, which was converted into a fortress during late antiquity and is now known as Castel Sant'Angelo.[37] From the beginning, the fortified Vatican complex was regarded as a new town, the Christian *Civitas leoniana*, the Leonine City, distinct from the old pagan *urbs*, Rome proper over the Tiber.[38] An inscription over one of the gates in the walls called it the *Arx poli*, the 'Fortress of Heaven'.[39]

Within the walls three roads ran east–west, two major, one minor. The principal one was the Porticus or Portica Sancti Petri, beginning and ending with an arch, which ran from the Pons Aelii (the bridge in front of Hadrian's mausoleum, now the Ponte S. Angelo) to St Peter's, the principal route for pilgrims coming from the city across the Tiber.[40] It probably followed the course of an earlier Roman road, running from the mausoleum, which became the major crossing point from the Campus Martius to the Vatican after the collapse of the Bridge of Nero, probably before the middle of the fourth century AD.[41] Its exact course is not certain.[42] The *porticus*, as the name implies, was probably flanked by colonnades of spolia columns, but by the twelfth century any unified structure is likely to have been replaced by a chain of contiguous colonnades or arcades of individual buildings lining the street, giving shelter to pedestrians,

---

[35] Sheila Gibson and Bryan Ward-Perkins, 'The Surviving Remains of the Leonine Wall', *Papers of the British School at Rome* 47 (1979), pp. 30–57, at pp. 31–3; *Le Liber Pontificalis. Texte, introduction et commentaire*, ed. Louis Duchesne, 2nd edn with additions, 3 vols (Paris, 1955–57), iii, pp. 123–5.

[36] See the excellent plan in Gabriella Villetti, 'Architetture di Borgo nel Medioevo', *L'Architettura della basilica di San Pietro: storia e costruzione*, ed. Gianfranco Spagnesi (Rome 1997), pp. 73–90 at 75, fig. 2.

[37] Amanda Claridge, *Rome: An Oxford Archaeological Guide*, 2nd edn (Oxford, 2010), pp. 410–15.

[38] Lepri, *L'urbanistica di Borgo*, pp. 57–8; see also Richard Krautheimer, *Rome: Profile of a City, 312–1308* (Princeton, 1980), p. 364 (note to p. 264).

[39] Adriano Prandi, 'Precisazioni e novità sulla civitas leoniana', *Miscellanea di studi storici: per le nozze di Gianni Jacovelli e Vita Castano, Massafra, VII-IV-MCMLXIX* (Fasano, 1969), pp. 107–29, at pp. 116–17.

[40] Louis Reekmans, 'Le développement topographique de la région du Vatican à la fin de l'antiquité et au début du Moyen Âge (300–850)', *Mélanges d'archéologie et d'histoire de l'art, offerts au Professeur Jacques Lavalleye* (Louvain, 1970), pp. 197–235, at pp. 206–7.

[41] Paolo Liverani, 'Pons Neronianus', *Lexicon topographicum urbis Romae*, ed. Margarethe Steinby, 6 vols (Rome, 1993–2000), iv, p. 111; Reekmans, 'Le développement', p. 202. Several Roman roads are known to have run through the Vatican area, including the *viae* Cornelia, Triumphalis and Aurelia and Aurelia Nova, but linking particular names to surviving tracts is largely conjectural: see Nevio Degrassi, 'La datazione e il percorso della via Aurelia e la via Aurelia Nova nella zona de Vaticano', *Rendiconti della Pontificia Accademia Romana di Archeologia* 61 (1988–89), pp. 309–42.

[42] Lepri, *L'urbanistica di Borgo*, p. 20.

similar to those surviving in Campus Martius on the other side of the Tiber and common throughout central and northern Italy.[43]

The second street, the Vicus Saxonum, followed the general line of the present Borgo Santo Spirito. It branched left shortly after the start of the Porticus/Portica S. Petri, ran past the south side of St Peter's and continued over the hill. It takes its name from the settlement of Anglo-Saxons in the area, already recorded during the reign of Pope John VII (705–7) before the reputed foundation of the earliest pilgrims' hostel in Rome by Ine, former king of the West Saxons, in 727: this was the supposed precursor of the hospital of Santo Spirito in Sassia, from which the name of the present street derives.[44] The area is first referred to as *burgus* (a word of Germanic origin) during the reign of Pope Paschal I (817–24), and later became the common name for the whole of the 'Leonine City'.[45] Hostels for Frisians and Franks were later established to the west, along the same route, which was almost certainly another tract of Roman road, probably originally leading from the bridge of Nero.[46]

The third minor road crossed the northern part of the Borgo.[47] It probably started near the north-west corner of the mausoleum of Hadrian and followed the line of the later Borgo S. Angelo, running close to the line of the northern tract of the Leonine wall. There is reference to a Via Hadriani in the area, a name that probably refers to Pope Hadrian I (772–95) rather than the emperor, although there is no specific mention of the road in the account of his works in the *Liber Pontificalis* (the collection of papal biographies compiled from the sixth century onwards).[48] The original goal was probably the complex of buildings that included the northern of two papal residences originally built by Pope Symmachus (498–514) flanking St Peter's, which became the nucleus of the

---

[43] Reekmans, 'Le développement', p. 207; Carlo Cecchelli, 'Roma medioevale', *Topografia e urbanistica di Roma*, ed. Ferdinando Castagnoli et al., Storia di Roma 22 (Bologna, 1958), pp. 189–34, at p. 241.

[44] In the thirteenth century, Matthew Paris related the story of how Ine built a *domus* to be called the *schola Anglorum* (*Chronica Maiora*, s.a. 727, ed. H. R. Luard, Rolls Series 27, 7 vols (London, 1872–84), i, pp. 330–1); see also G. J. Hoogewerff, 'Friezen, Franken en Saksen te Rome', *Mededeelingen van het Nederlandsch Historisch Instituut te Rome* 25 (1947), pp. 1–70, at pp. 5–10.

[45] *Liber Pontificalis*, ed. Duchesne, ii, pp. 53–4; Lepri, *L'urbanistica di Borgo*, p. 28.

[46] Reekmans, 'Le développement', p. 201; Hoogewerff, 'Friezen, Franken en Saksen', pp. 4–5.

[47] Rossella Motta, 'La topografia della Civitas Leoniana fra IX e XIV secolo: note sull'assetto viario e l'edilizia abitativa', *Saggi sulla storia del Borgo Vaticano in Roma*, ed. Ebe Giacometti (Rome, 1992), pp. 87–100, at p. 91; see also *Roma: le trasformazioni urbane nel Quattrocento*, ed. Giorgio Simoncini, 2 vols (Florence, 2004), i, p. 19.

[48] *Roma*, ed. Simoncini, i, p. 270; *Liber Pontificalis*, ed. Duchesne, ii, pp. 486–523. There is also a possibility that it refers to a road named after the emperor; a third-century AD Greek inscription from Ankara mentions the *viae Antoniana, Aureliana, Hadriana* and *Traiana* in Rome, all otherwise unknown; see M. Grazia Granino Cecere, 'Antoniniana via', *Lexicon topographicum urbis Romae: Suburbium*, ed. Adriano La Regina, 6 vols (Rome, 2001–08), i, pp. 75–6.

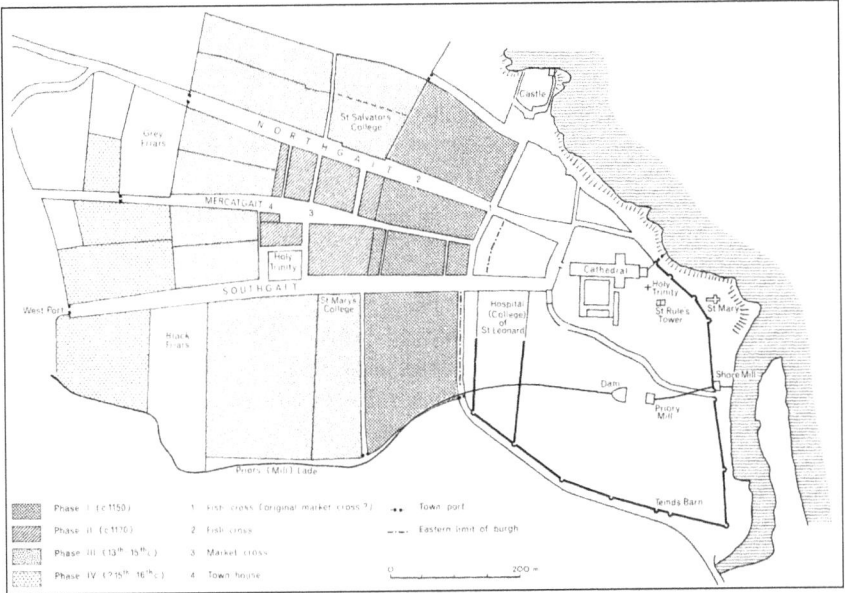

Figure 3.3: Conjectural Plan of the Development of the Burgh of St Andrews from N. P. Brooks and G. Whittington, 'Planning and Growth in the Medieval Scottish Burgh: The Example of St Andrews', *Transactions of the Institute of British Geographers* 2 (1977), pp. 278–95, figure 5.

future Vatican Palace.[49] The paucity of references to it during the Middle Ages implies that the road was always of lesser importance than the other two and had fallen into disuse at an early date. Only in the fifteenth century, when the Vatican palace was finally established as the principal seat of the papacy, did the need arise for restoring a northern route. In the programme of Pope Nicholas V (1447–55) for renewing the Borgo, three straight arcaded or colonnaded streets were envisaged, running in parallel from a new public square at Castel S. Angelo to the enlarged square in front of St Peter's and the palace.[50] The new Via Alessandrina, created by Pope Alexander VI (1492–1503) in time for the influx of pilgrims during the Jubilee or Holy Year of 1500, can be seen as the restoration of this northern link, providing a direct and quieter route to the palace than the two alternatives; but it did not follow for the most part any existing road.[51] Thus, any visitor to the Borgo during the twelfth century would most likely only be aware of two major streets.

The question not yet answered is why the founders of St Andrews should

---

[49] *Liber Pontificalis*, ed. Duchesne, i, p. 262.
[50] Christine Smith and Joseph F. O'Connor, *Building the Kingdom: Giannozzo Manetti on the Material and Spiritual Edifice* (Tempe, 2006), p. 390.
[51] *Roma*, ed. Simoncini, i, pp. 226–9.

want to imitate the Borgo. It has been argued recently that some of the Celtic monasteries with multiple churches were planned symbolically, with Iona and Clonmacnoise modelled on Jerusalem, and Armagh on Rome.[52] Besides the original shrine church of St Andrew, on the site of which St Rule's almost certainly stands and may preserve some of its fabric, FAB numbers seven other churches within the precinct of the monastery at Kinrimund, one of which, dedicated to the Blessed Virgin Mary, was probably the predecessor of the later medieval St Mary's on the Rock.[53] We also know that the original site of the parish church of the burgh, Holy Trinity, was north of St Rule's and east of the present cathedral, before the foundation of the present church in South Street in 1412.[54] The former's inconvenient location in respect of the new burgh, and the fact that the parish boundaries extended far beyond those of the burgh, suggest its prior existence.[55] There are also mentions in 1212 of a chapel of St Peter in the burgh near the sea and, in the later Middle Ages, of a chapel of St Anne in North Street.[56] Of the known names only that of St Peter and that of St Damian the Elder from FAB have an obvious Roman connection, though some of those in FAB may be misrecorded and we cannot be certain that they were the original dedications.[57]

Nevertheless it is conceivable that the Pictish monastery of Kinrimund was already conceived with Rome in mind, in which case the twelfth-century resemblance to the Borgo was the reworking of an old idea. Just as we have seen already with the cathedral (that there was no need to create a replica of Old St Peter's), the mere existence of two streets converging on the cathedral would be enough to evoke the Borgo. But was it merely a matter of formal symbolism or might there also have been a functional rationale in that the two-street plan could have been useful for the management of pilgrim traffic at major celebrations? In the case of Rome, there is remarkably little specific evidence of how pilgrims got around the city. Dante's famous comparison of the crowds passing in opposite directions in the eighth circle of Hell to the two-way system operating on the Ponte S. Angelo in the first Holy Year of 1300 is about all we have.[58] However, it

---

[52] Tomás O Carrigain, *Churches in Early Medieval Ireland: Architecture, Ritual and Memory* (New Haven and London, 2011), pp. 57–66, 74–5, 78–81.
[53] *PNF*, iii, p. 579.
[54] W. E. K. Rankin, *The Parish Church of the Holy Trinity, St Andrews, Pre-Reformation* (Edinburgh, 1955), p. 17.
[55] Matthew Hammond, 'Royal and Aristocratic Attitudes to Saints and the Virgin Mary in Twelfth- and Thirteenth-Century Scotland', *The Cult of the Saints and the Virgin Mary in Medieval Scotland*, ed. Steve Boardman and Eila Williamson (Woodbridge, 2010), pp. 61–85 at p. 70.
[56] *PNF*, iii, p. 427; Rankin, *The Parish Church of the Holy Trinity*, p. 69.
[57] *PNF*, iii, p. 599. St Damian is probably the brother of St Cosmas, who had a major cult in Rome.
[58] Dante, *Inferno*, Canto XVIII, lines 25–33. Herbert L. Kessler and Johanna Zacharias in *Rome 1300: On the Path of the Pilgrim* (New Haven and London, 2000), p. 184, refer to crowds in Via del Pellegrino on the opposite bank of the Tiber all going one way but fail to give a source.

is enough to make us realise that if the majority of pilgrims were heading up the Portica/Porticus S. Petri it would make sense for those leaving the basilica to head back down the Borgo S. Spirito towards the bridge rather than battle their way against the human tide coming towards them. Although 1300 postdates the planning of St Andrews, it is very probable that there were similar crowds in Rome at times in earlier years, since there is evidence that some sort of Holy Year already existed in Rome by the early twelfth century.[59] Thus, the planners of St Andrews might have been anticipating a comparable experience.

We have the first record of a pilgrim to Kinrimund in 965.[60] A century or so later, traffic had built up enough for Queen Margaret to establish a free ferry for pilgrims across the Firth of Forth; and about the same time, the 'basilica of Saint Andrew the apostle' was well enough known for a Welsh hagiographer to incorporate it into his Life of St Cadog.[61] By 1140 there was an official hostel for pilgrims at St Leonard's.[62]

David McRoberts suggested that North Street and South Street 'provide a circular route for a grand procession around the town, leaving undisturbed the booths and stalls in Market Street, where later in the day the merchants and itinerant showmen would provide food, trade, and entertainment for the concourse of pilgrims'.[63] He fails to explain which way the procession would have circulated, but clockwise tends to be more usual, which means pilgrims would have

---

[59] A bull of Pope Alexander III (1159–81), confirming to Santiago the privilege of holding a Holy Year in 1120, specifies that it was to be in the same manner and form as the church of Rome; but this has been seen as a later interpolation, given that the first Jubilee in Rome was in 1300; see Paolo Caucci von Saucken, 'Roma e Santiago di Compostella', *Romei e Giubilei. Il pellegrinaggio medievale a San Pietro (350–1350)*, ed. Mario D'Onofrio (Milan, 1999), pp. 65–72, at p. 69. However, there is a tradition that Boniface VIII met a centenarian whose father had attended a Jubilee in 1200; see Gary Dickson, 'The Crowd at the Feet of Pope Boniface VIII: Pilgrimage, Crusade and the First Roman Jubilee (1300)', *Journal of Medieval History* 25 (1999), pp. 279–307, at pp. 292–3.

[60] *Chronicon Scotorum*, s.a. [965.1], 'Aodh mac Maoilmithidh in perigrinatione moritur .i. hi Cind Ri Monaidh' ('Áed mac Máile Mithig dies on pilgrimage, that is, at Cennrígmonaid'), ed. Gearóid Mac Niocaill, published online at www.ucc.ie/celt/online/G100016/ (accessed 29 April 2013); see also James E. Fraser, 'Rochester, Hexham and Cennrígmonaid: the Movements of St Andrew in Britain, 604–747', *Saints' Cults in the Celtic World*, ed. Steve Boardman, John Reuben Davies and Eila Williamson (Woodbridge, 2009), pp. 1–17, at p. 4.

[61] For Queen Margaret's ferry see Turgot, *Vita S. Margaretae Scotorum reginae*, §9, ed. J. H. Hinde, *Symeonis Dunelmensis opera*, Surtees Society 51 (Durham, 1868), p. 247; *Early Sources of Scottish History, A.D. 500 to 1286*, trans. Alan Orr Anderson, 2 vols (Edinburgh, 1922; repr. with corrections and additions by M. O. Anderson, Stamford, 1990), ii, pp. 77–8. Lifris of Llancarfan, writing in 1091×1104, tells how Cadog (a supposed contemporary of Maelgwn of Gwynedd, d. 549) made a pilgrimage *ad basilicam sancti Andree apostoli*; *Vita S. Cadoci*, §26, ed. and trans. A. W. Wade-Evans, *Vitae Sanctorum Britanniae et Genealogiae* (Cardiff, 1944), pp. 24–140. For the dating of the text see John Reuben Davies, *The Book of Llandaf and the Norman Church in Wales* (Woodbridge, 2003), p. 76.

[62] For the history of St Leonard's see *PNF*, iii, pp. 527–8.

[63] McRoberts, 'The Glorious House of St Andrew', McRoberts, *St Andrews*, pp. 63–120, at p. 101.

approached the cathedral from North Street and left via South Street. This fits well with the cathedral itself, where the everyday entrance for laity would have been the north door. On major feasts the pilgrims could have approached the saint's shrine in the retrochoir from the north aisle of the nave and left via the south aisle, exiting perhaps from the usually closed west door to avoid a traffic jam.[64]

The only other place in Western Europe, outside Italy, which housed the relics of an apostle is Compostela, and it is to there that we now turn since its development shows some remarkable parallels to St Andrews.

Santiago de Compostela

THE earliest reference to the remains of St James the Great at Compostela goes back to the early ninth century.[65] Among the explanations for their presence was that St James had evangelised Galicia while alive but returned to Jerusalem where he was martyred about AD 45. His body was brought back by two of his disciples, the ship docking at Iría, a port 16 miles to the south, which later became the seat of a bishop and renamed Padrón, but the finding of the relics led to the relocation of the cathedral to Compostela around 860. From the mid eleventh century its bishops, especially Diego Gelmírez (bishop from 1100), used the relics to claim theirs was an apostolic see and argued for the independence of the church of the Christian Asturian kingdom from the metropolitan archbishopric of Toledo, which was under Moorish control.[66] In 1095 Pope Urban II (1088–99) put the diocese directly under the protection of the Holy See and renamed it in honour of St James.[67] In 1120, Pope Calixtus II (1119–24) finally raised it to metropolitan status, and granted the privilege of holding a Holy Year, allowing a pilgrimage to the *Civitas Sancti Jacobi* (the city of St James or Santiago) the same status as one to Rome or Jerusalem.[68] There was, moreover, a conscious attempt even before the twelfth century to emulate Rome in aspects of Compostela's liturgy, organisation, the dress of

---

[64] Sible de Blaauw (personal communication, Rome, 2012) thinks that the presence of more graffiti on the south (left-hand) side of the passage round St Peter's *confessio* suggests that the normal circulation route for pilgrims approaching the shrine was clockwise (St Peter's is oriented towards the west).

[65] R. A. Fletcher, *St James's Catapult: The Life and Times of Diego Gelmírez of Santiago de Compostela* (Oxford, 1984), p. 57; Robert Plötz, 'Traditiones Hispanicae beati Jacobi: les origins du culte de saint Jacques à Compostela', *Santiago de Compostela: 1000 ans de pèlerinage européen*, ed. Luis González Seara and Herman Liebaers, Europalia 85 España (Ghent, 1985), pp. 27–39; Plötz, 'Peregrinatio ad Limina Sancti Jacobi', *The Codex Calixtinus and the Shrine of St James*, ed. John Williams and Alison Stones (Tübingen, 1992), pp. 37–49.

[66] Fernando López Alsina, 'Santiago', *Il mondo dei pellegrinaggi: Roma, Santiago, Gerusalemme*, ed. Paolo Caucci von Saucken (Milan, 1999), pp. 299–320, at pp. 313–14; Fletcher, *St James's Catapult*, p. 196.

[67] Fletcher, *St James's Catapult*, p. 196.

[68] Fletcher, *St James's Catapult*, p. 199; López Alsina, 'Santiago', p. 313.

the cathedral chapter (with canons called cardinals), chapel dedications in the new cathedral, and the dedication of churches in the town.[69] Critically, for this argument, it appears that its town plan was consciously modelled on that of the Vatican Borgo. Originally there was a small lay settlement, the *villa*, clustered round the ninth-century shrine, which was a mausoleum standing in an ecclesiastical precinct including a church of St James, a baptistery and the church and monastery of San Pedro de Antealtares.[70] Gradually the settlement spread south, with two streets running parallel from the to meet the main road that ran from Iría to the south, the Rua de Vilar and the Vicus Francorum (Road of the Franks).[71] During the episcopate of Bishop Cresconio (1037–66), this enlarged settlement was enclosed within walls and in a document of 1105, when it became a *municipium* (a market town or burgh), the existing settlement was called the *villa burgensis*.[72] While this already sounds like the Borgo, by the early twelfth century, a third parallel street had been created to the east, the Vicus Novus (New Street).[73] This might be thought to invalidate the comparison with St Andrews but, in fact, the outer two streets, the Vicus Novus and Vicus Francorum, rapidly became the two principal streets.[74] We should also point to Bishop Diego's decision to replace the complex of older small churches and shrine with a large Romanesque cathedral begun around 1105.[75] It almost seems as if Santiago was a blueprint for the bishops of St Andrews to follow.

However, St Andrews fared less well, never achieving the popularity of Santiago, which, along with Rome, Cologne and Canterbury, was decreed one of the four major Western European pilgrimage destinations by the famous French inquisitor Bernard Gui (1261/62–1331).[76] English pressure prevented its bishops from achieving metropolitan status until 1472, and no special privileges were gained for pilgrims to St Andrews. We lack any information about numbers visiting the shrine, but one suspects some potential pilgrims were lured away by the quantity of reported miracles at the shrine of St Thomas Becket (canonised in 1174) at Canterbury.[77] There was also competition from

---

[69] Ibid., pp. 313–14; Fletcher, *St James's Catapult*, p. 169.
[70] José Suarez Otero, 'The Cult of St James at Compostela: From Antiquity to the Middle Ages. A Short Essay Dedicated to John Williams', *Boletín Avriense* 44 (2014), pp. 165–82 at pp. 170–1.
[71] Fernando López Alsina, *La ciudad de Santiago de Compostela en la alta Edad Media* (Santiago de Compostela, 1988), pp. 194–5, 256–7.
[72] Ibid., p. 145.
[73] Ibid., pp. 256–7; Fernando López Alsina, 'Compostelle, ville de Saint-Jacques', *Santiago de Compostela*, ed. González Seara and Liebaers, pp. 53–60; Arturo Franco Taboada, *Los orígenes de Compostela: una historia dibujada* (La Coruña, 1987), p. 52.
[74] E. A. Gutkind, *International History of City Development*, 8 vols (New York, 1964–72), iii, p. 344.
[75] Suarez Otero, 'The Cult of St James', pp. 172–4
[76] Bernard Gui, *Practica inquisitionis heretice pravitatis*, ed. Célestin Douais (Paris, 1886), p. 37.
[77] Diana Webb has discussed evidence for Dutch and Flemish pilgrimage to St Andrews; nine Flemish towns had St Andrews on their lists of pilgrimage destinations as punishments

Amalfi, which received the rest of the relics of St Andrew following the sack of Constantinople in 1204. In 1508, we have a record of a Scottish pilgrim going to Amalfi 'to visit St Andrew's grave'.[78] Nevertheless, the small Marian shrine of Whitekirk in East Lothian (to which Aeneas Sylvius Piccolomini, the future Pope Pius II, walked barefoot in 1435 in thanks for surviving a storm) is said to have had over 15,000 pilgrims in the year 1413.[79] As Whitekirk is only a few kilometres south of North Berwick, the southern end of one of the main ferry routes to St Andrews, it is likely that a large proportion of these 15,000 would have been on their way to or back from venerating the apostle's relics, and others would have come from the north and west of Scotland and from across the North Sea.[80] Averaged out over a year, the numbers might not seem impressive, but they would, of course, have been concentrated around major feast days, and so one can imagine that sometimes the cathedral was thronged with pilgrims, justifying its size.

Within a century, however, the paucity of pilgrims to St Andrews was used as an excuse for converting the old pilgrims' hostel into the third college of the university, St Leonard's.[81] The last time we have a report of someone visiting the relics is 1553; Marcus Wagner, the agent of the Lutheran Matthias Flacius Illyricus, who taught at Wittenberg, posed as a pilgrim, but was more interested in acquiring some of the few manuscripts to have survived the Scottish Reformation, now preserved in Wolfenbüttel, the most important being the St Andrews Music Book.[82] We should be grateful, but it seems an inglorious end to the centuries of pilgrimages to the 'Glorious House of St Andrew', built to rival St Peter's itself.[83] Only the gaunt ruins of the cathedral and, if we are right, the striking town plan now survive as a reminder of the bishops of St Andrews' ambitions to create a second Rome.

---

for crimes, whereas only eight list Canterbury; see *Pilgrims and Pilgrimage in the Medieval West* (London, 2001), pp. 60–1, 216, 226. See also David Ditchburn, '"Saints at the door don't make miracles"? The Contrasting Fortunes of Scottish Pilgrimage, c.1450–1550', *Sixteenth-century Scotland: Essays in Honour of Michael Lynch*, ed. Julian Goodare and Alasdair A. MacDonald (Leiden 2008), pp. 69–98, at 93–5.

[78] M. Livingstone, ed., *Registrum Secreti Sigilli Regum Scotorum: The Register of the Privy Seal of Scotland*, i: *A.D. 1488–1529* (Edinburgh, 1908), p. 235, no. 1606.

[79] See P. Hume Brown, *Early Travellers in Scotland* (Edinburgh, 1891), p. 25; Mark Hall, 'Wo/men only? Marian Devotion in Medieval Perth', *The Cult of the Saints*, ed. Boardman and Williamson, pp. 105–24, at p. 120.

[80] On the routes see Yeoman, *Pilgrimage in Medieval Scotland*, pp. 54–62.

[81] McRoberts, 'Glorious House', p. 102. On the general decline of St Andrews, see also Ditchburn, 'Saints at the door', pp. 69–70 and 93–5.

[82] McRoberts, 'Glorious House', p. 96.

[83] Prior James Haldenstone's description in 1418, cited ibid., p. 63.

CHAPTER FOUR

The Medieval Ecclesiastical Architecture of St Andrews as a Channel for the Introduction of New Ideas

Richard Fawcett

ST Andrews has – and almost certainly always has had – the greatest number of pre-Reformation ecclesiastical buildings of any Scottish burgh. Many of those buildings can be seen to have striven after strikingly innovative approaches to architectural design as a way of making a carefully calculated impression on the beholder.[1] Here it must be remembered that, through its scale and the degree of artistic originality, architecture has always had the potential to be one of the most potent expressions of status, and the commissioning of magnificent and thought-provoking buildings was one of the means by which the claims of the bishops and archbishops of St Andrews to primacy over their fellow prelates were bolstered. One of the fascinations of these buildings lies in trying to understand the choices underlying the complex sources of inspiration for their design.

'St Rule's' Church

THE oldest of St Andrews' churches to have survived in anything approaching an architecturally coherent form is that known as St Rule's, and as one of the first generation built to meet the needs of Scotland's revitalised church, its date of construction has been a keenly debated issue.[2] One of the most significant

---

[1] For more on these buildings see Richard Fawcett, *The Architecture of the Scottish Medieval Church, 1100–1560* (New Haven and London, 2011).

[2] St Rule's Church has been discussed in John Bilson, 'Wharram-le-Street Church, Yorkshire, and St Rule's Church, St Andrews', *Archaeologia* 73 (1923), pp. 55–72; *RCAHMS Fife*, pp. 228–30; H. M. Taylor and Joan Taylor, *Anglo-Saxon Architecture* (Cambridge, 1965), vol. 2, pp. 711–13; Ronald Gordon Cant, 'The Building of St Andrews Cathedral', McRoberts, *St Andrews*, pp. 11–12; Eric Fernie, 'Early Church Architecture in Scotland', *PSAS* 116 (1986), pp. 393–411; Stephen Heywood, 'The Church of St Rule, St Andrews', Higgitt, *St Andrews*, pp. 38–46; Neil M. Cameron, 'St Rule's Church in St Andrews, and Early Stone Architecture in Scotland', *PSAS* 124 (1994), pp. 367–78.

Figure 4.1: St Rule's Church, viewed from the north-west.

events for its construction to the form we now see was the election as bishop in 1123 or 1124 of Robert, the prior of the Augustinian house of Scone, who had previously been a member of the priory of Nostell in Yorkshire.[3] The expectation was that Robert would introduce a community of Augustinian canons

---

[3] *Fasti Ecclesiae Scoticanae Medii Aevi ad Annum 1638*, ed. D. E. R. Watt and A. L. Murray (Edinburgh, 2003), p. 378.

to supplant the existing community of Culdees, though this was not achieved until 1140, after royal pressure had been applied, shortly before which another Robert had been brought up from Nostell as prior.

At the time of Bishop Robert's election, the boundaries of the precinct on the headland are said to have been defined by twelve stone crosses, within which were seven churches in addition to those dedicated to St Andrew and to the Holy Trinity.[4] References to Bishop Robert enlarging a church and dedicating it to divine worship have been taken by some commentators to indicate that what we now see at St Rule's is an enlargement by Robert of one of those buildings already on the site when he came to St Andrews.[5] The architectural evidence does indeed indicate that the shell of the church is the result of two principal building operations, albeit with modifications dating from a range of later works, including the subdivision of the interior by Prior John Hepburn (1483–1526). The surviving parts consist of two small compartments, with a tower rising over the western of the compartments; on the evidence of the base courses it is possible that from the start there were further elements to east and west, though these must have been rebuilt at a second stage of operations.

The walls rise from a narrow base course and are constructed of carefully cut and squared ashlar. The eastern compartment is capped by a cornice and corbel table that continues at the same height around the south, west and north faces of the tower, showing that anything that may initially have been to the west of the tower can only have risen to a lower height than the compartment to its east. In both the south and north flanks of the eastern compartment are two double-splayed windows; their arches are externally cut into single blocks of stone, while internally their lower part is cut into coursed masonry below a voussoir-shaped keystone. In the east face of the tower is an arch of two orders that is so precisely fitted into the masonry that it is clearly an original feature. The belfry stage of the tower, which was presumably only reached after several years of construction, has a pair of lights to each face, with the arches cut into lintels. At the original wall head is a cornice and corbel table similar to that at the lower level.

The building's footprint is relatively small, and the chief impact was evidently intended to be created by excellent masonry and strongly vertical proportions: the walls of the eastern compartment rise to about 10.35m, while the tower soars to the extraordinary height for such a slender structure of almost 33m. The small scale of the plan, relatively attenuated proportions, and the form of the windows in the eastern compartment have invited comparison with Anglo-Saxon architecture south of the Border, with some suggesting dates as early as the first half of the eleventh century or the episcopate of Fothad (c.1070–93).[6] Such early dates are now generally deemed unlikely, though it might be tempting to wonder if

---

[4] A. A. M. Duncan, 'The Foundation of St Andrews Cathedral Priory, 1140', *SHR* 84:1 (2005), pp. 1–37; *PNF*, iii, pp. 405–22.

[5] '... ut ecclesia videlicet ampliaretur et cultui divino dedicaretur'; *PNF*, iii, p. 604.

[6] Taylor and Taylor, *Anglo-Saxon Architecture*, vol. 2, pp. 711–13; Cant, 'The Building of St Andrews Cathedral', p. 11.

Bishop Turgot (1107–15) could have started work on the church. However, the currently more widely accepted view is that Bishop Robert started building after his election in the early 1120s.

Whoever built the earlier parts, on stylistic grounds it is likely that it was indeed Bishop Robert who was responsible for enlarging the church in the second phase of works, possibly in anticipation of the eventual introduction of an Augustinian community in 1140. The chief survivors of this second phase are two major arches of similar design that were presumably associated with extensions of the church to both east and west: one is cut into the west wall of the tower and the other is through the east wall of the eastern compartment. The evidence for these arches being secondary insertions has been compromised by a well-intentioned but heavy-handed restoration programme carried out by the Barons of the Exchequer in 1789.[7] Nevertheless, their slightly awkward relationship with the surrounding masonry, together with the fact that the head of the west tower arch cuts into the corbel table on that side, leaves little doubt that they are not primary features.

These two arches have each been of two orders, with nook-shafts in the angles of the jambs between the two orders, as had also been the case in the east tower arch, and with a three-quarter shaft on the face of the inner order. But the arch orders are altogether more complex than the unadorned orders of the east tower arch, having in the outer order a quirked hollow to the face combined with an angle roll, and a half-roll to the soffit. It was pointed out as long ago as 1923 that this detail is strikingly like that to be seen on a smaller scale on the tower door of Wharram-le-Street in Yorkshire.[8] The significance of this stems from the fact that the church of Wharram had been granted at a date before 1129 to Bishop Robert's first monastic home, at Nostell Priory in Yorkshire, and it is likely that it represents work of the kind that was being produced under Nostell's aegis. It is therefore attractive to suspect that, in trying to give his church at St Andrews an added architectural *éclat*, Robert had sought advice on recruiting masons from his erstwhile brethren in Yorkshire. At a time when there were still relatively few masons in Scotland capable of meeting the rapidly expanding architectural needs of the Scottish Church, this was a course that many patrons of major building campaigns were choosing to follow if they were hoping to achieve architectural results of a high order.

The Start of Building the Cathedral

But for bishops who had claims to authority over their fellow prelates, and who had aspirations to archiepiscopal status, the church of St Rule must

---

[7] An inscribed tablet to the south of the eastern arch states: 'THIS WAS REPAIRD AT THE EXPENCE OF THE EXCHEQUER 1789 by R. Thomson'.

[8] Bilson, 'Wharram-le-Street Church, Yorkshire, and St Rule's Church, St Andrews', pp. 55–72.

soon have appeared irksomely small, and presumably once the episcopal revenues were on a firmer footing, a vast new cathedral was started a short distance to the north-west by Bishop Arnold, before his death in 1162.[9] The new cathedral was set out on a scale that was very much greater than that of any other Scottish cathedral, and must surely have been intended to leave Arnold's fellow bishops with little doubt as to his claims of supremacy.[10] As first planned, it was to have been over 97.5m in length, and while this is far short of the eventual length of, for example, London's St Paul's Cathedral of 178.6m or Winchester's 161.55m, it was by a considerable margin greater than the length of any other Scottish church built in the course of the Middle Ages. Of possibly greater significance is the fact that it approached York Minster's later twelfth-century length of around 107.7m; work on extending York had been started by Archbishop Roger of Pont-l'Evêque shortly before building at St Andrews was initiated.

As with St Rule's Church, Yorkshire was perhaps one of the areas to which Bishop Arnold looked for architectural inspiration for the design of his new cathedral, with some of the models being churches built for Archbishop Roger of York. This might seem rather odd, since relations between St Andrews and York were strained as a result of the vigorous prosecution of the claims of the archbishops of York to metropolitan authority over the Scottish Church. However, at a time when there were exciting new architectural ideas in the air, Yorkshire was a good area to look to for guidance, and it may be that, in taking some lead from the buildings of Archbishop Roger, Arnold and his successors were emphasising through the scale and quality of their architecture that St Andrews' bishops were fully the equals of York's archbishops.

The new cathedral was set out with an eastern limb that had a flat-ended aisleless termination of two bays at the far end of an aisled section of six bays, with stone vaulting over the aisles. Unusually for Scotland, the eastern parts of the cathedral were also designed to have high stone vaults over the central vessel, which is perhaps one of the clearest demonstrations of the high aspirations of its episcopal patrons, since such vaulting was costly and technically demanding to construct. It is likely that in the original arrangement the presbytery area, in which the high altar was located, was in the three eastern bays, with the canons' choir in the three or four western bays. Laterally projecting four-bay transepts had three chapels on the east side of each, with the innermost bay on each side opening into the choir aisles. West of the crossing at the junction of the main body and transepts was an aisled nave that was probably initially intended to be of fourteen bays, but that was eventually truncated to twelve bays with a two-bay narthex at the west end.

---

[9] *Chronicle of Melrose*, ed. A. O. Anderson et al. (London, 1936), p. 78.
[10] Recent studies of the cathedral include Cant, 'The Building of St Andrews Cathedral', pp. 11–32; Eric Cambridge, 'The Early Building History of St Andrews Cathedral', *Antiquaries Journal* 57 (1977), pp. 277–88; Malcolm Thurlby, 'St Andrews Cathedral and the Beginnings of Gothic Architecture in Northern Britain', Higgitt, *St Andrews*, pp. 47–60.

Figure 4.2: St Andrews Cathedral, the internal face of the east gable.

The combination of a flat-ended aisle-less eastern part and a longer aisled section may have its ultimate roots in one of the collegiate churches of the archbishops of York, at Southwell in Nottinghamshire, where work had probably started around 1108, though the idea had already been taken up in Scotland at the Augustinian house of Jedburgh in about 1138.[11] However, the eastern limb of St Andrews was much longer than either of those, presumably with the intention that all of the liturgically most important functions could be accommodated within an architecturally distinct limb, as had already been the case at Durham Cathedral, where work was started in 1093. Durham may also have been the inspiration for the decorative dado of intersecting blind arcading around the lower walls, of which there are traces along the east wall of the presbytery and more complete remains along the west side of the south transept. A more extended plan for the eastern limb was also a feature of Archbishop Roger's work at York, albeit without the aisle-less presbytery projection at the east end, and there were to be a number of other elements in the new cathedral at St Andrews that indicate an awareness of York.

While it must be stressed that St Andrews Cathedral has come down to us in such a fragmentary state that there is much we do not know about its earliest parts, it seems clear that the central vessel of the building was of three storeys throughout. If the proportions of the aisle-less presbytery were continued into the aisled choir, there would have been an arcade storey opening into the aisles at the lowest level, and we know that the arches were carried on piers of clustered-shaft form. Above this would have been a relatively tall gallery stage over the vaults of the aisles, and at the top there would have been a clearstorey of an approximately similar height to the gallery, pierced by windows to let light directly into the central vessel and with a passage in the wall thickness. It should be conceded that there is at least a possibility that the relative proportions of the three storeys in the aisled section were different from those in the aisle-less section, as was to be case, for example, at Tynemouth Priory in Northumberland some years later.[12] Analogies with York, however, suggest that the relative proportions in the presbytery are more likely to have continued down the eastern limb.

Archbishop Roger's eastern limb at York was probably started very soon after his election in 1154, and thus a few years before the start of work on St Andrews, though our understanding of it is even less complete than our knowledge of St Andrews, since it was replaced between 1361 and 1407.[13] But the survival of responds of clustered-shaft form and the indications from the transepts as

---

[11] Richard Fawcett, 'The Architectural Development of the Abbey Church', *Jedburgh Abbey: the Archaeology and Architecture*, ed. John Lewis and Gordon Ewart (Edinburgh, 1995), pp. 159–174; Malcolm Thurlby, 'Jedburgh Abbey, the Romanesque Fabric', *PSAS* 125 (1995), pp. 793–812.

[12] Richard Fawcett, 'The Architecture of Tynemouth Priory Church', *Newcastle and Northumberland: Roman and Medieval Architecture and Art*, ed. Jeremy Ashbee and Julian Luxford (Leeds, 2013), pp. 171–92.

[13] Sarah Brown, *'Our Magnificent Fabrick': York Minster, an Architectural History, c.1220–1500* (Swindon, 2003), pp. 169–93.

reconstructed after around 1225 that the relative proportions of the three storeys were similar to those of St Andrews all suggest that there were significant similarities between the two buildings. This view is supported by another of Archbishop Roger's buildings, the eastern limb of Ripon Minster, where work was started some years later than at York, but where we see the archbishop's architectural preferences in a far more complete state.[14] Amongst many parallels between Ripon and St Andrews are features such as the shared use of octofoil clustered-shaft piers, and the indentation from the main gable face of the end walls of the transept chapels. Many of the ideas seen at York and Ripon had originated in northern France, and had found their way to northern England through the medium of the churches built for the Cistercian monks who were active there, and whose original home was in Burgundy in eastern France.[15] Other ideas that may have reached St Andrews from the northern English Cistercians included the tiering of triplets of single-light windows, as can be seen to have existed in the east gable.

On this basis, we are able to understand St Andrews Cathedral as a building that, while incorporating a number of well-established approaches to design, was predominantly a building in the very latest fashion of northern English Gothic as it was beginning to take shape under the patronage of Archbishop Roger of York. As it rose, the new cathedral must have attracted the attention of a number of patrons, and it was to provide essential inspiration for the major operations that began on the nave of Jedburgh Abbey around the 1180s, and at William the Lion's great new Tironensian abbey of Arbroath, where the main campaign probably started in the later years of the twelfth century. At a time when, whatever the condition of state and ecclesiastical politics, northern England and lowland Scotland were essentially a single architectural province in which there was regular interchange of ideas, the solutions worked out at St Andrews may also have been a factor in the design of the choirs of Hexham and Lanercost priories.

Later Repairs to the Cathedral

THE cathedral as planned in the early 1160s must have stretched the available resources of the bishops and cathedral priory beyond the limit of what they

---

[14] Stuart Harrison and Paul Barker, 'Ripon Minster: an Archaeological Reconstruction of the 12th-Century Church', *Journal of the British Archaeological Association* 152 (1999), pp. 49–78.

[15] Peter Fergusson, *Architecture of Solitude: Cistercian Abbeys in Twelfth-Century England* (New Jersey, 1984); Christopher Wilson, 'The Cistercians as "Missionaries of Gothic"', *Cistercian Art and Architecture in the British Isles*, ed. Christopher Norton and David Park (Cambridge, 1986), pp. 86–116; Malcolm Thurlby, 'Roger of Pont l'Evêque, Archbishop of York (1154–81) and French Sources for the Beginnings of Gothic Architecture in Northern Britain', *England and the Continent in the Middle Ages*, ed. J. Mitchell (Stamford, 2000), pp. 35–47.

could easily afford, and completion of the less liturgically essential nave was a protracted process. Tragically, as work was nearing completion, the west front was blown down in a storm during the episcopate of William Wishart, probably the same storm that damaged Arbroath Abbey in 1272.[16] The cathedral was then completed to a truncated plan and a dedication was carried out in 1318.

Further major rebuilding was necessitated by yet another disaster: a fire that damaged much of the building in 1378. Prior Stephen Pay (1363–86) spent 2,200 marks on repairs that included the roof and the reconstruction of two piers of the south arcade. Work on the main body was continued by Priors Robert de Montrose (c.1386–94) and James Biset (1394–1416), with the latter starting the process of providing new furnishings, including choir stalls, to which canopies were added by Prior James de Haldenstone (1418–43). Haldenstone provided many further furnishings within what was said until then to have had the appearance of 'an empty, vast, deserted synagogue', and also rebuilt the upper part of the east gable with the attached vaulting. The finishing touches included the provision of an altar on the rood loft at the east end of the nave by Canon Walter Bower, who served the parish as its vicar.[17]

The most visible relics of this campaign are the upper parts of the west and east gables. The former has a band of blind arcading above the retained late thirteenth-century processional door, which relates closely to that above the outer arch of the nearby Pends Yett into the priory precinct, and is likely to be of a similar date. Above the west front arcading two levels of pairs of three-light traceried windows were installed. At the opposite end of the church, Prior Haldenstone's work can presumably be identified in a large three-light window corresponding to the gallery and clearstorey stages of the east limb, which has had a simple arrangement of the light-heads reaching up to the window arch.

Haldenstone's surviving work as represented by the east window now appears rather bland, but at one stage of the post-1378 operations it seems that an effort was made to have something architecturally out of the ordinary by employing a French-born mason. An inscription left by the mason John Morow at Melrose Abbey, which proclaims that he had been 'born in parysse certanly', records that at some stage in his career he had worked at 'santan[droys]'. The inscription goes on to list the other places at which he had worked in Scotland, which were: Glasgow, Melrose, Paisley, Nithsdale (almost certainly Lincluden) and Galloway (Whithorn).

In several of those buildings it is possible to trace a very distinctive approach to architectural design that corresponds with a short phase in French architecture represented in such buildings as the chapels added to the nave of Amiens Cathedral by Cardinal Jean de la Grange from 1373 and the earlier parts of the chapel in the château of Vincennes near Paris, which was started in about 1379 but with the main campaign around 1395–96. At Melrose Abbey, Lincluden Collegiate Church and Paisley Abbey that approach to design is seen in the use

---

[16] *Scotichronicon*, iii, p. 399; v, p. 385.
[17] *Scotichronicon*, iii, pp. 425–39.

of identical window tracery that displays a careful balance between curvilinear and bowed forms. In addition, at Melrose, Lincluden and Glasgow Cathedral his approach is reflected in the use of a type of corbel with a crouching figure holding a scroll, while at Melrose, Lincluden and Paisley it is evident in the use of closely similar mouldings.[18]

Unfortunately, so little has survived at St Andrews of the works dating from the repairs after 1378 that it would be difficult to identify Morow's contribution here with any confidence. Perhaps all that can be said is that parallels with buildings in France may be detectable in the way that the surviving window of the four inserted in the west front is stilted, so that the tracery field starts below the springing of the window arch, in a way that is very much more common in France than in England. Further possible parallels with France are perhaps discernible in the rebuilt piers of the nave arcades. No more than the sub-bases of a number of these have survived, and some of them appear to be modern reconstructions, but the continuous ogee moulding that runs around the upper edge of the sub-bases does bear comparison with a moulding favoured by Morow for arcade bases at Melrose, Lincluden and Paisley. Of possibly greater significance is the way in which the sub-bases are asymmetrically extended on the side towards the central vessel of the nave, presumably in order to support wall shafts that would have risen through the full height of the central vessel. As with the stilted windows, this is something that is more common in France than in the British Isles, though there could be no more than a tentative speculation that this feature is a survivor of Morow's work at the cathedral.

Work on the post-1378 repairs was presumably still in progress when, on the feast of St Kentigern in 1410, the south transept gable was blown down in a storm, damaging the adjacent dormitory and chapter house.[19] Surviving from the reconstruction that must have followed that collapse is the lower part of the south respond of the arcade that opened into the chapels on the east side of the transept. This is of semi-cylindrical form, and rises from a tall semi-circular base above a polygonal sub-base, with heads decorating the band between the two levels.

The survival of the respond suggests that the transept arcade had been at least partly reconstructed with cylindrical piers. Such piers had passed out of fashion for major Scottish churches after the mid twelfth century, but a new vogue for them appears to have begun in the nave of Aberdeen Cathedral, which was started by the second Bishop Alexander Kininmund (1355–80).[20] There the design of the crossing piers is of particular interest, since it almost certainly emulates a type of pier favoured in the duchy of Brabant, an area that had taken the lead in a revival of the use of cylindrical piers in the Low Countries, as seen

---

[18] Fawcett, *The Architecture of the Scottish Medieval Church*, pp. 236–42.
[19] *Scotichronicon*, viii, p. 75.
[20] J. Moir, ed., *Hectoris Boetii Murthlacensum et Aberdonensium Episcoporum Vitae* (Aberdeen, 1894), p. 24.

initially at St-Rombaut at Mechelen.²¹ The Aberdeen crossing piers have a massive cylindrical core, with large semi-cylindrical shafts on the cardinal axes and capitals set at a range of levels to support the arches that spring from those piers. This is a pier type that has its closest parallels in a number of Brabantine churches including St-Michel-et-St-Gudule in Brussels. In view of the Netherlandish debts displayed by Aberdeen's crossing piers, it appears likely that the simple cylindrical piers of the Aberdeen nave arcades were also taking their lead from the Netherlandish revived use of cylindrical piers.

It could be no more than a tentative suggestion that the arcade respond in the St Andrews transept shows the impact of ideas originating in the Low Countries that had already been demonstrated at Aberdeen. Nevertheless, at time when Scottish patrons were showing themselves to be more open to ideas emanating from mainland Europe, this should certainly be seen as worth considering, and it is a possibility that will perhaps find support when we move on to consider other buildings in St Andrews that may have taken a lead from Netherlandish prototypes. In this connection it should also be borne in mind that St Andrews' prelates were figures who operated on a European stage. Bishop Henry Wardlaw (1403–40), in whose time much of the cathedral reconstruction was carried out, is known to have passed through France to the papal court at Avignon for example, and is likely to have taken the opportunity to admire many buildings during his travels.²²

Holy Trinity Parish Church

IT was not only in the churches built under the direct control of its bishops that high architectural ambitions were displayed in St Andrews. Before the early fifteenth century the parish church had been within the precinct of the cathedral priory and was said to have been close to the east gable of the cathedral itself, where it may have perpetuated the location of one of the several churches that are known to have been within the precinct of Kinrymont.²³ Foundations located in the course of grave digging have suggested that it was probably to the south east of the cathedral and to the north of St Rule's Church.²⁴

The parish church had been appropriated to the cathedral priory by around 1163 and having it within the precinct perhaps facilitated control over parochial affairs by the priory.²⁵ Yet by the fifteenth century, when the precinct of the Augustinian priory was coming to be more completely enclosed by its splendid towered circuit of walls, this also had the disadvantage that the laity

---

[21] R. M. Lemaire, *Les Origines du Style Gothique en Brabant* (Antwerp and Zwolle, 1949), vol. 2.
[22] *Scotichronicon*, iii, p. 411.
[23] *Scotichronicon*, ix, p. 137, citing an addition to the Donibristle manuscript.
[24] David Hay Fleming, *St Andrews Cathedral Museum* (Edinburgh and London, 1931), plan 1, facing p. 2.
[25] Ian B. Cowan, *The Parishes of Medieval Scotland* (Edinburgh, 1967), p. 176.

Figure 4.3: Holy Trinity Parish Church by James Gordon of Rothiemay, *Andreopolis*, 1642.

had rights of access across the area that the canons were presumably increasingly regarding as their own space. It is also likely that the parishioners had aspirations for greater freedom in what they could do with their church, with the hope that it might become the principal architectural ornament of the expanding burgh.

On 14 November 1410, Sir William Lindsay of the Byres granted the parish a large site to the south of the market area in the burgh, and the new church was formally founded there in 1412.[26] In his charter Lindsay stated that he was giving the land so that the prior and convent together with the citizens and parishioners could build a new church, presumably with the assumption that the prior would be responsible for the chancel and the parishioners for the nave. It was specified that there was to be a row of pillars on each side – meaning that it was to be flanked by aisles – and the burgesses of St Andrews agreed to build a chapel with an altar dedicated to the Holy Trinity at the east end of the south aisle as a thank-offering to Sir William.

---

[26] St Andrews, Archives of the City of St Andrews, Charters, no. 16; *Scotichronicon*, viii, p. 83; W. E. K. Rankin, *The Parish Church of the Holy Trinity St Andrews* (Edinburgh and London, 1955), pp. 20–9.

Small-scale sketched depictions of the church in two post-Reformation views of the burgh probably show it still in its late medieval state. That attributed to John Geddy, of about 1580, shows it from the south, while that by James Gordon of 1642 shows it from the north.[27] These both indicate that it was cruciform with aisles running the full length of both nave and chancel, and Geddy shows the aisles with crenellated parapets. A clearstorey rose above the aisles and a transeptal chapel projected symmetrically on each side; the tall spired tower over the west end of the north aisle was a significant vertical addition to the burgh's skyline and there was a south porch over the principal entrance for layfolk. The main difference between the two views is that Geddy shows the transeptal chapels as rising little higher than the aisles, whereas Gordon shows them as rising to the same height as the central vessel of the main body, and there is now no way of knowing which was more accurate.

Any attempt to understand the architecture of the medieval church has to take account of the sequence of repairs and rebuilding it has undergone since the Reformation. Most significantly, under the direction of James Salisbury and Robert Balfour in 1798–1800 the church was almost completely rebuilt on the old foundations, apart from the tower, parts of the west front and a number of arcade piers. It seems that only part of the space was by then used for worship, and in that part a number of piers and arches were removed to allow wider and higher arches to be constructed that opened up the space into the heightened aisles.

In 1902–09 the building was heavily restored to a medieval appearance, albeit an appearance that bore only a partial relationship to what had been there in the Middle Ages. Internally, the only identifiable medieval fabric is now a number of nave piers, which are of cylindrical form, and it may be that the inspiration for the form of these piers was the south transept of the cathedral as rebuilt after 1410, with the ultimate source of the idea coming from the Netherlands. The reconstruction of the cathedral transept would presumably still have been in progress at the time that work was starting on Holy Trinity and the parish's leaders would have been closely aware of what was happening there, especially since the first vicar of the relocated parish church, William Bower, was also a canon of the cathedral priory.[28]

The importance of their parish church to the citizens of St Andrews is manifest in its ambitious scale. Although the churches of the great trading burghs of Aberdeen and Edinburgh had already grown to be imposing cruciform buildings by the later twelfth and late fourteenth centuries respectively, the parish church of St Andrews was probably the first of the major burgh churches to be built on a great scale and to a homogeneous design in the fifteenth century, predating the start of work on those of Haddington, Linlithgow, Perth and Stirling by some decades.[29] It is also an indicator of its significance for its founder and his heirs

---

[27] NLS, MS 20996.
[28] *Scotichronicon*, iii, pp. 438–9.
[29] See the plans fig. 2 in Richard Fawcett, 'The Churches of the Greater Medieval Cities', *The*

Figure 4.4: St Salvator's Collegiate Chapel, viewed from the south-east.

that there should have been considerations of founding a college within it from the start, and the failure of a petition of 27 May 1433, by the founder's son, is thought likely to have been due to opposition by the cathedral priory.[30] But if that petition had been successful, St Andrews would perhaps have been the first of the great burgh churches to have its clergy incorporated into a collegiate body.

St Salvator's College Chapel

A FURTHER lofty tower was to be added to St Andrews' skyline with the building of the chapel of St Salvator, which had its principal face towards North Street. The chapel was the great architectural focus of the new college founded by Bishop James Kennedy in 1450 and it was sufficiently complete to be dedicated for worship in 1460.[31] In its design we see how, in response to the wishes

---

Architecture of Scottish Cities: Essays in Honour of David Walker, ed. Deborah Mays (East Linton, 1997), pp. 13–25.

[30] Rankin, *The Parish Church of the Holy Trinity St Andrews*, p. 23; Registra Supplicationum in the Vatican Archives, Calendar of Entries held by Glasgow University School of Scottish History, vol. 286, fol. 221; Ian B. Cowan and David E. Easson, *Medieval Religious Houses, Scotland*, 2nd edn (London and New York, 1976), p. 228.

[31] Cant, *St Salvator*, pp. 54–60; A. Theiner, ed., *Vetera Monumenta Hibernorum et Scotorum* (Rome, 1864), no. dccciv.

of a highly cosmopolitan patron, ideas that were coming to be a part of the emerging Scottish repertoire of architectural forms might combine with ideas of Continental origin.

The chapel is an aisle-less rectangle of seven bays, terminating in a three-sided polygonal eastern apse. Along the south side and around the apse are substantial buttresses with image tabernacles at mid-height, between two levels of offsets. The tabernacles in the eastern bay are deflected inwards, perhaps because they housed images of the Virgin Annunciate and of the Archangel Gabriel; an additional corbel to the easternmost tabernacle may have supported the Virgin's lectern. The buttresses are capped by pinnacles, which are modern replacements in their present form, and between the buttresses are windows that occupy almost the full width available, within broadly curved reveals, though, as with the pinnacles, the tracery they contain is modern.

The main entrance door has a polygonal head, of a type that had been current in Scotland from around the 1430s, as at Torphichen Hospitaller church and Borthwick Castle. It is in the second bay from the west, where there is a shallow porch between the buttresses that is covered by a pointed barrel vault with ribs set out to a quadripartite pattern. Against the southern half of the west wall of the chapel is a tall tower, which is capped by a broached spire with two levels of lucarnes. Internally, the upper stages of the tower show extensive traces of burning that were probably suffered at the time of the siege of the castle of 1546–47, after which there may have been partial rebuilding. The entrance to the college quadrangle is through a barrel-vaulted passage at the base of the tower, the archway opening onto which is given added prominence by a plaque with Kennedy's arms flanked by a pair of tabernacles.

There was evidently a range along the north side of the chapel, which was entered through polygonal-headed doors in the second bay from the east and the second bay from the west. This range was of two storeys, with two windows that looked down into the chapel. It presumably contained sacristies at the lower level and a treasury above. In this there are analogies with the early sixteenth-century two-storey jewel house, library and sacristy range that was built along the south side of King's College Chapel in Aberdeen, a building that drew on St Salvator's Chapel for its plan.[32] The upper storey of the north range was accessed from an elevated door in the second bay from the east, the location of which presupposes that there must have been a gallery of some form in the two western bays, perhaps much as there is now. The function of such a gallery is not known, though there also appear to have been western galleries in the collegiate churches of Castle Semple and Innerpeffray, and it cannot be ruled out that there was a medieval west gallery at St Leonard's College Chapel, as there certainly was after 1578.

It has been generally assumed that the screen that would have separated the collegiate choir from the nave was between the fourth and fifth bays from

---

[32] Francis C. Eeles, *King's College Aberdeen* (Edinburgh and London, 1956).

the east, and this may indeed have been the case.[33] However, a screen in this position would have meant that the choir stalls covered a tomb in the fourth bay from the east, so it is perhaps more likely that the screen was between the third and fourth bays from the east. In some support of this, a small blocked window of clearly secondary construction is to be seen below the main window in the fourth bay from the east on the south side. By analogy with comparable windows at a number of other churches, including Fowlis Easter and Innerpeffray collegiate churches, of around 1452 and 1506 respectively, a possible function for that window would have been to light one of the altars in front of the screen.

The chapel is known to have been covered by a stone vault that was removed in 1773, and it is assumed that this was of the pointed barrel form that had come to be greatly favoured in Scotland; it also seems likely that it would have had a decorative application of ribs set out to a quadripartite pattern, as is the case in the south porch.[34] It must be conceded that there is no certainty that the main vault was ribbed, since at the church of Whitekirk the porch is ribbed but the vault over the chancel is not; but, on balance, in such a prestigious church as St Salvator's, ribbing seems more likely.

The pointed barrel vaults and polygonal-headed doors, amongst other features, show that St Salvator's Chapel was in step with the architectural vocabulary that was beginning to take shape in mid-fifteenth-century Scotland. The polygonal-apsed aisle-less plan was also to be favoured in Scotland for a range of buildings types, from monastic churches as at Crossraguel to small votive churches such as St Mungo's in Culross, and it was adopted for several collegiate churches including Seton and Biggar. It seems very likely that St Salvator's was the first example of this plan type, however, so we must ask from where the idea was derived.

Although a small number of English churches had such apses, including the Lady Chapel at Lichfield Cathedral and the church of St Michael in Coventry, they were so unusual south of the Border that, putting other considerations aside, an English source seems most unlikely. However, in France the plan had come to be widely adopted for a range of functions and was especially favoured for the private chapels of the monarchy, the prelates of the church and the great territorial landholders. Many of those private chapels were of two storeys, with the lower level allocated to lesser members of the household.[35] This plan in single-storey form also appears to have been favoured for the chapels of the colleges that were clustering around the university of Paris. One of those that survives was built as the chapel of the Collège de Beauvais, which dates from

---

[33] Cant, *St Salvator*, p. 106.
[34] Richard Fawcett, 'Barrel-Vaulted Churches in Late Medieval Scotland', *Architecture and Interpretation: Essays for Eric Fernie*, ed. Jill A. Franklin, T. A. Heslop and Christine Stevenson (Woodbridge, 2012), pp. 60–77.
[35] C. Billot, 'Les Saintes-Chapelles du xiiie au xvie Siècles', *L'Eglise et le Château: xe–xviiie Siècle*, ed. A. Chastel (Bordeaux, 1988), pp. 95–114.

1374 to 1380, but which has been greatly modified to meet the current needs of a Romanian Orthodox congregation.

A clearer image of one of these chapels in its medieval state can be gained from illustrations of the lost chapel of the Collège de Cluny, which was built in about 1269.[36] Although that chapel was considerably earlier than St Salvator's, the general proportions and the relationship of the windows to the buttressed walls appears to be significantly similar to what is seen at St Salvator's and it must be considered a possibility that it was from such a chapel that Kennedy borrowed the overall form of his own. Here it should be remembered that Kennedy had many connections with France.[37] At a date before 1431 his uncle, Hugh, had fought in France under Joan of Arc, and in 1436 Kennedy himself had been amongst the escort of Princess Margaret when she travelled to Tours for her marriage to the dauphin. John Kennedy, who was possibly a nephew, was an ambassador to France in 1456 and 1458 and had a prominent place in the university of Paris, which may be additionally significant when it is recalled that the constitutions of Paris were closely looked to in the formulation of St Salvator's own.[38] The founder's willingness to look to France in providing for his college is perhaps most clearly illustrated by the exquisite mace that he had made for it in 1461 by the goldsmith to the dauphin, Jean Mayelle, who was warden of the Paris goldsmiths in 1455, 1460 and 1467.[39]

The chapel has undergone many post-Reformation changes. In 1563 it was fitted out as a commissary court, before being brought back into ecclesiastical use two centuries later, when in 1759–61 it was repaired and fitted up to serve the parishioners of St Leonard's. Regrettably, in 1773 it was decided that the vault was in a dangerous condition and it was pulled down in a cavalier fashion that caused much collateral damage. A major campaign of restoration was initiated in the mid nineteenth century, when responsibility for the fabric of the Scottish universities was in the hands of the government's Office of Works. The Clerk of Works, William Nixon, refurnished the chapel and built the cloister along the north flank in 1845–49, obscuring evidence for the form of the north range in the process. His successor, Robert Matheson, inserted tracery in the window openings and replaced pinnacles on the buttresses in 1861–63. In 1904 the congregation of St Leonard's was decanted to a new church designed by Peter Macgregor Chalmers and St Salvator's once again became the university chapel. A further campaign of restoration was instigated in the 1920s, initially to the designs of Chalmers, and then by Reginald Fairlie, who installed the present screen and choir stalls in 1928–31.

The end result of all these operations is a very handsome interior, albeit one

---

[36] P. Anger, *Le Collège de Cluny* (Paris, 1916); Robert Branner, *St Louis and the Court Style* (London, 1965), pp. 90–1.
[37] Dunlop, *Kennedy*.
[38] Cant, *St Salvator*, p. 4.
[39] David McRoberts, 'Bishop Kennedy's Mace', *Innes Review* 25 (1974), pp. 153–8; Godfrey Evans, 'The Mace of St Salvator's College', Higgitt, *St Andrews*, pp. 197–212; see also Julian Luxford in this volume.

that bears relatively little resemblance to its likely medieval appearance; to visualise something of that lost appearance it is necessary to consult the late medieval inventories and to imagine where the items would have had their place in the collegiate worship.[40] Nevertheless, a number of important items do survive, including a pair of high quality fragmentary carvings of the Annunciation and Circumcision that may have been part of an elaborate altarpiece with scenes from the life of Christ.[41] The finest survivors of the medieval fixtures and fittings to remain in place are the large tomb in the north wall of the presbytery area, which it can be assumed was provided by the college's founder for himself, and the Sacrament House immediately to its east.[42] The tomb has suffered greatly, both as a consequence of the process of demolishing the vault and through erosion, and it has been conserved in a somewhat doctrinaire fashion with blocked-out detailing and steel joist supports; but despite all that it has suffered, it can still be appreciated as an extraordinary composition of the highest quality. There is no evidence that there was ever an effigy on the ledger slab within the deep recess of the tomb; indeed, there is nothing now visible on the tomb to associate it directly with the chapel's founder, other than an image corbel to its west that bears his arms. But there seems little reason to doubt that it was the founder's tomb, and a faded inscription at the back of the tomb has been read, perhaps a little over-optimistically, as 'Columen et decus et tutela hujus of[ficina]e mag[na]e/ Hic[c]e finit fanum qui largis co[n]tulit ortu[m]', which has been translated as 'The prop, ornament, and guardian of this great school here finishes the fane to which by his liberality he gave birth'.[43]

The tomb is a markedly vertical composition. Flanking the chest, which has a modern brass panel to its face and is capped by a ledger slab thought to be of Tournai marble, are the extended bases of multi-shafted flanking responds that are enriched with micro-architectural tabernacles between the shafts. Those responds frame a deep polygonal recess that was covered by a ribbed vault. At mid-height of the recess is a band of semi-vaulted tabernacle work, at the ends of which are doorways opening onto stairs that presumably lead to the heavenly mansions, and that are perhaps reminiscent of the flights of steps on Jean Mayelle's college mace. The responds rise to support the most lavish display of tabernacle work that is known to have existed in Scotland.

---

[40] Cant, *St Salvator*, pp. 107–63.
[41] James S. Richardson, 'Fragments of Altar Retables of Late Medieval Date in Scotland', *PSAS* 62 (1927–28), pp. 197–224, at pp. 214–16.
[42] Richard Fawcett, 'Aspects of Scottish Canopied Tomb Design', *Monuments and Monumentality across Medieval and Early Modern Europe*, ed. Michael Penman (Donington, 2013), pp. 129–42, at pp. 135–8; for measured drawings of the tomb, J. R. Walker, *Pre-Reformation Churches in Fife and Lothian* (Edinburgh, 1885); David McRoberts, 'Scottish Sacrament Houses', *Transactions of the Scottish Ecclesiological Society* 15 pt. 3 (1965), pp. 33–56, at p. 44.
[43] Robert Chalmers, 'Memorandum Respecting the Tomb of Bishop Kennedy in the Choir of St Salvator's College, St Andrews', *Archaeologia Scotica* 4:3 (1857), pp. 382–4 and pl. XXIX.

It is difficult to find close parallels for the design of the tomb. It has been suggested that it shows the impact of French ideas of tomb design, and, in view of the French sources that have been suggested for the chapel itself, and the French workmanship of the mace, it would be appealing to be able to confirm that idea.[44] However, no close parallels have so far been identified amongst what survives in France and there are none amongst the large collection of drawings of French tombs assembled by Roger de Gaignières.[45] One of the most striking features of the tomb is the tabernacle work at the summit, which is treated as a series of tall and slightly tubular turrets, rather than as spirelets that decrease in size as they ascend, and which is finished at the top with miniature traceried balustrades. Similar balustrading also runs along the edges of the semi-vaulting of the recess.

Some of the most precise analogies for such detailing may be found on a number of later fifteenth-century carved wooden altar retables that are known to have been manufactured in Brussels, examples of which may be seen at Korbeek-Dijle, Ham-sur-Heure, Villers-la-Ville and Zoutleeuw.[46] Taking account of the large numbers of church furnishings that are known to have been imported to Scotland from the Low Countries, and bearing in mind that Bishop Kennedy was himself a graduate of Leuven, would it be too much of a stretch of the imagination to wonder if the founder had imported the principal altarpiece for his chapel from the Netherlands and that he had chosen to have his tomb designed so that the two were stylistically homogeneous?[47] It is clear at churches where several of the furnishings survive that considerable pains might be taken to achieve artistic homogeneity. This is particularly well illustrated at Lincluden Collegiate Church, where Princess Margaret's tomb employs a similar repertoire of forms as the piscina and sedilia on the opposite side of the presbytery area. We should surely expect no less a wish for artistic unity from the patronage of Bishop Kennedy.

The location of the tomb on the north side of the presbytery area and the lack of prominent reference to the founder may suggest that it could have been intended to serve as an Easter Sepulchre as well as a burial place, where a consecrated host together with a representation of the crucified Christ could be ritually entombed between Good Friday and Easter Sunday. This possibility draws

---

[44] *RCAHMS Fife*, p. 244.
[45] Jean Adhémar, 'Catalogue des Tombeaux de Gaignières', *Gazette des Beaux-Arts* 84 (1974), and 88 (1976).
[46] Marjan Buyle and Christine Vanthillo, *Retables Flamands et Brabançons dans les Monuments Belges* (Brussels, 2000), pp. 129, 181, 223 and 233.
[47] *The Ledger of Andrew Halyburton, 1492–1503*, ed. Cosmo Innes (Edinburgh, 1867), lv–lxiii; David McRoberts, 'Notes on Scoto-Flemish Artistic Contacts', *Innes Review* 10 (1959), pp. 91–6; Lorne Campbell, 'Scottish Patrons and Netherlandish Painters in the Fifteenth and Sixteenth Centuries', *Scotland and the Low Countries 1124–1994*, ed. Grant G. Simpson (East Linton, 1996), pp. 89–103; David Ditchburn, *Scotland and Europe: The Medieval Kingdom and its Contacts with Christendom, 1214–1560* (East Linton, 2000), pp. 113–20.

some support from parallels with the Easter Sepulchre at the Norfolk church of Northwold, which similarly has two levels of tabernacle work, with the lower level helping to focus attention on the place where the receptacle for Christ's body would have been deposited. The vicarious sanctity that was deemed to be derived from close association with Christ's sacrificed body is known to have been an attraction for many individuals who were able to command a burial place in such a prominent location, and there are several cases in England of requests for a tomb that could also serve as an Easter Sepulchre.[48] Taking this into account, it is attractive to suspect at St Salvator's Chapel that the ledger slab was the Passion-tide location for the 'gret sepultur with an ymage off our Saluiour liand therewithin and ane swdour of quhit silk abon the sam' listed in the early sixteenth-century inventory.[49]

The possibility of such supplementary use for the tomb recess is given further credibility by the location immediately to the east of the tomb of a Sacrament House, where the consecrated host was reserved under normal circumstances, and it is easy to imagine the celebration of the Good Friday liturgy during which the host would be solemnly transferred from one to the other. It should be said, nevertheless, that the Sacrament House appears to be a secondary insertion, since it is slightly awkwardly fitted into the angle of the apse, and it must be conceded that the rather stolid angels who support the representation of the monstrance within which the host was reserved are of lower quality than the carvings of the tomb. Despite that, it is certain that it was for Kennedy that the Sacrament House was inserted, since his arms are prominently displayed on the cornice, along with those of the king.

The Dominican Church

ONE of St Andrews' more enigmatic medieval architectural fragments is the shell of the apsidal chapel that projected from the north side of the church of the Dominicans on South Street. A small oratory or hospice founded for the Dominicans at a date before 1464 provided a basis for a full mendicant establishment when it was decided on 16 November 1514 that funds left by Bishop William Elphinstone of Aberdeen should be allocated for this purpose.[50] The vignette on Geddy's aerial prospect appears to show the church with a rectangular main body and with a flat-gabled south transept of slight projection.[51] Excavations carried out by the St Andrews Antiquarian Society in 1909 located short sections of the north and south walls of the main body, indicating that the

---

[48] Pamela Sheingorn, *The Easter Sepulchre in England* (Kalamazoo, 1987), pp. 39–42.
[49] Cant, *St Salvator*, p. 162.
[50] Cowan and Easson, *Medieval Religious Houses*, pp. 119–20; *Registrum Episcopatus Aberdonensis*, ed. Cosmo Innes, vol. 2 (Edinburgh), pp. 310–12.
[51] NLS, MS 20996.

Figure 4.5: The North Chapel of the Dominican Church, viewed from the north-west.

internal width was about 25ft.[52] Since the south transept was evidently not of the same polygonal form as the north chapel, it may be suspected that the latter was an asymmetrical addition made around 1525, when Archbishop James Beaton gave permission to build out.

There was a limited vogue for laterally projecting apsidal chapels across Europe, which was reflected in a small number of Scottish examples. A single such chapel projects from the south side of the chancel of Arbuthnott church, where it was probably built to house the chaplainry of the Virgin founded in 1505 by Sir Robert Arbuthnott, and there is a symmetrical pair of such chapels against the flanks of Ladykirk church, which was erected by James IV between 1500 and 1507.[53] All three Scottish examples are covered by the pointed barrel vaults that had become such a characteristic feature of churches of moderate scale in Scotland since the later fourteenth century, though only at St Andrews and Ladykirk are the vaults decorated with ribs.[54]

[52] David Hay Fleming, *Hand-book to St Andrews* (St Andrews, 1924), p. 13.
[53] *Registrum Magni Sigilli Regum Scotorum*, ed. J. M. Thomson et al., 11 vols (Edinburgh, 1882–1914) [hereafter *RMS*], ii, no. 2867; *Accounts of the Lord High Treasurer of Scotland*, 12 vols (Edinburgh, 1877–1979) [hereafter *TA*], iii, pp. 82, 83, 87, 88, 295–9; *Exchequer Rolls of Scotland, 1264–1600*, ed. John Stuart et al., 23 vols (Edinburgh, 1878–1909) [hereafter *ER*], xi, p. 276.
[54] Fawcett, 'Barrel-Vaulted Churches in Late Medieval Scotland', pp. 60–77.

The most striking feature of the chapel of the St Andrews Dominicans is the tracery that filled the large windows in the north-east, north, north-west and west windows. Although only that in the north-west window, which was restored in 1913, is trustworthy, enough remained of the tracery stumps in the north window for that also to be reinstated with a sufficient degree of authenticity.[55] The leitmotif of the tracery is a pattern of uncusped loop-like forms that are paralleled in a number of other buildings of the early sixteenth century.[56] Those other buildings include the choir of Midcalder parish church, which was under construction at the time of a bond for its completion of 1542; the transepts of Tullibardine Chapel, which can be dated to after 1500 on heraldic evidence; and the transepts of Trinity College Chapel in Edinburgh, which can probably be associated with an indulgence of 1532.[57]

Apart from a number of examples in Ireland that may have taken their lead from Scotland, tracery of this kind is not found elsewhere in the British Isles. However, it is found in several churches in the coastal provinces of the Netherlands, where the use of brick as a principal building material fostered a tendency to simplification of forms. The churches in which such tracery is to be found varied in scale from the great Dominican church in The Hague, where the south aisle dates from around 1500, to village churches like that at Kapelle of the late fifteenth century.[58] At a time when the arts and architecture of the Low Countries appear to have been a significant source of inspiration for Scottish patrons and their masons, it is a clear possibility that the germ of the idea was provided by such windows.[59] In the case of the St Andrews Dominicans the case for architectural debts to the Netherlands may derive support from the fact that the foundation of the house was a particular project of the Provincial John Adamson, who was appointed to that office in 1510 after a visitation of the Scottish province by the Congregation of Holland.[60] Is it possible that the consequent contacts with Holland were fruitful in more ways than one?

---

[55] *Report of the Inspector of Ancient Monuments* (London, 1913), pp. 28–9.
[56] Richard Fawcett, 'Scottish Medieval Window Tracery', *Studies in Scottish Antiquity Presented to Stewart Cruden*, ed. David J. Breeze (Edinburgh, 1984), pp. 181–2.
[57] J. Robertson, 'Notice of a Deed by which Sir James Sandilands ... Binds Himself and his Heir to Complete the Vestry and Build the Nave, Steeple and Porch of the Parish Church of Mid-Calder', PSAS 3 (1857–60), pp. 160–71; *The Letters of James V*, ed. R. K. Hannay and D. Hay (Edinburgh, 1954), p. 217.
[58] Rijkscommissie voor de Monumentenbeschrijving, *Kunstreisboek voor Nederland*, 7th edn (Amsterdam, 1977), pp. 454, 532–3.
[59] Richard Fawcett, 'Architectural Links between Scotland and the Low Countries in the Later Middle Ages', *Utrecht, Britain and the Continent: Archaeology, Art and Architecture*, ed. Elisabeth de Bièvre (Leeds, 1996), pp. 172–82.
[60] *Rentale Dunkeldense*, ed. Robert Kerr Hannay (Edinburgh, 1915), p. 321; Anthony Ross, *Dogs of the Lord: The Story of the Dominican Order in Scotland* (unpaginated exhibition catalogue), (Edinburgh, 1981).

St Mary's College Chapel

AMONGST the latest pre-Reformation ecclesiastical buildings that were erected within the burgh, and about which we know anything, were two collegiate chapels: that of St Mary's College and that of St Leonard's College. A substantial part of the latter survives, albeit in a truncated and heavily restored state, but the former we only know only from a tiny sketch and some possible *ex-situ* fragments. It seems that the college of St Mary was planned with the intention of breathing new life into the college of St John that had been founded in 1419 and the Pedagogy established in 1430, though it had a rather faltering start after Archbishop James Beaton received papal permission for its foundation on 4 October 1525.[61] A bull of foundation was granted on 12 February 1538, but building work evidently progressed slowly, being continued by Cardinal David Beaton and Archbishop John Hamilton, and in fact construction of the collegiate buildings may never have been finished.

The chapel, which it is thought could have absorbed the existing chapel of St John's College, is likely to have been the substantial oriented building shown by Geddy on the north side of the courtyard, where Parliament Hall now stands.[62] That depiction is too small for great reliance to be placed upon it, but it appears to show a building with a south aisle, above which rose what may have been a clearstorey with traceried windows. The wall heads are shown as crenellated and there seem to be diagonal buttresses at the angles of the presumed south aisle. More concrete evidence survives in the form of a number of corbels and capitals that are thought to have originated in the chapel and that have been built into the walls of the Parliament Hall and the old library. One of those on the west side of the old library is a wall shaft capital decorated with the *Arma Christi* in the form of the five wounds and the crown of thorns. The most striking feature of the capital is that the shield is supported by a pair of winged *putti* of renaissance character.

Such *putti* are presumably of ultimately Italian parentage, though it may be suspected that the idea reached Scotland through the medium of France, in the same way that the classical additions to the architectural repertoire of the royal residences of Falkland and Stirling in the 1530s resulted from the involvement of French masons there.[63] One path by which the idea of shields supported by *putti* had reached France is illustrated by the tomb chest of 1499 at Tours Cathedral of the children of Charles VIII, which was a combined work of the Italian Girolamo da Fiesole and the French mason Michel Colombe. Although it must be admitted that the St Andrews *putti* appear to be somewhat over-nourished and consequently more earth-bound than any possible Italian or

---

[61] Cant, *University*, pp. 14–17, 33–8; Cowan and Easson, *Medieval Religious Houses*, pp. 232–3.
[62] NLS, MS 20996.
[63] John G. Dunbar, *Scottish Royal Palaces* (East Linton, 1999), pp. 27–39, 49–55.

Figure 4.6: A corbel with the *Arma Christi* thought to be from the chapel of St Mary's College.

French prototypes, it is easy to imagine how such motifs might have resulted from Scottish patrons being inspired by examples they had seen in France.

In the case of St Mary's Chapel, one the most likely potential patrons for these carvings is Cardinal David Beaton, who made many visits to France and was in high favour at the French royal court.[64] Of added significance is the recorded involvement of French masons at the college during Beaton's archiepiscopate. In 1539 French masons were paid for advice at the college, and in 1543–44 the mason Thomas French, whose father, John, may have been of French origin, and who had previously worked at Falkland, was in charge of the masons at the college.[65] Beaton's taste for renaissance detailing is further attested by a number of other carved fragments associated with his building operations in St Andrews. A stone thought to have originated at the castle has his motto 'INTEN[TIO]' in Roman capitals and the date 1544, while another stone that may also have come from the castle has had a shield supported by winged mermaids, with the tassels of what appears to have been a cardinal's hat.[66]

---

[64] Margaret H. B. Sanderson, *Cardinal of Scotland* (Edinburgh, 1986), p. 57.
[65] Dunbar, *Scottish Royal Palaces*, pp. 230, 238; *Rentale Sancti Andree AD 1538–1546*, ed. R. K. Hannay, Scottish History Society (Edinburgh, 1913) [hereafter *Rentale*], pp. 68, 198.
[66] Hay Fleming, *St Andrews Cathedral Museum*, p. 184.

Nevertheless, although there is every reason to assume that Beaton's work on the chapel would have been a vehicle for expressing his fashionably francophile tastes, his successor, Archbishop John Hamilton, who also worked on the chapel, was evidently similarly inclined towards French architectural fashions. His reconstruction of the upper walls of the frontispiece of the castle following the siege of 1546–47 appears to have terminated in a rich silhouette of French-inspired gabled dormers, below the central one of which is a frieze with the mullet or cinquefoil of his arms. Those same mullets are found on one of the surviving corbels thought to be from St Mary's College, now built into the south wall of Parliament Hall, on which they alternate with small heads beneath a band of anthemion decoration of ultimately classical derivation.

St Leonard's College Chapel

IF St Mary's College Chapel looked to France for its architectural detailing, as had evidently previously been the case with both a later phase of the cathedral operations and with St Salvator's College Chapel, at St Leonard's College there may have been some reflection of current fashions in England. Originating as a hospital of the Culdee community, the foundation was granted in 1140 to the newly established Augustinian priory for the reception and accommodation of pilgrims and visitors to St Andrews.[67] Its church had come to be regarded as parochial by 1413, but on 12 August 1512, it was re-founded as a college associated with the university by Archbishop Alexander Stewart and Prior John Hepburn, and the arms of the latter are displayed on a buttress near the mid-point of the south wall as it now stands.[68] There was a confirmation of the foundation by Cardinal David Beaton on 28 November 1545.[69]

The building has been modified on many occasions, both in the course of the Middle Ages and since the Reformation, as a consequence of which there is a great deal of uncertainty about the inter-relationships and dating of its constituent elements. Following on the difficulties in which the university found itself, in 1747 it was decided that the colleges of St Leonard's and St Salvator's should be united and concentrated in the buildings of the latter, and in 1761 St Leonard's Chapel was abandoned for worship. The roof of the chapel was removed and the tower demolished. Some reversal of the chapel's fortunes may have begun in 1853, when Principal Sir David Brewster cleared out the rubbish and vegetation that had accumulated within it and the windows were reopened. In 1910 the chapel was re-roofed and re-glazed, with the intention that it might serve as a hall of fame for members and benefactors of the university. Eventually, in 1948, it was decided the chapel should be restored for worship,

---

[67] Cowan and Easson, *Medieval Religious Houses*, p. 190.
[68] *St A. Liber*, pp. 15–18, 123; John Herkless and Robert Kerr Hannay, *The College of St Leonard* (Edinburgh and London, 1905), p. 128.
[69] Herkless and Hannay, *The College of St Leonard*, p. 144.

Figure 4.7: St Leonard's College Chapel, viewed from the south-east.

and the work was undertaken to the designs of Ian Lindsay and Partners, being completed in 1952.

As it presently stands, the chapel is a rectangular structure of 26.05m by 7.75m, with a rectangular sacristy of 8.6m by 3.75m projecting off the east end of its north wall. It is thought to have had an eventual medieval length of over 30m, with a tall tower rising from within the now demolished western part and a two-storeyed porch projecting from its south flank. It is possible that the core of the building incorporates some of the fabric of the Culdee hospital chapel of St Leonard. However, although the north wall certainly displays large amounts of cubical masonry of early character, during the restoration of 1948–52 it was deemed that the foundations beneath that wall were 'of late medieval character', suggesting that any earlier masonry was in secondary use.[70] It therefore appears that the earliest identifiable features should be associated with the college founded by Stewart and Hepburn in 1513.

The chapel as first rebuilt at that time is thought to have had its east wall on the line of the easternmost buttress against the south wall, the buttress that has the arms of Prior Hepburn set into its upper part, which is located about 8.5m west of the present east wall. At this earlier stage of its existence the chapel is presumed to have had a length of around 22m and to have abutted other

---

[70] Ronald Gordon Cant, *St Leonard's Chapel St Andrews*, 3rd edn (St Andrews, 1970), p. 7.

college buildings at its west end. On this basis, the easternmost window of the building before it was extended eastwards was the rectangular window immediately west of the buttress with Hepburn's arms. It is a three-light opening with cusped light heads, within reveals of cavetto profile to the jambs and a broad chamfer to the flat-arched head. West of this is a lintelled doorway with roll-moulded reveals that is known from a view of 1767 by John Oliphant to have been covered by a two-storeyed porch with a rectangular three-light window to its upper storey and a crow-stepped gable.[71]

West of this doorway is a sequence of a rectangular two-light window with similar mouldings to the three-light window further east, but with no cusping to the light head; this is followed by a two-tiered arrangement with a small slit window at the lower level that has a buttress immediately to its west and a larger upper window cutting into the wall-head cornice. West of that buttress there are again two tiers of windows with a rather compressed uncusped rectangular two-light lower window and an upper window similar to that to its east. Oliphant's view appears to suggest that there were two further upper windows in the demolished western part of the chapel, with two doorways at the lower level, albeit with no vertical alignment between those windows and doors.

The subsequent changes the chapel has undergone mean that it is difficult to be certain how far the pattern of windows and doors depicted by Oliphant reflected the early sixteenth-century liturgical arrangements. Perhaps the most likely interpretation is that the three-light window with cusped light heads lit the first presbytery area at the east end of the chapel and that the uncusped two-light window lit the choir, with the door between those two parts that was once covered by a porch serving as the entrance for the clergy. Corroboration for the possibility that the three-light window lit the presbytery comes from the existence of an aumbry internally, immediately to its east, since that is a feature which points to the proximity of an altar. On this basis the two-tiered arrangement of windows to the west of the choir window could have related to the screen between choir and nave, with the lower slit window lighting one of the altars in front of the screen and the upper window lighting the rood loft.

At some date prior to the Reformation the chapel was considerably augmented at both the east and west ends. At the west end the tower was inserted in a way that seems most unlikely to have been part of any original intention, since it left awkwardly narrow corridor-like spaces down each of its flanks. Taking account of the fact that the insertion of the tower at the west end would have significantly reduced the amount of usable space in the nave, it is likely that one of the reasons for the extension at the opposite end was to permit the presbytery and choir to be relocated further east, allowing the area that had initially housed the choir to be absorbed into the nave. The eastward extension increased the chapel's length by about 8.5m and a two-storeyed sacristy and treasury block was built on the north side of that extension. It is uncertain

---

[71] StAUL, John Oliphant, *St Andrews Delineated or Sixteen Views of the Ruins and Principal Buildings &c In and Near that City Drawn Anno Domini 1767*.

precisely where the division between choir and nave would have been located in this revised arrangement, though it may well be that it came to be associated with the door that it has been suggested was initially between the presbytery and choir.

Along its south flank the new eastward extension was lit by an arrangement of windows that was evidently intended to repeat as closely as possible the fenestration provided in the original presbytery and choir area: a rectangular three-light window to the east, with cusped light heads, and a rectangular two-light window with uncusped light heads to its west. The reveal mouldings of the earlier windows were also closely followed and it is only the slight differences in the treatment of the easternmost window's cusping that show the work is of a different date. Internally a second aumbry was provided to the east of the new easternmost window and there are the fragments of a piscina basin capped by a canopy head against the east jamb of the window. Architectural enrichment to the new presbytery area was provided by tabernacle work in the internal jambs of the easternmost window and by an elegant doorway into the sacristy that has a filleted roll flanked by diagonally-set cavettos to the reveals, with a basket arch cut into the lintel. The date of this phase of work is unknown, though an attractive possibility is that it was carried out at the time of the confirmation of the college's foundation by Cardinal David Beaton in 1544. It may be noted that the mouldings of the sacristy door are very like those of a door set in the blocking of the east tower arch of St Rule's Church, within the cathedral precinct.

So far as the fashion for rectangular mullioned windows with cusped light heads is concerned, this was almost certainly an import from England. Earlier examples may be seen in the galleries along the courtyard side of the south quarter of Linlithgow Palace, which probably date from the late fifteenth or early sixteenth century, and in a chapel of the Virgin as deliverer from damnation (*libera nos a penis inferni*) at Dunkeld Cathedral that is referred to in 1514.[72] As such, the windows represent an interesting reflection of ideas from south of the Border, at a time when a period of greater rapprochement with England meant that there was perhaps more receptivity to at least a limited range of English ideas than had been the case for some time previously.

So far as the smaller windows in the western part of the chapel are concerned, at least some of these may have been wholly or partly of post-Reformation date on the basis of the ogee-profile mouldings of their reveals. A possible date for those modifications is 1578, when the chapel was adapted for reformed worship. Other changes included the construction of a gallery for members of the college attending services in the nave, though it is possible that there had been a medieval west gallery, as also seems to have been the case in St Salvator's Chapel.

---

[72] Dunbar, *Scottish Royal Palaces*, p. 15; *Rentale Dunkeldense*, pp. xxxviii and 238.

The Castle Chapel

ST Leonard's Chapel may have created a vogue for rectangular mullioned windows in St Andrews, because four-light versions are depicted in the flank of the chapel on the south side of the chancel of Holy Trinity Parish Church, according to John Oliphant's drawing of the church. Similar windows are also depicted in John Slezer's view of the castle, where two windows and the jamb of a third are shown to the east of the old gate tower, in the range which is assumed to have had the chapel at first-floor level above a vaulted undercroft and an arcaded loggia.[73] No more than the partial jamb of the window next to the old gate tower of the castle now survives, and we cannot be sure of the details. Slezer shows them as rectangular two-light openings, with a square quatrefoil at the head of each light, above an uncusped light head, though it is possible that he has misrepresented trifoliate light heads like those in the three-light windows. No date for the castle windows is known. On stylistic grounds it might be thought that they pre-date the remodelling of the entrance front by Archbishop John Hamilton following the siege of 1546–47, since their ostensibly medieval character is so different from the French-inspired renaissance vocabulary of the entrance front. However, it could not be ruled out that the choice of windows with an 'ecclesiastical' appearance was prompted by a wish to express the religious function of this part of the castle. A preference for windows of medieval appearance in ecclesiastical buildings would continue for many years after the Reformation, even in such otherwise highly fashionable buildings as Dairsie Church of 1621 and Heriot's Hospital in Edinburgh of after 1627. On balance perhaps all that can be said is that the castle chapel windows are probably broadly contemporary with one of the sixteenth-century phases of work at St Leonard's Chapel.

Conclusion

IN the foregoing discussion an attempt has been made to demonstrate that the patrons who commissioned the large numbers of fine ecclesiastical buildings that were so prominent in the medieval burgh of St Andrews were prepared to go to great lengths to ensure that their buildings would make the desired impact on those who saw them. In the case of the cathedral and the parish church, this was achieved partly through setting out those buildings on a great scale, while the tall towers of St Rule's Church, the cathedral, the parish church and the chapels of the collegiate foundations of St Salvator and St Leonard must have given the burgh as a whole an exhilarating heavenward-reaching skyline. Of equal significance with size in creating a desired impact was the use of innovative architectural repertoires, through which could be demonstrated the cosmopolitan

---

[73] John Slezer, *Theatrum Scotiae* (London, 1693), pl. 15.

Figure 4.8: St Andrews Castle, the range to the east of the gatehouse tower thought to have contained the chapel, by John Slezer in *Theatrum Scotiae*, London, 1693.

outlook and wide terms of reference of patrons who understood where to recruit the master masons best able to express their ambitions architecturally.

In the twelfth-century works at St Rule's Church and the cathedral, it was chiefly from Scotland's nearest neighbour, England, that guidance was sought, albeit that guidance brought with it an awareness of ideas that were current in mainland Europe. After a lapse of some centuries, in the early sixteenth century, at a time of closer understanding with the southern neighbour after many years of hostilities, there was again a limited willingness to graft some ideas of English origin onto the native architectural stock. This may be seen in the use of a particular window type in St Leonard's College Chapel, Holy Trinity Parish Church and the chapel of the archbishop's castle.

Before that stage, however, the architectural patrons of St Andrews had already shown a willingness to look further afield, choosing to draw inspiration from France and the Low Countries, the areas of Continental Europe with which Scotland had developed the closest political, diplomatic, commercial and artistic relationships. In the later works at the cathedral it appears that a Parisian master mason, John Morow, was immediately involved, though it is now difficult to identify his contribution there with certainty. At the collegiate chapels of

St Salvator and St Mary, however, it seems that, while there was a wish to take a lead from Gallic forms, this was a selective process in which those forms were blended into the developing indigenous vocabulary.

A similar process was evidently operating in drawing ideas from the Netherlands. The first hint of this may be found in the early fifteenth-century repairs to the south transept of the cathedral, where the arcade was perhaps at least partly reconstructed with cylindrical piers of the type that were favoured in the Low Countries, and that were subsequently copied in the parish church. Further reflections of ideas from that part of the Continent have been suggested as an explanation for the detailing of the great tomb in St Salvator's College Chapel, and for the early sixteenth-century design of the windows in the Dominican Church. Something that is striking in several of these cases is that no inconsistency was seen in combining ideas from more than one source in attempting to achieve the desired effect.

One of the great tragedies for St Andrews, as for the rest of Scotland, is that the liturgical furnishings for which the churches were the intended receptacles, and which were the principal focus of the liturgical observance that took place within them, have been almost entirely lost. Hints at what has gone are to be seen at St Salvator's in the tomb and Sacrament House, and in the carved fragments thought to be from an altarpiece. But to build up a fuller picture we must look to the inventories of St Salvator's, to Bower's brief references to the late medieval furnishing of the cathedral, and to what we know of the parish church. Armed with that knowledge, we can see that St Andrews was the location for a concentration of church buildings in which the liturgy could be celebrated within architectural settings that were in the highest fashion of their day and that must have deeply impressed all visually receptive visitors to the city of the prelate who claimed leadership of Scotland's Church.

Glossary of Technical Terms

aisle: a space running alongside the main space of a church, and often separated from it by an arcade; in Scotland it can also be applied to a laterally projecting space.

anthemion: a foliate motif of classical origin, reflecting the radiating petals of a honeysuckle flower.

apse: a semi-circular or polygonal projection, commonly at the east end of the main space of a church.

arcade: a row of arches.

ashlar: masonry composed of carefully squared blocks.

aumbry: a cupboard, frequently set within the thickness of a wall, and sometimes with a rebate for a door or its frame.

barrel vault: a stone vault of rounded or pointed arched profile, and sometimes decorated with ribs in imitation of quadripartite vaulting.

base course: the projecting lowest external courses of a wall.

basket arch: an arch of flattened three-centred form.

blind arcade: a decorative row of arches that is unpierced by doors or windows.

broached spire: a spire with semi-pyramidal projections at the base of its diagonal faces.

buttress: a projection from a wall intended to strengthen it.

chancel: in a parish church the eastern compartment, containing the presbytery around the principal altar and the choir of the clergy.

choir stalls: the timber stalls occupied by the clergy during services and when not involved in activities around the high altar; they were frequently capped by enriched canopies.

clearstorey: an upper tier of windows in an aisled church that provided light for the central space.

corbel: a projecting block of stone intended to support a higher feature, and often treated decoratively.

corbel table: a row of corbels sometimes supporting a wall-head cornice or band of small-scale arcading.

crenellated: battlemented, with alternating merlons and embrasures.

crow-stepped gable: a gable of stepped form.

cusp: a triangular projection in window tracery.

double-splayed window: a window in which the jambs and arches are splayed both internally and externally.

Easter sepulchre: a decorated receptacle on the north side of the presbytery area where a consecrated host and figure of Christ were ritually entombed between Good Friday and Easter Sunday, as part of the commemoration and re-enactment of Christ's death and resurrection.

en délit shaft: a shaft that is laid against the natural bedding of the stone in order to achieve the required length.

gallery or tribune: the middle storey of a three-stage building, between the arcade and the clearstorey.

ledger slab: a flat stone slab most commonly laid on a tomb or over a burial.

loggia: an open structure, usually arcaded along one side, and set within or against a building.

lucarne: a small window, often gabled, opening through the faces of a spire.

micro-architecture: small-scale architectural detailing applied decoratively to a feature.

monstrance: a vessel, usually of precious metal, in which a consecrated host or a relic could be displayed to worshippers.

narthex: a porch or vestibule, usually extending across the whole or much of the entrance front of a church.

nave: the western limb of a church and the part that was most generally accessible to the laity, but also serving as a processional path for the clergy.

nook shaft: a shaft set within the re-entrant angle of a larger formation; it can be either coursed in with the adjacent masonry or *en délit* (free-standing).

ogee: an S-shaped double curve.

orders: in medieval architecture, the multiple stepped layers by which jambs and arches are built up in walls of some thickness.
pier: a free-standing upright member such as those that support the arches of an arcade.
pinnacle: a steeply pyramidal upper termination to a buttress or the outer angles of a building, often decorated with foliate crockets at the angles and capped by a foliate finial.
piscina: the basin in which the chalice and paten employed to hold the bread and wine at Mass were cleansed, and in which the officiating priest washed his hands; it was often set within an arched mural recess
presbytery: the area at the east end of the church around the high altar that was the province of the officiating clergy during the celebration of Mass.
putti: cherubs.
quadripartite vault: a stone vault in which each bay has a diagonal cross pattern of ribs, thus creating four triangular areas of webbing.
quirk: a v-shaped indentation between elements of a moulding formation.
respond: a half-pier at the end of an arcade.
retable or reredos: an upright feature behind an altar, often with carved or painted decoration relevant to the dedication of the altar.
reveal: the chamfered or moulded frame to a window or other opening.
roll moulding: an element in a moulding formation of rounded profile.
rood loft: a platform above the screen separating the east limb from the nave, associated with which there was a painted or carved representation of Christ's crucifixion.
Sacrament house: an aumbry to contain a consecrated host, bread that was believed to have become the body of Christ through the process of transubstantiation at Mass. It was usually located in the wall to the north of an altar and decorated with themes relevant to its function.
sedilia: the seats to the south of the altar where the celebrant at Mass and his assistants sat at certain points of the service. There were most commonly three seats, but might be two or four, and they were often surmounted by arches and gablets.
soffit: the under-surface of an arch or other feature.
sub-base: the lowest element of the base that supported a pier or shaft.
tabernacle: an enriched niche that was often intended to contain an image, but that might be purely decorative, especially if forming part of a micro-architectural ensemble.
transept: a laterally projecting arm at the junction of the east limb and nave of a church, giving it a symbolically significant cross shape and providing space for additional altars.
voussoir: a stone with two converging faces that forms part of an arch.
window tracery: the decorative patterns within the arch of some windows.

CHAPTER FIVE

When the Miracles Ceased: Shrine and Cult Management at St Andrews and Scottish Cathedrals in the Later Middle Ages

Tom Turpie

By the fifteenth century St Andrew had been firmly established as the patron saint of the Scots.¹ His image adorned coins and royal seals at home, while abroad altars and fraternities dedicated to the saint formed the focus for the communal identity of Scottish students and monks.² Paradoxically, at the same time belief in the efficacy of the relics of St Andrew, housed in their elaborate shrine in Fife, was on the wane. This development was part of a broader Western European trend in the later Middle Ages which saw a gradual decline in the importance and, perhaps as significantly, in the profits of long-established cathedral shrines.³ This decline was not indicative of a waning of interest in pilgrimage as an activity; in fact it may well have reached its peak in popularity in the two centuries between the first appearance of the Black Death and the Reformation.⁴ The decline resulted from what Richard Dobson has termed the 'widespread transfer of allegiance from the old to the new' that characterised late medieval popular piety.⁵ In England 'the new' included shrines focused on Marian and Passion devotion, the most popular of which were located at Walsingham and Hailes, and those of a range of uncanonised 'would be saints'

---

¹ Marinall Ash and Dauvit Broun, 'The Adoption of St Andrew as Patron Saint of Scotland', Higgitt, *St Andrew*, pp. 16–24.
² Donald E. R. Watt, 'Scottish Student Life Abroad in the Fourteenth Century', *Scottish Historical Review* 59 (1980), p. 7; Mark Dilworth, *The Scots in Franconia: A Century of Monasticism* (Edinburgh, 1974), p. 19.
³ Richard B. Dobson, 'Contrasting Cults: St Cuthbert of Durham and St Thomas of Canterbury in the Fifteenth Century', *Christianity and Community in the West: Essays for John Bossy*, ed. S. Ditchfield (Michigan, 2001), pp. 25–6; Ben Nilson, *Cathedral Shrines of Medieval England* (Woodbridge, 1998), pp. 176–9; Eamon Duffy, *The Stripping of the Altars* (London and New Haven, 1992), p. 195.
⁴ Eamon Duffy, 'The Dynamics of Pilgrimage in Late Medieval England', *Pilgrimage: The English Experience from Becket to Bunyan*, ed. C. Morris and P. Roberts (Cambridge, 2002), pp. 164–77.
⁵ Dobson, 'Contrasting Cults', p. 25.

like Henry VI (1423–71) at Windsor and Richard Scrope (d. 1405) in York.[6] Dobson has explored the strategies that the monastic communities at two of England's more venerable shrines, those of St Cuthbert at Durham and Thomas Becket at Canterbury, used to protect the status of their patron saints in this rapidly changing spiritual environment.[7] This essay will investigate similar efforts by the cathedral chapter at St Andrews to modernise the shrine of their patron saint, comparing the effectiveness of the techniques employed to those used by the custodians of other Scottish cathedral shrines in the later Middle Ages.

The shrine of St Andrew in Fife was at its peak of popularity from the late eleventh to the late thirteenth century. It was in this period that the confident claims made by the religious community at St Andrews that they possessed a thriving shrine, frequented by an international clientele, receive some corroboration from Welsh and English sources.[8] English visitors could still be found at the shrine on the eve of the Wars of Independence with groups of pilgrims recorded there in 1273 and 1285.[9] The shrine in St Andrews was also one of a small group patronised by Edward I (1272–1307) during his attempted conquest of Scotland, with the English king making a donation to the relics in 1304.[10] Following the wars, the only indication of foreign visitors to St Andrews comes in the form of penitential pilgrimages from Flanders and Brabant, most notably from Ypres and Antwerp. However, this form of spiritual punishment had apparently gone out of fashion by the end of the fifteenth century.[11] Efforts to promote the relics in Fife to a wider European audience may have been

---

[6] Robert N. Swanson, *Church and Society in Late Medieval England* (Oxford, 1989), pp. 287–90.
[7] Dobson, 'Contrasting Cults', pp. 24–43.
[8] These claims were made in the two St Andrews Foundation Legends, A which dated from c.1115 and B dated to 1140×53. See Marjorie O. Anderson, *Kings and Kingship in Early Scotland* (Edinburgh, 1980), pp. 258–60; *PNF*, iii, pp. 564–600; *Vitae Sanctorum Britanniae et Genealogiae*, ed. A. Wade-Evans (Cardiff, 1944), pp. 80, 82; *Libellus de Vita et Miraculis S. Godrici, Heremitae de Finchale. Auctore Reginaldo Monacho Dunelmensi. Adjicitur Appendix Miraculorum*, ed. Joseph Stevenson (Durham, 1847), pp. 28, 31, 219, 376, 426, 446; *Reginaldi Monachi Dunelmensis Libellus de Admirandis Beati Cuthberti Virtutibus quae Novellis Patratae sunt Temporibus*, ed. James Raine (Durham, 1835), pp. 56, 170, 218–19.
[9] Diana Webb, *Pilgrims and Pilgrimage in the Medieval West* (London, 1999), p. 217.
[10] *Calendar of Documents Relating to Scotland*, ed. J. Bain, 5 vols (Edinburgh, 1881–88) [hereafter *CDS*], ii, no. 8. Other shrines visited by the king and his son included those of SS Margaret (Dunfermline), Kentigern (Glasgow) and Ninian (Whithorn). *CDS*, ii, no. 1225, iv, nos. 448–9, 486, 487.
[11] David Ditchburn, *Scotland and Europe: The Medieval Kingdom and its Contacts with Christendom, 1214–1560*, i: *Religion, Culture and Commerce* (East Linton, 2000), p. 60, n. 123; David Ditchburn, '"Saints at the door don't make miracles"? The Contrasting Fortunes of Scottish Pilgrimage, c. 1450–1550', *Sixteenth-Century Scotland: Essays in Honour of Michael Lynch*, ed. J. Goodare and A. A. Macdonald (Leiden, 2008), pp. 93–5; David McRoberts, 'A St Andrews Pilgrimage Certificate of 1333 at Saint-Omer', McRoberts, *St Andrews*, pp. 155–6; Webb, *Pilgrims and Pilgrimage*, p. 218.

Figure 5.1: Pilgrim badge from St Andrews, c.1450–1500, found in Sluis.

hindered by the establishment of a popular shrine to Andrew at Amalfi on the south-eastern coast of Italy after 1208.[12] It is difficult to quantify the impact of the Anglo-Scottish wars on pilgrim traffic, but there is little evidence of large-scale international pilgrimage to the shrine from the fourteenth century.

Although the comprehensive shrine accounts that form the basis of English studies of pilgrimage have not survived for Scotland, there are a number of indications that by the late fourteenth century domestic pilgrimage to St Andrews was also on the wane.[13] The St Andrews shrine is conspicuous in its absence from references to popular Scottish shrines by foreign and domestic observers in the later Middle Ages, yet the raison d'être of institutions like St Andrews was the shrine of their patron saint.[14] This meant that the maintenance of steady pilgrimage traffic was essential in justifying their existence and protecting hard-

---

[12] Located on the south-west coast of Italy, in 1208 the shrine received relics of the apostle that had been looted from Constantinople following the sack of the city by Crusaders in 1204.

[13] Ditchburn, '"Saints at the door don't make miracles"', pp. 68, 92–5.

[14] For example William of Worcester who noted the popularity of Whithorn, Tain and the relics of the David Stewart, duke of Rothesay, and Sir David Lindsay of the Mount who complained of the impious behaviour of pilgrims visiting Musselburgh in the 1530s. *William Worcestre Itineraries*, ed. John H. Harvey (Oxford, 1969), pp. 6–7; *Poetical Works of Sir David Lyndsay of the Mount*, ed. David Laing (Edinburgh, 1879), iii, p. 40; Diana Webb, *Pilgrimage in Medieval England* (London, 2000), p. 65.

fought privileges. The shrine custodians at St Andrews were well aware of their responsibilities and did not sit idly by as pilgrim numbers began to stagnate. As for their counterparts at Durham and Canterbury, a number of promotional tools were available to the bishops of St Andrews and the Augustinian canons that formed the cathedral chapter. In the twelfth century the options available to shrine custodians can be seen in a series of campaigns instigated by the bishops of Glasgow. In an effort to promote the cult of St Kentigern these bishops translated the relics of Kentigern to an impressive new shrine, commissioned two new lives of the saint (the second by the professional hagiographer Jocelin of Furness), and may have attempted to have their patron formally canonised.[15] The incorporation of the doctrine of purgatory into official and popular practice, and the associated pull factor of papal-sanctioned indulgences, meant that shrine custodians in the later Middle Ages also had a number of new tools with which they might encourage pilgrimage to the tombs of their patrons.

The opportunity to modernise the shrine at St Andrews was provided by a fire that swept through the cathedral in 1378.[16] The chronicler Andrew Wyntoun, who was a contemporary observer of the resulting building work, suggested that the renovation was a collaborative project between the bishop, cathedral chapter and local secular leaders. Wyntoun noted that it was the bishop, Walter Trail (1385–1400), who supplied the wood beams, while the nine pillars of the church were engraved with the coats of arms of 'sum lords' who had contributed towards the restoration.[17] The bishop was also able to enlist royal help for the project. Robert II (1371–90) was keen to contribute to the work, well aware of the close relationship that his grandfather Robert I (1306–29) had developed with St Andrews.[18] Robert II, who would also have been keen to identify with what was by now a national saint, paid for masons to help reconstruct the building.[19] To further stimulate support for the project, Trail supplicated for and received a papal indulgence for those contributing to the work.[20] The restoration may have received a setback in 1410 when a storm blew down the south gable, damaged the dormitory, parlour and chapter house and fatally wounded the sub prior, Thomas de Cupar.[21] It was certainly

---

[15] Archibald A. M. Duncan, 'St Kentigern at Glasgow Cathedral in the Twelfth Century', *Medieval Art and Architecture in the Diocese of Glasgow*, ed. R. Fawcett (Leeds, 1998), pp. 9–22; Tom Turpie, 'A Casualty of War? Kentigern of Glasgow, Scottish Patron Saints and the Bruce/Comyn Conflict', *Bute: History and People*, ed. A. Ritchie (Lerwick, 2012), pp. 61–73.

[16] Ronald G. Cant, 'The Building of St Andrews Cathedral', McRoberts, *St Andrews*, pp. 28–9.

[17] *Original Chronicle of Andrew Wyntoun*, ed. F. J Amours (Edinburgh, 1903–14), vi, pp. 309–11.

[18] Geoffrey W. S. Barrow, *Robert Bruce and the Community of the Realm of Scotland* (Edinburgh, 2005), p. 318; *Scotichronicon*, ii, pp. 271–2.

[19] Payments to the masons are mentioned in the Exchequer Rolls in 1381 and 1384: *ER*, iii, pp. 70, 674.

[20] *Copiale*, pp. 115, 452.

[21] *Scotichronicon*, viii, p. 75.

not complete in 1418 when a further supplication to the papacy again cited damage caused by the fire.[22]

It may have been the need to provide funds for the renovation, as well as an awareness that pilgrim numbers were on the wane, that prompted sustained promotion of the shrine and relics in the fifteenth century. The second papal indulgence was followed by a concerted building campaign led by the prior, James Haldenstone (1418–43). As part of this campaign the shrine was remodelled and modernised in the style of the reliquary churches at Durham and Canterbury.[23] David McRoberts has equated this remodelling with the apparent growth in support for the cults of Scottish national saints in the fifteenth century.[24] The building of larger and more elaborate provision for pilgrims could reflect the popularity of a sacred centre.[25] However, as one commentator has emphasised, this type of rebuilding could also be a 'calculated investment'.[26] It is as an investment that Haldenstone appears to have viewed the work at St Andrews, with little evidence in the early 1400s that he had been forced into the action by the demands of excessive numbers of pilgrims. After the foundation of the university in 1413 the shrine of the apostle may no longer have been the primary attraction for visitors to the burgh. In 1419 a supplication by Henry Wardlaw (1403–40) for an indulgence to help towards rebuilding a bridge to the west of the town failed to mention the needs of pilgrims, emphasising instead the necessity of safeguarding the passage of students to the burgh.[27] Something of the low point that the shrine had reached by this time is also evident in a promotional letter sent by James Haldenstone to the Scottish bishops in the 1420s. In the letter Haldenstone stressed the national significance of the relics at St Andrews, urging his fellow churchmen to provide financial support for the fabric of the cathedral and to encourage their diocesan clergy to promote the shrine amongst their congregations.[28] The tone of desperation in the correspondence suggests that pilgrim income was no longer sufficient to cover costs or repair the damage caused by fire and storm.

Haldenstone and his successors seem to have been aware that in the new spiritual climate of the fifteenth century, the bones of St Andrew alone were no longer the draw for pilgrims that they had once been. Attempts were made to

---

[22] The letter mentions the cathedral was a victim of 'casualiter incendium'. *Copiale*, p. 116.
[23] For a description of the building work at St Andrews see David McRoberts, 'The Glorious House of St Andrew', McRoberts, *St Andrews*, pp. 69–70.
[24] David McRoberts, 'The Scottish Church and Nationalism in the Fifteenth Century', *Innes Review* 9 (1968), p. 9.
[25] Stephen Wilson makes the connection between successful cults and building programmes. Stephen Wilson, *Saints and their Cults: Studies in Religious Sociology, Folklore and History* (Cambridge, 1982), p. 28.
[26] Barbara Abou El Haj, *The Medieval Cult of Saints: Formations and Transformations* (Cambridge, 1986), p. 17.
[27] This was the Guardbridge, an important crossing over the River Eden. *Calendar of Scottish Supplications to Rome, 1418–22*, ed. Elizabeth Lindsay and Annie Cameron (Edinburgh, 1934), p. 109.
[28] *Copiale*, pp. 119–21, 454–6.

diversify the attractions for pilgrims in the cathedral and to bolster the cult of the apostle with saintly reinforcements.[29] Within the remodelling work of the 1420s greater prominence was given to the Lady Chapel, which now flanked the high altar.[30] Haldenstone would choose to be buried there in 1443, and in 1465 James Kennedy (1440–65) endowed a further chaplaincy at the Marian altar.[31] A statue of Mary was also placed alongside an image of Andrew that rested on the high altar.[32] In addition to this, efforts were made to connect the cathedral to the fashionable cult of St Michael.[33] Further papal indulgences, granted to help sustain the fabric of the cathedral in 1472 and 1487, were for pilgrims who visited on the feast of the archangel (29 September), to whom an altar was also dedicated in the nave of the cathedral.[34] The decision to make this connection with the popular cult of the archangel may have been prompted by an existing connection between St Andrews and the saint: in Foundation Legend B the relics of St Andrew were said to have arrived in Fife on the feast of St Michael.[35]

These efforts to diversify the attractions at the cathedral appear to have been a conscious policy with Kennedy and later Archbishop William Scheves (1476–97). Both, for example, depicted Mary and Michael alongside Andrew on their personal seals.[36] Scottish saints were also pressed into service to support Andrew. In a departure from previous chronicle accounts, Walter Bower included Triduana in the group of missionaries who had brought the bones of St Andrew to Scotland with St Regulus.[37] The shrine of Triduana at Restalrig reached its peak in popularity in the late fifteenth century following conspicuous patronage from James III (1460–88).[38] A place within the institutional history of St Andrews was also found for Duthac of Tain, a saint who too was the recipient of significant royal patronage in the late fifteenth century. Prior Haldenstone was involved in an attempt to have Duthac canonised in 1418, noting in the

---

[29] As Webb has stated it was 'prudent' for all churches to maintain as many attractions for pilgrims as possible. Webb, *Pilgrimage in Medieval England*, p. 78.

[30] McRoberts, 'The Glorious House of St Andrew', pp. 66–7.

[31] Ibid., pp. 66–7.

[32] The two statues of Andrew and Mary were known as the principal images in the cathedral. Ibid., pp. 68, 70.

[33] The perception that Michael was a particularly effective saint for souls in purgatory contributed to the broad popularity of the cult in Scotland. Audrey-Beth Fitch, *The Search for Salvation: Lay Faith in Scotland, 1480–1560* (Edinburgh, 2009), pp. 237–49.

[34] *Calendar of Entries in the Papal Registers Relating to Great Britain and Ireland: Papal Letters*, 20 vols (London, 1893–) [hereafter *CPL*], xii, p. 203, xiv, p. 178.

[35] *PNF*, iii, pp. 564–600.

[36] *Scottish Heraldic Seals*, ed. James Stevenson and Marguerite Wood, 3 vols (Glasgow, 1940), i, pp. 87–8.

[37] Bower's inclusion of Triduana in this party follows St Andrews Legend B where she is one of three virgin martyrs who were part of Regulus's missionary group. *Scotichronicon*, i, p. 315. In Wyntoun the saint had been part of another missionary group associated with Adrian of the Isle of May. *Chron. Wyntoun*, iv, p. 123.

[38] Helen Brown, 'Saint Triduana of Restalrig? Locating a Saint and her Cult in Late Medieval Lothian and Beyond', *Images of Medieval Sanctity: Essays in Honour of Gary Dickson*, ed. D. Strickland (Leiden, 2007), pp. 45–69.

supplication that the saint had been a bishop of St Andrews.[39] The chronicler Walter Bower was aware that this was not the case, but provided a connection between the diocese and the northern saint by identifying Duthac as the mentor of a late eleventh-century bishop called Maelbrigde.[40] A similar connection between St Andrews and a local saint was made by William Scheves, who promoted the shrine of St Palladius at Fordoun. According to the sixteenth-century historian Hector Boece, Scheves initiated a search for the relics of the saint and translated them to a more elaborate shrine.[41] There may well have been altars dedicated to these saints in St Andrews cathedral around which a localised worship was based. An altar dedicated to Duthac (before 1481), a chaplaincy in honour of Palladius, and a relic of Triduana were certainly present in the nearby church of the Holy Trinity in St Andrews.[42]

Although the shrine of St Andrew was struggling to attract pilgrims, the wider cult continued to flourish in fifteenth- and sixteenth-century Scotland. Predictably, dedications to Andrew were most commonly found in Fife, with altars in the burgh church of St Andrews (before 1456) and in the parish churches of Largo (1503), Cupar (1510) and Creich (1538).[43] Within the remainder of the diocese of St Andrews there were dedications to the apostle in all the large burgh churches: Dundee (1471), Edinburgh (1447), Haddington (before 1531), Linlithgow (before 1453), Perth (1466) and Stirling (before 1471).[44] Further altars in the diocese could be found at the abbeys of Cambuskenneth (before 1445) and Holyrood (before 1488).[45] Dedications to Andrew were less

---

[39] *Copiale*, pp. 4–6, 385.

[40] *Scotichronicon*, iii, p. 343.

[41] Boece mentions a search made by Archbishop Scheves of St Andrews for the relics of Palladius, which McRoberts places in around 1490. McRoberts, 'The Scottish Church and Nationalism', p. 10; *Chronicles of Scotland, Compiled by Hector Boece, Translated by John Bellenden*, ed. Edith Batho and R. W. Chambers, 2 vols (Edinburgh, 1938–41), i, p. 299.

[42] Unfortunately little information survives of the numerous altars in the cathedral during this period. The National Records of Scotland [hereafter NRS], Records of Thomson and Baxter, GD241/198; StAUL, Burgh Charters and Miscellaneous Writs, B65/23/88c; W. E. K. Rankin, *The Parish Church of the Holy Trinity St Andrews* (Edinburgh, 1955), pp. 76–7, 78–9; McRoberts, 'The Glorious House of St Andrew', pp. 79–83.

[43] There were two chaplains at the altar of St Andrew in Holy Trinity, the first founded by a cleric, John Scheves, in 1456, and the second by a David Dishington, a local burgess, in 1495. StAUL, Burgh Charters and Miscellaneous Writs, B65/23/38c, B65/23/135c. For Criech see *RMS*, ii, no. 1877; for Cupar, *RMS*, ii, no. 3 491; for Largo, *RMS*, ii, no. 2825.

[44] NRS, Scrymgeour of Wedderburn Writs, GD137/3768, Haddington Burgh: Court and Council Records 1530–55, B30/9/2, f. 16; *Perth Guildry Book, 1452–1601*, ed. Marion L. Stavert (Edinburgh, 1993), no. 111; *Abstract of the Protocol Book of the Burgh of Stirling, 1469–84* (Edinburgh, 1896), p. 41; *Registrum Cartarum Ecclesie Sancti Egidii de Edinburgh*, ed. David Laing (Edinburgh, 1859), no. 56; John Ferguson, *Ecclesia Antiqua or, the History of An Ancient Church (St Michael's, Linlithgow)* (Edinburgh, 1905), app. ii, no. 7.

[45] *Registrum Monasterii S. Marie de Cambuskenneth*, ed. William Fraser (Edinburgh, 1872), lxii. An inventory at Holyrood in 1493 mentioned the altar of St Andrew, *Historia*

common elsewhere in Scotland, apart from a small group in the city of Aberdeen. A relic of the apostle, encased in a silver cross, was part of the St Machar's reliquary collection from the late fourteenth century, having supposedly been gifted to Bishop Gilbert Greenlaw (1390–1421) by Robert II.[46] An altar in the cathedral church of Aberdeen was founded before 1436 and was patronised by a series of clergy from the cathedral chapter.[47] A further altar was founded in the burgh church of St Nicholas in 1450 by a burgess, Richard Rutherford, and received regular patronage from the townsmen of Aberdeen.[48] Outside of Aberdeen, and the diocese of St Andrews, altars dedicated to Andrew could be found in the cathedrals of Dunkeld (1500) and Glasgow (before 1426), and in the collegiate church of Peebles (before 1543).[49]

The cult of St Andrew had a broad clientele in Scotland, attracting patronage from local aristocrats like John Fouty and Andrew Wood, who founded the altars in Cupar and Largo, and from burgesses who were responsible for dedications in Aberdeen, Edinburgh, Perth and St Andrews.[50] However, its main patrons were the clergy who were responsible for the bulk of dedications to Andrew in this period.[51] The one recorded Scottish pilgrim to the shrine of the apostle at Amalfi near Naples also involved a cleric, James Watson, who was granted a safe conduct to pass to 'sanct andrea grafe' in 1507.[52] The popularity of the apostle amongst the wider church elite can also be seen in the appearance of imagery associated with the saint on the episcopal seals of Aberdeen and Ross from 1357.[53] While the emergence of Andrew as a patron of the Scottish kingdom was a gradual process, he had been closely identified with the national church since the conflict with York in the twelfth century. With St Andrews home to a university after 1413, it is unsurprising that clerics, some of whom

---

Miraculous Fundationa Monasteriii Sancte Crucis prope Edinburgh (1128), Bannatyne Miscellany II (Edinburgh, 1866), p. 9; *Protocol Book of James Young, 1485–1515*, ed. Gordon Donaldson (Edinburgh, 1952), nos. 138, 352, 997, 1832.

[46] *Registrum Episcopatus Aberdonensis*, ed. Cosmo Innes (Aberdeen, 1845), ii, pp. 127–53, 172–3.

[47] Ibid., i, pp. 314, 343.

[48] *Cartularium Ecclesie Sancti Nicholai Aberdonensis*, ed. James Cooper (Aberdeen, 1888–92), ii, pp. 92–4.

[49] John Durkan, 'Notes on Glasgow Cathedral', *Innes Review* 21 (1970), p. 58. According to Myln, Bishop George Brown (1484–1515) founded seven altars in Dunkeld dedicated to Andrew, Martin, Nicholas, Innocent, All Saints, Stephen and John the Baptist. *Vitae Dunkeldensis Ecclesiae Episcoporum by Alexandro Myln*, ed. Cosmo Innes (Edinburgh, 1831), p. 41. The Andrew altar was one of a number that formed prebends of the new college of Peebles in 1543. *RMS*, iii, no. 2921.

[50] These burgesses were Richard Rutherford (Aberdeen), Patrick Cockburn (Edinburgh), John Chalmers (Perth) and David Dishington (St Andrews).

[51] The exception to this were those altars founded by burgesses in Edinburgh and Aberdeen, and local nobles in Largo and Cupar.

[52] The safe-conduct identifies Watson as 'parson of Elcem', *Registrum Secreti Sigilli Regum Scotorum*, ed. Matthew Livingstone et al. (Edinburgh, 1908–82), i, no. 1606.

[53] *Scottish Heraldic Seals*, ed. Stevenson and Wood, i, pp. 122, 161.

were also alumni, should have been committed to his cult.[54] It would be this clerical interest, alongside his position as official patron of the kingdom, which ensured that while pilgrim numbers waned, the Andrew cult would remain a national rather than a local concern in late medieval Scotland.

Aside from St Andrews, three further Scottish cathedrals – Dunkeld, Glasgow and Whithorn – possessed the relics of major saints. The bishops of these dioceses, alongside the cathedral chapters, employed a similar range of techniques to that used by St Andrews to attract pilgrims in the late fourteenth and fifteenth centuries. For example, the cult of St Columba in eastern Scotland was split between two sites, Dunkeld, which held relics translated from Iona in 849 AD, and the abbey of Inchcolm in the Forth. While it has been suggested that the abbots of Inchcolm were behind attempts to renew interest in Columba in the later Middle Ages, the main instigators were the bishops of Dunkeld and their cathedral chapter.[55] The earliest signs of promotion can be traced to 1378 when John de Peebles (1378–90) successfully petitioned Clement VII (1378–94) for an indulgence of one year and forty days for pilgrims to Dunkeld, citing the ruinous condition of the church due to 'wars and pestilence'.[56] In 1419 Robert de Cardeny (1398–1437) elaborated on the problems of his diocese, which he described as 'largely mountainous and desert and often perilous for travellers', to gain a personal remission from Martin V (1417–31).[57] A further indulgence of ten years for pilgrims who visited the cathedral on the feast of Columba, or otherwise gave alms towards the restoration of the buildings, was obtained posthumously by James Bruce (1441–47) in 1448.[58]

In addition to these papal indulgences there were conspicuous efforts by successive bishops, and members of the chapter, to promote Columba by making personal grants and funding commemorations of the saint at Dunkeld and elsewhere. James Bruce, who died shortly before the indulgence was granted in 1448, bequeathed money to finance four new chaplainries in the cathedral.[59] His successor, Thomas Lauder (1452–75), decorated the church with a sequence of twenty murals depicting the miracles of St Columba and provided the high altar with two statues of the saint. Lauder was also involved in efforts to improve access to the church by the building of a bridge across the

---

[54] For example George Brown, who founded the altar in Dunkeld, was an alumnus of the university, *Vitae Dunkeldensis*, ed. Innes, p. 27.

[55] *Charters of the Abbey of Inchcolm*, ed. David Easson and Alastair Macdonald (Edinburgh, 1938), xxxii. The main promoter of the cult at Inchcolm was Walter Bower. Promotion of St Columba is one of the key themes in the *Scotichronicon* with Bower's patron saint emerging as the star of the Wars of Independence, regularly sending English troops and pirates to their deaths. *Scotichronicon*, ix, pp. 315–20, 339–47.

[56] *Calendar of Papal Letters to Scotland of Benedict XIII of Avignon (1394–1419)*, ed. Frank McGurk (Edinburgh, 1976), p. 27.

[57] *Calendar of Scottish Supplications to Rome*, ed. E. R. Lindsay, A. I. Cameron et al., 5 vols (Edinburgh, 1934–) [hereafter *CSSR*], i, p. 99.

[58] This petition was granted after Bruce's death in 1448, *CSSR*, v, no.199.

[59] Ibid., no.193.

Tay in 1461.⁶⁰ James Livingstone (1475–83), who succeeded Lauder, founded a chaplaincy in 1477 in the burgh church of St Giles, Edinburgh devoted to Columba, whom he described as 'patrono nostro'.⁶¹ A canon who witnessed Livingstone's grant in 1477 made his own contributions to the promotion of his patronal cult. David Meldrum, a graduate and later an official of the University of St Andrews, founded an altar in the Trinity church of that town in 1494, and gifted a paten with an image of Columba to Dunkeld cathedral.⁶² This process was continued by George Brown (1483–1515) who founded altars dedicated to Columba in Dundee and Perth, and named a new church bell at Dunkeld after the saint.⁶³

Easson has suggested that this campaign led to 'a new lease of life' for the Columban cult in the fifteenth century, pointing to the apparent renewal of the relationship between the saint and the Scottish monarchy.⁶⁴ This renewal of the bond between saint and crown dates from the reign of James IV (1488–1513), who, unlike his forebears, displayed a concern for both Dunkeld and Inchcolm, stating in 1497 his 'singular devotion [...] for St Columba'.⁶⁵ However, there are reasons to believe that the relationship between James and the saint was more political than personal. Aside from the gifts to Dunkeld and Inchcolm, the king did not include Columba in his general cycle of saintly devotions, while Columban shrines were not part of his regular pilgrimage itinerary.⁶⁶ On the whole there is little evidence that the promotional campaigns had an impact on pilgrim numbers at Dunkeld and Inchcolm. Both shrines were ignored by foreign and domestic observers in the later Middle Ages. Unlike Andrew, there is little evidence to suggest that the wider Columban cult in eastern and lowland Scotland was able to flourish while pilgrim numbers declined. Although there were a number of new altar dedications in honour of the saint in the fifteenth century, each one was founded by clergy with connections to Dunkeld or other centres of Columban worship.⁶⁷ In the *Aberdeen Breviary*, Columba, along with all the other diocesan patrons, was afforded a double feast.⁶⁸ It was this symbolic role as a diocesan patron and member of the pantheon of Scottish saints that

---

⁶⁰ *Vitae Dunkeldensis*, ed. Innes, pp. 23–4.
⁶¹ Ibid., p. 26; *Registrum Cartarum Ecclesie Sancti Egidii de Edinburgh*, ed. Innes, pp. 122–3.
⁶² Ibid., pp. 61–2; Rankin, *The Parish Church of Holy Trinity St Andrews*, pp. 74–5.
⁶³ *Vitae Dunkeldensis*, ed. Innes, pp. 45–6, 228, 243; Alexander Maxwell, *Old Dundee: Ecclesiastical, Burghal and Social, Prior to the Reformation* (Edinburgh, 1891), pp. 226, 243.
⁶⁴ *Charters of the Abbey of Inchcolm*, ed. Easson and Macdonald, xxxii–xxxiv.
⁶⁵ *RMS*, ii, no. 2347.
⁶⁶ These involved regular donations to the relics of his favourite saints, such as Duthac, Ninian and even Andrew, Margaret and Kentigern, and a small offering on the feast day at the nearest convenient light or location. Norman Macdougall, *James IV* (Edinburgh, 1989), pp. 196–219.
⁶⁷ The altars at Perth, Dundee, Edinburgh and St Andrews were founded by bishops and members of the cathedral chapter of Dunkeld.
⁶⁸ Leslie Macfarlane, *William Elphinstone and the Kingdom of Scotland, 1431–1514: The Struggle for Order* (Aberdeen, 1995), pp. 237–8.

prompted the patronage by James IV and survived into the sixteenth century, and while the popular eastern and lowland cult was in decline.

At Glasgow it was the bishops, supported by the secular canons that made up the cathedral chapter, who were the driving force behind the promotion of the shrine of St Kentigern. The catalyst for efforts to modernise the shrine may have been a major fire which swept through the cathedral sometime between 1387×1406, during the episcopate of Matthew Glendinning (1387–1408).[69] The earliest evidence of this promotion occurred in 1420 with a papal supplication by Bishop William Lauder (1408–25) to have the bones and relics of Kentigern translated into a 'chest of gold or silver so that they may be the more devoutly honoured by Christ's faithful'.[70] The translation does not seem to have been carried out, perhaps because, as the papal reply suggests, Kentigern's uncanonised status proved a stumbling block.[71] The campaign was continued by William Turnbull (1447–54), who used his close relationship with James II (1437–60) to promote the cult of his patron. In 1449 Turnbull was able to secure, with royal support, an indulgence by which visitors to Glasgow were able to enjoy some of the same spiritual benefits as those who visited Rome during the Papal Jubilee of 1450.[72] Although Turnbull may have been exaggerating the 'need of repair due to wars, upheavals and other calamities' – the avowed motivation behind the supplication – it is clear that activities of the 1420s had been unsuccessful in providing the resources to repair the cathedral.[73]

A second stage of promotion took place during the archiepiscopate of Robert Blacadder (1484–1508). Blacadder enjoyed a close relationship with James IV having supported the rebellion against his father in 1488. The archbishop (from 1492) endowed a new altar dedicated to his patron in Glasgow Cathedral and founded a chapel devoted to Kentigern at Culross in Fife in 1503.[74] Culross was the reputed birthplace of Kentigern and this personal dedication by Blacadder may have been part of a wider campaign by the archbishop to reactivate the cult in areas like western Fife, Moray and Alloa where there were churches, crosses and wells dedicated to the saint from the earlier period.[75] Blacadder also instigated a building campaign to further rejuvenate the shrine, with plans for an ambitious new aisle in his cathedral.[76] The promotional campaign at Glasgow

---

[69] John Durkan, 'The Great Fire at Glasgow Cathedral', *Innes Review* (1975), pp. 89–92.

[70] The supplication was dated 10 March 1420, *CSSR*, i, pp. 182–3.

[71] The papal reply to the supplication states that the indulgence would be agreed only if it was proved that the saint had been canonised.

[72] As the Auchinlek chronicle records, the indulgence was connected with the Papal Jubilee of 1450 so that 'thair myycht haf (as) in rome', printed in Christine McGladdery, *James II* (Edinburgh, 1990), p.163. The request was made on 11 January 1449,

[73] *CSSR*, v, no. 239.

[74] *RMS*, ii, no. 2723.

[75] In Glasgow Blacadder himself added a chaplaincy at the altar of St Kentigern founded by his brother Sir Patrick Blacadder of Tulliallan. *Registrum Episcopatus Glasguensis*, ed. C. Innes, 2 vols (Bannatyne and Maitland Clubs, 1843) [hereafter *Glas. Reg.*], ii, p. 486.

[76] The Blacadder Aisle was the last major building work completed at the cathedral; what remains today is a remnant of the plans that the archbishop had for a new east wing.

seems to have been more effective than those at St Andrews and Dunkeld with several indications that the shrine of St Kentigern retained an at least regional significance until the Reformation. In 1379 Thomas Walsingham described Scottish raiders praying to 'God and St Kentigern, St Romanus and St Andrew' in an attempt to ward off the plague, while the reputation of the shrine was known to English writers in the fifteenth century.[77] The 1449 indulgence was sufficiently lucrative to allow William Turnbull to lend James II £800 from the profits.[78] Glasgow was also noted as one of only three active Scottish shrines in the early sixteenth *Martyrology of Aberdeen*, and as late as 1550 the practice of bringing 'mad men, on fuit and horsse and byndis thame to saint Mongose cross' was condemned by Sir David Lindsay of the Mount.[79]

The shrine of St Ninian at Whithorn was presided over jointly by the bishops of Galloway and the Premonstratensian canons who served as the cathedral clergy, an arrangement not dissimilar to that at the shrine of the apostle in St Andrews. The situation was complicated in the fourteenth century by the allegiance of Galloway to the province of York, which meant that the bishops were often absent from Whithorn.[80] During that period it had been the canons that had controlled, and benefited from, the popularity of the cult and shrine. In the fifteenth century the canons, in often uneasy cooperation with the restored bishops, made a number of improvements to the shrine at Whithorn. This process began in 1406 when an indulgence was granted to help fund a new bridge over the river Bladnoch, an important crossing point on the route to Whithorn.[81] This extension to the infrastructure of the pilgrimage network in Galloway was matched by the repair and augmentation of the church at Whithorn, a process instigated by Bishop Eliseaus (1406–1412×15) in 1408.[82] In 1431 Prior Thomas (1413–31) personally built and founded the Lady Chapel, which

---

Norman Shead, 'Benefactions to the Medieval Cathedral and See of Glasgow', *Innes Review* 21 (1970), p. 15.

[77] *St Albans Chronicle*, i: *1376–94*, ed. John Taylor et al. (Oxford, 2003), pp. 310–11. The English spy John Hardyng suggested making an offering at Kentigern's shrine as part of any future English invasion of Scotland. *Early Travellers in Scotland*, ed. Peter Hume-Brown (Edinburgh, 1891), pp. 21–3.

[78] *CSSR*, v, no. 239. A grant to the cathedral by James II of fermes, revenues and profits from Bute, Arran and Cowal and burgh customs from Ayr, Irvine and Dumbarton was part of the repayment of this debt. *RMS*, ii, no. 542.

[79] The other two were Whithorn and Tain. *Kalenders of Scottish Saints*, ed. Alexander P. Forbes (Edinburgh, 1872), p. 127. The cross mentioned by Lindsay was probably the one located at Borthwick in East Lothian. *Poetical Works of Sir David Lyndsay*, ed. Laing, iii, p. 269.

[80] This led to a major conflict of loyalties during the Wars of Independence, which was exacerbated by the traditional support in the region for the Balliol family. See Richard Oram, '"In Obedience and Reverence": Whithorn and York c.1128–c.1250', *Innes Review* 42 (1991), pp. 83–101.

[81] *Calendar of Papal Letters to Scotland of Benedict XIII*, ed. McGurk, p. 156; *CSSR*, iv, no. 746.

[82] The mandate was enforced by a neutral party, the archdeacon of Glasgow: *Calendar of Papal Letters to Scotland of Benedict XIII*, ed. McGurk, pp. 173–4.

would become a further part of the pilgrim itinerary at Whithorn.[83] By the end of the fifteenth century these improvements saw a complex and sophisticated pilgrimage network at Whithorn. During the reign of James IV pilgrims could visit Ninian's cave at Glasserton, 5 miles from Whithorn, and the chapel on the hill near the town, possibly an early Christian site yet to be identified.[84] Once inside the church itself the pilgrim was greeted by an altar in the 'uter kirk', where a Ninian relic was displayed before moving on to the 'rude altar'. These were the preamble to the main event, the high altar, where the chief relics of St Ninian were displayed. After this the pilgrim would pass the Lady Chapel before descending into the crypt to view the empty tomb.

Although it lacked the space of large reliquary churches like Glasgow or St Andrews, the shrine of St Ninian was at the forefront of fashions in the display of relics in Western Europe. To provide a further attraction for pilgrims, William Douglas, prior from 1447–67, successfully petitioned Pius II (1458–64) and Paul II (1464–71) for indulgences in 1462 and 1466.[85] William had been able to enlist the support of Mary of Guelders and the young James III for these supplications. Royal cultivation of Whithorn and the Ninian cult was, initially at least, part of a wider process by which the crown tried to first interfere with, and after 1455 replace, Black Douglas lordship in the south-west. For the next century patronage of the saint and his shrine would become something of a royal custom, reaching its peak in the reign of James IV, who made annual pilgrimages to Whithorn.[86] A further notable element of the 1466 letter was its reference to 'the diverse miracles' that were occurring at the shrine.[87] From 1301 to the eve of the Reformation a range of sources from outside of Whithorn noted the miraculous reputation of the shrine and its saint.[88] It was this consistent reputation for the miraculous and royal support combined with active shrine custodians who took advantage of the available promotional tools to continually modernise their saint and shrine that explain the popularity of Whithorn in the later Middle Ages.

Despite their best efforts, the shrine custodians at St Andrews were unable to arrest the late medieval decline in pilgrim numbers. In 1512 a hospital, probably founded in 1144 to cater for pilgrims, was transformed into student accommodation for St Leonard's College. As Archbishop Alexander Stewart (1504–13)

---

[83] *CSSR*, iv, p. 175.

[84] This description of the arrangements at Whithorn come from James IV's pilgrimages in 1506–08. *TA*, i, p. 356, ii, pp. 80–1, 252, iii, pp. 280, 287, 292; Peter Yeoman, *Pilgrimage in Medieval Scotland* (London, 1999), p. 39.

[85] *CSSR*, v, no. 915, 1149.

[86] Tom Turpie, 'Scottish and British? The Scottish Church, Richard III and the Cult of St Ninian in Late Medieval Scotland and Northern England', *Medieval and Early Modern Representations of Authority in Scotland and Beyond*, ed. K. Buchanan, L. Dean and M. Penman (Aldershot, 2016), 226–45.

[87] *CSSR*, v, no. 1149.

[88] *CDS*, ii, no. 1225; *Letters of James V*, ed. Robert K. Hannay (Edinburgh, 1954), pp. 362–3.

explained, the pilgrim hospice was no longer needed as 'miracles and pilgrimages, as we may without impiety believe, had in a measure ceased'.[89] Scotland was not immune to the devotional fashions that swept through Western Europe in the later Middle Ages, as can be seen in the emergence of Our Lady, Holy Cross and Loreto shrines at Whitekirk, Peebles and Musselburgh. The 'would be saints' that characterised late medieval England were not a feature of the Scottish devotional landscape. The demand for novelty was instead filled by reinvented older cults like those of Duthac of Tain and Triduana of Restalrig, and shrines of adopted international saints like Katherine, Nicholas and Anthony. The response of the custodians of the shrines of Andrew, Columba, Kentigern and Ninian to this ever-changing spiritual climate had similar structural features, suggesting that even if they did not work together, they were able to learn and adapt from the example set by their rivals.[90] These structural features included the utilisation of indulgences, building campaigns and relic translations, alongside personal promotion by the bishops and cathedral chapter, in an effort to promote their cults and shrines.

Although individuals and communities were able to manipulate the cult of the saints, like any popular phenomenon it was subject to fashions often outside their control. This meant that the success of any promotional campaign was not inevitable, and despite the structural similarities between the responses of the four cathedral shrines, the results were considerably varied. The ability of Whithorn to attract healthy numbers of domestic and international visitors in the later Middle Ages is particularly striking when compared to the other cathedral shrines. Unlike their contemporaries, the custodians of the shrine of St Ninian seem to have been operating from a position of strength. Ninian was the most popular local saint in late medieval Scotland with a consistent reputation for performing miracles at the shrine and elsewhere from the fourteenth century to the Reformation. The custodians at Glasgow also appear to have had some success in attracting pilgrims to their shrine in the fifteenth and sixteenth centuries. What is again notable with regard to Kentigern is continuing references to his efficacy as an intercessor into the sixteenth century. This was a trait notably lacking from late medieval references to St Andrews and Dunkeld.[91] Once the relics of St Andrew and Columba were deemed to have lost their potency, habitual and potential new supplicants of the cult were able to turn instead to a host of fresh Marian and Passion shrines and flourishing regional saints like Ninian and Duthac. The communities at St Andrews and Dunkeld were no less committed to the cults of their patrons than their colleagues at Whithorn and

---

[89] *College of St. Leonard: Being Documents with Translations, Notes, and Historical Introductions*, ed. John Herkless and Robert K. Hannay (Edinburgh, 1905), p. 137.
[90] As Webb has shown, shrine custodians were well aware of each other and the promotional efforts of their rivals. Webb, *Pilgrimage in Medieval England*, p. 82.
[91] An exception to this is a miracle story involving Columba and an outbreak of pestilence in 1500. However, this was recorded in Myln's lives of the bishops of Dunkeld and was intended as much to praise the activities of George Brown, who oversaw the miracle, as Columba himself. *Vitae Dunkeldensis*, ed. Innes, p. 43.

Glasgow, as can be seen by their sustained efforts at promotion. However, like their English counterparts at Durham and Canterbury, with their patron saints no longer working miracles, the efforts of the bishops and canons were ultimately nothing more than an 'exercise in decline management'.[92]

---

[92] Dobson, 'Contrasting Cults', p. 41.

CHAPTER SIX

Religion, Ritual and the Rhythm of the Year in Later Medieval St Andrews

David Ditchburn

MEDIEVAL St Andrews was a town dominated by its ecclesiastical connections. That it was home to a cathedral and a wealthy Augustinian priory was hardly unique: Carlisle, Dublin and many other cities housed similar institutions. But unlike St Andrews, most cathedral towns were not directly dependent on their bishops.[1] Glasgow, Rosemarkie and probably Brechin were; and eight other Scottish burghs, including Dunfermline and Kirkcaldy, were answerable to a monastic house; but none matched the prominence or wealth of St Andrews.[2] The legal and political consequences for towns which were directly dependent on ecclesiastical overlords have been widely recognised by historians of Scotland, though (save for Glasgow) much less attention has been devoted to the social and economic consequences of that relationship – the subject with which this chapter is primarily concerned.[3]

Of course, all burghs had an ecclesiastical presence. In medieval Scotland, towns were the focal point of a single parish and usually the parish church was located within the town. Dependent chapels were often situated on the urban peripheries; and from the thirteenth century the urban landscape was further enhanced by the intrusion of mendicant establishments, the friars who lived in them charged particularly with care for the urban poor. In these respects the ecclesiastical topography of St Andrews was not unusual. In the early fifteenth century the parish church, originally located in the precincts of the priory,

---

[1] S. H. Rigby and Elizabeth Ewan, 'Government, Power and Authority, 1300–1540', *The Cambridge Urban History of Britain*, i: *600–1540*, ed. D. M. Palliser (Cambridge, 2000), pp. 291–312, at pp. 292–8.
[2] G. S. Pryde, *The Burghs of Scotland: A Critical List* (Glasgow, 1965), nos 83–120. For one indication of the town's wealth see Michael Lynch, 'Taxation of Burghs', *Atlas of Scottish History to 1707*, ed. P. G. B. McNeill and H. L. MacQueen (Edinburgh, 1976), pp. 308–11. By at least the later fifteenth century the town was unusually prominent in Baltic trade. See David Ditchburn, 'Trade with Northern Europe, 1297–1540', *The Scottish Town*, ed. Michael Lynch et al., pp. 161–79, at pp. 163–4.
[3] N. F. Shead, 'Glasgow: An Ecclesiastical Burgh', *The Scottish Town*, ed. Lynch et al., pp. 116–32.

99

was moved to South Street. There were several chapels in or near the town (including one in the castle) and two hospitals (dedicated to St Leonard and St Nicholas) had been founded in the twelfth century.[4] The friars came much later, which explains why they were based on the western fringes of the built environment: the Franciscans, established by 1463, were settled between Market Street and North Street while the Dominicans, whose presence did not become significant until the early sixteenth century, were located on South Street.[5] That St Andrews housed only two mendicant houses – both founded long after the thirteenth-century heyday of the mendicants – suggests that the town was small. However, the mendicant presence was perhaps inhibited by the Augustinian canons of the cathedral priory, whose order was also noted for its engagement with the secular world. There were other ecclesiastical institutions too. Secular canons inhabited the collegiate church of St Mary on the Rock.[6] And the university, founded by papal bull in 1413, was an essentially ecclesiastical institution with three constituent colleges (St Salvator's, St Leonard's and St Mary's) by the sixteenth century. Although none of these institutions was of a type unique to St Andrews, their sheer number did begin to make later medieval St Andrews distinctive, in Scotland at least.

We do not know exactly how many clerics lived in medieval St Andrews, but they and their immediate associates probably numbered in their hundreds. Twenty-four of the cathedral's canons succumbed to the Black Death in 1349.[7] The chronicler Walter Bower estimated that a third of mankind died during the 'first mortality' and, if his arithmetic was accurate, St Andrews was perhaps home to seventy-two canons or, if the death rate approached 50%, as it did in other countries, perhaps around fifty canons. This would make St Andrews Priory of a similar size to the English cathedral priories in Norwich and Winchester – and if St Andrews was similar in other respects to Benedictine Norwich, then once labourers, servants and visitors are included the priory's population would have extended to between 250 and 300 inhabitants.[8] Although the number of

---

[4] *Rentale*, pp. 179, 199, 224; Ian B. Cowan and David E. Easson, *Medieval Religious Houses, Scotland*, 2nd edn (London and New York, 1976), p. 190; Derek Hall, 'Archaeological Excavation at St Nicholas Farm, St Andrews, 1986–87', *TFAJ* 1 (1995), pp. 48–75; Jamie Hamilton and Ronan Toolis, 'Further Excavations at the Site of a Medieval Leper Hospital at St Nicholas, St Andrews', *TFAJ* 5 (1999), pp. 87–105; John Herkless and R. K. Hannay, *The College of St Leonard* (Edinburgh, 1905), pp. 8–18.

[5] Cowan and Easson, *Medieval Religious Houses*, pp. 119–20, 132–3; Brooks and Whittington, pp. 278–95, at pp. 286–9.

[6] Cowan and Easson, *Medieval Religious Houses*, pp. 225–6; G. W. S. Barrow, 'The Clergy at St Andrews', *The Kingdom of the Scots: Government, Church and Society from the Eleventh to the Fourteenth Century*, G. W. S. Barrow, 2nd edn (Edinburgh, 2003), pp. 187–202.

[7] *Scotichronicon*, vii, pp. 272–3.

[8] Philip Slavin, *Bread and Ale for the Brethren: The Provisioning of Norwich Cathedral Priory, 1260–1536* (Hatfield, 2012), pp. 8–14; Joan Greatrex, 'St Swithun's Priory in the Later Middle Ages', *Winchester Cathedral: Nine Hundred Years, 1093–1993*, ed. John Crook (Guildford, 1993), pp. 139–66, at pp. 144–5.

canons had dropped by the sixteenth century (to around forty), elsewhere in St Andrews clerics were, if anything, increasing. There may have been around twenty mendicants by the early sixteenth century, only some of whose names are now known, and perhaps up to a dozen or so secular clerics staffed St Mary's on the Rock, though they were not necessarily in constant residence.[9] A large body of clergymen also serviced the parish church – thirty priests are recorded in 1475.[10] We must factor in too those who staffed the chapels and hospitals, and a transient clerical population, including students who were in minor holy orders. The numbers studying in St Andrews were never as great as those who matriculated at the largest Continental universities, but perhaps extended to forty at any given time.[11] Other clergymen visited the town too, to attend church councils and conduct business in the ecclesiastical courts, to deliver financial dues or perhaps just to visit family, friends or saintly relics.

The demographic of medieval St Andrews was not, of course, constant. Recurrent outbreaks of plague (in addition to the fourteenth-century outbreaks, recorded at St Andrews in 1430, 1439, 1455, 1501, 1513, 1525, 1529, 1532 and 1539) caused the later medieval population generally to decline on its late thirteenth-century optimum, though in many towns post-plague immigration offset population loss.[12] However, even the largest Scottish towns were small by European standards. Aberdeen's population was probably only about 3,000 in 1408, the demographic nadir, rising to perhaps 4,000 by 1500; that of Dunfermline was about 1,000 in 1500.[13] St Andrews was probably smaller than Aberdeen but larger than Dunfermline, and by 1500 its numbers may well have slightly surpassed the 2,500–3,000 inhabitants estimated to have

---

[9] Cowan and Easson, *Medieval Religious Houses*, pp. 96, 120, 132, 225–6; Mark Dilworth, 'The Augustinian Chapter of St Andrews', McRoberts, *St Andrews*, pp. 121–36, at p. 132; Linda Dunbar, *Reforming the Scottish Church: John Winram (c.1492–1582) and the Example of Fife* (Aldershot, 2002), pp. 205–9. Ten Dominicans at St Andrews appended their name to an agreement of 1545 (*Calendar of the Laing Charters, AD 874–1837*, ed. John Anderson (Edinburgh, 1899), no. 494) though this was not necessarily the full complement of friars. See too J. P. Foggie, *Renaissance Religion in Urban Scotland: The Dominican Order, 1450–1560* (Leiden, 2003), esp. Appendix 3, pp. 255–322; W. M. Bryce, *The Scottish Grey Friars*, 2 vols (Edinburgh, 1909), i, pp. 287–98, esp. p. 289 n. 2.

[10] StAUL, B65/23/63c.

[11] The estimate of forty is provided by Isla Woodburn, 'Education and Episcopacy: Universities of Scotland in the Fifteenth Century' (unpublished PhD thesis, University of St Andrews, 2010), p. 33. For numbers at other universities see R. C. Schwinges, 'Admissions', *A History of the University in Europe*, i: *The Middle Ages*, ed. Hilde de Ridder Symoens (Cambridge, 1992), p. 189.

[12] *Acta Facultatis Artium Universitatis Sanctiandree, 1413–1588*, ed. A. I. Dunlop, 2 vols, Scottish History Society (Edinburgh, 1964) [hereafter *St Andrews Acta*], i, pp. 32, 51, 55, 57, 110n, 113n, 275–6, 307, 362, 387; *Rentale*, p. 162; Aberdeen, City Archive, Ms Council Register [hereafter ACR], xii, p. 689.

[13] R. E. Tyson, 'People in the Two Towns', *Aberdeen before 1800: A New History*, ed. E. P. Dennison, David Ditchburn and Michael Lynch (East Linton, 2002), pp. 111–28, at p. 108–9; E. P. D. Torrie, 'The Guild in Fifteenth-century Dunfermline', *Scottish Medieval Town*, ed. Lynch et al., pp. 245–60, at p. 246.

lived there in the early seventeenth century. By then the clerics, their coterie and the ecclesiastical business had gone, which probably adversely affected the town's population.[14] Before the Reformation the clerical and associated proportion of the town's population (even if only to be measured in hundreds) was thus significant. It was probably greater than the estimated 2–6% of the urban population elsewhere in the British Isles and perhaps closer to the 15% of the population in another Augustinian city, Carlisle.[15] Moreover, the ecclesiastical group stood out not just because of its distinctive legal standing but also because it was resolutely male. Home to no nuns, the clerical contingent probably ensured a significant gender imbalance in the town's population. This was perhaps exacerbated by the pilgrim influx. In other pilgrimage destinations, especially monastic centres where female access to shrines was often restricted, male visitors probably predominated. They certainly did among the exclusively male contingent of miscreants sentenced by the authorities of Ypres to visit St Andrews for penitential purposes in the later fourteenth century, some of whom were instructed to remain for a year.[16] There were implications to such a demographic. Rejuvenation depended, probably to a greater extent than in other Scottish towns, on clerical immigration.

There were other ways in which ecclesiastical interest and ideologies influenced both the physical shape of the town and its rhythms and routines. Planned towns of the twelfth century were often explicitly designed to reflect contemporary religious ideals.[17] Documentary evidence for St Andrews is thin, but Ian Campbell has argued that, with two major streets converging on a cathedral, St Andrews was consciously modelled on Rome.[18] But there are other, or additional, possibilities too. St Andrews and Jerusalem were compared as centres of pilgrimage in the eleventh century and the notion of Jerusalem as the ideal city perhaps motivated the town's planners, equipped with geometrical and spiritual knowledge, to shape the urban landscape with religious symbolism, as

---

[14] Geoffrey Parker, 'The "kirk by law established" and the Origins of "the taming of Scotland": St Andrews 1559–1600', *Perspectives in Scottish Social History: Essays in Honour of Rosalind Mitchison*, ed. Leah Leneman (Aberdeen, 1988), pp. 1–32, at pp. 1–2, 24–5.

[15] Gervase Rosser and E. P. Dennison, 'Urban Culture and the Church', *Urban History*, ed. Pallister, p. 350; N. P. Tanner, *The Church in Later Medieval Norwich, 1370–1532* (Toronto, 1984), p. 20; Henry Summerson, 'Medieval Carlisle: Cathedral and City from Foundation to Dissolution', *Carlisle and Cumbria: Roman and Medieval Architecture, Art and Archaeology*, ed. Mike McCarthy and David Weston (Leeds, 2004), pp. 29–38, at p. 36.

[16] Robert Bartlett, *Why Can the Dead Do Such Great Things? Saints and Worshippers from Martyrs to the Reformation* (Princeton, 2013), pp. 261–3, 346–7; *Registre aux sentences des échevin d'Ypres*, ed. Prosper de Pelsmaeker (Brussels, 1914), nos. 308 (at pp. 160–1), 375, 432, 780, 839.

[17] K. D. Lilley, 'Cities of God? Medieval Urban Forms and their Christian Symbolism', *Transactions of the Institute of British Geographers*, n. s. 29 (2004), pp. 296–313; K. D. Lilley, *City and Cosmos: The Medieval World in Urban Form* (London, 2009).

[18] Ian Campbell, 'Planning for Pilgrims: St Andrews as the Second Rome', *Innes Review* 64 (2013), pp. 1–22.

happened elsewhere. Jerusalem was a city 'which lieth four-square' (Revelation 21:16) and it was often cartographically depicted as a quadrangle. There and elsewhere (for example in Bristol and Dundee) streets were conceptualised in the shape of a cross, and in many towns streets were set straight in conformity with the Biblical precept to 'make the crooked places straight' (Isaiah 45:2). The topography of St Andrews, at first sight, is more difficult to explain in such terms. John Geddy's famous map of the town was published c.1580 but with its mendicant houses intact it reveals a pre-Reformation quadrangular townscape, bisected by straight streets. The map's inaccuracies have generally been regarded as error and distortion, rather than as deliberate and symbolic, but Geddy's reconfiguration does shape the town's original streets (North Street and South Street) into the form of two crosses (crossed by what are now Castle Street and Abbey Street).

All this is, of course, speculative, at least in so far as it applies to St Andrews; and we are only on slightly firmer ground in seeking to explore how the inhabitants of St Andrews engaged with the Christian symbolism of the townscape, if such it was. Elsewhere, from magnificent Florence to more modest Ayr – and perhaps in St Andrews too – streets were ritually cleansed in advance of significant religious festivals.[19] These festivals were often marked by public processions, which were in turn central to the process of both demarcating urban space and emphasising its sacred character. The Scottish sources are scant by comparison with those for other parts of Christendom, but for St Andrews we perhaps have an unusually early glimpse of such activity. The St Andrews Foundation Account B (FAB) states:

> Out of great devotion King Hungus and Bishop Regulus himself, and the other men went seven times round that very place, marked out by a clear sign. Having thus carried out the seven-fold circuit and perambulation, Bishop Regulus processed carrying above his head the relics of the holy apostle with all veneration, with his holy company following the bishop with songs and hymns. And the devout King Hungus followed them on foot, very devoutedly pouring out profound prayers and thanks to God. And the most noble aristocrats of all the realm followed the king. Thus they commended that place to God, and fortified it with royal permission <on 6 February>. As a sign of royal favour, the holy men erected 12 stone crosses at intervals around the circumference of the place; and they humbly begged God of heaven, that all who pray in that place with a devout mind and pure intention may obtain fulfilment of their petition.[20]

Set in the fourth century, to mark the arrival of St Andrew's relics, the description may be apocryphal. Perambulation did, however, have an ancient history.[21] Moreover, the passage may reflect the origins, or an attempt to identify

---

[19] R. C. Trexler, *Public Life in Renaissance Florence* (Ithaca, 1980), p. 76; *Ayr Burgh Accounts, 1534–1624*, ed. G. S. Pryde (Edinburgh, 1928), p. 20.
[20] *PNF*, iii, pp. 572–3, 578.
[21] C. J. Neville, 'The Perambulation of Land', *Land, Law and People in Medieval Scotland*, C. J. Neville (Edinburgh, 2010), pp. 42–3.

the origins, of a procession familiar to the twelfth century (when the text was composed) or to the early fourteenth century (when it was copied). Indeed, 6 February (the feast day of St Merinus/Merinach, who was credited with accompanying Andrew's relics to Scotland) remained a day of festivity in the fifteenth century, when it was recorded, and perhaps witnessed, by Abbot Bower.[22] The event described in FAB was, of course, more than a perambulation. In an apparent display of social cohesion, laymen, as well as clerics, were included, with the former placed towards the rear, a position normally reserved for the more important participants. The king was of humble disposition and on foot, rather than astride a horse. But this was not an inclusive occasion. There were neither women nor townsmen present, though those who erected the stone crosses (or who by the twelfth century perhaps re-enacted this endeavour) were likely to have come from the lower social orders associated with the priory. The clerical cast included those who possessed the relics of St Andrew, who from the twelfth-century were the Augustinian canons. It did not include other clergymen – most notably no mention is made of those who served the ancient Culdee establishment of St Mary's. This was, then, a clear and visual statement of Augustinian authority in St Andrews, even if that power was dependent on royal support and possession of Andrew's bones.

By the fifteenth century the Augustinian presence was neither new nor controversial, but the procession continued. If the beadle's arithmetic can be trusted, 400 clergy as well as lesser clerks and young monks now participated. The monastic singing recorded in FAB was accompanied by music and the chiming of bells and there was now a large audience of 'the people', presumably townspeople. An ecclesiastical procession had become a communal celebration. The authority of the church remained highly visible but it now depended on an aura of tradition and timelessness, rather than upon the fictitious King Hungus. Medieval rituals commemorated and confirmed, but they could also be adjusted to accord with developing circumstances.

It was, of course, no accident that this celebration took place in February. The month began with commemoration of St Brigid, a saint recognised in altar dedications in St Andrews, but also (according to FAB) one of seven saints in whose honour seven churches had been built after the arrival of the apostle's relics.[23] The feast of Candlemas, marking the purification of the Virgin after Christ's birth, fell on 2 February. This had been Christ's first public appearance when he was immediately recognised as 'a light for revelation to the Gentiles' (Luke 2:32). As elsewhere, candles were blessed in St Andrews to mark the occasion and, since St Andrews broadly followed the Sarum Rite in its liturgical observations, the candles were probably then taken in another procession.[24]

---

[22] *PNF*, iii, p. 586; *Scotichronicon*, viii, pp. 78–9, 184.
[23] StAUL, B65/1/1 (Black Book), fos. 3v–4v.
[24] NLS, Advocates' MS 34.1.8, fol. 152; *The Holyrood Ordinale: A Scottish Version of a Directory of English Augustinian Canons with Manual and Other Liturgical Forms*, ed. F. C. Eeles (Edinburgh, 1916), pp. 84–6. See too Ronald Hutton, *The Stations of the Sun: A*

In Aberdeen Candlemas was a day of secular celebration too.[25] If St Andrews staged similar festivities, then this might explain the seemingly happy coincidence by which the paperwork to inaugurate the new university arrived in St Andrews the day after the party (3 February), rather than during it. Bells tolled on 3 February to mark the arrival of the papal bulls and the clergy were then conveniently, but hardly spontaneously, assembled in a 'specially fitted up' refectory for the beginnings of the religious thanksgiving on 4 February. According to Bower, 'boundless merry-making' followed, accompanied by bonfires 'in the streets and open spaces of the city' and, of course, drinking.[26] The lay population, it would seem, now shared in the festivities.

Bower almost implied that the celebrations of 6 February were an addendum to the festivities marking the foundation of the university. It is more probable that the ecclesiastical establishment filled the gap between the partying of 2 and 6 February with a deliberately timed and carefully choreographed celebration to inaugurate the university. As the leading churchmen of St Andrews were no doubt aware, from their own studies abroad, relations between students and townspeople were often tense; here was a means by which the new and privileged institution might be moulded from the outset into the rhythms of what by the fifteenth century had become the town's traditional early February festivities.[27]

The inhabitants of St Andrews did not have long to wait before the next occasion on which religious ideals significantly influenced their routines. Fasternis Eve (Shrove Tuesday) was a day of dancing, singing and playing. In St Andrews, as elsewhere, recreational activities included football and cock-fighting, the latter perhaps because poultry were soon to be killed off in advance of Lent. Excess eggs were also used up to make festive cakes before the solemnities of Ash Wednesday ushered in Lent.[28] As late as 1564 the archbishop distributed ashes to the devout on this day and presumably this had been common practice in pre-Reformation St Andrews, as it was elsewhere in the Latin West.[29] The six weeks of Lent were a time of abstinence from both sex and food, in commemoration of the forty days which Christ spent in the desert.[30] Sundays and feast

---

History of the Ritual Year in Britain (Oxford, 1997), pp. 139–45. On the Sarum Rite and St Andrews, see David McRoberts, 'The Glorious House of St Andrews', McRoberts, *St Andrews*, p. 93; L. J. Macfarlane, *William Elphinstone and the Kingdom of Scotland, 1431–1514: The Struggle for Order* (Aberdeen, 1985), pp. 233–4.

[25] Aberdeen, City Archive, ACR, vol. 5/2, p. 661.
[26] *Scotichronicon*, viii, pp. 78–9, 184.
[27] Coincidentally, perhaps, later papal confirmations of St Salvator's College and St Mary's College were both dated to the same period in February, on the 5th and the 7th respectively. *CPL*, x, p. 88; Cant, *University*, p. 42.
[28] John Barbour, *The Bruce*, ed. A. A. M. Duncan (Edinburgh, 1997), p. 383; *The Poems of William Dunbar*, ed. J. L. Kinsley (Oxford, 1979), pp. 150–1; *St Andrews Acta*, i, p. 4; ii, pp. 266, 381, 459; *Rentale*, p. 115.
[29] *Calendar of State Papers Relating to Scotland and Mary, Queen of Scots*, ed. Joseph Bain et al., 13 vols (Edinburgh, 1898–1969), ii, no. 60 at p. 157.
[30] The regulations regarding sexual abstinence are discussed by J. A. Brundage, *Law, Sex and Christian Society in Medieval Europe* (Chicago, 1987), pp. 157–9.

days, such as the Annunciation (25 March, from when the new year in Scotland was calculated), were exempt from fasting.[31] But on other days dietary expectations were extensive. In recognition of the sinfulness of everything that walked on earth, meat and dairy products were removed from the menu of all but the most vulnerable. These stipulations were probably more easily adhered to than might be expected.

Fasting for shorter periods, on particular days of the week (especially Fridays but for some on Wednesdays and Saturdays too), was the norm throughout the year – so people were familiar with the concept. Moreover, Lent fell between February and April, when food supplies were especially precarious – this, in other words, was a sensible and timely means of rationing dwindling supplies. However, according to a parliamentary statute, by 1555 the 'insolent and evilly-minded' were ignoring the prohibition on eating meat – and the papacy had already relaxed the prohibition on consumption of milk, butter and cheese throughout the diocese of St Andrews in 1451.[32] We have little specific knowledge of how rigidly the populous of St Andrews adhered to the dietary expectations, but churchmen probably did try to observe them: in 1381 Bishop Landallis sought explicit papal approval for derogation from the rules on account of his 'advanced age'; but this was unusual.[33] Fasting by the population more generally was facilitated by easy access to permissible foodstuffs. Because they lived in water, and thus were associated with one of Christianity's most potent sources of purification, fish and crustaceans were exempt from the list of proscribed items. The priory possessed fishing rights as far away as the Tay and the Tweed and St Andrews fishermen were active in the Forth by at least 1222.[34] Although archaeological reports note little about fish remains in the town, it seems highly likely that, as in other Scottish burghs, a wide range of species was consumed.[35] Moreover, St Andrews was not far from freshwater fish in the River Eden; and just as importantly there were local sources of salt, the key ingredient required for preserving both meat and fish.[36] Besides fish, fruit

---

[31] 'Jahresanfänge im Spätmittelalter (um 1350)', *Grosser Historischer Weltatlas*, ed. Herman Bengtson et al., 3 vols (Munich, 1957–72), ii, p. 122.

[32] *Records of the Parliament of Scotland to 1707*, ed. K. M. Brown et al. (St Andrews, 2007–15) (www.rps.ac.uk) [hereafter *RPS*], A1555/6/10; *CPL*, x, p. 174

[33] *Calendar of Papal Letters to Scotland of Pope Clement VII of Avignon, 1378–94*, ed. Charles Burns (Edinburgh, 1976), p. 60.

[34] *St A. Liber*, pp. 54, 183, 201, 232, 324.

[35] Rains and Hall, *Excavations*. In Aberdeen there is evidence of the consumption of cod, godidae, ling, haddock, pollack, salmon and turbot. There is little evidence there of herring consumption, though herring and salmon bones often do not survive in the archaeological record. See *Aberdeen: An In-depth View of the City's Past*, ed. A. S. Cameron and J. A. Stones (Edinburgh, 2001), pp. 276–8. A substantial cargo of 15 lasts of herring (valued at £30 sterling) did, however, arrive in Hull on the *God's Grace* of St Andrews in 1520: London, The National Archives, E122/64/15, fol. 7r. For the apparent consumption of a beached whale, see *Rentale*, p. 125.

[36] *PNF*, iii, pp. 431, 439, 529–30. In 1541 salt was also shipped to St Andrews from Arbroath: *Rentale*, p. 123. See too *Scotichronicon*, iii, p. 423.

and vegetables were also permissible on fast days. Both clergy and laity might consume the produce of orchards and vegetable patches – and, although vegetables normally constituted only a minor component of diet, by at least 1557 peas dominated the menu on Carling Sunday, the fifth Sunday in Lent.[37] It seems probable that leeks were also consumed at Lent – and lettuce and onion were both planted in the archbishop's garden in 1539.[38]

The privations of Lent and other periods of fast (such as Advent and Ember Days, when clergy were ordained) bestowed great symbolic value on food. Of course, this was apparent not just in the periodic and regular ritual of fasting. Giving food was symbolically important too and the ecclesiastical establishment of St Andrews regularly sought to affirm its worth and authority through the distribution of alms, not only to the supposedly humble mendicant communities, but also directly to the town's secular poor.[39] However, the significance of these donations was not clear-cut and uncontested. Contemporary understanding of poverty changed over the course of the Middle Ages. Its meaning was, of course, a particular controversy among the mendicants, but confusion was also evident in the growing distinction made between the 'honest' secular poor (to whom Cardinal Beaton offered alms) and other laymen, such as the beggars and vagrants whose appearance in towns so frequently concerned parliament from the fifteenth century.[40] Moreover, the distribution of food in this economy of symbolic exchange was not simply one directional, from the elite to the governed. The latter reciprocated in their annual oblations, sometimes in kind, which were expected at Whitsun and Christmas, as well as in Lent.[41] Whether such ritualistic reciprocity genuinely consolidated the town's identity, or whether it became a cause for resentment and jealousy, is debatable. It is without doubt, however, that clerical hand-outs sometimes earned criticism rather than respect. Bower reported that Prior Haldenstone's donations to the disadvantaged were interpreted by some as largesse guided less by charity than by vanity – and clearly his gifts were distributed publically, allowing others to pass comment on his motives.[42]

Of course, Lent was not simply about abstinence. Fasting was designed to promote spiritual reflection in the lead up to Easter, the most important commemoration in the religious calendar. This was perhaps partly why students sat

---

[37] Bryce, *Grey Friars*, pp. 474–6; *CSSR*, i, p. 222; *Rentale*, pp. 109, 190. For other gardens in the town, see, for example, StAUL, B65/23/20c; B65/23/21c; B65/23/83c; B65/23/117c; B65/23/119c, all of which date from the fifteenth century. On monastic diet generally see Andrew Jotischky, *A Hermit's Cookbook: Monks, Food and Fasting in the Middle Ages* (London, 2011); and for Carling Sunday in St Andrews, see B65/23/331c.
[38] *Rentale*, p. 109.
[39] Ibid., pp. 82, 185–8, 200, 208.
[40] *RPS*, 1425/3/22; 1429/10/6; 1458/3/18; 1478/6/88.
[41] John Dowden, *The Medieval Church in Scotland: Its Constitutions, Organisation and Law* (Glasgow, 1910), pp. 179–83.
[42] *Scotichronicon*, iii, pp. 436–7.

examinations in Lent.⁴³ There were other signs too of the seriousness which marked the occasion. Bower noted that a richly embroidered veil, decorated with animals and other figures, was draped between the altar and the choir in the cathedral and it seems likely that, as elsewhere, saintly statues and crosses were hidden for Lent.⁴⁴ Palm Sunday marked the beginning of the climax of the Easter commemorations. Although we have no specific evidence regarding St Andrews, after the blessing of palms (in northern Europe usually represented by other foliage) this was normally another day of clerical and lay procession, devised to commemorate Christ's triumphal entry into Jerusalem.⁴⁵ The end of Holy Week was marked by Skire (Maundy) Thursday, when Augustinian canons washed the feet of thirteen poor in commemoration of the Last Supper; and new holy oils were consecrated for distribution to parishes throughout the diocese.⁴⁶ The next day, Good Friday (when Christ was crucified), was a major ecclesiastical occasion, as was Easter (marking the Resurrection). The week before Easter was, indeed, especially busy for secular priests, since the Fourth Lateran Council had stipulated in 1215 that the laity must confess and take the Eucharist at least once a year, usually at Easter – and, so far as we know, most did.⁴⁷

The form in which St Andreans marked Easter was probably similar to that observed elsewhere in the Latin West but in St Andrews there was no immediate lull thereafter. By at least the fourteenth century clergy from the archdeaconry of St Andrews arrived in town immediately after Easter for their annual assembly.⁴⁸ Their influx, with dues from their parishes, was a significant stimulus to the local economy. There were 124 parishes in the archdeaconry, to whose clergy must be added unbeneficed chaplains and the heads of religious houses, all of whom required food and accommodation for their stay of several days.⁴⁹ Business remained buoyant the following week. Some clergymen remained in town to attend the ecclesiastical court which resumed business on the second

---

⁴³ *St Andrews Acta*, pp. lxxxix–xcvii, cii–ciii, cvii.

⁴⁴ *Scotichronicon*, iii, pp. 422–3.

⁴⁵ Craig Wright, 'The Palm Sunday Procession in Medieval Chartres', *The Divine Office in the Latin Middle Ages*, ed. M. E. Fassler and R. A. Baltzer (Oxford, 2000), pp. 344–64. The Franciscans were obliged by their order to participate in processionals at both Candlemas and Palm Sunday; the Dominicans were similarly instructed, but on other feast days: Michel Huglo, 'The Cluniac Processional of Solesmes', *Divine Office*, ed. Fassler and Baltzer, pp. 205–12, at pp. 206–7.

⁴⁶ Eeles, *Holyrood Ordinale*, pp. 204–5. Although belonging to Holyrood, the ordinal 'perhaps describes what Augustinians generally did in Scotland' (ibid., p. xxiii). It is not clear how the poor were selected.

⁴⁷ Lateran IV, Canon 21 (X5.38.12) [www.fordham.edu/Halsall/basis/lateran4.asp, accessed 20 Aug. 2014].

⁴⁸ For clarification as to the nature of these assemblies, see Simon Ollivant, *The Court of the Official in Pre-Reformation Scotland* (Edinburgh, 1982), pp. 42–6. See too McRoberts, 'Glorious House', pp. 106–7.

⁴⁹ D. E. R. Watt, 'Parish Churches around 1300', *Atlas of Scottish History*, ed. McNeill and MacQueen, pp. 347–60, at p. 349.

Monday after Easter. This was the same day on which the Senzie (Synod) Fair began, lasting for a fortnight.[50] By the seventeenth century four other fairs (at Trinity, Lammas, Michaelmas and St Andrew's Day) were also held annually and all may have had pre-Reformation origins – or, if not, they were subsequently tagged on to days of longstanding festive significance in the St Andrews calendar.[51] Fairs were occasions when merchants from further afield, as well as from the town, gathered to do business. Because the range of items for sale was greater than those on offer at the weekly market, fairs might induce an influx of customers and revellers from landward areas. Margaret Moncur arrived from Anstruther, for example, four days before St Andrew's Day in 1559.[52] The fair constituted an opportunity to escape the routines and oversight of nearby communities and, with many strangers in its midst, of the town too. It was surely no coincidence that Bege Scot became aware of her husband's adultery at the Senzie Fair – an instance noted by the kirk session just after the Reformation, but surely not a unique happenstance at fair time, when sexual temptations and gossip were perhaps at their most acute in the aftermath of supposedly abstemious Lent.[53]

In May and June business and entertainment converged once again under a thick religious gloss. Pentecost (Whitsun), another moveable feast, fell four weeks after the conclusion of the Senzie Fair, between 10 May and 13 June. From at least 1381 an indulgence was offered to pilgrims who visited the cathedral during Whit week.[54] Trinity Sunday (which followed the next weekend) was the feast day of the parish church and a particular day of conviviality among the town's baxters. In 1538 an elaborate contraption, representing a cloud descending from Heaven, was prominent in the town's Trinity theatricals. It seems unlikely that such a construction was a one-off, designed solely to entertain a visiting queen, even if that is why its existence was recorded.[55] Sets of varying intricacy were a common feature of entertainments and processions across Christendom, both at Trinity and the following Thursday, which marked Corpus Christi. This celebration of the Eucharist was of widespread but recent recognition in the Latin West, dating only from the thirteenth century.[56] There were particular saints' days to mark too at this time of year. The Arts Faculty processed on the feast of St John (6 May); and in 1414 it sought to move the

---

[50] RPS, 1581/10/79.
[51] StAUL, B65/23/414c.
[52] *Register of the Minister, Elders and Deacons of the Christian Congregation of St Andrews, Comprising the Proceedings of the Kirk Session ..., 1559–1600*, ed. D. H. Fleming, 2 vols (Edinburgh, 1889–90) [hereafter *Reg. KS*], i, p. 23.
[53] Ibid., i, p. 245.
[54] *Letters Clement VII*, p. 62.
[55] The parish church was dedicated on 17 June 1243, the Wednesday after Trinity Sunday: W. E. K. Rankin, *The Parish Church of the Holy Trinity St Andrews* (Edinburgh and London, 1955), p. 17. See too StAUL, Ms DA890.S1B2 (Baxters' Book, 1548–1861), pp. 1–5; Robert Lindsay of Pitscottie, *Historie and Cronicles of Scotland*, ed. Æ. J. G. MacKay, 3 vols (Edinburgh, 1899–1911), i, pp. 378–81.
[56] Miri Rubin, *Corpus Christi: The Eucharist in Late Medieval Culture* (Cambridge, 1991).

charitable activities associated with the 'Boy Bishop', and an associated procession from castle to priory, from St Nicholas Day (6 December) to an alternative festal day associated with Nicholas on 9 May.[57] Spring was a season when social conventions were, it seemed, briefly overturned, as a boy was elected 'bishop' to oversee the revelries and as students disguised as royalty traversed the town on horseback.[58] It is probably also to this time of year that we can set the Robin Hood play which celebrated the famous English outlaw – his status rather than his nationality presumably explaining his attraction not just in St Andrews, but across Scotland.[59] All of these celebrations involved young men, though elsewhere craftsmen generally played a major role, especially in the Corpus Christi processions.[60] Whether they did in St Andrews too is not clear, though the guild structure to support the parades certainly existed.

Many of these springtime events (as well as those held on Shrove Tuesday) involved sections of the community which were normally subject to strict oversight by familial, burgh and ecclesiastical authorities. The establishment sometimes looked disapprovingly on what it witnessed. In 1415 the Arts Faculty sought to control student participation in the cock-fighting of Shrove Tuesday and subsequently in football, guising and other May games too.[61] The Robin Hood play survived parliamentary prohibition in 1552 only to fall foul of Protestant criticism in 1575.[62] Of course, no matter how raucous, popular entertainment did not really turn accepted authority on its head – and, indeed, it seems unlikely that Cardinal Beaton would have donated 27s to fund the Boy Bishop's activities in 1540 had this been a truly subversive occasion.[63] Rather, these were social diversions for young men in particular, but ones which directed their energies along routes that the authorities could control. The spectre of youth hanging around street corners with little to do and prone to commit violent sexual crime was unpleasantly familiar to many medieval towns – and, as far as the elite was concerned, best avoided.[64]

---

[57] *St Andrews Acta*, i, pp. 38, 79, 91; ii, pp. 322, 373–4.

[58] *St Andrews Acta*, i, pp. 37–8; A. J. Mill, *Mediaeval Plays in Scotland* (Edinburgh, 1927), pp. 21, 286; David McRoberts, 'The Boy Bishop in Scotland', *Innes Review* 19 (1968), pp. 80–2, at p. 80.

[59] E. P. Dennison, 'Robin Hood in Scotland', *Sixteenth-Century Scotland: Essays in Honour of Michael Lynch*, ed. Julian Goodare and A. A. MacDonald (Leiden, 2008), pp. 169–88, esp. pp. 173–4 and 183–4.

[60] E. P. D. Torrie, 'Power to the People? The Myth of the Medieval Burgh Community', *Scottish Power Centres from the Early Middle Ages to the Twentieth Century*, ed. Sally Foster, Allan Macinnes and Ranald MacInnes (Glasgow, 1998), pp. 100–31, at p. 113. See too B. R. McRee, 'Unity or Division? The Social Meaning of Guild Ceremonies in Urban Communities', *City and Spectacle in Medieval Europe*, ed. B. A. Hanawalt and K. L. Reyerson (Minneapolis, 1994), pp. 189–207.

[61] *St Andrews Acta*, i, pp. 4, 37–8; ii, pp. 266, 459.

[62] *RPS*, 1543/3/1; *Reg. KS*, i, pp. 396–7, 406.

[63] *Rentale*, p. 109. See too Andrea Thomas, *Princelie Majestie: The Court of James V of Scotland, 1528–1542* (Edinburgh, 2005), p. 122, for details on the 'maying' festivities, often staged in St Andrews, by James V's court.

[64] Jacques Rossiaud, *Medieval Prostitution* (Oxford, 1995), esp. pp. 12–26; Michael Rocke,

Spring was not just a time of fun. Rents were due too. Although Candlemas and Midsummer's Day marked some periods of account, it was at Whitsun that most people were expected to make their first payments of the year, with a second due usually at Martinmas (11 November).[65] There was latitude with the precise dates of payment, at least in some instances. From 1552 the annual rent from Lathockar was payable up to twenty days after Whitsun and Martinmas; and from 1555 the feuers of Priory Acres were instructed to pay their Whitsun dues 'apon the day of Sanct Johne the Baptist callit Mydsomerday or three day immediatlie preceeding the sammyn'; their Martinmas payment, meanwhile, was due on St Andrew's Day or three days before.[66]

As spring passed into summer St Andrews prepared for another influx of pilgrims. In 1290 Pope Nicholas IV had granted an indulgence to all who visited the cathedral on the Assumption (15 August) and during the following week. In the early fifteenth century there was an attempt to prolong the pilgrim season by proroguing an indulgence also granted for those who visited between the feast of SS Peter and Paul (29 June) and the Assumption.[67] The June indulgence would originally have concluded with the celebrations to mark the dedication of the cathedral on 5 July 1320 and the intention was perhaps to persuade pilgrims to visit in July since their numbers probably dwindled in August.[68] At most shrines the vast majority of pilgrims hailed from nearby. When sheep were shorn and the hay and cereal harvests gathered in, local pilgrims would have dwindled. Depending on the meteorological conditions in a given year, this would have occurred between August and October.[69] Even though most townspeople did not earn their livelihoods directly from agriculture, in physically and demographically small towns such as St Andrews the fields were close to the town's economic concerns. The land-owning elite, especially the ecclesiastical corporations, had to make arrangements for what to do with the produce of their fields and with their teinds (tithes), much of which was delivered in kind, even in the early sixteenth century.[70] Agricultural activity provided others too with employment, for instance in the barn and threshing-floor recorded in South Street in 1476.[71] Labourers perhaps temporarily joined the nearby rural workforce at its busiest moment in the year. Grain was shifted to the urban

---

'Gender and Sexual Culture in Renaissance Italy', *Gender and Society in Renaissance Italy*, ed. J. C. Brown and R. C. Davies (Harlow, 1998), pp. 150–70, at p. 164; N. Z. Davis, *Society and Culture in Early Modern France* (Oxford, 1997), pp. 97–123.

[65] E.g. StAUL, B65/23/20c; UYSL110/L/1; UYSL110/L/4; UYUC110/A1/1; UYUC110/A2/1; CSSR, i, 294; *Rentale*, pp. 96–7. For Candlemas and other dates of account, see, for example, Herkless and Hannay, *College of St Leonard*, p. 143.

[66] StAUL, B65/23/264c; B65/23/323c. My thanks to Bess Rhodes for drawing these examples to my attention.

[67] *CPL*, i, p. 520; *CSSR*, i, p. 10.

[68] *Scotichronicon*, vi, pp. 412–15.

[69] *RPS*, 1367/9/1; A1578/7/16; A1594/4/34.

[70] On teinds, the best general account remains Dowden, *Medieval Church*, pp. 162–78. See too *Rentale*, pp. xxx–xxxiii.

[71] StAUL, B65/23/65c; B65/23/72c.

granaries and brewhouses for the production of ale, while wool and animal skins were dispatched to urban craftsmen.[72] That the high points in the agricultural year had an impact on town life is evident from the experiences of Crail, Irvine and Stirling, all of which sought to move harvest-time fairs to quieter times of the year.[73] In St Andrews the fairs were more propitiously timed. There were, of course, days upon which the church decreed that people should refrain from labour: Lammas (1 August), St Lawrence's Day (10 August), the Assumption (15 August), St Bartholomew's Day (24 August), the Nativity of the Virgin (8 September), the Exaltation of the Holy Cross (14 September) and, of course, Sundays. But it is surely significant that from mid-August to late September the religious calendar was remarkably empty of prolonged festivity.

Other than in exceptional years, the harvest was gathered by late September and thereafter ecclesiastical influence on the calendar began to be reasserted. The feast of SS Cosmos and Damien, brothers skilled in medicine, fell on 27 September. More pertinently, Damien and another brother, Merinachus, had reputedly delivered Andrew's relics to Fife. According to the Aberdeen Breviary, 28 September marked the date of their arrival; and 29 September was the feast of St Michael, in whose honour (according to FAB) one of the original seven churches of St Andrews had been built. The concentration of religious festivals in early February was now paralleled in autumn. There were surely more processions, although we have no specific evidence of them, and latterly there was too the added bonus of an indulgence offered to pilgrims visiting at Michaelmas.[74] Every third year these indulgences were plenary, a benefit originally reserved almost exclusively for crusaders, though from 1300 they were also available to pilgrims at some major shrines. However, it was stipulated that the plenary indulgences offered in St Andrews (and indeed elsewhere, including Compostela) could not clash with Roman jubilees, which fell in 1475, 1500 and every twenty-five years thereafter. Some from St Andrews took advantage of the spiritual benefits on offer elsewhere.[75] But the incoming influx of pilgrims, often including royalty, probably more than outmatched the curious locals who ventured overseas.[76]

Other pre-harvest routines resumed in the autumn too. The burgh's head court and Fife's sheriff court usually reconvened on the first Monday after

---

[72] For granaries and brewhouses, see StAUL, B65/23/261c; B65/23/337c UYSL110/PW/100; *Rentale*, pp. 186, 200–1, 213, 224. The concept of 'counter-migration' from town to country has been little studied, though see John Leland, 'Leaving Town to Work for the Family: The Counter-Migration of Teenaged Servants in Fourteenth-Century England', *The Premodern Teenager: Youth in Society, 1150–1650*, ed. Konrad Eisenbichler (Toronto, 2002), pp. 323–34.

[73] RPS, 1578/7/14; 1581/10/80; 1607/3/25.

[74] CPL, xiii(1), pp. 202–3.

[75] StAUL, B65/23/34c; *The Sheriff Court Book of Fife, 1515–1522*, ed. W. C. Dickinson (Edinburgh, 1928), p. xxi; *St Andrews Formulare*, ed. Gordon Donaldson and C. Macrae, 2 vols (Edinburgh, 1942–44), i, nos. 76, 298, 300; CPL, x, p. 174 (which suggests that Bishop Kennedy visited Rome during the jubilee year of 1450).

[76] TA, i, p. 242; ii, p. 264; vi, p. 48.

Michaelmas. The ecclesiastical court also reassembled in early October, after a summer break which had begun in August, and students returned to their university studies. Early October was often a time when officials were newly appointed for the coming year and when the Arts Faculty elected its *quodlibetarius*.[77] The remainder of autumn was punctuated with several important feast days, including that of Triduana (8 October), another saint linked to the arrival of Andrew's relics, and Halloween/All Saints (31 October/1 November), a time traditionally associated with remembrance of the dead. There is little to suggest that the latter were days of extraordinary significance in St Andrews, but the dead were never far from public attention. Funerals, like weddings, were public affairs. Moreover, memories of the wealthier deceased were perpetuated not on their birthdays, but on the anniversaries of their death. Many bequests arranged for everlasting priestly prayers to be said, thereby easing the suffering of souls in purgatory, and for hand and church bells to chime, exhorting living laymen to join in these acts of remembrance.[78]

The next major occasion in the calendar fell on Martinmas (11 November), in terms of rents and dues the autumnal equivalent of Whitsun. But Martinmas also marked the start of winter, when animals were traditionally killed off to save on dwindling fodder. In St Andrews the cull was perhaps postponed until late November, in order to cater for the last big pilgrim influx of the year, on St Andrew's Day (30 November).[79] As elsewhere in Scotland, cows and sheep dominated animal husbandry in the area around St Andrews. Their slaughter brought work for urban labourers and craftsmen and profit for merchants who shipped wool and leather abroad. Our knowledge of the town's exports is limited: only occasionally, during episcopal vacancies, did the town's customers account at the crown's exchequer. But from the glimpses we have of trade during the 1360s, wool exports were usually at their greatest in the autumn – a busy time for traders since this was also when the wine imports of the new season would begin to arrive.[80] After Martinmas (or St Andrew's Day) fresh meat was scarce, though much would have been preserved with salt. Fresh rabbits and hares, which evaded the cull, remained available and perhaps became a more common feature of diet as the Middle Ages closed.[81] Rabbits had long since inhabited the Isle of May and by 1553 the archbishop had introduced them to the links, where they vied for space with footballers, golfers and other

---

[77] StAUL, B65/8/1 (Burgh Court Book, 1589–92), *passim*; Ollivant, *Court*, p. 47; *St Andrews Acta*, ii, pp. lxxxii, 97, 121, 125, 145, 157, 160, 364, 368.

[78] For example, see StAUL, B65/23/77c; B65/23/89c; B65/23/85c; and for bells B65/23/63c; B65/23/16c; B65/23/85c. The rituals of death are discussed in Mairi Cowan, *Death, Life and Religious Change in Scottish Towns, c.1350–1560* (Manchester, 2012), pp. 17–81.

[79] *CPL*, i, p. 520.

[80] *ER*, ii, pp. 20, 66, 240–1, 265–6.

[81] C. C. Dyer, 'Seasonal Patterns in Food Consumption in the Later Middle Ages', *Food in Medieval England: Diet and Nutrition*, ed. C. M. Woolgar, D. Serjeantson and T. Waldron (Oxford, 2006), pp. 201–14, at p. 206.

animals.[82] Warrens are depicted too on Geddy's map and, although they are absent from the medieval archaeology of other Scottish towns, rabbit bones do feature, if sparingly, in the archaeological record of St Andrews.[83]

By December St Andrews was in another period of lengthy fast, though the four weeks of Advent, as in Lent, were interspersed with moments of respite. For example, the feast of St Eloi, patron of the hammermen, fell on 1 December and that of St Aubert, of the baxters, on 11 December.[84] The Christmas festivities provided an extended contrast to the Advent fast, continuing beyond the feast of the Circumcision (1 January), which also marked a festival of ancient Roman origin, from which the tradition of exchanging presents derived. Although Bower hinted at excess when remarking that in 1425 James I 'kept the festivities [in St Andrews] going to include the feast of Epiphany' (Uphaliday, 6 January), this was normal practice at court.[85] Some of the court's Yuletide entertainments (including cards, dice, plays, mumming, dancing and carol singing) were probably mirrored, if more modestly, in towns too, before the resumption of business at the burgh head court on the first Monday after Epiphany signalled an end to the holidays.[86]

And so, after a quiet January, the year returned to February. It was not, of course, just the year that gravitated around familiar rituals and routines which were usually infused with religious significance. So did days and weeks, the former most intrusively through the chiming of church bells, which sounded at 5am to mark the start of the day.[87] Although modern notions of the 'working week' and 'weekend' had little resonance in the Middle Ages, Sunday was a day free from labour.[88] It was a day for attending church, but also for conviviality for it was often then that the various guilds assembled. While Saturday was normally a working day, almost fifty other days, randomly falling through the week, were of sufficient importance in the Christian calendar for labour to be

---

[82] StAUL, msdep106/1. See too *PNF*, iii, pp. 504, 513; *Rentale*, p. 206; StAUL, UYSM110/B4P1/2.

[83] Rains and Hall, *Excavations*, pp. 105–18; *Aberdeen*, ed. Cameron and Stones, pp. 271–2; G. W. I. Hodgson, 'The Animal Remains from Mediaeval Sites within Three Burghs on the Eastern Scottish Seaboard', *Site, Environment and Economy*, ed. Bruce Proudfoot (Oxford, 1983), pp. 3–32; C. Smith and G. W. I. Hodgson, 'Animal Bone', *Excavations in the Medieval Burgh of Perth, 1979–1981*, ed. Philip Holdsworth (Edinburgh, 1987), pp. 196–9.

[84] StAUL, Ms DA890.S1B2, pp. 10, 12, 13, 16, 18, 20; Rankin, *Holy Trinity*, pp. 70, 77. The celebrations of the craftsmen perhaps echoed those of their counterparts elsewhere, on whom see Cowan, *Death*, pp. 100–14; Margo Todd, 'Profane Pastimes and the Reformed Community: The Persistence of Popular Festivities in Early Modern Scotland', *Journal of British Studies* 39 (2000), pp. 123–56, at pp. 136–7.

[85] *Scotichronicon*, viii, pp. 255–6.

[86] *TA*, I, pp. ccxxxvii–ccxliv; R. L. Mackie, *King James IV of Scotland: A Brief Survey of his Life and Times* (Edinburgh, 1958), pp. 121–3; Thomas, *Princelie Majestie*, pp. 120–1.

[87] Rankin, *Holy Trinity*, p. 28. For the January head court, see for example, StAUL, B65/23/259c.

[88] StAUL, Ms DA890.S1B2 (Baxters' Book, 1548–1861), *passim*; Ms DA890.S1H2 (Hammermen's Book, 1553–1792), *passim*.

halted.[89] Judicial bodies observed these holidays too. The ecclesiastical courts met on most other weekdays and after the Reformation (but presumably before too) the burgh court usually met on Tuesdays and Fridays, and less regularly on other days.[90]

It seems almost inappropriate to reach conclusions about the ordering of a typical year since routine was, in some senses, timeless. Conclusions are further hampered by the paucity of evidence; only occasional glimpses survive of what happened in St Andrews and when. We may surmise further on the basis of occurrences elsewhere but there is no sustained data from St Andrews with which to engage. Still, it is reasonably clear that ecclesiastical influence was central to the fashion in which all medieval towns, including St Andrews, functioned. Ecclesiastical tentacles stretched far, partly because of the size, status and wealth of the clerical community and partly because the church was well capable of defending its interests through litigation and excommunication.[91] However, the clergy did not constitute a monolithic block which was immune from criticism. Disagreements between clergy, or between clergy and laity, were articulated in notices pinned to church doors, in graffiti, in oral abuse and in the bonfires which fanned heretics, usually in significant and liminal ecclesiastical locations.[92] Some laymen were sufficiently unbothered by the church's spiritual and temporal power that they simply thieved religious artefacts.[93] In a largely illiterate society display of all sorts was important. Still, the relationship between church and town was not consistently conflictual and most festivities were shared, albeit probably with contrasting emphasis, by both churchmen and laymen. While tensions could emerge amidst processions, marching could also regulate and mediate rivalries. And although processions could emerge as an expression of rivalry, after they had been repeated year-in, year-out their significance did not necessarily remain constant. The twelfth-century procession of 6 February probably had a quite different meaning to that of the fifteenth century. We may wonder too what happened to the feasts of several saints associated with the arrival of Andrew's relics. Regulus, Michael, Damien and Brigid remained core to the saintly repertoire of later medieval St Andrews – but others, such as Aneglas, are obscure, and probably were so even in the Middle Ages. Sometimes cults found no secular following and the church quietly dropped them. At harvest time too the church made accommodations with secular priorities. With

---

[89] *Statutes of the Scottish Church*, ed. David Patrick (Edinburgh, 1907), pp. 78–80.
[90] Ollivant, *Court*, p. 48 (The surviving data is largely for the Lothian archdeaconry, but similar practice might be expected in the St Andrews court, since it was in the same diocese.); StAUL, B65/8/1 (Burgh Court Book, 1589–92), *passim*.
[91] *Formulare*, ed. Donaldson and Macrae, i, no. 115.
[92] *Letters and Papers, Foreign & Domestic, of the Reign of Henry VIII*, iv, ed. J. S. Brewer, 4 pts (London, 1870–75; repr. Vaduz, 1965), no. 3021; *Scotichronicon*, iii, pp. 396–7; *Reg. KS*, i, pp. 36 (where the outburst was perhaps associated with traditional May exuberance); John Knox, *History of the Reformation in Scotland*, ed. W. C. Dickinson, 2 vols (Edinburgh, 1949), i, p. 13; Pitscottie, *Historie*, ii, pp. 80, 130–1, 135.
[93] *Copiale*, p. 138; *Formulare*, ed. Donaldson and Macrae, i, no. 93.

no large-scale industrial enterprises and an unusually prominent ecclesiastical complexion, the St Andrews calendar had not yet been secularised; neither was it divided, as supposedly in some English towns, between 'ritualistic' and 'secular' halves, from June to Christmas and back to June.[94] But there were compromises. After all, all towns, even ecclesiastical towns, were first and foremost about making money.

---

[94] Jacques Le Goff, *Time, Work and Culture in the Middle Ages* (Chicago, 1977), pp. 29–52; Charles Phythian-Adams, 'Ceremony and the Citizen: The Communal Year at Coventry, 1450–1550', *Crisis and Order in English Towns, 1500–1700: Essays In Urban History*, ed. Peter Clark and Paul Slack (London, 1972), pp. 57–85; D. M. Palliser, 'Civic Mentality and the Environment in Tudor York', *Northern History* 18 (1982), pp. 78–115.

CHAPTER SEVEN

Living in the Late Medieval Town of St Andrews

Elizabeth Ewan

PILGRIMS approaching St Andrews from the south-west in the late fifteenth century saw a place dominated by spires and towers, a place of religious piety and power and of higher learning. But between the impressive stone buildings of church and university lay the dwellings and properties of the ordinary inhabitants of the town. As the pilgrims drew closer, evidence of these people's lives began to appear. The Priory Acres, crofts of agricultural land around the edges of the city, were leased out to St Andrews burgesses from at least 1434, and had probably been worked by them long before that.[1] Some crofts lay just outside the town gates at the end of Market Street and South Street, in the areas known as Argyll and Dunsy dubs.[2] Argyll, one of the few urban suburbs in medieval Scotland, also had homes and dwellings, with some properties stretching from Argyll Street down to the water lade behind it.[3] Many people living here were craftworkers. As the pilgrims travelled towards the town, the reek and smoke of coal feeding hammermen's forges assailed the nose and eyes, while the sound of metal tools shaping nails, bars, horseshoes and other items of everyday life assaulted the ears. Crossing the Cowgait (City Road) and passing through the impressive gate (the West Port) into South Street, the pilgrims entered the western end and newest part of St Andrews, built up in the fourteenth and fifteenth centuries during the town's final phase of expansion.[4] A little further along on the north side of South Street, and encroaching on the street itself, were the

---

[1] *St A. Liber*, pp. 428–9. Many of these crofts were feued by the abbey to local citizens in 1555, StAUL, Burgh Charters and Miscellaneous Writs, B65/23/323.
[2] Now Doubledykes: R. G. Cant, 'St Andrews Street Names', *Three Decades of Historical Notes* (St Andrews, 1991), p. 10.
[3] StAUL, B65/23/121. Perth was the only other medieval town that had substantial suburbs in the medieval period.
[4] The present form of the West Port has been shaped by the rebuilding of the gate in 1589 but probably includes echoes of the medieval port. See Ronald Cant, 'The West Port of St Andrews', *Three Decades*, pp. 33–5. See also Brooks and Whittington, pp. 278–95. Archaeological excavation results have supported their conclusions about the timing of the westward expansion: Rains and Hall, *Excavations*, pp. 141–2.

churchyard and fine stone building and tower of the parish kirk, the collegiate church of Holy Trinity, founded in 1410 just before the university and a symbol of the townspeople's own confidence and identity.[5]

By the late fifteenth century, St Andrews had achieved its final medieval layout. Major building projects continued, with two new colleges established, the archbishop's castle strengthened and then partially destroyed, and the priory precinct wall doubled in height. The elevation of the see of St Andrews to an archbishopric in 1472 had brought even more status to the city, home to the relics of the kingdom's patron saint and one of its most important pilgrimage sites. St Andrews occupied a place in the kingdom's religious and intellectual life out of proportion to its small size, with a population of perhaps 2,000.[6] This chapter examines how townspeople in late medieval St Andrews lived their lives and how these lives were intertwined with the religious and educational establishments that surrounded them.

Unfortunately, the local government records which reveal much about individual lives in other Scottish towns are not extant for St Andrews before the 1580s, although a 1550s reference to 'the common book of the city' shows that they once did exist.[7] Nor are there any local notaries' registers (protocol books). The St Andrews records are dominated by documents produced by the church and the university, especially property transactions, which involved both lands and the annualrents generated by those lands. Some were grants which directly benefited the church or university; others concerned property that later became part of the endowment and so were preserved by the institution. However, because so many involved townspeople, they afford glimpses into their lives. Medieval properties lacked numbered street addresses, so the buildings, streets or other features that lay to north, south, east and west were used to describe their location. The transactions reveal the names of neighbours and the location of features such as craft workshops, arable crofts and watercourses. From them a picture can be built up of the layout of the town, the names of its streets and wynds, and the homes of its inhabitants, although the jigsaw has many missing pieces. Other sources of information include a small number of records from an Elgin notary who received his early training in St Andrews, the household accounts of Cardinal Beaton in the 1530s and 1540s, sixteenth-century craft books of baxters, cordiners and hammermen, and crown records. A few existing buildings contain medieval fabric, while for the physical conditions of life, increasing evidence is emerging from excavations carried out in the last few decades. The Geddy Map of the 1580s also provides evidence of the pre-Reformation town.

---

[5] StAUL, B65/23/16. See James R. Mackenzie and Colm J. Moloney, 'Medieval Development and the Cemetery of the Church of the Holy Trinity, Logies Lane, St Andrews', *TFAJ* 3 (1997), pp. 143, 153–4.

[6] This is an estimate as there are no records that give population figures for the medieval town.

[7] W. E. K. Rankin, *The Parish Church of the Holy Trinity St Andrews* (Edinburgh, 1955), p. 110.

Governing the City

THE parish church was not the only structure that proclaimed the status of the town. Market Street – the commercial hub – was dominated by the tolbooth, the centre of civic government and the burgh court. The council house lay on the west side, with the rest of the building serving as a toll-collecting centre and a gaol.[8] To the east the street widened out to form a marketplace. The tolbooth may have been situated deliberately to give protection from the west wind to those attending the market.[9] In the marketplace stood the market cross, symbolising the king's peace for all those trading there, and the tron, the public weighbeam. Weekly markets were supplemented by the Seinzie Fair, held in the fortnight after Easter, which brought traders from all over the country and abroad and was enlivened by games and festivities.[10]

There was no shortage of judicial bodies to regulate the townsfolk's lives. From 1452 the bishop and then archbishop had his own regality court with jurisdiction over secular matters, mainly criminal, normally reserved to the crown. The court of the official had jurisdiction over ecclesiastical matters involving layfolk, including marriage and morality. The prior and the archdeacon had their own barony courts, and there was a court of the university rector to deal with interactions between the townsfolk and university members. Craft guilds exercised authority over their members through their craft deacons. Outside the burgh, a few St Andrews citizens appeared in the sheriff court of Fife, which was held in Cupar.[11] The court that had the most influence over local people was the burgh court, presided over by the town officials, elected at the head court held just after Michaelmas (29 September).[12]

Local government was headed by a provost, usually a member of one of the town's prominent families, such as the Arthurs, Ramsays or Learmonths.[13] Three bailies and a council assisted him. Laws were enforced by sergeands and other officers with more specialised duties, including ale-tasters, wine-tasters,

---

[8] The council house was described as being at the west end of the tolbooth in 1564, StAUL, B65/23/348 and is possibly the western projection depicted in Geddy's map.

[9] Charles McKean, 'The Evolution of the Weather-Protected City', *Conservation and Change in Historic Towns*, ed. P. Dennison (York, 1999), p. 26.

[10] C. J. Lyon, *History of St Andrews, Episcopal, Monastic, Academic, and Civil*, 2 vols (Edinburgh, 1843), ii, pp. 371–2, confirmation of the former fair by James VI, 1581.

[11] For example, James Learmonth, the son of David Learmonth, provost of St Andrews, had to give lawborrows (surety for good behaviour) there on 30 April 1519, W. C. Dickinson, ed., *The Sheriff Court Book of Fife 1515–1522* (Edinburgh, 1928), p. 138. The sheriff court did not have jurisdiction over St Andrews citizens, but disputes involving others in Fife could be heard there.

[12] Although the city was part of the regality of the bishop of St Andrews, the right of the citizens to govern their own civil affairs was recognised, for example, in a 1485 act confirming the jurisdiction of the archbishop over his entire regality, StAUL, B65/23/103.

[13] Provosts are listed in Raymond Lamont-Brown, *St Andrews: City by the Northern Sea* (Edinburgh, 2006), pp. 248–52.

flesh-prisers (who checked the quality and price of meat sold at the market) and liners. A dean of guild, who oversaw cases relating to properties, was active by 1515 and possibly long before.[14] The common clerk, who was often the city's parish clerk as well, recorded council acts and the proceedings of the court. He was also responsible for looking after the clock. His was a longer-term appointment than that of the other officials, allowing him to bring knowledge of procedure and precedent to newly elected magistrates. For example, John Brown was appointed for life in 1447.[15] A common seal of the community was used from at least the mid thirteenth century to authenticate documents involving the community or to add weight to the transactions of individual citizens.[16]

As the town government records do not survive, the only glimpses of the magistrates' work can be found in a few extracts, occasional documents issued by them and indirect references.[17] For example, one responsibility of the burgh government was regularly to set the assize of bread and ale, the prices at which they could be sold, adjusting them according to the costs of the raw materials. The assize was mentioned in the foundation charter of the university, stipulating that its members were to be allowed to buy such goods at the same price as the townspeople.[18]

The main concerns of the local authorities were the regulation of trade and issues arising from property. However, from the fifteenth century onwards, St Andrews also faced additional concerns as a university town. The presence of young students on the streets could be disruptive to local people, as well as a source of profit. In April 1443 St Andrews wrote to Cologne, another university town, to enquire how it managed disputes between its inhabitants and the students. The Cologne magistrates replied in June, setting out the circumstances in which the town or the rector of the university could act.[19] The following year, arrangements were agreed between the town and the rector of St Andrews.[20] With the founders of St Salvator's and St Leonard's acknowledging the types of trouble their young students could get themselves into as 'nightwalkers, thieves or criminals of any kind' or 'a gamester, a calumniator [...] a drunkard, a peacebreaker and a brawler', the problems the town could face are clear.[21]

Earning a Living

As in many university towns, both medieval and modern, the presence of students could be both disruptive and beneficial. St Andrews' economy

---

[14] StAUL, B65/23/203.
[15] Rankin, *Holy Trinity*, p. 125.
[16] *St A. Liber*, pp. 284–5.
[17] StAUL, Records of St Salvator's College, UYSS110/S/10, extract from 1555.
[18] StAUL, Papal Bull confirming charter of Bishop Henry Wardlaw, 1413, UYUY100.
[19] StAUL, B65/23/30.
[20] Lyon, *St Andrews*, ii, pp. 231–4.
[21] Cant, *St Salvator*, p. 76; Lyon, *St Andrews*, ii, p. 252. See also *St Andrews Acta*, passim, for other problems caused by students in the town.

was similar to that of other towns, but it also had its own characteristics, arising out of its status as a major religious centre and site of learning. As well as supplying their neighbours, the townsfolk provided goods and services for the church and university men. Moreover, the town had frequent visitors, including pilgrims, nobles, foreign visitors and monarchs and their courts.

Royal visitors brought distractions and spectacle, although the visit of the English king Edward I, when he stripped the lead from the cathedral roof to make siege engines, was one the town could have done without. More pleasing was the visit of Robert I for the consecration of the newly finished cathedral in 1318.[22] St Andrews received many royal visits over the next two centuries. James IV liked to visit at Michaelmas; his sojourns often involved hawking, games and music, providing recreation and at least some temporary employment for the townspeople. Royal births and baptisms in the town and the attendant celebrations undoubtedly helped the local economy.[23]

The royal visit with perhaps the largest impact on the town came in 1538, when Marie de Guise, newly arrived from France, was honoured with a royal entry to the city, complete with an angel appearing out of a cloud to hand over the keys of the kingdom to her. Two days later the provost and burgesses escorted her around the town to visit the kirks, friaries and colleges. The diplomatic Marie remarked to the king (or at least was reported to have done so) that she had never seen in France or anywhere else 'sa mony goode faceis in sa lytill town as scho saw that day in Scotland'.[24] The king and queen remained in St Andrews for another forty days of jousts, entertainments and feasting, doubtless to the joy of the 'goode faceis' of St Andrews.

The shrine with its relics of St Andrew, at the east end of the cathedral, was a powerful draw for pilgrims. At various times, the papacy made pilgrimage even more attractive. In 1290 indulgences were granted for praying in the cathedral on various feast days including that of St Andrew. Perhaps this benefited William Bondolf of Dunkirk who came to the town in 1333 to gain expiation for manslaughter. From the early fifteenth century a plenary indulgence, which remitted all sins, was granted for those who came for the feast of St Michael, a particular attraction for the kings of Scots who venerated the saint.[25] In a more practical vein, Bishop Wardlaw built a stone bridge for pilgrims coming to the town at Guardbridge in 1419.[26]

The hospitals of St Leonard, beside the priory, and of St Nicholas, lying south of the burgh, functioned as resting-places for pilgrims as well as homes for the old, the poor and the sick, although high-status pilgrims might be put up in the

---

[22] R. G. Cant, 'The Building of St Andrews Cathedral', McRoberts, *St Andrews*, pp. 26–7.
[23] For example, *TA*, i, p. 242, Michaelmas 1495; *ER*, v, p. 607, baptism of the prince 1453.
[24] Robert Lindsay of Pitscottie, *The Historie and Cronicles of Scotland*, ed. Æ. J. G. MacKay, 3 vols (Edinburgh, 1899), pp. 378–81.
[25] Peter Yeoman, *Pilgrimage in Medieval Scotland* (London, 1999), pp. 65, 69.
[26] Lamont-Brown, *St Andrews*, p. 50; Lyon, *St Andrews*, i, pp. 211–12, questions whether Wardlaw or Bishop James Beaton built it, but suggests that Beaton's bridge may have been a rebuilding of an older structure.

prior's guesthouse near the Pends or the bishop's castle. There was possibly a decline in pilgrim numbers by the early sixteenth century, as stated by the founders of St Leonard's College, which took over the old hospital, although the fact that it was in their interests to say that the hospital was no longer needed suggests that the decline may not have been as great as they indicated.[27] However, visitors came to St Andrews for other reasons. For example, a steady stream of laypeople came to the bishop's court to have cases heard on testaments, marriages, widows' and children's rights, and contract and business disputes.[28] All of these visitors needed to be housed and fed while they were in the town.

St Andrews differed in status from most other ecclesiastical burghs. It shared the rights of royal burghs, including the right to trade in the staple goods of wool, wool-fells and hides and to export them overseas. From at least the early fourteenth century, merchants paid export duties on these goods to custumars who made annual reports to the royal Exchequer. As a result, the Exchequer Rolls provide a partial picture of the overseas trade of Scottish towns.

The harbour at St Andrews, at the mouth of the Kinness Burn, was not large and seems to have been mostly used for fishing boats, although it may have been enlarged in the sixteenth century when the baxters and other crafts paid money to the harbour works.[29] However, the Eden was also used as a port, expanding the opportunities for waterborne trade.[30] It is difficult to determine how busy St Andrews was as an overseas port. Two to five ships a year, as well as some smaller craft, were recorded as sailing overseas with goods subject to export customs in the later fourteenth century, although in the 1360s there were up to nine, but ships with other goods and those that arrived at St Andrews would not appear in the customs records.[31] The town's contacts with European towns such as Cologne and Bruges suggest that merchants from St Andrews were well known on the Continent. Some merchants shipped their goods from Dundee or other ports; possibly these were carried from St Andrews on one of the smaller boats that traded along the coast.[32] Such coastal trade was likely extensive, but has left only the occasional trace. For example, four barrels of salt were brought in a boat from Arbroath to St Andrews in 1541, while twenty hundredweight in lime came from Pittenweem in 1543–44, in a boat captained by a Pittenweem fisherman.[33]

Among the ships belonging to St Andrews merchants was *le Clement*, shipwrecked off the Norfolk coast in June 1388 where its cargo of wool, hides,

---

[27] For another argument for decline, see Ian Campbell, 'Planning for Pilgrims: St Andrews as the Second Rome', *Innes Review* 64:1 (2013), pp. 21–2.
[28] Margaret H. B. Sanderson, *Cardinal of Scotland, David Beaton c.1494–1546* (Edinburgh, 1986), p. 100.
[29] J. H. MacAdam, *The Baxter Books of St Andrews: A Record of Three Centuries* (Leith, 1903), p. 6.
[30] *ER*, iii, pp. 194, 207–8, 226, 258.
[31] *ER*, ii, pp. 136–8, 187–9, 240–1, 265–6; *ER*, iii, pp. 50–1, 96–7.
[32] *ER*, ii, pp. 265–6.
[33] *Rentale*, pp. 176–7.

blankets, some gold and other items was plundered by the local inhabitants.[34] Various bishops of St Andrews also had their own ships. Bishop Kennedy's ship, the *Marie*, laden with 125 tuns of wine and other merchandise belonging to the bishop, the king and various merchants was seized at Dover on its way back to St Andrews in 1453. The king sought restitution of the ship, but the case was complicated by the fact that an enterprising Englishman had commandeered it to transport thirty pilgrims to Santiago. Whether the wine was still in the ship for them to enjoy is not known.[35]

Robert III granted the whole customs revenue to the bishop and his successors in 1405.[36] Thereafter there are only occasional Exchequer returns for wool, wool-fells and hides, making it difficult to gauge the extent of St Andrews' export trade. Customs levied on woollen cloth brought some returns in the 1430s, as did customs on salmon in the 1480s.[37] Trade with England required safe conducts from the fourteenth century, and these continued into the fifteenth century. Richard Belle and William de Eglisham received several safe conducts from 1361 to 1368, including one in 1367 issued to both together, suggesting that they were partners.[38] Local merchants were involved in enough trade to win protection from James V in the early sixteenth century; he intervened in several disputes between merchants of St Andrews and various European towns, including Konigsberg, Stralsund and Antwerp.[39]

Merchants brought back many goods from abroad. Finds of English and European pottery in the later layers of some archaeological sites suggest increasing foreign contacts in the later Middle Ages. Some pottery came from containers, but other wares were imported for use. Local potters sometimes imitated the form or function of these foreign wares, for example the facemask jugs of Yorkshire or the dripping pans of Flanders.[40] Other imported goods included slates, tiles, and timber from the Baltic that was used in some of the more expensive houses, replacing diminishing supplies of Scottish timber.[41]

Trade was also carried out within the kingdom. Sometimes merchants came into conflict with other nearby towns over their respective trading rights. In 1354 David II confirmed the rights of St Andrews citizens to trade in wool, wool-fells and hides anywhere in Fife. A dispute with Cupar's inhabitants over

---

[34] *CDS*, iv, 381.
[35] Dunlop, *Kennedy*, pp. 350–1.
[36] *RMS*, i, App. ii, no. 1925. When customs were levied on woollen cloth, there were accounts from St Andrews custumars in the 1430s, *ER*, iv, pp. 501, 540, 618.
[37] *ER*, iv, pp. 501, 540, 618; *ER*, ix, pp. 77, 155.
[38] *Rotuli Scotiae in Turri Londinensi*, 2 vols (London, 1819), i, p. 915.
[39] *The Letters of James V*, ed. Robert Kerr Hannay (Edinburgh, 1954), pp. 23, 73–4, 179, 228, 320. Evidence from animal bone also suggests that the export trade may not have been insubstantial, Rains and Hall, *Excavations*, p. 115.
[40] Derek Hall, 'Blind Date – Scottish Medieval Pottery Industries', *TFAJ* 2 (1996), pp. 126–9. Local pottery in St Andrews may have come from Leuchars potteries, Rains and Hall, *Excavations*, p. 56.
[41] *ER*, vii, p. 79; Anne Crone and Coralie Mills, 'Timber in Scottish Buildings, 1450–1800: An Androchronological Perspective', *PSAS* 142 (2012), pp. 329–69.

this privilege, in which they tried to block St Andrews merchants from trading in their town, dragged on into the third decade of the fifteenth century, despite support for St Andrews from both king and parliament.[42] In 1485 the merchants clashed with the townspeople of Crail.[43]

The merchants were generally members of the town elite. Many served as provosts or bailies and some acquired substantial landed estates.[44] Merchants' seals give an indication of their sense of identity. The seals of many prominent men include a merchant's mark; in some seals this was a central feature, although in others it was combined with other significant or fashionable motifs. John Jackson's seal had a beaded circle surrounding his merchant's mark, while George Symson's included oblique crossing lines at the top and foliage off to the side.[45]

Merchants may have met the demand for expensive imported goods, but everyday supplies and even some luxury goods were produced locally. By 1557 the town had at least eight craft guilds: blacksmiths; wrights and carpenters; stonemasons; bakers; clothiers and tailors; tanners and cordiners; weavers; and dyers.[46] Of course, many more crafts and occupations existed. As well as the usual activities, St Andrews provided a home for less common occupations. From the early fifteenth century, stationers and parchment-makers in the town met students' and teachers' needs.[47] In the mid sixteenth century, John Scot set up a printing press.[48] Notaries and scribes found more work than in most towns its size due to the church, the university and the many courts. Moreover, the university trained such men, with many making their home in the town for a temporary period or permanently. The notary William Gray, who later practised in Elgin, held a chaplainry in St Salvator's in the mid sixteenth century, and the protocols from his early years in the town have survived.[49]

St Andrews had more stone buildings than most towns its size; these kept those in the building trade busy, both in construction and repair. The cathedral suffered from a major fire in 1378. The bishop's castle was heavily damaged during the wars of the fourteenth century, but from about 1385 Bishop Trail began a massive campaign of rebuilding. Such projects employed masons, glaziers, slaters, carpenters, woodworkers and a host of others. Although some were likely itinerant, the ongoing needs of the buildings ensured steady employment for many local people. Some even took on work elsewhere. On 16 February

---

[42] StAUL, B65/23/5, 6, 18, 23, 27.
[43] StAUL, B65/23/122.
[44] The appearances of Learmonth family members before the sheriff court were probably a result of disputes over lands outside the burgh, *Sheriff Court Book of Fife*, pp. 138, 141.
[45] StAUL, Records of St Leonard's College, UYSL110/PW47, 48.
[46] StAUL, B65/23/330.
[47] StAUL, UYUY100.
[48] Andrea Thomas, *Glory and Honour: The Renaissance in Scotland* (Edinburgh, 2013), p. 156.
[49] *The St Andrews portion of the Protocol Book of William Gray*, ed. Robert Smart (Edinburgh, 2015).

1394 William Plumber of Tweeddale, 'burgess of the city of Andirstoun', made a contract with the abbot of Arbroath, which had suffered severe fire damage in 1380, to thatch the great choir with lead and gutter it all about sufficiently with lead, and also lead the roof when it had been parapetted with stone.[50] There were enough masons for a guild of stonemasons to be founded by the mid sixteenth century.

Construction workers were employed on site, but many workshops were located on craftsmen's own properties, usually in the backlands, although activities such as cloth working might be carried out in booths fronting the streets.[51] Some industries, especially those needing fire and water, tended to be located in less built up areas. One of the most noisome was tanning, preparing hides for both export and local use, which required large pits where skins were soaked and processed. In the fourteenth century, a major tannery existed on the north side of the Swallowgait beside the castle, which was in a state of disrepair at the time. However, once rebuilding commenced in the 1380s, the large pits were in-filled and the tannery and its odours disappeared.[52] Not all tanneries were on the outskirts of town; in the fourteenth century there was also a tanning pit on the south side of North Street at Muttoes Lane.[53]

Many local industries made use of animal products. Skinners removed the hides not only of cattle but of other animals such as cats and dogs.[54] Horns and bones provided raw materials for hornworkers and boneworkers.[55] Tanned hides, if not exported, were used by leatherworkers such as cordiners. A sixteenth-century book from the cordiners' craft includes a list of deacons, cordiners, freemen and apprentices from 1524. There were also cobblers who repaired old shoes, but these were looked down upon by the cordiners. Whether Arnold Pattenmaker, probably a maker of wooden pattens worn underneath shoes to elevate feet off muddy streets, would have met their standards is unclear.[56]

Metalworking also needed fire and water. The hammermen's craft guild, which included most of the different types of metalworkers, was one of the wealthiest. By the mid sixteenth century it had about fifty members; with apprentices, there

---

[50] D. Hay Fleming, *The Doings of ane Antient Craft being an account of the Hammermen of St Andrews from Pre-Reformation Times until the End of Last Century* (Cupar, 1884), pp. 7–8.
[51] See Rankin, *Holy Trinity*, pp. 116, 118, for references to booths on South Street and Market Street, although it is not clear if they belonged to merchants or craftsmen.
[52] John H. Lewis, 'Excavations at St Andrews, Castlecliffe, 1988–90', *PSAS* 126 (1996), pp. 615–24.
[53] Rains and Hall, *Excavations*, pp. 21–5.
[54] Cat fur was used for trimming clothes. For evidence of cat skinning, see Colm Moloney and Louise M. Baker, 'Evidence for the Form and Nature of a Medieval Burgage Plot in St Andrews: An Archaeological Excavation of the Site of the Byre Theatre, Abbey Street, St Andrews', *TFAJ* 7 (2001), pp. 53, 73.
[55] Lewis, 'Castlecliffe', 679; *St Andrews Excavations*, pp. 89–90, 113.
[56] StAUL, Minute Book of the Cordiners Craft, MS DA890.S1B2 fol. 4r. Arnold Patinmaker was a citizen of St Andrews in 1404–09, StAUL, UYSL110/PW/9, 10

were about one hundred men working in the craft.[57] Its members probably included the local goldsmiths, one of whom made the earliest mace for the university around 1418.[58] The workshops for such delicate craftmanship were likely within the town. There were also leadworkers and coppersmiths, producing small items such as pins, buckles, rings, clamps and mounts.[59]

Several hammermen, mostly ironsmiths, lived and worked in Argyll Street, although metalworking took place in town as well.[60] They manufactured common articles such as iron nails, bars, staples, bolts, knives, candlesticks, locks, padlocks, fish-hooks and flesh-hooks. They produced horseshoes and other fittings for horses.[61] They may have worked closely with saddlers, who were also part of the hammermen craft. Alexander Napier, a saddler, was responsible for providing necessaries for Cardinal Beaton's horses and stables in 1543–44 and 1545; working with other smiths in his craft probably helped him.[62]

Some hammermen provided goods for more specialised markets. Some fragments of a coat of mail found near the castle perhaps came from a coat made locally, either for castle guards or for a local man participating in the regular wapinshawings or musters required of all adult men in the town.[63] Robert Smith in Argyll was paid by Cardinal Beaton for helping an engineer make a gun for the castle. St Andrews also provided a market for objects associated with more peaceful purposes, such as the pilgrim badges sold to visitors to show that they had reached the shrine of St Andrew.[64]

The production of woollen cloth provided employment for many women and men. Wool was processed through carding and combing, after which it was spun, activities usually carried out by women. Stone spindle whorls are common finds on St Andrews sites, suggesting the ubiquity of spinning. Even high-status women were accustomed to spinning; perhaps the finely decorated spindle whorls found near the castle belonged to them.[65] On the other hand, the spinner who took a thirteenth-century seal of Pope Clement and perforated it for re-use as a spindle whorl presumably did not recognise its significance.[66] Wool was then dyed, another process involving rather malodorous workshops. Finally it was woven by men such as Andrew Patersoune who had a property on

---

[57] StAUL, Minute book of the Hammermen of St Andrews, MS DA890.S1H2, fols 16v–19r; Fleming, *Hammermen*, p. 10.
[58] *St Andrews Acta*, i, pp. xv–vi.
[59] Rains and Hall, *Excavations*, pp. 24, 71–87.
[60] StAUL, Hammermen Book, fols 13r, 16v; Thomas Rees, Douglas Gordon and Alan Matthews, 'Excavations within the Graveyard of the Holy Trinity, St Andrews, Fife', *TFAJ* 14 (2008), pp. 64–5.
[61] *Rentale*, p. 14; Lewis, 'Castlecliffe', 640; Rains and Hall, *Excavations*, pp. 24, 64, 76–82, 85.
[62] *Rentale*, p. 200.
[63] Lewis, 'Castlecliffe', pp. 636, 637, 644.
[64] *Rentale*, p. 199; Lewis, 'Castlecliffe', pp. 638–9.
[65] Lewis, 'Castlecliffe', p. 644.
[66] Adrian Cox and Michael King, 'Recent Medieval Metalwork Finds from East Fife', *TFAJ* 3 (1997), p. 191.

South Street in 1479.[67] Flax was also spun to produce linen. One woman had a seal with what looks like a flax wheel on it; perhaps she was a flax spinner.[68]

The cloth was used by tailors, such as John Crag who lived in the town in 1471, who might also use imported cloth.[69] Parliamentary sumptuary laws in the fourteenth and fifteenth centuries decreed particular styles of dress for those of different social status, while student dress was also closely regulated by the university, so there was undoubtedly plenty of work.

Although St Andrews was an urban settlement, many inhabitants worked the land as well as carrying out more industrial pursuits. Several families leased croft lands for growing crops outside the three ports on South Street, Market Street and North Street. The area north of the Scores was extensively used for croft lands in the fifteenth century, although some of it was taken over as the castle was enlarged and took over property to the west.[70] Cattle were grazed on the links, an area which also afforded opportunities for playing at golf, football, shooting and other games, although the archbishop's rabbit warrens may have caused some tricky moments for participants.[71]

The backs of urban properties were often given over to vegetable gardens, orchards and poultry yards, and even the small-scale raising of crops. Some burgages included barns and threshing floors, doocots, corn-drying kilns and byres.[72] Geddy's map shows the long rigs and fields which stretched up to 225m from the road on the south side of South Street, as well as those on the north side of North Street.[73] Excavations of such properties have found rich layers of earth, ideal for cultivation. At one time it was thought that these 'garden soils' were deliberately brought into the town, as the population declined and more land was turned over to agricultural use. However, more recent work has indicated that these deep layers were built up from debris and organic matter deposited by the inhabitants over generations. Human waste, animal dung and vegetable matter, known as fulzie, was valuable for fertilising fields and was bought and sold by the inhabitants.[74]

Few urban families were self-sufficient in food and thus had to purchase supplies. The two staples of the urban diet were bread and ale. Corn-drying kilns and mills prepared grain for baking and brewing.[75] There was a mill in the

---

[67] StAUL, UYSS110/5/7; B65/23/83.
[68] *Calendar of Laing Charters AD 854–1837* (Edinburgh, 1899), no. 174.
[69] StAUL, UYSL110/PW/14; B65/23/54.
[70] The area was known as Castlecrofts from the fifteenth century, StAUL,UYSS110/P/3, UYSL110/PW/97.
[71] StAUL, B65/23/315; Records of St Mary's College, UYSM110/B3/P1.
[72] StAUL, B65/23/206,238; Moloney and Baker, 'Byre Theatre', pp. 55, 81; Ray Cachart, 'Excavations at 106–110 South Street, St Andrews', *TFAJ* 6 (2000), p. 133; Rains and Hall, *Excavations*, pp. 29–30.
[73] Cachart, '106–110 South St', p. 109.
[74] Stephen Carter, 'A Reassessment of the Origins of the St Andrews "Garden Soil"', *TFAJ* 7 (2001), pp. 87–92; Richard Oram, 'Waste Management and Peri-Urban Agriculture in the Early Modern Scottish Burgh', *Agricultural History Review* 59:1 (2011), pp. 1–17.
[75] Rains and Hall, *Excavations*, pp. 28–9; Moloney and Baker, 'Byre Theatre', pp. 55–6, 81.

priory grounds and in 1518 the priory and the city agreed to build another one close to the harbour. A windmill stood on Windmill Hill just to the west of the town and there were likely other mills along the Lade and the Kinnessburn. At least one miller, Laurence Bell, lived in Argyll in 1521.[76]

Baxters made up one of the largest guilds. By the mid sixteenth century there were forty-one baxters, with thirty-seven apprentices listed between 1548 and 1560.[77] The church and university provided good markets for their bread. St Leonard's students received four ounces of bread at 8 am every day, while for dinner they received eight ounces of bread.[78] The college may have had its own bakehouse, but it was also easy to purchase supplies, or at least have the baxters bake the flour which was made at the Abbey Mill. Baxters Wynd, running between South and Market Streets, seems to have housed a concentration of baxters. Several grants of bakehouses here were made in the late fifteenth and early sixteenth centuries.[79] Other bakehouses were situated elsewhere in the town, in Argyll and possibly at the hospital of St Nicholas.[80]

Oatcakes provided a cheap alternative to bread. Available in smaller sizes than loaves of bread, oatcakes were the food of the poor, although they were also eaten by those better-off, especially in times of church-ordered austerity. Most oatcake bakers in medieval Scottish towns were women, as little capital investment or time was required to make the product. This was probably the situation in St Andrews as well; the only 'cakebaker' who appears in the records is the wife of the castle gardener who was paid in 1540 for providing oatcakes in the previous Lent.[81]

St Andrews probably benefited from the export trade in hides, which brought cattle to the town. Animals were often slaughtered at the marketplace, although fleshers also went to individual homes on demand. Cleavers and axes, perhaps made by the hammermen, were used to separate meat from bones and marrow was also extracted.[82]

Fish was a crucial part of the medieval diet, especially with the many fish days decreed by the church. St Andrews, lying beside the sea, was well supplied. Haddock, cod and herring were abundant in local waters and could be eaten fresh or preserved by smoking or salting. Some fish, such as pollock, lay close to shore, while others were caught in deeper water by line and net fishing.[83] A

---

[76] Windmill Hill 1440, St AUL, UYSM110/B10/P1/1; R. N. Smart, 'Notes on the Water Mills of St Andrews', *Three Decades*, pp. 179–84.
[77] St AUL, St Andrews Baxters' Book, MS DA890.S1B2. The entries are printed in MacAdam, *Baxter Books*.
[78] Lyon, *St Andrews*, ii, p. 247.
[79] StAUL, B65/23/147, 162, 171, 274.
[80] StAUL, B65/23/316; Derek J. Hall, 'Archaeological Investigations at St Nicholas Farm, St Andrews, 1986–7', *TFAJ* 1 (1995), pp. 58–9.
[81] *Rentale*, pp. 115, 156–7.
[82] Mackenzie and Moloney, 'Byre Theatre', p. 157; Rains and Hall, *Excavations*, pp. 113–15.
[83] Cachart, '106–110 South St', pp. 128–30; Mackenzie and Moloney, 'Byre Theatre', pp. 73–5.

small fishing community lived in the north-east corner of the town, between the castle and the cathedral, plying their trade from the harbour and selling their wares at the Fish Cross in North Street.[84] Fishers' Vennel led from the narrow east end of Market Street north to the fisher community from at least 1479.[85]

Ale was the other staple of the medieval diet. The brewing trade was dominated by brewsters (women brewers) in most towns, although in St Andrews some brewing was done by the religious houses; the priory had its own brewhouse near one of its mills.[86] What appears to be a thirteenth- to fourteenth-century brewing complex where malting may have taken place as well was found in a South Street property.[87] A grant of land on Sea Street (now The Scores) in 1484 refers to 'le brewhouse'.[88] Cardinal Beaton employed Widow Fallowside for many years to supply his household with ale. The scale of her operations, with forty-one large barrels delivered to the castle brewhouse in 1545 as well as repairs made to other barrels, suggests she was employed full-time.[89] Most women brewed ale on a more part-time basis, fitting it around domestic responsibilities, although the location of one brewhouse just west of the tolbooth on Market Street may have benefited from a steady enough stream of customers to permit a more permanent operation.[90] Reports of drunken students suggest it was not difficult to find ale in the town, and it is likely that a number of brewsters ran alehouses.

In most families cooking was carried out by the wife and female servants. For those who did not have cooking facilities, it was possible to purchase cooked food. Larger households or institutions often employed their own cooks. William Thomson, cook for the priory, seems to have lived outside the priory walls as he held property in the town.[91] The St Leonard's statutes stipulated that all in the college were to speak in Latin except the cook and his boy. One hopes that they lived in the town, not the college, as otherwise opportunities for conversation would have been severely limited.[92]

Cooks were only one of many groups of townspeople providing services for others. The transport of goods from one place to another or up from the harbour to the town required the service of labourers and porters. Coal came by both land and sea, sometimes in large quantities such as the forty-four hundredweight of coals which were brought up from the harbour to the castle cellar in 1543.[93] Sometimes porters were employed for more unusual tasks, as in 1541

---

[84] StAUL, UYSL110/PW/74. They may also have sold their wares at the main market in Market Street.
[85] StAUL, B65/23/82.
[86] StAUL, B65/23/300.
[87] Cachart, '106–110 South St', pp. 112–16.
[88] St AUL, UYSL110/PW/56.
[89] *Rentale*, pp. 107, 121, 130, 141, 151, 188, 200, 224.
[90] StAUL, Hammermen Book, fol. 13r.
[91] Rankin, *Holy Trinity*, p. 118.
[92] Lyon, *St Andrews*, ii, p. 247.
[93] *Rentale*, pp. 168–9.

when payment was made to men for carrying to the castle the head and tail of a great whale killed near Byrehills.[94]

Certain service occupations, especially those related to domestic tasks, were dominated by women. Laundry was usually done by women. One washerwoman worked in the castle for two years to 1542, washing the altar linen. The only woman who was allowed to enter the College of St Leonard, except on special occasions, was the laundress, although she had to be aged at least fifty.[95] In their rules about the laundress, the authorities of St Leonard's, recognising human weakness, showed concern about their young students' physical desires. If anyone was convicted of going into the town at night or of unchastity he was to be expelled. This was a long-standing problem; similar prohibitions on students going into town at night were passed by the university from 1432.[96] It is likely that prostitution flourished in a town with such a large number of unmarried males, even if the majority were sworn to chastity. The trade may have increased with the founding of the university. In 1428 the bishop petitioned the pope for power to re-consecrate the churches, cemeteries and other ecclesiastical places of the city each time that they were 'violated by the effusion of blood or semen'.[97]

Another service was offered primarily to visitors. Some nobles and religious houses had their own accommodation available, but laypeople were more likely to find lodging with individual families. The 1413 university foundation charter spoke of the many hospices available in the town; in the early days of the university, students were taught in their masters' lodgings and would have required lodgings themselves.[98] The hospitals of St Nicholas and St Leonard offered some accommodation for travellers. There were also some inns, including one on the west side of Priors Wynd (Abbey Street) by 1493.[99] Some families may have specialised in providing lodging. At least two Englishmen stayed in Alexander Makesoun's house in 1539–40; as payment was made to his wife, she was probably in charge of the business. Another unnamed woman provided five months' lodging for two of Cardinal Beaton's French servants in 1543–44.[100]

House and Home

TOWNSPEOPLE'S houses and properties were places of business, but they were also markers of status and homes for families and households. As

---

[94] *Rentale*, p. 125.
[95] *Rentale*, p. 151; Lyon, *St Andrews*, ii, pp. 248.
[96] Lyon, *St Andrews*, ii, p. 252; *St Andrews Acta*, i, p. 38, ii, p. 322.
[97] *Calendar of Scottish Supplications to Rome 1423–1428*, ed. Annie Dunlop (Edinburgh, 1956), p. 185.
[98] Norman Reid, *Ever to Excel* (Dundee, 2011), p. 32.
[99] Lyon, *St Andrews*, ii, pp. 347–8. This may be the same as the 'Great Inns' mentioned in 1519, StAUL, UYSM110/B12/20.
[100] *Rentale*, pp. 93, 95, 180.

throughout Europe, land was central to wealth and status. The possession of a burgage was a qualification for acquiring the status of burgess, with its attendant rights and trading privileges. The liners, chosen yearly, were responsible for ensuring accurate boundaries between properties and resolving any disputes. The importance attached to these boundaries means that many have remained unchanged and can still be seen today. The burgages were generally long narrow strips of land, to allow as many buildings to have street frontage as possible. The Market Street burgages were considerably shorter, perhaps carved out of longer rigs which had stretched between the two older streets, as were those on roads running north–south. Reorganisation of settlement affected some properties. On the east side of Abbey Street older plots stretching to the west were truncated by the layout of new properties on the south side of South Street.[101] Some backlands, especially the longer ones, also housed additional occupants and their dwellings, but this was not as common in St Andrews as in other towns such as Aberdeen and Perth. Fences and gates at the end of the rigs on North and South Streets marked the boundary of the town; like most Scottish towns, St Andrews did not have a city wall, although it did have ports to control access to the main streets and the priory wall bounded it on the south-east.

Property transactions only rarely provide descriptions of the buildings located on them, although there are a few references to tiled roofs, stone walls, galleries and the like.[102] However, in the last few decades archaeological investigation has provided more insight into the habitations of the townspeople. St Andrews has been the site of more excavation than most other Scottish burghs, with the result that more and more about medieval life is being revealed. It is likely that most townsfolk in the fourteenth and fifteenth centuries lived in small wattle-and-daub or timber houses of one or two rooms, with a central hearth and a thatched roof. Some two-storey houses might have a stone ground floor or cellars, with a wooden floor above.[103] Workshops or shops often occupied the ground floor, with the family home above, perhaps reached by a forestair. Stone dwellings were not common in towns until the end of the Middle Ages, although some did exist by the fourteenth century. The number of stone houses may have increased earlier in St Andrews, perhaps aided by the presence of masons building and repairing church and university structures.[104] It is fitting that the earliest surviving image of a layman in St Andrews is the late fourteenth/early fifteenth-century effigy of a mason wearing a gown and hood, his feet on a mason's mallet, a hammer to the right and a mason's square to the left.[105] Parts of stone buildings such as St John's House (67–9 South Street), which replaced

---

[101] For example, Moloney and Baker, 'Byre Theatre', pp. 48–80. Excavations have supported the idea of Market Street as a later insertion between North and South Streets, Rains and Hall, *Excavations*, p. 141.
[102] StAUL, B65/23/327.
[103] Medieval cellars can be seen in St John's House, 71 South Street.
[104] Moloney and Baker, 'Byre Theatre', p. 80.
[105] National Museums of Scotland, *Angels, Nobles and Unicorns: Art and Patronage in Medieval Scotland* (Edinburgh, 1982), p. 68.

an earlier timber house, and the Old Student Union on North Street date back to the fifteenth century, and it is likely that medieval walls lie behind other more modern frontages.[106] The foundations of substantial stone buildings have been uncovered, some dating as far back as the thirteenth century, and more may yet be discovered, although others remain hidden under the more recent buildings lying above them. Ceramic roof tiles, found in large quantity in some excavations, also suggest the presence of substantial buildings.[107]

Most dwellings housed single families, with perhaps a few servants for domestic work and apprentices to help with the family business. Some more substantial houses were later divided into two or more dwellings, giving accommodation to more than one household, although this does not seem to have been as common in St Andrews as in larger towns such as Edinburgh.[108] An inner land (behind the frontage of the property) on the north side of South Street and the foreland of the innerland were held by two different owners.[109]

House furnishings are rarely mentioned in extant documents. Testaments, which sometimes describe moveable goods, only survive in large numbers from after 1550. However, a description of the contents of the inns on the west side of Prior's Wynd in 1493 gives some idea of the furnishing found in houses, at least those of the middling and wealthier townsfolk. Probably the largest moveable item in the house was a canopied and curtained 'standand' bed, a free-standing bed, usually for the parents of the household. Others might sleep on feather beds with bolsters and cushions, while box beds or rush mattresses served as sleeping places for servants and children. Tables included comptour boards, marked out to count money and settle accounts, and folding tables which could be put away when not in use. Seating was on benches, although a home might include one or two wooden chairs. Goods and clothes were stored in wooden kists, presses or langsadills (long benches with backs containing chests under the seat). Wooden cupboards, sometimes fixed to the wall, held plates, cooking utensils and food. Lighting came from rush or wax candles held in lamps or candlesticks, and in wealthier households hanging brass chandeliers, as well as from the hearth or fireplace. Iron grates for fireplaces are recorded in other properties such as a house on South Street in 1484.[110] At the hospital of St Nicholas, a fragment of a sixteenth-century Continental stove tile was found, suggesting that the inmates, or perhaps the staff, may have benefited from the latest Continental fashions.[111]

---

[106] N. P. Brooks, 'St John's House: its History and Archaeology', *Three Decades*, p. 91; Coralie Mills, 'Dendrochronology of Oak Timbers from Historic Buildings in St Andrews, Fife', *TFAJ* 6 (2000), p. 204.

[107] Rains and Hall, *Excavations*, pp. 90–2.

[108] Geoffrey Stell, 'Recording Scotland's Urban Buildings', *Conservation and Change*, ed. Dennison, p. 65; St John's House, built around 1450, was later subdivided, Brooks, 'St John's House', pp. 91–2.

[109] Rankin, *Holy Trinity*, p. 112.

[110] Lyon, *St Andrews*, ii, pp. 347–8; StAUL, B65/23/98; Brooks, 'St John's House', p. 91.

[111] James Hamilton and Ronan Toolis, 'Further Excavations at the Site of the Medieval Leper Hospital at St Nicholas Farm, St Andrews', *TFAJ* 5 (1999), pp. 93, 98.

Wives and Husbands, Daughters and Sons

St Andrews was unusual in the large proportion of single men in the town, most of them members of the church and, from the fifteenth century, the university, perhaps 10% or more of the population. They were housed in their own communities. The majority of laypeople lived in households, usually formed when a couple married and consisting of a single family and servants.

Marriage in the Middle Ages was a sacrament and therefore a matter for the church; marital cases probably made up a very large proportion of the work of the Official's Court in St Andrews, as they did in Lothian, although unfortunately few records survive.[112] Where property was involved, as it would be with most burgess families, betrothal and marriage were usually formal and public. The couple's parents (or the parties themselves if they were orphaned or widowed) agreed a marriage contract, promising certain lands and/or money to the couple once they had married. For example, on 15 February 1480 Robert Browin granted land in Market Street to Alexander Carstairs 'on account of the marriage contracted and solemnized in face of church' with Browin's daughter Elizabeth.[113] Women brought to the marriage a tocher or dowry, while the groom promised a terce or dower to sustain his widow if he died first. Legally, a widow was entitled to a third of her late husband's property, but marriage contracts could increase this portion. One way to do this was to grant lands to husband and wife in conjunct fee, which meant the survivor continued in possession on the other's death. On 4 November 1488 Walter Sawar granted to William Sawar, probably his son, and William's wife Agnes a tenement in conjunct fee as part of the marriage contracted between them.[114] If properties were acquired in this way after marriage, this also increased the proportion of lands to which a widow was entitled.

Upon marriage, a man's legal status remained the same, but that of the woman changed markedly. The husband was the legal head of the household, and all property and goods were under his administration, unless a contract specified otherwise. He controlled all family finances, although wives could spend necessary sums to provision and feed the household. The household was represented by the husband in court, meaning that married women are much less visible in official records than are married men. A man could alienate the property his wife had brought into the marriage, although if he did this without her consent, she was entitled to try to recover it in her widowhood. In most cases where property transactions involved the wife's property, it was specifically stated that it was done with her consent, in order to guarantee that there would be no later claims on it by her. Alexander Ramsay, having founded a new

---

[112] See Simon Ollivant, *The Court of the Official in Pre-Reformation Scotland* (Edinburgh, 1982).
[113] StAUL, B65/23/87.
[114] StAUL, B65/23/110.

chaplainry in Holy Trinity, granted it several annualrents in 1462, with the consent of Elizabeth Reid his spouse.[115]

The claims of a granter's family members to his property could be strong and sometimes threatened the security of the new holder of the land. Some parties tried to guard against this by being even more specific. Henry Scheves of Kilquhous, citizen of St Andrews, seems to have been particularly concerned about one grant of an annualrent to Mr Andrew Morrison in 1468, requiring his wife Janet Ramsay, son and heir John and brother Robert all to swear never to impugn the sale, under a penalty of £100 Scots to be paid to the altar of St Mary Magdalene. Moveover, leaving nothing to chance, Henry also swore that he would get his brother Mr William Scheves to swear likewise when he returned to Scotland, otherwise he himself would pay £20 to the altar.[116] As the recipient Andrew Morrison was qualified in both canon and civil law, perhaps it was he who insisted on such caution. In the later fifteenth century it began to become practice to question a wife away from the presence of her husband about her consent. When Henry Gilzam and his wife Christiana granted an annualrent to Walter Broun on 26 September 1482, Christiana was 'interrogated by the notary in the absence of her husband if she were compelled by him to make this resignation'. She swore on the gospels that she made it of her own free will and would never revoke it.[117]

In most families, children were likely to appear soon after marriage, as contraception was banned by the church (although perhaps practised in some form, such as through prolonged nursing). The care of children up to age seven, seen as the age when people first began to attain reason, fell largely to mothers, servants and elder sisters. Girls continued to be trained by their mothers after this, learning the domestic skills required to manage households of their own if they married. Boys had more options. They could attend school, begin learning a trade or start working for a living as servants. St Andrews had song schools, which taught basic reading and writing as well as the rudiments of music, and the more advanced grammar school, which taught Latin and other subjects, preparing some boys for university and perhaps a career in the church. Boys from song schools found employment as choristers in one of the many churches, including the parish church of Holy Trinity.[118]

In the fourteenth century, acquiring a university education meant going to England or the Continent, but local boys seeking higher learning in the fifteenth century did not have far to go. Entry to university was generally around the age of fifteen, but some new students were younger. In the early years of the university, students found individual lodgings, so St Andrews boys could presumably stay at home during their studies. As new buildings were erected and the statutes of the colleges insisted on residence for their

---

[115] StAUL, B65/23/41.
[116] StAUL, B65/23/50.
[117] *Laing Charters*, no. 187.
[118] StAUL, B65/23/141, StAUL, B65/23/242.

students, they may have moved out of the family home, although contacts likely continued.

Another route for boys was apprenticeship. Many apprentices are recorded in the books of the hammermen, baxters and cordiners. Parents paid an apprentice fee to a master craftsman, who gave the boy room, board and training for a period of years, usually with one extra year where he worked for wages before setting up on his own. The length of apprenticeship varied but terms of between five and seven years were common, although one unfortunate hammerman apprentice was bound for ten years.[119] Following apprenticeship, some boys worked as feed servants for a period.[120]

Many apprentices hoped to become masters of their craft. This involved demonstrating their proficiency to the masters, although sometimes there were other requirements. The hammermen, for example, insisted that masters be freemen of the city as well. Having been examined and found competent, the new master then swore the oath set down by the craft.[121] A hammerman swore to be loyal to God, kirk and St Eloy, the guild's patron, and 'never to hear or see any harm which might come to any brother or sister of the guild without giving them good warning of it', as well as to keep all the rules and articles of the guild. At the beginning of the Hammermen's Book is a stunning image of Christ at his crucifixion, complete with red blood from his wounds. It has been suggested that new masters took the oath with their hand lying on this image (see Fig. 7.1).[122]

Boys not entering apprenticeships or further education, and probably most girls, spent much of their teens in domestic service. Most families of middling or even lower status would have one or more servants, sometimes kin. A period of service acted as further training for girls in household tasks and responsibilities. For both boys and girls, service provided an opportunity to build up savings which allowed them to marry and create their own households, probably in their late teens or early twenties. At St Andrews, there were additional opportunities for service in the household of the bishop or the other religious houses.[123]

Most people worked their entire lives, or until illness or old age incapacitated them. However, a few made arrangements for a form of retirement. In May 1547 Laurence Hugone and Margaret Scot, his spouse, agreed with another couple, probably in return for a grant of property, that the couple would sustain Laurence and Margaret 'sufficientlie in meit and claithe induring ... [their] lyfetymes', as well as giving them a boll of barley yearly. This particular arrangement was not ironclad, however, as it broke down after Laurence's death. In 1557, Margaret assigned her rights to another man if he was able to recover them.[124]

Margaret Scot's troubles may have started with her widowhood. While

---

[119] StAUL, Hammermen Book, fol. 8r. The usual term for hammermen apprentices was five years and one more for food, ibid., fols. 7r, 8r.
[120] StAUL, Hammermen Book, fol. 15v.
[121] MacAdam, *Baxter Books*, p. 17, shows the traditional practice of the baxters.
[122] Fleming, *Hammermen*, p. 4; StAUL, Hammermen Book, fol. 1r.
[123] See *Rentale*, passim, for the servants in the cardinal's staff.
[124] *Protocol Book of William Gray*, ed. Smart, no. 11 note 28.

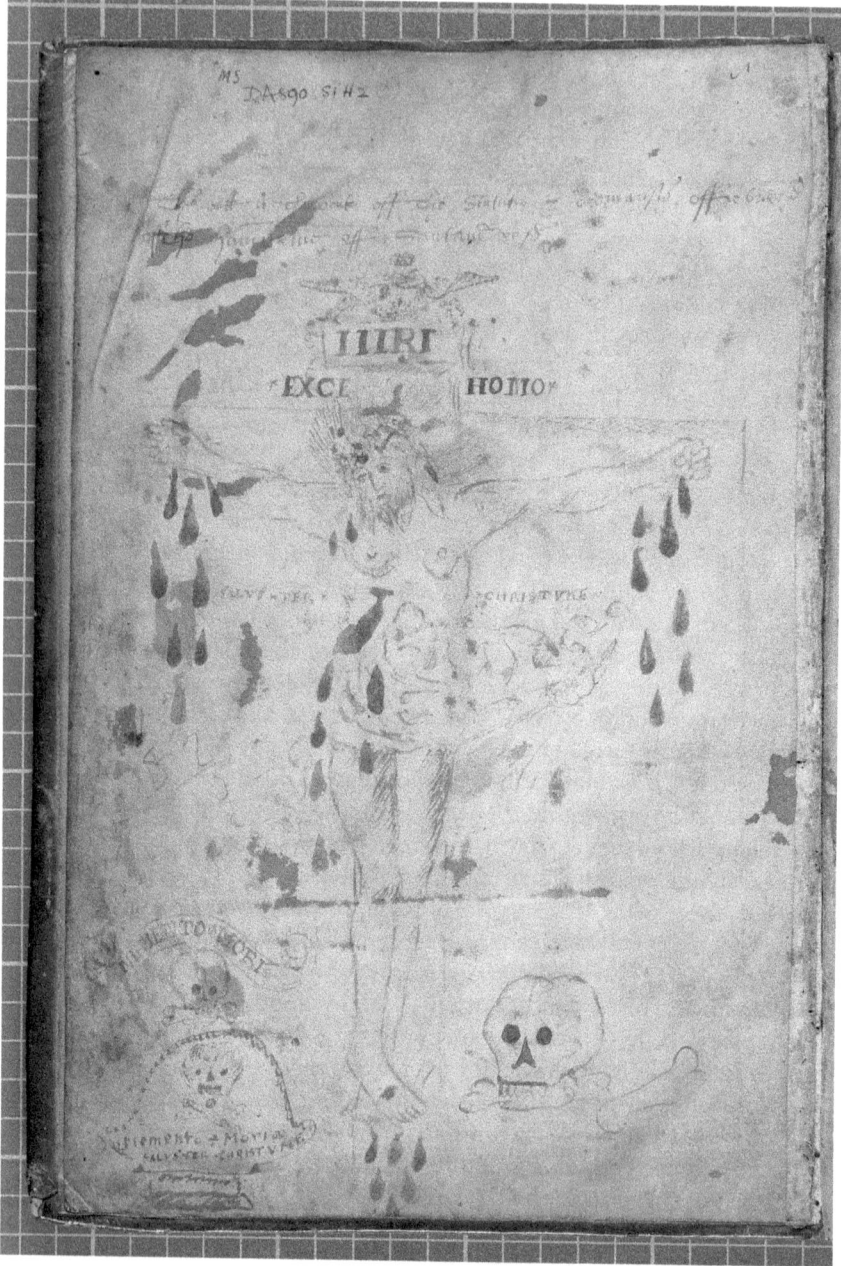

Figure 7.1: Image of the Crucifixion from the Minute Book of the Hammermen of St Andrews, 1553–1792.

widowhood restored a woman's independent legal rights, it could also be a period of vulnerability. There was some recognition of this among local authorities. When land in the priory acres was leased out to various citizens in 1527 for nineteen years, a special agreement was made that if a man died before the expiration of his lease, his widow could hold the land for the remaining term, unless she remarried.[125]

The priory was concerned about remarriage because different tenants could gain possession of the land through marriage to the widow. Occasionally husbands also tried to restrict their wives' remarriage. David Dishington, founding an altar to St Andrew in Holy Trinity in 1495, reserved the liferent of the property on South Street which he had donated to himself and to his wife Margaret Kennedy if she survived him, 'while she remains in honest widowhood without scandal, otherwise she is to be promptly ejected'.[126] In 1501, Margaret, by then widowed but presumably scandal-free, donated several annualrents to the same altar.[127] Given that the foundation specified prayers for many other family members as well as the founder, she was ensuring the spiritual health not just of her husband but of her extended kinsfolk as well.

Not all laymen and women in St Andrews married. Some may have stayed single all of their lives. Most single women probably continued to live with their families. Marion Williamson inherited property on the north side of Market Street from her father, but in 1469 she agreed to sell it to her mother who had married again after her father's death. Marion had her own seal, suggesting that she was of age to act independently. The sale may have been in return for maintenance in her mother's new household.[128] Some single women made their mark when planning the future of their own properties. Katherine Horsbruk, who held property on South Street near the church of St Leonard, granted it to Robert Armorer and his wife in 1460, but if they had no heirs, the next three heirs were to be specific women.[129]

One other option for women may have been more available in St Andrews than in most other towns. When Duncan Yellowlee, vicar of Crammond in Dunkeld diocese, founded a new chaplainry in Holy Trinity, on 10 July 1484, he specified that the chaplain was to have no concubine.[130] Despite such strictures, some clergy in St Andrews did form quasi-marital relationships with women who were known as their concubines. The most famous example is Marion Ogilvy, the mistress of Cardinal Beaton. Other lesser clergy also had concubines. The priest John Steel, chaplain of the Holy Rood, was ordered in 1534 to remove his mistress Agnes Scott from his premises.[131]

Concubines were marginalised by the church if not by their fellow

---

[125] StAUL, B65/23/245.
[126] StAUL, B65/23/97, 135.
[127] StAUL, B65/23/166, 169, 170.
[128] *Laing Charters*, no. 174.
[129] StAUL, UYSL110/PW/39.
[130] StAUL, B65/23/94.
[131] *Protocol Book of William Gray*, ed. Smart, no. 40.

townspeople. Another marginalised group was the poor. Like all medieval towns, St Andrews had its share of poor. Some lived in families; others scraped by on their own, relying on the charity of others or on institutions established to help them. The hospital of St Nicholas, lying near the East Sands, functioned from an early date as a leper hospital but by the sixteenth century it was referred to as a poor's hospital. A doorway found in the western boundary wall when the site was excavated was possibly a begging door used by inmates to solicit alms from passing pilgrims as the main route to St Andrews from the south went right by the hospital's walls. The hospital may have expanded in the sixteenth century.[132] The hospital of St Leonard offered further accommodation to poor travellers and the old and ill; by the late fifteenth century, it provided a home for elderly women. David Meldrum, official of St Andrews, at his death around 1510 bequeathed ten merks annually to sustain one poor person in the room called the cell of David Meldrum.[133] Presumably this person was ejected, along with the female inmates, when the hospital became the new college of St Leonard.

Some citizens provided concrete help to the poor. In 1476 Thomas Peirsoune gave to the town the forebooth of his tenement on South Street which he had made into an alms booth containing two beds called the 'cuche beddis' for poor people, as well as a yearly rent of 7s from his barn and threshing floor nearby to maintain the beds for all time for poor and disabled people destitute of food and clothing. The city magistrates were named patrons and visitors of the alms booth, responsible for admitting other poor persons when inmates died. One poor person was to be appointed as governor over the other inmates. Peirsoune also arranged that if his sister Marion Symson outlived him she was to have precedence over other poor in being given a place in the booth.[134]

Others relied on alms from those better off. James IV gave alms to the poor on a visit to St Andrews in August 1496 and probably on other visits as well.[135] Giving to the poor was a Christian duty or as Walter Mar, the chaplain of the altar of St Katherine in the parish church, put it, 'pious, useful and well nigh necessary'. People donating to the church for requiem masses and prayers for their soul often stipulated that alms should be given to the poor at the time of the funeral. Walter Mar asked for a mass for the dead to be said the day after the yearly anniversary of his death with thirty poor persons to receive 4d each. The same people would also receive 4d on four Saturdays throughout the year for the rest of their lives. Recognising that poverty could strike people of any status he also made provision for merchants and various craftsmen who might suffer

---

[132] Hall, 'Excavations at St Nicholas', pp. 49–75; Hamilton and Toolis, 'Further Excavations', p. 96; Derek Hall, '"Unto yone hospital at the tounis end": The Scottish Medieval Hospital', *TFAJ* 12 (2006), pp. 89–99.

[133] StAUL, B65/23/191.

[134] StAUL, B65/23/72.

[135] *TA*, i, p. 290; *Rentale*, p. 82. The cardinal gave the poor alms of meal in 1538 in return for their prayers for the late archbishop.

poverty, as long as it was for reasons other than 'bad management, luxuriousness, surfeiting, inebriety'.[136]

Many St Andrews townsfolk suffered from poverty; many more had to cope with disease and injury. Skeletons from the cemetery of Holy Trinity reveal a great deal about the health of the inhabitants, although the numbers studied thus far are not large. Among the health problems suffered were iron deficiency anaemia, malnutrition and dental disease. Arduous working conditions also affected health.[137] Many other diseases such as pneumonia leave little trace on skeletons but affected the townsfolk. Plague hit the town many times in the fourteenth to early sixteenth centuries. Leprosy was also a scourge; the hospital of St Nicholas functioned as a leper hospital from the twelfth century.

Town, Church and Identity

The fact that the medieval skeletons were found in the cemetery of Holy Trinity underlines the close connection of the townspeople with their parish church. Craft guilds had their own altars: St Obert for the baxters, St Eloy for the hammermen.[138] The town was patron of many of the altars in the church, some having been founded or given additional endowments by citizens and entrusted to the town after their death. Men such as John Arthur granted revenues to the choir of the church to organise anniversary masses for their souls after death, to lessen the time they might spend in purgatory. Arthur also ordered that a bellman should go through the street before each mass to exhort the townspeople to pray for his soul and the souls of others commemorated at the anniversaries.[139] Through such grants, the donor ensured that he or she was remembered not only in the church but throughout the town.

In 1495 an agreement was made between the prior and the town about the choir. In return for the repairs, the town sought the right of burial of 'honest dead folk' in the choir.[140] Burial near the high altar was seen as especially efficacious for salvation, but also demonstrated the social prestige of those interred there. This same combination of piety and social prestige can be seen in the efforts to reform the church services. In 1500 the town, as patron of many of the chaplainries, desired the choir to improve the standards of singing.[141] In 1527, it was agreed between the town and the choristers that they should keep divine service 'as well as any other choir does' in any parish kirk in Scotland.[142] In the same year, the town also arranged with the archbishop for redistribution

---

[136] StAUL, B65/23/330.
[137] Rees et al., 'Excavations in the Graveyard', pp. 58–63, 66; Mackenzie and Moloney, 'Cemetery of Holy Trinity', p. 9.
[138] MacAdam, *Baxter Books*, pp. 3, 9; StAUL, Hammermen Book, fol. 1r.
[139] StAUL, B65/23/90.
[140] StAUL, B65/23/134.
[141] Rankin, *Holy Trinity*, p. 128.
[142] Ibid., pp. 133–5.

of some of the revenues to the choir, so that Holy Trinity, which in age and importance took precedence over all other parish churches, should have 'the best and most ornate service' in any parish kirk in the kingdom.[143] Through this agreement, the people of St Andrews expressed their self-confidence in the town, and significantly they did so in close connection with the religious powers which surrounded them.

---

[143] StAUL, B65/23/240.

CHAPTER EIGHT

*The Burgh of St Andrews and its Inhabitants before the Wars of Independence**

Matthew Hammond

THANKS to the remarkable survival of the text of a charter of Robert, bishop of St Andrews (1127–59), our understanding of the foundation of a burgh as the kingdom's premier ecclesiastical centre, St Andrews, is better than for many much larger royal burghs.[1] Dating to between 1140 and 1159 (and possibly to 1152), Robert's charter relates that King David I (1124–53) had provided the bishop with one of his burgesses of Berwick-upon-Tweed, Mainard the Fleming, a man whom numismatic sources reveal was a royal moneyer there.[2]

---

* This work was produced under the auspices of the Leverhulme Trust-funded research project 'The Transformation of Gaelic Scotland in the Twelfth and Thirteenth Centuries', a partnership between the University of Glasgow and Kings College London. I would like to thank Dauvit Broun, Richard Fawcett, Douglas Speirs and Simon Taylor, with extra thanks to Rachel Hart, Muniments Archivist and Deputy Head of Special Collections, St Andrews University Library.

[1] *Scottish Episcopal Acta*, i: *The Twelfth Century*, ed. Norman Shead, Scottish History Society, Sixth Series, Volume 10 (Woodbridge, 2016) [hereafter *SEA*], no. 144 (H2/10/16; StAUL, 65/23/402). My thanks to Norman Shead for permitting me to use drafts of his new edition. All charter references include their unique 'H-numbers', employing the system used in the People of Medieval Scotland 1093–1314[hereafter PoMS] database. A full explanation of this system, as well as a concordance for the forthcoming acts of Alexander II (*RRS*, iii), can be found here: www.poms.ac.uk/information/. In order to save space, only the H-number is given rather than the full reference format, as follows: PoMS, H2/10/16 (http://db.poms.ac.uk/record/source/1256/; accessed 23 February 2015). Source pages can be found by removing the 'H' and entering the number into the Basic search box, choosing the 'source' result option. Occasionally, references are made in these footnotes to people in the PoMS database; these are given a 'PoMS number', as in 'PoMS, no. 2945'. Pages can be accessed by inserting the relevant number into the following full citation format: PoMS, no. 2945 (db.poms.ac.uk/record/person/2945/; accessed 23 February 2015). The PoMS database was used extensively in the writing of this chapter: Amanda Beam, John Bradley, Dauvit Broun, John Reuben Davies, Matthew Hammond, Michele Pasin (with others), *The People of Medieval Scotland, 1093 – 1314* (Glasgow and London, 2012), www.poms.ac.uk. [accessed Sept. 2014 to Feb. 2015].

[2] For the dating of this document and the circumstances behind its production, see Matthew Hammond, 'The Bishop, the Prior, and the Founding of St Andrews', *Innes Review* 66:1 (2015), pp. 72–101. For Mainard as a royal moneyer, see *The Charters of David I: The*

Figure 8.1: King Máel Coluim grants liberties and customs to the burgesses of St Andrews, 1153×62. Charter of Malcolm IV, St Andrews University Library, B65/23/1c.

It was Mainard who 'started to build and stock the said burgh from scratch', a task which prompted the bishop to make him the burgh's first grieve.³ The burgh was founded around the same time as the Augustinian cathedral priory, which A. A. M. Duncan has argued definitively dates to 1140.⁴ St Andrews was certainly the first episcopal burgh in the kingdom, and probably the second non-royal burgh, after the abbot of Holyrood's burgh of Canongate. In the 1140s its harbour would have made a convenient stopping point between the burgeoning trading centres at Berwick and Perth; by later in the century, how-

---

Written Acts of David I King of Scots, 1124–53 and of his Son Henry Earl of Northumberland, 1139–52, ed. G. W. S. Barrow (Woodbridge, 1999) [hereafter *Chrs David*], p. 165, no. 242.

³ *PNF*, iii, pp. 429–30. My thanks to Simon Taylor for allowing me to use his translation.

⁴ A. A. M. Duncan, 'The Foundation of St Andrews Cathedral Priory, 1140', *SHR* 84 (2005), pp. 1–37. The argument is made in Hammond, 'The Bishop, the Prior, and the Founding of St Andrews' that the burgh's founding may postdate the priory's establishment by a year or two.

ever, many other such ports acquired burghal status under the king and his relatives, notably Inverkeithing, Kinghorn, Crail and Dundee.[5] St Andrews' burgesses quickly acquired full parity with the king's, obtaining a charter in 1160 from King Máel Coluim (Malcolm IV, 1153–65) granting them the same rights as his own royal burgesses across the kingdom. Surviving as a contemporary single-sheet manuscript, this is the earliest surviving royal charter to a burgh in the kingdom (see figure 8.1).[6] A persistent theme of the burgh's early history was its tendency to keep pace with royal burghs in terms of developments in governance and trade.

Settlement and commerce had certainly preceded the burgh's foundation. As the seat of the kingdom's top bishop, with the shrine of St Andrew acting as a magnet for pilgrims, the church settlement on the headland had long been a place where people came together and mixed. Archaeologists have noted the significance of Kirkhill, near the harbour, as the centre of early settlement.[7] By the mid twelfth century, however, another, more secular, settlement, known as the 'Clochin' or *clachan*, may have been situated near the eastern end of North Street, a routeway which likely continued past the old parish church of Holy Trinity and the old church of St Andrew (the upstanding remains of which are St Rule's Tower), and thence to Kirkhill and the harbour.[8] Mainard also laid out a new street, South Street; its regular width suggests it was on more of a 'greenfield site', although there may have been a pre-existing routeway as well. Bishop Robert's charter to Mainard refers to this as 'the street of the burgesses' and it gave him land there; here was almost certainly the focus of the new merchant settlement, in juxtaposition to the more built-up area along North Street.[9] Burghal houses of this period tended to be set back from the street, with a forecourt allowing space for booths and other temporary structures. In this light, Mainard's task of 'creating' a street through the existing settlement may not have necessitated a great deal of new work.[10] In any event, this basic two-street layout clearly pre-dated the building of the new cathedral, suggesting that burgh and cathedral were likely not 'part of a single grandiose conception'.[11] It

---

[5] George Smith Pryde, *The Burghs of Scotland: A Critical List* (Oxford, 1965), although note opinion has changed on some of his dates.

[6] *RRS*, i, no. 166; StAUL, B65/23/1c (H1/5/43).

[7] Derek W. Hall, 'Pre-burghal St Andrews: Towards an Archaeological Research Design', *TFAJ* 1 (1995), pp. 23–7.

[8] *Scottish Episcopal Acta*, i: *The Twelfth Century*, ed. Norman Shead, Scottish History Society, sixth series 10 (Woodbridge, 2016) [hereafter *SEA*], no. 235 (H2/10/116; StAUL, B65/1/1 (The Black Book of St Andrews), fol. 35r). Brooks and Whittington, pp. 292–3. Richard Oram argues for a more conservative interpretation, noting that attempts to locate the 'Clochin' and 'Lambin's land' have been based on conjecture and that archaeological evidence for the development of Market Street may suggest a date as late as 1300. Richard Oram, *Domination and Lordship: Scotland 1070–1230* (Edinburgh, 2011), pp. 285–6.

[9] *SEA*, no. 144 (H2/10/16).

[10] Oram, *Domination and Lordship*, p. 290.

[11] Cf. Brooks and Whittington, p. 291.

is improbable that Bishop Robert, whose project centred around expanding the old church of St Andrew, and whose relationship with Prior Robert (1140–60) was very strained, would have asked Mainard to lay out the streets in reference to the new cathedral, which contemporaries attribute to his successor, Bishop Arnold (1160–62).[12] Moreover, it has been argued convincingly that the new cathedral was laid out on a grand scale, in direct competition with building works at York Minster, as part of, or in reaction to, the failed 1159 attempt to gain archiepiscopal status from the pope.[13] Furthermore, as the site of the large church was very likely to have been built up, it would have had to have been cleared: the building of the new pilgrim hospital on the site of St Leonard's by 1162 may be a clue to what had been there previously.[14]

Over the next decades, cathedral and burgh grew side-by-side. The building works attracted a number of craftsmen, quarrymen and other workers, whose skills were evidently highly valued by the burgesses. Bishop Richard (elected 1163, 1165–78) had to issue a charter to the burgesses forbidding them from taking these men away from their work on the cathedral without permission. The burgesses were apparently also taking part in that age-old custom of fleecing outsiders carrying cash, charging them fees to buy and sell in the town.[15] Land along North Street was being attracted into burgage as far west as what is now the golf clubhouse. Richard gave the priory land 'between Godric Sterecrag's land and Rathelpie, as far as the sea' for their work on the cathedral.[16] The bishop's sister also had land backing up to the sea; this must have been a North Street toft backing up to what is now the Scores.[17] By the end of the century, the marketplace, which may have been at the triangular area at the end of North Street, near the entrance to the new cathedral, had been moved to a new site, possibly its now familiar site between the two main streets, eventually allowing the creation of a third street, Market Street.[18] While the burgh may have been neglected during the troubled years of Bishop Hugh (1178–88), Bishop Roger (elected 1189, 1198–1202) restored the burgesses' rights to milling, common pasture and 'going out far and wide by the three ancient and customary exits from the

---

[12] Alan Orr Anderson, *Early Sources of Scottish History A.D. 500 to 1286* (Edinburgh, 1922), ii, p. 250; cf. Ian Campbell, 'Planning for Pilgrims: St Andrews as the Second Rome', *Innes Review* 64 (2013), pp. 1–22, at p. 10. For the tense atmosphere surrounding the priory's early history, see Duncan, 'Foundation', and Hammond, 'The Bishop, the Prior, and the Founding of St Andrews', infra.

[13] Malcolm Thurlby, 'St Andrews Cathedral Priory and the Beginnings of Gothic Architecture in Northern Britain', *Medieval Art and Architecture in the Diocese of St Andrews*, ed. John Higgitt (Leeds, 1994), pp. 47–60, at p. 52, pp. 54–6; Dauvit Broun, *Scottish Independence and the Idea of Britain* (Edinburgh, 2007), p. 137; Campbell, 'Planning for Pilgrims', pp. 16–17.

[14] The 'new hospital' is mentioned by Bishop Arnold (1160×62), implying a recent move. *SEA*, no. 152 (H2/10/34; *St A. Lib.*, 127).

[15] *SEA*, no. 200 (H2/10/74; *St A. Lib.*, 338).

[16] *SEA*, no. 195 (H2/10/89; *St A. Lib.*, 141).

[17] *SEA*, no. 183 (H2/10/73; *St A. Lib.*, 134).

[18] *SEA*, no. 235 (H2/10/116; StAUL, B65/1/1 (Black Book of St Andrews), fol. 35r.).

toun of St Andrews'.[19] In 1199, the bishop got papal sanction to build a new parish church 'to meet the increase of population in the parish of St Andrews'.[20] If this was followed through, it was probably an expansion of the existing church of the Holy Trinity near the cathedral. Nevertheless, it does demonstrate the burgh's flourishing in its first half century.

Trade and Government in the Burgh

CRUCIAL to the commercial success of any community of burgesses was the ability to buy and sell outside of the town itself. Royal burghs had access to trading zones over which the burgesses could enforce a monopoly and collect tolls and customs, underwritten by the king.[21] Burgesses in important royal centres like Perth and Aberdeen controlled buying and selling, at least in principle, across vast trading zones, but Fife, a less centralised county, was divided up into multiple monopoly regions. The earliest evidence for such a zone in Fife comes from the important south Fife burgh of Inverkeithing. Given burghal status by about 1160, Inverkeithing acquired the right to levy tolls and customs and control trade on land and on sea between the rivers Leven (which joins the Forth near Methil) and Devon (which joins the Forth at Tullibody, almost as far west as Stirling) in the 1160s or 1170s, a right which was renewed by kings Alexander II and III.[22] Kinghorn, also a royal burgh by about 1170, was located in the middle of this zone, suggesting its burgesses enjoyed only lesser privileges or that trade there was minimal.[23] Crail, a major trading centre, with a large marketplace laid out in the twelfth century and a two-week long annual fair, was held by Countess Ada, mother of kings Malcolm and William, until her death in 1178, and by Queen Ermengarde de Beaumont from 1186, likely until her death in 1233, despite attempts to transfer its lordship to the new Queen Joan in 1221.[24]

---

[19] *SEA*, no. 258 (H2/10/124; StAUL, B65/1/1, (Black Book of St Andrews), fol. 35r). Translation by Norman Shead.
[20] *CPL*, i, p. 5 (H2/137/4).
[21] G. W. S. Barrow, *Kingship and Unity: Scotland 1000–1306* (Edinburgh, 1981), p. 100.
[22] S. Taylor with G. Márkus, *The Place-Names of Fife, Volume One: West Fife between Leven and Forth* (Donington, 2006) [hereafter *PNF*, i], p. 378; *RRS*, i, nos. 212 (H1/5/78), 232 (H1/5/96); *RRS*, ii, no. 250 (H1/6/227); *Regesta Regum Scottorum III, The Acts of Alexander II King of Scots 1214– 1249*, ed. Keith Stringer (Edinburgh, forthcoming) [hereafter *RRS*, iii], no. 78 (H1/7/80; *Municipal Corporations (Scotland): Appendix to the General Report of the Commissioners* (London, 1835), p. 8); no. 44 (H1/8/42). I am very grateful to Professor Keith Stringer for giving me access to his as yet unpublished edition; conventional references are also given.
[23] *PNF*, i, pp. 391, 415; *RRS*, ii, no. 22 (H1/6/17).
[24] Duncan, *Making of the Kingdom*, pp. 469–70; *PNF*, iii, p. 18. *RRS*, iii, no. 60 (H1/7/60; *Foedera, Conventiones, Litterae et Cuiuscunque Generis Acta Publica*, ed. T. Rymer, Record Commission edition (London, 1816–69), I, i, p. 165). Kinghorn was also intended for Queen Joan in 1221. That Alexander II referred to 'our burgesses of Crail' in 1234 may suggest that he took over personal lordship of the burgh following Ermengarde's death in 1233. See *RRS*, iii, no. 205 (H1/7/212; *Liber S. Marie de Balmorinach*, ed. W. B. D. D.

A charter of King Robert I makes clear that Crail's trading zone picked up in the middle of the river Leven, where Inverkeithing's ended, extending around Fife Ness as far as Kenly water, the boundary with St Andrews St Leonard's parish.[25] The trading zone for north Fife was controlled by Cupar, a comital burgh of the earl of Fife by 1294 and probably long before (and a royal burgh later).[26] Its trading zone was described in 1428 as following 'ancient bounds and marches' from Ceres burn and the river Eden, marching with Inverkeithing's trading zone as far as Milnathort in Kinross-shire, evidently a major crossing point for roads leading to Perth, Stirling and east Fife. From there, Cupar's zone marched with Perth's north to the Tay by way of Arngask and MacDuff's Cross, a line not far off the modern boundary between Fife and Perthshire. Thus, Cupar controlled all of north Fife from the mouth of the river Eden to the border with Perthshire, as well as the Howe of Fife.[27] Piecing together the evidence for these other trading zones in Fife leaves a clear shadow impression of the St Andrews burgesses' monopoly zone, which extended from Kenly water in the east to the river Eden and the Ceres burn in the west. This meant that the exclusive trading zone of St Andrews was restricted to the areas held by the bishop, priory, hospital and *céli Dé*, covering the large parish of St Andrews St Leonard's (including at that time the later Cameron parish) and the barony of Kinninmonth, attached at a later time to Ceres parish.[28] However, the Cupar records suggest that the St Andrews burgesses' trading rights were not restricted to that zone, as a 1355 letter of David II went to some length to ensure that the 'ancient rights and privileges of the bishop and burgesses of St Andrews' were not curtailed in Cupar's zone, mentioning that Robert I and his predecessors had given the burgesses rights to sell wool, skins, hides and merchandise across Fife and Fothrif.[29] James I's 1428 charter also mentioned such rights, further suggesting that Dunfermline Abbey, which had its own monastic burgh, enjoyed similar liberties.[30] Thus when the burgesses went out 'far and wide', we have some sense of what this entailed.

The scant evidence available to us allows us to gain at least some sense of the connections a burgh like St Andrews had to its rural hinterland, as well as to other burghs. For St Andrews the most important links seem to have been with Berwick and Perth, as well as, later, Dundee and Aberdeen. But the highly significant trade with other realms, whether England, the Low Countries or elsewhere, often seems to fall off the documentary radar altogether. The value of this commerce could be considerable, but the dangers involved in conduct-

---

Turnbull, Abbotsford Club (Edinburgh, 1841) [hereafter *Balm. Lib.*], no. 35.)

[25] *Regesta Regum Scottorum V, The Acts of Robert I King of Scots 1306–1329*, ed. A. A. M. Duncan (Edinburgh, 1988) [hereafter *RRS*, v], no. 403; *PNF*, iii, pp. 185–7.

[26] S. Taylor with G. Márkus, *The Place-Names of Fife, Volume Four: North Fife between Eden and Tay* (Donington, 2010) [hereafter *PNF*, iv], p. 266.

[27] *PNF*, iv, pp. 266–7.

[28] *PNF*, iii, pp. 429–30.

[29] *Regesta Regum Scottorum VI, The Acts of David II King of Scots 1329–1371*, ed. B. Webster (Edinburgh 1982) [hereafter *RRS*, vi], no. 136; *PNF*, iv, p. 266.

[30] *PNF*, iv, p. 267; *PNF*, i, p. 284.

ing this trade could also be great. These points are brought vividly to light by a 1312 agreement between King Robert I and King Haakon V of Norway, which amongst other things dealt with the capture and imprisonment of burgesses and merchants of St Andrews, whose goods, worth 600 pounds, had been seized by officers of the Norwegian king.[31]

Therefore, commerce and trade were the raisons d'être of the burgh community, and the holding of a weekly market in the burgh was a vital source of income, both in terms of the goods the burgesses could sell and the fees and tolls they were able to charge stall-holders. Markets must have predated the establishment of burghs, especially near harbours and major land routes, to which the kings of Scots probably asserted increasing claims of authority in the twelfth century.[32] The bishop of St Andrews' market was mentioned in an early charter of King William I (1165–1214) granting the bishop of Brechin his own weekly market, understood at that time to be a gift of David I.[33] The history of the burghal market of St Andrews may hint at some competing power groups within the town. Bishop Roger's charter allowing the burgesses to move the market back to the 'land of Lambin', possibly the location of the later medieval mercat cross, noted that the market had been established there in the times of bishops Richard and Hugh.[34] Brooks and Whittington argued that the earlier bishops had merely begun the process of moving the market around 1170, but that the final move did not take place until Roger's time.[35] I would argue that the verb *statuo* in the phrase *ubi statutum fuerat* is more likely to convey the sense of an actual physical construction.[36] It is possible that the market had moved from the area where the *clachan* had been, presumably the triangular area near the new cathedral, to Lambin's land, then back to the *clachan* during the difficult period of Bishop Hugh (1178–8), perhaps under the influence of the priory or more conservative elements, and then back to the land of Lambin under Bishop Roger. This suggests that Mainard had not had enough clout or was unable to find a suitable site for the market in the area of the immigrant merchant settlement along the 'street of the burgesses' (South Street), and that the market had remained presumably where it already existed at that time, whether this was at the *clachan* or within the cathedral precinct. This is clear from the apparent fact that there was no 'public' or 'common' place set aside for a market at the outset, and that a burgess had to provide a suitable spot from his own privately held land. The vicissitudes of St Andrews' marketplace hint at a complex web of power agendas among individuals and institutions and remind us that the burgh was not constructed from a *tabula rasa* but instead had to be superimposed on existing constituencies.

---

[31] *RRS*, v, no. 25 (H4/1/6).
[32] Duncan, *Making of the Kingdom*, p. 472.
[33] *RRS*, ii, no. 115 (H1/6/99); Duncan, *Making of the Kingdom*, p. 470.
[34] *SEA*, no. 236 (H2/10/116; StAUL, B65/1/1 (The Black Book of St Andrews), fol. 35r.).
[35] Brooks and Whittington, p. 293.
[36] Compare to *SEA*, nos. 134 and 144.

Like the market, an annual fair, lasting several days, with traders from farther afield, may have predated the burgh's founding. It was common for royal burghs to have rights over fairs; Roxburgh's and Glasgow's fairs were likely the most important, but there were also fairs by the early fourteenth century (and in many cases well before then) at Aberdeen, Ayr, Coldingham, Crail, Dumbarton, Dundee, Kirkcaldy, Lanark, Stirling, as well as doubtless other places.[37] Even in episcopal burghs, the privilege of having an annual fair was given by the king, as William granted Glasgow's to Bishop Jocelin, 1189×95, and as renewed by Alexander II in 1215.[38] Whether the bishops of St Andrews had similar charters of privileges from the king for the St Andrews fair or whether it was already a well-established event (and the two are not mutually exclusive) is uncertain, but we do know it existed from chance mentions in various charters. The earliest of these dates from probably the 1220s or 1230s and flags up one of the important social functions of fairs, as a place to meet with family and friends. Richard of Liddel gave land to his nephew with the specification that he would render a pound of cumin or 3d to his uncle at the fair of St Andrews.[39] Similarly, shortly thereafter (1240×53), Duncan Ramsay was bound to pay the priory one pound of frankincense at the same fair.[40] In 1286, Constantine of Lochore, guardian of John son of Lord Alexander of Blair, leased the mill at Nydie to the priory until John came of age, in return for an annual payment of one pound of pepper at the fair.[41] While it was not uncommon to owe spices as customary renders, it must have been convenient to buy the spices at the fair itself. Beyond the simple transactions, the fair was clearly a nexus for the various ecclesiastical and lay elements of the community of east Fife.

The important economic role played by the burghs in the life of the kingdom allowed them to gain a certain degree of self-governance over time. The chief officers of the burgh were the *prepositi*, the grieves (a term sometimes translated as 'provosts').[42] In the twelfth century, the lord of the burgh, whether the king, a bishop, abbot, earl or baron, had the right to appoint grieves. This is obvious in Bishop Robert's charter, which makes it clear that he has appointed Mainard

---

[37] Barrow, *Kingship and Unity*, p. 96; Duncan, *Making of the Kingdom*, pp. 511–13; *CDS*, ii, nos. 1650, 1652, 1653, 1676b; *Early Records of the Burgh of Aberdeen*, ed. William Croft Dickinson (Scottish History Society, 1957), nos. 1 (H1/50/3), 2; *Regesta Regum Scottorum IV part one, The Acts of Alexander III King of Scots 1249–1286*, ed. C. J. Neville and Grant G. Simpson (Edinburgh, 2013) [hereafter *RRS*, iv], nos. 31, 87; London, BL Add. MS 33245, fol. 132 r-v (H3/296/3); *St A. Lib.*, p. 280 (H3/549/6); *RRS*, iii, nos. 25 (H1/7/25; *Glas. Reg.*, i, no. 132), 115 (H1/7/112; *RMS*, vii, no. 190(4)); *RRS*, ii, nos. 308 (H1/6/279), 442 (H1/6/409).

[38] *RRS*, ii, no. 308 (H1/6/279); *RRS*, iii, no. 25 (H1/7/25); *Liber S. Thome de Aberbrothoc*, ed. C. Innes and P. Chalmers, 2 vols (Edinburgh, 1848–56) [hereafter *Arb. Lib.*] i, no. 309 (H3/549/5).

[39] NRS, Gifts and Deposits, 45/27/95 (H3/347/1).

[40] *St A. Lib.*, p. 328 (H2/97/39).

[41] G. W. S. Barrow, 'Some East Fife Documents', *The Scottish Tradition: Essays in Honour of Ronald Gordon Cant*, ed. G. W. S. Barrow (Edinburgh, 1974), pp. 23–43, no. 10.

[42] Except at Berwick, which had a mayor.

as grieve.⁴³ At many royal burghs there was a power struggle between the sheriff and the grieves, with the latter in many places being drawn from the number of burgesses and taking over the duty of collecting the annual rents (the *firma* or *census*) for payment to the king.⁴⁴ In St Andrews this situation was probably less contentious, with the grieves presumably paying the burgh *ferme* to the bishop without any involvement from royal officials. As at some royal burghs, *prepositi* at St Andrews frequently acted in pairs. Peter the Fleming and Simon (I) appear jointly as grieves in the time of Bishop Richard, while Simon (II) and Laurence co-witnessed as grieves on four occasions in the first quarter of the thirteenth century.⁴⁵ As Duncan notes, by that time many burghal communities in Europe were able to achieve a degree of self-governance. It is impossible to know whether the St Andrews community gained the right to elect their own grieves, but it seems clear enough that they were selected in some way from the burgesses' own number.

What we can say without doubt is that the burgh had its own institutions and a sense of its own common identity. Probably the oldest of these institutions was the burgh court. While clear evidence of the court only survives from the middle of the thirteenth century, the business that the court handled would have been around from the early days of the burgh.⁴⁶ There are two charters relating to the sale of the land of Adam son of Odo of Kinninmonth on South Street to the cathedral priory, made in the 1240s and important enough to be witnessed by the bishop, archdeacon and earl of Fife, including his son John's consent and quitclaim. While no mention is made of the burgh court by name, the eight burgesses who witnessed both charters must have been the court's members or those of a subsidiary council.⁴⁷ In 1247, we see the burgh court acting by name in concert with the priory. Robert King, possibly a burgess of Aberdeen, left a certain piece of land to St Andrews Priory in his will, and an agreement was reached in court whereby Prior John supplied some land in Aberdeen for Robert's niece in compensation. The seals of the priory and of the burgh of St Andrews were attached to the indenture, and the document was witnessed by the chapter of St Andrews and the court of the same vill, in other words, the burgh court. This agreement must have been produced in St Andrews and the 'full court' must have been a combined court of the canons and the burgesses. The land which Robert King had bequeathed to the priory and to which Goda had sought claim surely must have been in the burgh of St Andrews.⁴⁸ The perquisite of the burgh court was matters affecting property

---

⁴³ *SEA*, no. 144 (H2/10/16; StAUL, 65/23/402).
⁴⁴ Duncan, *Making of the Kingdom*, pp. 482–3.
⁴⁵ *SEA*, no. 201 (H2/10/74; *St A. Lib.*, p. 338); *St A. Lib.*, pp. 262–3 (H3/173/8), pp. 272–3 (H3/632/8), pp. 276–7 (H3/551/2), pp. 315–16 (H4/9/2).
⁴⁶ Duncan, *Making of the Kingdom*, p. 482.
⁴⁷ *St A. Lib.*, p. 281 (H3/323/1); G. W. S. Barrow, 'The Early Charters of the Family of Kinninmonth of that Ilk', *The Study of Medieval Records*, ed. D. A. Bullough and R. L. Storey (Oxford, 1971), pp. 107–31, no. 13 (H3/323/2).
⁴⁸ NLS, Advocates' Manuscripts, 15.1.18, no. 37 (H4/21/4).

within the burgh's bounds. When Hugh of Nydie, son of Hugh of Nydie, the bishop's long-serving butler in the late twelfth century, sold his land in the vill to Prior John at some point between 1236 and 1258, the sale was not made in the priory's court but in the burgh's, the transaction corroborated by the common seal of the burgesses alongside the grantor's, and witnessed corporately by the 'whole court of the burgesses of St Andrews'.[49] The visual representation of the burgh's corporate identity and the tangible expression of its legal standing was of course the common seal. The kingdom's two leading burghs, Berwick and Perth, had common seals by the 1210s, and St Andrews seems to have acquired its own seal around the same time as many royal burghs, again suggesting parity in development.[50]

While the burgh may have had a corporate identity, not all the town's inhabitants had an equal say in its institutions. In theory there were two groups: those who had the legal rights inherent in free burgage tenure (the burgesses) and those who did not (such as the stallagers).[51] Burgesses held their land 'in free burgage', which allowed them to sell some property outright and to inherit and marry without payment of the feudal dues to which rural tenants were subjected.[52] Stall-holders paid fewer dues to the burgh court but did not have the rights of a burgess. They probably rented from the burgesses. A charter of Bishop Richard forbade burgesses from 'extorting stallage' from the men working on the cathedral, suggesting perhaps that 'extorting stallage' was something the burgesses were well skilled at.[53] Furthermore, there would have been another level 'below' that of the stallagers: the itinerant manual workers and servants. Indeed, even within the privileged group of burgesses, there was stratification based on wealth and power. One of the rights of the burgesses was the ability to elect members to an assize or *doussan* ('dozen'), usually consisting of twelve, although in reality membership was likely restricted to the elites. Probably originating in the early thirteenth century as a subcommittee of the burgh court, the development of this body is poorly understood. By the late thirteenth century, burgh laws required twelve men to swear an oath to the alderman to preserve the burgh customs, and these nascent burgh councils, with eighteen members at Perth and twelve elsewhere, seemed to exist in many royal burghs by the 1290s.[54] While delegations (councils?) from the royal burghs of Perth, Stirling, Roxburgh, Edinburgh, Jedburgh, Haddington, Peebles, Linlithgow, Montrose and Inverkeithing all travelled to Berwick to swear fealty to Edward I on 28 August 1296, the St Andrews burgesses, like

---

[49] *St A. Lib.*, pp. 284–5 (H3/445/3).
[50] Duncan, *Making of the Kingdom*, p. 484.
[51] Barrow, *Kingship and Unity*, pp. 102–3.
[52] Barrow, *Kingship and Unity*, pp. 98–9. Burgage tenure is mentioned as early as the 1170s: *SEA*, no. 196 (H2/10/89; *St A. Lib.*, 141). See also Hector L. MacQueen and William J. Windram, 'Laws and Courts in the Burghs', *The Scottish Medieval Town*, ed. Michael Lynch, Michael Spearman and Geoffrey Stell (Edinburgh, 1988), pp. 208–27.
[53] *SEA*, no. 200 (H2/10/74; *St A. Lib.*, p. 338).
[54] Duncan, *Making of the Kingdom*, pp. 487–8; Barrow, *Kingship and Unity*, p. 102.

other non-royal towns, stayed home.[55] In this, they were following the lead of their bishop and all the major office-holders of the diocese, who likewise failed to attend Edward's parliament. However, the 'burgesses and community of St Andrews' performed homage and swore fealty at St Andrews itself on the following day.[56] Although the detailed circumstances are unknown, the likelihood is that the burgh would have had to recognise Edward's lordship in order to carry on trading with the royal burghs.

On the ground, these courts and councils were controlled by a wealthy elite within the burgess community, who were defined by their membership in the guild merchant.[57] Bishop Roger granted his burgesses the right to form a guild merchant in 1198×99 in a charter that makes clear that Perth and Roxburgh already had guilds by that time.[58] Berwick almost certainly already had a guild, and royal burghs like Aberdeen and Stirling followed early in the thirteenth century.[59] In Geoffrey Barrow's turn of phrase, 'the gilds were a mixture of friendly society, burial club, trade union, drinking club, and religious brotherhood', and they helped to provide for the care of widows, orphans, the elderly, the infirm, the ill and the disabled of their constituent populations.[60] These social functions can mask the harder-edged fact that the guilds merchant provided the forum for the formation of power networks. For example, as Archie Duncan has shown, powerful commercial interests, such as importers of dyed cloth and of wine, were successful in lobbying the king to establish economic restriction beneficial to their trade.[61] Therefore, in the formation of a guild merchant, as well as the establishment of burgh courts and councils, a common seal, likely elected pairs of grieves and the holding of markets and fairs, not to mention the liberties conveyed by Malcolm IV, Scotland's first episcopal burgh followed closely the pattern of the kingdom's leading royal burghs.

---

[55] *Instrumenta Publica sive Processus super Fidelitatibus et Homagiis Scotorum Domino Regi Angliae Factis 1291–96*, ed. Thomas Thomson (Bannatyne Club, 1834) [hereafter *Instrumenta Publica*], pp. 121–4; *CDS*, ii, pp. 197–8.

[56] *CDS*, ii, no. 990, at p. 253.

[57] Duncan suggests that the guild actually chose the provosts, who were then merely rubber-stamped by the court. *Making of the Kingdom*, p. 494.

[58] *SEA*, no. 258 (H2/10/124; StAUL, B65/1/1 (Black Book of St Andrews), fol. 35r).

[59] Duncan, *Making of the Kingdom*, 488–9; *RRS*, ii, no. 467 (H1/6/434); *RRS*, iii, no. 7 (H1/7/7; Aberdeen Burgh Chrs., 5–8, no. 3), no. 127 (H1/7/124; R. Renwick, ed., *Charters and Other Documents Relating to the Royal Burgh of Stirling* (Glasgow, 1887–89), no. 7).

[60] Barrow, *Kingship and Unity*, p. 103.

[61] Duncan, *Making of the Kingdom*, pp. 491–2. Taverns were restricted to the benefit of the wine trade in the hinterlands of Perth, Inverness, Aberdeen and Stirling, if not others.

The Burgh and the St Andrews Church Establishment in the Thirteenth Century

IF the burgh followed royal patterns in its governance and institutions, its day-to-day existence was defined overwhelmingly by its relationship to St Andrews' ecclesiastical establishment. Remarkably, given the contentious role played by the priory in the early history of the burgh, it is with the cathedral priory that the burgesses would apparently form the closest bond over time.[62] Despite the fact that the burgesses were under the bishop's lordship and paid him their annual burgh ferme, what comes across in the sources is the close relationship between the burgh community and the cathedral priory. This pattern is no doubt partly due to the survival of the priory's cartulary and the loss of the episcopal registers; nevertheless, the paucity of burgesses attesting to the bishops' charters is remarkable. Instead, episcopal charters tend to be witnessed by clerks, chaplains, relatives, butlers and other members of the bishop's household. In part this must have been due to the fact that the episcopal household was often away from the city, either at the bishop's residence at Inchmurdo or making its way around the large diocese. Nevertheless, it is noteworthy that the two episcopal charters witnessed by more than two burgesses recorded gifts of land in Fife to the cathedral priory.[63] By contrast, burgesses and grieves of St Andrews were much more likely to witness charters to the priory, especially those made by lay donors. These were often gifts of land or privileges in Fife, such as Henry of Winton's gift of land in Lindores, or Margery de Lascelles' renewal of the church of Forgan, which was dated at St Andrews and where perhaps five or six of the seven witnesses were burgesses.[64] To a certain extent, this reveals how much the burgh community had become enmeshed in the landholding society of the county, even drawing them into the orbit of other religious houses. For example, Hugh of Kilmany's gift of land in Wester Kinnear to Balmerino Abbey was witnessed by two to four named burgesses of St Andrews and 'the community of the same vill'.[65] The connection here may have been through the Kinnear family, who were relatives of the Kinninmonths, the priory's stewards.[66] However, the relationship with St Andrews cathedral priory related even to gifts of property far beyond Fife. Grieves or burgesses witnessed, for example, charters of Alexander of Lamberton anent Bourtie in Aberdeenshire, of Waltheof of Strachan anent land in Strachan parish, Kincardineshire, of Roger Wyrfauk anent rights in Conveth parish, in the same county, of Christina Corbet anent a

---

[62] For the burgh's early history, see Hammond, 'The Bishop, the Prior, and the Founding of St Andrews'.
[63] *SEA*, no. 228 (H2/10/112; *St A. Lib.*, p. 45); *SEA*, no. 250 (H2/10/132; *St A. Lib.*, pp. 153–4).
[64] *St A. Lib.*, p. 273 (H3/610/1); date: possibly 1212×15; *St A. Lib.*, p. 109 (H3/337/6); date: 1266.
[65] *Balm. Lib.*, no. 18 (H3/314/1); date: ×1286.
[66] Barrow, 'Kinninmonth', pp. 110, 116.

serf named Martin son of Uviet, and of Robert of Bernham anent income from land in Berwick-upon-Tweed.[67] Burgesses even witnessed a charter in 1285 from the prior of St Andrews to Newbattle Abbey.[68] None of these related to land within the burgh of St Andrews or the business of the burgh court, as far as we can tell. It may have been that the burgesses were acting in some financial capacity in these dealings. These donations may have been made in the cathedral itself, making the involvement of the burgesses even more remarkable.

While the burgesses were involved in the priory's affairs in the thirteenth century, the priory sought to gain a meaningful existence within the bishop's burgh from the very outset, acquiring burgh tofts as early as Bishop Robert's day.[69] Bishop Richard, as a nephew of Alwine, Augustinian abbot of Holyrood and a royal chaplain, was clearly chosen as a compromise candidate to appease the canons of St Andrews, who claimed the right of election.[70] Unsurprisingly, under Richard, the priory made strong inroads into the burgh. The bishop gave the canons tofts either at that time or previously held by his sister Avis (or Hawise), by Archdeacon Matthew (and later Cuthbert the dean), Robert de Bonaire, William Brown and Master Herbert, not to mention probably drawing new land near Rathelpie into burgage.[71] Later, the priory's willingness to buy back burgh lands from families which had been in their service reflects on how desirable these properties were to them. In the 1240s, Prior John White bought land between St Leonard's and the street leading to the mill lade (i.e., Abbey Street) from Adam son of Odo, the priory's steward, part of whose timber house there was excavated in 1970.[72] The priory may have challenged Adam's right to inherit such land from his father; at any rate, they made sure they had a quitclaim from Adam's son John.[73] The priory seems to have taken a similar approach to land on the corner of North Street and Castle Street held by Hugh of Nydie, son of Hugh of Nydie, the butler, buying it for 9 marks of silver.[74]

The surviving evidence, partial as it is, suggests potentially little interest in the burgh on the part of the king and major lay lords and household officers, many of whom had houses in a number of royal burghs. Indeed, beyond the St Andrews church establishment, important as it was, even monastic landholding in the burgh was patchy and likely down to happenstance. For example, Dunfermline Abbey's toft in the burgh may have been the result of the munificence of Bishop

---

[67] *St A. Lib.*, pp. 267–8 (H3/331/4); date: 1222×38. *St A. Lib.*, pp. 276–67 (H3/551/2); date: 1219×40. *St A. Lib.*, p. 335 (H3/611/2); date: 1258×71. *St A. Lib.*, pp. 262–3 (H3/173/8); date: 1212×29. *St A. Lib.*, pp. 272–3 (H3/632/8); date: 1235×39.

[68] *Registrum Sancte Marie de Neubotle*, ed. Cosmo Innes (Edinburgh, 1849) [hereafter *Newb. Reg.*], no. 59 (H2/97/58).

[69] *SEA*, no. 135 (H2/10/18; *St A. Lib.*, p. 124). Given that the tofts had previous tenants, it is likely this happened later in Bishop Robert's rule.

[70] *SEA*, no. 174 (H2/10/47; London, BL Harley Ch.111.B.14).

[71] *SEA*, no. 183 (H2/10/73; *St A. Lib.*, p. 134); *SEA*, no. 229 (H2/10/113); *St A. Lib.*, pp. 149–52); *SEA*, no. 195 (H2/10/89; *St A. Lib.*, p. 141).

[72] *St A. Lib.*, p. 281 (H3/323/1); Brooks and Whittington, p. 291.

[73] Barrow, 'Kinninmonth', no. 13 (H3/323/2).

[74] *St A. Lib.*, pp. 284–5 (H3/445/3), date: 1236×58.

Richard, on the occasion that the abbey's possessions were confirmed at an assembly in St Andrews early in King William's reign.[75] Religious houses often held land and rights in royal burghs for commercial reasons, as bases for trade and sources of income.[76] St Andrews' early relationship with Scone, coupled with the importance of its trade with Perth, may explain Scone Abbey's acquisition of a toft in St Andrews from bishops Richard and Hugh.[77] In the mid thirteenth century, Balmerino Abbey had houses in St Andrews as well as in Crail, Dundee, Perth, Forfar and Roxburgh, but its proximity to St Andrews may have meant the small Cistercian abbey looked to the episcopal burgh as its primary commercial link.[78] The military orders had an interest in the burgh from its earliest days, and this was likely due to the draw of the apostle's shrine. The Templars had property near Crail, presumably in relation to the pilgrim trail.[79] Bishop Robert's charter of the tofts of Elfgar, Arnold and William the cook implies that the Templars held property in the burgh already by that date.[80] Peter Fleming held land on North Street in the 1170s from the Hospitallers; perhaps Bishop Robert had endowed lands on both military orders around the time of the Second Crusade shortly after the burgh's founding.[81] This impression is bolstered by King Malcolm's grand confirmation of the possessions and privileges of the cathedral priory, made at a large assembly at St Andrews, probably for the consecration of Bishop Arnold on 20 November 1160, where Richard of the Hospital of Jerusalem and Robert, brother of the Temple, were witnesses.[82]

The evidence of individual property holders in the burgh, such as we have, points to people with greater or lesser ties to the St Andrews church establishment. The archdeacons, deans of Christianity, *magistri* and others who were attached to the bishop rather than the monastic chapter would have needed accommodation and must have been involved to a certain extent in the economic life of the burgh. While Archdeacon Matthew had a toft with houses in the burgh in the early 1160s, the land that Archdeacon Ranulf successfully claimed in a cause heard by papal judges-delegate in 1202×06, against Hugh of Nydie and his nephew Jordan, was in Kilrymont outside the marches of the burgh.[83] Ranulf also managed to regain various lands, including land on the south side of the city, which had previously belonged to his predecessor, Walter of Roxburgh; these two acquisitions formed part of the later archdeacons' barony, with the

---

[75] *SEA*, no. 161 (H2/10/55; *Registrum de Dunfermelyn*, ed. C. Innes (Bannatyne Club, Edinburgh, 1842) [hereafter *Dunf. Reg.*], no. 95), date: 1165×72; *RRS*, ii, nos. 30, 31, 32, 33.
[76] Wendy B. Stevenson, 'The Monastic Presence in Scottish Burghs in the Twelfth and Thirteenth Centuries', *SHR* 60 (1981), pp. 97–118, at pp. 99 and 103.
[77] *SEA*, no. 225 (H2/10/109; *Scone Lib.*, no. 49), date: 1178×88.
[78] *Balm. Lib.*, no. 58 (H2/143/183).
[79] *PNF*, iii, 207, 227.
[80] *SEA*, no. 135 (H2/10/18; *St A. Lib.*, p. 124).
[81] *SEA*, no. 192 (H2/10/86; *St A. Lib.*, p. 139).
[82] *RRS*, i, no. 174 (H1/5/51).
[83] *SEA*, no. 181 (H2/10/43; *St A. Lib.*, pp. 132–3).

residence on the site of Dean's Court being outside of the burgh's bounds.[84] The land 'on the south side of the city, between the burns' was apparently outside of the burgh's bounds, but Walter the younger of Roxburgh, who seems to have inherited it from his uncle the archdeacon with the blessing of Bishop Hugh, may have been a burgess.[85] It is likely that many ecclesiastical figures had houses in the burgh; we know that Cuthbert, the dean of Christianity of Fife (d. ×1183), and his contemporary Master Herbert 'Scot' certainly did.[86] Bordering Cuthbert land's on the east was land that Master Máel Patraic, possibly master of the poor scholars, sold to the priory; this in turn was given to Hugh (of Nydie), the butler, and his heirs for 3s yearly.[87] As a domestic community for the church establishment and their lay servants, then, the burgh was simply carrying on the role of the pre-existing settlement, the main difference being greater commercial opportunities for such individuals.

Unfortunately, the monastic records that survive from this period are not likely to illuminate much landholding in the city by burgesses from other towns, although hints of links with Berwick, Roxburgh and Perth can be teased out. Our sole suggestion of a connection to Edinburgh is supplied by the name of one Robert de Bonaire, holder of a toft in the early 1160s; this is likely to be the man of that name who was a burgess of Edinburgh between 1170 and 1201.[88] Luckily, it is possible to delve a bit further into the types of lay landholders in Fife who held property in St Andrews. The families of Nydie and Kinninmonth, already mentioned, were local gentry who got their start through service to the church establishment. The Ramsays, a prolific family with ties to the Fife comital house, similarly had links to the burgh: William Ramsay of Clatto, possibly a burgess, may be the same person as (or the father of?) William of Clatto, a canon of the priory in 1270.[89] As with the Nydies and Kinninmonths, the Ramsays held some of their land from the church, in this case the bishop. John Ramsay of Gladney, who sold his land in Market Street shortly after 1300, took his toponymic from episcopal lands: the tenant of Gladney owed suit of court and an annual render of 15s to the bishop.[90] In the mid thirteenth century, Hugh of Nydie son of Hugh of Nydie's land on North Castle Street was

---

[84] Barrow, 'East Fife Documents', nos. 3 (H4/32/16) and 4 (H3/647/2) and notes, pp. 27–9.
[85] Note the likely burgess Robert of Roxburgh was possibly a relative of either Archdeacon Walter or his immediate successor, Archdeacon Hugh of Roxburgh. PoMS, no. 5211.
[86] *SEA*, no. 229 (H2/10/113); *St A. Lib.*, pp. 149–52).
[87] Barrow, 'East Fife Documents', no. 1 (H2/97/2).
[88] PoMS, no. 3148. Note that there was also a Robert de Bonaire, burgess of Roxburgh, possibly later. Given St Andrews' ties with Roxburgh, however, it is possible that he was the holder of the St Andrews toft, or indeed that they are all the same person.
[89] *Balm. Lib.*, no. 18 (H3/314/1); *Vetera Munimenta Hibernorum et Scotorum*, ed. A. Theiner (Rome, 1864), no. 276 (H2/150/7); *St A. Lib.*, p. 349 (H4/36/5). Duncan Ramsay held Clatto, 1240×53, when he got permission to have a chapel there from the priory with the consent of the bishop. *St A. Lib.*, p. 328 (H2/97/39).
[90] See Appendix; Barrow, 'East Fife Documents', nos. 8 and 9 with notes (H3/466/1&2); *PNF*, iv, pp. 289–90.

bounded by Malcolm of Kilspindie's on the corner of North Street and Richard Monypenny's to the north, with St Peter's Chapel on the other side. This prime location suggests these families were at the wealthier end of the spectrum for the burgh community.[91]

It is not surprising to find the Monypenny family holding land in the burgh. The surname was originally 'Manypenny', a nickname for a wealthy man (or, ironically, a poor one).[92] Richard, the first of the family on record in Scotland, witnessed charters of Thomas of Lundin and John of Methil, and his association with this John, a son of Michael the clerk, may be significant.[93] The surname could be read as suggesting a merchant background, and one charter is witnessed by at least two men with ties to Crail.[94] In 1263 or 1264, Richard's son John's wadset to Nicholas of Milton, clerk of the king's chamber, of the land of Morton in the holding of Blebo makes clear that Richard had purchased Morton, but from whom is not clear.[95] Blebo, in the parish of Kemback, was the centre of a medieval Scots shire and shared a mill with Kinninmonthshire.[96] The bishop gave all of his *cain* from Bleboshire to the priory by the 1160s, suggesting the shire was in the bishop's hand.[97] In the 1260s, Richard of Stickley, steward to Bishop Gamelin, was the lord of Blebo.[98] Kinninmonthshire had also belonged to the bishop, but was given by Bishop Robert to the priory, who then gave it to Matthew the archdeacon, after which it was feued to his brother Odo the steward, progenitor of the Kinninmonth family.[99] Furthermore, Clatto marched with Bleboshire to the north-east and was held by the Ramsays, a family who came to Fife in the service of the earls. The prior and convent of St Andrews referred to Clatto as 'in our parish of Lathrisk'.[100] Moreover, Methil, the vill of John son of Michael the clerk, close associate of Richard Monypenny, was held originally by the bishop.[101] The bishop was the lord of the Ramsay's lands at Gladney and

[91] *St A. Lib.*, pp. 284–5 (H3/445/3); Douglas Speirs, personal communication.
[92] P. H. Reaney and R. M. Wilson, *Dictionary of English Surnames*, revised edn (Oxford, 1997), p. 312.
[93] *St A. Lib.*, p. 269 (H3/403/1); *Melr. Lib.*, no. 215 (H£/403/8).
[94] *RMS*, iii, no. 2132 (5) (H3/369/9).
[95] Barrow, 'East Fife Documents', no. 7 (H3/410/1). Note that Michael of Stirling, burgess of St Andrews, is one of the witnesses.
[96] G. W. S. Barrow, 'Pre-feudal Scotland: Shires and Thanes', pp. 7–56 in his *The Kingdom of the Scots: Government, Church and Society from the Eleventh to the Fourteenth Century*, 2nd edn (Edinburgh, 2003), pp. 46, 49; *Atlas of Scottish History to 1707*, ed. Peter G. B. McNeill and Hector L. MacQueen (Edinburgh, 1996), p. 187.
[97] *RRS*, ii, no. 28 (H1/6/23); *PNF*, ii, pp. 191–2.
[98] Barrow, 'East Fife Documents', p. 34.
[99] *PNF*, ii, p. 92; Barrow, 'Kinninmonth', pp. 111–12.
[100] The Ramsay family's naming patterns suggest emulation of both the earls of Fife (Duncan, Malcolm) and the lords of Leuchars (Ness). Clatto was in the parish of Lathrisk, the lordship of which was held by the lords of Leuchars. However, Clatto was likely in the parish which was emerging as a separate parish under the chapel of Kettle, the lordship of which was held by the earls of Fife. See *PNF*, ii, p. 249.
[101] *CPL*, i, 30 (H2/137/53); *PNF*, i, pp. 582–3, 593–4; Michael the clerk may have been in the service of Earl Duncan II of Fife, *St A. Lib.*, pp. 40–1, 258–9, 260, 264, 264–5; *Carte*

Clatto, which, like Kinninmonth and Blebo, stretched along the western edge of the main block of territorial holdings of the St Andrews church establishment, intermingling with the patrimony of the earls of Fife. With the Ramsays and the Methil/ Wemyss family (and through them the Monypennys), we see families successfully navigating both sides of that border, as retainers and/or tenants of both the earl and the church. Indeed it may not be too radical to suggest that such families, traversing the divide between ecclesiastical and lay society, formed a kind of network, and that the burgesses of St Andrews, who themselves were (mostly) laymen (and women) operating in a 'world' defined by the church, were able to benefit by plugging themselves into this network. At the same time, these families would have benefited through their ties to the burgh, acquiring property and presumably business dealings there (as well as, perhaps, the special rights of burgesses). Merchant families sometimes made the jump from the burgh into the countryside, surely through making use of just this sort of network. The case of the Lambies will be examined later. The Monypennys were likely a similar case; while the wadset of Morton of Blebo was due to a debt John Monypenny owed Peter of Balfour, John was able to feu the land of Pitmilly in Kingsbarns parish from the priory, and the Monypennys remained lairds of Pitmilly for centuries to come.[102]

Malcolm of Kilspindie, Hugh of Nydie's neighbour on North Street (1236×58), flags up connections to the burgh from further afield. Kilspindie is in the province of Gowrie in Perthshire, 3 miles north-west of the Hay caput at Errol. Yet the Kilspindies were in a similar situation to the families we have already encountered. When, later in the century, Malcolm of Kilspindie son of Ralph of Kilspindie sold Kilspindie to Lord Nicholas Hay, lord of Errol, it was witnessed by the sheriff of Fife and various Fife landholders, and also stated that the bishop of St Andrews was the chief lord of Kilspindie.[103] A receipt by Malcolm dated at Dundee in 1295 clarifies this transaction was actually a sale.[104] At the Berwick parliament in 1296, Malcolm of Kilspindie, along with, amongst others, Odo of Kinninmonth, swore fealty as tenants of the bishop of St Andrews.[105] In addition to their status as episcopal tenants, a glance at the Kilspindie family's history reveals their links to the networks we have already encountered. Between 1206 and 1227, Adam son of Odo the steward acquired the neyf Samson son of Gilbert and his offspring from Scone Abbey; the charter is witnessed by Fife personages, including Thomas of Lundin of Fife and Duncan son of Adam, a member of the comital kindred, in addition to Malcolm *abb* of Kilspindie. As an *abb* or 'lay-abbot', he may have held the tenancy of

---

Monialium de Northberwic, ed. Cosmo Innes (Edinburgh, 1847), no. 3 (H3/16/2); *Registrum Monasterii S. Marie de Cambuskenneth*, ed. William Fraser (Grampian Club, Edinburgh, 1872) [hereafter *Camb. Reg.*], no. 36.
[102] *PNF*, iii, p. 383; Barrow, 'East Fife Documents', p. 34.
[103] 'Erroll Papers', *Spalding Miscellany*, ii (Spalding Club, 1842), no. 15 (H3/317/2).
[104] NRS, Register House Series, 1/6/23 (H3/317/3).
[105] *Instrumenta Publica*, pp. 147–8.

this church land hereditarily under the lordship of the bishop.[106] His association with the Kinninmonth family suggests that Malcolm the *abb* had pre-existing links with Fife. It is possible that this Malcolm was the same man, or alternatively the father or uncle, of the Lord Malcolm of Kilspindie who had a wife named Margery and a son named William mid-century. By this time, Malcolm and Margery were landholders in the burgh of Perth, where they gave a third of a toft to Lindores Abbey. This third of a toft had formerly belonged to William son of Lambin, burgess of St Andrews, from whom Malcolm presumably bought it.[107] The Kilspindies were part of a network that linked together the burghs of St Andrews and Perth with landholders in east and central Fife.

However, the ecclesiastical ties of this network, typified by the Kinninmonths and Kilspindies, also flag up the limitations of the burgh of St Andrews. While fairly central by sea, it was a backwater by land, and the king's household rarely visited. The exception to this rule seems to have been for consecrations of bishops and visits to the apostle's shrine, at which point local power figures obtained some royal charters.[108] There had been a royal hall at St Andrews c.1100, but this probably disappeared over the course of the twelfth century, perhaps in the laying out of the burgh. There is no indication up to the wars of independence in our admittedly spotty charter record of burgh holdings by the king or any of his household officers. Figures like the chamberlain and steward frequently had tofts or houses in royal burghs. It is perhaps more likely that the earls of Fife and the de Quincy earls of Winchester might have had residences there, but there is no surviving evidence of this or of other landholding by aristocrats.

Descendants of Mainard the Fleming

GIVEN Mainard the Fleming's standing as the burgh's first grieve, it is not surprising that his descendants maintained prominent positions in its government. Although no direct evidence of Mainard's children is recorded, Geoffrey Barrow's suggestion that Peter the Fleming, active in the 1160s and 1170s, was 'perhaps a son of Mainard' is accepted here with rather less reservation.[109] Peter held a toft in the burgh in the 1170s, but more importantly he is likely to be the Peter, grieve of St Andrews, who appears alongside another grieve, Simon (I),

---

[106] *Liber Ecclesie de Scon*, ed. C. Innes (Bannatyne and Maitland Clubs, Edinburgh, 1843) [hereafter *Scone Lib.*], no. 84 (H4/20/16).

[107] *The Chartulary of Lindores Abbey*, ed. J. Dowden (Edinburgh, 1903) [hereafter *Lind. Cart.*], no. 74 (H3/317/1); NRS, GD 160/112 (5) (H2/75/4).

[108] Relatively few surviving royal documents were dated at St Andrews: one of David I (*Chrs David*, no. 215), one of Earl Henry (ibid., no. 129), four of King Malcolm (*RRS*, i, nos 166, 174, 213, 240), eight of King William (*RRS*, ii, nos. 30–3, 109, 127, 329, 330), four of Alexander II (*RRS*, iii, nos 30, 214, 232, 233), one of Alexander III (*RRS*, iv, no. 19) and three of Robert I (*RRS*, v, nos 5, 11, 57).

[109] Barrow, *Kingship and Unity*, p. 92.

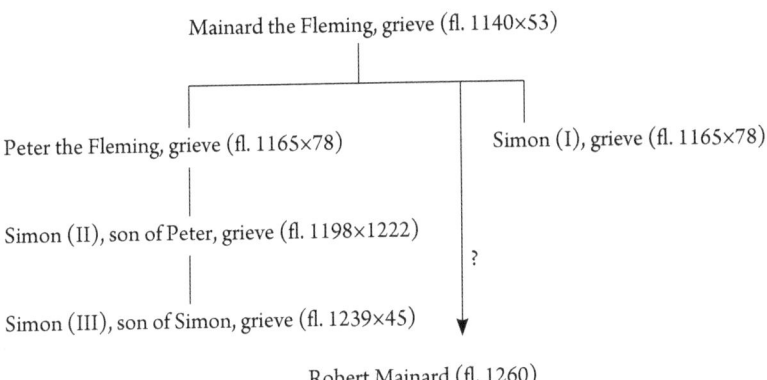

Chart 8.1: Conjectural family tree: descendants of Mainard the Fleming

as witness to a brieve of Bishop Richard between 1165 and 1178.[110] Peter's position as grieve increases the likelihood that he was the son or heir of Mainard. The pattern of two grieves appearing together in charter witness lists continues into the thirteenth century. A later Simon (II) and Laurence co-witness as grieves to three charters dating to the 1210 and 1220s.[111] This Simon (II) is likely to be identified with a Simon, son of Peter, who witnessed two charters, dated 1189×98 and 1200 respectively, as burgess of St Andrews.[112] However, it must be noted that it is also possible that Simon (II) the grieve may be a Simon son of Stephen, who witnessed a charter of Hugh of Nydie to Alexander of Blair, 1204×29, particularly if the Laurence son of Richard who witnesses that charter alongside him is to be identified with Laurence the grieve.[113] That Simon son of Peter was a burgess, combined with the fact that his father was grieve, militates in favour of the dynastic hypothesis espoused here. Thus, there appear to be three generations of the Fleming family acting as grieves – Mainard, Peter and Simon (II). Moreover, the use of the name Simon in the family suggests that Peter's contemporary, Simon (I), may also have been a relative, although this is much more speculative. A fourth generation may have continued the family's strong position in the burgh, with Simon (III), evidently a son of Simon (II), acting as burgess by the late 1230s and as grieve by the late 1240s.[114] Unfortunately, the trail runs cold at this point. In the absence of any names of grieves between 1250

---

[110] *SEA*, no. 192 (H2/10/86; *St A. Lib.*, p. 139); *SEA*, no. 200 (H2/10/74; *St A. Lib.*, p. 338).
[111] *St A. Lib.*, pp. 273, 315–16, 262–3 (H3/610/1; H4/9/2; H3/173/8).
[112] *SEA*, no. 228 (H2/10/112; *St A. Lib.*, p. 45); *SEA*, no. 250 (H2/10/132; *St A. Lib.*, pp. 153–4).
[113] It is just possible that this Simon's father was Stephen, the chamberlain of Bishop Hugh. PoMS, no. 3049. William Angus, ed., 'Miscellaneous Charters, 1165–1300', *Miscellany of the Scottish History Society*, iv (Scottish History Society, 1926), no. 4 (H3/16/12).
[114] *St A. Lib.*, pp. 272–3, 281, 284 (H3/632/8, H3/323/1, H3/245/5); Barrow, 'Kinninmonth', no. 13 (H3/323/2).

and after 1314, it is impossible to say whether the family retained its remarkable position. Indeed, there is no evidence that the family continued to use the name 'Fleming' after Peter, the likely son or heir of Mainard. However, given that Mainard is the only person known to have lived in the twelfth and thirteenth centuries in Scotland with that particular personal name, it is possible that the Robert Mainard who witnessed a charter of John of Denmuir alongside various east Fife landholders in 1260 was also a descendant of the first grieve.[115] Use of the name of a powerful progenitor as a surname, in this case Mainard, would certainly fit with the case of the burgh's second family, the Lambies.

Descendants of Lambin

THE only family to rival the position of Mainard's progeny were those descended from one Lambin who lived in the burgh in the second half of the twelfth century. Bishop-elect Roger's charter (1189×98) to the burgesses gave them their market on the land of Lambin, but also made clear that an earlier market had been held on Lambin's land in the times of Bishop Richard (1163–78) and Hugh (1178–88).[116] The positioning of the market on Lambin's land may suggest a level of power and wealth on his part. Furthermore, if the charter implies that Lambin held that land by the 1160s, he may have been among the first generation of settlers in the burgh. The name *Lambin* is a diminutive of the Old French personal name *Lambert*, itself derived from the Continental Germanic *Landberht*, as Robin is a diminutive of Robert.[117] Of the seven individuals named Lambin to appear in Scottish charters of this time, all but one (Lambin Asa, eponymous lord of Lamington in Lanarkshire) appear in a Fife context.[118] Many of these relate to the family of the St Andrews burgess Lambin. Furthermore, there are a few persons on record in Fife with similar names who may be connected. In 1202×06, papal judges-delegate settled a dispute between Ranulf the archdeacon of St Andrews and Hugh the steward and his nephew Jordan over lands lying to the west of the 'new work' (i.e., the new cathedral) towards the 'houses of Lamburc'.[119] This is the only mention of a 'Lamburc' in contemporary records, and it is not unlikely that this is the more formal name of the eponymous Lambin. If so, it would suggest that Lambin had built houses by about 1200 in a prime location, perhaps on South Castle Street towards the eastern limit of the burgh. This suggestion is strengthened by the witnessing

---

[115] *St A. Lib.*, p. 385 (H3/193/3).
[116] *SEA*, no. 236 (H2/10/116; StAUL, B65/1/1 (The Black Book of St Andrews), fol. 35r.)
[117] *The Durham Liber Vitae: London, British Library, MS Cotton Domitian A.VII: edition and digital facsimile with introduction, codicological, prosopographical and linguistic commentary, and indexes*, ed. David Rollason and Lynda Rollason, 3 vols (London, 2007), ii, p. 63.
[118] G. W. S. Barrow, *The Anglo-Norman Era in Scottish History: The Ford Lectures delivered in the University of Oxford in Hilary Term 1977* (Oxford, 1980), p. 45 and n. 66.
[119] Barrow, 'East Fife Documents', no. 3 (H4/32/16).

of a William 'son of Lambur' of a charter (1207×19) by Saer de Quincy, earl of Winchester and lord of Leuchars, to Cambuskenneth Abbey, alongside a number of Fife worthies.[120] In any event, the eponymous Lambin certainly had a son named William.

Lambin's son William was clearly a powerful man in east Fife circles. He witnessed eight charters in favour of St Andrews Priory, two dispute settlements and a lay charter of Hugh of Nydie.[121] William's long career spanned from the 1190s to the 1230s, and demonstrates the family's expanding interests into the countryside and to other burghs. William held a third of a toft in Perth, a small reminder of the vital trade links St Andrews maintained with the most important royal burgh and trading centre north of the Forth.[122] Remarkably, he often appears in witness lists ahead of current burgh grieves and members of Mainard's family, demonstrating that William may have managed to make the social leap from merchant burgess to landed gentry. William used his financial clout to acquire arable land around St Andrews, renting from Adam of Kinninmonth, the priory's steward, the ploughgate of Balrymonth south of the city, which Adam held from the priory for the term of his life.[123] William was able to set up on a more permanent footing when in 1235 King Alexander II confirmed an exchange made by William with Adam son of Adam of Letham, whereby William acquired the lands of Letham (in Cameron parish, Fife) for 25 marks and two burgage plots in St Andrews.[124] William's descendants became lairds of Letham, which became known as Lambieletham by (and probably well before) 1406.[125] Nevertheless, they also remained heavily involved in the burgh. William's son John had a charter from the provost of St Mary's for Letham and Carngour (formerly Kinninnis), 1273×86.[126] This John is likely to be the John 'dicto Lambin' who witnessed charters in 1266 and 1258×71.[127] If so, the patronymic surname Lambie was already becoming heritable by the late thirteenth century. Furthermore, if the 'William son of Lambur' who witnessed Saer de Quincy's charter can be identified with William son of Lambin, then the attestation of his own son 'Lambur' would be evidence for another son.[128]

Another branch of the family was descended from Andrew, son of the

---

[120] *Camb. Reg.*, no. 73 (H3/23/3).
[121] *St A. Lib.*, pp. 262–3, 267–8, 273, 278, 315–16 (H3/173/8; H3/331/4; H3/610/1; H3/15/108; H4/9/2); SEA, nos. 229, 251 (H2/10/112; H2/10/132); Barrow, 'East Fife Documents', no. 3 (H4/32/16); 'Miscellaneous Charters 1165–1300', ed. Angus, 312, no. 8 (H3/445/1).
[122] *Lind. Cart.*, no. 74 (H3/317/1).
[123] Barrow, 'Kinninmonth', no. 12 (H2/10/187). This was confirmed by Bishop William Malveisin, 1209×38, prob. mid 1220s×. The rent was one mark annually on Martinmas and Whitsun. It is not clear if this is Easter or Wester Balrymonth. *PNF*, iii, 449.
[124] *RRS*, iii, no. 233 (H1/7/239; NRS, Dalhousie Muniments, GD45/27/97).
[125] *PNF*, iii, pp. 111–12.
[126] Edinburgh University Library [hereafter EUL], Laing Charters, no. 3023 (H2/105/2). The late date of this charter may suggest that John had been born late in his father's life.
[127] *St A. Lib.*, pp. 109, 336; (H3/337/6, H3/611/2).
[128] *Camb. Reg.*, no. 73 (H3/23/3).

eponymous Lambin and brother of William, alongside whom he witnessed two charters in 1213 and 1204×29.[129] Andrew's son, also Lambin, a burgess of St Andrews, witnessed charters through the 1260s and 1270s.[130] In 1303, Gilbert Lambie and John Lambie were jurors in an inquest held at St Andrews; John was identified as a burgess of the city about a year later.[131] Their relation to previous generations is uncertain. The family maintained a significant role in St Andrews and east Fife through the rest of the Middle Ages. Alexander Lambie held Barns in Crail parish in the mid fourteenth century.[132] That the laird of Letham in 1406 was named John Lambie shows those lands stayed in the family; that he married the daughter of a burgess of St Andrews demonstrates their continuing involvement in the burgh.[133] There is ample further evidence for their continuing importance in the city. For example, in 1443, one Duncan Lambie was one of two citizens (along with Andrew Ramsay) sent to Cologne over university matters, and in the following year, one James Lambie was a common clerk of St Andrews.[134]

It must be noted that there were other Lambins active in Fife in the thirteenth century. First, Roger of Melcrether (in Forgan parish in north-east Fife) and his brother Lambin flourished in 1200×16.[135] Melcrether was a ploughgate in Naughton given by King Malcolm IV to St Andrews Priory, so this family must have been the priory's tenants or fermers there.[136] This St Andrews connection suggests some now undetectable influence from the eponymous twelfth-century Lambin. Second, Lambin son of Giles was a burgess of St Andrews who flourished between 1250 and 1266. While we know nothing of this Lambin or his family, his three witnessing acts are all alongside and directly following Lambin son of Andrew, implying a link, if only one of emulation.[137] Third, a Lambin son of Austin of Newburn swore fealty to Edward I in 1296. While there is no suggestion of a connection here, it is noteworthy that he was a tenant of the bishop of St Andrews.[138]

Before moving on, we should note the existence of a family called Lambie in Angus in the thirteenth century. The first to use the Lambie surname on record, excluding John 'called Lambin', is one Henry Lambie who was a burgess of

---

[129] 'Miscellaneous Charters 1165–1300', ed. Angus, no. 8 (H3/445/1); *St A. Lib.*, pp. 315–16 (H4/9/2).
[130] *St A. Lib.*, 109, 281, 335, 340–1 (H3/337/6, H3/323/1, H3/611/2, H3/414/6); Barrow, 'Kinninmonth', no. 13 (H3/323/2).
[131] *CDS*, ii, no. 1350 (H4/38/30); also no. 1646.
[132] *RMS*, i, App. 2, no. 932; *PNF*, iii, p. 193. See also George Black, *The Surnames of Scotland* (New York, 1946), p. 412.
[133] *PNF*, iii, p. 111; *Copiale*, p. 430.
[134] StAUL, B65/23/30c, B65/23/31c; B65/1/2 (Brown Book), pp. 214, 218.
[135] *St A. Lib.*, p. 275 (H3/337/3).
[136] *PNF*, iv, p. 424.
[137] *St A. Lib.*, pp. 109, 281, 335 (H3/337/6; H3/323/1; H3/611/2); Barrow, 'Kinninmonth', no. 13 (H3/323/2).
[138] *Instrumenta Publica*, pp. 147–8.

Dundee in about the 1270s.[139] Moreover, a Hervey Lambie witnessed a charter anent Dundee burghal land in 1281, among a list of probable burgesses;[140] mention is also made in a 1286 charter of land held by Hervey Lambie in Coupar Angus. The charter recorded a gift of a Hervey of Dundee to Balmerino Abbey and was witnessed by a Peter of Coupar of Dundee, so this charter is also firmly in a Dundee context.[141] Finally, a Richard of Lambiston was burgess of Dundee and witnessed three charters between 1268 and 1281.[142] The location of Lambiston is unknown, but the place-name was clearly formed from 'Lambin's toun' or 'Lambie's toun'.[143] The evidence is too scattered to make firmer suggestions about its ownership. There is no direct evidence linking these Dundee Lambies to the St Andrews family. It is certainly possible that the Angus Lambies were descended from another, unrecorded, eponymous Lambin. However, the transition of the name Lambie into a surname seems to have happened about the third quarter of the thirteenth century in both places. Given that William son of Lambin had land in Perth, it is not unlikely that the family also had a foothold in Dundee. We know that the Purrock family had land in Dundee (Warin Purrock, 1268) and in St Andrews (Adam Purrock, citizen, c.1300).[144] In the absence of further evidence, it is left to the reader to decide.

The Family of German

THE recurrent use of the personal name German may characterise another St Andrews family about whom we know substantially less than the Lambies. The forename German, rather than a marker of Teutonic identity, was a relatively rare saint's name and is found more often among churchmen, but also occasionally among laymen.[145] For example, a Nicholas son of German was a burgess of Glasgow in the mid thirteenth century.[146] The 'German' who witnessed Prior Walter's charter to Hugh the butler in 1189×98 was likely a burgess of St Andrews.[147] Given the rarity of the name, it is not unlikely that the German son of Leving, burgess of St Andrews, in the middle of the thirteenth

---

[139] *Highland Papers*, ii, ed. J. R. N. Macphail (Edinburgh, 1916), pp. 221–3. Note that Henry and Hervey Lambie might be the same person. The same conflation in names may take place with the cleric(s) Henry and/or Hervey of Dundee. PoMS, nos. 15004, 14163, 1973, 16366.
[140] *Balm. Lib.*, no. 33 (H3/635/2).
[141] *Balm. Lib.*, no. 44 (H2/41/17).
[142] *Balm. Lib.*, no. 32 (H3/274/5).
[143] It is possible, though not likely, that this place refers to Lamington LAN.
[144] *Balm. Lib.*, no. 32 (H3/274/5); see Appendix 4, below.
[145] David Hugh Farmer, *The Oxford Dictionary of Saints*, 5th edn (Oxford, 2003), pp. 217–18. The PoMS database indicates priors of Coldingham, Durham and Restenneth with this name, as well as another clerk (PoMS, nos. 463, 767, 464, 7334).
[146] PoMS, nos. 9502, 9503.
[147] Barrow, 'East Fife Documents', no. 1 (H2/97/2), noting that Barrow accepts the identification of five burgesses there, beginning with German.

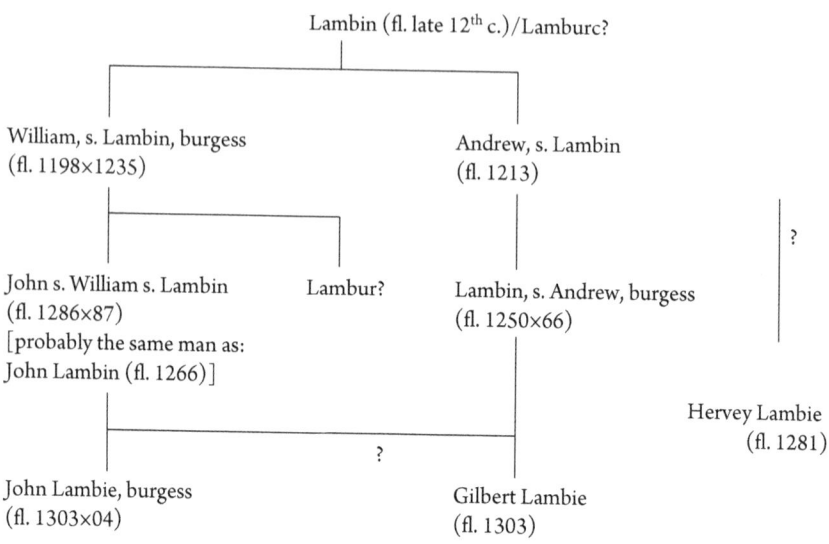

Chart 8.2: Conjectural family tree: descendants of Lambin

century, may have been a descendant.[148] This German witnessed five surviving charter texts alongside his fellow burgesses, and often in a prominent position in the list.[149] The personal name Leving is derived from the Old English forename *Leofwine*, common in the tenth and eleventh centuries at least.[150] Leving was also the name of the man who gave his name to Livingston in West Lothian, although there is nothing to suggest he was tied to the St Andrews family (if there was one).[151] However, it does seem possible that the Hugh son of Leving who held land in Newburn, Fife, in the mid thirteenth century could have been a brother or relative of German.[152]

The Family of Letham and Cultural Interaction

THE families descended from Mainard and Lambin were likely to have been French-speaking Flemings, but this does not mean that participation in the burgh of St Andrews and indeed in the trade networks linking St Andrews with larger burghs like Perth and Dundee was restricted to newcomers to the region. Readers will recall that William son of Lambin acquired the lands of

---

[148] PoMS, no. 12478 (http://db.poms.ac.uk/record/person/12478/; accessed 10 Jan. 2015)
[149] *St A. Lib.*, pp. 272–3; 276–7; 281; 335 (H3/632/8, H3/551/2, H3/323/1, H3/611/2); Barrow, 'Kinninmonth', no. 13 (H3/323/2).
[150] *Durham Liber Vitae*, ii, pp. 136–7.
[151] Barrow, *Anglo-Norman Era*, p. 36.
[152] *Dunf. Reg.*, nos. 314, 315 (H2/71/13 & 14).

Lambieletham from Adam son of Adam of Letham for a payment of 25 marks and two burgage plots in St Andrews, as King Alexander's 1235 confirmation describes.[153] As we have seen, between 1273 and 1286, Adam of Makerstoun, provost of the collegiate church of St Mary's on the Rock (which had acquired the lordship of Letham from the cathedral priory), gave the land of Letham and Kininnis (Carngour) to John son of William son of Lambin.[154] What interests us here is that the provost recounts that Adam son of Gilla Muire mac Martáin had held the land of his predecessors (that is, the *céli Dé*). Adam of Makerstoun's charter is harking back to the twelfth century, when the *céli Dé* held the lands; the Adam son of Gilla Muire mac Martáin can only have been the father of the Adam son of Adam of Letham alive in 1235. Thus we know that the Adam who made a deal with William son of Lambin was at least the fourth generation to have held the land of Letham.[155] Simon Taylor points out that neighbouring Gilmerton must have taken its name from Gilla Muire mac Martáin, who must have flourished in the late twelfth century.[156] However, this is not the last we hear of the Letham family. While the Lambie family were able to establish themselves on some countryside arable, Adam son of Adam of Letham was able to set himself up in St Andrews with the burgage plots he acquired. Another Adam of Letham appears in the documentary record towards the end of the thirteenth century. A charter of Robert of Wilton gave John son of Thomas Wallace his part of the land of Gladney in Fife, in around 1290.[157] The document is witnessed by the prior of St Andrews and a canon of St Mary's in St Andrews, as well as the sheriff of Fife and some people from Perth. The final name is Adam of Letham, and his name follows that of Michael of Stirling, a relatively prominent burgess of St Andrews from the 1260s to the 1280s.[158] Adam of Letham was listed among seventy-one burgesses and other inhabitants of Perth who swore fealty to Edward I in 1291.[159] It would appear from this evidence that the descendants of Gilla Muire mac Martáin thrived as merchants, first in St Andrews and latterly in Perth. Remarkably, they seem to have held on to the surname Letham, despite selling the land to the Lambies.

The notion that a family with deep roots in Fife, the sort of family to embrace Gaelic personal names (note that Adam could be used as a European 'equivalent' of the Gaelic name Áed), could succeed in the Europeanised surroundings of St Andrews should not surprise us. This is illustrated particularly well by the individual known as Baldwin the Scot, who witnessed three charters in

---

[153] *RRS*, iii, no 233.
[154] *PNF*, iii, pp. 112–13; EUL, Laing Charters, no. 3023 (H2/105/2).
[155] As Taylor points out, the *céli Dé* traded Letham and Kininnis (Carngour) to the priory for the two Strathkinnesses (one of which was named Balmartin after Adam of Letham's forebear). See *PNF*, iii, pp. 441–3.
[156] *PNF*, iii, pp. 103–4.
[157] Barrow, 'Kinninmonth', no. 11 (H2/137/10).
[158] PoMS, no. 5169.
[159] E. L. G. Stones and Grant G. Simpson, *Edward I and the Throne of Scotland 1290–1296: An Edition of the Record Sources for the Great Cause* (Oxford, 1978), ii, p. 125,

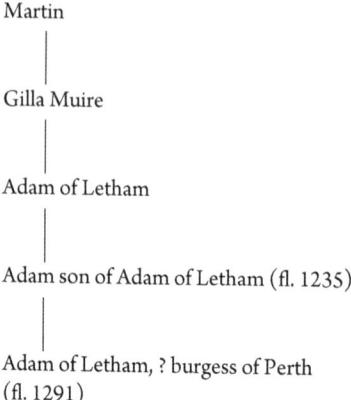

Chart 8.3: Conjectural Family Tree: Descendants of Gilla Muire mac Martáin

a St Andrews context either side of the year 1200.[160] We tend to find that ethnonymic by-names, like Fleming or Scot, are most often used when the bearer's forename and perhaps his or her language or accent suggest a different ethnic identity than the one flagged up with the by-name. In the case of Baldwin, we have a Germanic name particularly common in Flanders, so the addition of 'Scot' suggests that he was born in Scotland north of the Firth of Forth, or perhaps was a Gaelic speaker. Baldwin witnessed two charters as 'the Scot' and one charter as 'Baldwin son of Búadach'. His father was almost certainly the Búadach of Inchmurdo who witnessed two St Andrews documents between 1189 and 1199.[161] Inchmurdo was the chief episcopal residence, indicating strong links with the bishops.[162] Búadach was also the name of one of the two leaders of the bishop of St Andrews' army in c.1128.[163] As Simon Taylor highlights, the farm name Balbuthie (in Kilconquhar parish) means 'Búadach's farm'.[164] Taylor's suggestion that the Búadach of Balmakin (Carnbee parish), only about 3km from Balbuthie, who appears in 1266 is likely to be related to the eponymous Búadach of Balbuthie (perhaps Búadach of Inchmurdo?) is noteworthy.[165] I would go further and suggest that given the rarity of the personal name (these are the only three individuals in the People of Medieval Scotland 1093–1314 [PoMS] database to have it), it is likely that this name became an identity marker for the family. The emergence of the 'Scot' family of Balwearie may have led to Baldwin's descendants dropping that particular ethnonym. In addition to

---

[160] *SEA*, nos. 259, 255 (H2/10/124, 126); *St A. Lib.*, p. 329 (H/12/3).
[161] PoMS, no. 9065.
[162] *PNF*, v, pp. 231–2.
[163] PoMS, no. 9526
[164] *PNF*, iii, pp. 286–7.
[165] *PNF*, iii, pp. 143–4; 286–7. Note also Andrew of Balmakin in 1296.

this remarkable array of Búadachs, the name of Búadach of Inchmurdo's son, Baldwin the Scot, is striking: because the most likely scenario would have been a marriage between Búadach and a woman whose family used the name Baldwin, the most likely candidate would have been a Flemish or Northern French family in St Andrews. This provides an important reminder of the way that Gaelic, French, English, Flemish and Latin speakers would have pressed cheek by jowl on the crowded North and South Gaits of St Andrews in its first century.

Prosopographical Analysis

WITH the exception of some of the more distinctive personal names already mentioned, such as Lambin and German, the naming patterns of the St Andrews burgesses are unremarkable and completely typical of medieval Scottish burghs. The most common names were William and John, two of the most frequently attested forenames in Scottish charters generally, as were others which appear more than once, like Adam and Alexander.[166] The religious names on record reflect the interest in biblical personages which was characteristic of the era, with Simon, Peter, Thomas and, of course, Andrew in use. The use of saints' names is also unsurprising: Giles was particularly favoured in burghs, and there were parochial dedications to him in Edinburgh and Elgin, whereas Laurence had long been venerated in the kingdom. The significance of that name among St Andrews burgesses may be due to his church dedication at Berwick. It is noteworthy when considering Michael of Stirling that the castle chapel at Stirling was dedicated to Michael the Archangel.[167]

Second names, whether by-names or hereditary surnames, can offer a window into places of origin and 'national' or 'ethnic' identity, occupations, physical traits, parentage and other interesting details. References to various ethnolinguistic groups in St Andrews were sometimes made in the twelfth century. Bishop Richard's charter regarding the parish church of Holy Trinity mentions offerings from *Scotis quam de Francis et Anglicis et Flandrensibus* both within and outwith the burgh, with *Scotis* referring to people from *Scotia* or *Albania*, the land north of the Firth of Forth, and *Francis* and *Anglicis* defined by their maternal tongues rather than their political allegiance.[168] Given the high standing of Mainard the Fleming and Peter the Fleming, the appearance of *Flandrensibus* is not surprising.

---

[166] Matthew Hammond, 'Introduction: The Paradox of Medieval Scotland, 1093–1286', *New Perspectives on Medieval Scotland 1093–1286*, ed. Matthew Hammond (Woodbridge, 2013), pp. 1–52, esp. 30–48.

[167] Ian B. Cowan, 'The Emergence of the Urban Parish', *The Scottish Medieval Town*, ed. Lynch et al., pp. 82–98, at pp. 91–2; *Saints in Scottish Place Names* database (www.saintsplaces.gla.ac.uk).

[168] *SEA*, no. 182 (H2/10/43); Richard Sharpe, 'People and Languages in Eleventh- and Twelfth-Century Britain and Ireland: Reading the Charter Evidence', *The Reality Behind Charter Diplomatic in Anglo-Norman Britain*, ed. Dauvit Broun (Glasgow, 2011), pp. 1–119, at p. 102.

The name of the burgess Alexander *Francigena*, 'the Frenchman', belies his origins. It is not unlikely that Gilbert *Brito*, 'the Breton', who witnesses alongside William Lambin in 1202×06, was also part of the burgh community.[169] French, Flemish and Breton settlers were common in burghs and elsewhere in Britain and Ireland in the twelfth century. That these kinds of ethnic identifiers disappear thereafter in our sources is suggestive of the declining importance in such distinctions, probably due to growing linguistic homogeneity. Of course, we can also get a sense of whence the burgh's inhabitants came from locative or toponymic surnames. Burgesses across Scotland often have second names suggesting links with, for example, ports on the North Sea from East Anglia to Lincolnshire.[170] In the case of St Andrews, these names indicate associations with a variety of places in England and Scotland, but are sometimes hard to decipher. William 'Betham' may have roots in Beetham, Westmorland, or, more likely, if the 't' is to be read as a 'c', in Beckham, Norfolk.[171] The place-name indicated in the name of William 'de Haheness' is obscured, but Haynes in Bedfordshire can be very tentatively suggested. Michael of Stirling suggests links with an important royal burgh. However, St Andrews' special status as the burgh attached to the principal ecclesiastical centre and chief bishop's see also influenced the burgh's makeup. Robert of Roxburgh, a possible burgess in the 1190s, appears at the same time that Hugh of Roxburgh was archdeacon of St Andrews, while Hugh himself followed a Walter of Roxburgh in the same position.[172] Others, like John of Blebo or William Ramsay of Clatto, suggest ties closer to home in the county of Fife.[173]

In many burghs, it was not uncommon for burgess families to use the name of their home burgh, such as Perth, Dundee or Aberdeen, as a surname. This did not happen in St Andrews, at least as far as our evidence suggests. This was likely due to the use of the name 'of St Andrews' by a knightly family, as well as its use by people associated with the church establishment. As Grant Simpson has demonstrated, this knightly family were a cadet branch of the de Quincy family, who inherited Leuchars, Collessie and other lands in Scotland through Robert de Quincy's marriage to Orable daughter of Ness son of William. Lords Saer and Roger of St Andrews were brothers, nephews of Earl Saer de Quincy of Winchester in the early thirteenth century, and held land from him in Collessie, Fife, as well as various estates in England. As Simpson writes, 'Saer and Roger were presumably the sons of a sister of Earl Saer, whose name is unknown, by an equally mysterious father who used *de Sancto Andrea* as a surname.'[174] Simpson

---

[169] Barrow, 'East Fife Documents', no. 3 (H4/32/16).
[170] Matthew H. Hammond, 'A Prosopographical Analysis of Society in East Central Scotland, *circa* 1100 to 1260, with Special Reference to Ethnicity' (unpublished PhD thesis, University of Glasgow, 2005), pp. 106–9.
[171] Reaney and Wilson, *Dictionary of English Surnames*, p. 37.
[172] Barrow, 'East Fife Documents', no. 1 (H2/97/2); *Fasti Ecclesiae Scoticanae Medii Aevi Ad Annum 1638*, ed. D. E. R. Watt and A. L. Murray, rev. edn (Scottish Record Society, 2003), p. 393.
[173] PoMS, nos. 12477, 12441.
[174] Grant G. Simpson, 'The *Familia* of Roger de Quincy, Earl of Winchester and Constable

goes on to suggest a possible French St Andrew place-name as the eponym for the surname, but the Fife St Andrews is a much more likely candidate. A number of churchmen also used the by-name 'of St Andrews', especially those who had attained a high enough level of education to be known as *magister* ('master'). Adam, Henry, John, Patrick, Robert and Simon of St Andrews are all on record between the 1190s and the 1230s. Watt suggests that the Masters Robert and Simon 'of St Andrews' who appear in charters around 1200 may have been illegitimate sons of Bishop Roger (el. 1189, 1198–1202).[175] While these claims depend rather a lot on how old Bishop Roger was at the time of his election in 1189, the possibility should at least be considered that the brothers Saer and Roger of St Andrews, nephews of Earl Saer de Quincy, were the progeny of Bishop Roger and a daughter of Robert de Quincy and Orable.

As the reader may have observed in the names of some of the burgh's more prominent members, wealthier burgesses often preferred the use of a by-name of relationship, most often referring to the father, than some other kind of second name, especially the surnames of occupation, which often were associated with the lowlier and dirtier trades, with the notable exception of the wealthy and prestigious goldsmith. Such was clearly the case with men like Simon son of Peter, William son of Lambin and German son of Leving. Eventually, the 'son of' tended to be dropped, with the eponymous father's name eventually crystallising into a hereditary surname, as with Lambie. Thus the burgess Thomas Cnuth's surname suggests a male ancestor named Knut, a not uncommon name in Northern Britain; the surname later developed into Knott.[176] Men with metronymic by-names are generally assumed to have been illegitimate. This may have been the case with William son of Rohese, a possible burgess in 1258×71.[177] There must have been ample opportunities, in a town full of successful churchmen, for women of the burgh community to bring forth such sons. In the case of one burgess, Ranulf Hem (modern surname Heams), it is unclear to whom the bearer is related. The surname means 'uncle', but there is no way of knowing whose uncle he was, why that person mattered and indeed if the name even referred to Radulf or was already a heritable surname by that point (the 1240s).[178]

We have very few individuals with occupational surnames in our relatively short list of burgh inhabitants, and those we do have are quite typical. Aldred the baker, Gillanders the brewer and Ralph the cook witnessed a charter of

---

of Scotland', *Essays on the Nobility of Medieval Scotland*, ed. K. J. Stringer (Edinburgh 1985), pp. 102–30, at p. 113.

[175] D. E. R. Watt, *Biographical Dictionary of Scottish Graduates to A.D. 1410* (Oxford, 1977), pp. 475–6. It should be pointed out that Master Robert acted as a papal judge-delegate in 1198×1202, thus suggesting he was perhaps too old to be a son of Bishop Roger. It is always possible that previous bishops should be considered.

[176] *Balm. Lib.*, no. 18 (H3/314/1).

[177] *St A. Lib.*, p. 335 (H3/611/2).

[178] *St A. Lib.*, p. 281 (H3/323/1); Barrow, 'Kinninmonth', no. 13 (H3/323/2); P. H. Reaney, *The Origin of English Surnames* (London, 1967), p. 81. Note also Hugh Heam son of Constance, PoMS, no. 10892.

Bishop Roger, 1189×96, alongside such men as Gamel the doorward and Hugh the steward. These men were part of the episcopal household, and as such may have had dwellings within the burgh. Indeed, this raises the important question of how much the episcopal, monastic and burghal communities overlapped. Presumably someone like Aldred the baker travelled with the bishop when he was at his residence in Inchmurdo or throughout the diocese. But it is possible that someone like Gillanders the brewer sold his product in the town as well as providing for the episcopal table; sadly, it is just impossible to know. Similarly a Simon *blacarius* or corn-dealer of St Andrews witnessed a charter relating to Megginch in Perthshire; he was more likely to have handled renders of grain for the diocesan establishment rather than been a trader for the burgh.[179] More clearly within the burgh community were men like the burgess Adam the smith, active in the last quarter of the twelfth century.[180] A Herbert, janitor or gate-keeper of St Andrews, appears early in the thirteenth century, a reminder that securing the burgh's ports was key to security.[181] A burgess in 1285 was called R. the clerk, indicating an occupation that was crucial in any burgh, not just those held by bishops.[182] Finally we have the wonderfully descriptive moniker of Godric Sterecrag, whose land in the 1170s lay at the north-west end of the burgh, probably stretching to the sea. Bishop Richard gave land for the new work of the cathedral at that time which abutted the sea and was between Godric's land and Rathelpie, which was located around the site of the modern-day playing fields and new university buildings west of the bus station.[183] As the land for the cathedral use was in free burgage, Godric's land may also have been a burgh plot. His by-name suggests that Godric's job entailed steering ships around the dangerous crags north of the burgh, and his land seems to have backed up to rocks such as Doo Craigs. Given that the livelihood of the burgh depended on maritime trade, it is likely that Godric's job was important for the flourishing of the community.

A very few of our burgesses had second names derived from nicknames, with Laurence Bell and John Godsman appearing in the early fourteenth-century charter of John Ramsay printed in Appendix 4. Bell was a common surname for Scottish burgesses, with burgesses of Perth, Aberdeen and Crail holding the name.[184] There was a notary at St Andrews in 1248 named John Bell.[185] The

---

[179] *Holyrood Liber*, no. 66 (1) (H3/579/1).
[180] *SEA*, no. 193 (H2/10/86; *St A. Lib.*, 139); Barrow, 'East Fife Documents', no. 1 (H2/97/2).
[181] *St A. Lib.*, p. 278 (H3/15/108).
[182] *Newb. Reg.*, no. 59 (H2/10/279).
[183] *SEA*, no. 196 (H2/10/89; *St A. Lib.*, p. 141); *PNF*, iii, pp. 522–3.
[184] William Bell, 1266, possibly burgess; Laurence Bell, early fourteenth century; note William Bell and David Bell may have been burgesses of Crail; Alexander Bell, burgess of Perth; Adam Bell, probable burgess of Perth; John Bell, burgess of Perth; Walter Bell, apparently burgess of Aberdeen: PoMS, nos. 11490, 15926, 11491, 15459, 15407, 3471, 15245.
[185] *CPL*, i, p. 245 (H2/143/82); Black, *Surnames*, p. 67.

man who bought John Ramsay's land, Adam 'called *Purroc*', had a surname, now standardised as Purrock, which can be found elsewhere in Scotland. A Warin Purrock was likely a burgess of Dundee in the early thirteenth century.[186] Walter son of Robert Purrock was a landholder in Ayton, Berwickshire, between about 1259 and 1280, while a John Purrock was a son of William Scott in the same toun in 1283.[187] The Scott family established in Reston near Ayton in the second half of the thirteenth century was presumably descended from this same William 'the Scot', father of John Purrock, who flourished from the 1210s onwards.[188] 'Purrock' is a nickname. As Carole Hough has elucidated, *Purroc* was almost certainly a Middle English name for a kind of bird – the bittern, snipe or dunlin.[189] In this case, it is tempting to think that John Purrock took that name through marriage into the neighbouring Purrock family in Ayton. It is even more tempting to suggest that William 'the Scot' had that byname because he had travelled from north of Forth – perhaps east Fife? – and that Adam Purrock, citizen of St Andrews c.1300, may have been a member of this Berwickshire family, perhaps even William 'the Scot's grandson, and that his ties with St Andrews had been achieved through the family's historical ties, but this is pure speculation; it is just as possible that Adam was descended from Warin Purrock in Dundee or indeed from some completely unknown family.

In conclusion, the episcopal burgh of St Andrews was founded around the same time as the Augustinian cathedral priory and grew up side-by-side with it. The burgh was established with the support of the king and benefited in particular from early connections with Berwick and Perth, then the kingdom's two largest and wealthiest towns. Nevertheless, the new burgh incorporated a previously existing community, with new merchants from England, Flanders and elsewhere probably clustering along the eastern end of South Street. Despite initial teething difficulties, including apparently the inability to settle on a permanent place for the market, the burgh community grew up to serve the substantial ecclesiastical establishment centred on the kingdom's premier church centre. Although the burgesses gained full equality with the king's burgesses, and the burgh kept pace in terms of developments such as a court, council and guild merchant, trade was primarily with the east Fife hinterland. The priory was a substantial landholder in the town, and the burgesses established strong links, perhaps serving some financial function. At the same time, the burgh's success was largely underwritten by a network of gentry Fife landholders, tenants of both the church and the earls. The most successful of burghal families were able to join this network, while the more ambitious Fifers might acquire land in burgage and eventually attain burgess status. Thus, while the burgh

---

[186] *Arb. Lib.*, i, no. 136 (H3/635/1); *Balm. Lib.*, no. 32 (H3/274/5).
[187] PoMS, no. 8144; James Raine, *The History and Antiquities of North Durham* (London, 1852), App., no. 208 (H3/66/7).
[188] PoMS, no. 5349.
[189] Carole Hough, 'The Surname Purrock', *Notes and Queries* (Dec. 2003), pp. 375–7.

of St Andrews was founded by a Fleming and settled by speakers of English, French and other European tongues, it survived and thrived thanks to the deep connections that grew up with both the church establishment and the people of Fife.

CHAPTER NINE

The Archaeology of Medieval St Andrews

Derek W. Hall with Catherine Smith

IN the thirty-four years since the production of the St Andrews burgh survey, pressure from development has ensured that there have been several opportunities for archaeological investigations in the historic town.[1] This chapter on the archaeology of St Andrews thus aims to provide an accessible synthesis of this fieldwork in conjunction with burgh survey material.

St Andrews is a fairly compact and self-contained town. The original settlement was situated between the Kinness Burn and the sea, and slowly, by stages, the town expanded westward. By the sixteenth century, St Andrews had reached the limits defined by ports at South Street, Market Street and North Street. These three streets dominate the town plan. The cathedral and its precinct serve as a focus for the street plan and the three main streets converge on the headland with only Market Street stopping before the cathedral is reached. These can clearly be identified on Geddy's map of c.1580, which also shows the beginnings of suburban development outside the town walls at the west end of South Street. St Andrews has so far largely escaped the attentions of massive redevelopment and as such still retains its medieval streetscape. The considerable number of archaeological projects that have been carried out both within and on the fringes of the medieval town have indicated that the chances of good survival of archaeological deposits and structures are fairly high.

For our purposes, the medieval burgh has been subdivided into six areas and there is a seventh area that includes the site of the Leper hospital. The boundaries between areas are based on street frontages and natural features wherever possible.

Area 1 Golf Place/Links Crescent/City Road/Market Street/Greyfriars Garden/Murray Park/West Sands
Area 2 Murray Park/Greyfriars Garden/Market Street/Church Street/South Street/South Castle Street/North Castle Street/The Scores/Witch Lake

[1] A. T. Simpson and A. Stevenson, *Historic St Andrews: The Archaeological Implications of Development*, Scottish Burgh Survey (Glasgow, 1981).

Figure 9.1: Map of St Andrews showing archaeological area boundaries. After Munro 1997.

Area 3 Kennedy Gardens/Kinness Burn/Bridge Street/Alexandra Place/City Road
Area 4 Market Street/Church Street/Queens Gardens/Kinness Burn/Bridge Street/Alexandra Place
Area 5 South Street/Queens Gardens/Kinness Burn/Abbey Street
Area 6 North Castle Street/South Castle Street/Abbey Street/Abbey Walk/East Sands
Area 7 Kinness Burn/Woodburn Terrace/Arbitrary line to west of Priestden Place/Arbitrary line to south of Priestden Road/East Sands

The data recovered from St Andrews presents a vivid picture of a small medieval town on the east coast of Scotland. As with many archaeological excavations of a medieval date, in St Andrews ceramics tend to be the most common find. What is of interest is the evidence for a well-made local whiteware product, a native Scottish pottery produced in Fife, Lothian and Tweeddale between the twelfth and fifteenth centuries.[2] The presence of such a good, locally available

---

[2] D. W. Hall, 'The Pottery', Rains and Hall, *Excavations*, pp. 40–63; G. R. Haggarty

ceramic product may be the best explanation for the relatively low number of imported wares that have been recovered from excavations in the burgh. Aside from sherds of Yorkshire Type ware, which are ubiquitous on the east coast, vessels from other production centres are poorly represented. For example, so far there are virtually no German stonewares from any of the excavations in St Andrews, whereas in the likes of Perth and Dundee they are common finds.[3] Perhaps, as has been argued, St Andrews was poorly served from a trading point of view due to its harbour. What we still lack in St Andrews, in common with most of Scotland, are excavated pottery production sites, and future research could be usefully focused in this direction. Excavated iron and copper alloy objects from St Andrews include everyday items such as candlesticks, barrel padlocks, buckles, nails and horse fittings but so far there is no evidence for the manufacture of such material within the confines of the medieval burgh.[4]

Animal bone and environmental materials also account for considerable finds in the excavations. Although some medieval sites were excavated in St Andrews during the 1970s, reports were not published in full and nor is it likely that any faunal remains originating from them were retained. Certainly when these sites were reviewed and summarised in 1997 no animal bones came to light in the collections of Fife Museums.[5] The sites considered here are thus those from excavations that took place from the 1980s onwards. The excavations were mainly located within the core of the medieval burgh, with outliers at the Byre Theatre, Castlecliffe and St Nicholas Farm.[6] Hallow Hill, an early Christian long cist cemetery, is not considered here although animal bones were recovered from the ploughsoil and more significantly from one of the burials.[7] Although some of the urban sites produced only a very small quantity of animal bones they are included here as they corroborate the evidence of the larger sites as regards the species of animals to be found within the burgh. In the 1990s further assemblages may have been retrieved but in many cases were not analysed further, as for example those reported in *Discovery and Excavation in Scotland* but not elsewhere.[8]

---

and R. Will, 'Medieval Pottery', in J. Lewis, 'Excavations at St Andrews, Castlecliffe', *PSAS* 126 (1996), pp. 648–69.

[3] D. W. Hall, 'Pottery', in D. P. Bowler, A. Cox and C. Smith, 'Four Excavations in Perth 1979–84', *PSAS* 125 (1995), p. 952; D. W. Hall, 'The Pottery', in J. MacKenzie, 'Excavations at Green's Playhouse, Dundee', *TFAJ* 4 (1998), pp. 187–91.

[4] R. Maxwell, 'The Finds', Rains and Hall, *Excavations*, pp. 64–104; D. Caldwell, 'Small Finds', in J. Lewis, 'Excavations at St Andrews, Castlecliffe', *PSAS* 126 (1996), pp. 635–45.

[5] See Rains and Hall, *Excavations*.

[6] C. Smith, 'Animal Bone from 93 Market Street (Site code SA43)', *Scottish Urban Archaeological Trust Archive Report* (Perth, 2001); F. McCormick, 'Mammal Bones', in J. Lewis, 'Excavations at St Andrews, Castlecliffe', *PSAS* 126 (1996), pp. 669–71; C. Smith, 'The Animal Bone', in D. W. Hall, 'Archaeological Excavations at St Nicholas Farm, St Andrews, 1986–87', *TFAJ* 1 (1995) pp. 67–73.

[7] E. Proudfoot, 'Excavations in the Long Cist Cemetery on the Hallow Hill, St Andrews, Fife, 1975–7', *PSAS* 126 (1996), pp. 387–454.

[8] E. V. W. Proudfoot, '135 Market Street, St Andrews', *Discovery and Excavation in Scotland* [hereafter *DES*] (1990), p. 15; E. V. W. Proudfoot, '12 North Street, St Andrews',

Notably, domesticated species, particularly large mammals, predominated at sites in St Andrews. Cattle, sheep/goat and pig were the most frequently occurring species. While cattle and sheep/goats are almost equal at most of the sites within the burgh core, pig is always in a poor third place. Outside of the nucleus of the burgh, most notably at Castlecliffe, but also at the Byre Theatre site, Abbey Street, sheep/goats appear to predominate over cattle. It can be assumed that meat from cattle, sheep/goats and pigs contributed to the human diet, although their meat was only one of the reasons for keeping them. The observation that many of the cattle and sheep/goats were husbanded until they were older adults is probably a result of the trade in hides, wool and wool-fells since these commodities increase in value with the age of the animals which bear them. An optimum of about five years is indicated for good quality cattle hides. Older sheep continue to produce yearly clips of good quality wool so long as they are in a good state of health. The loss of incisor teeth, called 'broken mouth', usually occurring after the age of five or six years, was probably a common reason for culling sheep, since they are unable to feed adequately, lose condition and the quality of their wool decreases. Since pigs do not produce either wool or milk for human consumption, their primary function was to produce meat and fat, their hide being a valuable secondary product. Non-breeding pigs are thus liable to be slaughtered on reaching an optimum size and weight. Evidence from Scottish medieval sites has shown this to be between the ages of two and three years.[9]

Whether horses were eaten within the burgh is a vexed question. There is certainly evidence of horse bones having been butchered at the site of St Nicholas leper hospital and it has been suggested that horse meat, as well as other foodstuffs confiscated at the burgh markets, was considered fit for consumption by lepers.[10] There is some evidence from the Byre Theatre site that cats were skinned for their fur.[11] Both cat and dog bones from Castlecliffe showed evidence of knife cuts, presumably associated with skinning.[12] Skins of cats and dogs and other small fur-bearing mammals were valuable commodities and evidence of such trade has been noted wherever medieval burghs have been excavated in Scotland.[13]

Wild game species are almost uniformly absent from medieval sites in St Andrews. The only evidence for red deer (*Cervus elaphus*) was a single bone

---

DES (1992), p. 31.

[9] C. Smith, 'A Grumphy in the Sty: An Archaeological View of Pigs in Scotland, from their Earliest Domestication to the Agricultural Revolution', *PSAS* 130 (2000) p. 712.

[10] C. Smith, 'The Animal Bone', in Hall, 'Archaeological Excavations at St Nicholas Farm', pp. 67–73.

[11] C. Smith, 'The Animal Bone', in C. J. Moloney and L. Baker, 'Evidence for the Form and Nature of a Medieval Burgage Plot in St Andrews: An Archaeological Excavation on the Site of the Byre Theatre, Abbey Street, St Andrews', *TFAJ* 7 (2001), p. 73.

[12] McCormick, 'Mammal Bones', p. 670.

[13] C. Smith, 'Dogs, Cats and Horses in the Scottish Medieval Town', *PSAS* 128 (1998), pp. 977–8.

found at 134 Market Street and a piece of unattached antler from St Nicholas Farm. A single tooth of roe deer (*Capreolus capreolus*) was recovered from 133 Market Street. Positive evidence for wild boar was absent, although this is unsurprising given the fragmentary nature of the evidence and the fact that wild boar and domestic pigs are closely related. Hare (*Lepus capensis*), considered a lesser game animal, was recovered only at Kirkhill and South Castle Street. Wild game birds such as pheasant (*Phasianus colchicus*) and grey partridge (*Perdix perdix*) were few and occurred only at South Castle Street. Neither was there any evidence of the hawks which were necessary for the pursuit of game birds. Domesticated poultry, notably fowls (*Gallus gallus*) and geese (*Anser anser*), seem to have answered the everyday dietary needs of the populace. The lack of wild game in a burgh whose coat of arms bears a wild boar is therefore worthy of remark.[14] It seems likely that the sites excavated within the burgh may contain the refuse from everyday trade and commerce rather than the evidence of the bishops' sporting pursuits.

The presence of rabbit (*Oryctolagus cuniculus*) bones at several sites in St Andrews is complicated by the species' habit of burrowing and the possibility of bioturbation of archaeological deposits. In other words it cannot definitely be proven that any occurrence of rabbit remains has any connection with exploitation by humans unless the bones bear evidence of butchery. A radiocarbon date of 1320–1392AD derived from an unbutchered rabbit bone, a humerus from 52 South Street, is both unusual and early.[15] Rabbits are uncommonly found at any medieval site in Scotland, due perhaps to the difficulties of establishing the rabbit population in a cold, damp climate, and it is not until the post-medieval period that we see any firm archaeological evidence of their use, for example at the Holyrood Parliament site.[16] Rabbits are not thought to have become widespread in the Scottish Lowlands until as late as the mid eighteenth century.[17]

Marine resources appear to be under-represented in many of the excavated assemblages from St Andrews. While fish bones have been recovered from many of the sites, they have not always been retrieved by soil sampling (nor have all the bones been identified) and thus the results may be biased towards the larger species. However, at the Byre Theatre a soil sampling strategy was in place and the following economically significant members of the cod family were recovered: haddock (*Melanogrammus aeglefinus*), cod (*Gadus morhua*), saithe (*Pollachius virens*) and pollack (*Pollachius pollachius*). As well as these gadids, herring (*Clupea harengus*), flatfishes such as sole, dab and plaice

---

[14] Simpson and Stevenson, *Historic St Andrews*, frontispiece.
[15] C. Smith, 'The Animal Bone from 52 South Street, St Andrews', *Archive Report for Rathmell Archaeology*. Lab reference SUERC 54521/GU34507.
[16] C. Smith, 'Mammalian, Bird and Molluscan Remains', *Artefactual, Environmental and Archaeological Evidence from the Holyrood Parliament Site Excavations*, ed. Gordon G. Barclay and Anna Ritchie, *Scottish Archaeological Internet Report* 40 (2010), pp. 80, 81.
[17] A. Kitchener, 'Extinctions, Introductions and Colonisation of Scottish Mammals and Birds since the last Ice Age', *Species History in Scotland: Introductions and Extinctions Since the Ice Age*, ed. Robert A. Lambert (Edinburgh, 1998), p. 83.

(*Limanda limanda, Solea solea, Pleuronectes platessa*) and rays (*Rajidae*) were recovered.[18] A similar marine fish assemblage was recovered from Castlecliffe, with the addition of conger eel (*Conger conger*) and ling (*Molva molva*).[19] Fish bones occurred at most of the other sites reviewed here but were not identified to species. In addition, a few freshwater species of the Salmonidae (salmon/trout) and eel families were also represented at Castlecliffe.[20]

Other marine resources were cliff-nesting birds such as gannets (*Morus bassanus*) and guillemot (*Uria aalge*), which could have supplied both meat and eggs. Although the numbers of bones recovered from these species were very small, incidences of guillemots occurred at Byre Theatre and 133 Market Street and gannets at Cinema House, St Andrews War Memorial, Byre Theatre and St John's Court. Shore species such as the curlew (*Numenius arquata*) were noted at Castlecliffe.[21] Nowhere was the bird assemblage as large and varied as on the Isle of May, indicating an economic strategy quite different from the subsistence living to be encountered on an island, albeit roughly contemporaneous.[22] Marine mammals such as whales were also utilised at St Andrews. Two fragments of cetacean bone from Kirkhill and 106–110 South Street may have come from chance strandings of large species.

Marine molluscs should also be mentioned. These were frequent finds at most of the sites, although the number of shells was not always quantified. The species found at 133 Market Street are typical. Here, with the exception of a single shell of dog wulk (*Nucella lapillus*), all of the marine molluscs found at the site were edible. These were oyster (*Ostrea edulis*), cockle (*Cerastoderma* cf *edule*), *Arctica islandica*, limpet (*Patella* sp), buckie (*Buccinum ondatum*) and wulk/edible periwinkle (*Littorina littorea*). At St John's Court a similar range of species was found, with the addition of the mussel (*Mytilus edulis*). Oyster shells are frequently found at medieval urban sites throughout the north-east of Scotland. Although it is possible that they were exported in barrels from the Forth, they are so ubiquitous at sites such as Perth, Dundee, Arbroath, Montrose and St Andrews that there are fair grounds for suspecting they may represent an extinct oyster bed in the Tay.[23]

It has been argued elsewhere that the differences in relative frequencies of

---

[18] R. Ceron-Carrasco, 'The Fish Remains', in C. J. Moloney and L. Baker, 'Evidence for the Form and Nature of a Medieval Burgage Plot in St Andrews: An Archaeological Excavation on the Site of the Byre Theatre, Abbey Street, St Andrews', *TFAJ* 7 (2001), p. 73.

[19] S. Hamilton-Dyer, 'Bird and Fish Bones', in J. Lewis, 'Excavations at St Andrews, Castlecliffe, 1988–90', *PSAS* 126 (1996), p. 672.

[20] Ceron-Carrasco, 'The Fish Remains', p. 73.

[21] Hamilton-Dyer, 'Bird and Fish Bones', p. 671.

[22] C. Smith, 'The Bird Bone', *Excavations at St Ethernan's Monastery, Isle of May, Fife 1992–7*, ed. H. F. James and P. Yeoman (Perth, 2008), pp. 93–7.

[23] D. Heppel, C. Smith and D. McKay, 'The Mollusca', *The Perth High Street Archaeological Excavation 1975–1977, Fascicule 4: Living and Working in a Medieval Scottish Burgh: Environmental Remains and Miscellaneous Finds*, ed. L. M. Thoms and C. Smith (Perth, 2011), pp. 61–2.

the various species utilised (for example, a bias towards sheep/goats rather than cattle at some sites in St Andrews) is the result of large-scale sampling strategies carried out at sites excavated after the mid-1990s.[24] Elsewhere on the eastern Scottish seaboard, for example Perth and Aberdeen, cattle bones usually dominate the assemblages.[25] However, sampling bias does not appear to be the whole story. The Byre Theatre, Castlecliffe, Kirkhill and St Nicholas Farm sites lie somewhat outside of the core of medieval burgh and may thus not reflect all of the commercial activities of the butchery, skinning and preparation of large animal carcasses which typically occur at the heart of the burgh. Fish bones may be poorly represented at some sites because preparation may have been associated with sites nearer to the sea. Rather, the assemblages from outlying sites may illustrate a more domestic type of consumption. It has also been difficult, given the restrictions of watching briefs and rescue excavations, to assign absolute dates to all of the material recovered. The presence of turkey at South Castle Street, for example, indicates a date at least in the sixteenth century, when the species was first introduced to Britain. The rat bones (of indeterminate species) found at the Byre Theatre and in the solum of 52 South Street are also likely to be late in date, or intrusive, or both. Only through targeted excavation accompanied by large-scale sampling strategies can we build up a true picture of the economics of St Andrews as evidenced by the faunal remains.

On the basis of previous archaeological work in the burgh it is possible to identify questions that still require to be answered. For example, we currently have little idea of the nature and form of the secular buildings of the medieval burgh but limited evidence from excavations at the likes of Abbey Street and North Street suggests that they may have been timber. Recent work at 52 South Street suggests that the fabric of earlier medieval buildings may still survive in some of the standing buildings in the medieval burgh, and careful monitoring of building refurbishment or renewal is important. At several sites in the medieval core of the burgh a very distinctive horizon of deep soil has been located, sealing medieval deposits (see Market Street, North Street, South Street and Abbey Street in the appendix below). The archaeology of St Andrews is thus an important buried asset and needs to be better understood, curated and protected.

---

[24] Moloney and Baker, 'Evidence for the Form and Nature of a Medieval Burgage Plot in St Andrews', no. 2001.
[25] G. W. I. Hodgson, 'The Animal Remains from Medieval Sites within Three Burghs on the Eastern Scottish Seaboard', *Site, Environment and Economy*, ed. Bruce Proudfoot (London, 1983), pp. 3–32; G. W. I. Hodgson, C. Smith and A. Jones, 'The Mammal Bone', *The Perth High Street Archaeological Excavation 1975–1977. Fascicule 4: Living and Working in a Medieval Scottish Burgh: Environmental Remains and Miscellaneous Finds*, ed. L. M. Thoms and C. Smith (Perth, 2011), pp. 5–44.

Appendix: Excavation Details

Area 1 Golf Place/Links Crescent/City Road/Market Street/Greyfriars Garden/Murray Park/West Sands

This area lies beyond the western boundary of the medieval burgh and includes the site of the Franciscan friary. The discovery of the cinerary urns in the nineteenth century indicates that unexpected finds of prehistoric date may also be recovered in the area.

1. Step Rock excavations, NO 5070 1713
A limited excavation in 1981 located two uncoffined burials at the bottom of a midden deposit. Examination of the burials suggested they were between 35 and 45 years of age. Their date is unknown.[26]

2. Cinerary urns found 1864, NO 5044 1682
The Ordnance Survey map locates this findspot on the western side of City Road. Apart from a record of a further site visit by the Ordnance Survey in June 1964 there is no other information regarding this discovery. These vessels may have been of Bronze Age date.

3. Site of Franciscan friary, NO 5068 1682
The foundation date of this house of Observant Franciscan friars is uncertain but it is thought unlikely to be before 1463.[27] The best idea of the nature of the complex can be gained from Geddy's map of St Andrews, which shows the layout of the friary buildings. The cemetery is said to have been discovered in 1904 during building work on nearby houses.[28] Road works in Greyfriars Street in 2009 located four human burials and many fragments of disarticulated human bone apparently associated with the friary's graveyard.

4. St Mary's Place watching brief, NO 5062 1678
A watching brief by the Scottish Urban Archaeological Trust (SUAT) in 1992 located c.1.35m of garden soil above natural sand. Nothing relating to the Franciscan friary was located.[29]

5. West Park hotel watching brief, NO 506 167
A watching brief in 1971 recovered 200 sherds of medieval pottery from soil uplifted from this site during building operations.[30]

---

[26] F. W. Van de Veen, 'Step Rock, St Andrews', *DES* (1981), p. 11.
[27] I. Cowan and D. Easson, *Medieval Religious Houses of Scotland* (London, 1976), p. 132.
[28] R. Lamont Brown, *The Life and Times of St Andrews* (Edinburgh, 1989), p. 128.
[29] D. W. Hall, 'St Mary's Place, St Andrews', *DES* (1992), p. 31.
[30] J. Di Folco, 'West Park Hotel, St Andrews', *DES* (1971), p. 21.

Area 2 Murray Park/Greyfriars Garden/Market Street/Church Street/ South Street/South Castle Street/North Castle Street/The Scores/ Witch Lake

This area includes the northern half of the medieval burgh up to North Castle Street. It includes St Salvator's College, several late medieval and post-medieval buildings and the excavations at Johnston's Court and Cinema House, North Street and the Former Auction Hall, Market Street. Excavations in this part of the burgh have indicated that archaeological deposits may be very well preserved. This is especially true in the Market Street backlands where they may survive under deep garden soil. Preservation on the street frontages is harder to predict although good remains have been encountered (see no. 6). There has been less work on South Street and it is therefore much harder to assess the chances of preservation.

1. Site of North Port, NO 5071 1686
This stood in North Street at the north end of Greyfriars Garden and was demolished in 1838.[31]

2. 77 North Street, NO 5095 1685
The front of this building was remodelled in the late eighteenth century but the stairtower suggests an earlier origin. The north-west wing of this building, which has a vaulted ground floor, may date to the fifteenth century. It was owned by John Ray in 1459 and then Andrew Balfour in 1497. A large front block was added in the sixteenth century to give the building an L-plan.[32]

3. Johnston's Court, North Street excavations, NO 5085 1683
Excavations in 1974 located the remains of a boat-shaped timber building and an associated croft. This structure was superseded by a timber house built parallel to the street along the rig frontage.[33]

4. Cinema House, North Street excavations, NO 5090 1678
An excavation by the Scottish Urban Archaeological Trust (SUAT) in 1984 located a series of stratified deposits 1.5m deep spanning the late thirteenth to the nineteenth centuries. Parts of two plots fronting North Street were excavated to natural. Notable features included a clay-lined tanning pit, a well, a structure, hearth and furnace all of fourteenth-century date.[34]

---

[31] Lamont Brown, *The Life and Times of St Andrews*, p. 64.
[32] J. Gifford, *The Buildings of Scotland: Fife* (Harmondsworth, 1988), p. 395.
[33] Simpson and Stevenson, *Historic St Andrews*, p. 17.
[34] L. Ross, 'Cinema House', Rains and Hall, *Excavations*, pp. 22–5.

Figure 9.2: St Nicholas Farm excavation. General view of excavation of leper hospital bakehouse.

5. 135 Market Street excavations, NO 5077 1674

Excavations by St Andrews Heritage Services in 1990 located an earlier version of the building represented by two main rooms. Below this a possible kiln/furnace and an ash-filled pit with fragments of leather and fabric were located. A pit with bone and possibly thirteenth-century pottery was also recovered. Between the original S wall and the modern frontage a cobbled surface may have been an earlier surface of Market Street.[35]

6. 125 Market Street excavations and watching brief, NO 5081 1672

Excavations by the Scottish Urban Archaeological Trust (SUAT) in advance of an extensive redevelopment of a retail unit located a series of cut features c.1.1 m below ground surface. These features comprised three elongated hearths, from which quantities of slag debris were recovered, and two post-holes. Pottery sherds recovered in association with these features dates this period of probable industrial smithing activity to the thirteenth to fifteenth century. It is likely that this early phase dates from the period when Market Street was no more than a lane separating the backlands of North and South Street. This phase was sealed by a layer of orange/brown sandy loam garden soil which had a maximum thickness of 0.3 m. Pottery sherds, also dating from the thirteenth to fifteenth century, were recovered from this layer. Cutting the garden soil was the single course of a substantial stone wall 0.9m in width. This wall was aligned parallel to the existing street frontage, set c.2.5m back and represents the frontage of a sixteenth-/seventeenth-century stone building.

[35] Proudfoot, '135 Market Street', p. 15.

A watching brief on contractors' groundworks to the rear of the property, after partial demolition had taken place, revealed a large cut feature c.2m in width and 1.2m in depth. Thirteenth- to fifteenth-century pottery sherds were recovered from this feature. It was sealed by the medieval garden soil, identified during the excavation, and a disturbed, heavily contaminated layer of possible late medieval midden. A watching brief in a neighbouring pend, included in the redevelopment, revealed that the substantial frontage wall continued to the east. It too was cut through c.0.3m of medieval garden soil.[36]

7. St Salvator's College, NO 5100 1690
This college was founded in 1450 by James Kennedy, bishop of St Andrews. In 1452 the college was expanded by the founding of a chaplainry. The gate tower was probably originally built in the 1460s and was partially restored in the nineteenth century. To the left of the gate tower stands the Hebdomadar's Building, whose two lower storeys may also date to the 1460s. In front of it is a small cemetery which was laid out c.1459 when it extended further south.[37]

8. College Gate, North Street excavations, NO 510 168
Excavations by Nicholas Bogdan in 1972 suggested that this plot had been vacant until a chapel was erected in the nineteenth century.[38]

9. 38 North Street watching brief, NO 5115 1676
In a watching brief in 1992 the Scottish Urban Archaeological Trust (SUAT) recorded the top of archaeological deposits c.0.38m below the old floor surface.[39]

10. 30–32 North Street, NO 5118 1675
This small tenement has an early seventeenth-century core extended with later offshoots towards the street.[40]

11. 11 College Street, NO 5098 1678
This structure dates to c.1530 with a back jamb that was added in 1560.[41]

12. Former Auction Hall, Market Street excavations, NO 5111 1672
Limited excavations and a watching brief by the Scottish Urban Archaeological Trust (SUAT) in 1983 revealed over 1m of archaeological deposit. A neolithic/Bronze Age flint scraper was found as well as three sherds of Developed Stamford ware (a type of medieval pottery) dating possibly to the twelfth century. A series

---

[36] J. MacKenzie, '125 Market Street, St Andrews', *DES* (1995), p. 29.
[37] Gifford, *The Buildings of Scotland: Fife*, p. 375.
[38] D. W. Hall, 'Other Work', Rains and Hall, *Excavations*, p. 5.
[39] D. W. Hall, '38 North Street, St Andrews', *DES* (1992), p. 31.
[40] Gifford, *The Buildings of Scotland: Fife*, p. 375.
[41] Ibid., p. 18.

of substantial features consisting of pits and gullies cut into the natural subsoil contained possibly thirteenth-century pottery. These were sealed by a layer of garden soil 0.5 m-0.75m thick that was in turn sealed by the remains of a group of stone cottages, built in the sixteenth and seventeenth centuries and demolished in the nineteenth century before the hall was built.[42]

13. 26 Market Street excavations, NO 5110 1668
Excavations in 1974 confirmed that the earliest building on this site was late and probably sixteenth century. Prior to this, the land had been part of the croft, as thirteenth-century pottery confirmed. All of the building except the foundations, and a very minute area of floor, had been removed by later activity.[43]

14. 15 Church Street watching brief, NO 5096 1667
A watching brief by the Fife Archaeological Index in 1985 located a deposit of dark soil at least 1 m deep below the floor of this property.[44]

15. 99 South Street watching brief, NO 5096 1663
A watching brief by the Fife Archaeological Index recorded a Victorian cast-iron shop frontage below the 1950s one that was being replaced.[45]

16. 89 South Street watching brief, NO 5099 1664
A watching brief by the Fife Archaeological Index in 1989 recorded earlier building foundations to the rear of this structure. An area of burning was also noted at the south-east corner directly on the sand subsoil.[46]

17. 71 South Street, NO 5103 1665
This building was originally a tenement dating to c.1600 which was then remodelled c.1800.[47]

18. St John's House, 67–69 South Street, NO 5106 1663
This building was begun in 1450 as an L-plan building with the hall in the back wing. The front block was rebuilt c.1600, its upper floor was then jettied out on corbels at the rear, and it was raised from two to four storeys in the eighteenth century.[48]

19. 67–69 South Street excavations, NO 510 166
Excavations by Nick Brooks and Nicholas Bogdan in 1972–73 within and adjacent to a fifteenth-century cellar located a layer of cobbles set into the

---

[42] J. Wordsworth and P. R. Clark, 'Auction Hall', Rains and Hall, *Excavations*, pp. 17–21.
[43] Hall, 'Other Work', p. 5.
[44] E. V. W. Proudfoot, '15 Church Street, St Andrews', *DES* (1985), p. 15.
[45] E. V. W. Proudfoot, '99 South Street, St Andrews', *DES* (1992), p. 31.
[46] E. V. W. Proudfoot, '89 South Street, St Andrews', *DES* (1989), p. 16.
[47] Gifford, *The Buildings of Scotland: Fife*, p. 400.
[48] Ibid., p. 400.

natural sand. Medieval pottery was discovered lying on the surface of these cobbles.[49]

20. 69 South Street excavations, NO 5106 1663
Excavations by the Fife Archaeological Index in 1990 located earlier building foundations associated with twelfth- or thirteenth-century pottery. Above these the remains of two clay ovens were located and evidence of numerous alterations to the fabric of the building.[50]

21. 45c South Street watching brief, NO 5113 1664
A watching brief by the Fife Archaeological Index in 1992 recorded an inscribed carved stone of late medieval date built into the wall.[51]

Area 3 Kennedy Gardens/Kinness Burn/Bridge Street/Alexandra Place/City Road

By the time of Geddy's sixteenth-century map this area seems to have been fairly well developed. The single piece of archaeological work undertaken implies that there is the chance of finding good surviving archaeological deposits in those areas that have not been destroyed by building construction. The suburb of Argyle was a separate development to the medieval burgh of St Andrews and was once part of Rathelpie.[52]

1. Excavations at 50–52 Argyle Street, NO 5040 1652
Trial excavations by the Scottish Urban Archaeological Trust (SUAT) in advance of redevelopment in 1998 located features of medieval date at the rear of this property.[53] The ceramics from this site include the only sherd of fifteenth-century Spanish (Malagan) lustreware yet recovered from St Andrews.

Area 4 Market Street/Church Street/Queens Gardens/Kinness Burn/Bridge Street/Alexandra Place

This area includes the south-western part of the medieval burgh up to Queens Gardens and includes the sites of the Dominican friary, Holy Trinity Church, the Tolbooth, the market cross and several excavations and watching briefs. Archaeological excavation and observation in this area has indicated that deposit survival is liable to be very good. As with Area 2, deposits may survive sealed under deep deposits of garden soil. Recent monitoring in the grounds of Madras College (no. 9) seems to indicate that the remains of the Dominican

---

[49] Hall, 'Other Work', p. 5.
[50] C. Kelly and E. V. W. Proudfoot, '69 South Street', *DES* (1990), p. 15.
[51] E. V. W. Proudfoot, '45c South Street, St Andrews', *DES* (1992), p. 31.
[52] Lamont Brown, *The Life and Times of St Andrews*, p. 60.
[53] R. Cachart, '50–52 Argyle Street, St Andrews', *DES* (1998), p. 43.

friary survive largely untouched below modern ground level. Any proposed development work in the vicinity of Holy Trinity Church will require careful monitoring as skeletal remains survive close to modern ground surface. Archaeological evidence for the properties predating the laying out of Holy Trinity Church on this site in 1410–12 will also be recovered.

1. Site of Marketgate Port, NO 5060 1672
This stood at the western end of Market Street in line with the precinct wall of the Franciscan friary.

2. 9 and 10 Alexandra Place watching brief, NO 5058 1665
A watching brief by the Fife Archaeological Index in 1988 located a stone-lined well in the basement yard of 9 Alexandra Place. Massive stone foundations were also recorded underpinning both 9 and 10 Alexandra Place. It was noted that this stonework was of a different nature from the rest of the buildings and may have been reused from another building.[54]

3. 13 City Road trial excavations, NO 5059 1650
Trial excavations by EASE in 1995 and 1996 located a length of possible pre-Reformation property boundary wall close to the City Road frontage and a small group of residual medieval pottery. Most of the site had been severely truncated during the construction of the Drill Hall.[55]

4. Alexandra Place watching brief, NO 5061 1661
A watching brief by the Scottish Urban Archaeological Trust (SUAT) in 1991 located c.0.8m of garden soil across the site. Several features in the natural sand were sealed by this soil including a kiln/oven with a stone floor. A few sherds of medieval pottery were recovered from the garden soil.[56]

5. West Port, NO 5058 1671
This is the most substantial town gate surviving in Scotland. It is referred to in 1560 as 'Argailles Port' because the small suburb of Argyle lay just beyond it.[57]

6. West Port Garage, NO 5060 1646
No archaeological deposits were noted when the old petrol station was demolished. A house formerly stood on the site, but all features seem to have been destroyed when the petrol station was built. An artesian well was uncovered.[58]

---

[54] E. V. W. Proudfoot, '9 Alexandra Place, St Andrews', *DES* (1988), p. 12.
[55] H. Moore and G. Wilson, *Report on the Archaeological Assessment at 13 City Road, St Andrews* (EASE Archive report, 1995/96).
[56] D. W. Hall, 'Alexandra Place, St Andrews', *DES* (1991), p. 22.
[57] Simpson and Stevenson, *Historic St Andrews*, p. 7.
[58] C. Kelly and E. V. W. Proudfoot, 'West Port Garage, St Andrews', *DES* (1990), p. 15.

Figure 9.3: Deep garden soil, Alexandra Place. General view of medieval stone built corn dryer below deep garden soil (1991).

7. Imrie's Close excavations, NO 5062 1653
Excavations by James Kenworthy in 1975 located sixteenth-century and later deposits.[59]

8. 191 South Street watching brief, NO 5067 1653
A watching brief by the Fife Archaeological Index in 1990 recorded garden soil overlying natural sand.[60]

9. Site of Dominican Friary, NO 5075 1655
The foundation of the Dominican friary in St Andrews dates to shortly before 1464, and may be linked to the expansion of the University. In 1516 money left by Bishop Elphinstone of Aberdeen was used towards extensive building works in the friary. The only part of the friary that survives is a polygonal chapel that projected from the north side of the church. This part of the church projected out into South Street, and permission to encroach on the street was requested in 1525.[61] The remainder of the friary complex survives below the grassed area to the south of the chapel and possibly below Madras College. Geddy's sixteenth-century map shows the whole Dominican precinct as it survived prior to its demolition.

[59] Hall, 'Other Work', p. 5.
[60] E. V. W. Proudfoot, '191 South Street, St Andrews', *DES* (1990), p. 16.
[61] R. Fawcett, *Scottish Architecture from the Accession of the Stewarts to the Reformation 1371–1550* (Edinburgh, 1994).

10. Madras College watching brief, NO 5075 1655

A watching brief was undertaken by the Scottish Urban Archaeological Trust (SUAT) in 1995 on the excavation of trenches for floodlighting of the Blackfriars chapel and the college. This monitoring exercise located two areas of demolition rubble possibly indicating the size of the friary complex. Natural sand was located at a depth of c.0.5m at three locations around the Blackfriars Chapel. No human skeletal remains were recovered.[62]

11. 134 Market Street excavations, NO 5075 1680

Excavations by the Scottish Urban Archaeological Trust (SUAT) in 1985 located a sequence of medieval occupation dating from the thirteenth to the fifteenth centuries. The back end of a possible timber structure was located 22m south of the Market Street frontage associated with a corn dryer and a well. The timber building was superseded by a large well 2.6m deep containing pottery of fourteenth-century date. The well was replaced by two possible metalworking hearths which were in turn replaced by a stone building with a clay floor. All the medieval deposits were sealed by a 1.5m deep dump of garden soil which contained a large assemblage of medieval pottery. A series of parallel cultivation slots of eighteenth- or nineteenth-century date similar to those encountered at the Cinema House excavation were also discovered.[63]

12. 120–124 Market Street excavations, NO 5079 1668

Excavations by the Scottish Urban Archaeological Trust (SUAT) in 1985 located some medieval features cut into the natural sand. A possible corn dryer was discovered 52m south of the Market Street frontage containing badly damaged structural remains. A well, a property boundary and a pit were also excavated. The possible corn dryer produced a sherd of red painted Pingsdorf ware (twelfth century) pottery amongst a group of White Gritty wares (twelfth to fifteenth century). Truncated layers of garden soil similar to those located at 134 Market Street (see no. 10 above) were also excavated.[64]

13. Star Hotel, South Street watching brief, NO 5045 1633

A watching brief by the Fife Archaeological Index in 1982 recorded three human burials during building work on this site. Workmen reported that other burials had been found. These inhumations indicate the northern limit of the burial ground of Holy Trinity parish church.[65]

14. Site of Tolbooth, NO 5092 1675

The first documentary reference to a tolbooth is in 1144 when the Bishop of St Andrews acted as arbitrator in a dispute. It stood to the west of the market cross

---

[62] D. W. Hall, 'Madras College, South Street, St Andrews', *DES* (1995), p. 28.
[63] D. W. Hall, 'Market Street', Hall and Rains, *Excavations*, pp. 26–9.
[64] Hall, 'Market Street', pp. 26–9.
[65] E. V. W. Proudfoot, 'Star Hotel, South Street, St Andrews', *DES* (1982), p. 10.

in Market Street and was removed in 1862 when it was regarded as an 'incumbrance to the street'.[66]

15. Watching brief and excavations on resurfacing of Market Street, NO 5092 1675

A watching brief and limited excavations by Rathmell Archaeology Ltd in 2011 on the resurfacing of Market Street located the foundations of the medieval tolbooth.

16. Site of Market Cross, NO 5091 1673

There appears to have been an organised market in St Andrews by 1144.[67] The original site of the cross appears to have been in North Street at its junction with North and South Castle Streets and it was then moved in the 1190s to Market Street.[68]

17. 1 Church Square watching brief, NO 5088 1666

Pottery, glass and other items from a deep deposit of black soil were reported to the Fife Archaeological Index in 1985. Human bone was also reported, but not seen.[69]

18. Holy Trinity Church, NO 5086 1665

This church was built by Bishop Wardlaw in 1410–12 to replace the parish church in the cathedral precinct. Only the tower, two west arches and some piers remain from the original medieval building. It was restored by MacGregor Chalmers in 1907–09.[70]

19. Logies Lane excavations, NO 5085 1662

Excavations by the Scottish Urban Archaeological Trust (SUAT) in 1991 located 101 articulated human skeletons belonging to the graveyard of Holy Trinity Church. The stone foundations of a building were recorded on the South Street frontage and five earlier street surfaces were revealed under the present road surface in South Street. Finds included much disarticulated human bone and the first reconstructable example of a medieval White Gritty cooking pot.[71]

---

[66] Simpson and Stevenson, *Historic St Andrews*, p. 9.
[67] Ibid., p. 6.
[68] Brooks and Whittington, pp. 278–95.
[69] E. V. W. Proudfoot, '1 Church Square, St Andrews', *DES* (1985), p. 15.
[70] G. Pride, *The Kingdom of Fife: An Illustrated Architectural Guide* (Edinburgh, 1990), p. 127.
[71] J. MacKenzie and C. J. Moloney, 'Medieval Development and the Cemetery of the Church of the Holy Trinity, Logies Lane, St Andrews', *TFAJ* 3 (1991), pp. 143–60.

Figure 9.4: Logies Lane pot. Virtually complete cooking vessel from excavations in Logies Lane in 1991.

20. Church Square excavations, NO 5088 1666
Excavations by Rathmell Archaeology Ltd in advance of the construction of a lift shaft base in the Hay-Fleming Library (also on the site of Holy Trinity Church cemetery) revealed 76 human burials, all of probable fifteenth-century date.[72]

21. 141 South Street watching brief, NO 5074 1656
A watching brief by the Fife Archaeological Index in 1990 recorded three blocked windows and a moulded architectural fragment.[73]

22. 129 South Street watching brief, NO 5082 1663
A watching brief by the Fife Archaeological Index in 1985 recorded 1 m of archaeological deposit above natural sand. Below c.0.4m of dirty brown sandy soil was a dark soil layer which appeared to be burned; at the base of this layer irregular cuts of plough furrows could be seen.[74]

Area 5 South Street/Queens Gardens/Kinness Burn/Abbey Street

Excavations to the south of the South Street frontage suggest that the survival of archaeological deposits is liable to be good. Fife Council Archaeologist

---

[72] T. Rees, D. Gordon and A. Matthews, 'Excavations within the Graveyard of the Holy Trinity, St Andrews', *TFAJ* 14 (2008), pp. 56–68.
[73] E. V. W. Proudfoot, '141 South Street, St Andrews', *DES* (1990), p. 15.
[74] E. V. W. Proudfoot, '129 South Street, St Andrews', *DES* (1985), p. 15.

Douglas Speirs' work at 52 South Street also suggests that traces of earlier, potentially medieval, buildings may still survive incorporated into later standing structures.

1. 78 South Street watching brief, NO 5092 1659
A watching brief by the Scottish Urban Archaeological Trust (SUAT) in 1986 located natural sand at 1.4m below modern ground level. This was sealed by garden soil; no archaeological evidence was noted.[75]

2. 72 South Street watching brief, NO 5095 1661
A watching brief by the Fife Archaeological Index in 1990 located no archaeological deposits.[76]

3. St Mary's College, NO 5097 1655
This was founded as a hall for secular clergy by Archbishop James Beaton in 1538. Building work took place over the next five years and involved Thomas French as master mason and the French masons coming from Falkland. The college's west range survives and parts of it may be original sixteenth-century work.[77]

4. 58 South Street, NO 5110 1655
This building dates to the sixteenth century but has been extensively modernised.[78]

5. 46 South Street, NO 5112 1655
This was built c.1600 for the Balfours of Mountquhanie and then remodelled in 1723 for the principal of St Mary's College.[79]

6. South Court, South Street, NO 5115 1653
The northern, eastern and southern ranges were built by the Lamond family in the late sixteenth century and the east range extended to the south c.1660 by George Martine.[80]

7. 36–38 South Street, NO 5117 1655
This is a large sixteenth-century tenement that was owned by Prior John Hepburn in 1521. It was restored in 1968–72.[81]

---

[75] D. W. Hall, '78 South Street, St Andrews', *DES* (1986), p. 9.
[76] E. V. W. Proudfoot, '72 South Street, St Andrews', *DES* (1990), p. 15.
[77] Gifford, *The Buildings of Scotland: Fife*, p. 374.
[78] Ibid., p. 401.
[79] Ibid.
[80] Ibid.
[81] Ibid.

8. 52 South Street excavations

Excavations in 2012 located a cess pit which took the form of a stone-lined well, approximately 1 m square on plan by 1.7m in depth. It originally lay in garden/rig ground behind the medieval street frontage building and may have been housed within a small wooden structure. However, when the street front property was extended to the rear in the fourteenth century, the toilet was abandoned, sealed and built over. Upon excavation it was found to contain a rich and varied assemblage of waste representing a snapshot of the last weeks and months of its use. The bones of cow, sheep, pig, chicken, goose, jackdaw, rabbit and rat were all found along with the skeleton of a complete adult cat and two kittens. Fish bones, oyster, periwinkle and crab were also present. Iron objects, fire ash, cat faeces and an assemblage of fourteenth-century pottery including one fragmented but whole (probably Yorkshire) jug, two partially complete north-eastern English jugs (probably from Scarborough), plus extensive parts of at least three further locally produced vessels were also recovered.

9. 106–110 South Street excavations, NO 5086 1648

Excavations by the Scottish Urban Archaeological Trust (SUAT) in advance of redevelopment of the backlands of these properties on South Street located the remains of a medieval stone building some 40m back from the South Street frontage; evidence was recovered to suggest that this may have had an industrial function.[82]

Area 6 North Castle Street/South Castle Street/Abbey Street/Abbey Walk/East Sands

This area includes the cathedral precinct and the bounds of Kilrimont. It includes the site of the castle, the cathedral, St Rules Tower, St Mary on the Rock and many other important sites. The potential of this area is self-evident from the number of surviving monuments and the excavations that have taken place. The northern half of the cathedral precinct and the site of the castle are scheduled and are therefore less at threat from development. The precinct walls, The Pends and the remains of St Mary's Church are also protected. The remainder of the precinct is not protected and, as has been proved by recent fieldwork (nos 40 and 42), any development in this area may have serious archaeological implications. The site of St Peter's Chapel lies in an area that may be prone to redevelopment and development proposals should be closely monitored. Any opportunity to further define the limits of Early Christian Kilrimont should also be taken.[83]

---

[82] R. Cachart, 'Excavations at 106–110 South Street, St Andrews', *TFAJ* 6 (2000), pp. 109–35.

[83] D. W. Hall, 'Pre-Burghal St Andrews: Towards an Archaeological Research Design', *TFAJ* 1 (1995), pp. 23–7.

1. Port in Scores, NO 5119 1690
This port stood in the Swallowgait (now The Scores) and was demolished in 1698.[84]

2. St Andrews Castle, NO 5128 1692
This castle was founded by Bishop Roger in 1200 as the residence of the bishop, and later archbishop, of the diocese. There is as yet no evidence for occupation of this site before the early thirteenth century although it cannot be discounted. The surviving buildings date almost entirely from the sixteenth century although they overlie and incorporate earlier structures.[85]

3. Castlecliffe excavations, NO 5124 1692
An excavation by Nicholas Bogdan in 1975 cut a section across the castle ditch. It was discovered to have been severely landscaped and produced no finds.[86]

4. St Andrews Castle excavations, NO 5120 1689
Excavations by John Lewis between 1988 and 1990 located a number of phases of activity. The earliest phase was a group of features cut into the natural sand, one of which contained sherds from a Bronze Age beaker. Sealing this Prehistoric activity was a soil deposit which was cut by numerous postholes, post pits and beam slots. These features are undated. The remains of two stone buildings aligned east–west were excavated close to the frontage of The Scores. Four large pits were also located but could not be stratigraphically linked with either the timber or the stone structures. A shallow robber trench running east–west was located, post-dating the two stone structures, and may indicate the line of a boundary wall depicted on Geddy's map.[87]

5. Mine and countermine at the castle, NO 5126 1688
Outside the ditch, to the south-east of the Fore Tower, is the entrance to a mine begun by the castle's besiegers in 1546. It runs for about 19m towards the tower. Immediately to the east of the tower is the countermine made by the defenders.[88]

6. 33 North Castle Street excavations, NO 5126 1679
Excavations by Nicholas Bogdan in 1974 located medieval pits that produced a small amount of medieval pottery.[89]

---

[84] Lamont Brown, *The Life and Times of St Andrews*, p. 64.
[85] Simpson and Stevenson, *Historic St Andrews*, p. 41.
[86] Hall, 'Other Work', p. 5.
[87] J. Lewis, 'Excavations at St Andrews, Castlecliffe 1988–90', *PSAS* 126 (1996), pp. 605–88.
[88] Gifford, *The Buildings of Scotland: Fife*, p. 121.
[89] Hall, 'Other Work', pp. 5, 6.

7. 25 North Castle Street watching brief, NO 5123 1675
A watching brief, restricted excavation and survey by the Fife Archaeological Index in 1991 located the foundations of the previous house on this site and several earlier floor levels. At c.0.8m below present floor level numerous features were recorded cut into the natural sand. No dating evidence was recovered from these.[90]

8. 29 North Street excavations, NO 5125 1676
Excavations by the Scottish Urban Archaeological Trust (SUAT) in 1987 revealed stratigraphy dated by pottery from no earlier than the fourteenth century. A group of large sub-rectangular postholes lying c.6m back from the street frontage may indicate a substantial timber building, but with no clear evidence of internal or external features or surfaces.[91]

9. 25 North Street watching brief, NO 5126 1674
A watching brief by the Scottish Urban Archaeological Trust (SUAT) in 1991 recorded garden soil to a depth of 0.75 m. No archaeological deposits were recorded.[92]

10. Site of St Peter's Chapel, NO 5133 1681
It is claimed that documentary evidence suggests the existence of a chapel of St Peter in the Gregory Place area.[93] It is referred to as a 'capella' in the *Liber cartarum prioratus sancti Andreae*.[94] In the late nineteenth century several tons of hewn stones including pillar fragments were discovered in the garden of 3 North Street and Hay Fleming identified them as relating to St Peter's.[95] Several stone cists orientated east–west were found in the same garden and may represent a burial ground associated with the chapel.

11. 13–15 South Castle Street watching brief, NO 5120 1672
A watching brief by the Scottish Urban Archaeological Trust (SUAT) in 1994 recorded garden soil overlying a clay-bonded stone wall. This wall appears to represent a property boundary of modern date.[96]

12. 12 North Street trial excavations, NO 5125 1674
Trial excavations by the Fife Archaeological Index in 1992 located subsoil at a depth of c.0.95 m. Pottery of various dates, bottle and window glass, bone,

---

[90] E. V. W. Proudfoot, '25 North Castle Street, St Andrews', *DES* (1991), p. 23.
[91] P. R. Clark, 'North Street', Rains and Hall, *Excavations*, pp. 35–9.
[92] D. W. Hall, '25 North Street, St Andrews', *DES* (1991), p. 25.
[93] U. Hall, *St Andrew and Scotland* (St Andrews,1994), p. 57.
[94] *Liber cartarum prioratus sancti Andreae*, ed. T. Thomson (Bannatyne Club, 1841), pp. 284–5.
[95] David Hay Fleming, *Howkings in St Andrews Cathedral and its Precincts in 1904* (1904).
[96] J. MacKenzie, '13–15 South Castle Street, St Andrews', *DES* (1994), p. 21.

stone slates and a piece of grey pantile were found.[97] Further excavations in 1993 located a double pit dug into the natural sand. Its fill contained a shallow bronze bowl of uncertain purpose and quantities of animal bone and medieval pottery.[98]

13. Deans Court, NO 5132 1670
It has been suggested that the vaulted core of this building was part of the first archdeacon's house in the twelfth century. The house was acquired and remodelled by George Douglas in the sixteenth century.[99]

14. 1 South Street, NO 5130 1665
The front block of this building, known as The Roundel, probably dates to the sixteenth century. Parts of the remainder may be seventeenth-century remodelling.[100]

15. 7-9 South Castle Street excavations, NO 5120 1669
Excavations by the Scottish Urban Archaeological Trust (SUAT) in 1989 located evidence of continuous occupation in the later post-medieval period. Earlier features were sparse and badly disturbed by modern services.[101]

16. Abbey Street excavations, NO 5120 1664
Excavations in 1970 located the remains of a timber-founded medieval house on the South Street frontage. From the excavated ground plan it would seem that its northern gable faced the street.[102] The excavator suggested that this building could belong to one Adam Fitzodo and was built c.1180.

17. Queen Mary's House, NO 5128 1662
This building dates to the sixteenth century and was originally built to a U-plan. It contains sixteenth-century oak panelling in one of its second floor rooms.[103]

18. Queen Mary's House excavations, NO 5125 1662
Excavations by Nicholas Bogdan in 1974 located pits and ditches dated to the twelfth and thirteenth centuries by the pottery from their fills. Below these features ploughmarks were revealed in the natural subsoil.[104]

---

[97] Proudfoot, '12 North Street', p. 31.
[98] Ibid., p. 31.
[99] Pride, *The Kingdom of Fife*, p. 129.
[100] Gifford, *The Buildings of Scotland: Fife*, p. 399.
[101] A. Cox, 'South Castle Street', Rains and Hall, *Excavations*, pp. 31-4.
[102] N. P. Brooks, 'Urban Archaeology in Scotland', *European Towns their Archaeology and Early History*, ed. M. W. Barley (London, 1977), p. 28, fig. 2d.
[103] Gifford, *The Buildings of Scotland: Fife*, p. 399.
[104] Hall, 'Other Work', pp. 5, 6.

19. Byre Theatre, Abbey Street

Excavations by Headland Archaeology Ltd in advance of the extension of the Byre Theatre in 1998 located good surviving archaeological deposits associated with buildings on the Abbey Street frontage. An important group of medieval ceramic building material was recovered from one of the excavated pits.[105]

20. The Pends, NO 5132 1665

This served as the gateway to the Augustinian priory and dates to the fourteenth century.[106]

21. Cathedral and priory, NO 5142 1662

The cathedral church and priory of St Andrews is a successor to the adjacent church of St Regulus. The cathedral church was founded in 1160 but not consecrated until 1318. After the Reformation the cathedral was allowed to decay and is shown as roofless on Geddy's map.[107] St Andrews was one of only two cathedrals with a monastic foundation attached, the other being at Whithorn. The priory at St Andrews was under the control of the Augustinian canons.[108]

22. Cathedral Priory excavations, NO 514 166

Excavations by Historic Buildings and Monuments in 1987 were carried out to examine drainage in the cloister alley. Within the excavated areas no evidence of medieval occupation survived previous investigations.[109]

23. Site of Holy Trinity Church, NO 5147 1668

This is the original site of the parish church before it was moved to South Street in 1412. The earliest mention of this church is in an undated charter of Malcolm IV (1153–65) which records its transfer to Matthew, archdeacon of St Andrews. Hay Fleming located its probable position by recording the location of foundations identified in grave digging operations.[110]

24. Findspot of bowl and cover, NO 5144 1663

These were found in grave-digging operations in the late nineteenth century between the tower of St Rule's Church and the southern corner of the east gable of the cathedral. These objects lay at a depth of 5 feet (1.70m) below modern ground level in association with two fragments of Celtic cross slab. Comparison with an Irish example found in association with the Ardagh chalice suggests a date not later than the tenth century.[111]

---

[105] Moloney and Baker, 'Evidence for the Form and Nature of a Medieval Burgage Plot in St Andrews', pp. 49–85.
[106] Simpson and Stevenson, *Historic St Andrews*, p. 10.
[107] Ibid.
[108] Cowan and Easson, *Medieval Religious Houses*, p. 96.
[109] Hall, 'Other Work', p. 6.
[110] Simpson and Stevenson, *Historic St Andrews*, p. 28.
[111] Ibid., p. 19.

25. St Regulus' (St Rule's) Church, NO 5146 1662
The true date of this building remains the subject of some debate. On the literary evidence it was probably built between 1127 and 1144.[112] It may originally have been built to house the relics of the apostle Andrew and it has been claimed that it would also have served as a landmark for pilgrims.[113] It was superseded by the cathedral.

26. St Rule's Tower excavations, NO 5146 1662
A small trial excavation by Nicholas Bogdan in 1976 was carried out in advance of the reconstruction of the internal stair tower. A wall was discovered on an east–west alignment just to the north of the existing inner south wall of the tower associated with a floor level. These features post-dated an excavation of considerable size which had been cut into the boulder-filled foundations.[114]

27. Findspot of sarcophagus, NO 5149 1665
The remains of this important sculptured sarcophagus/altar tomb were discovered in 1833 during the excavation of a deep grave near St Rule's Church. The central fragment is decorated with a scene of the biblical King David struggling with a lion in the midst of a hunting scene. It has been dated to the eighth or ninth century and may have formerly held the relics of St Andrew.[115]

28. Site of St Magdalene's Chapel, NO 5146 1659
This stood on the south side of St Rule's Tower.[116] In 1911 part of a column base was recovered during grave-digging operations and was identified by Hay Fleming as part of this chapel.[117]

29. Site of Shore Port, NO 5147 1671
This port stood beside the north gate of the cathedral precinct. It is shown in different positions by Geddy (c.1580) and Gordon (1642), and the excavations at Kirkhill (see below) failed to locate it.

30. Kirkhill watching brief, NO 515 166
A watching brief by the Fife Archaeological Index located two skeletons from the early Christian cemetery at Kirkhill eroding from the cliff. The bones, which were in a poor condition, were in shallow graves dug in light gravel.[118]

---

[112] S. Cruden, *St Andrews Cathedral* (Edinburgh, 1986), p. 9 ; N. M. Cameron, 'St Rule's Church, St Andrews, and Early Stone-built Churches in Scotland', *PSAS* 124 (1994), pp. 367–74.
[113] Gifford, *The Buildings of Scotland: Fife*, p. 359.
[114] Hall, 'Other Work', pp. 5, 6.
[115] Cruden, *St Andrews Cathedral*, p. 29; *The St Andrews Sarcophagus: A Pictish Masterpiece and its International Connections*, ed. S. M. Foster (Dublin, 1998).
[116] Simpson and Stevenson, *Historic St Andrews*, p. 12.
[117] Fleming, 'Howkings in St Andrews Cathedral and Graveyard', p. 38.
[118] E. V. W. Proudfoot. 'Kirkhill, St Andrews', *DES* (1976), p. 33.

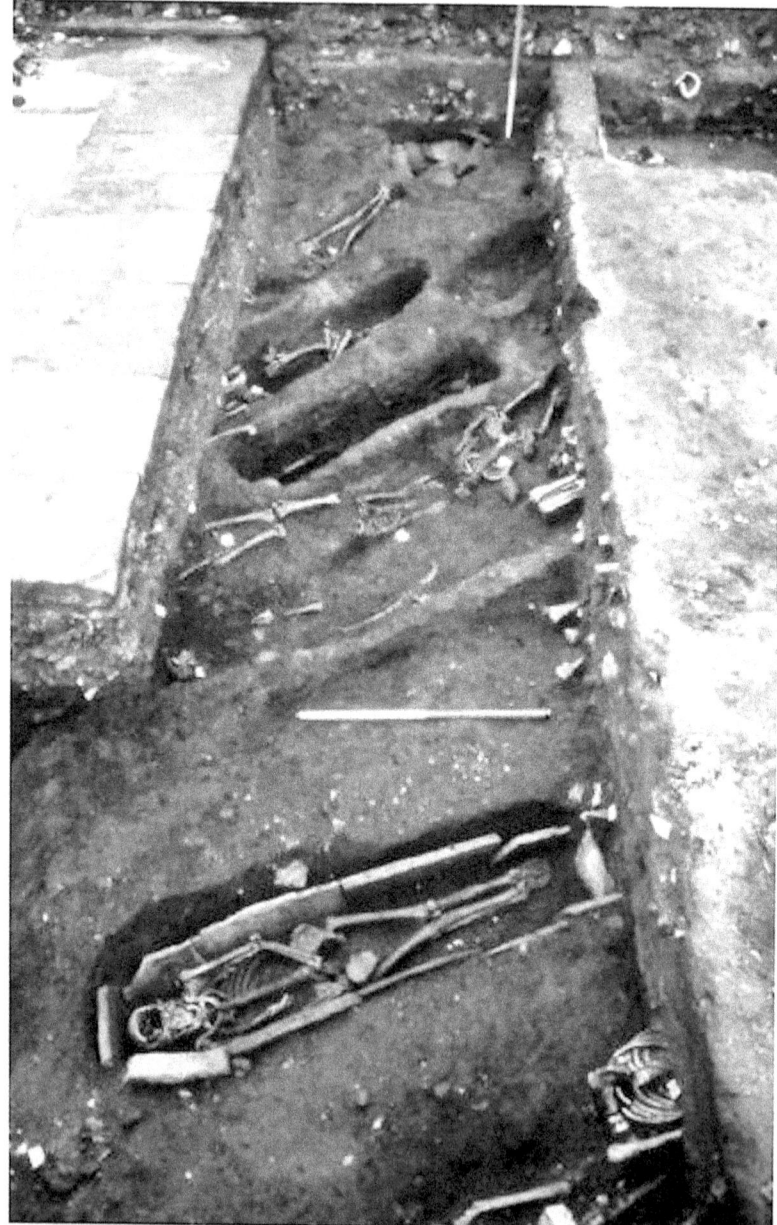

Figure 9.5: Kirkhill cists. General view of excavation of Early Christian long cists on Kirkhill in 1980 looking north.

31. Kirkhill watching brief, NO 515 166
Another grave from the early Christian cemetery was recorded in 1978 weathering out from the cliff.[119]

32. Kirkhill watching brief, NO 5151 1668
A short stretch of cobble edge and a large flat sandstone slab were recorded in 1979 in the path between the cathedral precinct wall and the cliff, west of St Mary on the Rock.[120]

33. Kirkhill excavations, NO 515 166
An excavation by the Urban Archaeology Unit (UAU) in 1980 was undertaken in advance of cliff consolidation. Two nineteenth-century gun platforms were exposed that had been cut into a cemetery. Over 300 skeletons of both sexes were uncovered and carbon dates suggest that the cemetery was first used in the ninth century AD. Apart from one wooden coffin and three stone long cists, all the burials were simple inhumations. Beneath the early medieval cemetery six crouched burials were discovered, three of them in short cists.[121]

34. Church of St Mary on the Rock, NO 5158 1666
The ruins of this church date to the twelfth and thirteenth centuries although it may occupy the site of a much earlier Culdee church. It was raised to the status of Chapel Royal in the thirteenth century.[122] The visible foundations were exposed in 1860 as a consequence of the construction of Napoleonic gun platforms on the cliff top. Its north transept was exposed and recorded in the excavations of 1980 (no. 33 above).

35. St Mary on the Rock watching brief, NO 515 166
Human bones and worked stones were recorded in 1984 during the laying of a gas main close to the remains of the church of St Mary on the Rock.[123]

36. St Mary on the Rock watching brief, NO 515 166
A watching brief by the Scottish Urban Archaeological Trust (SUAT) in 1987 on a new lighting trench observed demolition rubble below c.0.3m of topsoil and recovered some fragments of disarticulated human bone.[124]

37. The harbour, NO 5163 1665
A fishing harbour is on record from 1222 and it grew up in the shadow of the wall of the priory precinct. St Andrews appears to have always had a low status

---

[119] N. Q. Bogdan, 'Kirkhill, St Andrews', *DES* (1978), p. 7.
[120] Proudfoot, 'Kirkhill, St Andrews', p. 9.
[121] J. Wordsworth and P. R. Clark, 'Kirkhill', Rains and Hall, *Excavations*, pp. 7–16.
[122] Simpson and Stevenson, *Historic St Andrews*, p. 11.
[123] E. V. W. Proudfoot, 'St Mary on the Rock, St Andrews', *DES* (1984), p. 9.
[124] Hall, 'Other Work', p. 6.

as an overseas trading port. This appears, in part, to be due to the unsuitability of the harbour for handling large vessels. The Exchequer Rolls shows that goods were landed at Dundee and Inverkeithing and then carried overland to the burgh.[125]

38. St Leonard's Chapel and Hospital, NO 5126 1660
This hospital was formerly under Culdee control until 1144 when Bishop Robert assigned it to the Augustinian canons and endowed it for the reception of visitors and pilgrims.[126] Until 1248 it is referred to as the hospital of St Andrews but thereafter as St Leonard's. The chapel is the only surviving relic of this institution and has been the subject of many alterations.[127] Since 1881 the area and buildings have been the site of St Leonard's School.

39. St Leonard's Chapel watching brief, NO 5126 1660
A watching brief by the Scottish Urban Archaeological Trust (SUAT) and the Fife Archaeological Index in 1986 located two wall foundations c.0.2m below modern ground level and a paving stone c.0.4m below modern ground level. Medieval pottery and animal bone were recovered from the soil adjacent to the first wall. The wall was probably part of the original frontage of the chapel.[128]

40. Site of Abbey Guest Hall, NO 5135 1659
This building was erected during the first half of the thirteenth century and the remains of its eastern end wall are still visible in the playground of St Leonard's School. Its wall foundations were recorded in a watching brief (see no. 41). This building is shown on Geddy's map.[129]

41. St Leonard's School watching brief, NO 5133 1659
A watching brief by the Scottish Urban Archaeological Trust (SUAT) in 1985 located the foundations of a demolished stone building. 271 pieces from bell moulds were discovered inside this structure. The stone building located was almost certainly part of the Abbot's Guest Hall of the Augustinian Priory.[130]

42. Findspot of St Leonard's Shrine, NO 5139 1655
This was discovered in 1895 during the clearance of the site of St Rule's East. The shrine is cut from pale sandstone and decorated with three rows of splayed tegulae. It lay amongst forty stone cists containing human remains which were located to the east of the old gateway into the 'hospice'. It has been dated to the eleventh century.[131]

---

[125] Simpson and Stevenson, *Historic St Andrews*, p. 44.
[126] Cowan and Easson, *Medieval Religious Houses*, p. 190.
[127] Gifford, *The Buildings of Scotland: Fife*, p. 386.
[128] Hall, 'Other Work', p. 6.
[129] Simpson and Stevenson, *Historic St Andrews*, p. 10.
[130] D. W. Hall, 'St Leonard's School', Rains and Hall, *Excavations*, p. 30.
[131] Simpson and Stevenson, *Historic St Andrews*, p. 19.

43. St Leonard's School excavations, NO 5145 1653
Excavations by the Scottish Urban Archaeological Trust (SUAT) in 1990 located a ditch running north–south with a paved path running along its eastern side. To the east of the path lay the collapsed remains of a stone wall. No dating evidence was recovered. These features were sealed by deep deposits of garden soil. At the southern edge of the site the remains of a stone-built culvert possibly relating to the Abbey Mill pond were located.[132]

44. Mill Port, NO 5159 1652
This stands at the south-east end of The Pends and leads out to the harbour. It dates from the sixteenth century.[133]

45. St Leonard's School excavations, NO 514 165
Rescue excavations in 1970 by Nick Brooks recorded the fragmentary remains of three long-cist burials that were disturbed by building work.[134]

46. Site of Abbey Mill and dam, NO 5130 1650
The school building called St Katherine's stands on the site of the Abbey Mill. The mill is visible on Geddy's map and is still present on the Ordnance Survey map of 1895. The mill dam lay directly to the west of the mill in an area that is now the garden of The Hospice. The outline of the mill pond can be traced in existing garden features. Excavations in advance of an extension to The Hospice located part of the mill race (see no. 43 above).

47. Abbey precinct wall, NO 5134 1673 to NO 5160 1630 to NO 5134 1673
The priory precinct was first surrounded by a wall in the fourteenth century. In the early sixteenth century the wall was reconstructed by Priors John and Patrick Hepburn and most of their work still survives.[135] The precinct wall encloses an area of c.34 acres (14 ha) and of the sixteen towers recorded by Martine in 1683, only thirteen are now visible.[136]

48. Teinds Yett and barn, NO 5151 1639
This gateway leads out on to Abbey Walk and served the teinds (Tithe) barns which stood behind it within the precinct.[137] It dates to the sixteenth century.

---

[132] D. P. Bowler, 'St Leonard's School, St Andrews', *DES* (1990), p. 15.
[133] Pride, *The Kingdom of Fife*, p. 121.
[134] Hall, 'Other Work', p. 5.
[135] Gifford, *The Buildings of Scotland: Fife*, p. 367.
[136] Simpson and Stevenson, *Historic St Andrews*, p. 32.
[137] Gifford, *The Buildings of Scotland: Fife*, p. 367.

Area 7 Kinness Burn/Woodburn Terrace/Arbitrary line to west of Priestden Place/Arbitrary line to south of Priestden Road/East Sands

This area lies outside the burgh to the south-east and includes the site of the Leper Hospital of the Blessed Nicholas and a major prehistoric bronze hoard. The construction of the East Sands leisure complex effectively destroyed a considerable part of the leper hospital.[138] Elements of the later poor's hospital on the site were located in the excavations of 1997 (see no. 5 below). The discovery of the bronze hoard serves to indicate, as with Area 1, that unexpected prehistoric finds are liable to be discovered.

1. East Sands watching brief, NO 5185 1615
A watching brief by the Scottish Urban Archaeological Trust (SUAT) in 1987 located ploughsoil c.0.85m deep above natural sand. Nothing relating to the Leper Hospital of St Nicholas was located.[139]

2. Site of Leper Hospital of St Nicholas, NO 5157 1570
The foundation date of this institution is unknown but the first documentary reference to it is of twelfth-century date. From the available documentary evidence it appears to have been under secular control although it is not unlikely that the Augustinian canons were involved at some stage. In later references it is described as a poors' hospital, which may imply that leprosy was no longer such a problem. Its desertion date is also not known and there is reference to it in 1583.[140] Excavations in advance of the construction of the East Sands Leisure Centre have suggested that the complex occupied at least 2 acres.

3. St Nicholas Farm excavations, NO 5175 1585
Excavations by the Scottish Urban Archaeological Trust (SUAT) in 1986/87 located the eastern and western boundary walls of the Leper Hospital of St Nicholas. A blocked-up doorway was located in the western boundary wall which then had a multi-phase stone building constructed against it. In its final phase this building had a subcircular extension built against its southern end that may have been a bread oven.[141] Archaeological deposits below this structure produced fragments of disarticulated human bone which have been radiocarbon dated to 1530–1310 BC, AD 530–660, AD 130–390 and AD 430–650 respectively. These results may suggest the presence of an earlier graveyard on the hospital site.

---

[138] Hall, 'Archaeological Excavations at St Nicholas Farm', pp. 48–75.
[139] Hall, 'Other Work', p. 6.
[140] Cowan and Easson, *Medieval Religious Houses*, p. 190.
[141] Hall, 'Archaeological Excavations at St Nicholas Farm', pp. 48–75.

4. St Nicholas farmland trial excavations, NO 5170 1580
Trial excavations by the Scottish Urban Archaeological Trust (SUAT) in 1993 located further stretches of the leper hospital's western boundary wall and signs of extra-mural activity, apparently medieval in date.[142]

5. Further excavations at St Nicholas Farm, NO 518 158
An excavation was carried out prior to a housing development adjacent to the site of the medieval Leper Hospital of St Nicholas, in February and March 1997. Previous investigations had established the location of the precinct of the hospital under the car park of the East Sands Leisure Centre and the presence of possible extra-mural settlement further west in the field adjacent to the sewage treatment centre. The remains of a large structure, defined by a substantial drystone wall, 0.87m thick, on a WSW–ENE alignment and including a series of stratified decomposed organic layers and cobbled surfaces, were recorded. Green-glazed pottery, dating to the sixteenth century, was recovered from the foundation trench of this structure, immediately adjacent to the course of the St Nicholas Burn. At a later stage another slightly less substantial wall was constructed. These structures may belong to the redevelopment of the leper hospital in the sixteenth or seventeenth centuries. The partial remains of a cobbled surface, on the same alignment as the medieval Crail Road, also identified in previous work, were also recorded. This represented the only medieval activity apparent south of the present sewage works. A watching brief was carried out during topsoil stripping of the entire development area. In addition to several modern pits and animal burials, a heavily disturbed isolated long-cist burial was discovered and recorded. No human skeletal remains survived. No evidence of activity belonging to the earlier phase of the site, relating to the leper hospital, was recovered.[143]

6. St Nicholas Farm watching brief and excavation, NO 519 159
A watching brief and small excavation by St Andrews Heritage Services in 1994 located possible fragments of the eastern and southern precinct walls of the leper hospital.[144]

7. St Andrews Interceptor Sewer Pipeline watching brief, NO 516 153 to NO 516 155 to NO 519 159
A watching brief by St Andrews Heritage Services in 1994 located no archaeological remains.[145]

---

[142] C. J. Moloney, 'St Nicholas Farmland, St Andrews', *DES* (1993), p. 31.
[143] J. Hamilton and R. Toolis, 'Further Excavations at the Site of a Medieval Leper Hospital at St Nicholas Farm, St Andrews', *TFAJ* 5 (1999), pp. 87–105.
[144] Proudfoot, 'St Nicholas Farm, St Andrews', p. 21.
[145] E. V. W. Proudfoot, 'St Andrews Interceptor Sewer, St Andrews', *DES* (1994), p. 20.

8. Former line of Crail–St Andrews Road, NO 5200 1580

It appears that in the recent past the St Andrews to Crail road ran closer to the sea than it does now. This roadway is visible in Slezer's seventeenth-century view of St Andrews and is described by Henry: 'In those days the coast road left St Andrews by a route much further east than it does now.'[146] It seems likely that this was the pilgrims' route to St Andrews and that the blocked-up doorway located in the western boundary of the leper hospital led to it (see no. 3 above). Further excavations at St Nicholas Farm in 1997 (see no. 5 above) located possible fragments of this road line.

9. 18 Priestden Place, discovery of bronze hoard, NO 5135 1578

Excavations for a new house extension in 1990 located a substantial bronze hoard. The hoard included socketed axes, spearheads, knives, gouges and chisels, part of a sword, a scabbard, swan's neck sunflower head pins, bronze tweezers, many bronze rings and bracelets and three jet bracelets, beads and miscellaneous fragments. While this hoard is significant for its range and number of items, approximately dating to the ninth to eighth centuries BC, the presence of the remains of wooden handles, leather and cloth container fragments and string is particularly significant for interpretation of certain items and their use in this and other hoards.[147]

10. 18 Priestden Place excavations, NO 5135 1578

A small excavation by the Fife Archaeological Index in 1992 was undertaken immediately adjacent to the area where the bronze hoard (see no. 9) was found but no further traces were recovered.[148]

---

[146] D. Henry, *The Knights of St John with Other Medieval Institutions and their Buildings in St Andrews* (St Andrews, 1912), p. 196.
[147] E. V. W. Proudfoot, '18 Priestden Place, St Andrews', *DES* (1990), p. 16.
[148] E. V. W. Proudfoot, '18 Priestden Place, St Andrews', *DES* (1992), p. 31.

CHAPTER TEN

Prelates, Citizens and Landed Folk: St Andrews as a Centre of Lordship in the Late Middle Ages

Michael H. Brown

ON 19 January 1435 the hall of the prior's house in St Andrews Cathedral Priory was the setting for a ceremony. James Kinninmonth had presented his claim as heir to his father, who had died a month earlier. He sought legal possession of the family's ancestral lands at Kinninmonth, which lay 7 miles west of St Andrews, from the superiors of this property, the prior and canons of St Andrews Cathedral. These rights had been confirmed in the prior's court by an inquisition of fifteen 'noble and trustworthy men' from the local area. 'In the face of the whole court' James 'publically performed, made and solemnly swore a bodily oath of homage and fealty touching the Holy Gospels' to the prior as head of the cathedral community. In response, Prior James Haldenstone invested his kneeling vassal in the lands by a red staff held by his sergeant. The bailie, in charge of administering the priory's estates, then presented James Kinninmonth with sealed letters which promised the recipient full possession of his lands. This formal occasion took place before a gathering of impressive size. Present were the canons of the cathedral, other clergy, leading citizens of St Andrews, the sheriff of Fife, and local landowners numbered at 'around a hundred honest persons' by the record of the gathering.[1]

The record of this event, preserved in the letter book of Prior Haldenstone, provides a vivid account of the holding of his court. Describing the ceremony of homage and investiture, which were fundamental acts of landholding and social hierarchy across medieval Europe, it demonstrated that, amongst the numerous roles played by St Andrews in the Middle Ages, the city was also a centre of lordship. Alongside their spiritual and pastoral authority and duties, the great ecclesiastical charges and corporations of St Andrews were holders of wide earthly

---

[1] *Copiale*, pp. 111–14, no. 62. The Kinninmonth family had held 'Kynninmonth with its whole shire' by grant of the prior and convent of St Andrews since the twelfth century in connection with their role as hereditary stewards of the cathedral canons. See G. W. S. Barrow, 'The Early Charters of the Family of Kinninmonth of that ilk', *The Study of Medieval Records*, ed. D. A. Bullough and R. L. Storey (Oxford, 1971), nos 4, 7, 11. A second inquest for investing James Kinninmonth was held for lands near Lochore in west Fife at Cupar before the sheriff in May 1435: NLS, Ch. no. 9324.

rights.² In contrast to most of Scotland, in eastern Fife such baronial powers were overwhelmingly in the hands of ecclesiastical lords. The sixteenth-century Black Book of St Andrews recorded a ruling of the king's justiciars from 1309 which named three baronies within the *Cursus Apri*, the Boar's Raik.³ This was the territory around St Andrews which legend stated had been gifted to the church at its foundation. In it, baronial rights were held by the prior and canons, by the community of clerics in St Mary's Church (the former Culdee house) and by the bishop.⁴ The bishop's barony and its court held authority over the other two, reflecting the tradition that the priory and St Mary's had both received their property from the bishop.⁵ The prior of the cathedral and the provost of St Mary's were subject to the bishop's temporal lordship and cases could be appealed from their courts to that of their superior.⁶

The scale and scope of the bishop's temporal lordship was stated and extended in the so-called 'Golden Charter'. This grant from King James II to Bishop James Kennedy in June 1452 was made

> in praise of God and to the glory of his blessed mother, and to the honour of all saints, and especially of the blessed Andrew, brother of the chief of the apostles [and] patron of our kingdom; and for the exaltation and solace of the church of St Andrews, and the comfort and especial support of its prelates, the bishops.

The gift was also made in thanks for the birth of the king's first-born son in St Andrews Castle, 'the place and chief messuage of our same patron'. The charter confirmed the temporal properties of the bishop as 'one [...] free and special regality'. Within this private jurisdiction, the bishops possessed full powers of justice, even over the four pleas of the crown; robbery, rape, arson and murder. The charter also prevented the bishops' tenants between Forth and Tay from being brought before courts other than that of the bishops. The regality was also exempted from royal financial demands and services. While these liberties were broad, even by Scottish standards, James II also incorporated a long list of other episcopal estates into this regality of St Andrews.⁷ As well as the Boar's Raik, these possessions were spread more widely through the East Neuk of Fife and across the north and west of the sheriffdom. Even more striking was the inclusion of more distant estates, the Bishopshire, the area round Loch Leven, and

---

² For other examples C. D. Liddy, *The Bishopric of Durham in the Late Middle Ages* (Woodbridge, 2008); F. R. H. Du Boulay, *The Lordship of Canterbury* (London, 1966).
³ NRS, B65/23/4.
⁴ G. W. S. Barrow, 'The Cathedral Chapter of St Andrews and the Culdees in the Twelfth and Thirteenth Centuries', *Journal of Ecclesiastical History* 3 (1952), pp. 23–39.
⁵ Ash, 'The Administration', pp. 199–211.
⁶ The closest, well-studied parallel for St Andrews would seem to be the neighbouring (though cross-border) diocese of Durham. See Liddy, *Bishopric*; R. B. Dobson, *Durham Priory 1400–1450* (Cambridge, 1973); M. Threlfall-Jones, *Monks and Markets: Durham Cathedral Priory 1450–1520* (Oxford, 2005).
⁷ *RMS*, ii, no. 1444; *RPS*, 1479/10/12. The charter was confirmed by James III to Archbishop William Scheves in 1479 (the earlier grant is preserved within the text of the confirmation).

Muckhartshire in the Ochils, and the lands of Pittenweem Priory in this regality. Though the episcopal properties in Angus, in Aberdeenshire, at Tyninghame in Lothian and at Stow in Berwickshire remained separate, the charter extended the temporal power of the bishops at a time when the crown was bringing similar wide, private jurisdictions under royal control.[8]

The estates of the cathedral priory and the rights of the canons over these lands were a smaller version of the bishops' temporalities. As Elizabeth Rhodes has shown, the cathedral canons possessed property in eight burghs and were lords of numerous tenements in St Andrews. Within the Boar's Raik, the core lands of the regality of St Andrews, the prior and community possessed eighteen properties including the Priory Acres, a swathe of holdings to the south of the city. All these were held under the superiority of the bishop. In addition St Andrews Priory held other estates in the East Neuk and central Fife and in Angus, Aberdeenshire and Lothian.[9]

Like secular magnates, both the bishops and the priors relied on a network of officers and servants to run these estates. There seems to have been little change in the titles and duties of these men and the organisation of the temporalities between the fourteenth and sixteenth centuries. The financial accounts rendered for the lands of the bishop in 1328 following the death of Bishop William Lamberton and the evidence of the rentals for 1538–41 indicate clear continuity.[10] The rentals include salaries paid to bailies in the major detached estates of Monymusk and Keig in Aberdeenshire, and in Muckhartshire and Bishopshire (which were grouped together), and there are records of bailies operating in the episcopal estates in Angus.[11] South of the Forth, there were sergeants responsible for the bishops' courts in Kirkliston, Tyninghame and Stow. The same officers were also employed in the core estates. The rental records sergeants of Boarhills (Byrehills), Dairsie, Monimail and Scotscraig on the Tay, possibly supervised by the mair of Fife.[12] This arrangement of estates fitted in with the lands providing the bulk of rents and food renders in the rental and with the known episcopal houses. *Scotichronicon* gives a list of these residences which includes Inchmurdoch (at Boarhills), Dairsie and Monimail in Fife, and Muckhart, Kirkliston, Monymusk and Stow further afield.[13]

During the mid fourteenth century, when St Andrews Castle was in ruins, the

---

[8] A. Grant, 'Franchises North of the Border: Baronies and Regalities in Medieval Scotland', *Liberties and Identities in the Medieval British Isles*, ed. M. Prestwich (Woodbridge, 2008), pp. 155–99.
[9] E. S. G. Rhodes, 'The Estates of St Andrews Cathedral Priory, 1400–1450' (unpublished M.Litt dissertation, University of St Andrews, 2009).
[10] *ER*, i, pp. 109–10; *Rentale*, pp. 3–23.
[11] *History of the Carnegies, Earls of Southesk*, ed. W. Fraser, 2 vols (Edinburgh, 1867), nos 63, 66; NRS, GD45/27/80.
[12] *Rentale*, pp. 91–2.
[13] *Scotichronicon*, iii, p. 401.

normal residence of the bishops seems to have been Inchmurdoch.[14] Following the rebuilding of the castle by Bishop Walter Trail in the 1390s, the bishops and their households returned to their palace.[15] During the fifteenth and early sixteenth centuries the bishops and archbishops based their residence and administration in 'the place and chief messuage' of St Andrews Castle.[16] As well as the plentiful evidence of its role as a fortress palace in the rentals of 1538–43, there are scattered references to its function as a centre of temporal administration in the preceding century.[17] For example in July 1427 Bishop Henry Wardlaw's council met in the castle to arbitrate in a dispute over lands in Spott in East Lothian, while in March 1446 a resignation of lands held from Bishop Kennedy in Angus was made in the close of the castle of St Andrews.[18] It is reasonable to assume that the regality court of the bishops, at which his tenants were bound to appear, was also normally held in the castle. The holding of this court was the responsibility of the steward, who was the principal secular officer. An example of the steward fulfilling this role occurred in 1490 when an inquest of the archbishop's tenants before Henry Scheves, steward of the regality of St Andrews, recognised James Trail as heir to the lands of Blebo west of St Andrews.[19] More frequent were references to the stewards' role in formally giving sasine of lands to the tenants of the bishops, a function performed by the bailies in outlying areas.[20] There are two references in spring 1449 to the existence of a justiciar of the bishop. Both involved the holding of a perambulation of the boundaries between estates, and the justiciar, Alan Stewart, was also the steward by 1453, suggesting the two offices were closely related.[21] Lesser secular servants employed by the bishops and archbishops were the marshal, who was also referred to as master of the stable, and the constable and captain of St Andrews Castle, responsible for the running of the bishop's residence.[22]

In both the early fourteenth-century account and the rental of 1538–43 the chief financial officer of the bishops and archbishops was the chamberlain. These records were primarily the audit of the income and expenses managed by the officers. In 1328 there were separate chamberlains north and south of Forth and, while this was also the case in 1395, by the 1420s and 1430s Bishop Wardlaw seems to have employed a single chamberlain and the rental shows

---

[14] *Scotichronicon*, vii, pp. 330–1; *Memorials of the Family of Wemyss of Wemyss*, ed. W. Fraser, 2 vols (Edinburgh, 1888), ii, no. 22.
[15] *Scotichronicon*, iii, p. 409.
[16] Bishops Trail and Wardlaw both died in the castle while their predecessors had died in the cathedral priory, *Scotichronicon*, iii, pp. 405, 411.
[17] *Rentale*, pp. 58–9, 103, 121, 122, 222–4.
[18] *Southesk*, nos 66–7; NRS RH6/275. The charter issued by Kennedy the following day was simply placed at St Andrews and it can be assumed that this and other acts of the bishops were actually issued from the castle.
[19] NRS, GD7/1/3.
[20] NRS, GD7/1/1; GD20/1/11, 17, 18; *Southesk*, no. 33.
[21] StAUL UYSLL 110/C/1; NLS, 34.6.24 135v.
[22] *Southesk*, no. 66; *RMS*, ii, no. 244; NRS, GD18/419; GD82/44.

just one chief financial officer in the 1530s.²³ It is harder to find evidence for the writing office of the bishops and archbishops. A reference exists to the chancery of Archbishop William Scheves in 1491 but the names of chancellors or secretaries are largely absent, though there are numerous clerical witnesses to episcopal charters who could have fulfilled this role.²⁴ In terms of the running of the temporality, the most prominent ecclesiastical figure was the official of the diocese, responsible as the bishop's deputy in his consistory court. The overlap of temporal and ecclesiastical jurisdictions probably explains the frequent involvement of the official in dealings between the bishops and the tenants of the regality.²⁵

The other prelates of St Andrews similarly appointed officials to run their estates. Though the priors appointed a chamberlain, almoner, pittancer and terrar (an officer dealing with priory estates) from within the cathedral community, like the bishops they also relied on laymen to administer the property of the house.²⁶ A commission appointing a bailie for the estates of the priory both inside and outside the city of St Andrews indicates the duties of the post in the 1430s and can probably be applied to the functions of episcopal bailies. In these letters the prior gave the bailie

> our full power and authority special and general for the letting of lands, the raising of fermes and *cain*, for holding our courts, levying amercements and escheats [...] attaching our men and their servants with their goods [...] to our court [...] and those things which are known to pertain to the office.²⁷

Such terms spelled out the way in which local lordship over land and justice was exercised across late medieval Scotland. While the letter book of Prior Haldenstone reveals the management of the priory's property in the early fifteenth century via the holding of courts, leasing of lands and appointment of officials, there is similar evidence of the bishops and archbishops acting in the same roles.²⁸ In 1498 Archbishop James Stewart arbitrated in a dispute over the lands of Struthers in Fife.²⁹ In 1506 his successor, Alexander Stewart, exploited his powers as lord by granting the relief, mails and profits of Cragtoun in Aberdeenshire while they had been in the archbishops' hands due

---

23 *ER*, i, 109–10; NLS, Adv MSS 34.6.24, 141r; StAUL, B65/23/24c; *RMS*, ii, no. 244; Ash, 'The Administration', pp. 199–220.
24 NRS, GD20/1/17.
25 For example StAUL, B65/23/22c; NRS, GD18/419; GD20/1/13, 27; GD82/26, 45; RH6/416; Fraser, *Wemyss*, ii, no. 64.
26 *Copiale*, p. 113, no. 62; P. J. Murray, 'The Lay Administrators of Church Lands in the Fifteenth and Sixteenth Centuries', *SHR* 74 (1995), pp. 26–44.
27 *Copiale*, pp. 45–6, no. 24.
28 *Copiale*, p. 162, no. 94. It is striking that in the perambulations and other judicial actions involving the priory's estates the bishop's justiciar, steward or constable was present. *Copiale*, pp. 111–14, no. 62; StAUL UYSLL 110/C/1; NLS, 34.6.24 135v; NRS, GD247/365.
29 NRS, GD20/1/27.

to non-entry.[30] There survive numerous examples of the bishops and archbishops delivering legal sasine of fees to new tenants following the kind of inquest carried out in the prior's court in January 1435.[31] The duties of such tenants included attendance at the court of their superior as stated in a grant by Henry Wardlaw to Nicholas Hay in 1437.[32] This followed the resignation of the lands of Wester Foodie to Nicholas by his father, William Hay lord of Errol, an act to which the bishop consented and the sasine was delivered by his bailie.[33] An order for the bailie of Muckhart and Bishopshire to punish a man for the slaughter of the archbishop's sergeant is an isolated example of the kind of instructions which must have flowed between prelates in St Andrews and their servants in the administration of their estates and judicial authority.[34]

Did the extent and exercise of the rights possessed by the bishops and archbishops of St Andrews, especially in eastern Fife, translate into the kind of local dominance associated with other holders of similar landed and legal powers elsewhere in Scotland? For secular magnates, this dominance has been measured in terms of the leadership of local men. Not surprisingly, the obligation of the extensive group of lesser landowners in Fife who were tenants of the bishops provided the basis for lasting connections. The Monypennys of Kinkell (just to the south of St Andrews) with the lords of Magask and Kilmany (also in east Fife) acted as procurators for Bishop Kennedy in 1452.[35] The assizes for the perambulations of 1449 both included lists of local tenants of the bishop and were witnessed by others including the lords of Kinkell (again), of Pitcorthie, Cambo and Balcormo.[36] Witnesses to Kennedy's charters also included minor landowners from around St Andrews like Alexander Forsyth of Nydie and James Butler of Rumgally.[37] Many of the same names appear on acts dealing with the lands and rights of the priors, for example the homage received from James Kinninmonth and his subsequent legal dispute with his superior.[38] For local lords, like the Ramsays of Brackmont, who were tenants of the regality of St Andrews, the bishops, their officials and their courts provided the focal point for their access to land and justice.[39] Their papers include a formal bond of maintenance between Archbishop Andrew Foreman and William Ramsay of Brackmont in 1519 in which the latter was retained for life by his superior for a pension of £20.[40] This is an exceptional agreement which provides evidence of an archbishop acting as a lord by securing the service of a lay landowner but it is

---

[30] NRS, GD105/253. See also NRS, GD82/58.
[31] NRS, GD7/1/1; GD18/427, 433, 435; GD20/1/11, 15, 16, 18, 30.
[32] NRS, RH6/298.
[33] NRS, RH6/284, 286.
[34] NRS, GD150/1725.
[35] NRS, GD20/1/10.
[36] StAUL, UYSL 110/C/1.
[37] NRS, GD82/14.
[38] *Copiale*, pp. 111–14, no. 64; pp. 162–5, no. 94.
[39] NRS, GD82/14, 18, 20, 21, 26, 31, 45, 58, 59.
[40] NRS, GD82/312.

also an indication that personal service of the type paid for in the bond was not an automatic consequence of the obligations of a tenant.

Amidst such minor landowners, the vassals of the bishops of St Andrews also included families of wider interests and higher status. The Lindsays of the Byres, who were kinsmen of the earls of Crawford and possessed estates in Lothian, Fife and Stirlingshire, held Struthers, Kirkforthar and Letham from the bishops.[41] The Wemyss family were also significant landowners in Fife and were tenants of the bishops in Methil and elsewhere.[42] In the detached lands of Muckhartshire and Bishopshire to the west, the office of bailie and the management of lands seem to have been assigned frequently to the Douglas lords of Lochleven.[43] The relationship of the bishops with this baronial family seems to have created tensions. In 1443 Henry Douglas lord of Lochleven appealed to Rome in the course of dispute with Bishop Kennedy. Douglas claimed that the bishop had 'tried to despoil' him of a fishing in Loch Leven. Interestingly, Douglas complained that the bishop had refused royal judgement but sought to try the case as 'judge and party' in his own court.[44] This may indicate resentment at the regality powers possessed by the church of St Andrews, and Henry was again (or still) in dispute with the bishop, by now Patrick Graham, in 1467. This time he complained that when he presented himself in St Andrews Cathedral, before the altar of St Katherine the virgin, in answer to a legal summons, neither the bishop nor his representative appeared to accuse him.[45] However, despite these ongoing difficulties, Douglas's presence in St Andrews is further evidence of the significance of the city, its churches and the castle as centres of lordship. Henry's son, Robert, produced an instrument in the prior's chamber, while the connection of the Lindsays of the Byres with the city was much deeper. In 1410 William Lindsay of the Byres purchased and then donated the land on which the new parish church of Holy Trinity was constructed. In return for his gift, it was agreed between Lindsay and the citizens and community of St Andrews that a chapel within the new church should be 'adorned with the arms of the said Sir William'.[46] Spiritual benefits aside, Lindsay, whose castle at Struthers was much closer to Cupar, clearly sought to link himself to the city of St Andrews. This aspiration may be connected to Lindsay's tenurial connections with the bishop, whose consent was given to the agreement, and to his frequent presence in the city as a suitor at the regality court. It was at St Andrews, for example, that a marriage agreement was made between Lindsay's son, John, and John Lundie of that ilk for a match between their children. This agreement was made

[41] NRS, GD20/1/7, 11, 13, 15.
[42] Fraser, *Wemyss*, ii, nos 58, 68.
[43] NRS, GD150/1725; *Rentale*, pp. 92, 121, 137, 168, 176. James duke of Ross as archbishop of St Andrews assigned the leasing of Muckhart and the Bishopshire to Robert Douglas of Lochleven, 'our familiar servitor': *Registrum Honoris de Morton*, 2 vols, Bannatyne Club (Edinburgh, 1853), ii, no. 237.
[44] NRS, GD150/14 (k).
[45] NRS, GD150/138.
[46] StAUL, B65/23/16c.

on 20 January 1435, the day which followed the formal investiture of James Kinninmonth in the prior's court and may indicate that the presence of Lindsay and Lundie was determined by their obligation to attend this gathering.[47]

If St Andrews was a centre of lordship for the bishops and priors, this lordship encompassed not just landowners from eastern Fife but the citizens themselves. The bishop was, of course, the feudal superior of the city. The inhabitants benefited from his patronage and from the support of their lord in disputes. In 1363 Bishop William Landallis secured the citizens' right to buy wool and hides throughout Fife without paying customs to the king.[48] Seven years later the bishop also acted for the citizens in the dispute which arose from this right with the burgesses of Cupar. Lacking a similar advocate, Cupar's burgesses were punished for having 'molested' the citizens of St Andrews.[49] When a recurrence of this dispute was judged in 1432 St Andrews similarly enjoyed ecclesiastical support.[50] This close connection to princes of the church also had a personal element. Members of the urban elite, including several of the city's provosts, can be found as witnesses to episcopal acts. George Martine, who held the office in the mid-1450s, appeared as a witness to an agreement between two of Bishop James Kennedy's kinsmen, which was made in 1444 in the family's Ayrshire castle of Cassilis. The bishop, who was a guarantor of the agreement, clearly brought an entourage to the west coast which included Martine and perhaps other citizens of St Andrews.[51] The possibilities for citizens to benefit from their proximity to major ecclesiastical landowners can be demonstrated by the career of Martine's contemporary and neighbour William Bonar. Bonar was from an established St Andrews family. During the later 1430s he possessed the resources to lease estates from the priory at Greigston and Over Magask.[52] At the same time he was also bailie for the archdeacon of St Andrews' estates.[53] By the early 1450s Bonar had entered the king's service as comptroller, auditing the royal accounts and receiving his reward in the form of the lands of Easter Rossie in central Fife.[54] In the early sixteenth century, the leading family from St Andrews, the Learmonths, not only frequently held the office of provost but were also given hereditary right to the post of custumar of St Andrews in 1517.[55]

However, the advantages which flowed to these leading citizens via their access to clerical magnates were part of a two-way process. As in other burghs,

---

[47] NRS, GD160/291 no. 2; *Copiale*, pp. 111–14, no. 62. John Lindsay was on the jury which judged James Kinninmonth's claims against the priory in 1438 in the refectory of the monastery of St Andrews: *Copiale*, pp. 162–6, no. 94.
[48] StAUL, B65/23/6c.
[49] StAUL, B65/23/8c.
[50] StAUL, B65/23/23c, 27c.
[51] NRS, GD25/1/34. Martine also acted as the bishop's procurator in 1458: GD20/1/47.
[52] *Copiale*, pp. 127–8, no. 68; p. 149, no. 83.
[53] NLS, 34.6.24 136v.
[54] StAUL, MS 36, 929 3/1.
[55] NRS, GD241/204.

the majority of St Andrews' provosts were drawn from the urban elite. As well as William Bonar, George Martine and John and Robert Learmonth, this group included William Kinnaird, Robert Butler, Thomas Arthurson and Thomas and John Ramsay.[56] However, on a number of occasions official positions in the city were given to men whose principal significance was as members of the bishop's household. John Carmichael, who was provost between 1434 and 1436, Alan Stewart, who held the same office in 1453, and Alexander Kennedy, who was bailie in 1460, all owed their position to their close connection to the city's superior lord.[57]

The promotion of the bishops' connections in the city was on one level a natural consequence of their rights over St Andrews. However, it also formed part of a distinctive element in the character of ecclesiastical lordship over both city and regality which made it different from that exercised by lay magnates. The succession of bishops and priors introduced new personnel into the running of estates and jurisdictions. By comparison with secular lords, this transfer of office limited continuity at the heart of the household and administration of the bishopric and priory. Each new prelate brought with him a group of associates and especially kinsmen in whom he could place his trust. The role of the bishop's kin was a recurring feature of episcopal life in late medieval Scotland. This nepotism has generally been examined as a feature of ecclesiastical practice but it was equally significant in temporal government. In the thirteenth century, Bishop William Fraser relied heavily on his brother, Andrew, in terms of his temporal interests in Fife.[58] Walter Trail, who became bishop of St Andrews in 1385, similarly employed his brother, Thomas.[59] Both Bishop Henry Wardlaw and his successor, James Kennedy, can be shown to have assembled much more extensive networks of family connections. Wardlaw's cousins, Henry Wardlaw of Spot and William Wardlaw of Wilton and Torry, witnessed acts of Bishop Henry in St Andrews and in 1421 Thomas Wardlaw was the bishop's marshal. Bishop Wardlaw also employed his nephews. John Wemyss of Kilmany, who came from a family which held lands from St Andrews, was the husband of the bishop's niece, Janet.[60] Just after the death of Bishop Wardlaw in 1440, Wemyss and his wife secured confirmation of a charter in which Henry had appointed John as hereditary constable of St Andrews Castle and granted them both the lands associated with this office.[61] This grant was for 'loyal counsel and help to the bishop and church of St Andrews'. Wemyss probably succeeded John Carmichael in this office. Carmichael, who was called 'our neveu' by the

---

[56] *Copiale*, no. 100; StAUL, B65/23/19c, 20c, 29c, 31c, 38c, 97c, 134c; UYSS110/B/3.
[57] StAUL, B65/23/24c, 26c, 67c; UYSS110/R/11; UYSS110/PW/37–9, 120.
[58] M. H. Brown, 'Aristocratic Politics and the Crisis of Scottish Kingship, 1286–96', *SHR* 90 (2010), pp. 1–26.
[59] D. E. R. Watt, *A Biographical Dictionary of Scottish Graduates to AD 1410* (Oxford, 1977) [hereafter Watt, *Graduates*], p. 539.
[60] NRS, GD1/34/1.
[61] *RMS*, ii, no. 244.

bishop in 1433, was the son of Henry's sister.[62] From 1420 until the late 1430s Carmichael was captain and constable of St Andrews Castle and also acted as his uncle's agent in dealings with his tenants.[63] He combined these roles with spells as provost of the city.[64]

Given his extended network of family from Ayrshire, it is not surprising that James Kennedy similarly installed or supported kinsmen at the heart of his diocese. Two of these were clergy. Hugh Kennedy was Bishop James's uncle. After serving in France as a soldier, he was back in Scotland by the mid-1430s and was already provost of St Mary's Collegiate Church by the time of his nephew's appointment.[65] In the early 1450s he was also archdeacon of St Andrews and he was succeeded in both roles by his great-nephew, John Kennedy.[66] In 1457 another kinsman, master James Kennedy, was the bishop's chamberlain.[67] Like his predecessor, Bishop Kennedy looked to his kin for lay servants. By 1456 he had appointed his cousin Gilbert Kennedy of Kirkmichael as steward of the regality.[68] The bishop also advanced another kinsman. Alexander Kennedy was the bastard son of the bishop's uncle, Thomas Kennedy of Kirkoswald.[69] By 1459 Alexander was acting as constable of St Andrews Castle in the absence of John Wemyss. He also acted as bailie of the city and of the priory during the early 1460s, and in 1464, during Bishop Kennedy's period of pre-eminence on the council for James III, Alexander was sheriff of Fife.[70] Like Wardlaw, Kennedy promoted kinsmen to form the heart of his administration and council.

However, if the succession of a new bishop led to an influx of nephews and cousins, it did not lead to the disappearance of the old group of episcopal servants overnight. The rewards bestowed by bishops on their kin went beyond temporary office to include more lasting gifts in the form of land from within the episcopal temporalities. Thus James Trail who entered into the lands of Blebo west of St Andrews in 1458 was the descendant of Thomas Trail, Bishop Walter's brother.[71] Similarly Henry Wardlaw of Wilton received the lands of Torryburn in west Fife under the auspices of their superior, the bishop, and the same prelate included the lands of Lathockar in the hereditary grant of the constableship of St Andrews to his niece and her husband.[72] Bishop Kennedy's

---

[62] NRS, RH6/286.
[63] NRS, GD18/419, 420, 421; RH6/286; StAUL, B65/23/24c; *Copiale*, p. 169, no. 169.
[64] *Copiale*, pp. 111–14, no. 62.
[65] NRS, GD82/14; StAUL, UYSL110/B1; UYSM110/B12/4; D. E. R. Watt, *Fasti Ecclesiae Scoticanae Medii Aevi ad 1638*, Scottish Record Society (Edinburgh, 1969), p. 307.
[66] NRS, GD20/1/48, 52; Watt, *Fasti Ecclesiae Scoticanae*, p. 307.
[67] NRS, GD430/184.
[68] Fraser, *Wemyss*, ii, no. 58; Dunlop, *Kennedy*, p. 347.
[69] *RMS*, ii, nos 140, 1565.
[70] Martine, pp. 137–8; StAUL, UYSS110/B/2; UYSS/K/11; UYSS/PW/37, 38, 39, 44; *RMS*, ii, no. 812.
[71] NRS, GD7/1/1.
[72] *RMS*, ii, no. 244.

kinsman Alexander was rewarded with the lands of Urwell in the Bishopshire around Loch Leven.[73] As a result Trails, Wardlaws, Carmichaels, Kennedys and others continued to be landowners around St Andrews after the death of their episcopal patrons. Bishop Kennedy continued to rely on his predecessor's kinsmen. In 1454 Henry Wardlaw of Torry was still steward of the bishop's regality.[74]

The kinship ties of the bishops also left a mark on the city of St Andrews. Holding the provostship of St Andrews inevitably required the possession of property within the city. John Carmichael held tenements in South Street, Seagait and the land between North Street and the castle.[75] In 1462 Alexander Kennedy of Urwell received lands in Castle Street in an agreement with William Carmichael of Meadowfleet (perhaps a kinsman of John).[76] Wardlaw's other kinsmen obtained property in St Andrews during his episcopate. His marshal, Thomas Wardlaw, had a tenement in South Street and Henry Wardlaw of Wilton had rents from North Street and Castle Street.[77] The acquisition of urban property by clergy and their kin was not confined to the bishops and their relatives. In 1410 a long list of properties and rents in all parts of St Andrews was purchased by William Balmyle rector of Benholm, who had been chamberlain of Bishop Trail's estates north of Forth in the 1390s.[78] The leases to priory estates obtained by William Bonar, citizen and provost of St Andrews, in the late 1430s may have been facilitated by the influence of another William Bonar, undoubtedly a kinsman, who as a canon and the chamberlain of the priory had responsibility for the property of the cathedral.[79]

The most significant example of such a family network in fifteenth-century St Andrews was that started by John Scheves. Scheves was a central figure in the church and city of St Andrews between the 1410s and 1450s. He was official of St Andrews from 1411 to his death in 1456–57 and was named as a councillor of Bishops Wardlaw and Kennedy. John was also named by Walter Bower as one of the group of masters who commenced teaching at St Andrews prior to the formal foundation of the university and he briefly served as rector in 1418.[80]

---

[73] *RMS*, ii, no. 1565; StAUL, UYSS110/B/2.
[74] *Copiale*, 448; NRS RH6/334b; StAUL, UYSS110/R/11; *RMS*, ii, no. 244. Wemyss also appeared as a witness in 1458 along with Bishop Kennedy in a charter issued by John Kennedy, provost of St Mary's: NRS, GD20/1/48. Wardlaw of Torry was with the bishop at Cassilis in Ayrshire in 1444: NRS, GD25/1/34.
[75] StAUL, UYSL110/PW/27, 116; B65/23/39c. Carmichael's membership of the community was also signified by his payment for a column in the new parish church: StAUL, B65/23/24c.
[76] StAUL, UYSS110/PW/41, 42.
[77] StAUL, B65/23/29c; UYSS110/AQ/1; UYSM110/B12/2. John, William and Matthew Wardlaw also appear as citizens in the mid fifteenth century: StAUL, UYSS110/AQ/32, 36, 40.
[78] StAUL, B65/23/15; NLS Adv MSS 34.6.24, 141r.
[79] *Copiale*, p. 113, no. 62; pp. 129–30, no. 69; pp. 152–3, no. 86; p. 160, no. 91; p. 177, no. 102. Bonar succeeded James Haldenstone as prior in 1443.
[80] *Scotichronicon*, viii, pp. 76–9; Watt, *Graduates*, p. 480; NRS, GD209/21.

This role indicates close connections with the cathedral priory and Scheves accompanied Prior Haldenstone to the *curia* in 1419 to announce Scotland's adherence to Pope Martin V after the schism. He later acted as the prior's procurator at general council.[81] Scheves's long career as a leading cleric in St Andrews was accompanied by the acquisition of benefices in the dioceses of Aberdeen and Glasgow, as well as Arbuthnott in Angus, Kinaldy from St Mary's Church in St Andrews and Kilmany from the priory. Scheves also possessed links to the city of St Andrews. In 1432 he was removed for partiality from a commission of parliament enquiring into a boundary dispute between St Andrews and Cupar and Crail.[82] As well as possession of a tenement in the Seagait, in 1456, not long before his death, John founded a chaplaincy in the parish church at the altar of St Andrew, supporting it with rents from properties in South, Market and North Streets, Butler Wynd and the suburban district of Argyle.[83]

The terms of John Scheves's foundation stated that, after his death, the right to present to this chaplaincy would pass to Henry Scheves of Kilwhiss and his heirs, whom failing to his brother William. These brothers were obviously kinsmen of John. Their careers would be of major significance in later fifteenth-century St Andrews. It was later reported that William was illegitimate and his parents were not of baronial blood. It is possible from this that John Scheves was the father of both William and Henry.[84] If not, the charter is still clear evidence that Henry and William were John's heirs. That, by the 1460s, Henry was the possessor of property in Seagait and South Street suggests he had inherited some of John's tenements in St Andrews. In 1468 Henry was one of the bailies of the city, confirming his position as a significant member of the urban community. Like other leading citizens, Henry Scheves held an estate in Fife. Kilwhiss, near Auchtermuchty, had come into Henry's hands before 1456, possibly as a grant from the crown.[85]

The connections of Henry's brother William with St Andrews were on different lines. During the 1450s he was a student and then a faculty member at the university. Probably after 1461 he left St Andrews.[86] The sale of a rent by Henry Scheves in 1468 was formally consented to by Henry's wife and son and by another brother, Robert, but Henry had to promise to secure an oath from William 'when he should come to Scotland'.[87] Other evidence indicates William was studying on the Continent at Louvain and, perhaps, Paris.[88]

---

[81] *Copiale*, p. 24, no. 12; pp. 151–2, no. 85.
[82] StAUL, B65/23/23c.
[83] StAUL, B65/23/38c, 138c; UYSS110/P/3.
[84] Macdougall, *James III*, p. 146.
[85] One portion of Kilquhiss was held by the crown as part of the earldom of Fife: ER, v, pp. 466–70.
[86] StAUL, B65/23/39c; Macdougall, *James III*, p. 147. William was named as the recipient of payments from a tenement in the Seagait.
[87] StAUL, B65/23/50c.
[88] Macdougall, *James III*, pp. 264–6; J. Herkless and R. K. Hannay, *The Archbishops of St Andrews*, 4 vols (Edinburgh and London, 1907–15), i, pp. 80–3.

When he did return to Scotland it was to royal service. Duties as the physician to James III may have lacked formal status but they did provide ready access to royal favour. In 1474 this delivered to William Scheves the archdeaconry of St Andrews, apparently against the wishes of the archbishop, Patrick Graham.[89] By this point King James was already moving against Graham, whose securing of the archbishopric and other activities had alienated both the king and most of the leading clergy. In 1476 William Scheves was appointed as co-adjutor, effectively the administrator, of the see of St Andrews. He exercised this office in St Andrews, recording an agreement between the provost and community and the clergy of the parish church.[90] In October 1477 William Scheves concluded a bond of friendship with William Hay earl of Errol. Errol was both a vassal of the archbishops in Fife and an influential magnate in the northern parts of the diocese.[91] The alliance with the earl may well have been to counter any opposition to the further advancement of the king's favourite. In January 1478 Graham was deprived of his office and the next month William Scheves was created archbishop.[92] In October 1479 in parliament the new archbishop received a royal charter confirming the 'golden charter' and other rights received by his predecessors.[93]

As indicated above, the position of Henry Scheves within the urban community of St Andrews did not depend on his brother's ecclesiastical career. However, his appointment as provost of the city in 1475 coincided with the installation of William as archdeacon and the intensification of royal pressure on Patrick Graham.[94] After William's consecration as archbishop in 1479 Henry stepped into the established role of leading lay kinsman of the prelate, held by individuals like John Wemyss, John Carmichael and Alexander Kennedy. He acted as steward of regality; he was appointed as procurator for his brother on two occasions and possibly received a hereditary grant of the office of marshal of St Andrews.[95] He received direct rewards from the archbishop in the form of a grant of incomes from a list of properties in St Andrews.[96] The favour of the king towards his new archbishop's family was expressed through a grant of the lands of Demperston in north Fife to Henry's son and heir, John, in 1481.[97]

These roots in the city of St Andrews and the surrounding lands may have been helpful to Archbishop Scheves. The problems which rapidly emerged around his archiepiscopate derived instead from wider political events and continuing ecclesiastical discontent against the primacy of the archbishops of St

---

[89] StAUL, B65/23/75c; Herkless and Hannay, *Archbishops of St Andrews*, pp. 84–6.
[90] StAUL, B65/23/76c.
[91] NRS, RH1/6/97.
[92] Macdougall, *James III*, pp. 146–9.
[93] RPS, 1479/10/12.
[94] StAUL, B65/23/67c; UYSSL110/PW/120; Macdougall, *James III*, pp. 100–2.
[95] StAUL, UYSM110/B12/15, 16; NRS, GD7/1/3; GD 20/1/17–8; GD82/44; Fraser, *Wemyss*, ii, no. 71.
[96] StAUL, UYSL110/PW/58.
[97] *RMS*, ii, no.1467.

Andrews over the Scottish church.[98] In late 1482, with James III temporarily removed from power, there was an effort to force his familiar and counsellor William Scheves to resign the archbishopric. This was justified in personal terms as 'the prelates refuse to obey a man not of illustrious birth'.[99] The recovery of authority by his royal patron in 1483 allowed William Scheves to secure restoration of the archbishopric of St Andrews.[100] However it has been noted that Scheves' relationship with the king did not return to its previous intimacy.[101] One of the reasons for this new coolness may have involved a dispute over St Andrews Priory. The relationship between the bishops and their cathedral chapter in the fifteenth century is hard to gauge. There were no obvious conflicts and some signs of close interaction.[102] However the relationship was changed by the papal indult given by Nicholas V to Bishop James Kennedy which allowed the bishops of St Andrews the right to confirm all elections of abbots and priors in their diocese. From the beginning of his personal reign in 1469, James III sought to defend the indult as a means of increasing royal influence over the appointment of clergy via a pliable archbishop.[103]

In 1483, after the king had secured his restoration, Archbishop Scheves seems to have had an attack of independence. The death of Prior William Cameron had left a vacancy at the head of the cathedral chapter. The canons elected one of their number, Walter Monypenny, as the new prior. Monypenny's connections with St Andrews were more deeply rooted than those of Scheves. He was from the family of Monypenny of Kinkell whose lands were just south of St Andrews and were held from the bishops and priors.[104] Several of the family had been members of the cathedral chapter in the earlier fifteenth century and Walter Monypenny was prior of St Serf's Priory in Loch Leven (also known as Portmoak), a dependent house of St Andrews.[105] The election of Monypenny by the canons seems to have been confirmed by Archbishop Scheves. However, James III had other plans for St Andrews Priory. As part payment of the political debts incurred by the king in the recent crisis, James wished to assign the priory to John Hepburn. Hepburn was not a canon or other religious and appears only as a royal clerk before 1483. However, he was uncle to Patrick Hepburn lord

---

[98] Macdougall, *James III*, pp. 211, 220–1.
[99] *Scottish Formularies*, ed. A. A. M. Duncan, Stair Society (Edinburgh, 2011), p. 241, no. 29; p. 242, no. 32.
[100] Macdougall, *James III*, pp. 211–12, 224.
[101] Ibid., pp. 269–70.
[102] For example, in 1457 Bishop Kennedy acted as commissioner for Prior William Bonar during his absence from Scotland: NLS, Adv MS 15.1.18, no. 25.
[103] *RPS*, 1469/1. Macdougall, *James III*, pp. 101–2.
[104] StAUL, UYS110/B/3. Walter Monypenny of Kinkell (who may well have been Prior Walter's father) witnessed a charter of Bishop Wardlaw in 1436 and an act recording the retour of James Kinninmonth in 1435: NRS, GD18/421; *Copiale*, p. 111, no. 62. He was involved in the two perambulations of priory estates in 1449: NLS, Adv MS 34.6.25; StAUL, UYSL110/C/1.
[105] StAUL, B65/23/77c; B65/23/81c. These acts involved properties held by Walter in South Street and Priors Wynd, St Andrews.

Hailes whose support had been vital to the king during the preceding year.[106] In a series of letters to Pope Sixtus and other clergy, James III made clear his support for Hepburn's candidacy and claimed that the pope, and not the archbishop, had the right over the choice of prior.[107] The king sought to protect Hepburn from Monypenny's litigation which dragged on until 1486 and whose cost had impoverished the priory. 'Moveables have been smelted, immoveables have been alienated.'[108]

As a prior with royal support, appointed over the heads of his canons to an impoverished house, John Hepburn became prior of St Andrews in inauspicious circumstances. However, during his tenure of the office, which lasted nearly forty years, Hepburn proved to be one of the three late medieval prelates to leave his mark on St Andrews (along with Bishops Wardlaw and Kennedy). The reconstruction of the precinct wall which surrounded the priory and the foundation of a college for poor clerks, known as St Leonard's College, in 1512 were lasting reminders of his time as prior.[109] Though his effort to become archbishop in 1513 was thwarted, for much of his term as prior he overshadowed the holders of that office. Three times Hepburn acted as vicar-general of the archbishopric of St Andrews, running the archdiocese during a vacancy: in 1497 following the death of Scheves; in 1504–06 after the death of King James IV's brother, James duke of Ross; and finally, following the death of Andrew Foreman in 1521.[110] The key to Prior Hepburn's career was clearly rooted in the ruthless action of his family in 1488. Despite the efforts of King James III on his behalf, only a few years later John joined his brothers and nephew amongst the rebels who overthrew their royal lord. The Hepburns were central to the group who surrounded the new king, James IV. Within a fortnight of the change of ruler, Prior John had secured custody of Falkland Palace and, as keeper of the privy seal, was at the heart of government.[111] His influence was reflected in his inclusion amongst 'the maisterfull, parciall menys' named as the new king's councillors by their enemies in 1489.[112] Though their greed made them unpopular, John and his family managed to maintain their influence through James IV's reign.[113]

John Hepburn's rise did not wholly depend on broad political actions and affiliations. Like other bishops and priors of St Andrews, Hepburn sought

---

[106] Macdougall, *James III*, pp. 198, 292.
[107] *Formularies*, ed. Duncan, nos 19, 20, 21, 23, 26.
[108] Ibid., no. 34.
[109] *RMS*, ii, no. 3812; Cant, *University*, pp. 30–4; StAUL, UYSL110/A/1.
[110] NRS, GD20/1/25; GD150/1014; *RMS*, ii, no. 2789; *Calendar of the Laing Charters AD 854–1837*, ed. J. Anderson (Edinburgh, 1899), nos 327, 329, 333. There is also an interesting financial arrangement between Hepburn and Archbishop Alexander Stewart from 1506: NLS, Adv MS 15.1.18, no. 26.
[111] *RMS*, ii, nos 1732, 1739.
[112] Fraser, *Lennox*, ii, 130, no. 85. The same document, called 'the Lennox apologia', also claimed that these men planned to deprive Archbishop Scheves of his see.
[113] N. Macdougall, *James IV* (Edinburgh, 1989), pp. 51, 71.

friends amongst the landowners of eastern Fife. In particular, John found a long-standing local agent in William Lundie. Lundie was from a minor noble family who had held the barony of Lundin (Lundie) on the shores of the Forth since the twelfth century.[114] William was the eldest son of John Lundie of that ilk. More importantly, he was married to Elizabeth Hepburn, niece of Prior John.[115] Soon after Hepburn's appointment as prior there was a rearrangement of lands between William Lundie and his father. William and Elizabeth received the lands of the barony of Lundin and nearby Praytis and Balcormo in exchange for the lands of Benholm near Inverbervie in Kincardineshire which he had been given by his father fifteen years earlier.[116] The formal exchange occurred in the king's chamber in Edinburgh Castle in early January 1486.[117] However, nearly a year earlier, Elizabeth Hepburn had given her consent to the transaction in St Leonard's kirk in St Andrews, a church within the precincts of her uncle's priory.[118] This location suggests that John Hepburn was involved in an arrangement which installed his niece and her husband as landowners in Fife. By June 1487 William Lundie had been appointed as bailie of the priory, a position he held until at least 1513.[119] The link between the prior and his bailie was evident in the critical year of 1488. On 4 July 1488, just over three weeks after the death of James III, an indenture was produced arranging the marriage of Thomas son of William Lundie and Elizabeth Hepburn to Isabella daughter of James Boswell of Balmuto.[120] Along with the two fathers, Prior Hepburn was a third party to the agreement, which was made in St Andrews. This support for Lundie was also evident in early December 1488 when the young James IV made his first visit as king to St Andrews.[121] The young king granted William Lundie the lands of Kincraig near Elie.[122] At Cupar a fortnight later, the king gave William custody of lands forfeited by James III's disgraced favourite, John Ramsay.[123] In April 1489 William sought to endow his son Thomas with the lands of Praytis and appointed procurators to secure royal permission. These were headed by Prior John and his brother Alexander Hepburn of Whitsome.[124] Lundie's links of kinship to John Hepburn clearly provided the basis for growing influence in Fife and especially in St Andrews. This was reflected by the actions of Scheves's successor as archbishop, the king's brother James duke of Ross. He made grants to 'our lovit familiar squier', William Lundie, in 1498

---

[114] NRS, GD160/269.
[115] NRS, GD160/292/11.
[116] *RMS*, ii, nos 1631, 1633, 1634; NRS, GD160/292/ii. John Lundie's concern seems to have been to provide for Robert, his son by his second wife.
[117] NRS, GD4/6, 7.
[118] NRS, GD4/4; GD160/292/1.
[119] StAUL, UYSL110/PW/57, 58, 59, 62, 65, 71, 74, 81; StAUL, B65/23/125c, 169c.
[120] NRS, GD160/292/11.
[121] *RMS*, ii, nos 1803–5. Though Hepburn does not appear as a witness to the royal charters issued in St Andrews, it is very likely that he was present.
[122] NRS, GD160/292/10, 12.
[123] NRS, GD160/292/13.
[124] NRS, GD160/292/14, 18, 19.

which included properties in St Andrews and the wardship of a third of the barony of Leuchars.[125]

The promotion of William Lundie and his relations with Prior Hepburn show how bonds of kinship and ecclesiastical lordship functioned in fifteenth-century Scotland. Like other localities, the city of St Andrews and the baronies of its clergy which lay around it operated through networks of service and patronage. However, in eastern Fife this was shaped by the character of ecclesiastical office. The way in which prelates distributed property and office to their own kinsmen and friends brought new families and individuals to the landed class of both city and country. Bishops Trail, Wardlaw and Kennedy and Priors Haldenstone and Hepburn all drew on personal and family links in the running of their temporalities and the exercise of lordship. Their actions were not free from the kind of competition found in other localities. Prior Hepburn's clear influence over affairs in St Andrews must have involved the reduction of Archbishop Scheves's authority. There was admittedly no repeat of the open competition for control of the temporalities of St Andrews and custody of its castle which had followed the death of Bishop Walter Trail in 1401 and led to the arrest and death of David duke of Rothesay, the heir to the throne.[126] However, in the mid-1440s Bishop Kennedy faced a direct assault on his temporalities. This may have involved some tenants and neighbours of the bishop. Henry Douglas of Lochleven's complaint against Kennedy in 1443 was made in the house of David earl of Crawford in Dundee.[127] In early 1445 Crawford and others ravaged the lands of the bishop in the so-called 'herschip of Fife'.[128] At least one leading citizen of St Andrews, William Bonar, gave manrent to Earl Alexander at this time, specifically seeking protection for his lands in Fife and Angus. His act may indicate a wider submission to the magnate from the city and regality.[129] Though Kennedy famously excommunicated and cursed the earl, the episode was an indication of the vulnerability of episcopal lordship in the face of the hostility of a magnate like Crawford. Moreover, while Kennedy in the early 1460s and Prior Hepburn after 1488 clearly exercised influence over the office of sheriff and the government of Fife, these were exceptional periods. For most of the intervening time David earl of Crawford (grandson of Kennedy's persecutor) seems a more significant presence via his links to his brother Alexander Lindsay of Auchtemoonzie and his kinsmen the Lindsays of the Byres.[130] This influence was, though, nothing like that developed by the Neville family in the Durham Palatinate during the late Middle Ages.[131] If anything, despite the granting of the 'Golden Charter', it was the crown which

---

[125] NRS, GD160/293/1, 2.
[126] *Scotichronicon*, viii, 36–41; S. Boardman, *Early Stewart Kings* (East Linton, 1996), pp. 256–7, 279–80.
[127] NRS, GD150/14 (k).
[128] 'Auchinleck Chronicle', in C. McGladdery, *James II* (Edinburgh, 2015), p. 264.
[129] NRS, GD121/2/3/3.
[130] NRS, B13/22/9–10; *RMS*, ii, no. 1730.
[131] Liddy, *Bishopric*, pp. 34, 88–92.

seems to have been the most obvious focus for careers and patronage in eastern Fife.[132] The city and regality of St Andrews were, like the lands and tenants of the old earldom, part of the gradual transformation of Fife into one of the 'home counties' of the Scottish monarchy.

---

[132] M. Brown, 'Barbour's *Bruce* in the 1480s: Literature and Locality', *Barbour's Bruce and its Cultural Contexts: Politics, Chivalry and Literature in Late Medieval Scotland*, ed. S. Boardman and S. Foran (Cambridge, 2015).

CHAPTER ELEVEN

Augmenting Rentals: The Expansion of Church Property in St Andrews, c. 1400–1560

Bess Rhodes

THE fifteenth and early sixteenth centuries saw a flowering in Scottish urban piety, with recent research highlighting the vitality of Catholic religious observance in late medieval Scottish towns and cities.[1] During this period numerous new ecclesiastical foundations were established in burghs across the kingdom, whilst many existing churches were extended and developed.[2] The expansion in religious provision was accompanied (and partly enabled) by a growth in the amount of church property within Scottish towns. Throughout the late Middle Ages large plots of urban land were converted to religious purposes, and extensive portfolios of secular properties, such as houses and crofts, were acquired by ecclesiastical institutions. This increase in urban church landholding was particularly apparent in St Andrews, where it transformed both the appearance and the economy of the city.

Religious institutions and officials had played a part in St Andrews landholding at least since the burgh's formal foundation in the twelfth century.[3] Nevertheless, the late Middle Ages saw an increase both in the number of religious sites within the city and in the degree of financial burden ecclesiastical institutions placed on ordinary households. The layout of the urban settlement and the nature of the relationship between clergy and laity in St Andrews were redefined by the late mediaeval ecclesiastical expansion. This chapter aims to explore the extent of the fifteenth- and early sixteenth-century

---

[1] See, for example, Mairi Cowan, *Death, Life, and Religious Change in Scottish Towns, c. 1350–1560* (Manchester, 2012); Audrey-Beth Fitch, *The Search for Salvation: Lay Faith in Scotland, 1480–1560* (Edinburgh, 2009).
[2] For example, the fifteenth century saw the setting up of Trinity College in Edinburgh and the Observant Franciscan friaries in Aberdeen, Edinburgh and Glasgow. Major building work was also undertaken during this period at (amongst other places) St Giles' in Edinburgh, St Mary's in Dundee, St Nicholas' in Aberdeen and St John's in Perth. D. E. Easson, *Medieval Religious Houses: Scotland* (London, 1957), pp. 110–11, 179; Richard Fawcett, *The Architecture of the Scottish Medieval Church, 1100–1560* (New Haven, 2011), pp. 293–6, 309–13.
[3] *Early Scottish Charters*, ed. Archibald Lawrie (Glasgow, 1905), pp. 132–3.

growth in church property within St Andrews and its implications for the local community.

At the start of the fifteenth century the main religious foundations in St Andrews were the cathedral, the collegiate church of St Mary on the Rock, the parish church of Holy Trinity, and the hospitals of St Leonard and St Nicholas. With the exception of the old leper hospital of St Nicholas (which stood a little distance from the burgh) all of these foundations were located in a distinct ecclesiastical zone at the eastern end of the city.[4] To the west of the religious area lay the secular settlement of St Andrews, with its three main streets of South Gait, Market Gait and North Gait.[5] The extent of the pre-fifteenth-century development along these thoroughfares is uncertain. By 1400 South Gait was divided up into burgage plots at least as far west as Logies Lane, and probably beyond.[6] Some sections of North Gait and Market Gait were also divided into the small strips of land typical of medieval towns, although these streets were probably less densely inhabited than South Gait.[7]

The patchy nature of the surviving source material makes it impossible to reconstruct fully landholding in fourteenth-century St Andrews. Nevertheless, some broad trends can be uncovered. Officially, most properties within the secular settlement were held from the bishop of St Andrews, although a few plots towards the eastern end of North Gait and South Gait pertained to the archdeacon and the cathedral priory.[8] Thus in theory all St Andrews householders held their homes from an ecclesiastical institution or official. Yet the financial burden these religious landlords placed on local residents was often minimal. For example, the bishops of St Andrews sometimes limited their demands to a yearly

---

[4] Derek Hall, 'Archaeological Excavations at St Nicholas Farm, St Andrews, 1986–87', *TFAJ* 1 (1995), pp. 48–75.

[5] Brooks and Whittington, p. 285.

[6] Archaeological excavation has revealed evidence of pre-fifteenth century occupation on both the north and south sides of South Gait in the region of Logies Lane. James Mackenzie and Colm Moloney, 'Medieval Development and the Cemetery of the Church of the Holy Trinity, Logies Lane, St Andrews', *TFAJ* 3 (1997), pp. 143–60; Ray Cachart, 'Excavations at 106–110 South Street, St Andrews', *TFAJ* 6 (2000), pp. 109–35.

[7] Documentary evidence from the St Leonard's College pittance writs make it clear that by the end of the fourteenth century at least part of North Gait and Market Gait had been divided up into urban tenements. However, both written and archaeological evidence make it clear that by no means all of North Gait was built upon well into the early modern period. StAUL, UYSL110/PW series; Brooks and Whittington, p. 284.

[8] This pattern of landholding arose because the legal boundaries of the burgh of St Andrews did not match the area covered by the actual urban settlement of St Andrews. All properties within the official burgh of St Andrews were supposedly held from the bishop of St Andrews (by virtue of the bishops' role in founding the community). However, the eastern end of the settlement was technically outside the burgh and formed part of the baronies held (initially) by the cathedral priory and the clerics of St Mary on the Rock, and later by the cathedral and the archdeacon. Our understanding of the precise relationship between the different jurisdictions is rather confused and would benefit from more in-depth research.

payment of 2d.⁹ To put this figure in context, during the late fourteenth century a carcase of beef typically cost somewhere between 5s and 11s.¹⁰ Properties that were set in feu-ferme (a heritable form of tenure where the tenant paid a fixed yearly rent or feu-maill) were usually subject to rather heavier exactions. A charter from 1344 reveals that when the cathedral priory feued land in North Gait to a citizen of St Andrews named Matthew de Cornel an annual feu-maill of 6s 8d sterling was demanded.¹¹ However, during the late fourteenth century properties set in feu-ferme seem to have been the exception rather than the rule. There also appear to have been only a small number of rent-charges associated with St Andrews properties at this time. Rent-charges were a phenomenon whereby someone (often a religious institution) obtained the right to collect each year a set sum of money from the holder of a plot of land.¹² Aside from the right to collect the money due to them, owners of rent-charges normally had no other privileges concerning the property. The evidence for rent-charges in St Andrews before 1400 is sparse. In particular, it seems to have been extremely uncommon for more than one rent-charge to be levied on the same piece of land.¹³ Overall, the surviving St Andrews charters suggest that during the fourteenth century many St Andrews households were paying nominal sums to religious foundations. The church did have property rights within the residential and trading area of the burgh, but the degree of financial burden that religious organisations and officials placed on local households (at least through exactions concerning property) was limited.

This pattern changed fundamentally during the fifteenth and early sixteenth centuries. The years between 1400 and the outbreak of the Protestant Reformation saw a spate of religious activity in St Andrews. After several rather difficult decades in the mid to late fourteenth century, the church in St Andrews appears to have entered an era of growth and renewal.¹⁴ For instance, in the

---

⁹ When the burgh of St Andrews was founded Bishop Robert demanded from the first provost an annual payment of 4d for each virgate of land he held. It seems likely that this remained the standard scale for St Andrews burgh fermes (the annual fee paid by the occupants of each burgage plot to the burgh's lord). In the fourteenth and fifteenth centuries St Andrews burgage fermes are almost invariably recorded as being either 2d or 4d. See the series of charters StAUL, UYSL110/PW and B65/23; *Early Scottish Charters*, ed. Lawrie, p. 133.

¹⁰ Elizabeth Gemmill and Nicholas Mayhew, *Changing Values in Medieval Scotland: A Study of Prices, Money, Weights and Measures* (Cambridge, 1995), p. 236.

¹¹ StAUL, UYSL110/PW/6.

¹² Rent-charges were common in many parts of Western Europe. There has been extensive research into how they functioned in the Holy Roman Empire (and to an extent other regions of mainland Europe). However, there are currently very few studies exploring their role in Scotland. For an outline of some of the Continental research into rent-charges see Laurence Buck, 'The Reformation, Purgatory, and Perpetual Rents in the Revolt of 1525 at Frankfurt am Main', *Pietas et Societas: New Trends in Reformation Social History*, ed. Harold Grimm, Kyle Sessions and Philip Bebb (Kirksville, 1985), pp. 23–3.

¹³ As yet, no examples have been discovered of multiple rent-charges being attached to a property in St Andrews prior to 1400.

¹⁴ During the fourteenth century St Andrews (and in particular the Augustinian

early 1410s Scotland's earliest university was set up within the city.[15] In 1472 St Andrews became the seat of Scotland's first (and, for a brief time, only) archbishopric.[16] Major ecclesiastical building projects were also carried out during this period, and a series of new religious institutions were established.[17] Between 1400 and 1559 the number of major religious foundations in St Andrews almost doubled, and it is probable that the number of churchmen based within the city increased proportionately. St Andrews' ecclesiastical resurgence had direct consequences for landholding within the city. To facilitate the founding of new religious institutions and the expansion of existing ones, a number of secular sites in and beside the city were converted to religious purposes. Churchmen also acquired numerous houses within the burgh, both as residences for themselves and as sources of income. Meanwhile, the number of rent-charges paid by local residents to the city's religious organisations proliferated at an unprecedented rate. Even in isolation, each of these changes would have significantly altered the experience of landholding within St Andrews. Together they constituted a property revolution.

The most visible expression of the expansion of church property in St Andrews was the number of new religious sites within the burgh, most of which were located outside the traditional ecclesiastical area at the eastern end of the city. During the fifteenth and early sixteenth centuries residents of St Andrews witnessed the relocation of the parish church of Holy Trinity, the establishment of Dominican and Franciscan friaries, and the foundation of the university colleges of St John (later re-founded as St Mary's College), St Salvator and St Leonard. Of these institutions only the college of St Leonard was eventually situated in the traditional religious quarter; the rest were located either on former burgage plots or on green-field developments on the edge of the settlement.

The redrawing of St Andrews' ecclesiastical map can be broken into two key stages, the first in the 1410s and the second around 1450. The first phase commenced with the decision to move the main parish church of Holy Trinity from its historic location beside the cathedral to a site on the north side of South Gait. In November 1410 a local nobleman, Sir William Lindsay of the Byres, dedicated to God and 'the holy mother church' ('sancte matri ecclesie') a series of burgage plots on South Gait with the express aim of providing land for the con-

---

cathedral priory) suffered a series of disasters. Like most of Europe, St Andrews was affected by the Black Death, which in 1349 killed at least twenty-four of the cathedral's canons (the number of dead amongst the local laity being unknown). Two decades later, in 1368, the cathedral buildings were severely damaged by fire. Meanwhile, in 1394 disagreements amongst the St Andrews clergy became so embittered that the prior of the cathedral (Robert de Montrose) was murdered by a fellow canon. *Scotichronicon*, iii, pp. 272–3, 424–5, 426–9.

[15] Cant, *University*, p. 3.

[16] *Concilia Scotiae: Ecclesiae Scoticanae Statuta tam Provincialia quam Synodalia quae supersunt, MCCXXV–MDLIX*, ed. Joseph Robertson (Edinburgh, 1866), cx–cxi.

[17] For example, St Andrews Cathedral underwent extensive renovations during the early fifteenth century. David McRoberts, 'The Glorious House of St Andrew', McRoberts, *St Andrews*, pp. 66–7.

struction of a new and improved parish church.[18] It is probable that the relocating of the congregation of Holy Trinity was at least partly motivated by a desire for a larger church where more elaborate services could be celebrated. Yet it may also have reflected a wish to move the parish church closer to the residential and trading centre of the burgh. The new site was located on the city's most intensively developed street and right beside a vennel leading to the market cross.[19] Significantly, the site had previously been occupied. Sir William Lindsay's original charter of donation states that he purchased the land from Thomas de Butler and John Scissors, and recent archaeological excavation has found evidence of medieval stone buildings that pre-date the construction of the church.[20] The relocation of Holy Trinity was not a removal to some open space on the fringes of the city, but a deliberate repositioning of the church to the heart of the secular settlement of St Andrews.

Around the same time as construction of the new Holy Trinity Church was taking place the college of St John was established on the south side of South Gait on part of the plot now occupied by St Mary's College.[21] Like the parish church, St John's College was built on a town centre site that had probably previously been used for ordinary secular activities. In January 1419 Robert de Montrose (a canon at St Mary's on the Rock) granted scholars at the university a tenement of land on South Gait, bounded on the west by the property of Patrick Scissors and on the east by the property of Thomas Arthur, to enable the foundation of a college dedicated to God, St John the Evangelist and all the saints.[22] This was probably the first land within St Andrews owned by the newly formed university.[23] In common with other medieval university colleges, St John's was primarily a religious foundation. Robert de Montrose's charter of donation refers to the existence of a college chapel and specifies in some detail the services he wished to be celebrated there for the benefit of his soul. It is possible that the new chapel was located on the street frontage of the college. If this was so, it would mean that the chapel of St John and the relocated parish church were less than 100 metres apart. The existence of two new ecclesiastical buildings so close together had the potential to transform the appearance of South Gait and formed a major departure from the city's earlier tradition of locating religious institutions in the eastern part of the promontory on which the settlement stood. By the end of the 1420s St Andrews effectively had two religious focuses, one part way down South Gait, the other in the old ecclesiastical zone.[24]

---

[18] StAUL, B65/23/16.
[19] Ibid.
[20] Ibid.; Mackenzie and Moloney, 'Medieval Development and the Cemetery of the Church of the Holy Trinity', pp. 146–8.
[21] Cant, *University*, pp. 14–15.
[22] StAUL, UYUY150/1, ff. 64r-65v.
[23] Cant, *University*, p. 14.
[24] The significance of the South Gait centre was further enhanced in the 1430s when the university established teaching buildings known as the New Pedagogy adjacent to St John's College. StAUL, UYUY150/1, ff. 31r-32v.

This situation lasted until the middle years of the fifteenth century when the policies of Bishop James Kennedy brought further changes to St Andrews' ecclesiastical landscape. Bishop Kennedy was a graduate of Louvain University and for much of his career engaged actively with European church affairs.[25] He seems to have been influenced by changing Continental religious fashions and to have tried to implement them in St Andrews, most notably through his establishment of St Salvator's College at the beginning of the 1450s. The College of St Salvator was substantially modelled on English and Continental university colleges, and constituted by far the most ambitious project associated with the University of St Andrews up to that point.[26] Kennedy's new college had impressive stone buildings (including an elaborate Gothic chapel and an unusually tall bell tower) and covered a large area on the north side of North Gait. The college's site had previously been occupied by no fewer than six tenements, plus a series of crofts collectively known as 'Stanycroft'.[27] All of these properties were acquired by Kennedy in order to provide space for his religious and educational foundation.[28] The construction of St Salvator's thus entailed a change in the use of a significant section of one of St Andrews' three main streets.

However, the alterations of the mid fifteenth century were not limited to the setting up of St Salvator's College. This period probably also saw the establishment of two mendicant houses within St Andrews. Around 1458 Bishop Kennedy founded an Observant Franciscan friary in St Andrews.[29] The Observant Franciscans' vows of corporate (as well as individual) poverty meant that in the main they eschewed landed wealth. Nevertheless, they were willing to occupy substantial friaries.[30] The St Andrews Observant Franciscan house was located on land between North Gait and Market Gait towards the western edge of the city. The friary precinct appears to have been relatively extensive – at the time of the Reformation it was described as covering six roods of land.[31] The previous history of the site is unknown, but its location towards the edge of burgh suggests that it may have been cultivated land prior to the construction of the friary.[32]

---

[25] Dunlop, *Kennedy*, p. 7.
[26] Ibid., pp. 282–5.
[27] Cant, *St Salvator*, pp. 81, 99–103.
[28] Ibid., pp. 99–103.
[29] Dunlop, *Kennedy*, p. 297. For more on the Observant Franciscans see Christina A. Strauch, 'The Observant Franciscans in Scotland, c. 1457–1560' (unpublished PhD thesis, University of Edinburgh, 2007).
[30] Some Observant Franciscans may have had scruples even about owning religious houses. However, the St Andrews Observants appear to have owned their convent. In May 1559 (under increasing pressure from Protestant Reformers) the warden and vicar of the St Andrews Franciscans gave the site of their friary to the city. StAUL, B65/1/1, f. 31r; Dunlop, *Kennedy*, p. 298.
[31] StAUL, B65/1/1, f. 31r.
[32] Even in the 1530s the Franciscan friary was adjacent to crofts and gardens. For example, a charter from 1533 records that John Jackson's croft on the north side of Market Gait was bounded by the crofts of George Allanson on the west and the place of the friars minor on the east. StAUL, B65/23/269.

The St Andrews Dominican friary may also have been built on a green-field site, although the complex history of the Blackfriars in St Andrews makes it difficult to draw any firm conclusions on this issue.[33] The St Andrews Dominican friary was officially recognised as a convent around 1518.[34] However, by this date the Dominicans already had a lengthy record of involvement in St Andrews. There are regular references to a Dominican house or place in St Andrews from the mid fifteenth century onwards. For example, an extant charter from 4 August 1446 records that a citizen of St Andrews named John Michaels granted the house of the friars preachers in St Andrews an annual rent of 3s from a property in Argyle (the suburb which lay just to the west of the gateway to St Andrews now known as the West Port).[35] Similarly, a charter dated 15 May 1451 refers to the 'sacred house' of the 'friars preachers' in St Andrews.[36] The prevalence of post-1446 references to the St Andrews Dominican house, and the lack of earlier documentary evidence for its existence, strongly implies that the Blackfriars came to St Andrews during the city's fifteenth-century religious expansion.[37]

Perhaps unsurprisingly given the obscure origins of the friar preachers in St Andrews, the exact process by which the Dominicans acquired the site of their friary is unclear. It is likely that by the 1450s (and certainly by the start of the sixteenth century) the St Andrews Dominicans were based on a large plot towards the western end of South Gait.[38] Traditionally, it has been assumed that this land was unoccupied before its development as a friary and the limited archaeological investigation that has been undertaken on the site appears to support this interpretation.[39] Nevertheless, it should be noted that even if the Dominicans originally established themselves in an undeveloped area just outside the city, their friary quickly became part of the main settlement. By the late fifteenth century the St Andrews Dominicans' site was surrounded by ordinary secular

---

[33] For example, Brooks and Whittington assume that the Dominican friary was built on the edge of the burgh. Brooks and Whittington, p. 288.

[34] StAUL, B65/23/215.

[35] StAUL, B65/23/32.

[36] StAUL, B65/23/34.

[37] There is a tradition that the Dominicans established a house in St Andrews in the 1270s. However, there is a conspicuous absence of pre-fifteenth-century references to this foundation. Notably, St Andrews is not listed in any of the early lists of Dominican foundations in Scotland. Easson, *Medieval Religious Houses*, p. 101; Janet Foggie, *Renaissance Religion in Urban Scotland: The Dominican Order, 1450–1560* (Leiden, 2003), pp. 5–7.

[38] The site of the Dominican friary is still visible to this day thanks to the survival of part of the north transept of the church. There are references to the Dominicans owning land on South Gait dating from the 1460s onwards. StAUL, B65/23/46.

[39] The Blackfriars site has never been fully excavated. However, some archaeological investigation was undertaken by Derek Hall in 1995 when floodlights were installed by the remains of the friary church. Some of the trenches dug at this time revealed what appeared to be demolition rubble from the friary church at about 0.5m below ground level. Other trenches had no archaeological remains, but instead natural sand was reached at 0.52m below modern ground level. See note on RCAHMS website: canmore.rcahms.gov.uk/en/site/94440/details/st+andrews+south+street+dominican+monastery/.

burgage plots.[40] A religious community initially located on the margins of the burgh ended up occupying a substantial portion of a prime urban real estate.

In comparison to the religious properties developed during the 1410s, the ecclesiastical sites established during the mid fifteenth century were located in more peripheral areas of St Andrews. However, they still constituted a notable change to the appearance and plan of St Andrews. St Salvator's College, the Dominican friary and the Franciscan friary were all founded in places that had previously been devoid of major religious institutions. Crucially, the sites of these new institutions were also placed in such a way that they dominated the approaches to the city.[41] It did not matter whether a late fifteenth-century visitor came into St Andrews along North Gait, Market Gait or South Gait, one of their first sights would have been a religious foundation. No one could fail to observe the wealth and influence of the church.

The late medieval expansion in the number of religious institutions in St Andrews transformed the geography of the city. Rather than ecclesiastical foundations being confined to one quarter, they came to be scattered across the entire urban area. This brought St Andrews in line with typical English and Continental cities of the time, which normally had religious buildings dotted around in a variety of locations. To contemporaries the development of a range of different ecclesiastical sites probably made St Andrews appear more cosmopolitan and up-to-date. Certainly, there is some evidence that local elites were proud of the array of religious foundations within the city. For example, when in 1538 St Andrews served as the scene for Mary of Guise's formal welcome to Scotland, the new queen was taken on a tour of all of the city's ecclesiastical institutions before eventually being greeted by burgesses at the Tolbooth.[42] By the end of the Middle Ages the diversity of St Andrews' religious sites had become part of the city's public image.

However, the increase in religious sites may have had more concrete implications for St Andrews. It is possible that the take-over of large parts of the city by religious foundations encouraged the settlement of St Andrews to grow outwards. The fifteenth and early sixteenth centuries seem to have seen an expansion in the extent of the built-up area of St Andrews. Rentals compiled at the Reformation reveal that by the mid sixteenth century the whole extent of South Gait from the cathedral to the West Port (one of the main gateways marking entry to the city) was developed, and that there was significant building out-

---

[40] Indeed, when in the early sixteenth century the Dominicans wished to extend their convent westwards they had to acquire a tenement which had previously belonged to a St Andrews citizen named William Watson. StAUL, B65/23/253; B65/23/259.

[41] The tower of St Salvator's College dominates the western approaches to St Andrews to this day. The Dominican and Franciscan friaries were probably not quite as grand as St Salvator's College. However, the oldest surviving map of St Andrews depicts them as substantial buildings which overshadowed nearby secular properties. NLS, MS 20996.

[42] *The Historie and Cronicles of Scotland From the Slauchter of King James the First to the Ane Thousand Five Hundreith Thrie Scoir Fyftein Zeir, Written and Collected by Robert Lindesay of Pitscottie*, ed. A. J. G. Mackay, 3 vols (Edinburgh, 1899), i, p. 380.

side the port.[43] There also appears to have been some westwards development on Market Gait and (perhaps) North Gait.[44] This expansion may have been partly driven by population growth.[45] Yet it was probably also encouraged by the conversion of secular burgage plots to religious purposes. Ecclesiastical foundations' appropriation of large areas of St Andrews reduced the amount of land within the old settlement that was available for ordinary dwellings, and hence almost certainly increased the likelihood of secular development around the outskirts. An increase in religious sites necessitated an expansion in the size of the city.

However, the growth in church property within St Andrews was not restricted to the actual sites of ecclesiastical institutions. The fifteenth and (to an extent) early sixteenth centuries saw the church intensify its influence over ordinary burgage plots. Prior to 1400, although clerics and religious foundations played a role in landholding, they normally placed a limited financial burden on the inhabitants of secular tenements. This state of affairs was over-turned by the ecclesiastical expansion of the late Middle Ages. During the fifteenth and early sixteenth centuries religious institutions took over completely the ownership of a number of St Andrews burgage plots, and increased their financial rights regarding others via the phenomenon of rent-charges. Both developments ultimately enabled the church to exact much larger sums from the residents of St Andrews' secular properties.

St Andrews' churchmen increased their rights over the city's secular property through a combination of donations and purchases. During the late Middle Ages urban lands often formed part of the endowments given by the founder or other supporters to new St Andrews religious institutions. For example, in the 1450s the provost and canons of St Salvator's, as well as being granted the site of the college and extensive estates outside St Andrews, were given ten plots of land on the north side of the road now known as the Scores, plus a large burgage plot on the north side of South Gait.[46] These lands do not seem to have been previously held by religious foundations – the plots on the Scores had belonged to a man named David Trail, whilst the tenement on South Gait pertained to a citizen of St Andrews called James Arthur and his wife Janet Brown. Similarly, when St Leonard's College was founded in 1513, the masters, chaplains and students were given a series of houses in Priors Wynd (now known as Abbey

---

[43] StAUL, B65/1/1, ff. 39v-50v.
[44] Ibid.; Brooks and Whittington, p. 289.
[45] Unfortunately, the nature of the surviving source materials makes it extremely difficult to ascertain whether there was an overall growth (or decline) in the number of residents between 1400 and 1560. We currently lack any population figures for St Andrews before the seventeenth century (when extant tax and communion records make it possible to arrive at an approximate estimate of the inhabitants of the burgh). For seventeenth-century population figures see Geoffrey Parker, 'The "Kirk by Law Established" and the Origins of "The Taming of Scotland": St Andrews 1559–1600', *Perspectives in Scottish Social History*, ed. Leah Leneman (Aberdeen, 1988), p. 24.
[46] StAUL, UYSS110/P2; UYSS110/W/4.

Street) as well as tenements in South Gait and on the Scores.[47] Most of the plots granted to religious foundations were given as free alms – a specific form of tenure that gave the recipient complete control over the property. The church was thus acquiring the right to determine the future of these sites, and gaining the ability in effect to dictate the terms of contracts with any future tenants.

St Andrews burgage plots were frequently given to support chaplainries (the Scottish term for the small intercessory institutions normally referred to in England as chantries). The majority of chaplainries had quite limited holdings, but because there were so many of these institutions in late medieval St Andrews their impact on the city's property patterns was considerable. There is firm evidence that in the late 1550s there were at least twenty-nine chaplainries attached to Holy Trinity Church. The figures for other foundations are less certain. However, it has been suggested that St Salvator's College had a minimum of thirty chaplainries, and a similarly large number is posited for St Andrews Cathedral.[48] We also know that at least three chaplainries were attached to the College of St Leonard, and that at least one chaplainry was associated with the College of St John.[49] Therefore, it is likely that during the first half of the sixteenth century there were in the region of a hundred chaplainries based in St Andrews.

The overwhelming majority of these chaplainry institutions were founded in the years after 1400. For example, only three of the chaplainries attached to Holy Trinity appear to have existed before the church's move to South Gait – the rest were all established after 1412.[50] Likewise, all of the St Salvator's College chaplainries appear to post-date the foundation of the college. For the most part these new institutions were funded by income from urban lands and rent-charges. The endowments of a chaplainry dedicated to the Blessed Virgin Mary founded in Holy Trinity Church in 1501 were not untypical. The chaplainry's founder, a priest named John Bonar, initially donated a tenement in Ratton Row (the road now called South Castle Street) plus rent-charges bringing in £8 18s 8d per annum.[51] In 1504 John Bonar granted his chaplainry another tenement (this time located in Market Gait) and further rent-charges.[52] At the time of the Reformation the chaplainry was in possession of three tenements in St Andrews, as well as seven rent-charges bringing £11 8s each year.[53] Virtually

---

[47] StAUL, UYSL110/A/1. A number of these properties had formerly belonged to the Hospital of St Leonard.

[48] Cant, *St Salvator*, p. 24; McRoberts, 'The Glorious House of St Andrew', pp. 81–3.

[49] StAUL, UYSM110/B12/20; John Herkless and Robert Kerr Hannay, *The College of St Leonard* (Edinburgh, 1905), pp. 66–7.

[50] Of the Holy Trinity chaplainries, only those of St Fergus, the Holy Cross and Our Lady appear to have been in existence in 1412. W. E. K. Rankin, *The Parish Church of the Holy Trinity, St Andrews, Pre-Reformation* (Edinburgh, 1955), p. 24; F. C. Eeles, 'The Altar of St Fergus in Holy Trinity, St Andrews: A Sixteenth-Century MS. Rental and Inventory', *SHR* 2:7 (1905), pp. 260–7.

[51] StAUL, B65/23/171.

[52] StAUL, B65/23/179.

[53] StAUL, B65/1/1, ff. 39v–50v.

all of these endowments had been purchased by John Bonar specifically to support his new chaplainry.[54]

The church's increased rights over St Andrews tenements almost certainly had consequences for life in the burgh. Some of the secular properties the church acquired provided accommodation for clerics attached to institutions such as Holy Trinity Church and the university. A number of these religious residents appear to have been highly active in the development of their properties. For example, in the early fifteenth century James Braid, a priest serving at the altar of St Fergus in Holy Trinity Church, made extensive alterations to his chaplainry's house in Argyle.[55] Braid added to the property three rooms (one of which was designed for bathing), six fireplaces, a dovecot and a well. He also installed new drainage, dug trenches around the perimeter of the property and planted several trees. It is possible that affluent clerics such as Braid directly contributed to the improvement in the standard of housing that took place within St Andrews during the late Middle Ages.

A significant proportion of the secular properties that St Andrews' ecclesiastical institutions acquired would not have been lived in by churchmen. It is likely that many of these properties were simply leased out to local residents. However, as the sixteenth century progressed, and in particular during the 1550s, it became increasingly common for these properties to be set in feu-farm.[56] Whilst feuing had certain advantages for tenants (notably they enjoyed much greater security in tenure), these benefits were typically off-set by the quite substantial sums that landlords charged both for transition to this form of tenure and in annual feu-maills. The growing popularity of feu-farm tenure meant that by the mid-sixteenth century St Andrews householders were paying much larger sums each year to the church than had been typical for their predecessors. For example, in 1552 a tenement on the north side of South Gait belonging to the altar of the Blessed Virgin Mary was feued to David Rutherford and his wife Elizabeth Balfour in exchange for an annual payment of 10 merks (£6 13s 4d).[57] Such an amount formed a significant increase from even the feu-maills of the fourteenth century, which had normally consisted of a few shillings.[58]

[54] StAUL, B65/23/153–153; B65/23/157–161.
[55] Eeles, 'The Altar of St Fergus in Holy Trinity', pp. 260–7.
[56] See StAUL, B65/1/1 and B65/1/5.
[57] StAUL, B65/23/312. It is perhaps worthwhile noting that burgage plots on the north side of South Gait were generally smaller than those on the south side. The tenement taken on by Rutherford was almost certainly not even one of the larger or more desirable properties in St Andrews.
[58] Whilst some of the increase in the sums charged as feu-maills between about 1400 and 1550 was probably attributable to inflation, the rise cannot be blamed on that alone. For example, in the fourteenth century the annual maills paid on a St Andrews tenement were frequently similar to, or less than, the price of a carcase of beef. By the 1550s St Andrews feu-maills were commonly four or five times the contemporary value of a beef carcase (which in the mid sixteenth century was typically somewhere between £1 4s and £1 10s). Gemmill and Mayhew, *Changing Values in Medieval Scotland*, p. 248.

The growing financial burden placed on St Andrews households was, though, not confined to feu-maills. The fifteenth and sixteenth centuries saw a dramatic surge in the number of rent-charges levied within the city. Rent-charges formed a standard means of church finance in a number of European countries. However, they seem to have been particularly common in Scotland.[59] Certainly, they formed a key part of the funding of St Andrews' religious foundations during the later Middle Ages. There is reason to believe that all of St Andrews' major religious foundations drew at least some income from rent-charges during the later Middle Ages, and many intercessory institutions were reliant on rent-charges for the bulk of their funding.[60] Some of the rent-charges collected by St Andrews institutions were from rural estates, whilst others were levied on properties in other Scottish burghs such as Dundee and Linlithgow.[61] However, a large proportion of the rent-charges collected by St Andrews' religious foundations were from households based within the episcopal city itself. During the fifteenth and sixteenth centuries (largely as a result of the growing popularity of intercessory institutions) there was a rapid expansion in the number of rent-charges levied on tenements in St Andrews. Whilst references to rent-charges were relatively rare in the period preceding 1400, by the late fifteenth century they had become ubiquitous. By the early sixteenth century it was extremely unusual to find a property within the city that did not have at least one rent-charge associated with it. At the time of the Reformation, St Andrews Cathedral Priory was levying over 100 rent-charges from St Andrews tenements, whilst Holy Trinity Church was collecting more than 500 rent-charges from properties within the city.[62] To put this figure in context, in 1618 St Andrews had only 486 tax-paying households.[63] In the mid sixteenth century there were almost certainly more religious rent-charges than there were households.

The expansion in the number of rent-charges seems to have taken place with the consent (and at times the active support) of St Andrews residents. Rent-charges were acquired in three main ways: they could be purchased by

---

[59] Unfortunately the limited state of research into rent-charges in Scotland makes it hard to be certain of this point. Certainly rent-charges were very common in St Andrews during the fifteenth and sixteenth centuries and a perusal of the rentals of other urban religious institutions suggests that the phenomenon was widespread in other Scottish burghs. NRS, CH8/31.

[60] At the Reformation the cathedral, the church of St Mary on the Rock, Holy Trinity Church, the three university colleges, the hospital of St Nicholas, and the Dominican friary (not to mention the archbishop and the archdeacon of St Andrews) all derived part of their income from rent-charges. Even the Observant Franciscans appear to have had limited involvement with the phenomenon. An instrument of sasine from July 1495 records that the factor of the St Andrews Friars Minor of Observance transferred to Holy Trinity Church a rent-charge of 4s which had belonged to the friary. StAUL, B65/1/1; UYSS150/1–2; UYSL515; B65/23/136; *The Books of Assumption of the Thirds of Benefices*, ed. James Kirk (Oxford, 1995), pp. 1–21, 55, 64–7, 89.

[61] *The Books of Assumption*, ed. Kirk, pp. 11–12.

[62] StAUL, UYSL110/C2; B65/1/1, ff. 39v-50v.

[63] Parker, 'The "Kirk by Law Established"', p. 24.

the religious institution in question; pious donors could buy a rent-charge to give to their favoured religious foundation; or alternatively people could give a rent-charge levied from their own land.[64] The growth in rent-charges that St Andrews saw during the fifteenth and early sixteenth centuries could not have taken place without the co-operation of local householders.[65] Nevertheless, although a substantially voluntary process, the vast increase did result in much greater financial burdens being placed on households. In the 1550s it was not uncommon for three or more rent-charges to be levied on one household. For example, in 1553 the residents of a single tenement and bakehouse in the St Andrews suburb of Argyle were paying rents to the cathedral, St Leonard's College, the choir of Holy Trinity Church, the altars of St Ninian and the Blessed Virgin Mary (both of which were attached to Holy Trinity), and the Dominican friary.[66] When combined with the heavy feu-maills that some households were also paying, rent-charges could constitute a significant financial strain. By the end of the Middle Ages, the occupants of St Andrews properties were paying much more money to religious foundations for the privilege of living in their homes than had been typical in previous generations. At the same time, many local religious foundations vastly increased their revenues from property within the city. A rental compiled shortly after the Reformation reveals that in the mid sixteenth century the clerics of Holy Trinity Church were raising at least £434 per annum from St Andrews' houses and crofts – the rights to almost all of which had been gained since 1410.[67]

The growth in church property that the settlement of St Andrews saw during the later Middle Ages was part of a much broader expansion in the estates of the city's religious institutions. In the 150 years or so preceding the Scottish Reformation, ecclesiastical foundations based in St Andrews acquired the right to tithes from additional parish churches and significant properties in other Scottish towns and in the countryside.[68] However, the expansion in church wealth was particularly intense in the urban area of St Andrews. The city's patterns of ecclesiastical landholding changed dramatically between the beginning of the fifteenth century and the city's official conversion to Protestantism at the end of the 1550s. Most obviously, more of the settlement was occupied by the sites of religious foundations. However, the church had also substantially extended its rights over the city's secular properties and was levying much larger annual sums from local families. The expansion in St Andrews church estates

[64] See the StAUL, B65/23 series of charters.
[65] Relatively ordinary households often made gifts of rent-charges to religious foundations. For example, in 1536 a baker named Henry Law gave the altar of St Tobert in Holy Trinity Church (the baker's guild altar) an annual rent of 15s from his house on North Gait. StAUL, B65/23/273.
[66] The household was also paying an annual feu-maill of £3 5s to the altar of St Katherine in Holy Trinity Church. StAUL, B65/23/316.
[67] StAUL, B65/1/1, ff. 39v–50v.
[68] See (amongst others) the following series of documents: StAUL, B65/23; UYSL110; UYSM110; UYSS100; UYSS110.

seen both in the city itself and further afield was in many ways symptomatic of the vitality and prosperity that Scotland's ecclesiastical capital was enjoying at this date. Yet, it may also have held the seeds of the church's decline. So long as local residents were reasonably prosperous, the substantial wealth of the church in St Andrews seems to have been broadly accepted and, indeed, at times supported. However, in times of hardship there was more resistance to religious exactions. There is, for example, limited evidence from the 1550s of resistance to paying rent-charges in St Andrews.[69] These financial niggles could form points of conflict. When Protestantism began to become a serious issue in Scotland, the supposed greed of Catholic clerics was a convenient target for propaganda.[70] The church came to be portrayed by some Scots as a corrupt institution more concerned with revenues than redeeming souls. Indeed, in the early 1560s the Protestant poet Alexander Scott satirised the way in which chantry priests:

> tyrit God with tryfillis, tume trentalis,
> And daisit him with dalie dargeis,
> With owklie abitis to augment thair rentalis ...[71]
>
> [tire God with trifles, empty trentals,[72]
> And daze him with daily dirges,
> With weekly obits[73] to augment their rentals ...]

Such accusations may have found ready acceptance in households burdened with heavy ecclesiastical exactions. It is perhaps not insignificant that when, in the summer of 1559, John Knox wished to incite the citizens of St Andrews to reject Catholicism he chose as his text the expulsion of the money-changers from the temple of Jerusalem – a topic that probably had more than one resonance for local residents.[74]

---

[69] For example, during the 1550s the clerics of Holy Trinity Church sued several St Andrews residents for non-payment of rent-charges. StAUL, B65/1/1, ff. 39v–50v.

[70] Famously, during the winter of 1558/59 placards appeared on the doors of Scottish friaries condemning (amongst other things) the friars' greed and demanding the reallocation of their wealth to the poor. Yet condemnation of church wealth had been a stock part of Reformist rhetoric for some decades by that date. As early as the 1530s Reformist sympathisers in St Andrews had publicly criticised ecclesiastical avarice. *John Knox's History of the Reformation in Scotland*, ed. William Croft Dickinson, 2 vols (Edinburgh, 1949), i, pp. 16, 255–6.

[71] Alexander Scott, 'Ane New Yeir Gift to the Quene Mary Quhen Scho Come First Hame', *A Choice of Scottish Verse, 1470–1570*, ed. J. & M. MacQueen (London, 1972), p. 182.

[72] A trental was a cycle of thirty masses said for the souls of the dead.

[73] An obit was a service celebrated on the anniversary of someone's death.

[74] Dickinson, *John Knox's History*, i, p. 182.

CHAPTER TWELVE

The Prehistory of the University of St Andrews*

Norman H. Reid

ST Andrews, both medieval and modern, is characterised by the quest for knowledge. The modern university proudly markets its historical status with the conveniently ambiguous strapline 'Scotland's first university', and it is undoubtedly the case that the atmosphere, traditions and environment of a place which has been a seat of learning for centuries are amongst the attractions which draw scholars to the 'auld grey toun'. It is thus perhaps surprising that a degree of mystery still surrounds the foundation of the university, and that an event of such importance to Scotland's intellectual and cultural history remains relatively unexplored by historians. The first systematic attempt to describe both the motivation leading to the foundation and the process by which it was accomplished was not made until prompted by the 500th anniversary, celebrated (without obvious explanation of the choice of date) in 1911, apparently the first centenary to have been so honoured. However, since then remarkably little historiographical progress has been made regarding the events surrounding the foundation, which must of course be key to an understanding of the nature of the early institution and the town in which it was set.[1] Yet there are obvious inconsistencies and uncertainties in what has become the accepted version of events, which justify a sceptical re-examination of the evidence.

The contemporary sources at our disposal are sparse. Walter Bower, a

---

* The research for this article was conducted during research leave funded by the University of St Andrews and under a Senior Research Fellowship of its Institute of Scottish Historical Research, with research facilities provided by the Strathmartine Trust. I am also greatly indebted to my wife, Elspeth, and to my friends and colleagues Rachel Hart, Roger Mason, Robert Smart and Simon Taylor for their many helpful comments and suggestions.
[1] Several publications celebrating the rich past of the institution were produced around the 500th anniversary; the foundation was most notably discussed in three articles (all in the *Scottish Historical Review*, 1906 and 1911) written by James Maitland Anderson (1852–1927), who, during his long career with the university, held the posts of University Librarian and Keeper of Muniments, as well as Secretary of the University, Quaestor, and Secretary and Registrar of the General Council. His works will be fully cited below. Until recently, subsequent historians have largely accepted Anderson's conclusions.

fifteenth-century abbot of Inchcolm, an Augustinian house set on a small island in the Forth only some 35 miles from St Andrews, related in his celebrated *Scotichronicon* that in 1410 'after Whitsunday an institution of higher learning of university standing made a start in the city of St Andrew of Kilrymont in Scotland when Henry de Wardlaw was the bishop of St Andrews and James Bisset was the prior there'. He proceeded to name three masters, subsequently (*consequenter*) joined by five more, who taught theology, canon law and arts, and revealed that they taught for two-and-a-half years before 'at last' (*tandem*) on 3 February 1413/14, papal privileges confirming the university's status were received in St Andrews. He then described in great detail the celebrations which marked that event: a peal of bells of all the town's churches, a formal reading of the papal bulls before the clergy, liturgical ceremonies, celebration of mass, preaching and a large ceremonial procession of, Bower claimed, 'four hundred clergy besides lesser clerks and young monks'. Local colour is added by his further description of the 'boundless merry-making' and drinking around the bonfires that were lit in the streets (a wise precaution in St Andrews in February!).[2] Apart from the popular street-party, it is noteworthy that Bower's description of these events is of an entirely ecclesiastical affair: there is no reference even to the presence, let alone participation, of any representative of the nation's secular authorities who, as we shall see, had co-petitioned the pope for the cause of the celebration.

Bower's is a very closely contemporary account, written within thirty-five years of the events he describes.[3] It is rendered even more valuable because prior to gaining his abbacy in 1417, Bower was a canon of the priory of St Andrews, and was almost certainly one of those who lived through the terror of the partial collapse of the cathedral building in a great storm in the early weeks of 1410 (which caused significant damage to the conventual buildings and brought about the death of at least one canon).[4] It is probable that only a few months later he participated in the celebrations he described – one of the hundreds of clergy that walked in the procession 'for the glory of God and the praise and honour of the university'. The records, of course, cannot confirm this supposition, since only the records of the faculty of arts have survived, but it seems very likely that Bower was himself one of the university's early graduates; he was a bachelor of decreets (canon law) by 1417 and a bachelor of theology by 1420, neither of which has been traced to any other university.[5]

The documentary sources, although scanty, largely confirm Bower's story: on 28 February 1412, the best part of two years after the eight scholars are said to have started teaching, the bishop of St Andrews, Henry Wardlaw, issued a grant to the 'venerable men, the doctors, masters, bachelors, and all scholars dwelling

---

[2] *Scotichronicon*, viii, pp. 76–9; all references to Watt's edition of the text of *Scotichronicon* include both the Latin text (on even-numbered pages) and its parallel translation.
[3] For dating of the work, see *Scotichronicon*, ix, pp. 210–14.
[4] *The Heads of Religious Houses in Scotland from Twelfth to Sixteenth Centuries*, ed. D. E. R. Watt and N. F. Shead (Edinburgh, 2001), p. 106; *Scotichronicon*, viii, pp. 74–5.
[5] For a well-referenced biography of Walter Bower, see *Scotichronicon*, ix, pp. 204–8.

in our city of St Andrews'.[6] Making it clear that the grant was being given in response to a petition by the grantees, he described the institution thus:

> instituted and founded in fact by us, saving, however, the authority of the apostolic See, and by you under the favour of the divine clemency now laudably commenced, and which also, of and with the consent of our chapter of St Andrews, we over and above, by the tenor of these presents, institute and found.

That it might happily flourish in the teaching of medicine, canon and civil law and arts (curiously, theology is not mentioned), the bishop took the university under the protection of himself and his successors, and bestowed upon it a range of immunities and privileges in terms of trade, taxation and accommodation. As well as to the doctors, masters, bachelors and scholars, these privileges were extended to all the university's servants and suppliers ('your beadles, esquires, familiars and servitors, as also your writers, stationers, and parchment-makers, and their wives, children, and maid-servants'). These are the *suppositi*, the subordinate members, of a medieval university: it is being clarified, as is normal in such circumstances, that the privileges are to be effective for the entire university community.[7] Further than the grant of privileges, the document also goes into significant detail regarding the regulation of the relationship between the university and the town in terms of discipline, jurisdiction and the protection of rights, in all of which the secular authorities were made subordinate to those of the university and its ecclesiastical guardians.

Wardlaw stated that he had authenticated the document with the seal of the cathedral chapter, and then, in a separate statement, the prior and convent of St Andrews along with the two archdeacons of St Andrews and Lothian, formally convened as the chapter, gave their assent both to the foundation of the university and to the grant of privileges. The document makes no reference either to the constitution or to the internal organisation and administration of the university. Neither is it, in legal form, a charter. It is therefore inaccurate to describe it, as has been the usual custom, as a 'charter of foundation and incorporation'. There is no indication, however, of there having been any earlier document which is no longer extant, and so it is probably the case that this was indeed the first formal documentary act in the foundation of the university. It makes no claim to 'incorporate' in the legal sense and is self-avowedly a straightforward grant of privileges, issued at the specific request of the doctors, masters, bachelors and scholars of the city.

Towards the end of 1412 a formal petition was dispatched to the pope – now, with the benefit of hindsight, generally acknowledged to be the anti-pope – Benedict XIII, seeking his universal authority for the foundation of the

---

[6] Wardlaw's grant of privileges has not survived, but its text is recited within one of the papal bulls of August 1413. Quotations are from the original, StAUL, UYUY100; the translation is unpublished – anonymous, nineteenth century, revised by the author.

[7] *Universities in the Middle Ages*, ed. H. de Ridder-Symoens (Cambridge, 2003), p. 120.

Figure 12.1: The surviving papal bull of 28 August 1413.

university.[8] By long-acknowledged custom, only the papacy or the empire could authorise the award of degrees and thus the all-important universal licence to teach anywhere within the transnational education community, the *licencia ubique docendi*. The petition ran in the name of King James I and the bishop, prior, chapter and archdeacon of St Andrews, with the consent of the three estates of the kingdom. On 28 August 1413 the pope responded with a series of six papal bulls in which he authorised and formalised the foundation of the university, confirmed it in the privileges bestowed upon it by Wardlaw and made provision for its protection.[9] These were the documents which, having been

---

[8] The original petition has not survived. However, what appears to be a reasonably complete copy of its text is extant within the papal archives and was published by James Maitland Anderson as an appendix to 'James I of Scotland and the University of St Andrews', *SHR* 3 (1906), pp. 301–15, at pp. 313–14.

[9] Of the six bulls issued, only one has survived, that which confirms and recites Wardlaw's grant of privileges. There is a photograph and description of it in *Treasures of St Andrews University Library*, ed. Norman Reid et al. (London, 2010), pp. 112–13. However, all six are calendared in *Calendar of Papal Letters to Scotland of Benedict XIII of Avignon, 1394–1419*, ed. Francis McGurk (Edinburgh, 1976), pp. 276–8, and their texts are published in *Evidence, Oral and Documentary Taken and Received by the Commissioners … for Visiting the Universities of Scotland (St Andrews)* (London, 1837), Appendix Pt. 1, pp. 172–6.

expedited by the papal chancery in November, were carried to St Andrews and arrived in the following February to be received in the celebrations described by Bower.[10]

This, then, is the framework around which we have to build a more complete picture of the foundation of the university. As far back as 1906, James Maitland Anderson expressed curiosity about what lay behind Bower's obviously simplified narrative, which 'is quite satisfactory, so far as it goes [...] But it fails to answer many of the questions that arise in the mind of a serious inquirer into the genesis of so venerable and illustrious an institution.'[11] Anderson's own conclusions were that Scottish educational opportunities, hitherto sought abroad in the great Continental schools, particularly those of Paris and Orléans, were becoming limited. For many years, because of the endemic warfare between Scotland and England, few Scots had found their way to the English universities; from 1378 the Great Schism caused further discomfort in other parts of Europe, especially when in 1409, following the Council of Pisa, France withdrew from obedience to Benedict XIII. Anderson believed that 'as Scotland disregarded the decision of the council and continued to adhere to Benedict, Scottish students, whether pursuing their studies in England, France, or Italy, would be deemed schismatics and the need for a university at home would at once become a matter of extreme urgency'; as a result it was likely that rather than having been a carefully planned development, the university must have been 'called into existence to meet a sudden emergency'.[12]

Examining the biographies of the men whom he regarded as the key players – Bishop Wardlaw, the prior of St Andrews James Bisset, the archdeacon of St Andrews Thomas Stewart, and the king – Anderson came to the conclusion that the institution owed much to the coincidence of such a group of learned, well-educated men happening to be in power at the moment of necessity, and that the foundation was largely the result of their 'harmonious co-operation'. However, he seems to have assumed a somewhat leisurely and gentlemanly approach, at odds with the idea of a knee-jerk reaction to an emergency, when he claimed that 'all four were men of learning and culture, to whom the founding of a university must have been a congenial enterprise'.[13]

Anderson's picture, rooted firmly in the emergency created by the difficulties Scotland encountered through war with England and increasing schismatic isolation, has been largely accepted – although not entirely without question – by subsequent scholars.[14] His account has been enhanced by those who have made

---

[10] The date expedited is given in *CPL Benedict XIII*.
[11] Anderson, 'James I', p. 301. The following summary of Anderson's approach has been taken from that article and from his 'The Beginnings of St Andrews University, 1410–1418': two articles published in *SHR* 8 (1911), pp. 225–48 and 333–60 [hereafter, Anderson, 'Foundation'].
[12] Anderson, 'Foundation', p. 229.
[13] Ibid., p. 230.
[14] See, for example, H. Rashdall, *The Universities of Europe in the Middle Ages*, 2nd edn, ed. F. M. Powicke and A. B. Emden (Oxford, 1936), iii, pp. 302–3. A substantial challenge to

the further observation that the timing of the foundation of St Andrews places it firmly within the period when such 'national' universities were appearing with some regularity, especially on the periphery of Europe. Putting it very simplistically, the increasing fragmentation of Europe in the fourteenth and early fifteenth centuries (the effect both of schism and of dynastic rivalries which led to major conflicts such as the Hundred Years War) challenged the concept of the universality of education and compromised the ease of international travel and scholarship. The foundation in this period of universities in Heidelberg (1385), Cologne (1388), Erfurt (1392), Krakow (1400), Leipzig (1409), Buda (1410) and Turin (1412), as well as St Andrews, can be seen in the context of this developing regionalisation of education. The increasing cost of sending students abroad for education provided further motivation, in line with the demand for greater numbers of educated clergy and secular clerks.[15] This trend towards 'localisation' was evident throughout the fourteenth and early fifteenth centuries, irrespective of issues of schism or other political difficulties.[16]

It is instructive to look at a parallel foundation, that of the University of Louvain in 1425, only a little more than a decade after St Andrews. The reason given in the papal petition (made in the name of the duke of Brabant, the town authorities and the chapter of St Peter's in Louvain) was that, there being no university provision in the dioceses which lay within the duke's domains, 'many of those who live there must remain either deprived of science, or journey to faraway lands in order to fulfil the desire to deepen their knowledge'.[17] However, it seems clear that, as with the St Andrews petition, the complaint about the dangers of travel was largely formulaic and that there were other motivations. Cologne, founded in 1388, was after all within easy reach of Louvain. It is probable that equal, if not more weighty, considerations were a desire to control the influences to which students were exposed in an age of increasing theological controversy and a political imperative to limit the export of both intelligentsia

---

aspects of Anderson's view has recently been made by Isla Woodman in 'Education and Episcopacy: The Universities of Scotland in the Fifteenth Century' (unpublished PhD thesis, University of St Andrews, 2011).

[15] See, for example, Ridder-Symoens, *Universities*, pp. 97–102, 285ff., where there is some discussion of this issue specifically in relation to Scottish students.

[16] For example, Jacques Verger claims that 'from the fourteenth century on, university and state took various measures designed rather to discourage than to favour student mobility': Ibid., p. 40. See also discussion of the changing nature of nation-states in G. R. Potter, 'Some Characteristics of the Fourteenth Century', *Prague Essays*, ed. R.W. Seton-Watson (Oxford, 1949), pp. 19–28; R. N. Swanson, *Universities, Academics and the Great Schism* (Cambridge, 1979), pp. 11–12 sees the schism as a catalyst for this more general development.

[17] The petition, quoted from the text of the papal bull, in E. J. M. van Eijl, 'The Foundation of the University of Louvain', *The Universities in the Late Middle Ages*, ed. J. Ijsewijn and J. Paquet (Leuven, 1978), at pp. 32–3. Similar wording was used by the Emperor Charles IV in the 1344 foundation charter of the University of Prague: R. R. Betts, 'The University of Prague: The First Sixty Years', *Prague Essays*, ed. R. W. Seton-Watson (Oxford, 1949), p. 53.

and cash.[18] The parallels seem obvious and are not unique to Louvain: there can be no doubt, irrespective of any specific political or ecclesiastical exigencies, that the foundation of the university of St Andrews in the early fifteenth century was entirely consistent with broader European educational trends.

In summary, then, the received view of the foundation, based on Anderson's conclusions and developed through more recent scholarship, is that the Scots were increasingly excluded from educational opportunities beyond their borders, a difficult situation which became an emergency following French withdrawal from obedience to the Avignon papacy after the Council of Pisa. A local university was thus urgently required, a development which was in any case in accordance with broader European custom at the time. Coincidentally there happened to be a group of educated men in positions of authority in St Andrews at the right moment who were motivated to effect the foundation. Superficially, this seems a logical enough explanation of the narrative provided by Bower and supported by the documentary evidence. However, although these issues were no doubt influential to an extent, deeper examination of the evidence reveals that it remains at best an incomplete, and perhaps an entirely misleading, account.

The unsatisfactory nature of this argument is well exemplified by the lecture delivered in 1927 by J. H. Baxter, professor of Ecclesiastical History at St Andrews.[19] Baxter cited the difficulties caused by the schism and by the political situation in Paris as the primary reasons for what he inaccurately claimed was a total exodus of Scots from Paris; the difficulties of attending Oxford added to the picture, and thus 'there was little or no outlet for that stream of studious youths who for centuries had faced the long and hazardous journey to England or to France for learning's sake. A Scottish University became an indispensable necessity.' However, he also made the contradictory statement that even after the foundation 'St Andrews students are frequently found in the universities of the continent. When Paris had been rendered impossible by reason of the English occupation, the wandering tendencies of the Scot were not thereby checked.' He also recognised the increasing national fragmentation of Europe in this period, placed the founding of the university within that context, and noted the role played by both parliament and king in the foundation. He discussed the unusual failure to provide a satisfactory infrastructure before the beginning of operations, but did not manage to construct a coherent view of the foundation which made sense of these obvious inconsistencies in the narrative he appeared to accept.

Several immediate questions have to be posed. Why did the process of foundation take so long? If Wardlaw was indeed the prime instigator of the scheme, why was there such a delay in issuing any sort of documentation or official corroboration, or apparently any provision at all for the accommodation or maintenance of the new institution? Why was the supplication for papal confirmation

---

[18] van Eijl, 'Louvain', p. 33.
[19] J. H. Baxter, *St Andrews University Before the Reformation* (St Andrews, 1927), especially at pp. 5–7, 9–10.

apparently not made until over two years after the practical initiation of the university? Anderson himself made the point that the founders, including Wardlaw and Bisset, would indeed have known what it took to institute and maintain such an organisation – and yet apparently they did none of what was required, in either organisational or financial terms.[20] One must, therefore, question whether Wardlaw did indeed set the ball rolling, or whether the narrative proposed by Bower, which appears to regard him in that light, perhaps owes something to hindsight. Bower's point in his primary narrative about the foundation is that it happened when Wardlaw was bishop and Bisset was prior; at that point he does not claim that either of them was actually responsible for inviting the masters to begin teaching, or for instigating the process by which university status was achieved. He does say at another point, when eulogising Wardlaw, that 'it was he who as the prime founder brought the University to the city of St Andrews' – but as we shall see, exactly what that means may be open to question.[21]

If the foundation was the response to a sudden emergency after the Council of Pisa, there are also questions about how the masters, and indeed the students, were recruited. Returning to the example of Louvain, practical organisation did not take place there until after receipt of the papal bulls in response to the petition. Immediately thereafter, accommodation was identified, constitutional arrangements were made, teachers and other university officials were employed, and privileges similar to those granted by Wardlaw were given to the members of the new university. Importantly, marketing also took place. An open letter from the duke to princes, towns, bishops and abbots within his domains announced the opening of the university and was hung on church doors throughout the Netherlands.[22] Such organisation takes time, and there is no surviving evidence of any similarly deliberate attempt to attract either teachers or students to St Andrews in 1410/11, or to ensure that adequate practical arrangements were in place.

These considerations must raise suspicion that Bower's version of events, and the narrative that has been constructed around it and the meagre documentary evidence, is at best over-simplistic. Bower is clearly not quite accurate in some details. Most obviously, it seems that either his claim that there was a gap of two-and-a-half years between the start of teaching, which he places (in a priory under the shadow of a semi-ruinous cathedral) in May 1410, and the arrival of the papal bulls in February 1414 is miscalculated, or he has misdated

---

[20] 'At St Andrews the first doctors and masters, as well as the founders, were all true and patriotic Scotsman; and they brought with them to the new seat of learning not only ample knowledge of the subjects they undertook to teach, but likewise intimate acquaintance with the organisation and administration of the leading universities of their time.' Anderson, 'Foundation', p. 246.

[21] *Scotichronicon*, iii, pp. 410–11; Bower's acrostic epitaph on Wardlaw (ibid., pp. 410–13) further credits him: 'The schools founded on the Rymont stream are his noble achievement.'

[22] van Eijl, 'Louvain', pp. 38–40.

the commencement of teaching. If Bower is a year premature in his estimate of when teaching started, the issue of the two-and-a-half year wait for the arrival of the papal bulls is resolved, and the delay in Wardlaw's grant of privilege is less acute.[23] On the other hand, the suggestion that teaching did not start until 1411 deals a blow to the theory that the foundation was in response to the immediacy of concern about the effects of the Council of Pisa in 1409.

We also know that at least one of the masters whom Bower names as having been amongst the first group, William Fowlis, could not have been teaching in St Andrews in 1410, since he was not licensed in Paris until May 1411.[24] This may simply be another indication that Bower was mistaken in ascribing the start of teaching to 1410 or that the arrival of the teachers and the instigation of classes was a gradual process. (Fowlis is one of the five masters whom Bower states arrived *consequenter*, and so a possible interpretation is that the second group did indeed arrive a year later, and that the two-and-a-half years run from the date of their arrival, rather than that of the earlier group. It seems unlikely, however, given the way in which the events are described, that the gap between the arrivals of the two groups would have been as long as a year, or that Bower would have calculated his timing from the arrival of the second group rather than the first.) Either way, the date of Fowlis's degree has further significance for the interpretation of events: if Scots were so unwelcome in Paris and elsewhere after the Council of Pisa that the foundation of a national university became an urgent necessity, why was William Fowlis able to receive his degree in Paris in 1411; and why can over thirty further Scots be readily identified as scholars, bachelors and masters in the records of the English nation in the University of Paris between 1409 and 1411?[25] The contention that there was a purge of schismatic Scots from Paris in 1409/10 is unsupportable, and the proposition that the University of St Andrews was founded in response to the evaporation of overseas educational opportunity following the Council of Pisa is patently at odds with the documentary evidence. Indeed, in one of the papal bulls, Benedict XIII stated the situation quite explicitly: recognising that education necessarily crossed the boundaries of schismatic obedience, he made provision for Scots who had received their education at universities of the opposing papal obedience to be accepted for further study in St Andrews, either to graduate in St

---

[23] For notes about inconsistency between variant manuscripts and other issues relevant to Bower's chronology, see *Scotichronicon*, viii, pp. 184–5.

[24] *Liber Procuratorum Nationis Anglie (Alemanniae) in Universtate Parisiensi*, 1 (1333–1406), ed. H. Deniflé and A. Chatelain (Paris, 1894), p. 105.

[25] Many medieval universities were divided into 'nations', formal divisions of the institution that incorporated those studying there from particular geographical locations. The English nation in Paris was a division of the Faculty of Arts, comprising those Masters of Arts who emanated from the British Isles and most of northern and eastern Europe, including Germany, the Baltic states and Scandinavia. Although strictly speaking non-graduated scholars in arts were not members of the nation, their names were enrolled there, since they studied under the members of the nation. The nation's records offer a good, if not entirely complete, roll-call of Scots studying and teaching in Paris. For discussion of the nations in Paris, see Rashdall, *Universities*, i, pp. 311–20.

Andrews, or to have their degrees from elsewhere accepted.[26] Often regarded as a signal of the difficulties experienced by Scots overseas, this provision does indeed suggest that the issue of schism is not without influence;[27] more importantly, however, it reveals an acceptance that Scots would continue to pursue their education at other universities, irrespective of schismatic obedience.

This is unsurprising: most recent scholarship regarding educational relationships during the schism demonstrates that scholars' customary travel between universities and thus between obediences was less disrupted than might have been assumed. The schism was a major point of discussion and controversy between and within universities; opinions about the correct means of addressing the rift within Christendom varied widely, and ascendancy of one view or the other shifted within the institutions, creating greater or lesser comfort for adherents of both sides. The University of Paris, for example, the primary (but certainly not the only) home for Scots learning on the Continent, was sometimes at odds with the French monarchy over the schism; the English nation in Paris, in which in this period the Scots usually well-outnumbered the English, was often at odds with the rest of the university. Disputes raged, and it is true that sometimes individuals or groups were expelled or temporarily migrated elsewhere.[28] Such events were not always prompted by the schism, however: in 1411, when the English occupied Paris, it is said that the Scots left *en masse* for Cologne.[29] Certainly, there was an increase in Scottish numbers at Cologne in this period, and a corresponding reduction in numbers in Paris; but the exodus from Paris was far from total, as is demonstrated by the consistent presence of Scots in the records of the English nation during and after 1411/12. Patterns of travel certainly present a complex picture, but it is too simplistic to suggest that difficulties caused primarily by schismatic adherence created a crisis that could be addressed only by the hasty foundation of a local university.[30]

That Scots do not in fact seem to have been significantly discouraged from overseas travel for their education during the schism is demonstrated by scanning the pages of D. E. R. Watt's invaluable dictionary of Scottish graduates before 1410, which can provide approximate totals of the Scots known to have been attending universities in the pre-St Andrews era.[31] Starting in the 1370s, a

---

[26] *CPL Benedict XIII*, p. 277; *Evidence*, Appendix Pt. 1, p. 176.
[27] See, for example, R. Swanson 'The University of St Andrews and the Great Schism, 1410–1419', *Journal of Ecclesiastical History* 26 (1975), pp. 223–45, at p. 227.
[28] See Swanson, *Universities* for a study of the behaviour of universities during the schism.
[29] See, for example, Ridder-Symoens, *Universities*, p. 295.
[30] See, for example, Jacques Verger, 'Le recrutement géographique des Universités françaises au début du XVe siècle d'après les Suppliques de 1403', *Mélanges d'archéologie et d'histoire* 82 (1970), pp. 855–902, and especially at p. 868; Verger demonstrates that fluidity of movement continued during the schism and that the record of attendance is partially lacking, through such factors as the omission of 'schismatic' scholars from *rotuli* being sent to the papacy in search of benefices.
[31] Watt, *Graduates*. This survey was crude in its methodology – a simple process of turning the pages and counting relevant entries. Although the data cannot be complete, it suffices to demonstrate the point.

decade which it is fair to label 'pre-schismatic', one can count roughly one hundred Scots pursuing study outside of Scotland; in the 1380s, when Scotland is in tune with France, at least, in her obedience to the Avignon papacy, the numbers appear to dip to around seventy; but they rise again to over one hundred in the 1390s, and increase marginally between 1400 and 1410. This is not consistent with a picture of severe discomfiture. Looking at Paris alone, the records of the English nation (not a complete record of all the Scots in the university: usually neither the most senior scholars nor members of the mendicant orders were included within the nation) give us the names of over fifty Scots active in the university as teachers and/or scholars in the period 1410–20, when one might reasonably have expected a significant drop, given both the existence of a local university and the effect of the most difficult, dying years of the schism.[32] It is true that the figure for the period 1410–20 is a little lower than that for the previous decade, which offers almost seventy names; but we have already noted the politically motivated partial exodus from Paris to Cologne in 1411, and on the other hand in the pre-schismatic decade of the 1360s the English nation provides the names of only around thirty Scots. Deeper analysis of the figures (and, for example, the individual circumstances of the scholars themselves) would be required to draw any safe conclusions about the many reasons for such fluctuations, but the bare numbers are enough to be persuasive of the fact that we have to look elsewhere for an explanation of the emergence of St Andrews University.

The schism, as well as the long-standing war with England, would no doubt have played its part in limiting the attractiveness to Scots of an English university education from the late thirteenth century onwards. However, there is little evidence that even in earlier times Scots went to Oxford or Cambridge in significant numbers. Watt states that 'the Scots as a group have left no trace in these university communities', but neither did the natives of other countries attend the English universities in significant numbers: these universities were not as cosmopolitan in character as the great Continental ones; only a very small proportion of their students came from outside of England.[33] Paucity of evidence makes it difficult to be certain of numbers, but it is nonetheless clear that a trickle – if no more than that – of Scottish students did go to Oxford and Cambridge during the thirteenth century, and thereafter. Although we cannot know for certain how many of them were actually used, the fact that a fair number of safe-conducts for Scots travelling to study in England are enshrined within the *Rotuli Scotiae* for the second half of the fourteenth century must indicate that the doors, whilst perhaps not thrown open, were not locked and barred.[34]

---

[32] Gray Cowan Boyce, *The English-German Nation in the University of Paris during the Middle Ages* (Bruges, 1927), pp. 31–2.

[33] D. E. R. Watt, 'Scottish Student Life Abroad in the Fourteenth Century', SHR 59 (1980), pp. 3–21, at p. 3. On foreign attendance universities see, for example, Rashdall, *Universities*, iii, p. 236, and Ridder-Symoens, *Universities*, p. 296; see also the comment in ibid., p. 40, which suggests that only a few of the major Continental schools were in fact truly cosmopolitan.

[34] *Rotuli Scotiae in Turri Londinensi et in Domo Capitulari Westmonasteriensi Asservati,*

As long ago as 1975 Robert Swanson cast significant doubt on the centrality of the impact of schism to the foundation of the university: 'there is one slight flaw to this whole argument. There is no real evidence that, after Pisa, the Scots actually suffered any persecution.' Whilst not discounting the likelihood that the schism played some part, he nonetheless accepted that 'there must therefore have been some more pressing or convincing reason' for the foundation. He concluded that the dual purposes of 'nationalistic sentiment' and an attempt to contain the threat of heresy (which was stated quite explicitly in Wardlaw's grant of privileges) were major motivations, but that the 'sheer coincidence' of the presence in St Andrews of numerous academics who were firm in their adherence to Benedict XIII was ultimately of more importance.[35] This feels rather too close to Anderson's secondary conclusion, noted above, that the university owes its existence simply to the chance that the right people happened to be in the right place at the right time.

Yet happy coincidence seems rather too convenient an explanation for the emergence of the university. To construct a more satisfactory thesis we have to look beyond the immediate events of 1410–14 and consider the historical character of St Andrews. It has been often enough commented on that St Andrews was already a place of learning, but it is instructive to delve a little deeper. Inset within the cloister wall of the cathedral priory can still be seen two stone book presses: not an unusual feature in a medieval building of this type, but certainly a sign that this was indeed a place where learning and study were expected to take place. However, there is additional evidence about the importance of books in the priory. There are two early Scottish charters that mention books: they were both gifts to the priory of St Andrews. Remarkably, and perhaps uniquely amongst such documents in Scotland, the foundation charter of St Andrews priory, given by Bishop Robert in 1140, included a gift (not a legacy) of all of the bishop's books.[36] A few years later, around 1150, the monastery of St Serf on an island in Loch Leven was given to the priory so that it could be converted into an Augustinian house. The bishop's charter lists seventeen books that were being bestowed upon the priory amongst the other pertinents of the monastery.[37] It has been suggested that the books were given to the priory only nominally, remaining at Loch Leven as a resource of the new Augustinian house there, but even if this is the case, it nonetheless

---

2 vols (London, 1814–19). One student who did take up his safe conduct (*Rotuli Scotiae*, ii, p. 122) was John Scheves, one of those named by Bower in the first group of teachers in St Andrews, who was a graduate of both Oxford and Paris (Watt, *Graduates*, pp. 480–3). See also Woodman's comments about the attendance of Scots at Oxford and Cambridge in the 1360s: Woodman, 'Education and Episcopacy', p. 18 n. 35.

[35] '[...] and the Catholic faith, by an impregnable wall of doctors and masters, by whom thus surrounded she is enabled to withstand heresies and errors, grows strong'. Swanson, 'St Andrews', pp. 227, 229.

[36] *St A. Liber*, pp. 122–3. For the 1140 date, see A. A. M. Duncan, 'The Foundation of St Andrews Cathedral Priory, 1140', *SHR* 84 (2005), pp. 1–37.

[37] *St A. Liber*, p. 43.

Figure 12.2: The priory cloister book presses.

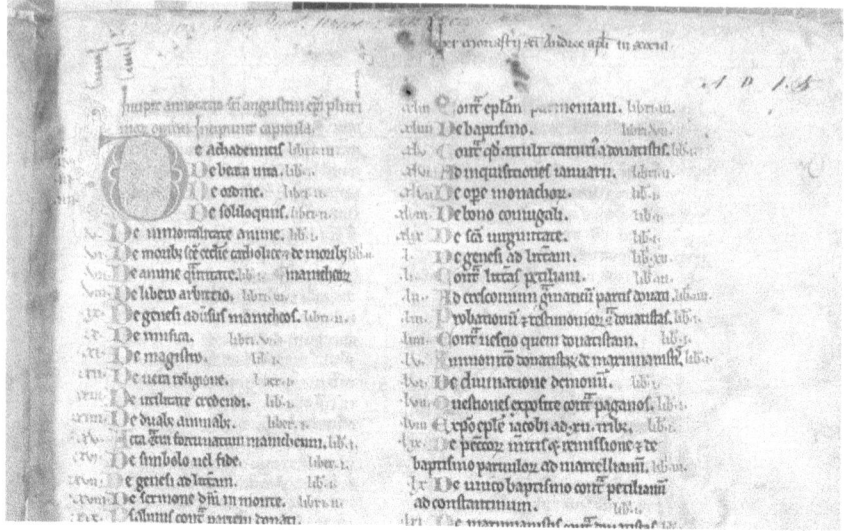

Figure 12.3: The priory's ownership inscription on the Augustine *Opera*.

reinforces the impression that books are of significant importance in the St Andrews context.[38]

By the late thirteenth century the priory of St Andrews had impressive holdings of books. The compilers of *Registrum Anglie*, a 'union catalogue' of works by selected authors held in religious houses throughout Britain, found amongst the priory's books no fewer than ninety-five texts that interested them.[39] They visited only seven houses in Scotland: the abbeys of Dunfermline, Holyrood, Jedburgh, Kelso, Melrose and Newbattle, and St Andrews priory.[40] Naturally, these were the establishments in which the compilers expected to find what they sought, and so presumably they represent the major book-collecting establishments of thirteenth-century Scotland. Dunfermline provided them with forty-six items of interest, Holyrood with twenty-eight and Newbattle with thirty-four. Only the wealthy abbeys of the borders had collections that could compete with St Andrews: in Jedburgh they listed eighty-two (all of them except six, however, being works of Augustine, unlike the broader-ranging collection in St Andrews); Kelso held ninety-six; and Melrose just topped the poll with 102. It is impossible to extrapolate the overall size of the collections from

---

[38] See the discussion of these books in *Scottish Libraries*, ed. John Higgitt (London, 2006), pp. 222–5. There is also an edition of the text and notes regarding the books in A. Lawrie, *Early Scottish Charters Prior to A.D. 1153* (Glasgow, 1905), pp. 210–11, 445–6.

[39] *Registrum Anglie de libris doctorum et auctorum veterum*, ed. R. A. B. Mynors, R. H. Rouse and M. A. Rouse (London, 1991), esp. pp. 306–7.

[40] Ibid., pp. 308, 307–8, 303–4, 304–5, 305–6 and 306, respectively. See also Higgitt, *Scottish Libraries*, pp. xxxvi–xxxix for comments regarding the Scottish element of *Registrum Anglie*, and the relevant libraries' entries therein.

Figure 12.4: The 'armariolo' inscription on the binding fragment in Franz Lambert's *Exegeseos Francisci Lamberti Avenionensis, in sanctam diui Ioannis Apocalypsim, libri VII* (Basel, 1539).

these figures: the compilers of *Registrum Anglie* were, after all, interested only in specific works. Nonetheless, it is clear that by the late thirteenth century St Andrews priory held a book collection that was amongst the nation's most significant. That it was organised in a way similar to the libraries of universities of the period is perhaps indicated by the fortunate survival of an ownership inscription from a twelfth- or thirteenth-century manuscript within the binding of a sixteenth-century book, bound within the priory of St Andrews and now held in St Andrews University Library. The inscription reads *Lib[e]r de [com]muni armariolo S[ancti] Andr[ee]* – 'a book from the common chest (or cupboard) of St Andrews', implying the usual division of books between those which were held, often for their lifetimes, by individual members of a community and those which were held communally for circulation amongst scholars.[41]

It is certain that this intellectual activity was not founded in 1140 with the

---

[41] This book (StAUL, Typ SwB.B39BL: Franz Lambert, *Exegeseos Francisci Lamberti Avenionensis, in sanctam diui Ioannis Apocalypsim, libri VII*, (Basel, 1539)), its binding and the manuscript fragment were discussed in a blogpost on 'Echoes from the Vault', 5 August 2011: https://standrewsrarebooks.wordpress.com/2011/08/05/52-weeks-of-fantastic-bindings-week-8/ (last accessed 27 Feb. 2015). For comments on the personal holding of such books, see Higgitt, *Scottish Libraries*, pp. liv–lv, in the context of his broader discussion of early libraries, pp. xlviii–lvii.

Augustinian priory. When Bishop Robert's predecessor Eadmer came from Canterbury to be 'Bishop of the Scots' in 1120, amongst those of the diocese who greeted him was a group of *scolastici*; and an early thirteenth-century document records an older agreement between the *pauperes scolares* of St Andrews, who claimed an ancient right to some revenues.[42] According to M. O. Anderson, these people 'no doubt represented an endowed body of students that had existed since the eleventh century or earlier'.[43] The payment awarded to them under the terms of the agreement was to be made to Laurence, the archdeacon of St Andrews and *ferlanus*, a title emanating from the Gaelic *Fer Léginn* which indicates the official holding overall responsibility for education within a monastic establishment. The scholars were represented in the negotiations by one 'Master Patrick, the master of the schools of the city of St Andrews' (*magistrum scolarum civitatis sancti Andree*). Master Patrick was one in a long line to hold such a position in St Andrews. His earliest named predecessor (although he too is said to have had 'forebears') is identified as Master Samuel in the earliest version of the St Andrews foundation legend, written c.1100.[44] His title was not unique: to quote only a couple of examples, around the same time one Berbeadh was 'rector of the schools of Abernethy' (*rectoris scolarum de Abyrnethyn*) and Master Thomas de Bennum, a canon of Aberdeen (and perhaps a little later a student in Bologna), held an identical title in Aberdeen in the early 1260s.[45] Such schools, probably (certainly in the case of Abernethy) within the ecclesiastical establishment, would have been analogous to the grammar schools that later provided preparatory education for students or aspiring

---

[42] For the pre-eminent status of the bishop of St Andrews ('... in many respects the ecclesiastical counterpart of the king of Scots'), see Ash, 'The Administration', p. vii; M. O. Anderson, 'St Andrews Before Alexander I', *The Scottish Tradition*, ed. G. W. S. Barrow (Edinburgh, 1974), pp. 1–13 at p. 5; *St A. Liber*, pp. 316–18.

[43] Anderson, 'St Andrews Before Alexander I', p. 5.

[44] Simon Taylor, 'Schools and Scholars in St Andrews and Beyond, c.1050 to c.1250', unpublished version of a conference paper at '600 Years of Town and Gown: Archaeology and History of St Andrews', 18 Feb. 2012. See also Taylor's essay in this volume, where he makes the point that the scale of the payment is large, thus presumably suggesting that the 'student community' was of significant size. Taylor speculates that Samuel, 'as a conspicuous man of learning', may have been the author of the foundation legend (version A), (see *PNF*, iii, pp. 413–14) which puts him also within the rich Gaelic learned tradition that thrived in eastern Scotland in this period.

[45] *St A. Liber*, pp. 115–16; *Arb. Lib.*, i, p. 193; Watt, *Graduates*, p. 40. There are also interesting earlier examples of similar schools, definitely outside of a cathedral establishment: Master Adam (as well as being a graduate – *Arb. Lib.*, i, p. 53) was the master of the schools of Perth (*Adam magister scolarum de Pert*) in the early thirteenth century, but was at the same time apparently a member of the chapter of St Andrews (Watt, *Graduates*, p. 446, citing *Paisley Registrum*, pp. 229–30 and *Dunfermline Registrum*, pp. 56–8; see also n. 66, below); and Allan was master of the schools of Ayr (*magister scolarum de Are*) (*Paisley Registrum*, pp. 168, 173, 174). On the St Andrews schools see the comment in Anderson, 'Foundation', p. 228, regarding the '*schola grammaticalis infra monasterium*'; and *St Andrews Acta*, p. 160. There is much useful discussion of early schooling in Scotland in the first chapter of John Durkan, *Scottish Schools and School-masters, 1560–1633*, ed. and rev. Jamie Reid-Baxter (Woodbridge, 2013).

students in many university towns. We know, too, that in 1386 James Stewart, a son of King Robert II, and another son of a noble, Gilbert Hay, went to St Andrews for their education – one was said in the Exchequer Rolls to be studying in St Andrews (*stante in studio apud Sanctum Andream*) and the other was in the schools there (*existe in scolis ibidem*). They were there for at least a couple of years, since there are similar entries in the accounts for 1384. In that year James Stewart was said simply to be living with the bishop of St Andrews (*existente cum domino episcopo Sancti Andree*), presumably indicating that the schools, in St Andrews at least, were indeed within the ecclesiastical domain.[46] Neither of these men was discovered by D. E. R. Watt to have been a pre-1410 graduate, but the school they were attending was clearly of high enough status to satisfy the needs of the nation's noble elite.

It is thus evident that there was significant and organised education taking place in St Andrews, perhaps by the eleventh century or earlier: certainly this was more than simply the devotional study of canon or culdee within the cloister. That there was a tradition of historical and literary work in St Andrews in the thirteenth century and earlier adds to our impression of an academically active community: *Veremundus*, a source quoted extensively by John of Fordun in his fourteenth-century *Chronica Gentis Scotorum*, has been convincingly identified with Richard Vairement, a member of the former culdee community of St Andrews.[47] The picture comes more sharply into focus when wider evidence is considered. One of the primary means of identifying Scottish graduates prior to the foundation of the University of St Andrews is by the designation *magister* in witness lists to charters and other official documents. A survey of documents issued by Scottish bishops can thus give some idea of the frequency with which they used graduates in such a capacity, and consequently can offer some information about the composition of the bishops' chapters and/or *familiae*, from which such witnesses were generally taken.

Such a survey, to be comprehensive, would be a major task, covering many documents recorded in a large number of sources. For the present purpose, a more limited exercise has been undertaken, using some of the readily available cartularies published in the nineteenth century by the Bannatyne Club and other historical clubs. Study has been restricted to documents dateable to between c.1140 and 1300, since to venture beyond these limits presents too great a variation in the amount of material available for the different dioceses. Starting with the most obvious source, the *St Andrews Liber*, one finds sixty-six charters or other official documents of the bishops of St Andrews dateable between the mid-twelfth and the end of the thirteenth century. Of these, only

---

[46] *ER*, iii, pp. 121, 138. Noted in Anderson, 'Foundation', p. 228.
[47] For an extensive discussion of *Veremundus*, see Dauvit Broun, *Scottish Independence and the Idea of Britain from the Picts to Alexander III* (Edinburgh, 2007), particularly ch. 9. There is detailed biographical information about Vairement in Watt, *Graduates*, pp. 559–60. Earlier work includes the writing of the St Andrews foundation legends: see *Kings, Clerics and Chronicles in Scotland 500–1297*, ed. Simon Taylor (Dublin, 2000), chs 7 and 8.

two have no witness lists, and so in search of graduates we have a sample of sixty-four. Only one of those sixty-four witness lists does not contain at least one graduate identified by the use of the term *magister*. The other sixty-three witness lists each include a minimum of one and a maximum of eight graduates. In total these documents provide the names of forty-seven individuals, and across the whole period the average number of graduates per witness list (the total number of graduate appearances divided by the number of witnessed documents, unhappily termed 'Graduate density' in table 12.1) is 2.92.

An obvious comparator is Scotland's 'second' bishopric, Glasgow. Even combining the documents found within the Glasgow bishop's register with those of several monastic cartularies, it is difficult to reach a sample as prolific as that of St Andrews.[48] Of thirty-six witnessed bishop's documents of the period, twelve have no graduates named in their witness lists; the maximum number of graduates found in any one list is five; there are twenty-seven named individuals; and the average number of graduates per witness list is 1.55. The disparity between this figure and that for St Andrews is startling. The pattern is repeated when one looks at other bishoprics. Figures for each of the bishoprics studied are given in the table below, but the key finding is that the bishoprics of Moray and Brechin present a smaller total number of graduates, who are used with less frequency than those in either Glasgow or St Andrews.[49] Although the numbers of charters noted from other dioceses (primarily Aberdeen, Dunkeld and Dunblane) are too low to contribute sensibly to the figures given below, it is clear that further study of those dioceses would in all probability demonstrate graduate prevalence as being similar to that in the bishoprics of Moray or Brechin.

Clearly, the statistical analysis in table 12.1 is crude: no attempt has been made to take account of factors such as the balance of documentation across the chronological period, the apparent preference of individual bishops, the nature or subject-matter of the documents, the locations in which they were issued, or the presence within the witness lists of men who were in fact graduates but were not identified as such. Nonetheless, it is clear that the bishop of St Andrews appears to have had many more graduates at his disposal for this type of purpose than even his nearest counterpart in Glasgow.[50] The impression becomes

---

[48] *Glas. Reg.* For this purpose additional documents have been taken from *Registrum Monasterii de Passelet* (Edinburgh, 1832), *Liber Sancte Marie de Melros* (Edinburgh, 1837), *Registrum Monasterii S. Marie de Cambuskenneth* (Edinburgh, 1872), and *Registrum Domus de Soltre, necnon Ecclesie Collegiate S. Trinitatis prope Edinburgh, etc.* (Edinburgh, 1861).

[49] Chosen for sampling because of easy availability of printed sources: *Registrum Episcopatus Moraviensis* (Edinburgh 1837) and *Arb. Lib.*, which offers a greater number of witnessed charters of the bishops of Brechin than does the *Registrum Episcopatus Brechinensis*, 2 vols (Aberdeen, 1856), the relevant entries of which are almost all repeated within the *Arb. Lib.*

[50] It is possible, of course, that the reason for the higher number of graduates used by the Glasgow bishops than by Brechin or Moray is that the diocese of Glasgow was the main competitor for St Andrews. There may have been an element of episcopal pride and rivalry involved in the composition of their chapters and *familiae*.

Table 12.1: Bishops' documents, c.1140–1300

Diocese	No. of documents which include witness lists	No. of witness lists without identified graduates	No. of witness lists with identified graduates	Total number of graduates	Maximum no. of graduates in one document	Graduate density
St Andrews	64	1	63	47	8	2.92
Glasgow	36	12	24	27	5	1.55
Moray	50	24	26	16	3	0.9
Brechin	27	15	12	8	3	0.78

even starker when the biographies of the named individuals provided in Watt's *Graduates* are considered. Of the bishop of Glasgow's graduate witnesses, at least nine out of the twenty-seven are known to have had previous connections with the priory of St Andrews or the bishop of St Andrews' *familia*.[51] The same is true for the bishop of Moray, at least three of whose sixteen graduate witnesses had previous St Andrews links; and for Brechin the figure is four out of the eight. Many of these men had careers which saw them active within several different dioceses: there was more mobility between dioceses than might have been assumed. Not infrequently, men appear in witness lists apparently out of the context of their 'home' diocese of the time, presumably having been drafted in for particular purposes because of their individual knowledge or skills. It is often difficult to ascertain why such cross-diocesan activity took place, but overall the evidence strengthens rather than weakens the impression that the diocesan administration of St Andrews held a powerfully dominant position with respect to its clergy's educational status.[52] The evidence to be found within the twelfth-century foundation legends of St Andrews that the city had long laid claim to archiepiscopal status over Scotia suggests that this educational dominance was a logical element of its clearly perceived ecclesiastical pre-eminence.[53]

In his extensive passage in praise of James Bisset, the St Andrews prior at the time of the foundation, Bower commends Bisset's encouragement of education amongst the canons. He tells us that it was no surprise that so many of them (including, explicitly, Bower himself) went on to distinguished careers, since Bisset 'arranged for two of his canons to become masters of theology [...]; two also qualified as licenciates and five as bachelors of decrees'.[54] He follows this statement by saying that:

> At that time, touched by the delightful mildness of a breeze from the south, the paradise of a cloister at St Andrews was experiencing spring with as many flowers as it abounded in distinguished men of virtue, when during the time of this prior the monastic company flourished in the sacred rites of the cloister. In the sphere of the preoccupations of Martha the scion of legal studies bloomed

[51] For example, Master Nicholas Moffat, archdeacon of Teviotdale from 1245–70, had previously been a clerk of Bishop William Malveisin of St Andrews (Watt, *Graduates*, pp. 399–400).
[52] This evidence accords well with the impression of the highly educated nature of the bishops' *familiae* and their close relationship to the royal chancery, presented in Ash, 'The Administration', ch. 8, and particularly at pp. 134–45. There is useful discussion of the households of Scottish bishops in Norman F. Shead, 'The Household and Chancery of the Bishops of Dunkeld, 1160s–1249', *Church, Chronicle and Learning in Medieval and Early Renaissance Scotland*, ed. Barbara E. Crawford (Edinburgh, 1999), pp. 123–34.
[53] See the discussion of the foundation legends in Dauvit Broun, 'The Church of St Andrews and its Foundation Legend in the Early Twelfth Century: Recovering the Full Text of Version A of the Foundation Legend', *Kings, Clerics and Chronicles*, ed. Simon Taylor (Dublin, 2000), pp. 108–14. Simon Taylor, 'The Coming of the Augustinians to St Andrews and Version B of the St Andrews Foundation Legend', ibid., pp. 115–23, gives further evidence of pretensions to superiority of the St Andrews diocese.
[54] *Scotichronicon*, iii, pp. 432–3.

again, and the seraphic enclosure reached boiling point in the theological branches of knowledge.[55]

In this curious passage, Bower seems to be making several points. First, given the generality of the chronological period he appears to be describing ('during the time of this prior'), as well as the generally poetic nature of the passage, it is difficult to take literally the mild southerly breeze; it is equally difficult, however, to explain his metaphor. Given that Bisset became prior in the year that King James I was born, it seems highly unlikely that Bower was reflecting on any encouragement of learning emanating from Scotland's royalty in English exile (even although James does appear to have played a personal role in the establishment of the university in 1410–13). However, it is possible that he was attributing some of the educational advancement of the period to men of learning (including Bisset and perhaps both of the bishops who were active in the see during his priorate, Walter Trail and Henry Wardlaw) who were returning from their education in England or on the Continent.[56] Whatever the interpretation of his southerly breeze, Bower does seem to be claiming that there was a *revival* of learning in the priory ('legal studies bloomed *again*' (*refloruit*)), particularly in the areas of theology and canon law. Bower's 'seraphic enclosure' (*seraphica indago*) and 'sphere of the preoccupations of Martha' (*Marthe sollicitudinibus*) are equally curious. Martha is said to have busied herself with domestic duties while her sister Mary listened to Christ's teaching, and Christian tradition thus uses the two sisters to typify respectively the active and contemplative approaches to belief.[57] It is not difficult to see in Bower's statement the division between 'active' legal and 'contemplative' theological studies. Bower's use of the word *indago* is interestingly architectural. Although it may have been chosen purely for the alliterative effect of *compago ... propago ... indago*, it is tempting nonetheless to consider that there might be a further layer of meaning. Might the 'seraphic enclosure' be a devotional space, implying that the cloister, the chapter house, or perhaps even the cathedral itself was the venue for the teaching of theology? The contrasting implication could be that law was being taught in the domestic ranges – perhaps in the refectory.[58] (It should be remembered that Bower's story of the celebrations accompanying the arrival of the papal bulls in

---

[55] *Sanctiandree tunc claustralis paradisus ad suavem spirantis austri clemenciam, quasi tot floribus vernabat, quot virtutum viris insignibus habundabat, quando in claustralibus cerimoniis, in diebus huius prioris viguit monastica compago. In Marthe sollicitudinibus refloruit juristica propago, et in scienciis theologicis efferbuit seraphica indago.* (Ibid.)

[56] See Watt, *Graduates*, pp. 539–42 (Trayl) and 564–9 (Wardlaw); Bower described Trayl as 'a very solid pillar of the church, a vehicle for eloquence, a repository of knowledge and defender of the church' (*columpna ecclesie robustissima vas eloquencie et thesaurus sciencie ac defensor ecclesie*) (*Scotichronicon*, viii, pp. 36–7), and, as we have seen, he credited Wardlaw with the foundation of the university.

[57] Luke 10: 38–42. I am grateful to Dr Robert Smart for pointing out this usage; see *The Oxford Dictionary of the Christian Church*, ed. F. L. Cross and E. A. Livingstone (Oxford, 1997), pp. 1043–4.

[58] I am grateful to Rachel Hart for this suggestion.

1414 has them being presented to the bishop and read aloud before a gathering of all the clergy in the refectory.) Such a suggestion perhaps also makes sense of a comment by the seventeenth-century historian George Martine, who stated that there had been a 'lycaeum' attached to the cathedral, of which there is no modern knowledge.[59]

The expression Bower used when describing the beginnings of the university is also curious. Translated in the modern edition as 'an institution of higher learning of university standing made a start in the city of St Andrew of Kilrymont in Scotland', the Latin is *incepit studium generale universitatis in civite Sancti Andr' de Kilreymonth in Scocia*. But the term *studium generale* has a very specific meaning: it is a fully fledged university, with papal approval and teaching in most, if not all, of the approved faculties. The term *universitas* is less specific, referring in this context to any gathering of teachers and students, formal or informal.[60] Certainly, by the fifteenth century it was not uncommon for the distinction to be blurred, and indeed the papal bull which founded the University of Cologne in 1388 referred to it as *universitas generalis studii*.[61] However, Bower's expression is ambiguous. The translator has assumed *universitatis* to be an adjectival qualifier of the *studium generale*, the subject of the phrase thus being *studium generale universitatis*. However, if *universitatis* is regarded as a genitive noun, an alternative translation (here using chevrons to emphasise the phrasing) could be 'there began the studium generale of the <university in the city of St Andrew>', tying the university to the city rather than to the *studium*. The second translation accords well with the notion that in St Andrews there was much more organised teaching already in progress than has hitherto been recognised, and suggests that Bower was making a deliberate distinction between the new *studium* and an existing *universitas*.[62]

As well as *universitas*, the term *civitas* requires consideration.[63] Noted above in relation to the 'grammar schools' often found in significant centres of population, this word has a connotation that should not be overlooked. In two of the examples noted, Adam and Allan were masters of the schools of Perth and Ayr respectively (*scolarum de Pert; scolarum de Are*). However, Patrick was 'master of the schools of the city of St Andrews' (*civitatis sancti Andree*). The *Revised Medieval Latin Wordlist* gives the meaning specifically as 'cathedral city', presumably explaining the modern convention that the existence of a cathedral

---

[59] Anderson, 'Foundation', p. 228, quoting G. Martine, *Reliquiae Divi Andreae* (St Andrews, 1797), p. 187.
[60] See the discussion of these terms in Ridder-Symoens, *Universities*, pp. 35–7.
[61] Anton G. Weiler, 'Les relations entre l'université de Louvain et l'université de Cologne au XVe siècle', *The Universities in the Late Middle Ages*, ed. J. Ijsewijn and J. Paquet (Leuven, 1978), pp. 49–81, at p. 49.
[62] This translation was suggested by Dunlop in *St Andrews Acta* (p. xii), but without noting its significance.
[63] I am grateful to Dr Barbara Crawford for pointing out the specificity of the meaning of *civitas*.

bestows the status of 'city' on a secular town.⁶⁴ However, there are examples of the use of the term where no secular town of any size existed, implying that the *civitas* was in fact the ecclesiastical establishment itself: 'the ecclesiastical concept of an episcopal city where the bishop had his seat'.⁶⁵ Thomas de Bennum's schools are not said to lie within the *civitas* of Aberdeen, as one might have expected in a town which was the seat of a bishop. However, Thomas was a canon of Aberdeen; Adam was a canon of St Andrews; and Allan, appointed as a papal judge-delegate along with the deans of Carrick and Cunningham in 1233/34, must also have been a figure of some standing within the Glasgow diocesan community.⁶⁶ These schools, it would seem, were the initial training-grounds for the clergy, established and run from (if not always within) the cathedral establishments. However, Master Patrick in St Andrews, a member of the community of St Mary's and with close associations to the bishop's *familia*, was running a school which was located quite specifically within the *civitas*, perhaps the forerunner of the school which still existed within the monastery as late as the mid-fifteenth century. That James Stewart and Gilbert Hay (neither of whom appears in the *Fasti* of the Scottish medieval church) attended these schools presumably indicates that in St Andrews at least the schools were not reserved entirely for those progressing towards clerical careers.

If Bower's use of the terms *civitas* and *universitas* were indeed quite specific, then they provide further evidence of well-established and high-status educational activity within the priory of St Andrews before the foundation of the university, evidence which is further strengthened by his assertion of the 'revival' of the teaching of law during Bisset's priorate and the apparent virtual monopoly of the graduate population of pre-fourteenth-century Scotland visible within the bishops' witness lists. Indeed, should we regard the specific references to books in the foundation charters for the priory as a hint that in fact learning was one of the primary purposes of its 1140 foundation? This, as the monastic foundation of the bishop of Scotland's cathedral, forming a very rare Scottish example (with Whithorn) of a cathedral chapter being made up of regular rather than secular canons, was perhaps designed to be the primary focus of the education of Scotland's clergy, standing upon foundations of earlier learning laid within the older culdee community.

The particularly learned nature of St Andrews in the opening years of the fifteenth century should therefore not be seen as a fortunate and timely aberration.

---

⁶⁴ R. E. Latham, *Revised Medieval Latin Wordlist from British and Irish Sources* (London, 1965), p. 89.
⁶⁵ Barbara Crawford, 'Birsay and the Early Earls and Bishops of Orkney', *Orkney Heritage* 2 (Kirkwall, 1983), pp. 97–118, at p. 104. The specific example cited by Dr Crawford is the eleventh-century establishment of a bishopric based on the Brough of Birsay on Orkney, described by Adam of Bremen as *civitatem Blasconam*.
⁶⁶ It is worth noting, too, that the more normal designation for the town of Perth in this period was 'St John's Town'; the ecclesiastical parish of 'Pert' was a living in the possession of the priory of St Andrews. I am grateful to Dr Robert Smart for reminding me of this point.

Rather, it is what should be expected. The eight teachers whom Bower notes as being there in 1410/11 were not there because they had been expelled from elsewhere, but because, having completed a particular phase of their education and all having backgrounds in the diocese of St Andrews, that is precisely where one would expect to find them: they had returned home to teach the next generation, some of whom would continue on to university and others of whom would content themselves with 'pre-university' training.[67] Following his description of the celebrations which accompanied the arrival of the papal bulls in February 1414, Bower commented that 'there is one thing in the university in recent times that is not only reprehensible but also needs changing, namely that when clerks begin to learn and obtain degrees within the schools, they soon leave the schools and thus demean the learning which ought to distinguish them'. Noting the life-long learning of the great scholars of classical times, he states that 'It is otherwise in the thinking of today's clerks who move in an undiscriminating manner to those schools from which they think they will share in some material gain.'[68] Is Bower, with hindsight, pointing to a disadvantage of having established Scotland's own university? Having opened up the opportunity to more Scots to gain degrees, the development had also pulled Scotland more firmly into the sphere of European higher education and had increased, rather than decreased, the mobility of Scottish students. Scholars who might in earlier times have studied within the St Andrews *universitas* and then remained there to teach, now had the opportunity to gain degrees there, and thus to travel onwards to continue their study elsewhere; and scholars who, having obtained degrees elsewhere, would formerly have come back to teach at home, as did the eight founding teachers, were now more likely to leave again for further study, or indeed not to return at all. This changing pattern of Scots' university attendance has been demonstrated by Isla Woodman in her recent PhD thesis on the education of the Scottish bishops: it was to become the common pattern for many Scots to undertake their arts study in St Andrews and then to follow it up with further study in the 'higher faculties' abroad.[69] However, it was not a universal pattern, and that Bower himself, who appears to have pursued his studies of both canon law and theology at home, is one of those who bucked the trend might imply that in his moralistic discourse there is an element of curmudgeonly resistance to change. Advanced in life – in his late fifties when writing and within a decade of his death – he may in part have been reflecting with mixed feelings on the increasing professionalisation of scholarly careers, but in doing so he provided a further hint of the nature of St Andrews in times past.

If the suggestion is correct that the appearance of the University of St

---

[67] The respective entries for seven of them in Watt, *Graduates*, demonstrate that they all either came originally from the St Andrews diocese, had previous career connections with it, or were canons of the priory. Only William Fowlis is uncertain in this respect, since nothing is known of him prior to his graduation in Paris in 1411.

[68] *Scotichronicon*, viii, pp. 78–81. On Bower as a moralist for his own times, see 'Bower as a source for his own times', ibid., ix, pp. 348–53.

[69] Woodman, 'Education and Episcopacy', especially in ch. 3.

Andrews is a much more gradual and perhaps inevitable development out of an existing *studium* than has previously been recognised, it should be possible to see parallels in other foundations of a similar date. The scope of the present work does not permit thorough exploration, but some superficial observations are relevant. The general consensus is that the University of St Andrews is based on the model of Paris. That is true, to the extent that it is a Parisian-style university, organised primarily around the authority of the masters, rather than a Bolognan-style university, based around the power of the students; but there are key elements of the organisation, particularly in relation to the respective positions of the rector and the deans of the faculties, which differ from the Paris model and more closely reflect the constitution of other European centres, particularly that of Cologne (upon which Louvain was specifically modelled), founded in 1388.[70] It is undoubtedly significant that when in the early 1440s the burgh authorities of St Andrews, in dispute with the university over its privileges, sent an embassy abroad to enquire as to how the relationship of town and university was regulated, it was not to Paris or Orléans they went but to Cologne, where for some years there had been a fair number of Scottish students. The answer they received was of sufficient weight, too, to persuade Bishop Kennedy to amend the town–gown relationship that his predecessor had established in the 1412 grant of privileges.[71] Cologne, despite a much greater influence of the secular authorities in its establishment, does reflect aspects of the St Andrews foundation experience.[72] Growing out of the celebrated *studium generale* established by the Dominicans in the mid-thirteenth century (in which, amongst others, Thomas Aquinas taught), which had close connections with the city as well as the religious houses, Cologne received papal authority in 1388 as a result of a petition from the city; but, as we shall see was also the case in St Andrews, the apparent removal of power from the religious establishment to a more autonomous institution was limited, the chancellorship remaining in the hands there of the cathedral provost (the archbishopric having been removed from the city in 1288), as in St Andrews it stayed in the hands of the bishop; and there was papal provision for canonry prebends for some of the university professors.[73] The monopoly previously held by the church in scholarly teaching was thus maintained within the newly established university. Cologne, with its key economic role in Scotland's trading heartland of the Low Countries, was an obvious target for Scottish students, who found the Scottish mercantile interests in that part of Europe at times a useful lifeline: it was one of the main

---

[70] See descriptions of the two primary models in Ridder-Symoens, *Universities*, pp. 109–12.
[71] The response, dated 28 June 1443, of the city council of Cologne to the enquiry sent by the burgh authorities of St Andrews survives within the St Andrews Burgh records: StAUL, B65/23/30c.
[72] The following passage on the history of Cologne is based on Rashdall, *Universities*, ii, pp. 254–7 and on the online short history of the university found at www.portal.uni-koeln.de/geschichte-archiv.html?&L=1 (last accessed 27 Feb. 2015).
[73] See Ridder-Symoens, *Universities*, pp. 152–3.

destinations for students who looked elsewhere for security during the civil strife which periodically beset Paris in the first quarter of the fifteenth century. It should be seen as no surprise that St Andrews' city fathers went to Cologne for help when it was needed; but it was perhaps a shared history that they sought, as well as mercantile camaraderie.

How, then, are we to understand the motivations which led to the foundation of the University of St Andrews, and to reconstruct a narrative which reconciles the analysis given above with the basic story provided by Bower and the surviving documentary evidence? As we have seen, by the early fifteenth century the movement towards the creation of 'national' universities was gaining momentum; and although it may have been less influential in the process than has previously been assumed, the effects of the schism cannot be entirely discounted.[74] It, along with secular political conflicts, must indeed have given rise to feelings of discomfort and insecurity. Although the formulaic nature of such appeals has been noted above, the dangers of overseas travel (never insignificant) may also have felt more immediate following the capture of James I at sea in 1406. There is also the important issue of cost: most students' studies were funded by the provision of benefices, church livings, with permission to hold them *in absentia* during periods of study.[75] As the power of Benedict XIII waned, it may have become more difficult to obtain such benefices: *rotuli* dispatched to the papal curia petitioning for benefices did not include individuals adherent to the rival obedience. Perhaps more significantly, in the early fifteenth century Scotland's economy faced serious challenges in the form of severe difficulties in the country's biggest export market, wool.[76] Given all of these pressures, then, it is unsurprising that the masters who were teaching in the priory in 1410/11 petitioned the bishop for privileges which would confer on them the status of a university, 'saving', as Wardlaw said in his grant, 'the authority of the Apostolic See'. By acceding to their wishes he did indeed do as he claimed and institute the university; and he formally confirmed it within his grant of privileges. He then further strengthened the establishment by preparing and sending the petition to the pope with the agreement of the important parties, including the king, who was

---

[74] There is a useful discussion of Scotland's position in the schism, including an assessment of the difficulties which it caused in relations with other countries, in David Ditchburn, '"Une grande ténacité doublée d'une loyauté remarquable": l'Écosse et le schism, 1378–1418'; *Le concile de Perpignan (15 novembre 1408–26 mars 1409)*, ed. H. Millet, *Études Roussillonnaises* 24 (Paris, 2009), pp. 137–46. On the foundation of St Andrews, Ditchburn accepts Swanson's view that the catalyst was the coincidental presence of an exceptional group of learned ecclesiastics, rather than the isolating effects of schism.

[75] See D. E. R. Watt, 'University Clerks and Rolls of Petitions for Benefices', *Speculum* 34 (1959), pp. 213–29.

[76] See Alexander Stevenson, 'Trade Between Scotland and the Low Countries in the Later Middle Ages' (unpublished PhD thesis, University of Aberdeen, 1982), especially at pp. 21–2, and pp. 25–7, where it is suggested that 'by the early 1400's [*sic*] Scottish wool exports were down by over fifty percent on the levels of the mid-1390's', with a consequent effect on the nation's economy which was 'little short of catastrophic'.

in exile but not *incommunicado*.[77] It is thus possible to dismiss the contention of a sudden schismatic emergency and yet to allow Wardlaw to retain his position as 'founder', whilst giving due recognition to the actions and aspirations of the masters and scholars themselves within an environment which in many ways was conducive to the movement towards a national university.

There is no doubt that by this time there was discussion amongst the Scottish ecclesiastical and political leadership regarding Scotland's continuing adherence to the Avignon papacy: certainly it was a hotly disputed issue within the university in the first few years of its existence. The wording of the petition sent by Wardlaw to Benedict XIII, making much of the schismatic difficulties Scotland faced, was doubtless designed to bolster the case of a nation struggling to maintain her loyalty in increasing isolation; and Wardlaw's explicit concern to combat the increasing spread of the heresies that would turn his church upside down over ensuing decades was yet another factor in encouraging him to take every possible measure to increase the local educational provision for the clergy. Scotland needed more clergy who were well educated and the provision of a home university would enable that expansion at a more manageable cost than continuing to send all students abroad. The intention was not to stem the flow of Scots to foreign universities – and as we have seen, that did not happen – but rather to increase educational provision by offering a home alternative.[78]

Theology, it seems, was already being thoroughly taught within the priory walls, perhaps in Bower's 'seraphic enclosure'; therefore Wardlaw did not specify it within his grant of privileges. However, he did specify canon law since, it seems, it had previously been taught and was about to be 'revived'. The faculties of canon law and theology doubtless continued, as they had always been, within the priory; they received no new constitution, no new administrative arrangements, and thus left no records other than what may have existed in the now lost records of the priory itself. It is known that there were very close links between the university and the priory: canons taught in these faculties, and the premises of the priory were the key locations both for teaching and for congregations in the early days of the university. James Haldenstone, who succeeded Bisset as prior of St Andrews in 1418, was also the dean of the faculty of theology. Indeed, as late as 1512, when the new College of St Leonard was founded, it was even then seen largely as an extension of the teaching activities of the priory.[79]

---

[77] For further information regarding James I's personal involvement, see Anderson, 'James I'.
[78] Although our interpretations differ in many respects, this conclusion echoes that of Woodman, 'Education and Episcopacy' – see, for example, her conclusion at pp. 231–2: '*studia generale* were introduced and developed in Scotland to facilitate access to higher education and not to reverse entirely traditional patterns of university going that continued to serve as a means of engaging with the intellectual developments of wider Europe'.
[79] For much valuable detail on the early relationships between the faculties, and between the university, its colleges and the priory, see the lengthy introduction to *St Andrews Acta* and Woodman, 'Education and Episcopacy', ch. 1. See also the comments on St Leonard's College by Roger Mason in this volume.

The faculty of arts was new to St Andrews and required new organisation and structure. Unlike the other faculties, therefore, it was formally established and, uniquely amongst the university's early faculties, has left detailed records in its very fine *Acta*.[80] There was no need in St Andrews to undertake the sort of marketing that characterised the grand opening of the University of Louvain: the students were there already. They were the same type of students that would have been taught in generations past: the young clergy and occasional high-status laymen who had received their education in the priory and schools of St Andrews for centuries. Isla Woodman commented that 'there is no evidence of the foundation being influenced by burgeoning intellectual and cultural interest among the laity of the kind that had given rise to the university at Cologne': indeed, the fundamental character of the foundation of St Andrews is of continuity rather than innovation.[81]

The nature of the student body in the earliest days of the university supports this contention. Of the first cohort of students, eleven in number, who became bachelors in 1413, the subsequent lives of only a few are traceable in any detail.[82] Some disappear from the records, and others can be seen to have pursued further study: seven became masters of arts of St Andrews in 1414 (and one more later, in 1416), and three received the further degrees of bachelor of decreets (Stephen Kerr) and bachelor of theology (Thomas Livingston and Alexander Methven), presumably in St Andrews.[83] Despite Bower's complaints about the hasty dispersal of graduates to other schools, only one of these men can be seen to have continued his studies elsewhere: Thomas Livingston matric-

---

[80] For a brief description of the *Acta*, see Woodman in *Treasures of St Andrews University Library*, ed. Norman H. Reid et al. (London, 2010), pp. 148–9. The common misconception that the faculty of arts was the only one which existed in St Andrews in any meaningful form (see, for example, the erroneous statements by Gietsztor that 'only arts students could follow a whole curriculum at a Scottish university' and by Garcia that Scottish law faculties were entirely inactive, in Ridder-Symoens, *Universities*, pp. 112, 389–90) is probably founded purely upon the survival of records only for that faculty. There is ample evidence, including, for example, the survival of a fine medieval mace for the faculty of canon law and the existence of a good number of canon law books (see Higgitt, *Scottish Libraries*, p. xlii, and the comment by John Durkan in the same volume, p. lxxii), which proves that the early university certainly comprised effective faculties of at least canon (and perhaps also civil) law and theology as well as arts. See also further comments on the faculties of civil law and of theology in Woodman, 'Education and Episcopacy', pp. 11, 26, 29–31, and the useful discussion of the early university (including comments on its monastic roots) by Ian Cowan, 'Church and Society', *Scottish Society in the Fifteenth Century*, ed. J. M. Brown (London, 1977) pp. 112–35, at pp. 125–9.

[81] Woodman, 'Education and Episcopacy', p. 26.

[82] Their names are given in *St Andrews Acta*, p. 1. The following passage and most of the citations noted within it rely entirely on biographical research, as yet unpublished, undertaken by Dr Robert Smart, which he has generously shared with me.

[83] John Homill, John Henderson, Stephen Kerr, Thomas Livingston, Andrew MacClauchane, Robert Tyninghame and William Yalulok (1414); Alexander Methven (1416); *St Andrews Acta*, pp. 5, 10; Kerr: CSSR, iv, p. 257; Livingston: CSSR, ii, pp. 8–9; Methven: ibid., p. 222.

ulated in Cologne in 1423, where he became a master of theology in 1425.[84] (Two of them, Andrew MacClauchane and Robert Tyninghame, had studied in Oxford prior to 1410/11.[85]) Four can be shown from later records to have remained in the University of St Andrews for longer periods: William Yalulok (1424); Alexander Methven (1430 and 1438); Thomas Livingston (1419); and Stephen Kerr (1429).[86] Post-university, most appear to have followed unspectacular ecclesiastical careers as vicars and canons throughout Scotland, with only one (Thomas Livingston) reaching the height of abbot (of Dundrennan) and bishop (of Dunkeld, to which see he was consecrated but did not gain possession).[87] One, John Homill, followed in the footsteps of the earlier Thomas de Bennum as the master of scholars in Aberdeen.[88] Only one of them, Thomas Livingston (who may have been a natural brother of Sir Alexander Livingston of Callander), seems likely to have had any elevated social background.[89] These men are not career or academic high fliers; they have not been specially recruited to kick-start the new university; rather, they are predominantly the same type of 'bread-and-butter' clergy from all over Scotland that had been educated in St Andrews for generations.

Looking back with hindsight, Bower correctly identified the formal beginnings of the university in the 1410/11 period, when that group of masters saw their opportunity to achieve something perhaps more effective and more contemporary, and persuaded Wardlaw that it was in his interest to grant them the privileges that would pave the way for a new form of education in St Andrews. By saying that the masters he named were 'the first to begin lecturing there' he meant, surely, that they were the first to teach under the new circumstances. If the beginning was indeed slow, these masters hatching their plot gradually over 1410 and 1411, the timings of Wardlaw's grant and of the subsequent developments are not without logic. If we take notice of the entirety of the story Bower tells us, in the several relevant passages, he does indeed describe the emergence of a *studium generale* out of the existing *universitas* of the city of St Andrews.

This fresh interpretation of the foundation of Scotland's first university undoubtedly remains work in progress. There are significant areas of study yet to be explored which cannot be included in the present article. For example, the relationship between the bishops of St Andrews and their chapters was often very fraught, leading to the bishops favouring the body of secular canons

---

[84] R. J. Lyall, 'Scottish Students and Masters at the Universities of Cologne and Louvain in the Fifteenth Century', *Innes Review* 36 (1985), p. 56.
[85] *St Andrews Acta*, p. 1.
[86] Ibid., pp. 18 (Yalulok), 29, 47 (Methven), 14 (Livingston), 24 (Kerr).
[87] *Heads of Religious Houses*, ed. Watt and Shead, pp. 64–5; *Fasti Ecclesiae Scoticanae Medii Aevi Ad Annum 1638*, ed. D. E. R. Watt and A. L. Murray (Edinburgh, 2003), p. 128. Livingston was also an influential presence in the Council of Basel in the 1430s.
[88] *Aberdeen Guild Court Records, 1437–1468*, ed. Elizabeth Gemmill (Edinburgh, 2005), p. 27.
[89] CSSR, ii, pp. 8–9.

which they encouraged to grow out of the old pre-priory culdee community; there were also severe tensions between Wardlaw, Bisset and the first rector, Lawrence of Lindores, which leads one to suspect that Anderson's happy picture of the protagonists 'congenially' founding their new university may obscure important elements of the truth.[90] Woodman also makes the intriguing suggestion that in founding the university Wardlaw saw an opportunity to revive his own status, which in the period of James I's exile had been under threat.[91] Beyond these local considerations, the entire question of the internal politics of Scotland in this context, still under an absentee king and fraught with tensions, must be examined. Were there further political and cultural considerations that motivated the king, the governor Albany and the three estates to support the petition to the pope?[92] In 1426, only two years after his return to Scotland from his protracted English exile, James I proposed moving the university to his new capital city, Perth.[93] In so doing, his intention must partly have been to reduce the stranglehold still exerted on the nation's education by the ecclesiastical establishment, perhaps another sign that the University of St Andrews was not as new an institution, nor as independent of the church, as the traditional interpretation of its foundation would have us believe. The increasing requirement for professional clerks within the royal administration, a role which had for long been largely supplied from amongst the St Andrews canons, may have been a motivation for the king in this, both to bring the source of clerical expertise physically closer to the court and to facilitate more secular influence over their education and training.[94]

Leaving these issues aside for others to investigate, it nonetheless seems that the story Walter Bower told in the *Scotichronicon* was not inaccurate, but was merely incomplete, and has been taken too literally by subsequent historians who have erected around it a wall of un-evidenced assumption. In fact, the story of the foundation is more complex, and yet at the same time more logical, than we have been led to believe. If we consider Bower's narrative in the light both of what we know about the nature of the tiny town of St Andrews and its crucially important ecclesiastical *civitas* over preceding centuries, and of the true story

---

[90] See Ash, 'The Administration', ch. 9. On Lindores, see Woodman, 'Education and Episcopacy', pp. 35–7 and 53–7.

[91] Ibid., pp. 14–16.

[92] The structure of Bower's narrative, placing the foundation of the university shortly after his discourse on the burning of the English 'heretic' James Resby in Perth in 1408 and immediately following his description of the battle of Harlaw, is not necessarily intended to link these events, but is undoubtedly an indication of issues which were of significance to the contemporary writer. Such a study would also further challenge the common assumption that Scotland's early universities were founded out of primarily diocesan concerns (see, for example, Swanson, 'St Andrews', pp. 235–6); the challenge to that assumption, which has not been repeated in this article, is central to Woodman's argument (see Woodman, 'Education and Episcopacy', pp. 8, 52, *passim*).

[93] See the discussion of this episode in *St Andrews Acta*, p. xviii.

[94] See Woodman's comment on the requirement for increasing numbers of educated royal clerks: 'Education and Episcopacy', pp. 75–6.

of Scotland's educational fortunes during the schism, we come much closer to an understanding that the creation of the University of St Andrews was not a response to a sudden emergency but was in fact a gradual process of evolution out of a centuries-old *universitas*.

CHAPTER THIRTEEN

*University, City and Society**

Roger A. Mason

No study of late medieval St Andrews would be complete without due consideration of the foundation and development of its university. Elsewhere in this volume Norman Reid explores the prehistory of higher learning in St Andrews and the complex circumstances of the establishment of a *studium generale* in the city in the years leading up to 1413. This chapter focuses rather on its subsequent development until the Reformation of 1560 and the foundation of its constituent colleges of St Salvator's (1450), St Leonard's (1512) and St Mary's (1538/54). As well as considering its internal evolution, however, what follows places the university in wider national and international contexts, looking at St Andrews' relations with subsequent Scottish university foundations at Glasgow (1451) and King's College, Aberdeen (1495) against a backdrop of what amounted to a revolution in European educational provision in the long fifteenth century. The sources for the study of St Andrews in this period are scrappy and limited, but sufficient records survive to allow us to offer some assessment of the university's impact on Scotland's ecclesiastical capital, while also considering the ramifications for the Scottish kingdom of the establishment of its first such centre of learning.[1]

As Norman Reid makes clear, the absence of a university in Scotland before 1413 does not mean the absence of higher education. Many of the religious

---

* My knowledge and understanding of the university's history is greatly indebted to the St Andrews History of the Universities Project, hosted by the St Andrews Institute of Scottish Historical Research between 2006 and 2012; I am grateful above all to Isla Woodman and Steven Reid for many illuminating conversations on the issues addressed in this chapter. It has also benefited from the critical eye of Norman Reid.
[1] For an overview of the university muniments and a guide to secondary reading, see Norman Reid, *Ever to Excel: An Illustrated History of the University of St Andrews* (Dundee, 2011), pp. 188–98. The key sources cited below are *Early Records of the University of St Andrews*, ed. J. M. Anderson, Scottish History Society (Edinburgh, 1926) [hereafter *Early Records*], *St Andrews Acta and Evidence, Oral and Documentary, taken by the Commissioners appointed by King George IV, for Visiting the Universities of Scotland, iii: St Andrews* (London, 1837) [hereafter *Evidence*].

houses that had been founded in the twelfth and thirteenth centuries, not least the Augustinian priory attached to St Andrews' Cathedral, were centres of learning with substantial libraries that provided education to a high level.[2] Scots also, and famously, joined the ranks of the wandering scholars who sought education abroad, at Paris in particular, the greatest of the northern European universities, but also at Orléans (where, unlike at Paris, civil law was taught and where, uniquely, a formal Scottish 'nation' was established) and Montpellier (the major centre for the study of medicine).[3] The foundation of three universities in Scotland in the fifteenth century did not put an end to this academic diaspora. Few Scots scholars attended the two English centres of learning at Oxford and Cambridge, dating from the twelfth and early thirteenth centuries, though both also experiencing substantial expansion in the era discussed here.[4] Nevertheless, a steady trickle of Scottish scholars continued to wend their way to the Continent, studying and teaching both at Europe's old universities and at the wave of new institutions whose foundations were contemporaneous with that of St Andrews, Glasgow and Aberdeen.

Such continued academic mobility did not mean that the Scottish universities were failing to fulfil the purposes for which they were founded. Fifteenth-century Scotland was a small kingdom with a small population (perhaps 750,000) and demand for higher education was modest in a country that was overwhelmingly rural and illiterate. There are indications that in the century after 1450 literacy was increasing among the landed elite, and that the clerical monopoly of learning was beginning to be challenged.[5] Nonetheless, the demand for university graduates still remained small, fuelled principally by the ecclesiastical establishment, centred on its senior and richest diocese of St Andrews and the royal administration of the Stewart dynasty, both of which required well-educated personnel to service their growing bureaucratic needs.

---

[2] See *Scottish Libraries*, ed. John Higgitt (London, 2006), esp. pp. 230–8 (on the Cathedral Priory).

[3] Watt, *Graduates*, identifies 550 Scots who studied furth of Scotland in the fourteenth century and a little short of a further eighty in the first decade of the fifteenth century; see also the same author's 'Scottish Student Life Abroad in the Fourteenth Century', *SHR* 59 (1980), pp. 3–21; and 'Scottish University Men of the Thirteenth and Fourteenth Centuries', *Scotland and Europe, 1200–1850*, ed. T. C. Smout (Edinburgh, 1986), pp. 1–18.

[4] The Scottish boast that by 1500 it had three universities compared to England's two is misplaced. By the time St Andrews was founded in 1413, Oxford already had seven colleges, and three more were created in the fifteenth century and another five in the sixteenth. Similarly, Cambridge was made up of six colleges in 1400, but another five were founded in each of the following two centuries. By 1600, in other words, Oxford had fifteen colleges and Cambridge sixteen. The foundation of Edinburgh's 'toun college' in 1583 and of Marischal College, Aberdeen in 1593 enhanced Scottish educational provision considerably, but it is misleading to consider that Scotland's five ancient universities, let alone its three earlier ones, were comparable in size and resources to England's two.

[5] See Roger A. Mason, 'Laicisation and the Law: The Reception of Humanism in Early Renaissance Scotland', *A Palace in the Wild: Essays on Vernacular Culture and Humanism in Late Medieval and Renaissance Scotland*, ed. L. Houwen et al. (Leuven, 2000), pp. 1–26.

As will become clear, the foundation of St Andrews did not so much hinder as promote intellectual exchange with the Continent, and its masters and students remained abreast of the revolutionary intellectual transformations that we associate with the Renaissance and the Reformation. While these developments are considered in some detail, there are additional questions that this chapter seeks to address. Who went to university, and why? What were they taught? What careers did they subsequently pursue? Did the different St Andrews' colleges serve different purposes? Were later university foundations at Glasgow and Aberdeen rivals to St Andrews or complementary to it? Before attempting to answer these questions, however, a brief introduction to the late medieval university is appropriate.

Late Medieval Universities

LATE medieval universities were essentially ecclesiastical institutions, run for and by the clergy, and requiring papal sanction through the issuing of bulls conferring the right to establish a *studium generale*.[6] Normally such institutions of higher learning were made up of a faculty of arts and four higher faculties of theology, civil law, canon law and medicine. Papal recognition as a *studium generale* gave a university the right to award master's degrees and doctorates and to give its MA graduates licence *ubique docendi* ('to teach anywhere'), the universally recognised qualification to teach at any of Europe's universities. Students usually went through the arts faculty before proceeding, if they chose to do so, to the higher faculties, though direct entry into law faculties was increasingly common. Boys (and it was an exclusively male preserve) went to university aged as young as thirteen or fourteen – what would now be considered high-school age – and undertook foundation courses in Latin grammar, logic (dialectic) and rhetoric – the three basic disciplines known as the *trivium*. Latin was the *lingua franca* of the middle ages (and long after), essential for politics and diplomacy as well as for higher learning, so a sound grounding in the language was a *sine qua non* of university education. Similarly, dialectic was viewed both as a key tool for organising knowledge and as an essential skill applicable to all other disciplines, not least the higher disciplines of law, medicine and especially theology. Finally, rhetoric, the art and science of speaking and writing effectively, was likewise a critical communication skill, transferable to a variety of learned and non-learned contexts.

The foundation courses in the *trivium* were originally followed by study of a further four subjects – the *quadrivium* – made up of arithmetic, geometry, music and astronomy. By the later middle ages, however, this curriculum had

---

[6] This and the following paragraph draw heavily on the standard modern survey: *A History of the University in Europe*, i: *Universities in the Middle Ages*, ed. H. de Ridder-Symoens (Cambridge, 1992); though see also H. Rashdall, *The Universities of Europe in the Middle Ages*, rev. and ed. F. M. Powicke and A. B. Emden, 3 vols (Oxford, 1936).

given way to one in which the skills of the *trivium* were applied to three different branches of philosophy: natural philosophy (physics), moral philosophy and metaphysics. Much of this curriculum – what came to be known by the generic term scholasticism – was grounded in the works of the ancient Greek thinker Aristotle, whose extraordinary range of writings on all these branches of philosophical thought as well as on logic and rhetoric had long been lost to the Christian west but were re-discovered via Arabic sources in the twelfth and thirteenth centuries. Translated into Latin, Aristotle's writings were glossed and harmonised with Judaeo-Christian tradition by such great scholastic thinkers as Albert the Great, Thomas Aquinas, William of Occam and John Duns Scotus, each of whom attracted followers of their particular brand of scholasticism who have in turn become known as Albertists, Thomists, Occamists and Scotists.

Intellectual disputes and rivalries between the followers of these various schools of thought frequently divided academic communities and had an impact on St Andrews and the other Scottish universities just as they did on their counterparts across Europe. John Duns Scotus (1266–1308), who, as his name suggests, may well have hailed from Duns in Berwickshire, had a particularly distinguished group of Scottish followers in what has become known as the 'circle' of John Mair of Haddington (1465–1550).[7] Mair was a Parisian-trained logician, philosopher and theologian who taught and studied for two decades at the Sorbonne before returning to Scotland in 1518 to take up posts first at Glasgow and then at St Andrews where he taught from 1523 to 1525 and again from 1531 until his death in 1550. However, Mair's stature and reputation as a scholar working in the Scotist tradition may give an exaggerated impression of how influential Scotus was in the fifteenth-century Scottish universities. The importance of this lies in the different world views that adherence to these various schools of thought implied and that informed the teaching of the three branches of undergraduate philosophy.

Scotus is generally considered a transitional figure between what became known as the *via antiqua* of the great Dominican theologians Albert the Great (1190–1280) and Thomas Aquinas (1226–74) and the *via moderna*, the new approach to theology and philosophy pioneered by the English Franciscan William of Occam (c.1285–1349). The subsequent intellectual debate between 'moderns' and 'ancients' is often characterised as one between 'nominalists' and 'realists' respectively. However, defining them solely in terms of the issue of universals – whether or not an entity exists independently of the particulars in which it is instantiated – does not always work. In this respect, Scotus was in fact a realist. Yet there was a broad range of radical scholastic thinking, owing much to Scotus as well as Occam, and often described as nominalist, which questioned the prevailing orthodoxies associated with the *via antiqua*.

---

[7] For this and what follows, see Alexander Broadie, *The Circle of John Mair: Logic and Logicians in Pre-Reformation Scotland* (Oxford, 1985); Alexander Broadie, *The Shadow of Scotus: Philosophy and Faith in Pre-Reformation Scotland* (Edinburgh, 1995); Alexander Broadie, *A History of Scottish Philosophy* (Edinburgh, 2009), chs 2–4.

Albertists and Thomists, for example, stressed the rationality – and thus knowability – of God's creation and developed an ordered, hierarchical and, in social and political terms, conservative understanding of the world around them. In contrast, Scotists and Occamists argued that God was inscrutable, unpredictable and inaccessible to reason. As a result they privileged faith over reason, circumscribing man's ability to subject God's creation to rational analysis, dichotomising man's intellect and his will, and creating a more contingent and anxious world than the more comfortably ordered cosmos of the Thomists and Albertists.[8] Consequently, while proponents of the *via antiqua* tended to see political authority as a necessary part of God's creation and were sympathetic to the growth of papal – and royal – authority, adherents of the *via moderna* were more likely to stress the importance of human volition in political society and to sympathise with both ecclesiastical conciliarism and the doctrines of popular sovereignty and the consent of the community which were developed to underpin challenges to royal as well as papal absolutism.

Such issues were of immediate topical significance when St Andrews was founded in the midst of the Great Schism, which was only ended by acceptance of the authority of the decrees of the General Council of the church that met at Constance between 1414 and 1418. While the ideological debates engendered by the schism are clearly important, there are more mundane questions that also demand attention, not least the ends that a university education was designed to achieve and the prospects it opened up for those who benefited from it. First and foremost, the arts curriculum was intended both to educate an orthodox clerical caste who could be trusted with a parish ministry and, for those who wanted to pursue a higher degree, as essential preparation for the study of theology, the queen of sciences. The great scholastic thinkers mentioned above – Albert, Aquinas, Occam and Scotus – were all theologians who spent their lives in academia. But a doctorate in theology took at least twelve years to complete, few wanted it, and fewer still were intellectually capable of attaining it. At a more pragmatic level, it is not surprising that legal studies proved much more popular than theology among ambitious young men who saw a law degree as a means of social mobility and advancement.[9] The demand for personnel learned in the law, both the canon law of the church and Roman civil law as codified by the Emperor Justinian in the sixth century, expanded exponentially as the middle ages progressed. Graduates with legal training were needed to service the increasingly complex ecclesiastical bureaucracy that radiated out from the papal curia and the burgeoning needs of temporal authorities – kings, princes and urban communities – whose own governmental machinery was likewise

---

[8] For the sources of this bald summary, see the wide range of essays in *The Cambridge History of Later Medieval Philosophy*, ed. Norman Kretzman et al. (Cambridge, 1982), and *The Cambridge History of Medieval Philosophy*, ed. Robert Pasnau, 2 vols (Cambridge, 2009), esp. ii, part VII.

[9] A theme explored in Jacques Verger, *Men of Learning in Europe at the End of the Middle Ages*, trans. Lisa Neal and Steven Rendall (Notre Dame, 1997).

growing rapidly and demanding a greater than ever reservoir of educated civil servants to enable it to function effectively.[10]

These novel demands for educated personnel, and especially clerks learned in the law, go a long way towards explaining the vast increase in university provision in the fifteenth century. Against a backdrop of schism in the church, the threat of the collapse of a united western Christendom, and the emergence of more powerful and bureaucratised dynastic states, the demand for educated graduates could not be met by existing institutions, even greatly expanded ones such as Paris, Oxford and Cambridge. As a result, the late fourteenth and fifteenth centuries were the great age of university foundations. In the 1360s there were about thirty universities in Europe ranging from Lisbon and Salamanca in the west to Prague and Vienna in the east, and from Oxford, Cambridge and Paris in the north to Bologna in the south. By 1500, there were over sixty, with new foundations in Scandinavia (Uppsala and Copenhagen), Germany (Leipzig, Heidelberg and Cologne) and the Low Countries (Louvain) as well as Spain, France and Italy. The establishment of a *studium generale* at St Andrews, and subsequent Scottish foundations at Glasgow and Aberdeen, were part of this European-wide development and are best seen in this broader context.

St Andrews: Early Development

THE foundation of St Andrews by Bishop Henry Wardlaw was accomplished through a complex series of grants and charters made by him and the Avignonese pope, Benedict XIII, in 1412 and 1413. The establishment of the new university was a protracted and somewhat opaque business that is examined in great depth by Norman Reid elsewhere in this volume.[11] Suffice it to say here that, given the Parisian education of its founder, and of those who petitioned for its establishment, it is no surprise that the new foundation owed much in terms of organisation, governance and curriculum to the example of Paris. While Bishop Wardlaw had granted the masters and students a range of trading privileges and tax exemptions – in effect recognising them as a self-governing corporation or *universitas* – the papal bulls sanctioned the establishment of a *studium generale* made up of the standard five faculties.[12] Although the bishop of St Andrews was not formally designated as chancellor of the new foundation, he was generally regarded as such, holding ultimate jurisdiction over it, and it was only he (or his deputy) who could confer a master's degree and thus grant a

---

[10] For a broad perspective on these themes, see John Watts, *The Making of Polities: Europe, 1300–1500* (Cambridge, 2009).
[11] In addition to Norman Reid's chapter, see Isla Woodman, 'Education and Episcopacy: The Universities of Scotland in the Fifteenth Century' (unpublished PhD thesis, University of St Andrews, 2011), ch. 1, where the relevant secondary literature is discussed.
[12] For the details that follow, see Cant, *University*, pp. 7–16; see also Dunlop's lengthy and invaluable introduction to *St Andrews Acta*.

Figure 13.1: Image of the seal matrix of the university, 1414×18, reversed.

licence *ubique docendi*. The university's internal affairs, however, were presided over by a *rector* who was elected annually by a general congregation (*comitia*) of the university. As in Paris, the *comitia* was notionally divided into four 'nations' – originally *Albania, Angusia, Laudonia* and *Britannia* – each headed by a *procurator*. However, the 'nations' appear in the records only sporadically.[13] More important were the faculties, of which the faculty of arts was by far the largest and most important, and also the only one for which extensive records survive. This can give the impression that theology, law and medicine were of only marginal importance – that the university was little more than an arts college – but this is misleading. Although there are only very occasional traces of medicine being taught, there is clear evidence that students were pursuing higher study in canon and civil law as well as theology from the earliest days of the university, and that this built on traditions of higher study that were already well established in the priory.[14]

[13] See *Early Records*, pp. ix–xi.
[14] The evidence is considered in *St Andrews Acta*, pp. cxxxix–clix; see also Norman Reid's chapter in this volume.

The faculties appointed a *decanus* (dean), usually on an annual basis, whose job it was to supervise and regulate all matters relating to teaching and examining. At St Andrews, the first dean of the arts faculty, Laurence of Lindores (c.1374–1437), who succeeded in monopolising the post for at least a decade, proved an immensely powerful figure, with a strong sense of the importance and prestige of his position: it was he who advanced the funds in 1418 for the making of the earliest surviving university mace, a symbol of the corporate identity of the arts faculty as well as of the authority of its dean.[15] As we shall see, Lindores was equally dominant in theological instruction, but in the arts faculty he presided over the characteristic 'regenting' system by which individual masters (those who had graduated with a master's degree and were thus licensed to teach) took a group of students through the entire curriculum.[16] As students paid their regents rather than the university for instruction this could lead to unseemly rivalry among the masters who were effectively touting for business, often to fund their own higher studies in law or theology. Nonetheless, regenting remained the standard practice in arts teaching at St Andrews for over three centuries (it was abolished, along with teaching in Latin, only in 1747). Regents thus taught their students the foundation disciplines of grammar, logic and rhetoric, while taking them through the philosophy curriculum, grounded in Aristotle's works, and presenting them, first, as 'determinants' who after three years of study might graduate as bachelors of arts, and second, as 'licentiates' or 'intrants' who after a further year's study could graduate as masters of arts. Critical parts of the examination process for these degrees took the form of oral disputations (in Latin) in which students were expected to display their mastery of the curriculum, and the skills of logic and rhetoric, in conducting philosophical arguments before an assembly of fellow students and their masters.[17] Late medieval graduates were, like Lindores himself, both highly articulate and very argumentative.

A forceful – not to say over-bearing – personality, Lindores was not surprisingly at the heart of the two issues that dogged the new foundation from the very outset. The first was that it was chronically under-funded. Masters and students had been accorded a range of privileges by papal and episcopal authority, but precious little funds were made available to sustain them and they had no premises beyond the precincts of the Augustinian priory that serviced the cathedral. It was in the priory, or in the adjacent St Leonard's Hospital, that teaching initially took place. It was only in 1419 that the otherwise obscure Robert of Montrose, rector of the nearby parish of Cults, gifted a tenement in South Street – close to the site of what is now St Mary's College – to endow a

---

[15] Lawrence Moonan, 'Lindores, Lawrence (d. 1437)', *Oxford Dictionary of National Biography* (Oxford, 2004) [www.oxforddnb.com/view/article/53487, accessed 1 Dec. 2014] takes a more charitable view of Lindores' temperament than do historians of the university more generally.
[16] *St Andrews Acta*, pp. cxxiii–cxxvi.
[17] The curriculum and examining procedures are outlined in detail in *St Andrews Acta*, pp. lxxvii–cxvi.

College of St John to house 'theologians and artists' with Lindores as 'master, rector and governor'.[18] The foundation of such a college might have resulted in tension between it and the arts faculty, but Lindores' position as both master of the college and dean of the faculty clearly obviated this. There was, however, considerable friction between Lindores and the university's chancellor, Bishop Wardlaw. It seems likely that this was increased by the second issue that dogged St Andrews in its early years: that is, ferocious intellectual in-fighting among its senior personnel.[19]

There seems little doubt that it was not the apparently mild-mannered Wardlaw who dominated the university in its early years, but the more forceful Lindores.[20] Before arriving in St Andrews, Lindores had already carved out a reputation for himself as a formidable exponent of the *via moderna*, following the influential teachings of the Parisian nominalist Jean Buridan (c.1300–c.1358). His dominance of the arts faculty is evident in 1418 when the teaching of Albertism, the form of moderate realism favoured by more conservative academics such as Wardlaw himself, was banned in favour of the doctrine of Buridan.[21] But Lindores' position as dean was neither continuous nor unchallengeable. In 1430, for example, William Turnbull (the future bishop of Glasgow and founder of Glasgow University) was appointed head of the faculty in his place.[22] Turnbull had graduated MA from St Andrews a decade earlier in 1420 and there is some evidence that as a regent-master he shared Wardlaw's preference for Albertism and led the opposition to Lindores' insistence on its suppression. It may have been in an attempt to reduce Lindores' dominance over the university that, in the same year that Turnbull was appointed dean, Wardlaw granted a tenement immediately to the west of St John's College as a further endowment of what he envisaged as a common pedagogy, under Turnbull's decanal guidance.[23] This would have eliminated the need for masters to hold private pedagogies in their own lodgings, while also superseding Montrose's earlier grant with its provision that Lindores took charge of the college. The plan did not succeed and Turnbull left St Andrews for the newly founded University of Louvain in Brabant, an avowed centre of Albertist teaching, accompanied by (among others) William Elphinstone senior, whose son would found King's College Aberdeen, and the young James

---

[18] *Evidence*, p. 350; *St Andrews Acta*, p. xviii.
[19] Although it has not been possible to pursue this theme here, the politics of the university were almost certainly complicated still further by the interests and ambitions of successive priors, initially James Bisset, and from 1417 to 1443, James Haldenstone. On the latter, see *Copiale*.
[20] C. A. McGladdery, 'Wardlaw, Henry (c.1365–1440)', *Oxford Dictionary of National Biography* (Oxford, 2004) [www.oxforddnb.com/view/article/28722, accessed 1 Dec. 2014].
[21] *St Andrews Acta*, p. 12 (16 Feb. 1418): '... doctrina Alberti adhuc non legatur in isto Studio sed Buridani'.
[22] *St Andrews Acta*, p. 25; John Durkan, 'William Turnbull, Bishop of Glasgow', *Innes Review* 2 (1951), pp. 1–61, at pp. 8–10.
[23] *Evidence*, p. 351; *St Andrews Acta*, pp. 26–8.

Kennedy, Wardlaw's successor as bishop of St Andrews and founder of St Salvator's College.²⁴

Meanwhile the academic feuding that blighted the university's early years did not go unnoticed by the king. In 1426, newly returned from captivity in England and bent on the reassertion of royal authority, James I sought papal approval for moving the university wholesale to Perth, closer to the heart of royal authority. Although this initiative was not pursued, the king did continue to interfere in university affairs, not least in 1432 when he confirmed the university's privileges while also, in the wake of Turnbull's unsuccessful academic coup, lending royal support to Lindores' efforts to maintain his authority over the now expanded St John's College, more commonly known simply as the Pedagogy.²⁵ For Wardlaw it was a philosophical as well as a political defeat: Lindores' brand of Buridanist teaching continued to dominate the arts faculty. The following year, Lindores' authority was further and very publicly demonstrated when, as Papal Inquisitor for Heretical Pravity, a title he had held since 1408, he presided over the trial and execution by burning of the Bohemian Hussite Pavel Kravař.²⁶ This was the first such execution that St Andrews had witnessed – in 1408 the English Wycliffite priest James Resby had been burned at Perth – but it was a reminder of the threat of heresy which the new university was avowedly founded to counter and the prestige and power that accrued to Lindores as the enforcer of doctrinal orthodoxy.²⁷ Bishop Wardlaw's reaction to Lindores' death in 1437 – or indeed to that of James I the same year – is not recorded. However, it is surely no coincidence that the next year, amid renewed quarrels between proponents of the *via moderna* and the *via antiqua*, the faculty of arts finally lifted the ban on the teaching of Albertism.²⁸

When Wardlaw himself died in 1440, the university he had founded was hardly in a healthy state. Its masters were at daggers drawn over the curriculum, its buildings were inadequate and poorly funded, and discipline was lax. As noted above, his successor as bishop of St Andrews was James Kennedy (c.1408–65), a nephew of James I, who had graduated MA from St Andrews in 1429, but had left St Andrews for Louvain in 1431 with his senior colleague, William Turnbull.²⁹ It was thus as an Albertist with jaundiced memories of

---

²⁴ On the immediate Scottish interest in Louvain, founded in 1425 and with strong links to Cologne, see R. J. Lyall, 'Scottish Students and Masters at the Universities of Cologne and Louvain in the Fifteenth Century', *Innes Review* 36 (1985), pp. 55–73, at pp. 58–9.
²⁵ *St Andrews Acta*, pp. xix–xx.
²⁶ Paul Vyšný, 'A Hussite in Scotland: The Mission of Pavel Kravař to St Andrews in 1433', *SHR* 82 (2003), pp. 1–19.
²⁷ On the significance to Wardlaw's foundation of the threat of Lollardy, see Woodman, 'Education and Episcopacy', pp. 25–6.
²⁸ *St Andrews Acta*, pp. xviii–xx, xxv–xxvi, 48–9.
²⁹ Dunlop, *Kennedy*; Norman Macdougall, 'Kennedy, James (c.1408–1465)', *Oxford Dictionary of National Biography* (Oxford, 2004) [www.oxforddnb.com/view/article/15372, accessed 1 Dec. 2014], suggests that Kennedy's reasons for leaving were as much political as intellectual.

in-fighting in the arts faculty that Kennedy returned to St Andrews as its bishop in 1440. It was presumably deliberate policy that both he and Turnbull, who was appointed bishop of Glasgow in 1447, sought to embed the more conservative and pro-papal teachings that they had imbibed at Louvain at new institutions in their respective dioceses. However, rather than focusing his energies and resources on the Pedagogy on South Street, Kennedy determined to establish a wholly new college occupying a large and prominent site on the town's North Street. Founded in 1450, the building of St Salvator's was still in progress when Kennedy died in 1465. While only the chapel now survives, and within it Kennedy's own tomb, the foundation was on a far grander scale than the Pedagogy, albeit still quite modest by contemporary standards.[30] Kennedy appropriated the teinds of four Fife parishes (Cults, Kemback, Dunino and Kilmany) to provide for six poor scholars and six teaching staff, all presided over by a provost, a total complement of thirteen that deliberately echoed Christ and the twelve apostles. Fittingly, St Salvator's was founded as a college of arts and theology (all its staff were to be either masters of theology or masters of arts pursuing higher degrees in theology) and the appointment of John Athilmer, a Cologne-educated Albertist, as its first provost clearly indicated Kennedy's desire to establish a better endowed and theologically more conservative alternative to the Pedagogy.[31]

That Kennedy's new college at St Andrews was founded within a year of his old friend William Turnbull's new *studium generale* at Glasgow was more than coincidental.[32] In fact, the papal bulls authorising their establishment were issued by Nicholas V within a month of each other in January–February 1451. There seems little reason to doubt that, in the wake of the Great and Little Schisms in the church, they colluded in their efforts to promote the more conservative and pro-papalist doctrines of Albert the Great. Indeed, several of the masters recruited to teach at Glasgow, including its principal regent and first vice-chancellor, Duncan Bunch, were graduates of Cologne with strong associations with Kennedy and St Andrews.[33] However, while Kennedy's focus at St Salvator's was exclusively on arts and theology,

---

[30] According to Cant, *St Salvator*, pp. 3–4, Kennedy modelled it on New College Oxford, founded in 1379 by Bishop William of Wykeham, like Kennedy an ecclesiastical politician and statesman who rose to become Chancellor of England, just as Kennedy was chancellor of Scotland. However, Wykeham's foundation was on far grander scale, providing funds to support one hundred students and masters (not to mention a further endowment of a feeder school at Winchester).

[31] On Athilmer and Cologne, see Lyall, 'Scottish Students and Masters at Cologne and Louvain', pp. 56ff., and Woodman, 'Education and Episcopacy', p. 58. Cologne was the resting-place of Albert the Great and its university, founded in 1388, was a realist stronghold where debates between Albertists and Thomists were more usual than debates between proponents of the *via antiqua* and the *via moderna*.

[32] For this and what follows, see Woodman, 'Education and Episcopacy', pp. 53–63; Durkan, 'William Turnbull', pp. 31–2, 34ff.

[33] Bunch graduated from Cologne in 1447 and was in St Andrews from 1448 to 1450 before moving to Glasgow; see Durkan, 'William Turnbull', pp. 42–4.

Turnbull's Glasgow placed more emphasis on legal studies. Turnbull himself had migrated from Louvain to Pavia to study canon law (he attained a doctorate in 1439) before his return to Scotland where he became a counsellor to James II and bishop of Glasgow in 1447. His interest in government may well have prompted him to promote the teaching of law at Glasgow and, had he lived longer (he died in 1454, just three years after his university's foundation) Glasgow might well have developed as the major centre for legal study in Scotland, with St Andrews taking the lead in theology. As it was, Glasgow suffered the same problem of chronic under-funding as early St Andrews and, without its founding patron, its subsequent development was halting, and (one might add) somewhat obscure owing to the paucity of surviving records.[34]

Two key points emerge from this that are worth further emphasis. The first is that, while some Scottish intellectuals continued to promote the *via moderna* after Lindores' death in 1437, it was no longer a dominant force in Scottish academia. By the mid-fifteenth century, in common with a more general European trend, the prevalent doctrinal orthodoxy was the moderate realism of Albert the Great which was becoming entrenched not just at St Andrews but also at Turnbull's Glasgow. Academic in-fighting did of course continue, but it was driven less by the philosophical issues that had preoccupied earlier generations of students and masters than by personal animosities compounded by ecclesiastical politics.[35] John Athilmer, for example, Kennedy's hand-picked provost of St Salvator's, proved as contentious a figure as Laurence of Lindores, if for different reasons. His attempts to promote the interests of his college led to constant tension with the arts faculty and its associated Pedagogy and ultimately to attempts to free St Salvator's from the faculty's jurisdiction. To this end, in 1469 Athilmer obtained a papal bull granting the college the right to administer its own examinations – thus freeing it from faculty control – prompting two of its masters publicly to defy the dean by staging a walk-out from a general faculty meeting. In a still less edifying example of the breakdown of collegiality, the dean was subsequently attacked in the street by a student armed with a sword and knife and subjected to an intimidating assault under cover of darkness by a rampaging pack of St Salvator's men armed with bows and arrows. The feud dragged on for some years. However, by the time

---

[34] John Durkan and James Kirk, *The University of Glasgow, 1451–1577* (Glasgow, 1977), esp. chs 1–2.

[35] It is interesting in this context that John Ireland, possibly a native of St Andrews, who graduated BA in 1456, left the university before obtaining his licentiate following a dispute with the faculty in 1458. His subsequent academic career in Paris included playing a key role in opposing the ban on nominalist texts that was imposed in 1474 and lasted for seven years. While there is no evidence that his earlier altercation at St Andrews was rooted in doctrinal issues rather than simply in a combative temperament, it is not inconceivable that he took exception to the Albertist orthodoxy represented by the likes of Athilmer. On his career, see J. H. Burns, 'John Ireland: Theology and Public Affairs in the Late Fifteenth Century', *Innes Review* 41 (1990), pp. 151–81.

of Athilmer's death in 1473, the faculty had emerged victorious and the college had been forced to acknowledge its place within the governing structures of the university.[36]

Such internal disputes can have done little to enhance St Andrews' reputation as Scotland's premier place of learning, and the unstable nature of James III's kingship and the lengthy controversy over the bishopric's elevation in 1472 to archiepiscopal status were hardly conducive to investment in education. Even under a sympathetic archbishop such as William Scheves (1479–97), himself a former student and master at the university, only modest progress was made in improving facilities and funding.[37] Moreover, and this is the second key point that is worth further thought, after 1450 St Andrews had a rival in the form of Turnbull's Glasgow. Whatever pretensions St Andrews might have had to be a national centre of learning were undercut by Turnbull's decision – apparently supported by his friend Kennedy – to establish a second *studium generale*, complete with all five faculties, within his own diocese on the other side of the country. This regional pattern of educational provision was confirmed and extended in 1495 when William Elphinstone, bishop of Aberdeen, followed the lead of his episcopal predecessors in seeking papal approval for a third *studium generale* in his northern diocese. Just as Turnbull was an alumnus of St Andrews, so Elphinstone was a graduate of Glasgow (1462), where his father was among the earliest teachers of law, and where his philosophical training was rooted in the Albertist realism that Kennedy and Turnbull had sought to promote. Subsequently, Elphinstone studied canon law at Paris and civil law at Orléans before becoming a key royal counsellor to both James III and especially James IV. His foundation of King's College in 1495 proclaimed his loyalty to the crown at the same time as it extended still further the regional character of Scottish university provision.[38]

The result, in contrast to the concentration of colleges in Oxford and Cambridge, was a geographically dispersed system, one that mirrored the more decentralised nature of the Scottish kingdom. The downside of this was that none of the three Scottish universities ever achieved the critical mass that would have allowed it to develop into a major centre of learning, attracting students and masters from outside Scotland. The incorporated students and masters were almost exclusively Scots and, throughout the late medieval period (and, indeed,

---

[36] For details of these incidents, see *St Andrews Acta*, pp. xxviii–xxxii; Cant, *St Salvator*, pp. 33–5.

[37] Scheves graduated BA in 1455 and MA in 1456 (*St Andrews Acta*, pp. 103, 111); for his career, see Norman Macdougall, 'Scheves, William (b. in or before 1440, d. 1497)', *Oxford Dictionary of National Biography* (Oxford, 2004) [www.oxforddnb.com/view/article/24806, accessed 15 Dec. 2014].

[38] The fullest account of the foundation and early development of King's College is in Leslie J. MacFarlane, *William Elphinstone and the Kingdom of Scotland 1431–1514* (Aberdeen, 1995), ch. 7; see also J. M. Fletcher, 'The Foundation of the University of Aberdeen in its European Context', *The Universities of Aberdeen and Europe: the First Three Centuries*, ed. P. Dukes (Aberdeen, 1995), pp. 9–56.

well beyond), it remained common for Scots to graduate as licentiates from one of their home institutions and then to venture overseas for further study. As a result, the Scottish universities remained small and, in terms of fully functioning higher faculties, under-developed institutions. Between 1413 and 1463, the number of arts students graduating from St Andrews averaged twenty-one per year (thirteen BAs and eight MAs) rising to thirty-four (twenty BAs and fourteen MAs) in the following half century up to 1513. Even at the end of the fifteenth century, therefore, the full complement of masters and students in any given year – including those who were incorporated but never graduated – was probably not much greater than 100 (see table 13.1). These numbers increased slightly in the five decades between 1513 and 1563, peaking in the 1520s and 1530s before falling away sharply in the troubled 1540s. However, at no time is the university population likely to have exceeded 150 (including those pursuing higher degrees for whom no graduation rolls survive). Comparable figures for Glasgow and Aberdeen do not exist, but they almost certainly had fewer students than St Andrews. The Scottish universities were small institutions, adequate for servicing basic domestic needs – indeed, serving a critical function in providing higher education in relatively cheap local colleges – but unlikely to attract international attention.

Humanism, Scholasticism and the Founding of St Leonard's

Elphinstone's new foundation at Aberdeen is often linked to what has become known as the 'Education Act' of 1496 and the statutory requirement that 'wealthy' barons and freeholders send their sons to grammar school from the age of eight or nine and then to 'the schools of art and law, so that they may have knowledge and understanding of the laws, through which justice may reign universally throughout the realm'.[39] This emphasis on legal training can be seen as an effort to reach beyond the conventional pool of clerical careerists who had traditionally served as administrators in church and state – and which Turnbull's Glasgow foundation was intended to augment – and to encourage the lay elite to embrace similar educational opportunities. Evidence relating to the education of the laity in this period is very patchy, but just as local grammar schools were increasingly widespread in pre-Reformation Scotland (and not simply a product of Protestant reform), so the universities were catering for increasing numbers of students of landed background who had no intention of embarking on a clerical career.[40] At St Andrews, for example, there was a notable increase in the number of students incorporated in the decade or so after 1496 and the fact that many of them did not go on to graduate suggests that this was an influx

---

[39] RPS, A1496/6/4.
[40] See *Scottish Schools and Schoolmasters, 1560–1633*, ed. John Durkan (Woodbridge, 2013), which brings together the available evidence on pre-Reformation schools as well as their immediate post-Reformation successors and equivalents.

Table 13.1: Graduation and incorporation data 1413–1573, by decade.

Decade	BA	MA	Notes	Incorporation
1413–23	83	37	Plague 1420–22	–
1423–33	72	66		–
1433–43	142	80	Plague 1439–42	–
1443–53	134	97		–
1453–63	131	85	Foundation of St Salvator's and Glasgow	–
50-year average	11.2	7.3	Weighted for lost years (5): 12.5 and 8.1	
1463–73	257	176		
1473–83	185	133		
1483–93	201	142		320
1493–1503	144	110	Plague 1502–03; foundation of Aberdeen 1495	192
1503–13	155	98	Plague 1503–4	304
50-year average	18.8	13.2	Weighted for lost years (2): 19.6 and 13.7	29 (average 28 years)
1513–23	157	129		259
1523–33	210	169	Foundation of St Leonard's	376
1533–43	267	208		436
1543–53	32	12	Rough Wooing – no records 1545–51	198
1553–63	101	57	Foundation of St Mary's; no records 1558–63	323
50-year average	15.3	11.5	Weighted for lost years (10): 19.2 and 14.3	40 (average 40 years)
1563–73	189	127		387
Totals	2,426	1,726		

Note:

Details of matriculation (more properly 'incorporation') exist only from 1473 (though 1474–83 and several later years are missing) and do not give a clear sense of the numbers at the university in any given year. Students and masters were required to matriculate only once rather than annually and other anomalies render any statistics based on the records approximate at best (the problems are discussed at length in the introduction to *Early Records*). That said, the figures for incorporations presented here are broadly in line with figures for graduation and bear out a guesstimate of a total university population of 100 before 1513 rising to 150 thereafter. The figures for incorporations do not necessarily take full account of students pursuing higher degrees in law and theology for whom there is no surviving evidence of graduations. However, it is unlikely that they would add more than a handful to the overall numbers.

Source: graduation data are drawn from *St Andrews Acta*; incorporation data from *Early Records* (there is only one list of incorporations prior to 1483). The weighted 50-year averages take account of 'lost years' when graduations and incorporations did not take place due to plague or other circumstances. Thus, for example, the weighted averages for 1413 to 1463 are based on 45 rather than 50 years.

of laymen less interested in a degree than in acquiring basic proficiency in 'art and law'.[41]

It was for precisely this lay elite that, across Europe, contemporary humanists were developing a curriculum – the *studia humanitatis* – that played down the significance of logic (the traditional foundation discipline of scholastic study) and put greater emphasis on rhetoric (the *ars dictaminis* or the art of speaking and writing well) that was perceived as more fitting for an educated gentleman.[42] Training in the martial arts remained *de rigueur* for those of noble status, but the lay elite were also being forced to adapt to new roles as learned counsellors to kings, as diplomats and politicians, dedicated to the welfare of the crown and community. In this context the *ars dictaminis* as practised in classical Rome – and familiarity with classical history, poetry and moral philosophy – was of more practical use than the conventional scholastic curriculum.[43] Universities, however, are deeply conservative institutions where effecting change in the face of entrenched intellectual tradition can prove extremely difficult. In establishing a new institution, Elphinstone perhaps had more opportunity to be innovative and he is well known for appointing Hector Boece, a friend of Desiderius Erasmus, the doyen of Northern European humanists, as grammarian and then principal of King's College. Yet, while Boece was an accomplished Latin stylist and author of the first humanist history of Scotland – the *Scotorum Historia* (Paris, 1527) – he was also enough of a scholastic logician to publish a textbook on the subject.[44] In fact, Aberdeen retained a largely traditional arts curriculum and, while Elphinstone provided for the teaching of civil as well as canon law, and the king himself endowed a chair of medicine, the college principal was still expected to teach theology and provision was made for a total of seven theology students.[45]

But what of St Andrews? What impact did the so-called 'new learning' have on Scotland's oldest university? It is indicative of both entrenched conservatism and awareness of novel intellectual trends that in 1498 the faculty formally prohibited regents from adopting 'the new curriculum' or teaching 'the new way' without proper consultation with the dean and the facul-

---

[41] *St Andrews Acta*, pp. xl–xli. The recurrence of plague between 1502 and 1504 may have prevented a greater influx of students post 1496 (see table 13.1).

[42] For this development in a Scottish context, see Mason, 'Laicisation and the Law', and Roger A. Mason, *Kingship and the Commonweal: Political Thought in Renaissance and Reformation Scotland* (Edinburgh, 1998), ch. 3.

[43] For a useful overview of this kind of study and its implications, see Charles Nauert, *Humanism and the Culture of Renaissance Europe*, 2nd edn (Cambridge, 2006).

[44] On Boece, see John Durkan, 'Early Humanism and King's College Aberdeen', *Aberdeen University Review* 48 (1979–80), pp. 259–79; Nicola Royan, 'Boece, Hector (c.1465–1536)', *Oxford Dictionary of National Biography* (Oxford, 2004) [www.oxforddnb.com/view/article/2760, accessed 13 Dec. 2014].

[45] Of all the new Scottish foundations, King's College was probably the best endowed, Elphinstone annexing the revenues of parishes across his diocese to fund a total foundation of forty-two masters and students. See Macfarlane, *Elphinstone*, pp. 309–17.

ty.[46] Unfortunately, the records do not expand on these enigmatic phrases, although they do suggest that the novel approaches advocated by humanists might be welcomed in some quarters but met with suspicion in others. There is some evidence – perhaps prompting the faculty's decree – that individual scholars were making available tuition in subjects such as 'the poetic art of oratory' in extra-curricular lectures and informal discussion groups.[47] It is noteworthy, moreover, that on his death in 1496, Alexander Inglis, a doctor of both canon and civil law who became archdeacon of St Andrews, bequeathed a small but select collection of classical texts to the university, including works by Virgil, Ovid and Cicero.[48] It is not known where Inglis went to university, but it is inconceivable that the many Scottish scholars who studied in Cologne, Louvain and Paris at the turn of the fifteenth century were untouched by humanist learning even if the formal curricula at these institutions remained essentially scholastic. Hector Boece, for example, was not the only Scot to have shared accommodation at the Collège de Montaigu in Paris with Erasmus. So too did James IV's long-serving secretary Patrick Paniter, an accomplished humanist who, in addition to writing the king's diplomatic correspondence in appropriately fashionable classical Latin, also took responsibility for educating the king's illegitimate son, Alexander, appointed archbishop of St Andrews in 1505 at the tender age of twelve.[49]

Scandalous though the king's promotion of his adolescent son may have been, he did at least go to considerable lengths to ensure that Alexander received the best possible education.[50] By all accounts a studious and intellectually gifted boy, his early schooling at the hands of Paniter was followed by a three-year sojourn in Italy, much of it in Siena and Rome in the company of Erasmus who was hired as his tutor and who was evidently deeply impressed by his young charge.[51] On his return to Scotland in 1510 the archbishop was immediately drafted into his father's government as chancellor, sitting regularly on the king's council, but he also took a keen interest in the university at the heart of his diocese. Initially, he appears to have sought to revitalise the perennially under-endowed and ailing Pedagogy. However, Alexander was not yet master of his own house: still not consecrated as archbishop, the bulk of his

---

[46] *St Andrews Acta*, p. 267 (7 May 1498): '[…] ordinatum erat […] quod regentes Facultatis Arcium non legerent neque inciperent novos cursus sive novam viam ad placitum illorum nisi prius habita matura deliberacione Decani et Facultatis Arcium'.

[47] *St Andrews Acta*, pp. xl–xli, lxxxv.

[48] Higgitt, *Scottish Libraries*, pp. 382–4.

[49] J. A. Gould, 'Panter, Patrick (c.1470–1519)', *Oxford Dictionary of National Biography* (Oxford, 2004) [www.oxforddnb.com/view/article/21234, accessed 9 Dec. 2014]. His Latin is commended for its 'Corinthian glitter' in *The Letters of James IV, 1505–13*, ed. R. K. Hannay and R. L. Mackie (Edinburgh, 1953), p. xxxiii.

[50] For a recent sketch of his career, see Trevor Chalmers, 'Stewart, Alexander (c.1493–1513)', *Oxford Dictionary of National Biography* (Oxford, 2004) [www.oxforddnb.com/view/article/26454, accessed 9 Dec. 2014].

[51] He wrote a touching panegyric to his former pupil, translated in John Herkless and R. K. Hannay, *The Archbishops of St Andrews*, 5 vols (London, 1907–15), i, pp. 262–4.

episcopal revenues were being diverted into the royal coffers, and he was able to make only piecemeal contributions to reviving the Pedagogy's fortunes. He was faced, moreover, with a forceful rival in St Andrews itself in the shape of Prior John Hepburn, a scion of a leading noble family who had been head of the cathedral priory since 1483, and who may well have resented Alexander's elevation to the primatial see.[52] Unlike the archbishop, Hepburn had full control over the priory's considerable resources and, in the ancient hospital and church of St Leonard, lying within the priory's precincts, abutting the town at the east end of South Street, he had an institution that could be readily adapted to serve educational needs. The archbishop fell in with the prior's plans and, in 1513, a charter was issued in their joint names establishing a 'College of Poor Clerks of the Church of St Andrews', known from an early date simply as St Leonard's.[53]

Later that year Alexander was killed fighting at his father's side at the battle of Flodden and we will never know what impact he might have had on the fortunes of the university had he lived longer than his twenty years. As it was, Prior Hepburn, though frustrated in his efforts to seize the vacant archbishopric for himself, was given free rein to shape the college in his own image.[54] As a result, St Leonard's was essentially an extension, intellectually as well as physically, of the priory, its emphasis exclusively on arts and theology, designed to suit the needs of the regular clergy and promoting the austere piety associated with reforming Augustinian principles. Far better endowed than St Salvator's, let alone the Pedagogy, it provided for twenty poor scholars as well as masters drawn primarily from the canons of the cathedral.[55] Fittingly the character of the college was thoroughly monastic, possibly inspired by the notably austere ethos of the same Collège de Montaigu that in the 1490s had been home to Paniter, Boece and Erasmus. Erasmus later expressed his extreme dislike of the regime he experienced there and one wonders if his protégé would have shared the vision of monastic discipline that Hepburn set out in his famous statutes detailing, as he put it in the preface, 'a short order of life for the poor Scholars, Priests and Regents of the College'.[56] The statutes provide a unique insight into

---

[52] *St Andrews Acta*, pp. xliii–xlvii.

[53] Herkless and Hannay, *College of St Leonard*, pp. 136–44: a translation of the charter of James IV dated 23 February 1513 that incorporated those issued by the archbishop and the prior dated 20 August 1512 and 1 February 1513 respectively. Hepburn and Stewart, unlike the founders of St Salvator's and St Mary's (or indeed the university), did not seek papal sanction for their foundation.

[54] J. H. Burns, 'Hepburn, John (c.1460–1525)', *Oxford Dictionary of National Biography* (Oxford, 2004) [www.oxforddnb.com/view/article/13004, accessed 9 Dec. 2014], says surprisingly little about the foundation of St Leonard's, for which the extensive introduction to Herkless and Hannay, *College of St Leonard*, remains the standard authority.

[55] The endowment was complex, but included the properties (not just the teinds) with which St Leonard's church and hospital was already generously provided; see Herkless and Hannay, *College of St Leonard*, pp. 92–6, and for the lands and rents specified in Hepburn's charter, ibid., pp. 140–1.

[56] Herkless and Hannay, *College of St Leonard*, p. 159. In his colloquy 'Ichthyophagia,

the life of the college community, ranging from the basic admission criteria – 'sobriety of character', skill in Latin and familiarity with Gregorian chant – to the daily round of religious services students and masters were to observe and the food and drink on which they were to dine.[57] Under the disciplinary eye of the *hebdomadar* (a supervisory role performed weekly in rotation by the masters), students were to rise at five in the summer and five-thirty in the winter, and between morning mass at six, Vespers at three and Salve at nine, they were to apply themselves to study.[58] Only Latin was to be spoken in the college, and while students were allowed out once a week to enjoy 'honest games' on the links, they were permitted to do so only as a group, wearing their gowns and hoods for easy identification, under the supervision of a master.[59] Students were strictly forbidden to meet with women of the town and women were equally forbidden to set foot in the college, 'save the common laundress, who must be fifty years at the least'.[60] Students were also expected to perform some menial tasks themselves, taking turns helping in the kitchens and with the cleaning, while twice a year at Christmas and Easter all the boys were to lend a hand clearing the windows, altars and walls 'of spiders' webs and other filth'.[61]

Hepburn did not specify a detailed curriculum, but the statutes do refer to masters being required to give classes in 'Grammar, Verse, Rhetoric, or out of the books of Solomon'; while students, 'before they proceed to the degree of master', were 'to hear Logic, Physics, Philosophy, Metaphysics, and the books of Ethics, or at least in place of these some one of the books of Solomon'.[62] Leaving aside the marked preference for the wisdom of Solomon, these stipulations do not indicate any obvious concession to the kind of humanistic training that Alexander Stewart had received. Hepburn's intellectual world appears more traditionally scholastic and Aristotelian. Interestingly, the statutes do make explicit reference to the college being open to 'the sons of noblemen or of others', but the presence of lay students was not allowed to compromise the college's traditional curriculum or monastic discipline.[63] On the contrary, Hepburn insisted that such students must conform in every way to the regimen imposed on the foundationers – the 'poor scholars' – who formed the core of the community. Thus he went out of his way to forbid the wearing of secular garb – multi-coloured caps and tunics that were fashionably short or 'slashed'

---

or Fish-Eating', Erasmus recalled with horror the ascetic conditions he had suffered at 'Vinegar College' under John Standonck; see *The Whole Familiar Colloquies of Erasmus*, trans. N. Bailey (Glasgow, 1877), pp. 285–6.

[57] Herkless and Hannay, *College of St Leonard*, pp. 160–3.
[58] Ibid., pp. 163–6.
[59] Ibid., pp. 167–8.
[60] Ibid., p. 167; though later, with reference to attending to the sick, the statutes also make allowance for the ministrations within the college of 'a Matron of no less than fifty years, a good woman of unblemished character and repute': ibid., p. 176.
[61] Ibid., p. 166.
[62] Ibid., pp. 163–4.
[63] Ibid., p. 171.

– as well as outlawing long hair and beards.[64] In terms that give a clear insight in to how students were accustomed to behaving, at least when discipline was lax, Hepburn laid down that: 'They are not to frequent the town. They must by no means leave the place [the college] without permission; they are not to hold feastings at night, wear knives or weapons of offence within the walls, play dice at all, or football, or any other dishonest or dangerous games.'[65] Given that Hepburn insisted that students at St Leonard's had to be aged between fifteen and twenty-one, the disciplinary challenges were not far to seek.

One final point worth noting about the statutes is that they refer to the wider context of the university on only one occasion. Hepburn seems to have envisaged his college as being self-contained, answerable to the prior rather than the archbishop, and the authority – indeed, existence – of the university is recognised only with reference to bachelors processing formally to the 'Paedagogium' for their MA examinations and 'inception' (graduation).[66] These were solemn occasions when the new licentiates were placed in a master's chair and capped with a *birettum*, signifying the beginning (hence 'inception') rather than the end of their academic careers. In return, they were expected to thank the examiners and witnesses with gifts of bonnets and gloves as well as communal banquets that were sometimes more convivial than the faculty was willing to tolerate.[67] In fact, feasting was a regular feature of university life, used to relieve the tedium of quotidian fare, while also celebrating the corporate identity of the university and its constituent colleges through, for example, the commemoration of their patron saints.[68] Hepburn evidently wished to subject such feast days to greater regulation and restraint, and also to limit the recreational activities in which students traditionally indulged. Folk plays, cock fighting, golf and archery were all part-and-parcel of the colourful world of St Andrews' students and it is unlikely that Hepburn's statutes eradicated them entirely, even in St Leonard's. Indeed, in 1537, a decade or so after his death, the faculty had to deal with a serious breach of the peace caused by inter-college football rivalry.[69]

As with the foundation of St Salvator's, so the foundation of St Leonard's was followed by some years of instability and friction as the new college found its place in the wider structures – academic and administrative – of the university. In this case, tensions were exacerbated by the political dislocation that accompanied James V's long minority and by Hepburn's own failed attempts to gain promotion to the archbishopric. It was only in 1520 that the prior belatedly relinquished his claim to succeed Alexander Stewart and recognised Andrew Forman as archbishop. However, Forman's death in 1521 led Hepburn to revive

---

[64] Ibid., p. 171.
[65] Ibid., p. 172.
[66] Ibid., pp. 167–8.
[67] *St Andrews Acta*, p. cxix.
[68] *St Andrews Acta*, pp. cxxxi–cxxxiv.
[69] The dispute involved all three colleges: *St Andrews Acta*, pp. cxxxii, 380–1 (19 Feb. 1537). In Nov. 1497 students had been forbidden to play 'ad pilam pedalem' on pain of excommunication (ibid., pp. 265–6).

his claim, only to be disappointed once again by the translation to St Andrews of James Beaton, archbishop of Glasgow since 1509. Despite such political and personal wrangling, by the time of his own death in 1525, Hepburn's college of St Leonard had become as fully integrated with the university as St Salvator's. Yet, beneath any such surface calm, the intellectual life of the university was being quickened and disturbed, not just by humanist ideas, but also by the assault on Catholic verities launched by Martin Luther in 1517 and soon convulsing Europe as a whole.

Reform and Renewal: The Foundation of St Mary's College

It is probably no more than coincidence that in 1525, the year of Hepburn's death, the new Archbishop Beaton petitioned the pope for permission to establish 'a College of St Mary for the teaching of Theology, Law, Physic and other liberal disciplines'.[70] In so far as this was yet another attempt by an incumbent primate to revivify the fortunes of the Pedagogy, it is perhaps not surprising that in the short term it came to nothing. But Beaton's ambitions for the university had already been signalled by his invitation to John Mair to transfer from Glasgow to teach arts and theology in the St Andrews Pedagogy. Mair was yet another of that distinguished group of Scots who had studied at the Collège de Montaigu in the 1490s, but unlike Boece and Paniter, he had remained in Paris where in the first two decades of the sixteenth century he established a formidable reputation for himself as one of the leading academics of his generation.[71] It was a considerable coup for Beaton to persuade such an intellectual luminary to swap the Sorbonne for Glasgow in 1518 and subsequently in 1523 to move to St Andrews. In some respects, it also ran counter to the prevailing doctrinal orthodoxies, for Mair was an exponent of the *via moderna*, an acknowledged admirer of Occam and especially Scotus, whose teaching did not always square with the Albertism that had come to prevail in the Scottish universities and in which Beaton himself, as a St Andrews student in the 1490s, had presumably been trained.[72] Perhaps the new archbishop calculated that Mair's stellar reputation, and hence his ability to attract high calibre masters as well as students to St Andrews, was worth the risk.[73]

---

[70] *St Andrews Acta*, p. liv.
[71] For his biography, see John Durkan, 'John Major: After 400 Years', *Innes Review* 1 (1950), pp. 131–9; J. H. Burns, 'New Light on John Major', *Innes Review* 5 (1954), pp. 83–100, and Alexander Broadie, 'Mair, John (c.1467–1550)', *Oxford Dictionary of National Biography* (Oxford, 2004) [www.oxforddnb.com/view/article/17843, accessed 12 Dec. 2014].
[72] James K. Cameron, 'Beaton, James (c.1473–1539)', *Oxford Dictionary of National Biography* (Oxford, 2004) [www.oxforddnb.com/view/article/1824, accessed 12 Dec. 2014]; he graduated from St Andrews BA in 1492 and MA the following year.
[73] As far as students were concerned, it paid off: numbers graduating in the Pedagogy in 1525–26 show a marked increase, and the same happened in the years following Mair's appointment to St Salvator's in 1531.

However that may be, it was also the case that the main focus of intellectual debate had shifted and was now less to do with the relative merits of different schools of medieval philosophy than with the wholesale attack on scholasticism *per se* being mounted by humanists who were increasingly dismissive of the unreconstructed aims and methods of the 'schoolmen'. In conservative academic eyes, Mair was a safe as well as a distinguished pair of hands, his commitment to traditional scholastic disciplines unwavering, yet famous enough to be lampooned by François Rabelais as the author of a treatise on how to make sausages.[74] In fact, Mair may not have been quite as unsympathetic to humanism as Rabelais – a former pupil – suggests. While in Paris he attended the first Greek classes to be taught there and, in the 1520s, possibly in response to the humanist mantra *ad fontes* ('back to the sources!'), Mair also made an unexpected departure from the conventional approach to theological commentary. In his youth he had cut his theological teeth commenting in the customary manner on the four books of Peter Lombard's *Sentences*.[75] In 1529, however, he published his *In quatuor evangelia expositiones*, commenting directly on the four Gospels themselves, a method of theological exposition that was extremely rare among his scholastic predecessors. That said, the approach was more innovative than the content. Mair shared neither the humanists' interest in philology (his earlier brush with Greek does not appear to have had any lasting impact on his scholarship) nor their more heterodox theological views. Deeply wedded to traditional Catholic theology, his suspicion of humanism's corrosive influence was only hardened by the rapid rise of Protestant dissent. His last published work (a commentary on Aristotle's *Nicomachean Ethics*) was dedicated in 1530 to his old friend Cardinal Thomas Wolsey in terms that make clear that his prime concern was now less the threat posed to the Catholic faith by Erasmian humanism than the growing challenge of Lutheran heresy.[76]

Mair wrote his last books in Paris, whence he had returned in 1526 only two years after his move from Glasgow to St Andrews. His motives for leaving remain obscure, as does what prompted his final return to St Andrews in 1531, this time to St Salvator's where he was appointed Provost in 1534 and

---

[74] 'Majoris de modo faciendi Puddinos' is among the lengthy list of books that Pantagruel encounters in the library of St Victor in Paris, beginning with (in Sir Thomas Urquhart of Cromarty's translation) 'The for Godsake of Salvation' and 'The Codpiece of the Law'. Urquhart chose not to translate the title of his countryman's treatise. See *The Second Book of the Works of Mr. Francis Rabelais ... treating of the Heroick Deeds and Sayings of the Good Pantagruel* (London, 1653), pp. 36–8 (book II, ch. 7).

[75] In the twelfth century, Peter the Lombard had brought together biblical passages and *sententia* (opinions) from the church fathers covering all aspects of Christian theology in his *Libri Quatuor Sententiae*. Commentary on his four books remained the standard method of theological exposition from the time of Albert and Aquinas to that of Mair and beyond.

[76] Alexander Broadie, 'Mair, John (c.1467–1550)', *Oxford Dictionary of National Biography* (Oxford, 2004) [www.oxforddnb.com/view/article/17843, accessed 12 Dec. 2014]. I am grateful to Professor Broadie for advice on the points discussed in this paragraph.

where he would remain until his death in 1550. The young George Buchanan, who accompanied Mair to Paris in 1526, later recalled the dangerously febrile religious atmosphere they encountered in the French capital, which he attributed to 'the Lutheran sectaries who were already spreading their doctrines far and wide'.[77] By leaving Paris, Mair may have hoped to escape these inflammatory confessional controversies. If so, he did not succeed. Ironically, he had first been incorporated into the University of St Andrews in 1523 on the same day as the young Patrick Hamilton, a member of a powerful noble family headed by the first earl of Arran, and a recent graduate of the University of Paris, who has the distinction of being the first Scot to be executed for embracing Lutheran ideas.[78] Hamilton was closely associated with St Leonard's College where, perhaps influenced by the long-serving regent and principal, Gavin Logie, reformed ideas appear to have been discussed more openly than elsewhere in the university. It was due to Logie that, according to the later Protestant historian David Calderwood, those who embraced Protestantism were said to have 'drunken of Sanct Leonard's well'.[79] But Archbishop Beaton unwittingly facilitated discussion of the new heresies. For in 1525, the year Mair left for Paris, he was responsible for steering through the Scottish parliament legislation that outlawed the import of Lutheran books and expressly forbade the discussion of Lutheran ideas *except* 'among clerks in the schools'.[80] Hamilton evidently took advantage of this dispensation, but instead of disputing Lutheran doctrines in order to refute them, he came to embrace them, prompting Beaton to launch an inquiry into his behaviour in 1527. Rather than face his accusers, Hamilton fled to Germany and the newly founded Lutheran University of Marburg where he took part in disputations that formed the basis of his influential vernacular Protestant primer, 'Patrick's Places'. But it was not long before he returned

---

[77] Unlike Mair, Buchanan probably found the intellectual debates exhilarating, and he parted company with his mentor during these years in Paris. See his brief autobiography written in 1580 and translated in *The Trial of George Buchanan before the Lisbon Inquisition*, ed. J. M. Aitken (Edinburgh, 1939), pp. xiv–xxvii.

[78] For their incorporation on 9 June 1523, see *Early Records*, pp. 218–19.

[79] David Calderwood, *The History of the Kirk of Scotland*, ed. T. Thomson, 8 vols (Edinburgh, 1842–49), i, pp. 82–3, 141–3; Calderwood was probably elaborating on a passage in Knox's *History of the Reformation in Scotland*, in *The Works of John Knox*, ed. David Laing, 6 vols (Edinburgh, 1846–64), i, p. 36: 'And so within schort space many begane to call in dowbt that which befoir thei held for a certane veritie, in so much that the Universitie of Sanctandrose, and Sanct Leonardis Colledge principallie, by the labouris of Maistir Gawin Logy, and the novises of the Abbay, by the Suppriour [John Winram] begane to smell somwhat of the veritie, and to espy the vanitie of the receaved superstitioun.'

[80] *RPS*, 1525/7/2: the act stipulates that 'no manner of stranger who happens to arrive with their ships within any part of this realm bring with them any books or works of the said Luther, his disciples or servants, dispute or rehearse his heresies or opinions, unless it be to disprove them, and that by clerks in the schools only'. The significance of this clause is explored in Elizabeth Tapscott, 'Propaganda and Persuasion in the Early Scottish Reformation, c.1527–1557' (unpublished PhD thesis, University of St Andrews, 2013), ch. 1.

to Scotland, initially to his family lands around Linlithgow, but thence to St Andrews, summoned by the archbishop to answer the charges against him. Hamilton may have anticipated that, under the protection of the 1525 legislation, his intellectual prowess, not to mention his family connections, would ensure he was spared the fate of a convicted heretic. If so, he was quickly disabused, and on 29 February 1528 he was burned at the stake in the shadow of St Salvator's imposing bell tower.[81]

According to John Knox, a servant of Beaton's warned the archbishop that 'the reek of Patrick Hamilton infected as many as it blew upon'.[82] However, while Hamilton did convert others both before and as a result of his death, the new Protestant doctrines did not simply sweep the board in Scotland. It would be another three decades before the Reformation of 1559–60 destroyed the old religious order.[83] The reformers may have read it as a sign from God that St Andrews suffered a severe outbreak of the plague in the year following Hamilton's execution. Yet, by the time Mair returned to the city in 1531, some degree of stability had returned – in fact, the 1520s and 1530s mark a highpoint in terms of incorporations and graduations – though there is little evidence of investment in buildings or facilities. The Pedagogy does not seem to have benefited at all from Beaton's earlier interest in establishing a new college, while Mair's appointment as Provost of St Salvator's in 1534 followed hard on the heels of a visitation that revealed what has been described as 'an appalling state of neglect, decay and filth'.[84] The task of reform and meeting new intellectual challenges was not made any easier by the young king, James V, who had taken personal control of the kingdom in 1528, and for whom the price of remaining true to Rome was papal approval of massive ecclesiastical taxes and increased royal interference in church appointments – among them that of his five year-old bastard son James, the future Protestant earl of Moray, as titular head of the St Andrews Priory. Such appointments did little to enhance the church's reputation in the eyes of its critics, while despite an uneasy relationship with James V, Beaton's heavy involvement in politics and diplomacy left him little enough time to devote to the university. As old age took its toll, the archbishop's nephew David Beaton was appointed his coadjutor (assistant) in 1538, and would duly succeed him the following year. But it was in fact two other young nephews of James Beaton, the brothers John and Archibald Hay, who were

---

[81] The fullest most recent treatment of Hamilton's career and significance is Martin Dotterweich, 'The Emergence of Evangelical Theology in Scotland to 1550' (unpublished PhD thesis, University of Edinburgh, 2002), ch. 3; see also Iain Torrance, 'Hamilton, Patrick (1504?–1528)', *Oxford Dictionary of National Biography* (Oxford, 2004) [www.oxforddnb.com/view/article/12116, accessed 12 Dec. 2014] and the sources cited there.

[82] Knox, *History*, in *Works*, i, pp. 41–2.

[83] For recent overviews, see Alec Ryrie, *The Origins of the Scottish Reformation* (Manchester, 2006) and Jane Dawson, *Scotland Re-Formed, 1488–1587* (Edinburgh, 2007).

[84] *St Andrews Acta*, pp. liii–liv.

Table 13.2: BA graduation by college 1483–1573.

Decade	Total	Pedagogy	St Salvator's	St Leonard's	St Mary's	Unspecified
1483–93	201	27	27	–	–	147
1493–1503	144	50	89	–	–	5
1503–13	155	54	101	–	–	–
1513–23	157	29	77	51	–	–
1523–33	210	58	48	104	–	–
1533–43	267	–	138	129	–	–
1543–53	32	–	12	13	–	7
1553–63	101	–	35	36	25	5
1563–73	189	–	49	59	71	10

Source: *St Andrews Acta* (before the 1480s, colleges are not specified).

responsible for instigating yet another attempt to found (or re-found) St Mary's College in place of the apparently now moribund Pedagogy.[85]

Both the Hay brothers were recent MA graduates of Paris where they had become thoroughly imbued with advanced humanist thinking. However, whereas John returned to Scotland in 1536 and was at once admitted to the St Andrews arts faculty and appointed a regent-master, Archibald stayed in Paris where in 1538 he published a short but important pamphlet, *Oratio pro collegii erectione*, dedicated to his uncle.[86] The *Oratio* set out in accomplished humanist Latin not only a plan for establishing a college dedicated to the pursuit of 'polite letters' (*politiores literas*) – the study of logic is notably absent from his proposed curriculum – but also a higher faculty of theology that rather than being devoted to traditional scholastic pursuits would instead take the biblical languages (Hebrew and Greek as well as Latin) as the main focus of its studies. In other words, Hay was advocating the establishment of a trilingual college, such as had been founded in Louvain in 1517, Alcala in 1528 and Paris (the Collège de France) in 1530. In many ways, Hay's *Oratio* epitomised the evangelical humanist programme that, while remaining well within the bounds of Catholic orthodoxy, sought to counter the Protestant appropriation of Scripture and to provide a sound education for Catholic clergy and laity alike. It is not clear how much impact – if any – the *Oratio* had on Archbishop Beaton, but Archibald's brother John was meanwhile making successful efforts to push their uncle

---

[85] While Mair's appointment to the Pedagogy had led to a surge of students studying there in the mid-1520s, after 1533 it vanishes entirely from the lists of graduands in the *St Andrews Acta* (see table 13.2).

[86] See Euan Cameron, 'Archibald Hay's *Elegantiae*: Writings of a Scots Humanist at the Collège de Montaigu in the Time of Budé and Beda', *Acta Conventus Neo-Latini Turonensis*, ed. J.-C. Margolin (Paris, 1980), pp. 277–301, and J. K. Cameron, 'A Trilingual College for Scotland: The Founding of St Mary's College', *In Divers Manners: A St Mary's Miscellany*, ed. D. W. D. Shaw (St Andrews, 1990), pp. 29–42. Cf. Euan Cameron, 'Hay, Archibald (d. 1547)', *Oxford Dictionary of National Biography* (Oxford, 2004) [www.oxforddnb.com/view/article/12709, accessed 12 Dec. 2014].

towards founding a new college. While John arranged that his own parsonage of Tyninghame together with that of Tannadice be appropriated to endow the new college, Beaton supplicated the papacy and in February 1538 was granted by Pope Paul III authority to erect a college dedicated to the Assumption of Mary the Virgin.[87]

The new college was planned on an ambitious scale, but one that specifically looked to Elphinstone's foundation at King's College Aberdeen as its model rather than to Archibald Hay's vision of a trilingual institution. Thus it was in effect founded as a *studium generale* with the potential to develop all five of the traditional faculties, though emphasis was placed primarily on arts, theology and canon law as a means of educating a new generation of secular clergy. The college was also potentially self-contained in terms of its examining and degree-awarding powers. Its immediate prospects, however, were not good. In 1538, as the papal foundation bull made its way from Rome, plague once again struck St Andrews. Moreover, towards the end of the year James Beaton fell ill, and practical arrangements for establishing the college had to be hurriedly made in conjunction with his designated successor David Beaton. At a ceremony in the bishop's palace on 7 February 1539 Robert Bannerman, principal regent in the Pedagogy since 1526, was appointed provost and theologian of the new college, and provision was also made for the appointment of a canon lawyer, a civil lawyer and four arts regents. A week later James Beaton died, leaving St Mary's in the hands of his nephew David, who just two months before, in December 1538, had been made a cardinal in recognition of his key role in keeping James V and his kingdom true to the Catholic faith.[88]

The cardinal's succession to the primatial see was marked by a flurry of activity and considerable sums were expended on building work on the Pedagogy, presumably in anticipation of its new role – and name – as St Mary's College.[89] However, while it had a full complement of staff, the records give no indication that it was recruiting any students. Moreover, its future, like that of the university as a whole, was seriously threatened by the death of James V in 1542 and the conflict between England and France for control of Scotland that ensued. Cardinal Beaton emerged as a key defender of Scotland's traditional alliances with France and the papacy, protecting the interests of the late king's daughter, the infant Mary Queen of Scots, against Henry VIII and the Protestant heresy that was taking root in England. St Andrews, as Scotland's ecclesiastical capital, and Beaton's backyard, found itself at the eye of an increasingly destructive storm. Since the execution of Patrick Hamilton in 1528, heresy trials had taken place sporadically in St Andrews, with its learned doctors – notably John Mair –

---

[87] For this and what follows in the next paragraph, see *St Andrews Acta*, pp. lv–lvi; *Evidence*, pp. 357–8.

[88] His career is well documented in Margaret Sanderson, *Cardinal of Scotland: David Beaton, c. 1494–1546* (Edinburgh, 1986).

[89] *St Andrews Acta*, p. lvi. Beaton apparently employed French masons, presumably borrowed from Falkland where they were overseeing the king's building programme on the royal palace.

being asked to pronounce judgement on those who were suspected of embracing Protestant ideas or harbouring Protestant sympathies.[90] The trial and execution of George Wishart in 1546, therefore, was not an entirely novel experience for the town's citizenry. However, the assassination of Cardinal Beaton two months later certainly was, while the subsequent siege of the castle and the military operations that attended its fall to the French fourteen months later were as unprecedented as their implications were profound. The university was not directly involved in these events, but it suffered the fall-out in terms of material damage and economic loss in the same way as the city as a whole. Henry VIII's chilling instructions that the cardinal's town be destroyed 'so the upper stone be the nether [...] sparing no creature alive within the same' were fortunately not fulfilled to the letter.[91] Nonetheless, dearth and disease stalked the streets, students were scarce, St Salvator's suffered badly from a fire in 1547, and the university maces were taken to the archbishop's country residence at Monimail for safety.[92] It is no surprise that the records of the faculty of arts are largely silent between 1545 and 1551. The university was more or less closed for business for six years.

Emblematic of the dashed hopes of the decade was Archibald Hay's tragically brief return to Scotland in 1545 where he joined his brother as an incorporated master at St Andrews. Archibald had renewed his campaign for the establishment of a trilingual college at the university in 1540 in a lengthy panegyric addressed to Cardinal Beaton on his succession to their uncle James as archbishop.[93] Praising him in the most fulsome terms, he also called upon him to establish a college devoted not to the idle speculations of the schoolmen but to the study of Scripture and the scriptural languages, the basis of true Christian piety. In 1546 Hay was given the opportunity to make his educational vision a reality when he was appointed Bannerman's successor as principal of St Mary's. That promise was left unfulfilled when he was killed in 1547, very possibly fighting an invading English army at the battle of Pinkie where the Scots suffered a heavy defeat in September of that year.[94] It would be his successor as principal of St Mary's, John Douglas, together with Beaton's successor as archbishop of St Andrews, John Hamilton, who would finally establish the new college on a firm footing in the more stable years that followed the 1550 peace settlement between England and France and the withdrawal of English forces from Scotland.

---

[90] Jane Dawson, 'The Scottish Reformation and the Theatre of Martyrdom', *Martyrs and Martyrologies*, ed. Diana Wood (Oxford, 1993), pp. 259–70. Indeed, according to John Knox, who might well have had first-hand experience as a student in St Andrews, Mair's word 'then was holden as ane oracle, in materis of religioun'; Knox, *History*, in *Works*, i, p. 37.

[91] *The Hamilton Papers*, ed. J. Bain, 2 vols (Edinburgh, 1890–2), ii, p. 326 (no. 207), the English Privy Council to the earl of Hertford, 10 April 1544.

[92] *St Andrews Acta*, pp. lxi–lxii. The situation led the rector to petition the governor complaining that the university was 'sa desolate and destitute bayth of rederris, techarris, and auditouris that it is near perist and meritis nocht to be callit ane universiteis'. *Early Records*, pp. xx–xxi.

[93] *Ad ... D. Davidem Betoun ... gratulatorius panegyricus* (Paris, 1540).

[94] *St Andrews Acta*, p. lxii; Cameron, 'A Trilingual College', pp. 41–2.

The death of the octogenarian John Mair in 1550 is an apt enough symbol of the passing of an old intellectual order. Both Douglas and Hamilton had been deeply touched by the new learning of the humanists of which Mair had been so suspicious, and would bring this to bear on the revitalised university of the 1550s. Both men were graduates of St Leonard's, Douglas being among the first of its students to be granted a licence in 1517. Thereafter he pursued a remarkably varied academic career primarily in Paris where his association with Archibald Hay led to his being appointed his successor as principal of St Mary's in 1547.[95] He would prove a dominant force in the university for the next twenty-five years, not only as principal of one of its constituent colleges, but also as its rector, a post to which he was elected on no fewer than twenty-three occasions between 1552 and his death in 1574. As this suggests, Douglas rode out the Reformation storm of 1559–60, emerging as a leading light of the Protestant movement, and succeeding Hamilton as archbishop of St Andrews when the latter was finally executed in 1572. For his part, Hamilton remained loyal to the family interests into which he was born. The illegitimate son of the first earl of Arran, he entered St Leonard's College in 1528, intriguingly the same year that his kinsman Patrick suffered at the stake, and remained there until 1537.[96] He was destined for a career in politics rather than academia, and became the close confidant of his half-brother the second earl of Arran (from 1550 duke of Châtelherault) who acted as governor of Scotland on behalf of Mary Queen of Scots between 1543 and 1554. His appointment as Beaton's successor was a political one and did not go uncontested. However, Hamilton proved a highly effective archbishop, well attuned to the Catholic reforming ideas that were becoming more widespread in Europe and presiding over a series of councils of the Scottish church that sought to remedy many of the problems identified by the church's Protestant critics, including the inadequacy of its educational provision.[97]

The re-foundation of St Mary's should be seen in the context of this Catholic reforming programme. Hamilton and Douglas wasted little time in putting long-delayed plans into effect. Additional land to the west of the old Pedagogy's properties in South Street was acquired – the site thus taking on the dimensions it has today – while Hay's endowment of the college from the teinds of the parishes of Tyningham and Tannadice was supplemented in 1550 by a further grant

---

[95] On Douglas, see J. K. Cameron, 'St Mary's College, 1547–1574 – The Second Foundation: The Principalship of John Douglas', In Divers Manners, ed. Shaw, pp. 43–57; D. F. Wright, 'Douglas, John (c.1500–1574)', Oxford Dictionary of National Biography (Oxford, 2004) [www.oxforddnb.com/view/article/55907, accessed 15 Dec. 2014].

[96] Janet P. Foggie, 'Hamilton, John (1510/11–1571)', Oxford Dictionary of National Biography (Oxford, 2004) [www.oxforddnb.com/view/article/12102, accessed 15 Dec. 2014].

[97] On the church councils, see Alec Ryrie, 'Reform without Frontiers in the Last Years of Catholic Scotland', English Historical Review 119 (2004), pp. 27–56; and J. K. Cameron, '"Catholic Reform" in Germany and in the pre-1560 Church in Scotland', Records of the Scottish Church History Society 20 (1978–80), pp. 105–17.

of the parish of Conveth and subsequently by Inchbriok and Tarvit. As building work recommenced, Hamilton petitioned the pope once again and in 1552 Julius III duly issued a bull granting him the necessary permission on the basis of which the archbishop drew up his own foundation charter dated 25 February 1554.[98] Not surprisingly, Hamilton's *nova erectio* owes something both to James Beaton's original plan of 1538 and to the Catholic reforming impulse that lay behind Hay's proposals. While not a trilingual college, the new St Mary's was a well-endowed institution dedicated to arts and theology and intended to support a total of thirty-six students and masters. Its senior positions were to be held by three theologians and a canon lawyer, and provision was made for eight theology students who would participate in the study and teaching of scripture and scriptural exposition. While it is not made explicit, the wording perhaps suggests the intention that biblical study would take account of Hay's emphasis on trilingualism. In addition, five arts regents were to be appointed, three of whom would guide students in the traditional way through the four years of the philosophy curriculum (though the details of the curriculum are sadly not specified), while the two others would devote themselves to teaching grammar and rhetoric. Finally, domestic staff aside, sixteen poor students – foundationers – completed the college roll.[99]

This was a college on a grander scale than any St Andrews had seen in the past and one that immediately began to benefit student recruitment across the university. Moreover, in finally absorbing the Pedagogy into the collegiate structure of the university, it also put an end to the latter's increasingly anomalous existence. As early as 1555, student numbers had recovered. The 1520s and 1530s had witnessed the largest cohorts of students progressing through the baccalaureate to become masters. Between 1523 and 1543, following the founding of St Leonard's, an average of twenty-four bachelors and nineteen masters graduated every year, surpassing the previous highest averages of twenty-two and fifteen between 1463 and 1483, in the wake of the founding of St Salvator's. The averages for the four years between 1554 and 1558 are roughly comparable – twenty-three and thirteen per year – indicating that Hamilton's reforms and the final establishment of St Mary's had immediate impact. Yet dark clouds loomed on the horizon. In April 1558, an eighty-two-year-old Protestant, Walter Mylne, in exile in Germany from the late 1530s to 1556, was arrested and brought before the archbishop, assorted members of the church hierarchy and sundry doctors of theology in St Andrews. When he persisted in denouncing the mass, denying transubstantiation and defending clerical marriage, he was condemned to death as a heretic and burned at the stake outside the priory on 28 April 1558. It was perhaps a sign of changing times that the town's provost refused to cooperate with the ecclesiastical authorities in Mylne's trial, while the citizenry refused to supply the timber, rope and tar needed for the execution. Indeed, in its aftermath, they made a cairn of stones as a memorial on the site of the burning.[100]

---

[98] *Evidence*, pp. 360–6.
[99] Cant, *University*, pp. 44–5; Cameron, 'Second Foundation', p. 48.
[100] Richard L. Greaves, 'Mylne, Walter (c.1476–1558)', *Oxford Dictionary of National*

Conclusion

IF hardly a revitalised institution on the eve of the Reformation, St Andrews by the mid-1550s was showing clear signs of a strong recovery after the trauma of the 1540s. This was not an institution teetering on the brink of collapse. Yet, like the Catholic church of which it was an integral part, the university was not without its problems – problems that its Protestant critics could easily exploit. Not the least of them was the manner in which its constituent colleges, and the students and masters who populated them, were funded. The financial arrangements made by successive founders relied heavily on the appropriation of parish revenues, thus depleting the resources that might have made a parish living an attractive career option for a university graduate. As it was, few graduates were content with a poorly rewarded parochial charge, and the less accomplished vicars who took their places fed still further the laity's perennial anti-clericalism. Protestant reformers set great store by education, though the extent to which they were able to realise their vision for St Andrews, or the Scottish universities as a whole, is another matter altogether.[101] They did succeed in transforming the city of which the university had become such an integral part. Although a relatively small institution, its master and students comprised a sizeable constituency in a St Andrews community that numbered no more than 2,000, or at most 3,000, souls.[102] Part of the fabric of the kingdom's ecclesiastical capital, its three colleges were landmarks on a cityscape dominated by religious institutions. Moreover, as Scotland's premier centre of learning, the university's contribution to the broader evolution of the Scottish kingdom in the late medieval period is incalculable. Small and functional though it was, the university played a vital role in educating the clerical elite and, increasingly, its lay equivalent. At the same time it linked the Scottish intelligentsia to Continental centres of learning through the peripatetic careers of those who took advantage of their licence *ubique docendi* but returned to St Andrews to teach successive generations of students. If the history of the pre-Reformation university is a rocky one, it is also fundamental to the history of the kingdom it served.

Biography (Oxford, 2004) [www.oxforddnb.com/view/article/19704, accessed 12 Dec. 2014].

[101] Explored at length in Steven Reid, *Humanism and Calvinism: Andrew Melville and the Universities of Scotland, 1560–1625* (Aldershot, 2010).

[102] The best study of the town in this period is Elizabeth Rhodes, 'The Reformation in the Burgh of St Andrews: Property, Piety and Power' (unpublished PhD thesis, University of St Andrews, 2013).

CHAPTER FOURTEEN

The Medieval Maces of the University of St Andrews

Julian Luxford

WHILE the University of St Andrews has lost almost all of its medieval paraphernalia, the deliberate preservation of three fifteenth-century ceremonial maces is a redeeming counterexample to what have been branded past 'acts of non-custodianship'.[1] One of these maces was made for the faculty of Arts between 1416 and 1419, another for the faculty of Canon Law (or Decreets) at an unknown date and the third for the College of St Salvator in 1461. That of the Arts faculty also appears to have served, at least occasionally, as a rector's mace and to have represented the authority of the university in common. With the exception of the regalia and plate of the bishops of Winchester now at Oxford, this is the most coherent and artistically important set of ceremonial metalwork to survive from a medieval British institution (see figure 14.1).

There can be no doubt that from an early date the maces have benefited from special care. In 1544, during the period of the so-called 'Rough Wooing', two of them were looked after privately by trusted masters of Arts, and all three were being stored for safekeeping in St Andrews Castle around 1559.[2] But even allowing for the respect shown them as symbols of corporate worth, their preservation in such good condition is extraordinary. While the early maces of the university of Aberdeen were destroyed, and that of Glasgow was at different times robbed of its imagery and sent to France for safekeeping, the St Andrews maces have not only survived but have also kept the images of saints considered so objectionable in other settings without, apparently, ever having left north-east Fife. That they were used in 'frequent attendance on common and daily funerals' in the town in the eighteenth century suggests these images were painted or varnished over at some stage, as to bury the dead in open view of

---

[1] R. N. Smart, 'The University Treasures', *The Alumnus Chronicle* 62 (1971), pp. 13–17, at p. 14. It is sometimes said that St Andrews has more surviving pre-Reformation maces than any other university, but this is false: Krakow also has three, Greifswald and Halle four each and Rostock five, one of them now in the Cloisters Museum in New York.

[2] *St Andrews Acta*, i, p. lxi n. 5. For storage in the castle see J. Durkan, 'St Salvator's College, Castle Inventory', *Innes Review* 16 (1965), pp. 128–30.

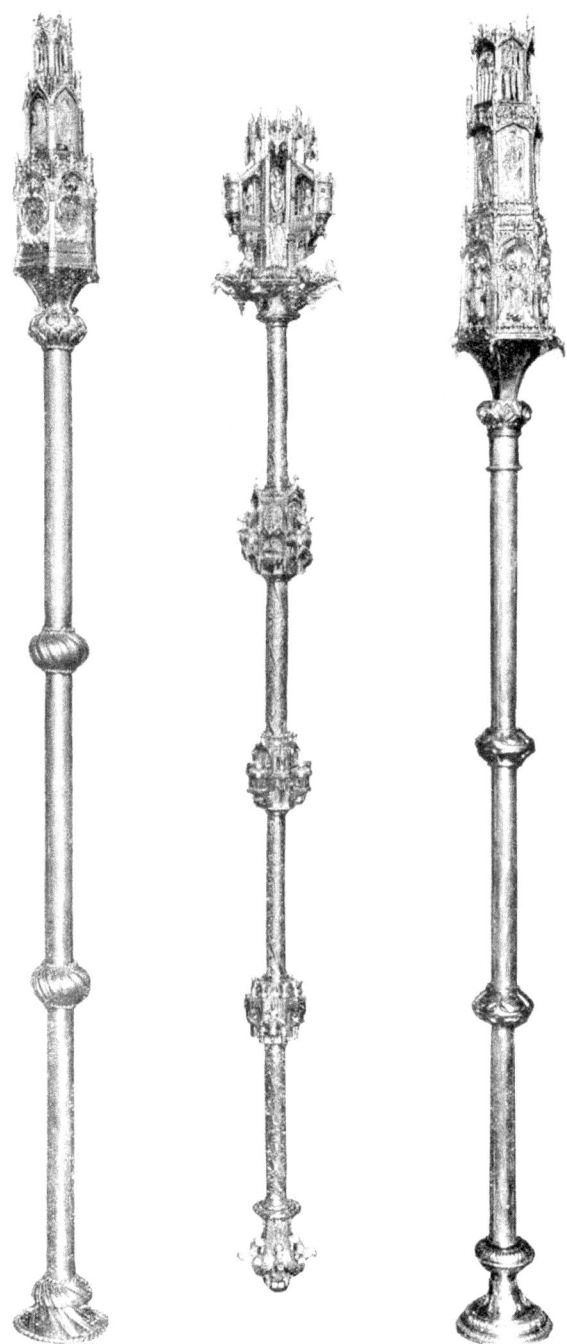

Figure 14.1: The St Andrews maces, with the Arts faculty mace on the left, the St Salvator's College mace in the centre and the Canon Law faculty mace on the right.

the Virgin Mary and other saints would have represented an unconscionable affront to prevailing ideology.[3] Moreover, the maces' materials alone must have proved tempting when, as often, cash was short, and the fact that they escaped the melting pot that claimed all of the other ecclesiastical silver from medieval St Andrews can be attributed to good luck as well as good management.

The number, form, imagery and original uses of these compelling objects all require explanation, and it is the purpose of this essay to address them, taking each mace in turn and seeing what it will yield of its history when set against the wider development of its type and whatever documentation survives for it. This is attempted in two parts. In the first, the terminology and typology of academic maces will be briefly examined, and the quantity and function of maces and related objects at medieval St Andrews will be considered. In the second, a short analysis of each mace will be provided, building on previous work; a detailed and perceptive article of 1892 by Alexander Brook kindled scholarly interest in the maces, and there has been a steady trickle of scholarship over the last sixty years.[4] However, the subject is not exhausted. Most of what has been written to date is insular in its focus on the objects and their place in the culture of the University of St Andrews, and does not attempt anything more contextually ambitious than comparisons with the surviving mace of the university of Glasgow, which was made in the 1460s and designed to look like the Arts faculty mace. The only notable exceptions to this are the catalogues of academic maces by Walter Paatz and Günter and Ingeburg Vorbrodt, which allow one to compare what St Andrews has with existing and lost examples made for other European universities.[5] In fact, the maces are as variously and attractively ramified in historical terms as most of the ceremonial metalwork that has survived from the Middle Ages, and as such many possible approaches could be taken to develop understanding of them.

Terms, Types and Uses

ALTHOUGH 'mace' may not seem an obvious term for these objects, its use is historically justified with respect to ceremonial staves which, like those of St Andrews, have large, complex heads. In fact, at least four terms are used in medieval Latin documents of the staves employed at universities: *virga*, anglicised as verge, which means reed, rod or wand; *baculum*, which is commonly translated

---

[3] For the maces' use at funerals see A. J. S. Brook, 'An Account of the Maces of the Universities of St Andrews, Glasgow, Aberdeen, and Edinburgh, the College of Justice, the City of Edinburgh, &c.', *PSAS* 26 (1892), p. 474.

[4] Brook, 'Account'. Further literature is cited in due course.

[5] W. Paatz, *Sceptrum Universitatis: die europäischen Universitätsszepter* (Heidelberg, 1953); G. Vorbrodt, I. Vorbrodt and W. Paatz, *Corpus Sceptrorum: die akademischen Szepter und Stäbe in Europa*, 2 vols in 3 (Heidelberg, 1971–79). J. Miethke and J. M. Fritz, *Mittelalterliche Universitätszepter: Meisterwerke europäischer Goldschmiedekunst der Gotik* (Heidelberg, 1986) is briefer.

as staff and is the normal medieval term for a prelate's crosier; *sceptrum*, which seems often to have been preferred in German-speaking territories; and *massa*, or mace.⁶ Of these, *virga* is the most common, and was the term used by the Arts faculty at St Andrews for its own mace.⁷ When the three St Andrews maces were listed in early Scots-language inventories, the term used was the cognate *wand* (pluralised as *wandis*).⁸ *Sceptrum* is formally appropriate where, as often, an academic mace was long and thin, with no massy projections (so that it resembles a monarch's sceptre), and also because the word has connotations of authority and dominion in harmony with the functions of these objects. Notably it is the only one of the four terms not found in St Andrews records. As well as *virga*, an account of 1560–62 of one of the bursars of the Arts faculty mentions 10s spent 'pro reparatur baculo' ('for the repair of the staff'), and an inscription in Scots on the St Salvator's mace refers to the object as 'þis masse'.⁹ In the context of this inscription – the mace was made by a Frenchman in Paris and the vernacular wording, if not added in Scotland, must have been supplied by the Scots patron or his agent – the term is a Gallicism. 'Masse' is used again in a French-language document, discussed further below, about another grand academic mace bought from the same goldsmith (or his son) by the English-German nation in the university of Paris in 1494. The word is also found in Latin as a synonym for *sceptrum*.¹⁰ It occurs in another record of the English-German nation, mentioning a 'massa sive virga' ('mace or rod') used by a sub-beadle.¹¹ This record, though it may refer to something relatively modest, expresses an ambiguity about what such objects should be called that persists in modern scholarship. Yet the fact that the word is used as an identifying label on one of the St Andrews maces, and continued in use in the workshop that made this object, is enough to justify the preference for it over 'staff' or 'sceptre', which are the obvious alternatives. Another reason for using the term is the formal association of these large-headed maces with the military objects of the same name. Indeed, the St Salvator's mace in particular is closer in form to some of the secular ceremonial maces once in existence than it is to the sceptres of German academic preference. Jean Fouquet, among the most naturalistic of all medieval illuminators, painted a scene from a treason trial held in Paris in 1458 in which the court serjeants hold maces with large, highly elaborate architectonic heads.¹²

---

⁶ On terminology more widely see Paatz, *Sceptrum Universitatis*, pp. 33–6; reprised in *Corpus Sceptrorum*, ii, pp. 16–20.
⁷ For example, *St Andrews Acta*, i, pp. 6, 13, 15, 26, 44, 50; ii, pp. 117, 120 (*bis*), 127; StAUL, UY412, fols 35r, 197v.
⁸ Cant, *St Salvator*, p. 161; Durkan, 'St Salvator's College', p. 129. The inventories date from c.1500, 1537–47 and c.1559.
⁹ StAUL, UY412, fol. 46r.
¹⁰ For example, *Corpus Sceptrorum*, vol. I/i, p. 258.
¹¹ *Liber receptorum nationis Anglicanae (Alemanniae) in Universitate Parisiensis*, ed. A. I. Gabriel and G. C. Boyce (Paris, 1964), col. 425.
¹² E. Inglis, *Jean Fouquet and the Invention of France: Art and Nation after the Hundred Years War* (New Haven and London, 2011), pp. 14–15, 124.

Ornamental staves of various sorts were a ritual requirement of medieval universities and their faculties, colleges and nations, and hundreds of such objects once existed. Records of lost examples and the abundance of institutions needing ceremonial representation show that even the stately variety, of which there are now thirty-eight dating from before or around 1560, must originally have numbered, at a cautious estimate, over one hundred.[13] (Here it will be remembered that St Andrews, with its three imposing examples, whilst third in the British Isles, was only forty-sixth in order of foundation among European universities, and was always relatively small.)[14] Their use at all European universities is certain, even though the patterns of survival favour the German-speaking territories and Scotland to the extent that no such object survives from England, France or Spain, while from Italy only a fragment of a single fifteenth-century mace is known to exist. These grand staves fall into two basic categories. The first and more common sort, which it is reasonable to call the sceptre type, is uniformly slim, with an ornamented grip and small head embellished with foliage, a cast image, heraldry or a combination of these things. The other is the mace type, with a larger, ostentatious head shaped like a miniature tabernacle and usually incorporating cast or engraved imagery. Only eight such objects survive – two from Heidelberg and two from Erfurt in addition to those of St Andrews and Glasgow – but various lost examples are documented.[15] All of these ceremonial staves were made of silver and had gilded components. The rods by which they were held were reinforced with base metal or wood, and embellished with ornamental bands to disguise and strengthen their jointing.

The variety of existing and documented examples shows that unlike the processional cross or crosier, the elaborate academic staff had no fixed, essential form. This is explained by the fact that it emerged abruptly, probably in the fourteenth century, rather than according to a protracted process of evolution. While the formal derivation of the sceptre type from secular regalia is clear enough, the form of the mace type has multiple antecedents. It has an atavistic relationship to the military mace, but at a shorter remove it is clearly dependent on such things as the crosier, image tabernacle, donor's model (a diminutive building, usually resembling a church, held by a founder in sculpted and painted images), reliquary and censer. The degree of dependence on objects like these varies according to the shape of the head. The mace type of academic staff has two different sorts of head, one richly canopied, open in the middle and displaying a three-dimensional image or images (for example, the St Salvator's mace; the surviving university and Arts faculty maces from Heidelberg), the other closed and usually hexagonal. Examples of the second type include the

---

[13] The figure is based on *Corpus Sceptrorum*, vol. I/ii, plus the Cloisters Museum mace (see n. 1 above). Some of these maces have later additions, and in two cases only heads survive.

[14] *A History of the University in Europe*, ed. H. de Ridder-Symoens, 2 vols (Cambridge, 1992–96), i, pp. 62–4 (not counting *studia* which may never have been universities).

[15] The Erfurt maces may originally have come from Prague: *Corpus Sceptrorum*, vol. I/i, p. 63.

faculty maces from St Andrews, the maces of Glasgow and Erfurt universities (the latter four-sided), and lost maces from Avignon and Cologne (both university maces), Louvain (Arts faculty mace) and Paris (mace of the faculty of Medicine). In a particularly opulent lost example known only from its inclusion in an eighteenth-century painting, these types were combined in an open-sided hexagon surrounded by miniature piers and containing a cast image of the Virgin Mary with the Christchild.[16] Such spatially open, inhabited heads must have reminded contemporaries of the devotional and cultic images that stood in contemporary churches and must have seemed particularly captivating in their reduction and preciousness. Closed, hexagonal heads owe a clearer debt to liturgical and pastoral staves, which commonly incorporated polygonal knops below their crosses or crooks. Some shorter handled sceptres not associated with universities also seem to have had large microarchitectural terminations; the miniature by Fouquet shows examples, and another was represented in a mural of c.1355–63 in St Stephen's Chapel at Westminster. Although nothing quite like this appears to have survived, such objects may also have influenced the design of academic maces.[17]

These sorts of objects were heavily invested with ideas about religion and authority and thus their formal relationship to the maces inevitably embodied ideology; it is pointless to disaggregate the two strands of influence. Where incorporated into the design of academic maces, the conceptually freighted forms of the episcopal staff, for example, or the monstrance, or the elevated image in its Gothic housing worked to express the dignity and importance of academic institutions that were themselves integral to the church. The ideological associations of form could have specific as well as general resonances. In representing a miniature golden building, for example, the head of the St Salvator's mace had the potential to evoke the Heavenly Jerusalem (it incorporates a figure of Christ surrounded by angels), an image tabernacle on a larger scale, and also the fact that the man who had it made, and whose name and initials were engraved on it in a perpetual declaration of largesse, was the founder and builder of the architectural complex in which it was kept and used.[18] This exquisite example of votive architecture served to remind viewers of a larger operation of patronage that ultimately transcended the college to nourish the university and the church in common. Finally, the agency of goldsmiths is to be considered alongside the influence of patrons as a critical factor in the generation of the mace type. The impression arising from surviving artists' contracts is that while patrons voiced a desire for luxury and were often specific about imagery, heraldry and the wording of inscriptions, they left it to practitioners to come up with overall designs.

---

[16] *Corpus Sceptrorum*, vol. I/i, pp. 15, 119, 146, 190–1 (lost maces); vol. II, pl. VI (mace in painting).

[17] J. Stratford, *Richard II and the English Royal Treasure* (Woodbridge, 2012), pl. 14. For similar objects in German stained glass of c.1540 see *Corpus Sceptrorum*, vol. II, pl. V.

[18] See in general on these issues J. M. Fritz, *Goldschmiedekunst der Gotik in Mitteleuropa* (Munich, 1982), pp. 56–7; E. S. Klinkenberg, *Compressed Meanings: the Donor's Model in Medieval Art to Around 1300* (Turnhout, 2009), pp. 249–51 and *passim*.

In attempting to gratify patrons, these men naturally drew on both their experience of devising intricate, beautiful objects of various kinds and their knowledge of the cultural significance of these objects. Even where goldsmiths were asked to imitate or improve upon exemplars, as happened with the Canon Law mace at St Andrews and also the Glasgow mace, the exercise of their judgement marked the development of the type in clear ways rather than resulting in facsimiles. Explicit replication only occurred where a pair of sceptres was made simultaneously to suit local custom, as with the Erfurt maces and various examples of the sceptre type.

These observations relate to a category of academic mace that may be called 'solemn', the term applied to the Arts faculty mace of St Andrews in a record of 1437.[19] Of course, there were other grades of mace as well. At Vienna, a distinction existed in the fifteenth century between the *sceptrum majus* and a lesser sceptre of the Arts faculty. Both were made of gilded silver, but the lesser sceptre, which was used 'pro actibus minoris' (that is, for events of modest importance), was presumably smaller or plainer than its counterpart. At Louvain, the rector also had a large and a small sceptre, and it is likely that each had specific and independent uses.[20] Many maces inferior to the solemn category are documented at other universities. Records of repair like that about the Arts faculty's *baculum* cited above could refer to either a solemn or a lesser object, but where connected with a secondary beadle, the latter is usually meant.[21] This is the case with the Parisian 'virga sive massa minoris bedelli' already mentioned, the mace (*baculum*) of the 'inferior' beadle of the Arts faculty at Oxford repaired in 1450 at the cost of 2s, and various others.[22] Responsibility for bearing solemn maces fell to the superior beadles of universities, faculties and colleges. As each sub-beadle can also be assumed to have had a designated mace – the Oxford mace mentioned here was repaired so that it could be handed over to a new sub-beadle on his admission – one can begin to estimate the quantity of lesser maces possessed by an institution where the number of its sub-beadles is known.[23] For example, each of the four nations in the university of Paris had a superior and an inferior beadle, and this was also the case with the three faculties at Oxford. Cambridge is recorded to have had three principal (or 'esquire') beadles.[24] To the total numbers of eight and six that arise from this must be

---

[19] *St Andrews Acta*, ii, p. 44.
[20] *Corpus Sceptrorum*, vol. I/i, pp. 146, 257–8.
[21] Although not consistently: the sub-beadle of the medical faculty at Paris had an ostentatious mace with a hexagonal head displaying figure-work: ibid., vol. I/i, p. 190.
[22] *The Register of the University of Oxford*, i, ed. C. W. Boase (Oxford, 1885), p. 294.
[23] See also G. C. Boyce, *The English-German Nation in the University of Paris During the Middle Ages* (Bruges, 1927), pp. 68–9.
[24] *University in Europe*, i, p. 115; *Statuta Antiqua Universitatis Oxoniensis*, ed. S. Gibson (Oxford, 1931), pp. lxxvii–lxxviii; H. P. Stokes, *The Esquire Bedells of the University of Cambridge* (Cambridge, 1911), pp. 9–10, 15; A. P. Humphry, 'On the Maces of the Esquire Bedells, and the Mace Formerly Borne by the Yeoman Bedell', *Communications of the Cambridge Antiquarian Society* 4 (1879), pp. 207–18.

added whatever rectorial, collegiate or (as at Paris) independent faculty maces there once were.

At St Andrews in the Middle Ages, the office of sub-beadle does not appear to have existed. No such officer is mentioned in the business minutes or bursars' accounts of the Arts faculty, or in the acts of the rectors, although this is not an expansive source. The existing statutes of the faculties of Theology and Arts are equally silent. Indeed, the pre-Reformation documents consistently assume a single beadle: the records of the Arts bursars first refer to an 'archipedello', as opposed to a 'pedello', in 1704.[25] On this basis, the assumption will be that St Andrews lacked the lesser maces recorded elsewhere. However, it has been observed that the faculty of Arts must have possessed some sort of minor instrument, which its beadle carried on ordinary occasions. Something like the cane staff with silver trimmings that served the rector at Glasgow for everyday use is to be envisaged here.[26] The only support for this in the faculty's records is the use of the term 'virgam solempnem' for its mace, but the idea makes a certain amount of common sense as well. The qualification suggests that the Arts mace was specifically intended for solemn occasions, and rationed use of this sort is a logical assumption in light of its preciousness and the trouble involved in fetching it from under lock and key. Moreover, it must have been realised that quotidian use would reduce its impact on viewers. If this is correct then something else was used to represent the authority of the dean in the course of his ordinary duties. As the customs of Arts in this regard are likely to have been shared by the other faculties, the same hypothesis can be extended to them, although it is not clear that Theology ever possessed a solemn mace of its own (indeed, the faculty's small size, an absence of documentation and the efforts of mace-preservation combine to suggest that it did not). All that is mentioned for Theology is a *virga*, perhaps of silver, in its revised statutes of 1560, and this may refer to a borrowed mace: it has been shown that in 1457 a theologian had custody of the Arts mace and another wanted it to magnify his inaugural lecture.[27] Nevertheless, Theology must have had an instrument of some sort, given that it had its own dean and beadle. At the University of Caen the theologians had a simple wooden staff 'to show their humility'; perhaps their counterparts at St Andrews were similarly modest.[28] The only other indication that lesser maces existed at St Andrews is the mid-sixteenth-century description of the

[25] StAUL, UY412, fol. 180v.
[26] *St Andrews Acta*, i, p. 15 n. 3; Brook, 'Account', p. 481 (Glasgow staff).
[27] Doctoral candidates in Theology were preceded by a beadle 'cum virgis et clavis argenteis' (the key at least was of silver): *The Statutes of the Faculty of Arts and the Faculty of Theology at the Period of the Reformation*, ed. R. K. Hannay (St Andrews, 1910), p. 131; *St Andrews Acta*, i, pp. cxlvi–cxlvii (on 1457). For a sense of the relationship of beadle and mace to inaugural lecturer, see the late fifteenth-century image in N. Thorp, *The Glory of the Page: Medieval and Renaissance Illuminated Manuscripts from Glasgow University Library* (London, 1987), p. 35.
[28] For Theology's deans see *St Andrews Acta*, i, p. cxlvi; *Corpus Sceptrorum*, vol. I/i, p. 37 (Caen).

St Salvator's mace as 'byschop James kendeis best wand'.[29] This certainly suggests that there were others, but none appears in the college inventories.

These observations raise the issue of how the St Andrews maces functioned. The subject has been little considered in the past, and not without reason. For one thing, documented instances of use are few and only exist for the Arts mace. As the faculty beadles generated no independent records, their movements are relatively obscure, and patterns of use correspondingly difficult to extrapolate. For another, it is hard to know precisely what counted as a fitting occasion for the use of a solemn mace as opposed to a lesser instrument. While some public and solemn ceremonies clearly required the highest levels of corporate representation, others, such as faculty congregations, did not so obviously do so. Even when a ceremony was sufficiently important to warrant a solemn mace, uncertainty respecting precedence can complicate assumptions about use. For example, where the rector and deans of faculty were present together, as at the annual congregations of the university held in the refectory of the cathedral priory, it is not obvious that the deans were able to assert their dignity through display of their respective maces. The rector himself, whose superiority to the dean of Arts was volunteered by the same faculty, almost certainly did not have a solemn mace of his own, and it would be strange to think that he would be pleased to sit among hierarchical inferiors who manifestly did.[30]

Related to this question is whether or not the faculty maces, and in particular that of Arts, commonly served the rector, and hence the university in general. Shared use of this sort occurred elsewhere: at Caen, for example, the fifteenth-century mace of the Law faculty, a solemn object of gilded silver, doubled as the university mace.[31] The rectors of St Andrews served for a single year and realised little income from their office. They had, as a matter of forensic necessity, their own seal, but there was little obvious incentive for any one of them to commission an object whose use he would not enjoy for long, or indeed – if its making was protracted – at all; and there is no evidence that the chancellor or anyone else ever gifted a university mace, as happened, for example, at Krakow.[32] It is well known that from an early period the rector had at least some call on the Arts mace. He wanted to have it for the general council of the Scottish Church at Perth in 1418 where the university renounced its obedience to Benedict XIII, and it was certainly taken when he sent ambassadors to treat with James I in 1430. The rector was also permitted to borrow it for the use of another embassy to Perth in 1437.[33] If the Arts faculty had considered itself in sole moral and legal possession of its mace then one might expect the busi-

---

[29] Durkan, 'St Salvator's College', p. 129.
[30] *St Andrews Acta*, ii, pp. 291–2. On the effect on hierarchical dignity of ceremonial staves see e.g. *The Victoria History of the County of Worcester*, ed. J. W. Willis-Bund, H. A. Doubleday and W. Page, 4 vols (London, 1901–24), ii, pp. 36–7.
[31] *Corpus Sceptrorum*, vol. I/i, p. 37.
[32] For a rector's seal as early as 1417 see *St Andrews Acta*, i, p. lxxviii. The donor at Krakow was Cardinal Zbigniew Oleśnicki (d. 1455): *Corpus Sceptrorum*, vol. I/i, p. 124.
[33] *St Andrews Acta*, i, pp. xvi, xix n. 1, cxlvii, 12–13, 26, 44.

ness memoranda which record these concessions to mention what sureties the university was offering against the object's loss, or at least indicate that sureties had been made. When the rector of Paris university borrowed the mace of the English-German nation in 1415 to represent his institution at the Council of Constance, he was obliged to put his seal to a detailed set of guarantees.[34] For St Andrews there is nothing of this sort, and the impression one gets is that the Arts mace was commissioned on the understanding that it would be available for the use of the rectors *ad hoc* during a period when university and faculty were still closely conflated.[35] The fact that the iconography of the university seal – St Andrew and the heraldry of Benedict XIII, Scotland and Henry Wardlaw – was incorporated into the mace is lasting evidence of this conflation.

A long-lived aspect of the faculty–university relationship that has a bearing on the functional status of the Arts mace is the sharing of beadles. Two long-serving Arts beadles of the early sixteenth century are recorded to have held the same office simultaneously for the university, and there is evidence that this arrangement was traditional. In a minute of 1457, the faculty denied that the rector should have untrammelled access to its beadle, and appealed to the established 'manner and custom' by which such access had previously operated. This, Annie Dunlop has argued, was a plank in a larger campaign to assert the independence of the faculty, which included commissioning a seal for the use of its dean, requesting the return of its mace from a master of Theology and refusing the mace's use at an inaugural lecture.[36] Yet it clearly did not put an end to the joint operation of the beadle, and only two independent university beadles are recorded before 1540.[37] Whatever prerogative the rector had over the beadle did not automatically extend to the mace. The beadle never had ultimate custody of the object; this rested with the dean until 1437, then with the dean, bursar and senior master (who are stated to have held the keys to the faculty's safes in 1458), and at some later date the sacristan of St Salvator's College.[38] Furthermore, it is most unlikely that all of the beadle's duties for the rector involved ceremony: beadles were effectively the factotums of high university officers.[39] However, where they did involve it, the beadle must have carried something as he walked in front of and announced the rector. As there was probably no distinct solemn university mace, this was either some lesser object permanently at the rector's disposal or else an item of faculty property.

---

[34] *Index chronologicus chartarum pertinentum ad historiam Universitatis Parisiensis*, ed. C. Jourdain (Paris, 1862), p. 234 (no. 1092).
[35] For this conflation see *St Andrews Acta*, i, pp. xiv–xv, cxli.
[36] Whether it was regularly used at inaugural lectures is unknown, but if these lectures were part of the inception process then it was. For the relationship of the inaugural lecture to inception see A. I. Cameron, 'Scottish Students at Paris University, 1466–1492', *Juridical Review* 48 (1936), pp. 228–55 at p. 242.
[37] *St Andrews Acta*, i, pp. xxvi, cxxviii, cxlvi–cxlvii, ccxlix; ii, pp. 119–23; on the beadles see also *Copiale*, pp. 452–3.
[38] *St Andrews Acta*, ii, p. 127 (safes).
[39] See *University in Europe*, i, pp. 126–7.

The likelihood is that the rector did have a dedicated staff of some sort, but that it was insufficiently pompous to represent him at some events beyond and probably within the university. When it was, he called on the Arts mace, and perhaps also, once it had been made, that of Canon Law.

Whatever the difficulties of these considerations, it is more or less certain (if undocumented) that the Arts mace was produced at the solemn annual ceremonies associated with the act of licence (where graduands of the faculty of Arts were empowered to teach, examine and otherwise serve in the university and elsewhere), inception (the formal process by which graduands were enthroned and 'wedded' to academic life) and the Feast of St John before the Latin Gate on 6 May (when the faculty celebrated its patron saint), as well as at other important liturgical feasts officially observed (in the cathedral or elsewhere) by representatives of the faculty. It may also have been present at the Quodlibetal disputations in which the faculty had an investment; and other regular uses to set beside occasional ones might be added to this conservative list without great risk.[40] The Canon Law mace is likely to have been put to the same sorts of uses. However, the function of the St Salvator's mace is more obscure because the college worked in a different way from a faculty, meaning that one cannot make educated guesses based on what is known of Arts. It is unknown, for example, whether the mace was the sole prerogative of the provost and his representatives or also served the other senior officials of the college, the licentiate and the bachelor. Like the provost, these men had to preach in public regularly and perform a range of other duties as college representatives.[41] Its use may have been more domestic and more liturgical than that of the other maces: Ronald Cant imagined it, or some other mace, in the hands of a verger going before the provost at high mass on Sundays.[42] Ultimately, James Kennedy may have considered it a desirably grand but not highly functional accessory to his foundation.

While the maces themselves are things, and assert their object-status candidly to the modern viewer in terms of form, materials and imagery, their original significance was largely symbolic.[43] At a basic level, they advertised the unity, dignity, piety and authority maintained or pretended to by the institutions they represented. They did this through their images and heraldry, but mainly by evoking concepts of elevation, beauty, integrity and costliness, and associating these with an institution through the man – rector, dean, provost, ambassador etc. – they were carried and placed in front of. Their significance to given people in given situations varied, but this essential function was calculated and constant. The main situational factor affecting what may be called

---

[40] *St Andrews Acta*, i, pp. xcviii–cxvii (licence), cxvii–cxxi (inception), cxxvi (Quodlibet disputations), cxxxiii–cxxxiv (Feast of St John); *Statutes of the Faculty of Arts*, pp. 44–56.

[41] For these senior officers see Cant, *St Salvator*, pp. 55–9 and *passim*.

[42] Ibid., p. 146.

[43] For a formulaic sense of the symbolic connotations (Parisian, thirteenth-century) see L. J. Bataillon, 'The Tradition of Nicholas of Biard's *Distinctiones*', *Viator* 25 (1994), pp. 245–88 at pp. 273–5.

their symbolic function must have been how they were viewed, whether at some remove, elevated and in motion, and thus as an extension of the beadle's body, or close up, when stationary, in a way that permitted identification of their iconography and appreciation of the qualities of their designs. Both perspectives were obviously envisaged by their patrons, for whom the parts as well as the whole must have been a source of pleasure. The following individualised discussion of the St Andrews maces privileges close viewing with this broader consideration in mind.

The Faculty Maces

THE maces of the Arts and Canon Law faculties are close to one another in form and materials (see figures 14.2 and 14.3). There is a marked difference in artistic quality, although they would have looked similarly impressive at a distance. They have plain silver rods, with flanged feet and prominent, ornamental bands – what in the fifteenth century were called 'junctures' (*juncturae*) – to mask and reinforce the joints.[44] Their gilded heads are hexagonal and rise in three tapering stages on coved necks. Both have cast figures of angels at the lowest level, engraved images of saints at the intermediate stage and a tabernacle with miniature, traceried windows at the top. A formal link to prelatal crosiers has often been pointed out, and it has even been thought, incongruously, that the better quality mace was originally made as a crosier and subsequently modified.[45] Grand crosiers sometimes incorporated knops of three polygonal stages and displayed engraved and (or) cast images on their ascending facets. Whoever designed the earlier of these maces – of which the later is patently a free copy – knew about the form, iconography and resonances of such objects. However, the openwork canopies at the top do not obviously relate to crosier design. They more closely resemble a censer like the one from Ramsey Abbey in Cambridgeshire, and also the cage-like settings for miniature images found in surviving Continental metalwork, which tantalised the viewer by simultaneously concealing and revealing what they contained.[46] There is no evidence that

---

[44] For *juncturae* see e.g. A. Way, 'Indenture for Making a Pastoral Staff for William Curteys, Abbot of St. Edmunds', *Proceedings of the Suffolk Institute of Archaeology and History* 1 (1850), pp. 160–5 at p. 163.

[45] Cant, *University*, 3rd edn (St Andrews, 1992), p. 194. Apart from anything else, the aperture at the top is too small to have admitted a proportionately sized crook: compare E. Taburet-Delahaye, *L'orfèvrerie gothique (XIIIe-début XVe siècle) au Musée du Cluny* (Paris, 1989), pp. 134–7 (no. 49).

[46] *Age of Chivalry: Art in Plantagenet England, 1200–1400*, ed. J. J. G. Alexander and P. Binski (London, 1987), pp. 240–1 (no. 121) (Ramsey censer). See also *Studi di oreficeria*, ed. A. R. C. Masetti (Rome, 1996), pp. 149–58; *Oreficerie e smalti in Europa fra XII e XV secoloi*, ed. A. R. C. Masetti (Pisa, 1997), pp. 83–95. In the fifteenth century, Lincoln Cathedral acquired gilded silver staves for use in the choir which had hexagonal heads with enamelled images, and also miniature windows at the top. In these cases, the heads seem to have been of two rather than three stages, but the formal relationship to the St

Figure 14.2: The head of the Arts faculty mace.

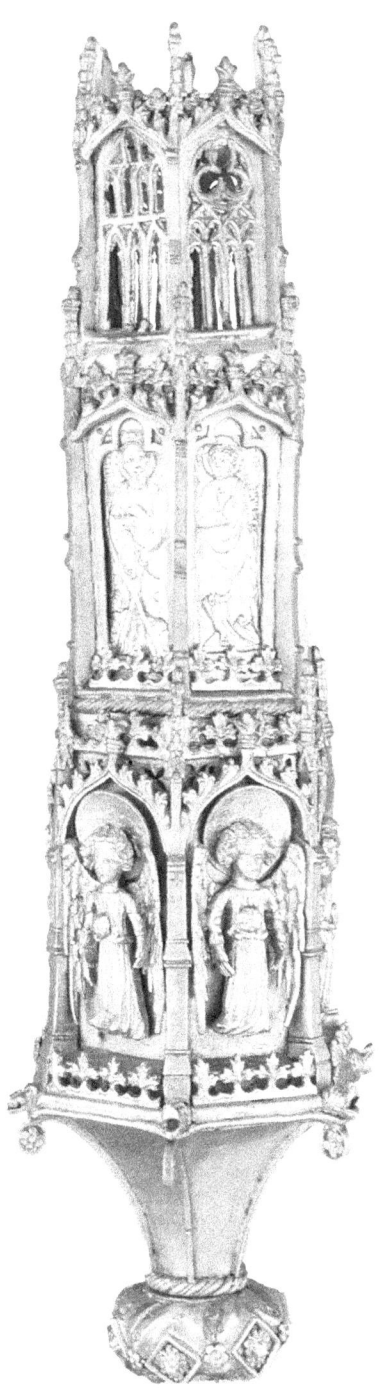

Figure 14.3: The head of the Canon Law faculty mace.

either mace contained a cast figure, but the higher quality one, which terminated in a now-lost foliate finial, has an upper stage that looks more like a tabernacle or censer for incorporating a slanting roof with imitation tiles, and was designed by a goldsmith whose creativity was informed by such things.

The university used to display the higher quality mace as the Canon Law mace and the other as that of Arts. Alexander Brook contradicted this interpretation on various grounds in 1892, but uncertainty lingered, and Ronald Cant was among a number of scholars to insist on the university's attribution.[47] In the wake of an article by M. A. Michael published in 1994, the present consensus is that the higher quality mace was made for Arts, and that is how it is now labelled in the university museum.[48] Although there is no incontrovertible argument for this conclusion, the balance of probabilities favours it. The minutes of the Arts faculty record the commission and manufacture of an expensive, obviously solemn mace between January 1416 and December 1419.[49] Nothing is revealed of quality, only cost; and the total expenditure of 45 merks and 20d is not obviously excessive for the lesser quality mace.[50] However, the style of the cast angels and engraved figures on this mace looks later than 1420. One's inclination, though informed by nothing more graspable than professional instinct, is to date them at least a quarter of a century later.[51] Admittedly, medieval art's susceptibility to dating on the basis of style usually decreases as its quality does, so this is not an easily testable assertion. But Michael buttressed it by pointing out, given that the form and detail of one mace derives from the other, how unlikely it is that an object of high artistic quality would be based on something manifestly inferior.[52] Exceptions to this are rare in surviving medieval art, and it is equally unusual to be able to attribute an imaginative design of the sort embodied in the faculty maces to a mediocre artist.[53] This is a very difficult argument to get around. One could always ignore the stylistic evidence and contend that the superior quality mace was made for Canon Law before the lesser quality one was made for Arts, but nothing in the faculty minutes suggests that the exemplar for the Arts mace was present in St Andrews. The goldsmith certainly

---

Andrews maces was evidently clear: C. Wordsworth, 'Inventories of Plate, Vestments, &c., belonging to the Cathedral Church of the Blessed Mary of Lincoln', *Archaeologia* 53 (1892), pp. 1–83 at pp. 21–2.

[47] Brook, 'Account', pp. 456–9; Cant, *University*, pp. 13, 194–5; see also Smart, 'University Treasures', pp. 14–15.

[48] M. A. Michael, 'The First Maces of St Andrews University', Higgitt, *St Andrews*, pp. 184–96. For further support of the current attribution see H. C. Rawson, 'Treasures of the University: An Examination of the Identification, Presentation and Responses to Artefacts of Significance at the University of St Andrews, from 1410 to the Mid-19th Century' (unpublished PhD thesis, University of St Andrews, 2010), pp. 81–8.

[49] *St Andrews Acta*, i, pp. 6 (*bis*), 9, 13, 15–16; Michael, 'First Maces', pp. 191–2.

[50] Compare Brook, 'Account', p. 457.

[51] Compare Michael, 'First Maces', p. 194.

[52] Ibid., p. 191.

[53] In theory, of course, the design may not have been original to either faculty mace. The maker of the earlier one may have known similar objects, now lost.

was not: an appeal made in 1418 that he either come to the town to finish the mace or send what he could of it shows that he was based elsewhere.[54] It would be possible to meet this by supposing that a geographically remote goldsmith designed the Arts mace on the basis of drawings of its Canon Law counterpart. Such drawings have never been considered with respect to this problem, but they must have been used, unless the earlier mace was sent for use as a sort of studio model for the later one, but, whether or not the corporate owner would have allowed this, this is not how medieval goldsmiths worked. However, there are other objections to support the current attribution, including the fact that the strength, leadership and financial liquidity of Arts make it a more likely candidate than Canon Law to have commissioned the first mace. While Canon Law was provided for at the foundation of the university, and existed in some form at an early date, it does not appear to have had the status likely to have led it to commission a mace before 1420.[55] Again, the better quality mace displays the heraldry of an individual – Archibald, fourth earl of Douglas (d. 1424) – who helped to procure the Arts mace.[56] Douglas may also have supported Canon Law, but if he did, then, unlike his support for Arts, this is undocumented. When these objections are taken together, the hypothesis that Canon Law had a mace before Arts, which is required for the identification of the higher quality object with Canon Law on the grounds that the lesser quality mace is later, looks distinctly uneconomical.

By contrast, there is no obvious reason for doubting that the object documented in the minutes of the faculty of Arts is the higher quality mace. The only possible objection, in fact specious, relies on three assumptions of varying cogency: first that the higher quality mace was made in Paris, second that the lesser quality one is of Scottish manufacture and third that the Arts faculty's mace was taken to the church council at Perth on 2 and 3 October 1418.[57] The Arts mace is known to have been unfinished on 9 August 1418, when it was decided, as mentioned above, to send someone to the goldsmith. It is thought that a period of fewer than two months would have been insufficient to fetch it from Paris and finish it. But a mace made in Scotland could have been obtained and completed in such a time: *ergo*, the lesser quality mace is that of Arts. The flaw in this reasoning is that, *pace* Dunlop, there is no evidence the Arts mace was actually taken to Perth in 1418.[58] In fact, it seems not to have been finished for another year or so. A later memorandum of the Arts faculty dated 9 December 1419 mentions its total cost, including a sum for locally procured charcoal. This was presumably for firing a furnace for assembling the rod and

---

[54] Compare *St Andrews Acta*, i, p. 13.
[55] Ibid., i, pp. cxlix–clvii; Cant, *University*, p. 13.
[56] Documented in *St Andrews Acta*, i, p. 16.
[57] Thus the maces are commonly called the 'French' and 'Scottish' maces, terms which beg a question at issue.
[58] As noted by Rawson, 'Treasures of the University', pp. 75, 86; compare *St Andrews Acta*, i, p. xvi n. 1.

fitting the head to the mace: the head may have been procured separately.[59] If the mace had been completed before the Council at Perth then this information would have appeared in the minutes of an earlier faculty meeting (there were four in the year from October 1418). It is thus more logical to suppose that the old university attribution of the lesser quality mace to Arts was premised on some mistake. In light of this, what follows assumes that the aesthetically more refined mace is the earlier of the two and that it was made for Arts.

The Arts mace is a little over 4ft long (about 49.5in, or 1254mm) (see figure 14.2). It has been repaired, apparently extensively, at various times: in 1721, the expenses of the bursar of Arts included £15 10s 'for remaking the faculty's mace', while the same official laid out £12 in 1657 'for mending the silver insignia', which may also have included it.[60] One of these repairs probably involved replacement of the rod. Inspection reveals that all of the foliate finials at the heads of the arches enclosing the angels and saints have been renewed, along with various other details including one of the shields and – unevenly – the arcs of some of the arches at the second stage. However, the general appearance and most of the details of the mace are original. Its base and lower two junctures have a helical pattern common in contemporary metalwork, while the juncture just below the head displays tongue-shaped motifs and fleurons. All of these elements are bordered by delicate cable-work bands. The angels of the lower stage, which rest on knobbly silver clouds, are demi-figures of a sort exceedingly popular in fifteenth-century art. They are couched within shallow-headed ogee arches, whose curvature answers that of their wings, and the arches are separated by miniature, stepped buttresses with pinnacles. Each angel holds a shield displaying, with one exception, the heraldry of someone associated or at least associable with the nascent university, and by extension its Arts faculty. The anomalous heraldry represents Archbishop John Spottiswood (d. 1639), and must replace the arms of Benedict XIII, which have the place of honour above St Andrew on the common seal engraved for the university some time in or before 1418.[61] Benedict's arms, and those of Scotland, Henry Wardlaw (d. 1430) and Robert Stewart, first duke of Albany and governor of the realm from 1406 until his death in 1420, are straightforward expressions of deference to men with either a practical or Olympian role in founding the university. The arms of Archibald, fourth earl of Douglas, represent an individual known to have supported the Arts faculty directly, while those of Alexander Stewart, earl of Mar (d. 1435), respond to some less obvious but (as noted by Michael) expected act of support.[62] Although reattached at some stage, the original shields are expertly

---

[59] *St Andrews Acta*, i, pp. 9 ('capitis virge' distinctly), 15–16 (9 December 1419); Brook, 'Account', p. 459 (charcoals for firing a local furnace).

[60] StAUL, UY412, fols 133v ('*Item pro emendatione insignium [sic] argenteorum – 12 lib.*'), 197v ('*It. pro refacienda virga facultatis* – 15: 10: 00').

[61] On the seal see *Treasures of St Andrews University Library* (London, 2010), pp. 60–1 (text by Rachel Hart). Similarly, Pope Martin V was represented as founder of the university on the Arts faculty mace from Louvain: *Corpus Sceptrorum*, vol. I/i, p. 146.

[62] Michael, 'First Maces', p. 190. The blazon of the fifteenth-century shields men-

fitted to their settings. The fact that neither the royal arms nor those of Wardlaw, as bishop of St Andrews, is located underneath the engraved figure of St Andrew tends to suggest that their order has been changed. To people with opportunity to scrutinise it, the heraldry declared the strength and quality of the university and faculty's allies. While heraldry was included on academic maces elsewhere, the number of coats of arms here is exceeded by surviving examples only on two fifteenth-century maces from Krakow.[63]

The six standing figures represented on the second stage are the Virgin Mary holding the Christchild, and SS Michael, Margaret of Antioch, John the Baptist, Andrew and Ninian (see figure 14.4). The Michael alone has been deliberately damaged, so that its face is now indistinct: it is not obvious when or why it was singled out like this. All of the figures are shallowly and expertly engraved on silver plates fitted within ogee arches. Each is framed by a border, and the lines articulating these borders are uneven in their duct, although this was originally less noticeable than it is now. The backgrounds were formerly enamelled green and blue, so that the silver figures themselves stood out within silver borders, but only slight traces of this refinement survive. If, as suggested previously, these figures were censored at some stage then the process of revealing them again might have caused the loss. The enamelling technique used here is a mixture of *basse taille*, in which translucent enamel is applied to shallowly engraved surfaces, and translucent enamel on its own without any engraving under it. There are differences of style and handling between the figures, suggesting the involvement of more than one artist. The St Andrew is particularly detailed, perhaps due to his importance to the patron, and has a stolidity and breadth of treatment familiar from contemporary Italian art. By contrast, the Virgin and Michael are handled in a more mannered way, and look almost bland in their lack of hatching. Their draperies have broad folds and fussy outlines, and they have the smaller head-to-body ratio common in French imagery of the early fifteenth century. The variations of treatment may reveal a desire to expedite the commission. While all the figures are confidently executed and of high quality, the panels with the Virgin, Michael and the Baptist have no background hatching around the figures. It must have been realised that enamel would adhere less durably to these smooth surfaces, and that this was a less than ideal way to leave

---

tioned here is: *per fess, in the upper part a crescent reversed* (Benedict XIII); *a lion rampant within a double tressure flory and counterflory* (Scotland); *on a fess between three mascles, three cross crosslets fitché* (Wardlaw); *quarterly, first and fourth a lion rampant, second and third a fess chequy under a label of four points* (Robert Stewart); *quarterly, first a heart under a fess with three stars, second a lion rampant, third three stars, fourth a cross saltire and chief* (Douglas); *quarterly, first and fourth a bend dexter between six cross crosslets fitché, second and third a fess chequy between three crowns* (Alexander Stewart). There is room for argument about exactly who the lay magnates' arms represent, but these are the most likely identifications: see Brook, 'Account', pp. 447–8; Michael, 'First Maces', pp. 188, 190; Rawson, 'Treasures of the University', p. 79.

[63] *Corpus Sceptrorum*, vol. I/i, pp. 123–6 (Krakow), 146 (Louvain: a lost mace of 1430 with eighteen heraldic shields).

Figure 14.4: The engraved images of saints on the Arts faculty mace. Clockwise, from top left: SS Andrew, Ninian, Margaret, the Virgin Mary and Christchild, SS John the Baptist, Michael.

them. This, as well as the lack of detailing in some of the figures themselves, creates an impression of rapid or even incomplete execution.

As the choice of figures is extremely unlikely to have been left to the goldsmith, it is reasonable to seek its explanation in patronal interests. While some academic institutions had 'intellectual' saints like Catherine, Jerome and Paul put onto their maces, and Catherine in particular was identified with Arts (she was included on Arts faculty maces at Louvain, Heidelberg, Tübingen and Vienna), this was not done at St Andrews. Similarly absent are the non-saintly figures of patrons or paragons connected with specific disciplines, as formerly represented on lost maces from Louvain (Aristotle, Boethius, a founder, a patron) and Paris (Avicenna, Hippocrates, Galen), and also on some medieval academic seals. This sort of imagery must have been known to those who ordered the mace: a concrete indication of the fact is that the dean of Arts at St Andrews had a seal designed for him in 1457 showing 'a woman carrying a sphere in her hand', which seems to have been meant for Philosophy or some such allegorical figure related to the liberal arts.[64] But it was not chosen, and the faculty's patron saint, John the Evangelist, is also missing: he was adopted in 1419, marginally too late for inclusion.[65] The saints that were chosen are nevertheless perfectly appropriate to the context of the mace's commission. Andrew is self-explanatory in Scotland and at St Andrews: his large book relates to the evangelism and adherence to Christ for which he was martyred (its sacredness as a symbol of Christ is shown by the fact that even he does not touch it with the skin of a bare hand) and is also a straightforward reference to the book-dependant vocation of faculty and university. The Virgin and Christchild are generically suitable to any such setting for combining the two figures of greatest doctrinal and devotional importance to medieval people. Ninian, holding chains to signify his status as a helper of prisoners, probably owes his inclusion to the fact that (in George Hay's words) he 'enjoyed a measure of veneration all but equalling that accorded to St Andrew' in late medieval Scotland.[66] This figure has also been identified as St Leonard, another ally of prisoners but not properly shown with a prelate's ornaments unless conflated with the sainted abbot of the same name.[67] As such conflation is conceivable, and because there was a church of St Leonard in St Andrews that the Arts faculty sometimes used

---

[64] *Corpus Sceptrorum*, vol. I/i, pp. 146, 190; for the seal see *St Andrews Acta*, ii, p. 120 ('sigillum haberet sculptam in se Dominam in sua manu portantem speram'). Pace previous opinion (e.g. *Statutes of the Faculty of Arts*, p. 23), this description is too mere for the Virgin Mary, and the iconography is inappropriate for her unless one assumes an unmentioned figure of the Christchild. See also J. Durkan, 'The Cultural Background in Sixteenth-Century Scotland', *Innes Review* 10 (1959), pp. 382–439 at 401.

[65] *St Andrews Acta*, i, pp. xviii, cxxxiii. Later, in 1478, the bursar of Arts paid 20s for a painting (*pictura*) of John the Evangelist: StAUL, UY412, fol. 8r.

[66] G. Hay, 'A Scottish Altarpiece in Copenhagen', *Innes Review* 7 (1956), pp. 5–10 (at p. 5); also J. Higgitt, *'Imageis Maid With Mennis Hand': Saints, Images, Belief and Identity in Later Medieval Scotland* (Whithorn, 2003), pp. 8–10. There was an altar dedicated to St Ninian in the parish church of the Holy Trinity at St Andrews.

[67] Michael, 'First Maces', p. 24; *St Andrews Acta*, i, pp. 3, 5, 12, 21, 25–9, 31, 33.

for meetings in the years before 1433, this alternative is possible. A preacher of unparalleled eloquence, John the Baptist was again generically appropriate to a teaching institution: he is represented elsewhere on the mace from Rostock now in New York, and was on a lost mace of the University of Avignon.[68] At St Andrews, his denunciation of evil (Mark 6:17–19; Luke 3:19) also made him fitting as an adversary of the heresy that the university was deliberately founded to combat.[69] With this in mind, it may be relevant to acknowledge the attitude of Lawrence Lindores, who was first rector, first dean of Arts and an influential figure for the procurement of the mace (he made a loan to the faculty of 10 merks towards the object's head, and it remained in his personal possession until his death in 1437).[70] Lindores also functioned as the first inquisitor-general for Scotland (from 1408 to 1437), instigating two heresy trials that ended in burnings, one of them in St Andrews.[71] The practical threat of heresy may in fact have been modest, but what matters in historical terms is the perception of the threat, and this was clearly acute. According to an oath ratified by a meeting of the Arts faculty in June 1417, when the mace was being made, incepting students had to swear to defend the Church 'contra insultum Lollardorum'.[72] This anxiety adequately explains the presence of SS Margaret and Michael on the mace, both of whom are shown destroying beasts symbolic of evil and deceit and both identified in the *Golden Legend* as scourges of the Devil.[73]

Finally, it should be noted that the question of where the Arts mace was made is unanswerable on current evidence. The old idea that it is Parisian makes sense in stylistic terms, and also cultural ones, as the figures documented in connection with it – Douglas, Lindores and Wardlaw – all lived in Paris for extended periods. Lindores and Wardlaw both belonged to the English nation in Paris university and must have known the solemn mace conceded to the rector in 1415 for use at Constance, or perhaps its predecessor.[74] However, as scholars often point out, goldsmiths moved about in the fifteenth century.[75] Even if attri-

---

[68] *Corpus Sceptrorum*, vol. I/i, p. 15.
[69] *St Andrews Acta*, i, p. ix; R. Swanson, 'The University of St Andrews and the Great Schism, 1410–1419', *Journal of Ecclesiastical History* 26 (1975), pp. 223–45 at p. 229.
[70] *St Andrews Acta*, i, pp. xvii n. 4, xxi, 9, 45–6.
[71] L. Moonan, 'Lindores, Lawrence (d. 1437)', *Oxford Dictionary of National Biography* (Oxford, 2004) [www.oxforddnb.com/view/article/53487, accessed 24 Sept. 2014].
[72] *St Andrews Acta*, i, pp. 11–12 (oath); *Copiale*, pp. 382–4; compare E. Poleg, 'The Earliest Evidence for Anti-Lollard Polemics in Medieval Scotland', *Innes Review* 64 (2013), pp. 227–34.
[73] *Legenda Aurea*, ed. G. P. Maggioni, 2 vols (Florence, 1998–99), i, pp. 616–20; ii, pp. 986–1001.
[74] Lindores even had a student there named Johannes Aurifaber, which may indicate some connection to goldsmiths even if the named individual was no practising craftsman: L. Moonan, 'The Scientific Writings of Lawrence of Lindores (d. 1437)', *Classica et Medievalia* 38 (1987), pp. 217–66 at p. 242.
[75] See *inter alia* Michael, 'First Maces', p. 186; Stratford, *English Royal Treasure*, p. 70.

bution to an artist trained in Paris could be established, and the possibility of a Netherlandish, German, English or Scottish goldsmith excluded, the maker could still have been based in Bruges, or for that matter Edinburgh. The instincts that militate against Scottish residence are not necessarily sound: James I 'brocht oute of Ingland and Flanderis ingenious men of sindry craftis to instruct his pepill in vertewis occupacioun', and the fact that there were at least 140 goldsmiths in Paris alone in 1455 is enough to suggest that others may have left to seek their fortunes elsewhere.[76] As no fresh documentary discoveries about the mace can be expected, any positive solution to this impasse would have to rest on stylistic or technical analysis. But stylistic analysis, at least, is unlikely ever to serve here, because, in addition to the possibility of an immigrant designer, the mace's figures belong to the phase of Gothic art known as the International Style, whose distinguishing characteristics were reproduced by artists working across much of Europe.

The mace of the Canon Law faculty can be dealt with more briefly (see figure 14.3). Knowledge of its original ownership rests solely on the record of a 'beddell wand of siluer [...] for the facultie of Canoun', kept with the Arts and St Salvator's mace in the college chapel c.1537–47. At 50in (1283mm), it is marginally longer than the Arts mace, and its head is taller and wider. The main design difference is that the upper two stages of the head do not telescope as obviously as they do on their counterpart, but are closer to each other in width: whether or not this calculated variation is thought an improvement, it results in a larger and arguably more imposing head. On the whole, however, the overall design and most of the details are obviously derivative, even if the detailing of the head is consistently grosser, to the extent that manufacture by a Scottish goldsmith seems likely on the grounds that nobody would have sent abroad for something of this quality. The base is similarly flanged out to provide stability when the mace was being held stationary for long periods, and the rod is constructed in the same way, with similar bulbous junctures, although the decorative treatment of these junctures is different and the intermediate ones may be later substitutions. The base itself is certainly a replacement, apparently of the sixteenth century, but the form of base seen on the Arts mace has been preserved. The necking is also coved, though it rises more steeply, and the lowest stage again has cast angels set in depressed ogee arches. In this case, the angels are draped, full-length figures with disproportionately large heads and haloes.[77] They do not float on silver clouds: this feature of the Arts mace, while replicated on that from Glasgow, presented too great a technical challenge to the goldsmith. The angels' arms are splayed out as if to accommodate shields, and they

---

[76] L. Campbell, 'Scottish Patrons and Netherlandish Painters in the Fifteenth and Sixteenth Centuries', *Scotland and the Low Countries 1124–1994*, ed. G. G. Simpson (East Linton, 1996), pp. 89–103 (quotation at p. 89); H. Nocq, *Le Poinçon de Paris*, 5 vols (Paris, 1968), iv, p. 134.

[77] One halo displays a seventeenth-century goldsmith's mark, demonstrating later repair: G. Dalgleish and H. S. Fothringham, *Silver Made in Scotland* (Edinburgh, 2008), p. 163.

have holes in their breasts (filled in relatively recently with little foliate bosses), which look like fixing-points.[78] If there were shields then these were smaller than the ones on the Arts mace, and they covered up the carefully rendered folds of the angels' albs. At the second stage, the arches over the figures of saints are much shallower than those on the Arts mace, and at the third, the tracery designs of the miniature windows are different and also varied: on the Arts mace all but one of the windows are identical. This upper stage was apparently never closed off with a miniature roof and finial, so that it recalls the fenestrated 'lantern' stages of some late medieval church towers. The direct influence of monumental architecture is unlikely: the difference looks more like an imaginative variation on the Arts mace by a goldsmith who had been asked by his patrons to surpass his model.

The saints at the second stage are technically, stylistically and in three cases iconographically different from those of the Arts mace (see figure 14.5). Their silver plates are not married as competently to the architecture of the head, and they were apparently never enamelled, even though their backgrounds are hatched in a way that would help enamel to bond.[79] The awkwardness of the faces and draperies is shared by some mid- and later fifteenth-century Scottish manuscript painting (for example, that of Andrew Lundy's primer and the Arbuthnott hours), although such comparisons are meant to suggest only the engraver's place in a regional artistic domain and not his practice of more than one craft. Once again, the figures of the Virgin and Christchild, St Andrew and St John the Baptist are present. Minor differences include the Virgin's jewelled crown, the smaller size of Andrew's cross and the fact that the Baptist holds the Lamb of God in his left rather than his right hand. Here, too, the Lamb nestles on a book, as it did increasingly in fifteenth-century art. The other three figures are the Holy Trinity (in the form known as the 'Throne of Grace', with the crucified Christ held between the knees of the seated God the Father), St Peter and St Kentigern, the latter identifiable by the salmon he holds in reference to a miracle involving the recovery of a royal ring from the fish's gut. Again, the iconography must have been suggested by the patron, and so the variation is likely to reflect the interests and identity of the Canon Law faculty. In its reference, the Trinity is probably no more specific than the Virgin and Christchild, and this may also go for Peter, an immensely popular saint who together with Andrew functions as a *pars pro toto* figure for the twelve apostles.[80] The apostles were commonly shown together on crosiers, and also on some grand processional crosses like the one owned by St Salvator's College.[81] Kentigern may reveal a personal identification with Glasgow cathedral, where this saint was spiritual

---

[78] The holes were empty in 1892: Brook, 'Account', p. 453.
[79] Compare Michael, 'First Maces', pp. 190, 193: a microscopic examination might help to decide the matter.
[80] A Throne of Grace Trinity was on a fifteenth-century mace at Paris, and St Peter on maces at Avignon, Cologne and Louvain: *Corpus Sceptrorum*, vol. I/i, pp. 15, 119, 146, 190.
[81] Cant, *St Salvator*, p. 159.

Figure 14.5: The engraved images of saints on the Canon Law faculty mace. Clockwise, from top left: SS Andrew, Peter, the Holy Trinity, SS John the Baptist, Kentigern and the Virgin Mary and Christchild.

patron and focus of an important relic-cult. Perhaps, then, the mace was made under the aegis of John Feldew, who was a master of Canon Law and dean of faculty in 1457, and also a canon of Glasgow cathedral. If this is the case then John the Baptist takes on additional significance here as a name-saint, and also spiritual patron of Markinch church, where Feldew was a long-serving vicar.[82]

The St Salvator's Mace

WHILE its broader symbolic connotations were similar to those of its faculty counterparts, the college mace of St Salvator's is strikingly different in conception (see figure 14.6). It is the shortest of the three, at about 3ft 10in long (1162mm), but its form and embellishment are extravagantly picturesque. This is unquestionably the most magnificent medieval academic mace in existence, and was probably never surpassed by any object in its class, although the processional cross of the University of Cambridge, which served at academic as well as distinctly religious ceremonies, was at least as grand.[83] It intentionally exudes the magnificence of the patron and institution it was made to represent. In this case, there is nothing ambiguous about patronage, provenance or date of manufacture because inscriptions on a flange above the base terminal and a circular pendant formerly attached to it with a chain document these things (see figure 14.7). It is worth noting that although this pendant is called 'ane sell' in the college inventory of c.1500, and a similar chained pendant on a lost mace of the University of Paris has also been described as a 'petit scel', it cannot actually have been used as such, because its letters are not reversed and its inscription unsuitable for authenticating anything other than the origins of the mace itself.[84]

Neither inscription has obvious precedence over the other: where one is mostly in Latin and names the patron, the other is integral to the mace. That on the flange is in Scots and reads: '+ iohne maiel govldsm[i]che and verlete ofe chamer til þe lorde þe dalfyne [/] hes made þis masse in þe toune of paris þe 3er of our lorde m cccc lx i'. Here are the name of the goldsmith (Jean Maiel), the fact that he was a royal servant and the place and date of the mace's making. The cross delimiting this circular inscription looks like an inducement to the medieval viewer, who knew the motif from its inclusion in prayers and commemorative inscriptions elsewhere, to intercede for those named. The inscription on the pendant is in French and Latin, and set out in lines, as on a page: 'avisses a la fin [/] Jacobus [/] kanedi illustris [/] san[c]tiandree antistes [/] ac fv[n]dator. collegii s[anc]ti [/] salvatoris cvi me dona[/]vit me fecit fieri p[ar]

---

[82] *Copiale*, pp. 406–7.
[83] H. P. Stokes, *The Chaplains and Chapel of the University of Cambridge (1256–1568)* (Cambridge, 1906), pp. 24–6, 62, 76–9.
[84] Cant, *St Salvator*, p. 161; P. A. J. de Moncets, *De l'origine des appariteurs des universités et de leurs masses* (Paris, 1782), p. 74: the pendant on the Paris mace displayed three fleurs-de-lys.

Figure 14.6: The head of St Salvator's college mace.

Figure 14.7: Inscription of the pendant formerly attached by a chain to the college mace.

isi[/]vs an[n]o d[omi]ni M [/] cccc l x i' (see figure 14.7). ('Consider the end carefully: James Kennedy, an illustrious bishop of St Andrews and founder of the college of Saint Salvator, who donated me, had me made in Paris in the year of our Lord 1461.')[85] The fact repeated here, that the mace was made in Paris, was evidently considered a point of prestige: a proof of quality, refinement and patronal reach. Another assertion of Kennedy's patronage is found on the rod, which is chased all over with the initials *I K* (for 'Iacobus Kanedi'). It has been argued that these cannot be Kennedy's initials because they are crowned and that this motif would have represented a treasonous imposture, even though the bishop had royal blood in him. The alternative offered is *I H* (for 'Ih[esus]' or 'Ihesus hominum [salvator]'), which would correspond to the college's ded-

---

[85] For facsimiles of the inscriptions see Brook, 'Account', p. 466; G. Evans, 'The Mace of St Salvator's College', Higgitt, *St Andrews*, pp. 197–212 at p. 198.

Figure 14.8: Figure of apocalyptic Christ within the head of the St Salvator's College mace.

ication.⁸⁶ But this idea can be put to rest. First, and definitively to my mind, the final minim is indented in a way that allows the second letter to be read as a *k* but not an *h* (or for that matter an *s*). Second, the initials *I K* were also on a red satin cope that Kennedy gave to his college, showing that he considered them effective for commemorative purposes and used them elsewhere.⁸⁷ Third, as Godfrey Evans noted in his article on the mace, *IH* is not a usual abbreviation of the holy name.⁸⁸ The trigrams *IHC* and *IHS*, crowned or uncrowned (both frequently occur), are normal and would have been equally possible for Maiel to execute. Finally, there are precedents for grand churchmen having their crowned initials put onto ostentatious objects, even where they had no blood relation to a monarch. For example, Abbot Walter Monington (d. 1375) gave a set of blue vestments spangled with the capital letters *W M*, crowned and in gold circles, for use at the high altar of Glastonbury Abbey, and the great missal made for Westminster Abbey in 1383–84 displays the initials of its patron, Nicholas

---

⁸⁶ D. McRoberts, 'The Glorious House of St Andrew', *Innes Review* 25 (1974), pp. 95–158 at p. 154; Evans, 'Mace of St Salvator's', pp. 206–8.
⁸⁷ Cant, *St Salvator*, p. 153.
⁸⁸ Evans, 'Mace of St Salvator's', pp. 207–8.

Litlyngton, under a crown as part of the full-page crucifixion miniature on folio 157v and also on other pages of the manuscript.[89]

While the full significance of these inscriptions cannot be discussed here, a couple of points deserve notice for what they bring to the understanding of the mace. Kennedy's austere motto, 'Avisses a la fin', which is still displayed over the tower-arch leading into the college, has a semantic inflection that integrates it cleverly with the iconography of the mace's head. As well as meaning 'awareness' and 'careful consideration', the Old French word *avisement* had connotations of forensic deliberation and judgement. In the head of the mace, Christ is represented specifically as the apocalyptic Judge, standing on a globe with an open mantle and palms turned outwards to display his wounds (see figure 14.8). He is surrounded by angels holding the instruments of the passion that represented the portentous 'sign of the Son of Man in Heaven' (Matthew 24:30) in later medieval art.[90] In this context, the motto's admonishment to the reader-viewer to meditate reflexively on the ultimate fate of his soul is sharply emphasised by a vision of what he would encounter at the Last Judgement. A sober pun is also involved, for in looking at this scene on the head of the mace one is considering the physical end of the object. A second point relates to the goldsmith Jean Maiel, whom Kennedy may or may not have known personally (the mace is likely to have been commissioned through an agent). While Paris was well supplied with goldsmiths at the time, this man may have recommended himself to Kennedy's attention, or the attention of an adviser, for his nominal relationship to the prince, who became King Louis XI in the year the mace was made. Kennedy was, after all, in the market for something of unusual magnificence. With regard to Maiel's status, the fact that he appears to have served thrice as a guardian of the Paris guild of goldsmiths should not be overemphasised: there were six guardians in any one year, and the job was probably considered as onerous as it was prestigious.[91] Moreover, goldsmiths seem customarily to have been honoured with the title of royal valet (their products being a constant royal requirement), and as any king or prince had numerous valets simultaneously, there is no reason to suspect that Maiel shared his patron's itinerary or was unusually distinguished in any

---

[89] J. M. Luxford, 'Nichil ornatus in domo domini pretermittens: the Professional Patronage of Walter of Monington, Abbot of Glastonbury', *Patrons and Professionals*, ed. P. Binski and E. A. New (Donington, 2012), pp. 237–60 at p. 249; L. F. Sandler, *Gothic Manuscripts 1285–1385: A Survey of Manuscripts Illuminated in the British Isles* 5, 2 vols (London, 1986), i, fig. 402.

[90] It is true that Christ is not seated in judgement here, but no other context is available for representing him with a globe at his feet, showing his wounds and surrounded by the instruments of the passion. The idea that this is Christ as the Man of Sorrows (e.g. *Corpus Sceptrorum*, vol. I/i, p. 222) is disqualified by the globe and the imperious bearing of the figure.

[91] P. Lacroix and F. Seré, *Le livre d'or des métiers: histoire de orfèvrerie-joaillerie* [...] *de la France et de la Belgique* (Paris, 1850), pp. 158, 159. In 1455 a 'Jean Hahiert' is recorded, in 1460 a 'Jean Mayelle' and in 1467 a 'Jean Mayet'.

way other than the practice of his craft.⁹² But in this capacity he certainly was distinguished, and it was probably his reputation that later led the English-German nation in the university of Paris to order a solemn mace of their own from either him or his son. In January 1494, Jehan Mahiel, living in the rue de la Voirrerie, released to the nation a silver-gilt mace ('masse'), for the design and making of which he and his son were paid 24 gold écus. This had been ordered through a deputy in the previous year; and the nation had a party ('dejantaculo') to celebrate its completion. According to another memorandum of 1493, the nation allotted a smaller sum 'to our goldsmith': no name is given here, but if, as seems likely, Maiel is intended, then he may have been a regular employee of the nation.⁹³ This is worth mentioning here because regular work for this particular institution, with its longstanding Scottish connections, could have brought Maiel to Kennedy's attention. Alternatively, a reputation as a mace-maker gained in part through the college mace may have recommended him to the English-German nation. Such networks of influence and patronage are generally obscure, but in this case the coincidence encourages speculation. Whatever doubts one might have that a goldsmith of the period worked at the top of his game for over three decades are insufficient to imply that the document of 1494 refers to a son of the same name, but even if it does, the indications are that Maiel of Paris was known for the production of grand academic maces.

Like its faculty counterparts, the college mace has been variously restored. A second pendant kept with it records that it was repaired in 1685, and at least eight of its minor figures were either missing or badly damaged when it was described in 1843.⁹⁴ Altogether, the mace originally incorporated at least forty-one figures, including ten crouching lions, of which nine or more are currently missing. Nineteen of these were on the head, and the rest occupied a series of three intricate junctures on the rod, and also the base terminal, which has four of the lions. The junctures are designed as receptacles for miniature figures. Their decorative vocabulary is almost confusing in its variety, incorporating arches, foliate pinnacles, circular bastions, battlements and windows with blind tracery. They must have made the mace challenging to carry and store. Some of their detailing looks post-medieval, and several of the figures certainly are. The surviving figures represent bare-headed men, none tonsured, who pray, read from books or scrolls, or listen with their hands cupped behind their ears. There are also three figures of angels holding up round objects on the upper juncture. The imagery alludes in a general way to intercession, learning and sermonising, all functions of the college, and may,

---

⁹² For other goldsmith-*valets de chamber* see for example: D. Gaborit-Chopin, 'Le bâton cantoral de la Sainte-Chapelle', *Bulletin Monumental* 132 (1974), pp. 67–81 at p. 80–1 (Hennequin and Jehan de Vivier, 1377–8); É. Kovács, *L'âge d'or de l'orfèvrerie parisienne au temps des princes de Valois* (Budapest, 2004), pp. 355, 390 (Herman Ruissel, 1390, 1399).

⁹³ *Index chronologicus*, p. 308 (no. 1497); *Liber receptorum*, cols 719, 731.

⁹⁴ C. J. Lyon, *History of St Andrews*, 2 vols (Edinburgh, 1843), ii, p. 199.

as others have argued, reflect the actual staffing of the institution (though without the provost).[95] Nine of the figures can be identified as scholars and three more of similar appearance may have occupied now-empty receptacles on the middle juncture.

The head, a fantasy of inhabited microarchitecture, is now missing three of the figures most important to its original appearance. They stood highest of all, in castellated turrets, and were probably angels blowing trumpets to signal the Last Judgement. Six of the remaining figures are lions which project on ragged, lopped branches, and there are three chained, gesticulating wild men holding clubs: between the wild men's legs are shields with the heraldry of the see of St Andrews, James Kennedy and the college.[96] In this context, these rampant figures represent guardians of Christ and his angels. The same idea is visible in the combination of lions and wild men commonly found on late medieval font stems and church porches in eastern England. On a larger scale, a whole tribe of chained, shield-bearing wild men flanks the processional entrance to the collegiate church of San Gregorio at Valladolid in Spain, guarding in grotesque and romantic fashion the sacred space beyond them.[97] Around the tabernacle containing Christ are three relatively large figures, one wearing a crown, another a mitre and the third dressed in a cap and long, vertically pleated gown with a belt and purse at the waist. They have previously been said to represent the three estates of medieval society: the clergy, nobility and commoners.[98] This suggestion can be associated directly with the judging figure of Christ through a popular late medieval English sermon on the three estates which declares that representatives of each will be summoned to the Last Judgement in the person of priests, temporal lords and ordinary Christians.[99] A compatible idea is that these figures represent the three men mentioned in the inscriptions, Kennedy, the dauphin and Maiel. Goldsmiths of the mid fifteenth century did dress like the third figure on the evidence of contemporary painting: the same cap and pleated garment are represented in Petrus Christus's *Goldsmith and a Young Couple* (painted in Bruges in 1449), and purses on belts are attributes

---

[95] Evans, 'Mace of St Salvator's', pp. 208–9. This idea has parallels elsewhere. Compare, for example, the seal of Trinity Hall, Cambridge (die made *c.* 1351), which includes as part of its design a shield of the founder with the heads of the twenty foundational scholars growing out of it on a vine.

[96] On the heraldry see Brook, 'Account', p. 461; Evans, 'Mace of St Salvator's', p. 201. The blazon is: *a saltire within a tressure flory and counterflory* (St Andrews); *a chevron between three cross crosslets fitché, with a double tressure flory and counterflory* (Kennedy); *an imperial orb within a tressure flory and counterflory* (college).

[97] A. E. Nichols, *The Early Art of Norfolk: A Subject-List of Extant and Lost Art Including Items Relevant to Early Drama* (Kalamazoo, 2002), pp. 267–8; T. Husband, *The Wild Man: Medieval Myth and Symbolism* (New York, 1980), p. 7.

[98] W. Coutts, *James Kennedy, Bishop of St Andrews: His Church, Tomb and Mace* (St Andrews, 1901), p. 40; McRoberts, 'Glorious House', p. 155; Evans, 'Mace of St Salvator's', pp. 205–6.

[99] *A Repertorium of Middle English Prose Sermons*, ed. V. O'Mara and S. Paul, 4 vols (Turnhout, 2007), i, pp. 54–61.

of goldsmiths in other contemporary works of art.[100] If this is the case then the intention was commemorative, and also to suggest the blessed status of those associable with the mace's production.

While their prominence means that the large figures on the head demand interpretation, the more detailed symbolic analyses of the mace's images and architecture offered in the past seem to me largely overstated. The goal of medieval art was rarely to present its viewers with a riddle. Objects of this kind were typically designed to convey abstract and general ideas rather than specific, complicated messages: their symbolism is almost always open. The little golden lions dotted over the mace can be summoned to illustrate the point. To the sort of viewer abroad in the university in the 1460s, these may have embodied the power and regality of Christ and (or) a general notion of Solomonic grandeur and wisdom responsive to 3 Kings 10:11–25, the outstanding account of sumptuous art patronage in the Bible which mentions the gold-plated *leunculi* that decorated King Solomon's throne. They would hardly, however, have suggested that Kennedy or anyone else represented by the mace was a type of either Christ or Solomon. Over and above a desire to advertise the college's dedication and purpose, and to encapsulate the patron's motto, the motive for such a complex design was apparently that of inspiring curiosity, wonder and admiration in the viewer in a way that contributed to the fame of Kennedy and his institution. The same motives governed the designs of many high quality works of late medieval art, among which the tabernacles in some of the borders of the Sherborne missal (c.1400) make particularly good comparisons with the college mace.[101] Several of the fantasy-productions of Parisian and Netherlandish goldsmiths illustrate the tendency with special clarity. Surviving examples include the works now known as the Esztergom Calvary, the *Goldenes Rössl* and the Holy Thorn reliquary, all made in Paris around 1400 for royal patrons and presumably a type of object Maiel knew.[102] The desire to astonish is also present in the Daedalian composition of Kennedy's tomb in the college chapel, called by one late medieval writer 'the most magnificent tomb in the whole world'.[103] This is the impression Kennedy sought to create through such lavish patronage of art.

There is a congenial irony in the fact that objects first commissioned to advertise the arrival of their owners on the academic scene have become symbols of six centuries of history. The maces' initial purpose to demonstrate the unity and autonomy of fledgling, still plastic institutions contributed with each public showing to the consolidation that eventually secured the university's future. In retrospect, they emerge as still points in the diachronic process

---

[100] J. Cherry, *Medieval Goldsmiths* (London, 2011), pp. 39, 89–91; Nocq, *Poinçon de Paris*, iii, pl. between pp. 128 and 129.
[101] J. Backhouse, *The Sherborne Missal* (London, 1999), pp. 11, 22, 26, 38, 58.
[102] Kovács, *L'âge d'or*, p. 18; Stratford, *English Royal Treasure*, pls 8–10; E. Panofsky, *Early Netherlandish Painting: Its Origins and Character*, 2 vols (Harvard, 1971), i, pp. 68–9.
[103] *Scotichronicon*, iii, p. 492 ('preclarissimo tumulo tocius orbis').

which has led the university to where it is today, and also as constituents of that process to the extent that they acted upon the minds of its agents. They have, in other words, a dual nature: as well as being museum pieces lodged behind bullet-proof glass, they are restless with historical life. Taken singly or together, the maces are the most evocative surviving reminders of the vitality of material display to the university's founders, and they rise above all the lost books and forgotten acts to declare in shining images the ultimate values of these grave, ambitious men.

CHAPTER FIFTEEN

Heresy, Inquisition and Late Medieval St Andrews

Katie Stevenson

By the late Middle Ages St Andrews was a major ecclesiastical centre and was home to an associated intellectual community that was to become the foundation of a university. Such a vibrant mix of scholars and clerics made St Andrews an obvious destination for heretical and heterodox thinkers who wished to engage with intellectual circles in the town on matters of doctrine and the principles of Church authority. Evidence indicates that the principal heresies of the late Middle Ages were preached in St Andrews and the eradication and avoidance of heretical thought played a considerable role in early university life. To combat the inherent attraction of St Andrews for those who sought to question orthodoxy, there quickly emerged formal channels of inquisition, with St Andrews providing the structural focal point. Indeed, the rector of the university, Laurence of Lindores, was appointed as first Papal Inquisitor of Heretical Pravity in Scotland. Lindores tried many cases of heresy in both the town and diocese of St Andrews, several of which resulted in public executions but the vast majority of which did not. This essay will explore the links between the university, the Church and the detection of heresy in the town and the diocese of St Andrews.

The closing decades of the fourteenth century and the first of the fifteenth century saw considerable tensions within the late medieval Church. Pluralism and the abuse of benefices were rife, the protracted Great Schism drove the Church into near-terminal disarray, and European alliances were under strain as adherences and bonds were tested. In this climate heterodoxy and heresy flourished, particularly amongst those who sought reform of the Church to resolve its crisis. Considerable scholarly attention on these matters has been focused on England and Bohemia, because the principal heresies of late medieval Europe, Lollardy and Hussitism, grew out of these areas. Yet, despite it being known that heresy and the fear of heresy were features of medieval life in Scotland, the patchy and fragmentary archival record has hindered significant study of the subject. Moreover, the medieval evidence has been shoehorned into the narrative arc of the Scottish Reformation rather than considered in its own historical context.¹ Indeed, while the Protestant martyr Patrick Hamilton is commemorated in St Andrews with a stone memorial in the pavement outside St Salvator's Chapel, where he was burned for his Lutheran heresies in 1528, earlier figures have received no such recognition.² This essay thus seeks to reconsider and recover the evidence, arguing that St Andrews is especially important in the history of heresy in late medieval Scotland.

While scholars have tended to focus on Lollardy's southward trajectory from Oxford in the latter part of the fourteenth century, particularly towards London, it is not in the least bit surprising that John Wyclif's theology and teachings gained a foothold in Scotland.³ Indeed, there were several channels by which Lollard ideas could readily be circulated and discussed. First, there was a reasonably consistent stream of Scots matriculating at Oxford during the height of Wyclif's influence there, many of whom subsequently returned to Scotland, to destinations including both the town and the diocese of St Andrews. Balliol College, where Wyclif was master from c.1360, was the principal attraction for a substantial number of those Scots; from 1364 to 1379 Balliol seems to have been the exclusive destination for Scottish students.⁴

A further avenue for awareness and engagement was by the small but notable influx of English clerics from 1378. Within the first few years of the Schism, evidence indicates that there was a marked increase in English clerics appearing

---

¹ See, for example, James Edward McGoldrick, *Luther's Scottish Connection* (London and Toronto, 1989). The best work to date is Alec Ryrie, *The Origins of the Scottish Reformation* (Manchester, 2006), esp. ch. 1; and Margaret H. B. Sanderson, *Ayrshire and the Reformation: People and Change, 1490–1600* (East Linton, 1997). For more on the shaping of 'national' stories of reformation and counter-reformation see *The Reformation in National Context*, ed. Bob Scribner, Roy Porter and Mikuláš Teich (Cambridge, 1994).

² On Hamilton see EUL, Dd.10.74, *Alexandri Alesii Scotti Responsio ad Cochlei Calumnias* (Leipzig, 1551); John Foxe, *The Unabridged Acts and Monuments Online* or *TAMO* (1576 edition) (Sheffield, 2011), 1563 edition, book 3, pp. 511–12. See also Joe Carvalho, *Patrick Hamilton, 1504–1528: The Stephen of Scotland* (Burrelton, 2009); *The Reception of Continental Reformation in Britain*, ed. Polly Ha and Patrick Collinson (Oxford, 2010).

³ The Midlands and pockets in the north have also received attention, but these are not dominant strands in discussions about the spread of Lollardy. See, for example, *Lollardy and the Gentry in the Later Middle Ages*, ed. Margaret Aston and Colin Richmond (Stroud, 1997); J. A. F. Thomson, *The Later Lollards, 1414–1520* (Oxford, 1965); Anne Hudson, *Studies in the Transmission of Wyclif's Writings* (Aldershot, 2008); Hudson, *Lollards and their Books* (London, 1985), pp. 141–63. For more see: *Lollards and their Influence in Late Medieval England*, ed. Fiona Somerset, Jill C. Havens and Derrick G. Pitard (Woodbridge, 2003).

⁴ *Rotuli Scotiae in Turri Londinensi et in Domo Capitulari Westmonasteriensi Asservati*, i: *Temporibus Regum Angliae Edwardi I. Edwardi II. Edwardi III* (London, 1814), pp. 808–9, 815–16, 822, 825–6, 829, 849, 851, 859, 877, 881, 886, 891, 896; *Rotuli Scotiae in Turri Londinensi et in Domo Capitulari Westmonasteriensi Asservati*, ii: *Temporibus Regum Angliae Ric. II. Hen. IV. V. VI. Ed. IV. Ric. III. Hen. VII. VIII* (London, 1819), pp. 8, 20, 45–6, 100; J. I. Catto, 'Wyclif and Wycliffism at Oxford, 1356–1430', *The History of the University of Oxford*, ii: *Late Medieval Oxford*, ed. J. I. Catto and Ralph Evans (Oxford, 1992), pp. 175–261.

in Scottish churches, including amongst the canons of the cathedral priory in St Andrews. This might suggest that St Andrews was a refuge for supporters of the restored Avignon papacy, which was not without bitter controversy.[5] Whether or not there were Lollard sympathisers amongst the English clerics remains entirely speculative, but it is not beyond the realms of possibility that their arrival would have at least increased awareness of the heresy, for Lollardy was nothing if not topical in these years. Indeed, the Schism coincided with the production of an English vernacular Bible, and, with the regular movement of books from Oxford to Scotland, it is not implausible that the English vernacular Bible was known.[6] Perhaps of more pertinence was the English law *De heretico comburendo* passed in 1401, a strict censorship law that demanded the burning of heretics at the stake.[7] The law had immediate effects and in that same year a follower of Jerome of Prague – a student of Wyclif and chief follower of Jan Hus – fled across the Scottish border to avoid prosecution by English authorities. By early 1403 three English priests sheltering at Kelso Abbey in the diocese of St Andrews had been accused of heresy by the bishop of Durham and warrants had been issued for their arrests.[8] This, of course, might be read as evidence of schismatic adherence rather than reformist views, and yet, in that same year the first Scottish inquisitor was appointed by the Avignon papacy, which certainly indicates a serious concern with the spread of heresy and demonstrates a robust response to this fear from the Church.[9]

It is apparent that there were a variety of points of contact between heretics and the communities in St Andrews in the late fourteenth century and a coterminous concern to prevent the spread of heresy through the diocese and Scotland more widely. In 1388 James Dardani, a clerk of the Roman papal court (and thus, it should be noted, not the obedience to which Scotland adhered at this time), was appointed by Urban VI as nuncio to hear and examine the accounts of inquisitions of heresy in Scotland.[10] Within a decade the duke of Rothesay, lieutenant for his father Robert III, was awarded the explicit right to restrain heretics at the request of Church authorities.[11] Concern continued to grow

---

[5] A. Francis Steuart, 'Scotland and the Papacy during the Great Schism', *SHR* 4 (1907), p. 147.

[6] On regular movement of books from Oxford to Scotland see Eyal Poleg, 'The Earliest Evidence for Anti-Lollard Polemics in Medieval Scotland', *Innes Review* 64:2 (2013), p. 233. For more in general see: Kantik Ghosh, *The Wycliffite Heresy: Authority and the Interpretation of Texts* (Cambridge, 2002); Fiona Somerset, *Clerical Discourse and Lay Audience in Late Medieval England* (Cambridge, 1998).

[7] On this act see A. K. McHardy, '*De Heretico Comburendo*, 1401', *Lollardy and the Gentry in the Later Middle Ages*, ed. Margaret Aston and C. Richmond (Stroud, 1997), pp. 112–26.

[8] *Liber S. Marie de Calchou: Registrum Cartarum Abbacie Tironensis de Kelso, 1113–1567*, ed. Cosmo Innes (Edinburgh, 1846), ii, pp. 435–6 (no. 538), 436–7 (no. 539).

[9] Isla Woodman, 'Education and Episcopacy: The Universities of Scotland in the Fifteenth Century' (unpublished PhD thesis, University of St Andrews, 2011), p. 25.

[10] *CPL*, iv, p. 267.

[11] *RPS*, 1399/1/3. For more on Robert III and David, duke of Rothesay, see Stephen Boardman, *The Early Stewart Kings: Robert II and Robert III, 1371–1406* (East Linton, 1996).

as heretical thinking gained firmer ground in pockets of Europe, now including not only England but also Bohemia. The Hussite movement in Prague, centred on the teachings of the outspoken reformer Jan Hus, was drawn to some of the same theological arguments as the Lollards and the movements were in regular communication.[12] The events in Prague were of international significance and were played out in a European arena that was focused on resolving the Great Schism, which naturally drew the attention of religious authorities across Europe. Widespread disarray in the Church and the existence of competing papal authorities combined with the strengthening in reformist movements that explicitly criticised the corruption of the clergy and, amongst other beliefs, held that the clergy was inessential to communion with God. It was not long before Scottish churchmen were condemning Hus, while sophisticated underground communication networks developed between heretics in Bohemia and sympathisers in Scotland.

Regular contact between heretics and sympathisers in Scotland was of grave concern. Indeed, at the same time as the governor of Scotland, Robert Stewart, duke of Albany, was praised for being 'a constante Catholyk / All lollaris he laythit and herrrotyk', the new university was founded in St Andrews with the explicit aim 'to counteract the heresy of the times'.[13] It is entirely logical that the episcopal centre of St Andrews became the principal focal point for concern with heresy, as it was not only the premier bishopric of the kingdom, a major site of pilgrimage where both the apostle and local Scottish saints were venerated, and home to several ecclesiastical foundations that coexisted with the cathedral and its priory, but also a thriving intellectual centre, with frequent preaching, debate and circulation of books. Both the space and the audience for orthodox and heterodox preaching could be found in St Andrews. Thus, what appears to have been the rather sudden and unplanned foundation of the university can be seen not only as a direct response to the general need for a degree-awarding body in an established intellectual centre, but also as a means of creating a body of men properly equipped to staff the Church in a period of complex pressure. A crucial aspect of this latter role was the need to maintain orthodoxy through the parish system. It is no coincidence then that the man appointed to several senior leadership roles in the early administration of the university, as well as the

---

[12] See for example Michael Van Dussen, *From England to Bohemia: Heresy and Communication in the Later Middle Ages* (Cambridge, 2012).

[13] *The Original Chronicle of Andrew of Wyntoun: Printed on Parallel Pages from the Cottonian and Wemyss MSS., with the Variants and Other Texts*, ed. F. J. Amours (Edinburgh, 1908), vi, p. 417; Karen J. Hunt, 'The Governorship of the First Duke of Albany: 1406–1420' (unpublished PhD thesis, University of Edinburgh, 1998); StAUL, UYUY152/3, fols 19–22r. For more on the foundation of the university see: J. Maitland Anderson, 'James I of Scotland and the University of St Andrews', *SHR* 3 (1906), pp. 301–15; J. Maitland Anderson, 'The Beginnings of St Andrews University, 1410–1418', *SHR* 8 (1911), pp. 225–48, 333–60; Hastings Rashdall, *The Universities of Europe in the Middle Ages: A New Edition in Three Volumes*, ed. F. M. Powicke and A. B. Emden (Oxford, 1987), ii, p. 302; Woodman, 'Education and Episcopacy', esp. pp. 25–7.

teaching of theology and canon law, was also the principal inquisitor, Laurence of Lindores.[14]

As the papal bulls from Benedict XIII arrived to confirm the foundation of the university in St Andrews in early 1413, pressure was mounting to resolve the Schism. The Council of Constance was called in 1414 to seek an end to the dispute and restore the unity of the Church. A secondary agenda was to direct a unified attack on John Wyclif and Jan Hus. The evidence from Constance hints at a perception of a more serious problem in Scotland than scholars have been inclined to acknowledge. Indeed, Dietrich von Nieheim, a German chronicler of the Schism, reported that Wycliffite doctrines were being widely circulated in Scotland, England, Bohemia and Moravia.[15] The following year Jean d'Achéry, ambassador of the University of Paris at Constance, called upon the pope and council to deal with doctrinal errors 'being sown most widely in the kingdoms of Bohemia and Scotland'.[16] Of course, this cannot be detached from Scotland's continued adherence to the Avignon line and the relatively small Scottish presence at Constance. Nevertheless, the theologian Jean Gerson, procurator of the French nation at the University of Paris, in that same year complained about the influence of Wycliffism in Scotland in his work on the literal interpretation of Scripture. 'There is opposition to the truth, in England, in Scotland, in the university of Prague and in Germany, and even, shameful as it is to admit it, in France. [...] And these sowers of heresy, and enemies of truth [...] claim that their sayings are founded upon holy scripture, and on its literal sense.'[17] Increasingly aware of the rumours of the state of belief in Scotland, Benedict XIII called upon Henry de Lichton, bishop of Moray, to investigate whether or not heresies were being spread through his diocese in the north-east of Scotland.[18] It is not unreasonable to presume that the bishop of St Andrews was called upon to do the same.

In summer 1416 the Schism was still unresolved, the Hussite revolution was increasing in intensity after the execution of Jan Hus at Constance in 1415, and the convicted English Lollard John Oldcastle was at large and in close contact with some in the south of Scotland.[19] It was in this climate that in St Andrews

---

[14] On Lindores see Anderson, 'The Beginnings of St Andrews University', pp. 235–40; Woodman, 'Education and Episcopacy', *passim*; Lawrence Moonan, 'Lawrence of Lindores (d.1437) on "Life in the Living Being"' (unpublished PhD thesis, University of Louvain, 1966); Lawrence Moonan, 'The Scientific Writings of Laurence of Lindores (d.1437)', *Classica et Mediaevalia* 39 (1988–9), pp. 273–217; J. H. Baxter, 'The Philosopher Laurence of Lindores', *Philosophical Quarterly* 5: 21 (1955), pp. 348–54.

[15] Dietrich von Nieheim, 'Super reformacione ecclesie', in *Forschungen und Quellen zur Geschichte des Konstanzer Konzils*, ed. Heinrich Finke (Münster, 1889), p. 269.

[16] Vatican City, Biblioteca Apostolica Vaticana, MS Pal. lat. 595, fols 102r–103v.

[17] Margaret Deanesly, *The Lollard Bible and Other Medieval Biblical Versions* (Cambridge, 1920), pp. 105–6n, 359; Thomson, *The Later Lollards*, p. 203.

[18] Vatican City, Archivum Secretum Vaticanum, Registra Vaticana 332, fol. 51v; *Copiale*, pp. 253–4; Reid, 'The Lollards in Pre-Reformation Scotland', p. 272.

[19] Oldcastle may have had long-established connections with families operating in the south of Scotland for in autumn 1400 he had been stationed at the then English garrison at Roxburgh Castle in the Scottish borders. *CDS*, iv, p. 118 (no. 567). In 1413 Oldcastle had

the Papal Inquisitor, Laurence of Lindores, used his position and influence in the new university to insist upon a set of revised oaths for new masters of arts who would be teaching bachelors students.[20] Teaching in significantly smaller cohorts was mandated, in order to encourage better knowledge of the students and their thinking, but most crucially, the new masters undertook an oath to defend the Church against the assault of the Lollards and to resist their adherents.[21] When James I was eventually released from English captivity in 1424, one of his early concerns was to respond to the perceived threat of heresy: in parliament on 12 March 1425 it was declared that a general inquisition to root out all 'lollardis and heretykis' should be carried out in every diocese in the kingdom.[22] Yet despite the near resolution of the Schism and the end of the Hussite wars, the fear of heresy remained a serious concern to the Scottish clergy in the 1440s and beyond. In a letter written by James Ogilvie, a former master of arts at the University of St Andrews to that same university in 1441, he remarked that the treachery of heretics had long afflicted the Church in Scotland.[23] The 1440s also witnessed Walter Bower, a chronicler and the abbot of Inchcolm Abbey (situated fairly close to St Andrews), penning a violent attack against Wyclif and Lollardy and expressing his serious reservations and anxieties about the continued presence (however genuine) of widespread heretical thinking in the kingdom. In a long and impassioned diatribe he revealed that 'writings of this heretic [Wyclif] are still retained by some Lollards in Scotland and are carefully preserved at the instigation of the Devil by the kind of men in whose view "stolen water is sweeter and bread got by stealth more pleasant"'.[24] Bower laid

> been convicted as a heretic and refused to recant, quickly escaping the authorities and declaring himself in open rebellion of the king. During his time as an outlaw Oldcastle and his supporters were implicated in several attempts to release James I and to reinstate to the English throne Richard II, at that point believed to be living under the protection of the duke of Albany in Scotland. London, The National Archives, KB 27/624, Rex m. 9r; KB 27/595, Rex m. 3v; BL, Cotton MS, Cleopatra F IV, f. 109; *Calendar of Letter-Books of the City of London*, ed. Reginald R. Sharpe (London, 1899–1912), i, pp. 165–6; *Chronica Monasterii S. Albani: Ypodigma Neustriae, A Thoma Walsingham, Quondam Monacho Monasterii S. Albani, Conscriptum*, ed. Henry Thomas Riley (London, 1876), p. 482. See also Margaret Aston, *Lollards and Reformers: Images and Literacy in Late Medieval Religion* (London, 1984), pp. 26–8; Nigel Saul, *Richard II* (New Haven, 1997), p. 427; Sanderson, *Ayrshire and the Reformation*, p. 37.
>
> [20] On student life in medieval St Andrews more generally see James Robb, 'Student Life in St Andrews before 1450 AD', *SHR* 9 (1912), pp. 347–60.
> [21] StAUL, UYUY411, fol. 3v; *St Andrews Acta*, pp. clxxvii, 11–12.
> [22] *RPS*, 1425/3/4.
> [23] *Copiale*, p. 208. Of course, an element of this attack was against schismatics: the tone of the letter was no doubt influenced by Ogilvie's personal situation for in July 1440 he had been elected to the see of St Andrews by Felix V, who in 1439 was elected as pope by the Council of Basel. Ogilvie's letter was a petition for the university to adhere to the decisions of Basel, and related to his difficulties in obtaining possession of the see of St Andrews, which had been granted in June 1440 to James Kennedy by the Roman Pope Eugenius IV. For more on the Scots and Basel see J. H. Burns, 'Scottish Churchmen and the Council of Basle', *Innes Review* 13 (1962), pp. 3–53, 157–89.
> [24] *Scotichronicon*, viii, pp. 68–9.

considerable stress on what he argued was the most pernicious and dangerous aspect of Lollardy, that 'those who have once been tainted with and become rooted in the school of this most infamous doctrine scarcely ever return to the faith'.[25]

James Kennedy, the bishop of St Andrews from 1440, oversaw measures to continue to provide for the defence of the Church against heresy.[26] In 1450 he founded St Salvator's College at St Andrews for the teaching of theology, with the stated purpose of strengthening the faithful and eradicating heresy.[27] When nearly two decades later in 1469 Kennedy's foundation of St Salvator's was granted degree-awarding powers (explicitly distinct from those of the University of St Andrews), Pope Paul II decreed that the study of theology was necessary in the college 'for the extirpation of certain heresies which the old enemy of the human race has sown in those parts'.[28] Further university establishments followed the foundation of St Salvator's. In 1451 William Turnbull, bishop of Glasgow, received papal permission to erect the University of Glasgow, a response to the 'urgent need for an educated class, particularly of laymen to administer the royal and franchisal courts, and for sound theologians to combat and contain Lollardy'.[29] A third university foundation – that of Aberdeen in 1495 – at the instigation of the bishop of Aberdeen, had the faculty of theology as its centrepiece and the defence of Christian orthodoxy at its heart.[30] The cleric and poet Walter Kennedy, great-nephew of James Kennedy, bishop of St Andrews, wrote at this time that:

> The schip of faith tempestrous wind and rane
> Dryvis in the see of lollerdry that blawis.[31]

Concerns escalated in St Andrews, which by 1500 was reputed to be 'strongly impregnated with heretical ideas'.[32]

---

[25] Ibid.
[26] For more on Kennedy see: Norman Macdougall, 'Bishop James Kennedy of St Andrews: A Reassessment of his Political Career', *Church, Politics and Society: Scotland 1408–1929*, ed. Norman Macdougall (Edinburgh, 1983), pp. 1–22; Dunlop, *Kennedy*.
[27] StAUL, UYSS110/A/2; UYSS110/A/3, transcribed in Cant, *St Salvator*, pp. 54–6. It has been suggested that Kennedy was inspired by the success of the bishop of Winchester William of Wykeham's foundation of the New College at Oxford in 1379, for Wykeham and Kennedy's careers shared similarities and Wykeham was also 'alarmed at the spiritual decline of the secular clergy and the growth of heresy'. Cant, *St Salvator*, p. 3; Dunlop, *Kennedy*, pp. 283–4. For more on the foundation of New College, Oxford, see R. L. Storey, 'The Foundation and the Medieval College, 1379–1530', *New College Oxford, 1379–1979*, ed. John Buxton and Penry Williams (Oxford, 1979), pp. 3–43.
[28] *CPL*, xii, p. 313.
[29] Leslie J. Macfarlane, *William Elphinstone and the Kingdom of Scotland, 1431–1514: The Struggle for Order* (Aberdeen, 1985), p. 21.
[30] Ibid., pp. 304–5.
[31] Quotation from NLS, Adv. MS 1.1.6, ff. 52v–53r; all extant versions are transcribed in Walter Kennedy, 'At matyne hour, in myddis of the nycht', *The Poems of Walter Kennedy*, ed. Nicole Meier (Woodbridge, 2008), pp. 10, 11, 12.
[32] Reid, 'The Lollards in Pre-Reformation Scotland', p. 279.

The veracity of these assertions, which might be deemed to be somewhat hyperbolic, is nuanced by the fact that historians are still uncovering evidence of both anti-heretical and heretical writings in Scotland. A recent discovery in the margins of the Traquair Bible – which, by the last decades of the fourteenth century, was in the diocese of St Andrews at Culross Abbey – firmly roots concern with heresy to twenty years earlier than the first recorded burning of a heretic.[33] Around 1390, and possibly not long after the bible arrived at Culross, a short anti-Lollard sentence was added as a marginal gloss to Ezekiel 33:6, and the same phrase was repeated in an empty space at the end of the manuscript by a different hand in the mid fifteenth century.[34] Eyal Poleg has argued that the 1390 marginal commentary is in direct reference to the subject of the adjacent biblical text, where Ezekiel rebukes negligent watchmen (here read as the clergy):

> if the watchman see the sword coming, and sound not the trumpet: and the people look not to themselves, and the sword come, and cut off a soul from among them: he indeed is taken away in his iniquity, but I will require his blood at the hand of the watchman.[35]

What makes the commentary particularly remarkable is its conscious engagement with John Wyclif's use of the same verse from Ezekiel to argue 'in what way a watchman negligent in his office is an underlying cause of trial to the people, and a traitor of his guard', referring here to the heretical tenet that spiritual power was subject to temporal authority.[36] Moreover, Ezekiel 33 had considerable resonance with reformers and inquisitors alike: the chapter, for example, was drawn upon in 1415 by both the heretic Jerome of Prague and his examiner Robert Hallum, president of the English nation at the Council of Constance.[37]

The Traquair marginalia adds to a small group of survivals from what can now be identified as a fairly substantial lost corpus of writings against heresy. The works that are known to be lost from St Andrews are suggestive of a vibrant intellectual culture and a full engagement with canon law and heterodox theologies. During his tenure as Papal Inquisitor, for instance, Laurence of Lindores wrote a number of tracts against Lollardy. None appear to have survived, but three are identified in other works: *Election and the Power of the Elect*; *An Examination of the Heretical Lollards who Spread throughout the Realm*; and *The*

---

[33] Poleg, 'The Earliest Evidence for Anti-Lollard Polemics in Medieval Scotland', pp. 228, 233–4. The Traquair Bible is now in the private collection of Traquair House, Peeblesshire. Although only two surviving works can be traced to Culross Abbey, we know that it was an important intellectual hub and centre of manuscript production in medieval Scotland. See London, Lambeth Palace Library MS 440, fol. 2r; John Higgitt, *Scottish Libraries* (London, 2006), pp. 167, 222, 387–8.

[34] Poleg, 'The Earliest Evidence for Anti-Lollard Polemics in Medieval Scotland', p. 234.

[35] Ibid., pp. 227–34, 239.

[36] Ibid., pp. 231–2.

[37] Matthew Spinka, *Jan Hus: A Biography* (Princeton, 1968), p. 247. On Hallum see *A Biographical Register of the University of Oxford* (Oxford, 1957–59), ii, pp. 854–5.

Process of Peter Krek, the English Heresiarch.[38] It is quite possible that copies of these tracts will one day be uncovered, for Lindores' writings were widely circulated and copied amongst students on the Continent (including in Prague during the rise of Hus), where his commentaries on Aristotle's *Physics* and *De Anima* – based on lectures he gave at the University of Paris – achieved considerable academic renown.[39]

Traces of arguments against heresy and trial proceedings of accused heretics have survived in some contemporary sources. In 1419, for example, an inquisition took place in the diocese of St Andrews into the heresies of Robert Harding, an English friar and master of theology. Harding had been appointed by the governor, Robert, duke of Albany, to argue and promote the case for continued obedience to Avignon at the Council of Perth in October 1418, which was called to discuss the outcome of the Council of Constance, the cause of significant ruptures in the political and ecclesiastical community.[40] During the council Harding revealed ten errors of thought and he was accused of heresy by Master John Elward, rector of the University of St Andrews.[41] John Fogo, master of theology at St Andrews and afterwards abbot of Melrose, wrote a polemical letter against Harding, which the chronicler Walter Bower declared an 'impressive refutation of Harding's case'. Fogo remained constant in his vehement resistance to heresy and in the early 1430s he wrote a book, which has not survived, against the heresies of Pavel Kravař, the Hussite evangelist who was burned at the stake in St Andrews.[42]

Of the heretical tracts that were circulating, virtually all have been lost because of the very nature of the inquisitorial process, which saw the burning of heretical writings as the only way of destroying the venomous errors contained therein. Indeed, during the trial of James Resby in 1408, Laurence of Lindores dramatically refuted Resby's writings, 'putting them into the fire and burning them', although – perhaps somewhat hopefully – the nineteenth-century historian

---

[38] Thomas Dempster, *Historia Ecclesiastica Gentis Scotorum* (Edinburgh, 1829) ii, p. 443.
[39] Krakow, Krakow University MS 2095 (BB XVIII 5) dating to 1406; Krakow University MS 705 (DD I 13) dating to 1417; Krakow University MS 2099 (BB XVIII 9), fols 1–73, dating to 1433; Erfurt, Erfurt University Library, MS 342, fols 1–179v, dating to 1436; Lübeck, Stadtbibliothek, MS lat. 141, dating to 1443; Krakow, Krakow University MS 1892 (BB XIX 1), dating to 1444; Munich, Bavarian State Library, MS Lat. 26974, dating to 1472; and two undated manuscripts, Krakow University MS 709 (CC VIII 44) and Erfurt MS quart. 317, fols 161–290. This is not an exhaustive list of Lindores manuscripts and there are almost certainly more to be found: there is some indication that Dublin, Trinity College Library EE.e.53, No. 4, might be an early printed version. For more see J. H. Baxter, 'Four "New" Medieval Scottish Authors', *SHR* 25 (1928), pp. 92–5. It is entirely plausible that sermons (which have barely been touched by historians) delivered by Thomas Livingston before the Council of Basel may reveal concerns with heresy. For more on Livingston at Basel see: Burns, 'Scottish Churchmen and the Council of Basle', pp. 6–7.
[40] *Scotichronicon*, viii, pp. 86–91.
[41] Ibid., pp. 88–9.
[42] Ibid., pp. 90–3.

Bellensheim suggested that copies were preserved by his followers and were being read at the time of the Reformation.[43] Likewise, when Pavel Kravař was burned at the stake in St Andrews in 1433, so too were his writings. A flavour of these might survive in three radical reformist treatises, *De anatomia Antichristi*, *De regno Antichristi* and *Sermones de Antichristi*, once erroneously ascribed to Jan Hus, then suggested to be the work of Kravař (although this attribution has also been recently disputed and the authorship is now unclear).[44] The recantation in 1435 of one St Andrews master, Robert Gardiner, included a wholehearted promise to seek, destroy and annihilate any copies of his heretical orations.[45]

The absence of ecclesiastical and inquisitorial court records has obscured the existence of much of the inquisitorial structure. Nevertheless, there is sufficient evidence in the existing record to confirm its place in the history of the Church in Scotland and it seems that the diocesan structures were crucial in the practice of inquisition. Parliament of 1425, for example, instructed 'that each bishop should cause an inquiry to be made by the inquisitors of heresy', who were to then be dealt with according to the laws of the Church in inquisitorial courts.[46] Writing in the 1440s, the chronicler Walter Bower remarked that 'whenever Lollardy or the Lollard heresy begins to sprout heresies of this kind in a kingdom, the inquisitors must strive to cut it down, calling for the help of the secular arm if need be'.[47] Papal inquisitors – who were often drawn from the Dominican order – worked alongside bishops in rooting out heresy.[48] But, in the case of Laurence of Lindores, the precise nature of his inquisitorial work cannot be extracted from his wider duties at the new University of St Andrews, where he was the principal theologian and held numerous senior posts within university administration.[49] Indeed, it is entirely plausible that Lindores' successes as an inquisitor contributed to these very appointments. In many ways Lindores' position in the university has obscured discussion of inquisition in St Andrews, for the survival of substantial early records of the university has

---

[43] Ibid., pp. 68–9.
[44] Matthew Spinka, 'Paul Kravař and the Lollard-Hussite Relations', *Church History* 25 (1956), pp. 19–21. Lawrence Moonan argues that these texts should not be attributed to Kravař on the sole basis of the arguments put forward by earlier scholars. See Lawrence Moonan, 'Pavel Kravař, and Some Writings Once Attributed to Him', *Innes Review* 27:1 (1976), pp. 3–23.
[45] StAUL, UYUY411.
[46] RPS, 1425/3/4. It has been argued that this act may have been inspired by the English Suppression of Heresy act of 1414 (2 Henry V, c. 7, *Statutes of the Realm*, ii, pp. 181–4). Thomson, *The Later Lollards*, p. 203.
[47] *Scotichronicon*, viii, pp. 280–1.
[48] On the Dominicans in Scotland see Janet P. Foggie, *Renaissance Religion in Urban Scotland: The Dominican Order, 1450–1560* (Leiden, 2003). For more on inquisitors see for example: *Praedicatores, Inquisitores*, i: *The Dominicans and the Medieval Inquisition*, ed. Wolfram Hoyer (Rome, 2004); Karen Sullivan, *The Inner Lives of Medieval Inquisitors* (Chicago, 2011); Christine Caldwell Ames, *Righteous Persecution: Inquisition, Dominicans, and Christianity in the Middle Ages* (Philadelphia, 2009).
[49] See for example *St Andrews Acta*, pp. 21, 29–30, 33; StAUL, UYUY411.

skewed studies of Lindores' life in that direction. Yet he was evidently an active and forceful inquisitor in the diocese and by 1408 – several years before the foundation of the university – he had already condemned a heretic to burning at the stake. The trial of James Resby, an English Wycliffite priest, took place after his arrest at Perth in 1408 for preaching Lollard heresies. Lindores' arguments against two of Resby's forty tenets were laid out by the chronicler Abbot Walter Bower, and it is clear from his account that Lindores prosecuted Resby with great enthusiasm.[50]

Over the course of the next decade there was a notable rise in the detection and prosecution of heresy in the town and diocese of St Andrews. In 1418 Laurence of Lindores was again in court at Perth, bringing charges against Robert Harding, the English friar who was accused after the Council of Perth.[51] From Bower's account we learn something more about the range and weight of the personnel involved in these trials. James Haldenstone, prior of the cathedral chapter of St Andrews, was also present and later took Laurence of Lindores to task for failing to condemn Harding during the trial.[52] In his rebuke, Haldenstone demonstrates substantial knowledge of the problems and argues that the heresies that James Resby first sowed in the kingdom had taken root and grown in the hearts of some. Moreover, he argued that Lindores had failed in his position as inquisitor and been careless with suppressing dangerous preachers such as Harding. Haldenstone chides: 'error cui non resistitur approbatur'.[53]

The pressure mounted and the inquisitorial structures expanded to deal with an increasing caseload. Around 1424 John Shaw, a monk from Dunfermline Abbey, was challenged by the academic authorities in St Andrews for unorthodox comments on the sentences of Peter Lombard, the standard textbook of theology at medieval universities. Again James Haldenstone was integral to the detection of this case, as the then dean of the faculty of theology; the trial was held in that faculty, ending with little more than the chastisement of Shaw's master, William de Spalding, and a recommendation for more robust policing of heterodox ideas amongst the student body.[54] Shaw appears to have emerged unscathed and went on to hold clerical appointments at Dunfermline and Urquhart. What this incident illustrates is the impulse to bring forward charges of heresy with haste in situations where there was little

---

[50] *Scotichronicon*, viii, pp. 66–73. See also *Registrum Episcopatus Glasguensis: Munimenta Ecclesie Metropolitane Glasguensis a Sede Restaurata Seculo Ineunte XII ad Reformatam Religionem* (Edinburgh, 1843), ii, p. 316, a brief chronicle in list form with entries dating 1067–1413. For more on Resby's trial see Lawrence Moonan, 'The Inquisitor's Arguments Against Resby, in 1408', *Innes Review* 47:2 (1996), pp. 127–35.

[51] Papal bulls – one to Lindores and one to the university – were expedited by Martin V from Florence on 11 July 1419 authorising Lindores to seize and detain Harding and make him desist. Notarial copies of the bulls are preserved in StAUL, UYUY150/1, fols 42v–44r. A transcription of two bulls is printed in Anderson, 'The Beginnings of St Andrews University', pp. 358–60. See also *Scotichronicon*, viii, pp. 88–9.

[52] *Copiale*, pp. 3–4; Spinka, 'Paul Kravař and the Lollard-Hussite Relations', p. 18.

[53] *Copiale*, pp. 3–4.

[54] Ibid., pp. 71–2.

evidence of real dissidence but where there might have been potential for serious consequences.

It is not until 1433 that the next case of heresy is recorded, this time a Hussite from Bohemia, Pavel Kravař. St Andrews was again the focus; Henry Wardlaw, the bishop of St Andrews, brought the accusations against Kravař and Laurence of Lindores, still in post as inquisitor, led the trial. Despite the loss of two extant records of the trial sometime after 1627, we can deduce that it is highly likely that an ecclesiastical council was called to hear the case, and it is possible that amongst its members were James Haldenstone, prior of St Andrews, and John de Crannach, bishop of Brechin, who may have known Kravař during their overlapping time in the English nation at the University of Paris.[55] Kravař was 'convicted, condemned, put to the fire and burned to ashes' on 23 July 1433, 'silenced by that venerable man Master Laurence of Lindores [...] who gave heretics or Lollards no peace anywhere in the kingdom'.[56]

Pavel Kravař, a Bohemian physician who had studied arts at Paris and medicine at Montpellier, came to St Andrews to win support for the Hussite cause at the Council of Basel. He had almost certainly read Quentin Folkhyrde's *Nova Scocie*, four reformist open letters written in 1410 by a small landholder in the parish of Lesmahagow,[57] which were translated into Czech and circulated amongst Hussite sympathisers.[58] He may also have been familiar with the philosophical works of Laurence of Lindores, which were used at the University of Prague.[59] Kravař arrived in St Andrews with letters from several Hussites in

---

[55] The two trial copies are recorded as extant in 1627 by Thomas Dempster, *Historia Ecclesiastica Gentis Scotorum*, ed. David Irving (Edinburgh, 1829). Kravař was recorded in the *Liber procuratorum* of the English nation at the University of Paris in 1415, which included scholars from central and eastern Europe, and a number of Scots, including John de Crannach, who was one of the most distinguished and well-known teachers in the faculty of arts. *Auctarium Chartularii Universitatis Parisiensis: Liber procuratorum Nationis Anglicanae (Alemanniae) in Universitate Parisiensi. Ab anno 1406 usque ad annum 1466*, ed. Henricus Denifle and Aemilius Chatelaine (Paris, 1937), pp. 190, 196, 197. Other scots that coincided with Kravař were William Croyser, Thomas Lauder, Patrick Young and John Borthwick.

[56] *Scotichronicon*, viii, pp. 276–81.

[57] While Lesmahagow Parish Church was in the diocese of Glasgow, Lesmahagow Priory was a dependent of Kelso Abbey in the diocese of St Andrews, which raises tantalising questions about the importance of Lesmahagow in the history of heresy and heterodoxy in medieval Scotland. For more on Folkhyrde and Lesmahagow see Sanderson, *Ayrshire and the Reformation*, p. 37.

[58] The Latin letters are in Prague, Archiv Univerzity Karlovy, MS 1925, fols 391v–393v; Bautzen, Archivverbund Stadtarchiv und Staatsfilialarchiv, MS VIII° 7a. The Czech translations of 1415 are in Vienna, Österreichische Nationalbibliothek, Cod. 4916, Han-Verschiedene: Theologische Sammelhandschrift, fols 5r–11v. Transcriptions can be found in Jan Sedlák, *M. Jan Hus* (Prague, 1915), appendix xiv, pp. 182–96; *Copiale*, pp. 230–6. See also Michael Van Dussen, 'Conveying Heresy: "A Certayne Student" and the Lollard-Hussite Fellowship', *Viator* 38:2 (2007), p. 217; Van Dussen, *From England to Bohemia*, pp. 66–7; MacNab, 'Bohemia and the Scottish Lollards', esp. pp. 11–16.

[59] Baxter, 'Four "New" Medieval Scottish Authors', pp. 92–3; Moonan, 'Pavel Kravař, and Some Writings Once Attributed to Him', pp. 8–9.

Prague recommending him as an 'outstanding' physician.[60] His purpose in St Andrews, one chronicler tells us, was 'to corrupt the kingdom of the Scots'.[61] One Hussite method of propagating messages was to send emissaries and manifestos to the potential locations of sympathisers. Indeed, almost contemporary manifestos, issued in 1430 and 1431, that proclaimed the basic tenets of Hussite belief and appealed for secular powers to fight against corrupt clergy, spread throughout Germany, France, Spain and England.[62] The four articles of Prague, the 'bedrock of the Hussite programme', were reiterated therein; and it is almost without question that Kravař would have expounded their virtues.[63] The timing is suggestive that St Andrews was also an intended destination for such manifestos and the town was, in every way, an attractive destination. It is not unreasonable to assume that Kravař expected to meet a receptive group of sympathisers in St Andrews. Moreover, the Hussites 'detested all branches of the religious orders, abhorred pilgrimages, and scorned the holy orders of the church and its power of the keys', and thus St Andrews was an obvious target for reformist preaching.[64]

The heightened awareness of the problems of heresy in St Andrews no doubt led to the prosecution two years later of Robert Gardiner, who was charged by the university with lecturing heresies within the faculty of canon law. On 27 October 1435 charges were laid against him by Laurence of Lindores before a council of university and ecclesiastical dignitaries. Gardiner quickly recanted and declared that he would never again support these propositions nor defend them in public or private.[65]

Scholars have often assumed that on Lindores' death the position of Papal Inquisitor lapsed; no further burnings took place until the sixteenth century, for instance, but this has somewhat obscured the picture. The fear of and concern with rooting out heresy was still an important priority, regardless of the actual number of instances of genuine heretical thought being detected. Three subsequent Papal Inquisitors were appointed: George Newton, rector of Bothwell

---

[60] *Scotichronicon*, viii, p. 277; Paul Vyšný, 'A Hussite in Scotland: The Mission of Pavel Kravař to St Andrews in 1433', *SHR* 82:1 (2003), pp. 1–19.
[61] *Scotichronicon*, viii, pp. 276–7.
[62] *Husitské Manifesty*, ed. Amedeo Molnár (Prague, 1986); 'Manifesty města Prahy z doby husitské', ed. František M. Bartõs, *Sborník příspěvků k dějinám hlavního města Prahy* 7 (1933), pp. 253–309; J. Prokes, 'Taborske manifesty z r 1430 a 1431', *Casopis Matice Moravske* 52 (1928), pp. 1–28. For more on Hussite propaganda see Thomas A. Fudge, *The Magnificent Ride: The First Reformation in Hussite Bohemia* (Aldershot, 1998), pp. 178–274; Josef Macek, *The Hussite Movement in Bohemia* (London, 1965).
[63] Vyšný, 'A Hussite in Scotland', p. 18; E. F. Jacob, 'The Bohemians at the Council of Basel, 1433', *Prague Essays: Presented by a Group of British Historians to the Caroline University of Prague on the Occasion of its Six-hundredth Anniversary*, ed. R. W. Seton-Watson (Oxford, 1949), pp. 81–123; Howard Kaminsky, *A History of the Hussite Revolution* (Eugene, 2004), pp. 369–75.
[64] *Scotichronicon*, viii, pp. 278–9.
[65] *St Andrews Acta*, pp. clxxxi, 39–41; Anderson, 'The Beginnings of St Andrews University', p. 239.

(and nephew of Henry Wardlaw, bishop of St Andrews), was inquisitor from Lindores' death in 1437; Robert de Essy, vicar of Auchterhouse, was inquisitor by December 1493; and James Haldenstone, prior of the cathedral chapter of St Andrews, held the post of inquisitor by May 1440.[66] Of these three, Haldenstone in particular had long played a prominent role in inquisition and it was reputed that he 'refuted heretics fiercely every day'. In December 1436, when Lindores was still in post, Haldenstone received a letter that attacked him personally for persecuting heretics with such vigour. This letter brought about a new inquisitorial strand, for the letter claimed to be from the house of Archibald Douglas, fifth earl of Douglas, but Haldenstone found this claim to lack credibility. Instead, he suspected it was written by one of the canons of the cathedral priory, whereupon he instructed his subprior to seek out the author of the letter from amongst the canons and extract a confession.[67]

No evidence of papal-appointed inquisitors has survived after Haldenstone's death in 1443, although it seems probable that the bishop of St Andrews retained authority over the detection of heresy in the diocese. Certainly the charge of heresy retained currency, despite its ever-widening application, and in a politically motivated attempt to oust the first archbishop of St Andrews from his post, heresy was amongst the accusations laid against Patrick Graham in the late 1470s.[68]

St Andrews was thus the heart of the detection and discussion of heresy in late medieval Scotland. And it is clear why St Andrews would have attracted heterodox, heretical and reformist thinkers: it had a convenient coastal location for access; there were relics of an apostle that attracted pilgrims from all over Europe; and it was the premier ecclesiastical centre of the kingdom, the seat of the premier bishop, a centre of learning, and the home of many religious houses. It is also evident that in that context, robust and prominent anti-heretical detection and teaching were a significant part of life in late medieval St Andrews.

---

[66] StAUL, UYUY411; *St Andrews Acta*, p. 89; *CPL*, viii, pp. 578–9.
[67] *Copiale*, pp. 136–7.
[68] *CPL*, xiii, p. 226; J. A. F. Thomson, 'Some New Light on the Elevation of Patrick Graham', *SHR* 40 (1961), pp. 87–8; Leslie Macfarlane, 'The Primacy of the Scottish Church, 1472–1521', *Innes Review* 20:2 (1969), esp. pp. 111–12; Norman Macdougall, *James III: A Political Study* (Edinburgh, 1982), pp. 104–7; John Herkless and Robert Kerr Hannay, *The Archbishops of St Andrews*, volume 1 (Edinburgh, 1907), pp. 1–79.

APPENDIX ONE

*The St Andrews Foundation Account**

Simon Taylor

THE two Latin texts translated in appendices 1 and 2 are (1) the St Andrews Foundation Account B [hereafter FAB], also known as the longer St Andrews Foundation Legend or Foundation Legend B, and (2) the Augustinian's Account [hereafter AA]. They are generally treated as two separate entities, but were conceived of as one text by their mid-twelfth-century compiler, who was almost certainly Robert, first prior of the cathedral priory of St Andrews. A crucial and unique text for understanding the politics of church and state in the period in which it was compiled, it also presents a twelfth-century version and vision of the early history of both. There is a no less important shorter St Andrews Foundation Account, known as Foundation Account A [hereafter FAA].[1] Only the translation of FAB is given here. For the Latin text with full editorial apparatus, the reader is referred to *PNF*, iii, Appendix 1, where this translation can also be found.

FAB and AA survive as a continuous text only in an eighteenth-century copy of the lost St Andrews Register (London, BL Harleian MS 4628, fos 224v to 238r) [hereafter H]. This manuscript is described by Marjorie Anderson,[2] and the two texts are printed in W. F. Skene's *Chronicles of the Picts: Chronicles of the Scots* (Edinburgh, 1867), no. XXXI (pp. 183–93) [hereafter S], with no break between the two (FAB pp. 183–8, AA pp. 188–93). In the copy of the St Andrews Register, and presumably also in the Register itself, now lost, FAB is

---

* Several scholars have over the years made important contributions to the translations here, in particular Philip Burton, formerly of the School of Classics, University of St Andrews, now of Classics, Ancient History and Archaeology, University of Birmingham, for his indispensable help with editing and translating both FAB (Appendix 1) and AA (Appendix 2) when these texts were being prepared for publication in *PNF*, iii. Other scholars who helped with various aspects of the process are mentioned by name in *PNF*, iii, Preface, p. xi. I am also most grateful to the Carnegie Trust for their financial support, which several years ago allowed me to examine the Wolfenbüttel manuscript containing the two earliest versions of the longer Foundation Account (FAB).
[1] For more on FAA, see D. Broun, 'The Church of St Andrews and its Foundation Legend in the Early Twelfth Century: Recovering the Full Text of Version A of the Foundation Legend', *Kings, Clerics and Chronicles in Scotland, 500–1297*, ed. S. Taylor (Dublin, 2000), pp. 108–14.
[2] Marjorie O. Anderson, 'St Andrews before Alexander I', *The Scottish Tradition*, ed. G. W. S. Barrow (Edinburgh, 1974), pp. 1–13, at pp. 10–11.

immediately preceded (on fo. 224v) by a list of priors headed by Prior Robert himself (1140) and ending with the succession of John of Forfar in 1313. The fact that Prior John is the last in this list, and that the year of his death (1321) is not given, suggests that the list was compiled during his priorship. It also suggests that this is when the combined text of FAB and AA, which as we have seen immediately follows the succession of priors, was copied into the Register. It is probably significant that it was also during John's priorship that the cathedral church of St Andrews was consecrated, with great ceremony, on 5 July 1318. This was not only a major celebration of the cult of Andrew, who by this time had become Scotland's patron saint; it was also 'in part, at least, a vindication of Scottish independence'.[3] It would therefore have been an ideal time to re-copy older manuscripts dealing with what was regarded as the very beginnings of the Scottish Church.

While AA exists only in H (fos 230v to 238r), FAB exists in two other versions which were copied in St Andrews by the same hand into a single manuscript sometime in the early 1300s, and it is quite possible that they belong to this same burst of activity concerning the early history of the church of St Andrews around the time of the consecration of the cathedral in 1318. The two versions are contained in Wolfenbüttel MS, Cod. Guelf. 1108 Helmst, the first version on fos 28v–30v (hereafter W1), the second version on fos 32v–35r (hereafter W2). For his edition Skene had access only to H. In 1974 Marjorie Anderson described W1 and W2, collating them against H and S,[4] but it was not until 2010 that a complete edition and translation appeared in print (*PNF*, iii, pp. 567–79).

The St Andrews Foundation Account as found in FAB purports to have been written in the mid ninth century by Thana or Chana son of Dubabrach at Meigle. It forms an introduction or preamble to the Augustinian's Account (AA), which can be dated between 1140 and 1153. In its present form FAB was almost certainly compiled at the same time, and by the same writer. However, FAB consists of the splicing together of several texts, one of which may go back to the period claimed for it by the colophon, that is to say to the mid ninth century. It is striking, for instance, that several of the places in FAB have two names, an earlier and a later one. These are: 'the place which is called Ardchinnechena<n> within the harbour now called Queen's Ferry'; the place 'which had been called' Muchros, 'now' Kilrymont; *Doldauha* 'now called' Kindrochit (later known as Braemar); *Monethatha* 'now called' Mondynes; and Naughton MacIrb (*Hyhatnachten Machehirb*), 'which is now called' Naughton. There are probably several different motivations behind such usage. It is very likely that some of these name-forms do indeed go back to Pictish times, and were found by the compiler in his source or sources. They were then identified with 'modern' places to make the geography of the narrative more accessible and credible to a

---

[3] Ronald G. Cant, 'The Building of St Andrews Cathedral', McRoberts, *St Andrews*, pp. 11–32, at p. 27.
[4] Anderson, 'St Andrews before Alexander I', pp. 10–13.

twelfth-century audience. Others, however, in particular Muchros, may represent a deliberate attempt to give the text a spurious antiquity.

FAB remained an important document throughout the medieval period. Besides the two early fourteenth-century copies made at St Andrews (W1 and W2), the later fourteenth-century chronicler John Fordun, or rather his source, the 'proto-Fordun', clearly had access to a version of FAB for his account of the arrival of St Andrew's relics in Scotland.[5] He followed it especially closely in the list of names of St Regulus's companions. Fordun was, in the mid fifteenth century, copied and expanded upon by Abbot Walter Bower in his *Scotichronicon*, the list of companions appearing in chapter 59.[6] The readings both of Fordun MS A (F) and *Scotichronicon* CCCC MS 171 (C), probably also the best witness of Fordun's chronicle, have been noted in the edition of the text (*PNF*, iii, pp. 567–75). Furthermore, Prior James Haldenstone of St Andrews (1417–43) quotes almost verbatim from FAB in his fund-raising letter for the fabric of St Andrews church.[7]

The following translation is based on W1, with variant readings from W2, H and (where appropriate) S. The sigla used are:

C Corpus Christi College, Cambridge (CCCC) MS 171 (*Scotichronicon*).

F John of Fordun's Chronicle (MS A), Wolfenbüttel MS, Cod. Guelf. 538 Helmst.[8]

H British Museum, Harleian MS 4628, fos 224v to 238r (18th century). This is prefaced to the so-called Augustinian's Account; the combined texts are printed in William F. Skene's *Chronicles of the Picts: Chronicles of the Scots* (Edinburgh 1867), no. XXXI (pp. 183–93) (hereafter S); it is obvious that Skene had access only to H.

S Skene *Chron. Picts-Scots* no. XXXI (pp. 183–88). See also under H.

W1 Wolfenbüttel MS, Cod. Guelf. 1108 Helmst, fos 28v–30v [late 13th–early 14th c.; same hand as W2]

W2 Wolfenbüttel MS, Cod. Guelf. 1108 Helmst, fos 32v–35r [late 13th–early 14th c.; same hand as W1]

Translation of FAB

The place-names are taken from W1. Those parts in W2 only have been placed within angled brackets < >. Those parts shared by W2 and H, but which are not in W1, have been placed within curly brackets { }.

---

[5] See Dauvit Broun, *Scottish Independence and the Idea of Britain from the Picts to Alexander III* (Edinburgh, 2007), pp. 227–9.

[6] Bk 2, chs 58–60, i, pp. 310–17. See also *Scotichronicon*, i, p. 404, where the editors make no mention of W1 or W2.

[7] *Copiale*, no. 65, p. 120; see FAB Text §2 (*PNF*, iii, p. 568); also Commentary to FAB Translation §1, below).

[8] For full details, see Dauvit Broun, *The Irish Identity of the Kingdom of the Scots* (Woodbridge, 1999), p. 20).

§1. In the year of the incarnation of our Lord Jesus Christ 345 Constantius grandson of Constantine son of Helena gathered a great army to plunder the city of Patras in order to avenge the execution of the blessed Andrew the Apostle of Christ, and to remove from there his remains. But on the third night, before the emperor entered the city with his army, an angel of God descending from Heaven appeared to the holy men who were guarding the remains of St Andrew the Apostle, and ordered the holy bishop Regulus to go with his clerics to the sarcophagus, in which were deposited the bones of the blessed Andrew, and to take from there three fingers of his right hand, and the arm between the elbow and the shoulder, and his knee-cap, and one of his teeth. They took these parts of his remains, just as the angel had commanded them, and put them in a very secret place. The following day after these relics had been put away, Emperor Constantius came at dawn with his army and plundered both the city and the province; and took with him to Rome the casket in which he found the rest of the bones of the holy apostle had been placed. On his arrival there he ravaged the island of the Tiber, and the Colosseum, and took with him from there to Constantinople the bones of St Luke the Evangelist, and of Timothy the disciple of the blessed Paul the apostle, along with the remains of the blessed Andrew.

§2. At that time Hungus son of Forso, the great king of the Picts, gathered his army against Athelstan the king of the Saxons, and pitched camp at the mouth of the river Tyne. That very night, before the two armies met, the blessed Andrew appeared to Hungus king of the Picts in his sleep, saying to him that the apostle himself would on the following day overcome the enemy army in such a way that Hungus would triumph fully over his enemies. To whom the king said; 'Who are you? And where do you come from?' The blessed Andrew replied saying, 'I am Andrew, apostle of Christ, and now I have come from Heaven, sent by God, to reveal to you that tomorrow I will overcome your enemies, and subjugate them to you, and having obtained a happy victory you will return home unharmed with your army, and my remains will be brought into your kingdom, and the place to which they will be brought with all honour and veneration will be famous until the last day of time.' With these words he vanished. So the king, on waking from his dream, told his men what the blessed Andrew had revealed to him while he slept. When they heard these things, the people of the Picts rejoiced and swore that they would with all diligence and for all time show veneration to the blessed Andrew, if those things which he had shown to their king were brought about. On the following day the Picts, made joyful by the Apostle's promise, prepared for battle; and having divided up the army they set seven ranks around their king. The Saxons divided up their army and took up a close formation around their king Athelstan in fourteen ranks. When battle was joined the Saxons, immediately deprived of all courage, by God's will, and with the holy apostle Andrew intervening on the side of the Picts, turned in flight. The head of Athelstan, king of the Saxons, was cut off, and countless Saxons were slaughtered. And King Hungus, possessed of victory, returning with no small army to his own land, ordered Athelstan's head to be brought with him and he had it fixed on a wooden stake in the place which is called *Ardchinnechena<n>* within the harbour now called Queen's Ferry. After this victory, obtained by heavenly means, the Saxons never dared attack the Picts.

§3. After a few days had passed after the happy victory of this war, the angel of God again came from Heaven to the blessed bishop Regulus, whom he addressed thus: 'By command of God on high do not delay to go to northern parts, towards the rising sun, with the remains of Andrew the disciple of Christ which at our warning you recently kept back; and in whatever place the ship which will carry you and your company across the sea is wrecked, with no danger to you or your companions, there you will lay the foundations of a church in the name of the Lord and of his Apostle Andrew. For that place will be for you and your companions your resting place forever, and there will be your resurrection on the day of the last judgment.' And Bishop Regulus, according to the precept of the angel, accompanied by holy men, with the remains of the holy apostle, sailed towards the north, and for the space of one and a half years, driven by many violent storm winds, founded an oratory in honour of St Andrew wherever throughout the islands of the sea of Greece he was brought to land. And so the holy men, having suffered innumerable toils along the sea coasts, with God as their guide, directed their sail towards the north, and landed on the night of St Michael in the land of the Picts, at a place which had been called Muchros, but is now called Kilrymont. Muchros means 'wood of pigs'. After the ship in which they were sailing had been wrecked on the rocks, they pitched tents for themselves there and fixed in the ground a cross which they had brought with them from Patras as a sign of the sacred things which they had brought, and as a protection against the snares of demons. And there they remained for seven days and as many nights. And leaving the older men there, St Damian and his brother Merinach, to guard the place, Regulus and the other men went to Forteviot with the relics of the most holy apostle Andrew, and there they found the three sons of King Hungus, Eoganán and Nechtan and Finguine Garb, and because their father was at that time on an expedition in Argyll, for whose life the sons were much concerned, they gave a tenth part of the city of Forteviot to God and St Andrew. Having erected a cross there the holy men blessed the place and those who dwelt there, the sons of the king.

§4. Then they went to *Monethatha*, which is now called Mondynes, and there the queen Finchem gave birth to a daughter to King Hungus, who was called Mouren. The body of the virgin Mouren is buried at Kilrymont, and no-one was buried there before her. Queen Finchem gave the house in which she had given birth to her daughter Mouren to God and St Andrew, and all the royal enclosure for ever. And having erected a cross there, they blessed the queen and that place. Then they crossed the mountains, i.e. the Mounth, and came to a place which was called *Doldauha* but is now called Kindrochit-Alian [Braemar]. There Hungus the great king of the Picts, on his way back from his expedition, met the holy men, and prostrated himself with all humility and reverence in front of the relics of St Andrew the Apostle when they were shown to him; and all the noble Picts who were with him prostrated themselves in front of the relics like their humble king. And the king gave to God and the holy apostle Andrew that place i.e. *Doldauha*, and built a church on the spot where the bare relics had been shown him. Then the king with the holy men crossed the mountains i.e. the Mounth and came to Mondynes. And there he built a church in honour of God and the blessed Apostle. And so the king with his holy men came to Forteviot, and there he built a basilica to God and the Apostle. Afterwards King Hungus, with the holy men, came to Kilrymont, and, going round the big site of the place, offered it to God and to St Andrew the Apostle to build there basilicas and oratories.

§5. Out of great devotion King Hungus and Bishop Regulus himself, and the other men went seven times round that very place, marked out by a clear sign. Having thus carried out the seven-fold circuit and perambulation, Bishop Regulus processed carrying above his head the relics of the holy apostle with all veneration, with his holy company following the bishop with songs and hymns. And the devout King Hungus followed them on foot, very devoutly pouring out profound prayers and thanks to God. And the most noble aristocrats of all the realm followed the king. Thus they commended that place to God, and fortified it with royal permission <on 6 February>. As a sign of royal favour, the holy men erected 12 stone crosses at intervals around the circumference of the place; and they humbly begged God of heaven, that all who pray in that place with a devout mind and pure intention may obtain the fulfilment of their petition.

Afterwards King Hungus gave to the church of the holy apostle as a *parochia* whatever land is between the sea which is called the Firth of Forth, as far as the sea which is called Firth of Tay; and in the adjacent province along its bounds from Largo, as far as Ceres <of the Dogs or of the Cains?>; and from Ceres as far as Naughton MacIrb (*Hyhatnachten Machehirb*), which land is now called Naughton. And the king gave this place, that is Kilrymont, to God and St Andrew his apostle, with waters, with fields, with meadows, with pastures, with muirs, with woods in alms for ever; and he endowed that place with such liberty that its inhabitants will always be free and quit of hosting, and of castle- and bridge-work, and of the trouble of all secular exactions.

§6. Bishop Regulus sang the prayer Alleluia so that God might forever protect that place given in alms, and guard it in honour of the apostle. As a reminder of the liberty granted King Hungus seized a divot and in front of his Pictish nobles bore it as far as the altar of St Andrew, and on it he placed that same divot as an offering. This was done in the presence of these witnesses: Talorc son of Iarnbodb, Nechtan son of Chelturan, Gartnait son of Dubnach, Drust son of Wythrossi, Nacthaleth son of Gigherti, Shinach son of Litheren, Oengus son of Foichele, Feradach son of Finlaech, Fiachna Finn son of Bolg, Gilunineruh son of Taran, Demene son of Chinganena, Dubtalorg son of Bargoit. Those witnesses are born of royal stock.

Afterwards in Kilrymont the holy men built seven churches. One in honour of St Regulus; the second in honour of St Aneglas {the deacon}; the third in honour of St Michael the Archangel; the fourth in honour of St Mary the virgin; the fifth in honour of the honourable St Damian the elder; the sixth in honour of St Brigid the virgin; the seventh in honour of a certain Mouren the virgin, and in that church were 50 virgins born of royal stock, all dedicated to God, having taken the veil at eleven years of age, and all buried in the eastern part of that church.

These are the names of those men who brought the holy relics of St Andrew the apostle to Scotland: Bishop Regulus, Gelasius the deacon, Matheus the hermit, St Damian the priest and Merinachus his brother, Nermus and Chusemus from the island of Crete, Mirenus and Chubaculus the deacon, Natchabeus and Silicius his brother, seven hermits from the island of Tiber(is), Felix, Saranus, Mauritius, Madianus, Philipphus, Eugenius, Lucius; and three virgins from Collossia, viz Triduana, Potentia, Emeria. These virgins are buried in the church of St Anaglas.

Cano son of Dubabrach wrote this record for King Uurad son of Bargoit in the estate of Meigle.

End of Foundation Account B

Commentary

This section contains comments on individual names and passages in the above text, drawn mainly from the section called 'Notes' in *PNF*, iii, pp. 579–600.

§1. FAB's account of the first translation of the corporeal relics of Andrew derives ultimately from St Jerome, although it has been changed in some details. According to Jerome, Constantius, the son of Constantine, takes the relics of Timothy from Rome to Constantinople in 356, while he takes those of Andrew and Luke from Rome to Constantinople in 357. FAB, in contrast, calls Constantius grandson (*nepos*) of Constantine, and it has the bones of Luke and Timothy brought to Constantinople in the same expedition.[9] Constantius was in fact the son of Constantine, and was emperor of the eastern Empire 337–61. The Fordun text, unlike FAB, has the correct relationship between the two emperors.

Patras: The modern Greek city of Patrai. The tradition which connects Andrew with Patrai seems to be no older than the fourth century.[10]

---

[9] Ursula Hall, *St Andrew and Scotland* (St Andrews, 1994), p. 27; Anderson, 'St Andrews before Alexander I', p. 7 n. 57.

[10] See Hall, *St Andrew*, pp. 10–12. For later evidence of the cult of Andrew at Patrai, see ibid., pp. 81–2.

the bones of the blessed apostle: a detailed list of the apostle's bones to be found at St Andrews is given by several late medieval writers. When Prior James Haldenstone writes in the early fifteenth century of the relics that form the basis of St Andrews' claim to precedence over the other Scottish churches, it is clear that he is drawing on this text: 'the right arm ... from the shoulder to the elbow, and three fingers of his right hand, and his right knee-cap, with one tooth and another bone from his glorious head'.[11] This last bone, 'another bone from his glorious head', is the only one which is not mentioned in FAB. Note that in another context Haldenstone quotes almost verbatim from FAB (for full details, see *PNF*, iii, p. 568 n. 44).

St Andrew's arm was an object of special veneration: to it Edward I and his queen each offered a jewel on March 13 and 19 respectively, 1304.[12]

Rome: this detour to Rome derives at least partly from Jerome: 'The relics (*Reliquiae*) of Timothy the Apostle were brought to Constantinople' (356 AD);[13] and 'After Constantius had been to Rome, the bones of Andrew the Apostle and Luke the Evangelist were received by the citizens of Constantinople with wonderful acclaim (*a Constantinopolitanis miro favore*)'[14] (357 AD). Similarly, Jerome writes in *Liber de Viris Illustribus* cap. 7: 'In the 20th year of Constans,[15] the bones of Luke with the relics (*reliquiis*) of Andrew the Apostle were translated to Constantinople (*Constantinopolim*).'[16]

island of Tiber and Colossia: These may be Tiber Island (the only island in the River Tiber at Rome) and the Colosseum, also in Rome. They seem to have been added by the writer of FAB to add local colour, as they are not to be found in earlier accounts of the removal of Andrew's relics by Constantius. Both names are repeated at the end of FAB, but in a different context: amongst those who accompanied Regulus to Scotland were seven hermits (all named) 'from

---

[11] 'brachium dextrum ... ab humero usque ad cubitum, et tres digiti manus eius dextre, et patella de genu eius dextro, cum uno dente et alio osse de capite eius glorioso' (*Copiale*, no. 65, p. 120).

[12] *Calendar of Documents relating to Scotland*, ed. J. Bain et al., 5 vols (Edinburgh 1881–1986), iv, p. 486.

[13] *Patrologia Latina*, ed. J. P. Migne, 221 vols (Paris 1844–64) (hereafter *PL*), xxvii, pp. 687–8.

[14] *PL*, xxvii, pp. 689–90; translation from Anderson, 'St Andrews before Alexander I', p. 7 n. 57. Jerome's text is also quoted in the Annals of Ulster (*Annals of Ulster (to 1131)*, ed. S. Mac Airt and G. Mac Niocaill (Dublin, 1983) (hereafter AU) under the year (of the world) 4396 (with *Constantinapolitanis* for *Constantinopolitanis*), being wrongly translated by the modern editors as: 'When Constantius had entered Rome, the bones of the apostle Andrew and of Lucas the evangelist were brought by great favour from Constantinople' (AU, p. 33).

[15] An error for Constantius, emperor 337–61, ruling jointly in the first part of his reign with his brothers Constans (337–50) and Constantine II (337–40), all sons of Emperor Constantine I.

[16] *PL*, xxvii, p. 689.

the island of Tiber(is)'; and three virgins (all named) from Collossia. See §6, below, under **Tiberis** and **Collossia**.

§2. **Hungus son of Forso**: This represents the Pictish Unust/Unuist/Onuist son of Uurguist,[17] Old Gaelic Oengus mac Fergusso (alternatively Forgosso, which may lie behind *Forso*) and English Angus son of Fergus. There were two Pictish kings of this name and this patronymic: Unust I c.729–61 and Unust II (king of the Picts 820–34). Within the terms of FAB, it appears that Unust II is meant, since one of his sons is Howonam (= Eoganan/Uuen), the name of Unust II's son, who ruled as king of Picts 836–39. This is certainly the interpretation put upon the Legend by various king lists (for which see next paragraph), as well as by Fordun and Wyntoun. However, A. O. Anderson writes that these legends 'probably have as their basis the establishment of a monastery near St Andrews during the reign of Angus [I]' (*Early Sources of Scottish History, AD 500 to 1286* (Edinburgh, 1922), i, p. 267), conceding that it is possible that the relics were brought to Scotland during the reign of Angus II, that the monastery was enlarged, or a new church [or churches] built. For the likelihood that in fact both the establishment of the church and the acquisition of relics belong to the era of Unust I, see pp. 00, above.

Marjorie Anderson, in her ground-breaking book *Kings and Kingship in Early Scotland* (published 1973, revised edition 1980), examines this whole matter in more detail. She distinguishes two groups of lists containing the names and reign-lengths of Pictish kings, the so-called Pictish Regnal Lists, List P and List Q.[18] List Q was attached to a Scottish Regnal List in the reign of Alexander II (1214–49), to form the source of F, I, D and K, and lists used by Fordun and Wyntoun.[19] List P, with strong Abernethy connections, tended to preserve Pictish forms of names ungaelicised, while Q, with strong St Andrews connections, generally preferred to use Gaelic forms of names (ibid., pp. 96, 102). In fact, after 724 Q uses only Gaelic forms of names, with one notable exception: this is the name of the king known variously as Angus II son of Fergus, Oengus II mac Fergusa (Old Gaelic) or Unust II son of Uurguist (Pictish), who reigned from 820 to 834. His name appears in Q as Hungus, and beside his name and reign-length a note is added to the effect that he built Kilrymont (ibid.,

---

[17] For a discussion of the spelling of these Pictish name-forms, see Katherine Forsyth (with an appendix by John T. Koch), 'Evidence of a Lost Pictish Source in the *Historia Regum Anglorum* of Symeon of Durham', *Kings, Clerics and Chronicles in Scotland, 500–1297*, ed. S. Taylor (Dublin, 2000), pp. 19–34, at p. 24.

[18] P is often now referred to as *Series Longior* (SL) i.e. the longer list, Q as *Series Brevior* (SB), using Molly Miller's designations ('Matriliny by treaty: the Pictish foundation-legend', *Ireland in Early Mediaeval Europe: Studies in Memory of Kathleen Hughes*, ed. Dorothy Whitelock, Rosamund McKitterick and David N. Dumville (Cambridge, 1982), pp. 133–61).

[19] *Kings and Kingship*, p. 77. These make up the so-called X group of Scottish Regnal Lists. Each letter represents a separate copy of the regnal list, with no copy earlier than the twelfth century. Full details can be found in the chapter entitled 'The Scottish Regnal Lists' (*Kings and Kingship*, pp. 44–76).

pp. 97–8).²⁰ As Anderson points out, it can hardly be coincidence that both FAA and FAB call the founder king by this same name (Ungus or Hungus). This survival of the Pictish form may have been due to textual, oral or liturgical tradition maintained at St Andrews itself, but, as she quite correctly points out, it does little to help us decide which of the two kings called Unust son of Uurguist was the actual founder of the church of St Andrew (ibid., pp. 98–9).

Athelstan the king of the Saxons: No English king of this name died during the reign of either of the Pictish kings called Unust. Fordun, followed by Bower, confuses the matter still further by dating the battle to 802 and identifying Athelstan with the son of Aethelwulf king of Wessex (and thus the brother of King Alfred). This Athelstan, king of Kent, Sussex, Surrey and Essex, died 851×56.²¹ For the suggestion that the king in question may have been the mid-eighth-century Mercian king Æthelbald, see Woolf, 'Onuist Son of Uurguist', p. 39.

Tyne: Wyntoun (*Chron. Wyntoun*, VI, ch. 7 (ii, p. 82)) is the first to explicitly identify the Tyne with the East Lothian river of that name as opposed to the northern English Tyne. Fordun (IV, ch. 13) locates the battle on the Tyne, implying that it is in East Lothian because he tells us that Athelstan was no longer in his own country. Both Wyntoun loc. cit. and Bower (*Scotichronicon*) loc. cit. use the place-name Athelstaneford ELO as further evidence for this location, although Athelstaneford is not on the Tyne but on the upper reaches of the Peffer Burn. The personal name Alstan or Elstan, which appears in the earliest forms of the name, is the later Middle English (and Older Scots) development of OE Æþelstān. These forms are:

firma molendini de *Alstaneford'* 1213, *RRS*, ii, no. 517 [original document]
ecclesia de *Elstanford* c.1250, *Dunf. Reg.*, no. 313
Elstanfurd 1420, *Chron. Wyntoun*, ii, 82
Athelstanford c.1440, *Scotichronicon*, bk 4, ch. 13 (vol. ii)

Bower's expanded form shows conscious archaising on his or his source's part, and this tradition has survived in the modern written form. The modern local pronunciation, however, is Elstanford, with stress on the first syllable, and descends directly from the earliest written forms.

For the suggestion that the original battle which may lie behind this story lay

---

[20] 'Hungus f. Fergusane ix annis reg[navit]. Iste edificavit *Kilremonth*' (D, Anderson, *Kings and Kingship*, 1980 edn, p. 266); 'Hungus fil. Fergusa x an. Hic aedificavit Kilremont' (F, Harleian 4628; *Kings and Kingship*, p. 273); 'Hungus fitz Fergusa .x. aunz, cesty edifia *Kelrimonech* ore *saint Andrew*, quel temps veint Fegulus [for 'Regulus'] od sez discipl' al eglis de saint Andrew' ('at which time Regulus and his disciples came to the church of St Andrew') (K, *Scalacronica*, mid-fourteenth century, *Kings and Kingship*, p. 287 (text), p. 66 (commentary)).

[21] See *Scotichroniconi*, ii (bk 4, ch. 13) and notes to pp. 461–2.

far to the south, in the English Midlands, see Woolf, 'Onuist Son of Uurguist', p. 39.

the place to which they will be brought with all honour and veneration will be famous until the last day: Bower's version of this story (*Scotichronicon*, bk 4, ch. 14) does not mention the arrival of the relics of Andrew. For a comparison of different versions of this story, see A. O. Anderson, *Early Sources of Scottish History, AD 500 to 1286* (Edinburgh, 1922), i, pp. 266–7.

Ardchinnechena<n> or **Ardchinnechena<m>**: A Gaelic place-name, the first two elements certainly represent *àird* and *cinn*, gen. of *ceann*, 'height/promontory of (the) head'. The third element is obscure, but it may be Gaelic *cù* (genitive singular *coin*) 'dog', the whole name thus meaning 'height of the head of the dog',[22] the dog perhaps a derogatory metaphor for Athelstan. While the place-name may indeed contain the dog-word, it is very unlikely that this was the origin of the name; rather we are dealing with an elaborate *dindsenchus* or place-name story which has been cleverly woven into the wider narrative. Ardchinnechena<n> would seem to refer to the rocky height above North Queensferry. Fordun, Wyntoun and Bower all draw on this account. Fordun (IV, chapter 14) states that the head was fixed on a stake at the top of a rock 'in the middle of the Scottish sea (i.e. the Firth of Forth)' (in medio maris Scottice). Wyntoun (iv, p. 171) has:

> Than bere it [hys hede] to the Qwenys-ferry
> In to that crage he gert but lete ['without delay']
> That hewyd apon a stayke be sete.

This also suggests the height at North Queensferry, at the Fife or north end of the Forth Rail Bridge. Bower (*Scotichronicon*, bk 4, ch. 14), taking his lead from Fordun, adds 'at a certain island beside Queen's Ferry which is called Inchgarvie' (apud quandam insulam juxta Portum Regine que *Inchgerri* vocatur). Inchgarvie is the small rocky island immediately below the Forth Rail Bridge, on the south (Lothian) side (Dalmeny parish).[23]

Queen's Ferry: Literally 'the Queen's Harbour' or 'Port'. This is of course another anachronism, since the eponymous queen is Margaret, who died in 1093. The earliest form of this name recorded by MacDonald is in 1184, as *Passagium Sancte Margarete Regine*. His earliest form with *Portus* is from 1364.[24] The Gaelic name for Queensferry is recorded in the seventeenth century as *Caschilis*, for *cas chaolas* 'steep strait' (see PNF, i, p. 382).

---

[22] Unfortunately W2 omits this line, so there is less certainty than is usual as to the underlying reading.
[23] Adapted from *PNF*, i, pp. 381–2.
[24] Angus MacDonald, *The Place-Names of West Lothian* (Edinburgh and London 1941), p. 11. See also *PNF*, i, p. 380.

§3. **night of St Michael** (nocte S. Michaelis):[25] Michaelmas is 29 September. McRoberts points out that St Andrews had one of the earliest recorded dedications to the archangel in Britain.[26] In the later Middle Ages, the most important indulgence at St Andrews seems to have been that granted for the feast of St Michael and its octave, and was known in Scots as 'the Michaelmas pardon'.[27]

Kilrymont: For a full discussion of this name, see *PNF*, iii, s.n. The earliest datable form of this name with Gaelic *cill* 'church' as opposed to original *ceann* 'head, end' as the first or generic element is 1128×36. As M. O. Anderson points out, '*Kil*-forms in various literary texts are to be attributed to scribes who wrote later than the 1130s' ('St Andrews before Alexander I', p. 1).

Muchros means 'wood of pigs': For more details on Muchros # (St Andrews and St Leonards parish), see *PNF*, iii, s.n. The translation of *ros* as 'grove, wood' (*nemus*) reflects Irish usage rather than that of eastern Scotland, where it means exclusively 'promontory, head-land'. Muckersie (*Mucrosin*), a medieval parish beside Forteviot PER, also contains these elements, with the addition of a locational suffix *-in* 'pig-promontory place'. This suggests that someone responsible for a recension of the text was familiar with Irish Gaelic. In fact Muchros was almost certainly an earlier or alternative name for the headland on which St Andrews Cathedral and Priory now stand.

Apart from two places in Ireland called Muckross, there is also Moccas (Court) on the Wye, Herefordshire SO358433, earlier *Mochros*, which plays an important role in the Life of St Dubricius (Dyfrig), the alleged founder of the diocese of Llandaff (in Cardiff).[28]

Merinach: Boece 1527 has 6 February as the day of 'Merinus a monk of Paisley' (Merini monachi Basiliani), who, arriving along with St Regulus, brought the precious relics of the father St Andrew the apostle protector of the realm.[29]

---

[25] McRoberts, *St Andrews*, pp. 63–120, at p. 94, translates this 'on the eve of St Michael's feast day', i.e. the day before the feast day, although Latin *vigilia* is the usual word for 'eve'. The early sixteenth-century *Breviarium Aberdonense* (Edinburgh, 1510, hereafter *BA*) (under 30 March, the feast of St Regulus) also interprets it thus, stating that Regulus and his companions arrived in the land of the Scots on 28 September (*quarto kalendas Octobris*). For a new edition and translation of the Scottish material in *BA*, see Alan Macquarrie with Rachel Butter (and contributions by Simon Taylor and Gilbert Márkus), *Legends of the Scottish Saints: Readings, Hymns and Prayers for the Commemorations of Scottish Saints in the Aberdeen Breviary* (Dublin, 2012). The office for St Regulus or Rule is on pp. 94–7 (text and translation).

[26] McRoberts, *St Andrews*, p. 94.

[27] McRoberts, *St Andrews*, pp. 94–5; for more on the cult of St Michael in Scotland, see David McRoberts, 'Cult of St Michael in Scotland', *Millénaire Monastique du Mont St Michel*, ed. M. Baudot (Paris, 1971) 3, pp. 471–9.

[28] For full details, see *PNF*, iii, pp. 584–5.

[29] Cited by A. P. Forbes in his *Kalendars of Scottish Saints* (Edinburgh, 1872), p. 191). It is found in Thomas Dempster's *Menologium Scotorum* (1622), reprinted in Forbes,

This would seem to be Mirren,[30] one of the patron saints of Paisley Abbey. *Breviarium Aberdonense* [*BA*] at 15 September has the acts of Merinus, and links him closely with Bangor, Co. Down.[31]

It is unlikely to have anything to do with the north Fife Cistercian Abbey of Balmerino for several reasons: firstly there does not appear to have been a religious foundation there until the founding of the monastery by Queen Ermengard in the late 1220s; secondly the forms of the name are *Balmurinach* or *Balmorinach* consistently through the medieval period (see *PNF*, iv, s.n.); and thirdly no such saint is recorded in documents originating at Balmerino.

Fortevieth: Forteviot lay in St Andrews diocese, deanery of Gowrie. The form of the name is consistent with a twelfth-century or later date for the text as it now stands. The disyllabic first element, from Gaelic *foithir*, probably an adaptation of a Pictish word meaning 'territory' (for which see *PNF*, v, Elements Glossary, s.v.), is clearly seen in tenth-century forms such as *Fothiurtabaicht* (Anderson, *Kings and Kingship*, p. 250), and is even discernible in the mid-twelfth-century *Fetherteuiet* 1162×64 (*RRS*, I, no. 256, an original document). However, at the same date, it is being recorded with a monosyllabic first element, as in *Ferteuieth* (1165×69, *RRS*, ii, no. 28, also an original document).

Forteviot is obviously considered very important by the compiler of FAB, presumably because of its early connections with the kings Cinaed I and Domnall I, with which he would be familiar from the same chronicles from which he extracted other names and places. It is the first place visited by St Regulus and his companions, along with the relics of St Andrew, after landing in St Andrews. We have no evidence for the medieval dedication of the church there but, as with Kindrochit (Braemar), where Regulus finally meets King Hungus and shows him the relics, and which certainly had an Andrew dedication, Forteviot church, too, may well have been dedicated to that saint.[32]

The church itself seems to have been the subject of some controversy, at least in the later Middle Ages, with rights in it being contested between Cambuskenneth Abbey and St Andrews Cathedral. For more details see *PNF*, iii, pp. 586–7.[33]

Kalendars, item X (pp. 177–229). He gives the source of this simply as Hector Boethius, *Historicus Scotorum* (i.e. Boece 1527). February 6th was associated with the arrival of the relics of St Andrew in Scotland in FAB W2 §5 (q.v.) and in *Scotichronicon* (bk 15, ch. 22 (viii, p. 79, line 34).

[30] W. J. Watson gives the Gaelic form of this name as Mearán (*CPNS*, 274).

[31] For a new edition and translation of the office of St Mirren (Sanctus Merinus) in *BA*, see Macquarrie et al., *Legends of the Scottish Saints*, pp. 212–15; for full notes on the saint, see ibid., pp. 392–3, which lists other probable or possible traces of his cult in Scotland as Kirkmirran, Kelton KCB (NX799549); St Mirrin's Well, Kilsyth STL (NS720780) and Cill Mhearáin, Clyne (Strathbrora) SUT.

[32] The modern parish kirk of Forteviot is dedicated to Andrew. I am grateful to Nick Evans for discussions on Forteviot.

[33] Leslie Alcock has suggested that the iconography on the famous Forteviot arch represented the three sons of Hungus with the cross that Regulus is said to have erected

The three sons are called **Howonam** (Pictish Uuen, Gaelic Eog(h)anan, whence Ewan: Uuen son of Unust was the king of the Picts who died in 839);[34] **Nechtan**, the Gaelic form of Pictish *Naiton*, the name of several Pictish kings, the most famous being Naiton son of Dargart (died 732); and **Phinguinegarf(e)**, the Gaelic name Fin(n)guine + epithet *garbh* 'rough'.[35]

§4. **Mondynes**: Fordoun parish KCD (St Andrews diocese, Mearns deanery); there can be no doubt that Mondynes correctly identifies '*Monethatha* which is now called *Monithi*'.[36] The patronage of the church there lay in royal hands until the reign of Robert I, when the king gave it to the church of St Andrew after the consecration of St Andrews Cathedral on 5 July 1318 in gratitude for his victory at Bannockburn (see *RRS*, v, no. 500, quoting *Scotichronicon*, bk 12, ch. 37 (vi, p. 413)). This gift of the church of a place which plays such an important role in FAB, and made at the time of the consecration, which was a great national event, is especially significant in the light of the suggestion put forward, above p. 00, that at least one version of FAB was re-copied at this time. Royal connections with Mondynes were strong: Donnchad II's murder at Mondynes in 1094 suggests there may have been a royal residence there at that time; and the king was disposing of demesne land there in the 1180s in a grant to Arbroath Abbey (*RRS*, ii, no. 277). However, an important agreement between Bishop William Malveisin of St Andrews on the one hand and the abbey of Arbroath on the other, which can be dated to 1219×26,[37] shows that the bishops of St Andrews, too, had an interest in Mondynes. The agreement settled a controversy which had arisen between the bishop and abbey 'anent the lands, rents and conveths of Fyvie ABD, Tarves ABD, Inverboyndie BNF, Montbrey, now part of Boyndie parish BNF, Gamrie BNF, Inverugie (St Fergus) ABD and Mondynes KCD' (super de *Fiuin* et de *Tharueis* de *Inuirbond*' de *Mumbee* de *Gamerin* de *Inuirugin* de *Monedin* terris et redditibus et coneuetis earumdem). Bishop William quitclaims all his rights to these lands except for 'the old rent from Mondynes' (antiquo redditu de *Monedin*), which is put at 3s 6d, as well as the portion of conveth[38] (right of hospitality) which the bishop was wont to exercise at Banchory (*Bencorin*; probably Banchory-Ternan, which lay in

---

there ('Forteviot: a Pictish and Scottish Royal Church and Palace', *The Early Church in Western Britain and Ireland*, ed. S. M. Pearce (Oxford, 1982), pp. 211–390). Note, however, that he makes no mention of this in his book *Kings and Warriors, Craftsmen and Priests in Northern Britain AD 550–850* (Edinburgh, 2003).

[34] See Anderson, *Early Sources*, i, p. 268.

[35] Fin(n)guine is the name borne by two important figures in early eighth-century Pictavia, one the half-brother of King Naiton, for details of whom see James Fraser, *From Caledonia to Pictland: Scotland to 795* (Edinburgh, 2009), pp. 272–3, 291–2.

[36] This identification was first made in *PNF*, iii, p. 587, to which the reader is referred for a full discussion, and rejection, of other candidates.

[37] *Arb. Lib.*, i, no. 169.

[38] A tribute due to the king or other lord in respect of his lordship, specifically hospitality, entertainment and accommodation, or some payment in lieu of these (*RRS*, ii, p. 52).

Aberdeen diocese). The other piece of evidence for a St Andrews interest in the royal estate of Mondynes is of course FAB itself.

As to the name, it is mentioned relatively early in the record because of the royal death there in 1094. From the various late witnesses to this event, *Monathedhen emerges as the best reading of this place-name.[39]

The *Extracta e Variis Cronicis Scocie* (published by the Abbotsford Club, 1842) has under 1094: 'Duncanus ... in regem susceptus. Qui dolo Douenaldi auxilio comitis de *Mernis* nomine Malpedir, apud *Monathechin* alias *Monythyne* cesus est' (*Chron. Extracta*, 63). This source is a fifteenth- or sixteenth-century compilation which has obviously used sources with both the older and the more recent form of the place of King Duncan II's murder, and has reconciled the two just as FAB has done.[40]

For a detailed analysis of this name, see *PNF*, iii, p. 589.

Finchem, Old Gaelic Findcaem: in O'Donnell's *Betha Colaim Chille* (completed in 1532), Findchaemh is the name of Mochonna or Macarius's mother (St Machar of Aberdeen). His father's name is Fiachna, king of Ireland.[41] The Scots version (fourteenth century) gives the names as *Synchene* and *Syaconus*.[42]

Mouren: this would appear to be the G female name Muirenn. It was borne by several important Irish women, two of them with tenuous Scottish connections. These are:

1) Muirenn daughter of the Leinster overking Cellach of Cualu (genitive Cualann), a territory covering the foothills of the Dublin Mountains. This famous king, who died 715 (Annals of Ulster [AU]), was the last Uí Máile king of Leinster.[43] He himself is mentioned in Annals of Ulster three times (704, 709 and 715), which also record the deaths of eight of his children, from 709 to 748: four sons and four daughters, including Caintigern[44] in 734 and Muirenn in 748. The name of Muirenn's sister Caintigern is closely associated with Inchcailloch, the island in Loch Lomond, the importance of which as an

---

[39] For full details of early forms, see *PNF*, iii, p. 588 n. 265.
[40] A. O. Anderson, in his introduction, writes laconically of this source: 'This is a 15th–16th c. compilation seldom referred to here.' (*Early Sources* i, p. lv).
[41] Brian Lacey's translation of Manus O'Donnell's *Betha Colaim Chille*, *The Life of Colum Cille* (Dublin, 1998), p. 134.
[42] *The Legends of SS Ninian and Machor from an Unique MS. in the Scottish Dialect of the Fourteenth Century*, ed. W. M. Metcalfe (Paisley, 1904), pp. 85–134.
[43] For more on him, see Alfred P. Smyth, *Celtic Leinster: Towards an Historical Geography of Early Irish Civilization AD 500–1600* (Dublin, 1982), pp. 65, 67, 81.
[44] AU 733.4: 'Caintigern, daughter of Cellach of Cualu, dies' (Caintigernd ingen Ceallaig Cualann moritur). For more on Caintigern (Kentigerna) as a possible candidate, in legend at least, for the mother of the Scottish St Fillan, see S. Taylor, 'The Cult of St Fillan in Scotland', *The North Sea World in the Middle Ages: Studies in the Cultural History of North-Western Europe*, ed. T. R. Liszka and L. E. M. Walker (Dublin, 2001), pp. 175–210, at pp. 181–2.

early religious centre can be deduced both from its name ('nun island') and from the fact that it was the centre of a medieval parish.[45] Furthermore the biggest of the islands in Loch Lomond, only c.2km south-west of Inchcailloch, is Inchmurrin, 'Muirenn's island', in the neighbouring parish of Kilmaronock DNB.[46]

(2) Muirenn daughter of Congalach, abbess of Kildare (comarba Brigti), died 979 (AU 978.1). Her father was presumably the Irish high king Congalach son of Maolmithigh (Mael Mithig), who was killed in 956. Her uncle, Congalach's brother Aodh (Aed), died on pilgrimage in St Andrews (hi Cind ri[g]monaidh) in 965 (Anderson, *Early Sources*, i, 472; see also above, p. 00). Her predecessor at Kildare was also called Muirenn. She belonged to different kindred, and it looks as if Congalach was involved in intruding his daughter into the abbey.

And having erected a cross there (at Mondynes), they blessed the queen and that place. This is one of several crosses mentioned in the text, and probably points to the existence of a Pictish cross-slab or some other early Christian carved monument here at the time of the compilation of the text.

Mounth: If this refers to the Mounth in its modern, more limited, sense, as the eastern outlier of the Grampians which reaches the North Sea north of Stonehaven, rather than to the Grampians as a whole, then the identification of *Monithi* with Mondynes is further strengthened, since it lies immediately south of the Mounth.

Doldauha: The place where Hungus first met the relics, and prostrated himself before them. It appears to be a genuine name, containing Pictish **dol* 'water-meadow, haugh'; this was borrowed into Gaelic as *dail* with the same meaning, occurring in many place-names north of the Forth as *Dal-*. Its Pictish form gives us such place-names as Dull PER and Dollar CLA. The second element represents MIr *dabcha* the genitive singular of *dabach*, Scottish Gaelic *dabhach*, 'davoch'. Although Gaelic in form, there is little doubt that its use as a land-measurement or assessment term in Scotland has been influenced by a Pictish cognate.[47] So the meaning is 'haugh of the davoch'. Its later name Kindrochit represents modern Braemar, or at least the settlement on the east bank of the Clunie, where the ruins of Kindrochit Castle are still to be seen. Kindrochit was also a medieval parish, whose church was dedicated to St Andrew (see **Kindrochit-Alian**, below).

The same name, but referring to a different place, appears in two *Moray Reg.*

---

[45] See S. Taylor, 'The Cult of St Fillan', pp. 183–4.
[46] For a fuller account of the life of Muirenn daughter of Cellach, and her possible links with the Britons of the Lennox, see *PNF*, iii, pp. 590–1.
[47] For more discussion and references, see *PNF*, v, Elements Glossary, s.v.

charters, nos. 3[48] and 31, as *Duldauach*, now Culdoich, Croy & Dalcross INV (NH75 43).[49]

Kindrochit-Alian (*Chendrohedalian*): Kindrochit is G *ceann* + *drochaid* 'bridge-end', pointing to the existence of a bridge over the gorge of the River Clunie from at the very latest the early twelfth century. This was the former name of Braemar parish ABD, now united with Crathie; although it lies in Aberdeen diocese, it has links with the church of St Andrews, not only through its dedication to Andrew (attested in an early thirteenth-century charter *St A. Liber*, p. 367) but also through its links with the priory of Monymusk, itself closely connected with the church at St Andrews. Donnchad (Duncan) earl of Mar (1214–34) granted to the canons of the church of St Mary of Monymusk the church of St Andrew of Kindrochit with its teinds. This grant was confirmed to the canons by Gilbert bishop of Aberdeen (1228–39), so seems to have been made 1228×34 (*St A. Liber*, pp. 367–8). This is of course too late for FAB, but it may well be simply formalising an earlier link to Monymusk. This was not the only church belonging to Monymusk which was dedicated to Andrew: its church of Alford ABD was too (*St A. Liber*, p. 372).

Monymusk is also mentioned as a manor of the bishop of St Andrews during the episcopate of William Lamberton (1298–1328) by Bower, who lists it along with nine other such estates, all of which bar Monymusk lie within the bishopric of St Andrews (*Scotichronicon*, bk 6, ch. 43 (iii, p. 401)).

The suffix *alian* is the name of the river at Braemar, now called the Clunie. The river is called *Alien* in *St A. Liber*, pp. 367, 368.

the bare relics: i.e., the relics taken out of their protective box or shrine.

§5. with his holy company following the bishop with songs (and) hymns: This translates *suo sacro conuentu episcopum cum cantibus ymnidicis sequente* (W1, W2); H, S has *comitibus* for *cantibus*, so would translate: 'with his companions singing hymns'. *(h)ymnidicus* (adj. nom. sing. m.) means 'singing hymns'.

on 6 February: This date appears only in W2. It clearly had Andrean associations in Ireland from a relatively early period, since the early ninth-century verse martyrology *Félire Óengusso* (hereafter *FO*)[50] records under 6 February: *Andreas ard a ordan*. The editor of *FO*, Whitley Stokes, translates this 'Andreas, high his rank!', but it is better translated 'high his ordination'. This is certainly how the (probably twelfth-century) Notes to *FO* interpret it, with the gloss 'Ordinatio eius est in Patrias …' (*FO*, p. 68). It certainly does not refer to his crucifixion, which *FO* commemorates under 30 November. The Martyrology

---

[48] Edited as *RRS*, ii, no. 142, where it is dated 1172×74.
[49] See note in *RRS*, ii, p. 215.
[50] *Félire Óengusso Céli Dé: The Martyrology of Oengus the Culdee*, ed. Whitley Stokes, Henry Bradshaw Society 29 (London 1905; reprinted Dublin 1984).

of Tallaght,[51] which is roughly contemporary with *FO*, makes no mention of Andrew at 6 February, but under 9 May celebrates the festival of the relics of the apostles Thomas, John and Andrew, a festival not mentioned in *FO* or its Notes. *BA* under 9 May has the translation of St Andrew, which it describes as the day when Constantius son of Emperor Constantine brought the remains of Andrew to Constantinople.[52]

From a passing reference in Bower (*Scotichronicon*, bk 15, ch. 22 (viii, p. 79, line 34)), 6 February was celebrated at St Andrews in the early fifteenth century as the date of the arrival of the relics. McRoberts refers to this as 'an additional feastday related to the famous relics';[53] while the notes in *Scotichronicon* (viii, p. 186) call it 'presumably a regular local feast'. Boece 1527 has 6 February as the day 'of Merinus a monk of Paisley' (Merini monachi Basiliani), who, arriving along with St Regulus, brought the precious relics of the father St Andrew the apostle protector of the realm (cited Forbes, *Kalendars*, 191). This is Merinach, mentioned above and below. The calendar of David Chambers (Camerarius) (early seventeenth century) has at 6 February: 'Hic Sanctus relictâ Scotiâ Apostolorum limina, quae in summa apud Scotos semper veneratione fuere, inuisenda suscepit' (cited Forbes, *Kalendars*, 234).[54]

stone crosses: For a note on these crosses, see above, **Foundation Accounts**.

called the Firth of Forth: This translates W1 *Ihwdenemur*. For a full discussion of this British and probably Pictish word for the Firth of Forth, see *PNF*, iii, p. 593; see also *PNF*, i, p. 41).

Firth of Tay: This is W1 *Slethemur*, a unique, and probably Pictish-derived, name for the Firth of Tay.

from Largo: Largo, a parish on the Firth of Forth. The form of this name (*Largau*, W1, W2) is late, the original final palatal fricative (written *ch*) surviving in other recorded forms at least until c.1300 (see *PNF*, ii, s.n.).

Ceres <of the Cains *or* of the Dogs > (*Sires*, W1; *Sereis canum*, W2; *Sireis canum*, H, S): The more likely explanation of *canum* is a genitive plural of a Latinised form of Gaelic *càin* 'cain, tribute'. However, *canum* is also the genitive plural of Latin *canis* 'dog', and so may be related to the small land-holding of Casconity # (Ceres), which lies on the old main road running south-west from

---

[51] *The Martyrology of Tallaght*, ed. R. I. Best and H. J. Lawlor (London, 1931).
[52] Macquarrie et al., *Legends of the Scottish Saints*, pp. 118–21; see also the notes ibid., pp. 323–4, which discuss *BA*'s various offices relating to St Andrew and their relationship to FAA and FAB. This relationship is further explored in the notes to the office of St Regulus or Rule (ibid., pp. 411–13).
[53] McRoberts, *St Andrews*, p. 93.
[54] 'Here the saint, having left Scotia, undertook to visit the apostles' shrines, which were held in the utmost veneration by the Scots.'

Ceres towards Struthers (NO390107), and which may contain an oblique form of Old Gaelic *cú* 'dog, hound' (see *PNF*, ii, s.n.).

The addition of *canum* in W2 shows that W2 cannot be a copy of W1.

as far as *Hyhatnachten Machehirb*, which land is now called Naughton: *Hyhatnachten* appears to contain the same elements which make up the place-name Naughton, G *àth Nechtain* 'Nechtan's ford', the name of the place which the text goes on to state is its modern name (*Hadhnachten*). The first syllable of the older name is puzzling. One explanation is that it is a misunderstanding of a Gaelic text which had **hynatnachten* for **i nAtnachten* 'in or at **Athnachten*', with the preposition *i* 'in' causing regular nasalisation expressed as *n* before the initial vowel or consonant of the following noun. Naughton was formerly the name of Forgan parish FIF. It is now the name of an estate in Balmerino parish, to which parish the lands of Naughton were transferred in 1650. The name consistently appears with the G generic *àth* 'ford' until the fourteenth century (see *PNF*, iv, s.n. for full details). 'Nechtan's ford' no doubt refers to the ford over the Motray Water (NO416241) which later became known as Sandford, and which in turn gave its name to the neighbouring estate of Sandford, now St Fort, Forgan parish.

Naughton was clearly an early and important territorial name. The question arises as to who the eponymous Nechtan might be. It is the first territory along the Tay eastwards of Abernethy which did not belong to Abernethy's early ecclesiastical lordship (see *PNF*, iv, p. 146). An early foundation legend links a King Nechtan (the Gaelicised form of Pictish *Naiton*) with the founding of the church at Abernethy, possibly as early as the early seventh century (see Anderson, *Kings and Kingship*, pp. 93, 247), and it may be that this land retained the king's name as a marker of the land by the Tay which remained in royal hands after the establishment and endowment of the church of Abernethy.

That this estate is named after the alleged founder of the church of Abernethy is remarkably corroborated by *Hyhatnachten*'s affix *Machehirb*, which must represent *mac Irb* 'son of Irb': the father of the Nechtan who according to the foundation legend established the first church at Abernethy and whose father is called variously *Erp*, *Erip*, *Wirp*, *Irb* etc. (see Anderson, *Kings and Kingship*, pp. 92–3).

All the land east of this line from Largo to Naughton (from the Forth to the Tay) was given as a parish or *parochia* to the church of St Andrews: that is land for which St Andrews had direct pastoral responsibility. This boundary would seem to bear no relation to any obvious boundaries, either ecclesiastical or secular. However, the southern part (from Ceres to Largo) corresponds very closely to the eastern march of the liberties of the burgh of Cupar as described in a 1428 charter,[55] which is also the western march of the liberties of the episcopal burgh of St Andrews. This latter burgh, founded c.1160, seems to have taken as the boundary of its trading liberty a much older boundary which may in fact go back

---

[55] StAUL, B13/22/3.

to a very early secular, tribal unit,[56] and which we see described in this alleged grant by King Hungus to the newly founded church of St Andrew. However spurious that grant might be, the remarkably archaic forms of some of the place-names – *Ihwdenemur* and *Slethemur* – strongly suggest not only that this border itself is genuinely much older than the time at which the Augustinian's Account was written, but also that it was recorded in written form at a much earlier date.

For full text and translation of the 1428 document describing the burgh liberty boundary of Cupar, see *PNF*, iii, p. 595 and *PNF*, iv, pp. 266–7.

free and quit of hosting, and of castle- and bridge-work, and of the care of all secular exactions: The only comparable passage in a Scottish document regarding the burdens of castle- and bridge-work, so common in an Anglo-Saxon context, can be found in the charter relating to the Culdees of Lochleven, which purports to relate to a grant of land made by King MacBethad (Macbeth) and Queen Gruoch of Kirkness, Portmoak parish KNR, although in that document hunting replaces castle-work (*St A. Liber*, p. 114; for full details, see *PNF*, iii, pp. 595–6).

§6. the prayer Alleluia: compare the account of the founding of Abernethy by King Nechtan in King List A in the Poppleton MS (Anderson, *Kings and Kingship*, p. 247), in which Darlugdach, abbess of Kildare, 'sang an Alleluia over that sacrifice (*hostiam* i.e. Abernethy)'. This similarity was also noted ibid., p. 92.

The following 'witness list' is discussed by Anderson (*Kings and Kingship*, pp. 99–100), who states that most of its names can be found in King List Q and P, 'as though a regnal list had been used by an author of the legend as a quarry' (ibid., p. 99). She goes on to say that the corruptness of the forms makes it difficult to relate them to any particular extant version, but in most cases they seem to be closer to List Q than to P. List Q, already discussed under §2 **Hungus son of Forso** above, was attached to a Scottish list in 1214×49 to form the source of F, I, D, K, as well as of the lists used by Fordun and Wyntoun, and shows a Gaelicisation of names.[57] Despite the corrupt nature of the forms in FAB, this Gaelicisation is also evident e.g. in the frequent use of *F/Ph* for Pictish *U*; also the form *Nechtan* as opposed to *Naiton* etc.[58] Furthermore, Q 'seems to have been connected with St Andrews or at least with the orbit of the St Andrews bishopric' (Anderson, *Kings and Kingship*, p. 102). In one case, however, the compiler of the witness list seems to have used the Annals rather than the king list as his 'quarry', since Ythernbuthib (Iarnbodb) occurs only in the Annals, not in any king list (see above). Anderson (*Kings and Kingship*, p. 100) includes

---

[56] Perhaps that of the Nidwari or *Nith people, whose name has been preserved in Newburn (parish) (*PNF*, ii, s.n., and perhaps in Nydie near St Andrews (*PNF*, iii, s.n.).
[57] This is Anderson's Scottish Regnal List Group X, for more on which see §2 Note on Hungus son of Forso, above.
[58] See K. H. Jackson, 'The Pictish Language', *The Problem of the Picts*, ed. F. T. Wainwright (Edinburgh, 1955; reprinted Perth, 1980), pp. 129–66, at pp. 163, 164–5.

Duptalarch (Dubtalorc) in this category, but this name does occur in the King Lists, see below s.n.

Thalarg: a common Pictish name, sometimes in the diminutive 'Talorgan'; six kings of that name are found in King List F (see Anderson, *Kings and Kingship*, pp. 272–3), none of whom has a father whose name in any way resembles Iarnbodb (see next note).

son of Yther[n]buthib: Iarnbodb, mentioned in AU s.a. 642 (son of Gartnait) (Anderson, *Early Sources*, i, pp. 168–9. See Anderson, *Kings and Kingship*, p. 100 (also p. 14 and note). The name does not occur in any of the Regnal Lists.

Pherathach son of Phinleich: That is Feredach son of Finlaech.

Phihacnanfin: This probably represents the Gaelic personal name Fiachna, with the epithet *finn* (G *fionn*) 'white, fair'. Perhaps the best known bearer of this name was Fiachna Lurgan, son of Baetán son of Eochaid, of the Dál nAraide and king of the Ulaid c.588–626 (Anderson, *Kings and Kingship*, p. 149).

Duptalarch: cf Dubtalorc Annals of Ulster s.a. 781, where the death is recorded of Dubt(h)olargg king of the Picts on this side of the Mounth ('citra monot(h)'). But he is also found in the King Lists (e.g. F, for which see Anderson, *Kings and Kingship*, p. 273).

son of Bargoth: It is perhaps significant that this is also the name of the father of the king (Urad) who is mentioned in the dating clause at the end of FAB, and so the last name in the text.

seven churches: For a short comment on these churches, see M. O. Anderson's 'The Celtic Church in Kinrimund', p. 2. There are two possible reasons why the chapel of St Peter, mentioned in a charter dated 1212 as lying near the sea in the burgh of St Andrews (*St A. Liber*, p. 315), is not included in these seven churches: either it was founded after FAB had been put into its final form; or, since it lay in the burgh, it was not deemed part of the original settlement of *Kinrymont, which was considered to have lain within the old church precincts.

Aneglas: this name is reminiscent of the fictitious saint Anglas in Tarves parish ABD, derived from a misunderstanding of the place-name 'Oenglas', for which see Watson, *CPNS*, pp. 318–19. The church of St Aneglas at St Andrews is mentioned again below, as the burial place of the three virgins from Collossia who accompanied Regulus to Scotland, namely Triduana, Potentia and Emeria. The possibility exists that this is in fact the Gaelic *an eaglais* 'the church', misunderstood at some stage in the transmission or recording of this version of the Foundation Account. He is only mentioned as the name of the patron of one of the seven churches of St Andrews, not as one of the companions of Regulus.

When he is first mentioned (in the list of the seven churches of St Andrews) he is given (by W2 and H only) the title of deacon (*diaconus*). The only other deacons mentioned in the text are the two who accompanied Regulus from Greece, namely Gelasius and Chubacls' (or Thubaculus etc.). The church of Keig, near Monymusk ABD, was dedicated to St Diaconus (*St A. Liber*, p. 372, dated 1245). The parish of Keig, while lying in the diocese of Aberdeen, was in the gift of the bishop of St Andrews, since Bishop William Malveisin of St Andrews (1202–38) granted it to the priory of Monymusk (*St A. Liber*, p. 366). The bishops also held at least some of the lands of Keig, as two acres of their lands of Keig around the cemetery, between the two burns of *Conglassy* and *Puthachin*, stretching to the south as far as the Don (*Don*), are granted by Bishop David of Bernham to Monymusk Priory 1239×54 (*St A. Liber*, p. 366).

St Michael the Archangel: According to the Scottish Chronicle, also known as the Chronicle of the Kings of Alba, 'which may have been written during the tenth century and possibly at St Andrews' (Anderson, 1974, p. 3), Marcán son of Breodalach (Marcan filius Breodalaig) was killed in the church of St Michael during the reign of King Culen (966–71) (Anderson, *Kings and Kingship*, p. 252). It does not state where this church was, but Anderson (1974, 3) suggests it may have been in St Andrews, in the church mentioned here. Note also that St Regulus is said to have landed at St Andrews on St Michael's night, 29 September (see §3 **night of St Michael**, above).

Damian: commemorated with his twin Cosmas on 27 September (*BA*; also Butler, *Lives*, which has no other early Damian). For various other saints of this name in both Irish and Roman martyrologies, see *PNF*, iii, p. 599. None of these has any trace of Damian's FAB epithet *senior*. Cosmas and Damian are from Cilicia, but Syria later became the centre of their cult. For Cilicia, see **Silicius** below.

Gelasius: commemorated 19 August in *Mart. Tallaght*.

Silicius: cf Cilicius, inhabitant of Cilicia (a province in south-east Asia Minor, now Ejalet Itschil). Neither Silicius nor Cilicius is in *Mart. Tallaght* or *FO*.

Tiberis: mentioned also in the opening section of FAB, in a Roman context, where it presumably refers to Tiber Island. In this context it may refer to the same place, or to Tiberias on the Sea of Galilee (see *Scotichronicon*, i, p. 404).

Collossia: mentioned also in the opening section of FAB, where it may refer to the Colosseum in Rome (see §1 **island of Tiber and Colossia**, above). It must refer to a different place here, perhaps Colossae, the oldest of the three major cities (with Laodicea and Hierapolis) in the Lycus Valley in south-west Phrygia (now Turkey), well known in the Christian West from Paul's Epistle to the Colossians (*ad Colossenses* Vulgate; *eis qui sunt Colossis*, ibid., 1: 2.).

Triduana: This is one of the earliest mentions of Triduana. *BA* (for 8 October)[59] draws on either FAB itself or on one of its sources, since it, too, has her born in *Colosia*, and coming to Scotland with Regulus, associating her with the two virgins Potencia and Emeria. Departing from FAB, *BA* then has her, along with Potencia and Emeria, living a holy life in the wilderness beside Rescobie ANG. *BA*'s readings for St Bonifacius (16 March) have Boniface accompanied on his journey to Scotland by a large company, amongst whom were 'two shining (*preclare*) virgins, the abbesses, Crescentia and Triduana' (*Lectio* vii).[60] The reading for Triduana associates her with Rescobie ANG,[61] then with Dunfallandy in Atholl PER, and finally with Restalrig by Leith, which was the centre of her cult in the later Middle Ages. Triduana means 'three-day fast' in Latin (Watson, *CPNS*, p. 334), and may have developed from a misunderstood Latin liturgical text or saint's life.[62]

Potentia: One of the three virgins from Collossia who accompanied Regulus to Scotland, and who were buried in the church of St Aneglas in St Andrews. See also under **Triduana**, above. She is not in *Oxford Dictionary of Saints* (*ODS*), nor is she mentioned in MacKinlay 1914 or Forbes, *Kalendars*. She may have evolved, however, from Potenc/tiana, a from of the name Pudenc/tiana, a spurious early Roman martyr who was widely celebrated in the medieval Church on 19 May (see *ODS* under Pudentiana). For example, *Kelso Lib.* no. 279, a general confirmation charter to Kelso Abbey by Walter bishop of Glasgow, is dated at Ancrum in the year 1232 'die Potenciane Virginis'. 19 May was also the feast of St Dunstan, and there is some variation in liturgical calendars between the two saints, with the fifteenth-century Drummond Missal, the Culross Psalter (c.1470), the fifteenth-century Calendar of Fearn, and *BA* preferring Potenciana, while the fourteenth-century Herdmanstoun Breviary has Dunstan for 19 May; and the fifteenth-century Arbuthnott missal has both.[63] In *BA*'s Litany of Saints she appears as *Sancta Potentiana* amongst the saints invoked every Thursday during Lent. In that Litany she is immediately preceded by *Sancta Eremenciana* (see under **Emeria**, below), followed by *Sancta Oportuna*, *Sancta Sophia* and *Sancta Triduana*. The list continues with Saints *Iuliana*, *Beatrix*, *Kennera* and *Crescentia*, the last saint to be named in the Lenten Thursday litany.[64]

Emeria: the third of the virgins from **Collossia**; a form of Erementiana or Eremenciana, the name of an early Roman martyr who became associated with

---

[59] Macquarrie et al., *Legends of Scottish Saints*, pp. 240–2 (text and translation).
[60] Ibid., p. 87. Also amongst Boniface's companions are seven named bishops, none of whose names is similar to those of St Regulus's companions.
[61] The bishops of St Andrews had direct landed and jurisdictional rights in Rescobie ANG. For example, in 1329 mention is made of a mair (a court official) of the bishop there (*ER*, i, 109). For more details, see Ash, 'The Administration', pp. 206–7.
[62] See Macquarrie et al., *Legends of Scottish Saints*, pp. 420–1 for a discussion of the nature and distribution of her cult in medieval Scotland.
[63] I am grateful to Eila Williamson for her help with the contents of this note.
[64] See Macquarrie et al., *Legends of Scottish Saints*, p. lv.

St Agnes and whose feast-day was celebrated on 23 January, two days after Agnes (*ODS*, 161). She is associated with **Triduana** and **Potentia** in *BA*'s office for Triduana (8 October), for details of which, see under **Triduana**, above. She is also invoked (as *Sancta Eremenciana*) in *BA*'s Litany of Saints, for details of which see under **Potentia**, above.

Dubabrath: cf *DIL gorm-abrach* 'dark-lashed' from *abra* n. m (later often with inorganic fem.), 'eyelash, eyelid', often compounded with colour-words.[65]

King Uurad son of Bargoit: in Gaelic-language sources he is known as Ferat. He was king of the Picts 839–42. He is discussed by Anderson, *Kings and Kingship*, p. 195. The name (in the form *Uoret*) also appears in the inscription on the fine Pictish cross-slab at St Vigeans by Arbroath, although there is no certainty as to his identity.[66]

monimentum/monumentum: It is possible that it refers to a genuine document which records a grant to the church of St Andrew in the mid-ninth century, and which has been inflated and incorporated into the narrative by the compiler of FAB. In AA §3 (for which see below, Appendix 2) the same word (*monumentum*) is used to refer to Alexander I's act of having an Arab steed led to the altar of St Andrew to symbolise and fix the memory of his grants of lands and rights to the church there. This mirrors, in grander fashion, King Hungus's act of carrying a divot to the same altar to symbolise basically the same grant (FAB §6).[67]

Meigle: the existence of a royal residence here in the ninth century is suggested by the relatively small amount of biblical iconography on the rich collection of stones found around the kirk.[68]

---

[65] See Marinell Ash and Dauvit Broun, 'The Adoption of St Andrew as Patron Saint of Scotland', *Medieval Art and Architecture in the Diocese of St Andrews*, ed. J. Higgitt (Tring, 1994), pp. 16–24, at p. 20 and note.

[66] T. O. Clancy's interpretation of the line in which his name occurs as 'in the reign of Uoret' is no longer tenable ('The Drostan Stone: a new reading', *PSAS* 123, pp. 345–53). It hinged on the reading of *ipe Uoret* as *ire Uoret*, but Clancy himself would agree that it reads *ipe* (T. O. Clancy, pers. comm.).

[67] Alan Macquarrie misinterpreted this word as a stone monument, seeing it as interpolated, and as evidence of a royal burial at Meigle ('Early Christian religious houses in Scotland', *Pastoral Care Before the Parish*, ed. J. Blair and R. Sharpe (Leicester, 1992), pp. 110–33, at p. 123).

[68] Anna Ritchie, 'Meigle and Lay Patronage in Tayside in the 9th and 10th Centuries AD', *Tayside and Fife Archaeological Journal* 1 (1995), pp. 1–10, at p. 4.

APPENDIX TWO

The Augustinian's Account

Simon Taylor

THE Augustinian's Account (AA) is a unique document, containing as it does an eye-witness account of the coming of the Augustinians to St Andrews in 1140, their relationship with the existing ecclesiastical establishment, and the delicate and difficult business of creating a viable community of religious.[1] It was originally envisaged as the second part of a longer text, the first part of which is now known as St Andrews Foundation Account B (FAB), the translation of which is given in Appendix 1. As with FAB, AA was first fully edited and translated in 2012, in *PNF*, iii, pp. 600–6 (text) and pp. 606–15 (translation with notes).[2] What follows is a slightly revised and updated version of that translation with notes.

The manuscript details of AA are discussed in the opening section of Appendix 1. Unlike the longer Foundation Account (FAB), AA exists in only one manuscript, an early eighteenth-century copy made of material from the lost St Andrews Register (British Museum, Harleian MS 4628, fos 230v–238r). Together FAB and AA occupy fos 224v–238r (H). The text of AA is printed in Skene's *Chronicles of the Picts: Chronicles of the Scots* (Edinburgh, 1867), no. XXXI (pp. 188–93) (S).

Modern punctuation and capitalisation are used throughout. Square brackets denote words or letters not in H (or not legible in H), but which have been added or changed to improve the sense. Section-numbers are not original, but have been added for editorial purposes.

Note also that some of the text has been used by Walter Bower in *Scotichronicon*, iii, bk 6, ch. 24.

---

[1] There is a remarkable collection of Cistercian foundation accounts from the north of England from such abbeys as Fountains (founded 1132) and Byland (founded about the same time), but, though drawing on eye-witness reports, they are written by second- or third-generation monks in the late twelfth and early thirteenth centuries (Antonia Gransden, *Historical Writing in England c.550 to c.1307* (London, 1974; reprinted London, 1996), pp. 287ff). As far as I am aware, this is the only foundation account written by someone who was personally intimately involved in that foundation.

[2] For a recent important article on the church in St Andrews at this time, which draws heavily on AA, see A. A. M. Duncan, 'The Foundation of St Andrews Cathedral Priory, 1140', *SHR* 84 (1) (2005), pp. 1–37.

APPENDIX TWO

Translation of the Augustinian's Account

§1. These things, as we have said before, we have transcribed just as we found written in old books of the Picts. Most Scots affirm that the blessed Apostle Andrew was here alive in the flesh; taking as proof of their assertion the fact that he got as his lot the land of the Picts, that is Scythia,[3] to preach in; and for this reason he held this place dear above all places; and what he did not fulfil while alive, he might fulfil after he had been released from the flesh. Because we have not found this written down,[4] we are strongly inclined neither to deny or to affirm it. But since mention has been made of the miracles and wonders which God through His holy apostle has done and is doing, and since an occasion has offered itself to write some of these things, we have determined to write, by God's gift, the things that we have either found written down or have heard from trustworthy informers or have even observed for ourselves; and this the brothers have asked us[5] to do. In the meantime, however, we have put this off until we may finish what has been begun.[6]

§2. So when the kingdom of the Picts had been completely destroyed, and had been seized by the Scots, the property and estates of the church [at St Andrews] waxed or waned in turn in proportion to the devotion kings and princes had for the holy apostle. About which things it must not be told individually, but only those things which relate to us are to be dealt with in abridged form.[7] There was a royal city called Rymont, royal hill,[8] which the above-mentioned[9] King

---

[3] Literally '(the) Scythian (land)'. Already by the third century the idea had developed amongst Christians that the Apostles had drawn lots for areas to evangelise, and that Andrew had been allotted Scythia (Ursula Hall, *St Andrew and Scotland* (St Andrews, 1994), p. 4). Bede is the first to record the origin legend that the Picts came from Scythia (*HE*, i, 1). This tradition seems to have arisen through a misunderstanding of Virgil (see Watson, *CPNS*, pp. 60–1 for more details). The superficial similarity between the names *Scythia* and *Scotia* probably helped later to strengthen the perceived connection between Andrew and Scotland. Our author distances himself somewhat from this whole question. However, the statement that Andrew was allotted the mission to the Scythians and the Picts, and that he was in Scotland in person, is found in the shorter Foundation Legend (FAA). That St Andrew was in Scotland in person is also implied in the Declaration of Arbroath of 1320 (Hall, *St Andrew*, p. 125).

[4] This would seem to suggest that the author either did not know FAA, or was intentionally ignoring it.

[5] Reading *nos* for MS *non*.

[6] The account of miracles wrought by St Andrew at St Andrews as envisaged in this statement has not survived. Perhaps it was never written. Thus the 'Augustinian's Account' must be seen as incomplete.

[7] *compendiose*; compare *compendiose tractanda* with the opening words of the introduction to the Lochleven material in the *St Andrews Liber* (*St A. Liber*, p. 113): *Sub compendiosi sermonis tractatu* ('By using an abridged mode of expression').

[8] *Erat autem regia urbs Rymont, regius mons, dicta*: 'royal hill' here is the writer's interpretation of *Rymont*. In FAB §3 Forteviot PER is described as *urbs*.

[9] In FAB, for which see Appendix 1.

Hungus gave to God and the holy apostle. And when the saints whom we have mentioned above, who had arrived with the relics of the blessed apostle, had been removed from their present life, along with their disciples and imitators, religious worship died out there as it was a barbarous and uncouth people. But there continued[10] in the church of St Andrew, such as it was then, by carnal succession thirteen whom they call Culdees,[11] who were living more according to their own judgement and human tradition, than according to the statutes of the holy fathers. Indeed they still live like this; and they have certain things in common which are less in amount and value, while they have as their own the things which are greater in amount and value, as each of them is able to acquire gifts, either from friends who are united to them by some personal tie,[12] such as kindred or connection, or from those whose *anmcharait*, that is soulfriends,[13] they [the Culdees] are, or in whatever other ways.[14] After they are made Culdees, they are not allowed to keep their wives in their houses, nor any other women from whom evil suspicion may arise.

§3. Moreover,[15] there were seven *personae*,[16] who divided among themselves the

[10] W. Reeves translates *Habebantur* as 'There were kept up' (*The Culdees of the British Islands* (1864, reprinted 1994), p. 37). In this work, which predates Skene's edition (S) by three years, Reeves gives the text and translation of that part of AA which deals with the Culdees.

[11] *Keledeos*. An abbot Eoghan (Ewinus) is the last witness in a charter of Bishop Richard anent the parish kirk of the Holy Trinity (St Andrews) 1165×69 (*St A. Liber*, p. 133). He is presumably head of this Culdee community. See also Ballewyne #, a local place-name which probably contains this personal name (*PNF*, iii, p. 441).

[12] translating *necessitudo*, which can mean 'close connection, friendship, intimacy'.

[13] i.e. 'spiritual advisers, confessors'. *Anmcharae* (nominative plural *anmcharait*) is the usual word for 'confessor' in Old Irish ecclesiastical literature, including that connected with the Culdees. See for example the Prose Rule of the Culdees (Reeves, *The Culdees*, pp. 88, 89). The Old Irish Rule of Mochutu, also known as the Rule of Fothad na Canóine (who died 819), states that a confessor (*anmcharae*) should not accept alms from sinners who fail to do his bidding, and should show no favour to those who give donations (*edbarta*) (C. Etchingham, *Church Organisation in Ireland AD 650 to 1000* (Maynooth, 1999), p. 261).

[14] i.e. from whatever other sources.

[15] Translating *nihilominus*; Reeves (*The Culdees*, p. 37) alludes to the use of this word (which occurs twice in the text) as evidence of a similarity of style between this text and the foundation charter of St Andrews priory (*St A. Liber*, p. 123).

[16] M. O. Anderson translates this as 'individuals' ('The Celtic Church in Kinrimund', p. 9). Lawrie (*Early Scottish Charters*, pp. 390–1) suggests that these seven persons represented the seven churches mentioned in FAB, and Dauvit Broun would translate 'incumbents' (pers. comm.). Ash discusses this term, suggesting that it may simply imply persons with individual rights and legal status ('The Administration', p. 217, note 1). She also says that it has been suggested that the term describes the descendants of priests (loc. cit., no reference given). Reeves translates the word as 'beneficiaries' and sees them as including 'the bishop, the eleemosynary establishment [including the hospital] and the representatives of the abbot and other greater officers, now secularised' (*The Culdees*, pp. 37, 39). Mentioning the abbot confuses the issue somewhat, as at this time he would have belonged to the Culdee establishment, which Reeves sees (rightly, I think) as quite

offerings of the altar;[17] of which seven portions the bishop used to enjoy only one, and the hospital another; the remaining five were apportioned to the other five, who performed no duty whatsoever to the altar or the church, except that they provided, according to their custom, hospitality for pilgrims and strangers, when more than six arrived, determining by lot whom or how many each of them was to receive.[18] Indeed the hospital had continual accommodation for a number not exceeding six; but from the time that, by God's gift, it came into the possession of the canons, till the present it has received all who come to it.[19] The canons have also determined that if anyone should arrive who is sick, or who falls ill there, his care is to be undertaken in all necessities according to the resources of the house, until he recovers his health or dies. But if he has any property, let him do what he wants with it and let him dispose[20] of it as he will since in that house nothing will be demanded of him. Also a chaplain has been appointed by the canons to look after both the sick and the dying, and two brothers, who look after the house, receive strangers, and minister to the sick; but who do not eat or drink there, nor do they receive their clothing there.[21] Moreover, the canons have granted for this purpose the tenths of their own labours, and the remains of their food. If there is anything necessary in their cellar for either the healthy or the sick which cannot be had from the hospital, let it be given without objection. The above-mentioned *personae* also had their own revenues and possessions; which, when they died, their wives, whom they openly kept, and their sons and daughters, their relatives or their sons-in-law, divided amongst themselves, even the very offerings of the altar at which they did not serve; it would be shameful to speak of this were it not for the fact that they had been allowed to do it.[22] Nor

---

separate. A. A. M. Duncan retains the Latin word *persona* in his discussion, and sees them as the successors to the original clergy established at the church at its foundation ('The Foundation', p. 4). See also next note.

[17] This must be the altar of the church of St Andrew. According to Bishop Robert's foundation charter for the Augustinian priory at St Andrews dated c.1140 (*St A. Liber*, p. 123), two portions were given to the canons (a grant also mentioned below §7) and one to the hospital. In a charter dated 1152×59 Bishop Robert gives all six portions to the priory, retaining only his own single portion (*St A. Liber*, p. 125a). Bishop Arnold, in a charter dated 1160×61, conveys all seven portions to the canons (*St A. Liber*, p. 129). See Duncan, 'The Foundation', pp. 4–5, 10–11 for detailed discussion.

[18] *præter quam perigrin[o]s et hospites, cum plures quam sex adventarunt, more suo hospitio suscipiebant sortem mittentes quis quos vel quot reciperet*. The wording of part of this is reminiscent of *St A. Liber*, p. 123: 'for the reception of strangers and pilgrims' (*in suscepcionem hospitum et peregrinorum*). See also next note.

[19] The hospital was given to the priory by Bishop Robert 'for the reception of strangers and pilgrims' (see previous note), along with its one portion, and with land, animals and revenues, by Bishop Robert in the priory's foundation charter c.1140, *St A. Liber*, p. 123. By 1162 a new hospital had been built, since it is mentioned in a charter of Bishop Arnold (1160×62 *St A. Liber*, p. 127).

[20] Reading *disponat* for MS *disponit*.

[21] Literally 'nor are they clothed there'. In other words the two brothers do not use the revenues of the hospital for their own food, drink or clothing.

[22] Reading *licuisset* for MS *libuisset*. This would put the blame on the system rather than

could so great an evil be removed until the time of King Alexander of happy memory, a special friend of the holy church of God; who magnified the church of the blessed apostle Andrew with estates and revenues, loaded it with many and valuable gifts,[23] and endowed it with liberties and customs which were of his royal gift, to be held as royal possessions. Also the land which is called The Boar's Raik,[24] which King Hungus, whom we mentioned above, had given to God and the holy apostle Andrew when the relics of the blessed apostle Andrew had been brought,[25] and which had afterwards been taken away,[26] he also established to its pristine condition [or 'anew'];[27] with the specific purpose and on condition that the religious life[28] should be established in that church for the maintenance of divine worship. For there was no-one who served the altar of the blessed apostle, nor was mass celebrated there, except when the king or the bishop came there, which happened rarely. For the Culdees celebrated their office after their own fashion in a corner of the church, which [church] was very small.[29] Of which royal donation there are many witnesses still living, and this donation his brother Earl David also confirmed, whom the king had constituted

   on the individuals within the system. Reeves translates: 'a profanation which one would blush to speak of, if they had not chosen to practise' (*The Culdees*, p. 38).
[23] This contrasts with the picture painted by Eadmer of the lands of the bishopric being wholly drained during Alexander I's reign. Rather than two conflicting accounts here, it is more likely that Alexander's beneficent actions towards the church in St Andrews belong to the very end of his reign, between Eadmer's return to Canterbury in 1121 and the king's death in 1124. See Anderson, 'The Celtic Church in Kinrimund', p. 9.
[24] This is the standard Scots translation of *Cursus Apri*, which is often translated into English as 'Boar's Chase' but is more correctly 'Boar's Run or Range'. There must have been a Gaelic name underlying it, which has been lost. It is not mentioned in FAA or FAB. For full details, see Appendix 3.
[25] Note the difference between this clause and the equivalent in C, which does not mention King Hungus.
[26] Reading *ablata* for MS *oblata* 'offered', suggested by Anderson, 'The Celtic Church in Kinrimund', p. 9, n. 68.
[27] M. O. Anderson considers the *Scotichronicon* reading *ex integro restituit* 'restored ...' preferable to H's *ex integro instituit* ('The Celtic Church in Kinrimund', p. 9, n. 68). Watt et al. translate 'restored in its entirety' (*Scotichronicon*, iii, p. 345). However, *ex integro* can also mean 'anew'. A. A. M. Duncan would translate 'established or gave anew', suggesting that the grant of the lands making up the Boar's Raik was a new grant made by Alexander I, but was taken back by him 'presumably because his purpose [of establishing Augustinian canons at St Andrews] was then unattainable'. However; he later restored the gift, the Arab steed episode representing that restoration ('The Foundation', pp. 5–7).
[28] Watt et al. translate *religio* 'religious community' (*Scotichronicon*, iii, p. 345).
[29] Or 'in a corner of a church which was very small', which is how Reeves translates this (*The Culdees*, p. 38), implying that this took place in a different church from the one which contained the altar of St Andrew. Marjorie Anderson compares this with the situation in Toul (near Nancy, Meurthe-et-Moselle, France) in the mid-tenth century, when the bishop there supported a number of Irish at his own expense and allowed them to assemble daily in his chapel, worshipping 'in the manner of their own land' ('The Celtic Church in Kinrimund', p. 9). This is not a very useful comparison, as the Culdees at St Andrews were part of the indigenous church structure, not dependent on the favour of an individual bishop.

his heir and successor in the kingdom, as he is today. As a royal record[30] of his gift the king ordered to be led to the altar an Arab steed, with its own bridle, saddle, shield and silver lance,[31] and covered with a large, precious cloth; and he ordered the church to be invested with all the aforementioned royal gifts, liberties and customs; he also gave Turkish arms of a different kind, which are still kept[32] in the church of St Andrew, along with its [the steed's] shield and saddle to commemorate[33] royal munificence. They are shown to people coming from all the airts, so that what is so frequently brought to mind will not be forgotten in any way. It was of course in the days of this King Alexander, near the end of his earthly life, that sir Robert the first prior of the church of Scone, which the same king had also given to the canons and had enriched with many gifts and estates, was elected to the bishopric of the Scots.[34] So indeed from ancient times they have been called bishops of St Andrew, and in both ancient and modern writings they are found called 'High Archbishops' or 'High Bishops of the Scots'. Which is why Bishop Fothad, a man of the greatest authority, caused to be written on the cover of a gospel-book[35] these lines:

> Fothad, who is the High Bishop to the Scots,
> made this cover for an ancestral gospel-book.[36]

So now in ordinary and common speech they are called *Escop*[37] *Alban*, that is 'Bishops of Alba'. And they have been called, and are (still) called this on

---

[30] *Ob cujus etiam donationis monumentum regium equum Arabicum*: *regium* 'royal' may qualify *equum* ('horse, steed') rather than 'record'; it would then read 'As a record of his gift the king ordered ... a royal Arab steed etc.'. It is in this latter sense that it was understood by Walter Bower (*Scotichronicon*, bk 6, ch. 24, iii, pp. 344–5). Even within the relatively short text of the Foundation Account the adjective *regius* is found both preceding and following the noun it qualifies.

[31] 'a silver lance which is now the shaft of a cross', *Scotichronicon*, bk 6, ch. 24; see also McRoberts, *St Andrews*, p. 68, who gives the reference for this piece of information as the John Law Chronicle (an abridgement of the *Scotichronicon*) fo. 13, for the text of which see John Durkan, 'St Andrews in the John Law Chronicle', McRoberts, *St Andrews*, pp. 137–50, at p. 145.

[32] Reading *conservantur* for MS *conserventur*.

[33] Literally 'in memory of' (*in memoriam*).

[34] Sometime between 25 December 1123 and 31 January 1124 (*Fasti Ecclesiae Scoticanae Medii Aevi Ad Annum 1638*, ed. D. E. R. Watt and A. L. Murray, Scottish Record Society (revised edn, Edinburgh 2003), p. 378).

[35] For more on such ornate book-covers (Irish *cumdach*), see J. Anderson, *Scotland in Early Christian Times* (i) (Edinburgh, 1881), pp. 145–7; and George and Isabel Henderson, *The Art of the Picts: Sculpture and Metalwork in Early Medieval Scotland* (London, 2004), p. 215. None has survived in Scotland.

[36] This verse is also quoted by *Scotichronicon*, bk 6, ch. 24, and translated by Wyntoun, both of whom attribute it to Fothad I bishop of St Andrews mid tenth century. However, as the notes in *Scotichronicon*, iii, p. 463 point out, it might equally well be Fothad II (died 1093), quoting from Marjorie O. Anderson, 'St Andrews before Alexander I', *The Scottish Tradition*, ed. G. W. S. Barrow (Edinburgh, 1974), p. 4.

[37] According to *Dictionary of the Irish Language* this is a later (Middle Irish) form, the earlier form being *epscop*. It bears no relation to Irish *escop* 'large vessel or measure for wine' (from Latin *scyphus*)!

account of their pre-eminence by all the bishops of the Scots, who are called after the places over which they preside.

§4. But before the consecration of that (bishop-)elect the said King Alexander, having died, left his brother King David, who was the only one of the brothers still alive, and who is still alive, heir not so much to the kingdom as to his devotion towards the church of God and towards the protection of the poor. For he is, and will remain, fully occupied in bringing to a conclusion with God's help what his brother the often-mentioned king had begun. He founded very many churches and monasteries of both monks and canons as well as of nuns; and conferred upon them many benefices. Moreover, he has done many works of mercy towards the servants and hand-maidens of Christ, which it is not within our ability to narrate. He brought it about that the head of the church of St Andrew the aforementioned sir Robert be consecrated by Thurstan archbishop of York of blessed memory,[38] without profession,[39] or any exaction whatsoever, saving only the dignity of both churches, and the authority of the holy and apostolic see.[40] Therefore, once the bishop had been ordained and had returned to his own see, he applied himself zealously to accomplish what he cherished in his heart,[41] namely the work of enlarging the church and dedicating it to divine worship. But both before and after his ordination Satan opposed him in many things; he sustained many injuries and insults, according to what the apostle said: 'all who want to live piously in Christ suffer persecution'.[42] He spent the seventh small portion of the altar, which was due to him, and which he took away from his own uses, on work on the church. But since the outlay[43] was small, the building was also being constructed in a small way,[44] until, with God's help and next with King David's assent, offerings were recovered for the uses of the church, extracted from the hands of lay people, both men and women.[45] Thereafter the more that he might have to hand to give, the faster the work went.

---

[38] Robert was consecrated bishop of St Andrews on or just before 17 July 1127 (*Fasti*, p. 378). Thurstan died in February 1140.
[39] i.e. of obedience. This is confirmed by *Chrs. David*, no. 29.
[40] See also A. O. Anderson, *Scottish Annals from English Chroniclers*, pp. 164–6. Note that '1128' on pp. 164–5 should read '1127', the year of the consecration.
[41] 'what he had much at heart' (Neil Cameron, 'St Rule's Church, St Andrews, and early stone-built churches in Scotland', *PSAS* 124 (1994), pp. 367–78, at pp. 371–2).
[42] 2 Timothy 3:12: 'Et omnes qui pie volunt vivere in Christo Iesu, persecutionem patientur' (Vulgate).
[43] *impensa* 'outlay, cost, charge, expense; payment' is a feminine singular noun (Lewis and Short's Latin Dictionary; *Medieval Latin Word List* (*MLWL*). Here it is neuter plural, unless it is assumed that Latin *erant* 'were' is a copyist's error for *erat* 'was'.
[44] 'limited way' (Cameron, 'St Rule's Church', pp. 371–2). Perhaps in the sense 'on a small scale'.
[45] *donec Domino cooperante et proxime rege David annuente oblationes in manibus laicorum tam virorum quam mulierum exceptæ in usus ecclesiæ sunt receptæ*; I am grateful to Professor A. A. M. Duncan for help in elucidating this clause.

§5. Therefore, having begun the foundations of the church, and now having completed the greater part, and having started some houses, and having finished some (others), along with a cloister, in such a way that now residents[46] could be introduced who might not ask for too many things, and who in the meantime might wait with patience, he [Bishop Robert] asked sir Athelwold[47] bishop of Carlisle by letters and by messengers, as well as by the personal intervention of King David, to grant him from the church[48] of St Oswald,[49] of which the bishop himself was head by right of prior, a person with whom he might share his work, and whom he might set up as prior for the canons whom he was arranging to establish in the church of St Andrew. Since it seemed to him more intimate and sweeter to receive a person from that church where[50] he had devoted himself to God and had taken the habit of the religious life, also whence as the first prior he had been sent to the church of Scone; from which, as we have said above,[51] he had been elected and taken as bishop, than to receive a person from elsewhere. But he did not ask for just any person, but for brother Robert, not indeed well known by renown or way of life but only by name, whom those who knew him considered suitable for this work[52] according to what [the bishop had heard] from his friends and members of his household.[53] Therefore he asked for him and he received him, nor from that church could anything be denied him or should be denied him that he might reasonably request.

§6. The above-mentioned brother Robert by order of the lord bishop dwelt at St Andrew's[54] for some considerable time,[55] and without any canons, but not

---

[46] reading *habitatores* for MS *habitationes*.
[47] *Adeboldum*; his name appears variously – usually known as Adelulf or Aldulf; bishop of Carlisle 1133–57, occurs as prior of Nostell 1122, retained priorship of Nostell till 1153 (D. Knowles, C. N. L. Brooke and Vera C. M. London, *The Heads of Religious Houses, England and Wales 940–1216* (Cambridge, 1972), p. 178).
[48] reading ablative *ecclesia* for accusative *ecclesiam*.
[49] The Augustinian priory of Nostell, Yorkshire, founded c.1114, but full regular life perhaps not introduced until 1122 (D. Knowles and R. N. Hadcock, *Medieval Religious Houses: England and Wales* (Harlow, 1971), under Nostell).
[50] reading *ubi* for MS *ibi*.
[51] See §3, above.
[52] cf. 2 Corinthians 2:16.
[53] *Nec tamen quamlibet postulavit personam, sed fratrem Robertum, non quidem fama notum vel conversione sed tantum nomine, quem juxta quod ab amicis et familiaribus suis qui eum noverunt ad hoc idoneum estimabant.* This clumsy sentence might read better if *estimabant* is taken as a copyist's error for *estimabat*, with Bishop Robert as subject. It could then be translated: 'whom, according to what [Bishop Robert had heard] from his [Bishop Robert's] friends and from members of his household who knew him [Prior Robert], he [Bishop Robert] considered suitable for this work'.
[54] The church rather than the settlement, which was still at this time known as Kilrymont.
[55] Duncan suggests that Prior Robert could have come to St Andrews at any time after late 1138, following a reconciliation between Bishop Athelwold and David I at Michaelmas (29 September) of that year ('The Foundation', p. 9).

without clerks, with the lord bishop providing the necessaries for him and his men. He had no power over the church, nor did he want any, until the Lord would give him what he desired, a community for the service of God. But he did not trust in himself in any way, but putting himself entirely into the hands of God, and submitting himself to His ordinance, he assiduously beseeched God that He would deign to visit and console him, and to grant him[56] to lay a foundation for the religious life such that the building built upon it should be strong and abiding, just as he had decreed in his heart. He did not want in any way to enter into the work of outsiders[57] (which might perhaps have been easy for him), to gather to himself brothers from other and diverse churches, lest different brothers, taking different views, wishing to appear to be a somebody, should not coalesce into unity, and thus the fabric of the building should suffer harm before the foundation was laid. If, however, God should send him men who were prepared[58] to live in the way in which he himself was minded to live,[59] he would receive them warmly.[60]

§7. Meanwhile with Brother Robert staying there by order of the bishop, as has been said, but with the lord bishop carrying out somewhat sluggishly the business which he had begun, the king came to St Andrew's, along with his son Earl Henry the king designate to pray, and with them many of the earls and potentates of the land.[61] The next day, having heard mass and having observed the customary hours and made the customary offering,[62] the king coming into

---

[56] reading *sibi* or *se* for MS *si*.
[57] *Nequaquam in alienos labores intrare volebat*; this is an allusion to John's Gospel (4:38): 'I sent you to harvest what you had not worked for: others laboured, and you have entered into their labour.' (*Ego misi vos metere quod vos non laborastis: alii laboraverunt, et vos in labores eorum introistis*).
[58] reading *paratos* for *paratis*.
[59] *Si quos tamen modo quo ipse disponebat vivere parat[o]s ei Deus* /H fo. 237r/ *adduceret, eos benigne susciperet*. Duncan translates 'in the way in which he was laying down', suggesting that he (*ipse*) might refer to God. He also suggests perhaps emending *quo* to *quod* ('The Foundation', p. 10 and n. 33).
[60] Duncan argues that the 'outsiders' are canons from Scone, supported by the bishop, while the implicit 'insiders' are the *céli Dé* (Culdees) of St Andrews, whom Robert hopes to recruit to his newly established Augustinian priory, along with their property and rents ('The Foundation', pp. 10, 13, 24). I am not entirely convinced, as I find it surprising the writer would describe as outsiders fellow-Augustinians from the sister-house of Scone.
[61] These would appear to have included Duncan (I) earl of Fife, William the chaplain, probably later bishop of Moray, Herbert the chamberlain, Alwin mac Arkill (the king's *rannaire* or food-distributor) and Malothen the marischal. All of these witness Earl Henry's charter (*Chrs. David*, no. 129) issued at Kilrymont (St Andrews) confirming to Prior Robert and his canons the gifts made to them by Bishop Robert and King David. Duncan would argue that this was issued at the time of the visit of King David and Earl Henry to St Andrews described here ('The Foundation', p. 18).
[62] *oblatio* 'offering made during mass' (see Dowden, *Medieval Church in Scotland*, pp. 180ff.). Duncan translates 'mass and the hours having been heard by custom, and offering made'

the cloister, such as it then was, along with those who had come with him, and once everyone had settled down, he explained[63] to them firstly many things of little importance, then finally the main reason why he had come. He therefore arraigned[64] the bishop since he had not hastened on the work and service of God so that he might establish the religious life[65] in the church of the blessed Andrew, even though the bishop had declared himself minded to do so, and as King Alexander had decreed. And when after many disputes the lord bishop argued that he was not permitted either to diminish or disperse the property of the bishop, lest perchance what had been conferred on the servants of God by him should be taken away from them by his successor,[66] the king replies saying that from the land called the Boar's Raik,[67] which was not the bishopric's, which King Alexander his brother had dedicated to God and to St Andrew for that very purpose, namely that in his (St Andrew's) church the religious life[68] might be established, he (the bishop) should endow them sufficiently, and both he and his son would confirm [it][69] and would help towards stocking the land; which they in fact did, and compelled certain others by oath to help.[70] Then the lord bishop, as if of his own free will but in fact under constraint,[71] by the advice and consent of the king and his son and of the other barons who were present, transferred into the hands of brother Robert some portion[72] of the lands

---

from text emended from *audita missa et horis ex more et oblatione factis* to *auditis missa et horis ex more, et oblatione facta* ('The Foundation', 14 and n. 50).

[63] *apperuit* for *aperuit*, from *aperio* 'I open, disclose, explain' etc..

[64] *convenit*; Duncan translates 'summoned', stating that this meaning is given in *MLWL*, although it 'does not seem to mean "summon" in classical Latin' ('The Foundation', p. 14 and n. 51). I have chosen the classical meaning 'arraign, sue, bring an action against' (see Lewis and Short's Latin Dictionary). Both interpretations make sense and the choice of one or the other simply gives a different emphasis to the passage rather than fundamentally altering the meaning.

[65] 'institute religious life' (*ut ... constitueret religionem*), Duncan 2005, 14.

[66] *ne forte a successore suo a servis Dei auferret[ur] quod ipsis ab eo conferretur*. This clause is ambiguous, as it could also be translated 'lest perchance what had been conferred on the servants of God by him should be taken away from his successor by them'. This latter interpretation lies behind Duncan's paraphrase 'the bishop argued that he could not deprive his successors of episcopal endowments' ('The Foundation', p. 15).

[67] For which see §3, above, and Appendix 3.

[68] Latin *religionem*.

[69] I owe the suggestion that *concedere* means 'to confirm' rather than 'to grant' to Professor Duncan (pers. comm.).

[70] Duncan, 'The Foundation', 15: 'the bishop argued that he could not deprive his successors of episcopal endowments, to which the king replied "saying that he [the bishop] should endow them sufficiently from the land called the Boar's Raik, which (*quae*, i.e. the land) was not the see's and which King Alexander had dedicated to God and the saint for that very purpose – that the religious life might be established in his [the saint's] church"'.

[71] This translates the difficult phrase *quasi sponte coactus*; Duncan is probably correct in suggesting that a second *quasi* has been omitted after *sponte*, translating 'partly freely, partly under compulsion' ('The Foundation', p. 16 and n. 58).

[72] Duncan suggests emending *quamlibuit* 'any portion whatsoever' to *quamlibet*, '"a portion at his (the bishop's) choice" i.e. not all his lands', ('The Foundation', p. 16).

of the *personae*[73] which had come into his (the bishop's) hands on their deaths, from which the brothers who came there to serve God ought to have been maintained in the meantime.[74] Nor however did he act more sluggishly regarding the work on the church, but he busied himself[75] in every way so that he might complete the work more swiftly. On that day Robert the priest, of pious memory, the uterine brother of the lord Bishop, renouncing the world with heart, voice and deed in order to serve God in the church of the blessed Andrew following the canonical rule of our holy father Augustine, gave himself into the hands of Brother Robert the prior, with his church of Tyninghame,[76] with the agreement of the lord bishop, so completely that the canons should have either that church or fifty shillings per year.

End of AA

From *Scotichronicon*, bk 6, ch. 24 (MS C) (see §3 above) [translation from Watt et al., iii, p. 345]

In 1122 [1124] Robert prior of Scone was elected to the see on the urging of King Alexander. He [the king] restored in its entirety the land called the Boar's Chase, which had been taken away from the church of St Andrew, on condition that a religious community was established there, as had been previously arranged by King Alexander [in a ceremony involving] the king's Arabian steed with its special harness and saddle, covered with a voluminous and precious caparison, along with a shield and silver lance (which now forms the shaft of a cross) – all these things the king in the presence of the magnates of the land had brought up to the altar, and he had the church invested with, and given sasine of, the said liberties and royal customs. David his brother, then an earl, was present there and confirmed this gift.

---

[73] These are the *personae* mentioned above §3, q.v.
[74] Lawrie, *Early Scottish Charters*, p. 391 describes this portion as 'two-sevenths of the altar oblations'. These are no doubt the two portions which belong to 'the two parsonages [or 'personages', as translated by Anderson, 'The Celtic Church in Kinrimund', p. 9, Latin *p<er>sonagiis*] which the canons hold', as described in the priory's foundation charter given by Bishop Robert c.1140 (*St A. Liber*, p. 123).
[75] *satagere*: can also mean 'to busy oneself ostentatiously'; the verb is used of Martha in the Martha and Mary story. Is this a subtle dig at the bishop? It is also the verb used of King David in §4, above.
[76] No such gift (of either the church or 50s) appears in the early charters or bulls of the priory, and the church continued to belong to the episcopal mensa, so the involvement of the priory is not entirely clear (see I. B. Cowan, *The Parishes of Medieval Scotland* (Edinburgh, 1967) under Tyninghame).

APPENDIX THREE

The Boar's Raik

Simon Taylor

MEANING 'the boar's run or range', the Boar's Raik was the name applied to a large tract of lands in east Fife which from an early date supported church life and organisation at St Andrews. Its early forms include the following: *Cursus Apri* c.1140×50 AA §3, §7 [18th c.; see Appendix 2 for full context]; infra *Cursum Apri* 1212 *St A. Liber*, p. 315 [lands belonging to the archdeanery of St Andrews outwith the burgh of St Andrews within the Boar's Raik acquired by St Andrews Priory]; carrucate terre infra *Cursum Apri* c.1220 Terrier C [in the hands of the bishop of St Andrews; see *PNF*, iii, pp. 617, 619 and n. 39]; infra *Cursum Apri* 1309 Black Book of St Andrews, fo. xxxiv r; the *Baris Raik* c.1420 *Chron. Wyntoun*, iv, 374, 390.

According to the Augustinian's Account (AA), probably written in the 1140s by Robert, the first prior of the Augustinian Priory of St Andrews (see Appendix 2), the Boar's Raik was originally given to the church of St Andrews at its foundation by King Hungus, and restored by Alexander I 'with the indisputable purpose and understanding that a religious society should be established in that church for the maintenance of divine worship' (AA §3). The Augustinian's Account also states that this grant was re-activated by David I when the Augustinian house at St Andrews, founded in 1140, was languishing through lack of funds, cleverly emphasising the fact that the Boar's Raik was not part of the bishop's lands, and could therefore be diverted to the Augustinians without in any way diminishing the bishop's estates (AA §7). M. O. Anderson suggests that the bishop may have held the lands of the Boar's Raik not as bishop but as the representative of the old abbots.[1] From the careful wording of Bishop Robert's 1140 foundation charter for the Augustinian priory (*St A. Liber*, p. 123) it would seem that the list of seventeen lands (eighteen if we assume that Balgove has been omitted in error) and two mills which are grouped together at the start of the bishop's grant represent the lands of the Boar's Raik, although that designation is not used.

In an important article on the foundation of St Andrews Priory, A. A. M. Duncan suggests a more nuanced history of the giving and withholding of the lands of the Boar's Raik by Alexander I (1107–24), stating 'that Alexander

---

[1] Marjorie O. Anderson, 'St Andrews before Alexander I', *The Scottish Tradition*, ed. G. W. S. Barrow (Edinburgh, 1974), p. 5.

and his queen had previously given the Boar's Raik for Augustinian canons, a gift recorded in the lost register of St Andrews: *Oblatio Alexandri primi regis et Sybillae uxoris eius*.[2] But he had taken it back, presumably because his purpose was then unattainable, i.e. before or in the time of Eadmer, bishop-elect, who recounts the exhaustion of the see's lands at Alexander's hands.[3] The "Arab steed" episode was restoration of that gift, made before magnates, recorded in a narrative[4] which also referred to the election of Robert as bishop, possibly to explain that he could not carry out the foundation until consecrated' ('The Foundation of St Andrews Cathedral Priory, 1140', *SHR* 84 (1) (2005), pp. 1–37, at pp. 6–7).

Marjorie Anderson states that the 'places said to be within the Boar's Raik show that it was more or less co-extensive with the modern parishes of St Andrews and St Leonards (SSL), Dunino, Cameron, Ceres, and Kemback (KMB)'.[5] This definition, however, is too generous. Ceres (CER) can almost certainly be excluded from this list, as none of the lands assignable to the Boar's Raik in the twelfth or early thirteenth century appears to be in that parish by its medieval boundaries. Dunino (DNO) was also excluded, since Stravithie, which was in the Boar's Raik, and now occupies the most northerly part of DNO, was in SSL until the 1640s (see DNO Introduction, *Other Parish Boundary Changes*). In fact, Reskes # KMB, and possibly *Douachredin*, if it is indeed Dirdum KMB, are the only properties in the Boar's Raik not in the medieval parish of St Andrews.

It should also be stressed that the lands of the Boar's Raik do not constitute a continuous block of territory. The longer Foundation Account of St Andrews (FAB), discussed below and given in full in Appendix 1, which forms a preamble to the Augustinian's Account, claims that the lands given by King Ungus to the newly established church of St Andrew occupied all of Fife east of a line from Naughton near Balmerino on the Tay to Largo on the Forth. This is of course much greater in extent than the Boar's Raik, which is probably why that name is not used to apply to Ungus's grant. In fact, at least south of the Eden, the boundary of the lands allegedly given by Ungus corresponds closely to the boundary of the trading liberties of St Andrews and Cupar.[6]

The most complete medieval list of lands within the Boar's Raik is to be found in the St Andrews Terrier (C), under the heading 'the carucates of land within the Boar's Raik'.[7]

---

[2] *St A. Liber*, p. xxvi, no. 10. 'The offering made by King Alexander I and by his wife Sybill.'
[3] Eadmer, *Historia Novorum in Anglia*, ed. M. Rule, Rolls Series 81 (London, 1884), p. 284, and for Alexander's excuses, p. 287; *Scottish Annals*, pp. 143, 145–46.
[4] The narrative referred to is AA §3.
[5] Anderson, 'St Andrews before Alexander I', p. 5 and note 43; see also George Martine, *Reliquiae Divi Andreae or the state of the venerable and primitial see of St Andrews. ... With some historicall memoirs of some of the most famous prelates and primates thereof. By a true (though unworthy) sone of the church* (St Andrews, 1797) [written 1683], p. 93.
[6] For a fuller discussion of these boundaries, see Appendix 2, §5 notes Naughton.
[7] *carucatae terrae infra Cursum Apri*.

Thomas Randolf's inquisition of 1309[8] states that there are only three baronial jurisdictions within the Boar's Raik, namely those of the bishop of St Andrews, of the prior of St Andrews Priory, and of the Culdees.[9] This shows that the Boar's Raik still had a well-defined legal, as well as geographical, identity in the fourteenth century.

Watson (*CPNS*, pp. 397–8) considers that the name refers to some famous, possibly mythological, boar-hunt, such as is found in Gaelic and Welsh legend. This was also the opinion of Hector Boece, writing in the early sixteenth century, who says that the name arose because a huge boar, which had been terrorising the area, was finally attacked by an armed crowd, and 'fleeing through this area [i.e. the Boar's Raik] was pierced to death' (as quoted by Martine, *Reliquiae*, p. 94). Boece goes on to state that the boar's immense tusks, 'sixteen fingers long and four wide', were preserved in the cathedral, fixed to the choir stalls by small chains.[10]

The famous earthwork in Ireland called in English 'The Black Pig's Dyke', which dates to c.100 BC, is also known in parts as 'The Black Pig's Race', and according to local folklore it was created by a supernatural black pig when it was being hunted to death.[11] This raises the question as to whether there were earthworks in the St Andrews area which may have given rise to the name by a similar thought-process.[12] There does not appear to be anything relevant in the National Monuments Record of Scotland, but it is worth bearing the possibility of earthworks in mind when reassessing the archaeological remains of the St Andrews area, especially along the marches of The Boar's Raik.

Many place-names in the vicinity of The Black Pig's Dyke which contain Irish

---

[8] *Et inventum est et solemniter in communi publicatum quod infra Cursum Apri non sunt nisi tres baronie viz baronia domini Episcopi Sancti Andree, baronia domini Prioris Sancti Andree et baronia Kalediorum*, which baronies with their inhabitants are held immediately subject of the bishop of St Andrews and his church and of no other, and owe him suit of court, Black Book of St Andrews fo. xxxiv r.

[9] Ash states that this inquisition shows that even when the Boar's Raik became priory lands the bishop retained a superior jurisdiction in it ('The Administration', p. 202).

[10] In the context of Alexander I's endowments of the church of St Andrew, Boece writes: 'Auxit quoque facultates sacrae aedis D. Andreae cum aliis quibusdam praediis, tunc eo agro, cui nomen est *Apricursus* ab apro immensae magnitudinis, qui edita et hominum et pecorum ingenti strage saepe nequicquam a venatoribus magno ipsorum malo petitus, tandem ab armata multitudine inuasus, per hunc agrum profugiens, confossus est. Extant immanis huius beluae indicia ad Diui Andreae: dentes (quos maxillis exertos habent) admirandae magnitudinis, longitudinis enim sunt sexdecim digitorum, et latitudinis quatuor, religati catenulis ad sellas D. Andreae' (*Scotorum Historiae a prima gentis origine* (Paris, 1527). Text and translation available of 2nd edn (Paris, 1575), posted 26 February 2010 by Dana F. Sutton, University of California, www.philological.bham.ac.uk/boece.

[11] A. Walsh, 'Excavating the Black Pig's Dyke', *Emania* 3 (1987), pp. 5–11, at p. 11; and F. Williams, 'The Black Pig and Linear Earthworks', *Emania* 3 (1987), pp. 12–19.

[12] The so-called Danes' Dyke at Fife Ness, Crail, is too far away for it to be relevant here.

muc 'pig' are attributed by *dindsenchus* to this mythical pig and its final chase.[13] It is almost certain that the early, and long obsolete, Gaelic name for the area around St Andrews, Muchros ('pig promontory', for which see p. 356, above), is linked to the name Boar's Raik.

Taken in conjunction with the other important swine-place-name in this area, Denork (Cameron),[14] it is possible that we are dealing ultimately with some kind of tribal emblem going back to Pictish times. Such a mythological boar hunt as posited above would be compatible with this, although it may equally belong to a later stratum of *dindsenchus* after the emblematic significance had been forgotten.

---

[13] Williams, 'The Black Pig', p. 16.
[14] See *PNF*, iii, s.n.

APPENDIX FOUR

University of St Andrews Library, UYSL 110/6/4[1]

Matthew Hammond

A:

OMNIBUS hoc scriptum uisuris uel audituris Johannes de Ramesay dominus de Gledny eternam in domino salutem· Noueritis me dedisse concessisse ac pure et plenarie uendidisse· Ade dicto Purroc' Ciui Ciuitatis Sancti Andree illam dimidiam perticate terre cum pertinenciis in uico fori ciuitatis eiusdem que iacet inter terram dicti Ade ex parte orientali ex parte una et terram quam tenet Willelmus filius Symonis ex parte occidentali ex parte altera pro quadam pecunie summa mihi in mea maxima et urgente necessitate numerata tenendam et habendam predicto Ade heredibus et assignatis suis quibuscunque adeo libere quiete pacifice et honorifice· sicut aliquis ciuis aliquam terram infra ciuitate predicta de domino nostro Episcopo liberius et quietius tenet seu possidet quoquo modo· Reddendo inde annuatim domino meo Episcopo duos denarios sterlingorum ad terminos in ciuitate consuetos· Ego uero et heredes mei concessionem et uendicionem predictas predicto Ade sic factas contra omnes homines et feminas warandizabimus acquietabimus et in perpetuum defendemus Et si contingat quod absit me uel aliquem heredem meorum concessioni et uendicioni predictis aliquo modo contrauenire obligo me et heredes meos ad solucionem centum solidorum sterlingorum fabrice ecclesie Sancti Andree cathedralis amplicandorum In cuius rei testimonium Sigillum meum una cum sigillo communi Ciuitatis supradicte presentibus est appensum Testibus Dominis Stephano Pay'· Gilberto Withman· Roberto Cathill' Ecclesie cathedralis Sancti Andree canonicis· Laurencio Bell'· Johanne Goddisman · Johanne Lambi· supradicte ciuitatis Ciuibus et multis aliis

To all who see or hear this writing, John of Ramsey, lord of Gladney, eternal salvation in the Lord. Know that I have given, granted, and wholly and fully sold to Adam called Purrock, citizen of the city of St Andrews, that half perch of land with pertinents in the market street of the same city, which lies between the

---

[1] I would like to acknowledge gratefully the advice of John Reuben Davies, Simon Taylor, Gilbert Markus and Dauvit Broun on the diplomatic and palaeography of this charter.

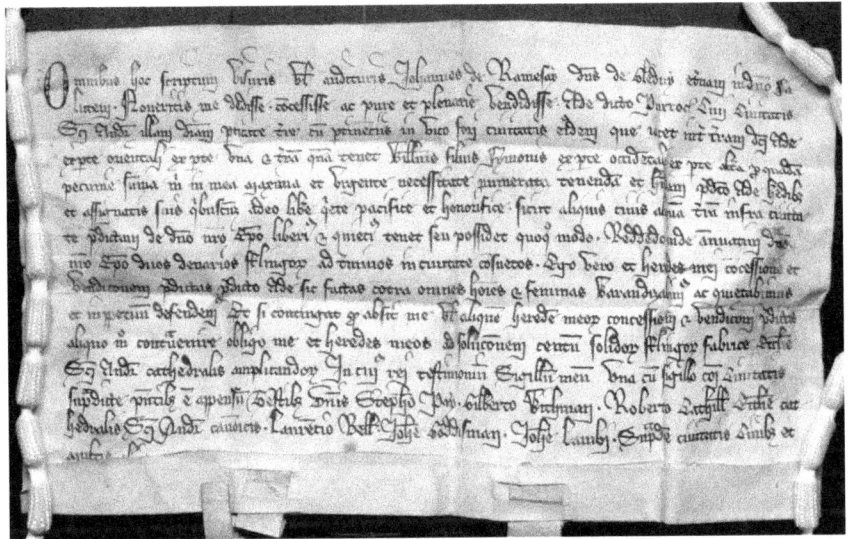

Figure A4.1: Charter of sale of land on Market Street to Adam Purrock, citizen, version 1.

said Adam's land on the east side, on one side, and the land that William son of Simon holds on the west side, on the other side, for a certain sum of money paid to me in my great and urgent need, to be held and had by the aforesaid Adam, his heirs and his assignees whosoever they be, as freely, quietly, peaceably, and honourably as any citizen freely and quietly holds or possesses any land of our lord bishop by whatever means, by rendering thereupon annually to my lord Bishop two sterling pennies at the customary terms in the city. And I and my heirs shall warrant, acquit, and defend forever against all men and women the aforesaid grant and sale as made to the aforesaid Adam. And in case it happens that I or my heirs should contravene the aforesaid grant and sale in any way (far be it), I bind myself and my heirs to the payment of 100 sterling shillings for the extension of the fabric of the cathedral church of St Andrew. As testimony of this matter, my seal together with the common seal of the City aforementioned is appended to these presents. As witnesses, the lords Stephen Pay, Gilbert Whitman, Robert Cattell, canons of the cathedral church of St Andrew, Laurence Bell, John Godsman, John Lambie, citizens of the aforesaid City, and many others.

B:

Omnibus hoc scriptum uisuris uel audituris Johannes de Ramesay d*omi*nus de Gledny eter*n*am in d*omi*no salutem· Noueritis me dedisse · concessisse ac pure et plenarie uendidisse· Ade dicto Purroc' Ciui Ciuitatis S*an*cti Andree illam d*imid*iam p*er*ticate t*er*re c*um* pertinenciis in uico fori ciuitatis eiu*s*dem

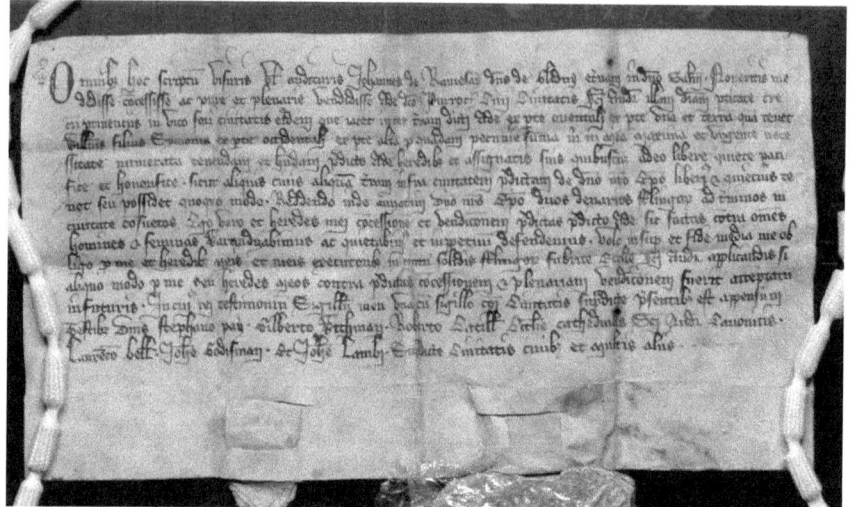

Figure A4.2: Charter of sale of land on Market Street to Adam Purrock, citizen, version 2.

que iacet inter terram dicti Ade ex parte orientali ex parte una et terram quam tenet Willelmus filius Symonis ex parte occidentali ex parte altera pro quadam pecunie summa mihi in mea maxima et urgente necessitate numerata tenendam et habendam predicto Ade heredibus et assignatis suis quibuscunque adeo libere quiete pacifice et honorifice· sicut aliquis ciuis aliquam terram infra ciuitate predicta de domino nostro Episcopo liberius et quietius tenet seu possidet quoquo modo· Reddendo inde annuatim domino meo Episcopo duos denarios sterlingorum ad terminos in ciuitate consuetos· Ego uero et heredes mei concessionem et uendicionem predictas predicto Ade sic factas contra omnes homines et feminas warandizabimus acquietabimus et in perpetuum defendemus · Uolo in super et fide media me obligo pro me et heredibus meis et meis executoribus in centum solidis sterlingorum fabrice ecclesie Sancti Andr' applicandis[2] si aliquo modo per me seu heredes meos contra predictas concessionem et plenariam vendicionem fuerit acceptatum in futuris · In cuius rei testimonium Sigillum meum una cum sigillo communi Ciuitatis supradicte presentibus est appensum Testibus Dominis Stephano Pay'· Gilberto Withman· Roberto Catill' Ecclesie cathedralis Sancti Andree Canonicis· Laurencio bell'· Johanne Godisman · Et Johanne Lambi· supradicte Ciuitatis ciuibus et multis aliis

To all who see or hear this writing, John of Ramsey, lord of Gladney, eternal salvation in the Lord. Know that I have given, granted, and wholly and fully sold to Adam called Purrock, citizen of the city of St Andrews, that half perch of land with pertinents in the market street of the same city, which lies between

---

[2] Sic, *applicandorum* is clearly intended, as written in version A.

the said Adam's land on the east side, on one side, and the land that William son of Simon holds on the west side, on the other side, for a certain sum of money paid to me in my great and urgent need, to be held and had by the aforesaid Adam, his heirs and his assignees whosoever they be, as freely, quietly, peaceably, and honourably as any citizen freely and quietly holds or possesses any land of our lord bishop by whatever means, by rendering thereupon annually to my lord Bishop two sterling pennies at the customary terms in the city. And I and my heirs shall warrant, acquit, and defend forever against all men and women the aforesaid grant and sale as made to the aforesaid Adam. I will, moreover, and bind myself with plighted troth, for myself and my heirs and my executors, for a hundred shillings sterling to be put towards the fabric of the church of St Andrews if in the future there should be an attack by any means by me or my heirs against the aforesaid grant and full sale. As testimony of this matter, my seal together with the common seal of the City aforementioned is appended to these presents. As witnesses, the lords Stephen Pay, Gilbert Whitman, Robert Cattell, canons of the cathedral church of St Andrew, Laurence Bell, John Godsman, John Lambie, citizens of the aforesaid City, and many others.

Notes

Date: Probably early fourteenth century, based on the palaeography and the grantor and witnesses (see below). There is no place-date, but the subject matter and witness list suggests that it surely must have been St Andrews.

On individuals: Many of the individuals whose names appear in these charters do not appear anywhere else in contemporary records. The grantor, John Ramsay, lord of Gladney, witnessed a charter of Joan daughter of Robert of Balcurvie to Alexander de Bethune (Beaton) dating to the early fourteenth century (StAUL, MS 37490, no. 1; *PNF*, ii, pp. 56–7). Of the witnesses, the citizens John Godsman and John Lambie were jurors in an inquest held at St Andrews on 19 March 1303 (*CDS*, ii, no. 1350; H4/38/30).

On surnames: The surname Pay comes either from Middle English *pe* ('peacock') or the rare Old English personal name *Pega* or *Pæga*; Whitman is from the ME personal name *Whytman*; 'Cathill' and 'Catill' appear to be renderings of the surname Cattell, a relationship name based on a diminutive form of the personal name *Catelin*; 'Bell' in this case is likely from the ME *bel* ('fair, fine') from Old French *bel* ('beautiful, fair'); 'Godsman' is from the Continental Germanic personal name *Godesman* ('man of God'), probably as a nickname for a man noted for his piety; 'Lambie' is from the personal name *Lambin*, itself a diminutive of the OFr personal name *Lambert*.

Index

Aberardy, John, of Balcormo 210
Aberdeen 7, 12, 13, 14, 101, 131, 146, 148, 178–9
  Bishops of 254
  Breviary 93
  Cathedral 60, 91
  Parish Church of St Nicholas 63, 91
  University of 269, 270, 273, 298, 337
    King's College 268, 276, 280, 281–3, 293
    Chapel 65
Abernethy, Perthshire 5
Acca, Bishop of Hexham 28
Achéry, Jean d' 335
Ada de Warenne, mother of Kings Malcolm IV and William I (d. 1178) 145
Adam master of the school of Perth 258–9
Adam son of Gilla Muire mac Martain 165
Adamson, John, Provincial of the Dominicans 72
Aebbe founder of monastery at Coldingham 30
Aedán mac Gabráin, sixth-century king 25
Agricultural activity in St Andrews 111
Albert the Great, Dominican scholar 271
  Followers of 272, 276–80
Alcala, University of 292
Alexander VI, Pope (1492–1503) 45
Alexander I, King of Scots (1107–24) 6, 21
Alexander II, King of Scots (1214–49) 161
Allan, master of the schools of Ayr 258–9
Alloa, Clackmannanshire 94
All Saints (Halloween), Feast of (31 October) 113
Alwine Abbot of Holyrood 153
Amalfi, Italy, Shrine of Saint Andrew at 86, 91
Amiens Cathedral 59
Anderson, James Maitland 241
Anderson, M.O. 31, 252
Animal remains 175–7, 192
Animal skins see hides
Annunciation, Feast of the (25th March) 106
Anselm, Archbishop of Canterbury (d. 1109) 6
Anstruther, Fife 109
Antwerp, Brabant 85, 123
Aodh son of Maolmithigh 23
Aquinas, Thomas, Dominican and philosopher 261, 271
  Followers of (Thomists) 272
Arbroath 122
  Abbot of 125

Arbuthnott Church, Kincardineshire 71, 216
Arbuthnott Hours 320
Arbuthnott, Sir Robert 71
Argyll, suburb of St Andrews 117, 126, 128, 185, 216, 229, 233, 235
Aristotle 271, 275
  Nichomahean Ethics 289
Armagh, as ecclesiastical centre 16, 40, 46
Arnold, Bishop of St Andrews (d. 1162) 36, 55, 144, 154
Arthur family 119, 213
  James 231
  John 139
Ash, Marinell 7
Assumption, Feast of the (15 August) 111, 112
Athilmer, John, Provost of St Salvator's 278–80
Augustinian Canons 7, 52–53
Avignon Papacy 243, 263, 332, 339
Avignon University, mace of 303, 318
Avis sister of Bishop Richard of St Andrews 153
Ayr 103, 148

Balcormo, Fife 220
Baldwin son of Búadach 166
Balfour, Elizabeth 233
Balfour, James 63
Balfour, Peter of, 157
Balmerino Abbey, Fife 154
Balmyle, William, rector of Benholm 215
Balrymonth, Fife 161
Baltic, trade with 123
Barrow, G.W.S., 33, 151
Basel, Council of (1431–49) 342
Baxters, Guild of 114, 118, 122, 124, 128, 139
Baxter, J.H. 243
Beaton, David, Cardinal, Archbishop of St Andrews (d. 1546) 73, 74–75, 77, 107, 110, 118, 126, 129, 130, 137, 291, 293–4
Beaton, James, Archbishop of St Andrews (d. 1538) 73, 139, 191, 288, 290, 291–3
Bell, John, notary 170
Bell, Laurence, miller 128
Belle, Richard 123
Benedict XIII, Pope (1394–1423) 239–41, 245–7, 262, 263, 273, 306, 314, 335

INDEX

Bennum, Thomas de, rector of schools of Aberdeen 252, 259, 265
Berdeabh 'rector of the schools of Abernethy' 252
Bernham, David, Bishop of St Andrews (d. 1253) 9
Bernham, Robert burgess of Berwick 153
Berwick-upon-Tweed 7, 40, 141, 142, 146, 150, 155, 157
Biset, James, Prior of St Andrews (d. 1416) 59, 238, 241, 244, 256-7, 263, 266
Blacadder, Robert, Archbishop of Glasgow (d. 1508) 94
Blackfriars (Dominican Friary) in St Andrews 1, 13, 14, 15, 100, 185, 187, 226, 229, 230, 235
   Church 70-92
Bladnoch, River, new bridge 95
Blair, Alexander of 159
   John son of Alexander 148
Blebo, Fife 156-7
   Morton of 157
Boarhills (Byrehills), Fife 32, 130, 207
Boar's Raik (*Cursus Apri*), Ecclesiastical Lordship of, 6, 7, 11, 206, 207 see appendix 3
Boece, Hector, Principal of King's College, Aberdeen 283, 284, 285, 288
Bohemia, Kingdom of 333-4
Bologna University 273
Bonaire, Robert 153, 155
Bonar, John 232-3
Bonar, William, provost of St Andrews, royal comptroller 212, 213, 215, 221
Bonar, William, chamberlain and prior of St Andrews 215
Bondolf, William, of Dunkirk 121
Borthwick Castle, Midlothian 65
Boswell, Isabella 220
Boswell, James, of Balmuto 220
Bower, Walter, Abbot of Inchcolm, chronicler 21, 81, 90, 100, 104, 105, 107, 215, 238, 241, 245, 256-8, 263, 265, 267, 336, 339, 340
   Account of the foundation of the University of St Andrews 238-9, 244, 258
Bower, William, canon of St Andrews Priory and vicar of Holy Trinity, St Andrews 59, 63
'Boy Bishop' festivities 109-110
Brabant, Duchy of 60, 85, 242
Braid, James 233
Brandub mac Echach, sixth-century king of Leinster 25
Brechin, Angus 99, 147
   Bishop of 147
Brega, Ireland 20
Brewing in St Andrews 112, 129
Brewster, Sir David, Principal of St Andrews University 75
Bristol 103
Brook, Alexander 300, 312
Brooks N.P. and G. Whittington 40, 147
Broun, Walter 134

Browin, Robert 133
Brown, George, Bishop of Dunkeld (d. 1515) 93
Brown, John, common clerk of St Andrews 120
Brown, William 153
Bruce, James, Bishop of Dunkeld (d. 1447) 93
Bruges, Flanders 122
Brussels 69
   Church of St-Michel-et St Gudule in 60
Búadach of Balmakin 166-7
Buchanan, George, scholar and reformer (d. 1582) 290
Buda, University of 242
Bunch, Duncan, Vice-chancellor of Glasgow 278
Burgage plots 127, 131, 150
Burgh of St Andrews (urban corporation and settlement) 4, 10, 16, 36, 40-42, 117-140, 141-72, 223-36
   Archaeology of 173-204
   Pre-burghal settlement ('Clochin' (*clachan*)) 11, 25, 143, 147
   Foundation of 10-12, 141-3
   Government of 119-120, 151
   Guilds 151
   Head court of 112, 119, 149, 151
   Liberty (trading zone) 145-6
   Market 13-14, 62, 147, 189
      Cross 189
   Occupations in 124
   Officials of 118, 119-20, 148-9
   Rights of burgesses 144-5
   Tolbooth (council house) 14, 119, 185, 188, 230
Burgundy, France 58
Buridan, Doctrine of 276
Butler of Rumgally, James 210
Butler, Thomas 227
Byre Theatre, excavation at 176, 177-8, 196

Caen, University of 305-6
Cairns, Fife 32
Cairnsmill Burn 20
Calderwood, David, Protestant historian 290
Calixtus II, Pope (1119-1124) 48
Cambridge, University of 247, 273, 280, 304, 322
Cambuskenneth Abbey, Stirlingshire 90, 161
Cameron, Fife 32
Candlemas, Feast of (2nd February) 104-105, 110
Canongate, burgh of (Edinburgh) 142
Cant, Ronald 3, 308, 312
Canterbury, Archbishops of 21, 39, 49
   Shrine of St Thomas at 85, 86, 88, 98
Cardeny, Robert, Bishop of Dunkeld (d. 1437) 92
Carling Sunday (fifth Sunday in Lent) 107
Carlisle 99, 101
Carmichael, John, constable of St Andrews Castle, provost of St Andrews 213-4, 217
Carmichael, William, of Meadowfleet 215
Carngour, Fife 32, 161
Carron, Fife 29
Carstairs, Alexander 133

389

INDEX

Cassilis Castle, Ayrshire 212
Castlecliffe, excavation at 175, 176, 177, 193
Castle Semple, Renfrewshire 65
Cathróe, Life of, 23, 25
Cattle 127
Cellach Bishop of St Andrews 21
Cennrígmonaid (*Cindrighmonaidh*), early name for St Andrews 4–5, 16, 20–22, 25–26, 40, 46
Ceres, Fife 32
Cistercian architecture 58
Chalmers, Peter Macgregor 67
Charles VIII, King of France (1483–1498) 73
Christmas festivities 114
Cinema House, Archaeological excavation 178, 181
Clatto, Fife 156–7
Clement VII, Pope (1378–94) 92
Clothmaking 126–7
Coal 129
Coldingham, Monastery of, Berwickshire 30, 148
Cologne, 49, 120, 122, 162
   University of 17, 242, 246, 258, 261–2, 265, 273, 278, 284, 303
Colombe, Michel, mason 73
Constance, Council of 272, 307, 318, 335, 338–9
Constantine II (Cústantin mac Aeda) King of Scots (900–943) 21, 22, 31
Constantinople 29
Constantius II, Roman Emperor (337–61) 4
Copenhagen, University of 17, 273
Corbet, Christina 152
Cordiners, Guild of 118, 124, 125
Cornel, Matthew de 225
Corpus Christi, Feast of 109, 110
Crafts and craftsmen 112, 113, 118
   Guilds 124, 151
Crag, John, tailor 127
Crail, Fife 4, 26, 124, 143, 145, 146, 148, 154, 216
Crannach, John, Bishop of Brechin 342
Creich, Fife 90
Crossraguel Abbey, Ayrshire 65
Culdees (*céli Dé*), house of, at St Andrews 6, 7–8, 12, 22–23, 31–33, 53, 165
   See also St Mary on the Rock
Culross, Fife 90, 94
   Abbey 338
   St Mungo's Church 66
Cults, Fife 278
Cupar, Fife 90, 119, 123, 146, 211, 212, 216, 220
Cupar, Thomas de, Sub-prior of St Andrews (d. 1410) 87

Dairsie, Fife
   Bishop's manor 207
   Parish Church 79
Dardani, James 333
David I, King of Scots (1124–1153) 7, 12, 25, 31, 39, 41, 141, 147
David II, King of Scots (1329–71) 123, 146

Diego Gelmirez Bishop of Santiago (d. c. 1139) 48–49
Diet 106–107
Dishington, David 137
Dominican Order of Friars 16, 340
   Dominican Church, St Andrews see Blackfriars
Douglas, Archibald, 4th Earl of Douglas (d. 1424) 313–4, 318
Douglas, Archibald, 5th Earl of Douglas (d. 1439) 344
Douglas, Henry, lord of Lochleven 211, 221
Douglas, John, Principal of St Mary's College 294–5
Douglas, Robert, lord of Lochleven 211
Douglas, William, Prior of Galloway (d. 1467) 96
Dover 123
Dublin 99
Dumbarton 148
Dunblane, Bishops of 254
Duncan, A.A.M. 7, 142, 149, 151
Duncan son of Adam 157
Dundee 14, 103, 143, 146, 148, 154, 175, 234
   Church of St Mary's 90
Dunfermline 13, 24, 25, 99, 101, 146
   Abbey 39, 153, 250
Dunino, Fife 26, 278
Dunkeld 5, 97, 254
   Bridge at 93–4
   Cathedral 78, 91, 92
Dunlop, Annie I. 307
Duns Scotus, John 271
   Followers of 272
Durham, as ecclesiastical centre 16–17, 85, 86, 88, 98, 221, 333
   Cathedral 57

Eadmer of Canterbury, Bishop of St Andrews (d. 1121) 21, 33, 252
Easter 107–108
Eden, River 18, 106, 122, 146
Edinburgh 13, 14, 41, 42, 132, 150
   Castle 220
   Church of St Giles 63, 90, 93
   Heriot's Hospital 79
Edward I, King of England (1272–1307) 85, 121, 151, 162
Egilsham, William 123
Elgin 124
Eliseus, Bishop of Galloway (d. 1412 x 1415) 95
Elphinstone, William, senior 276
Elphinstone, William, Bishop of Aberdeen (d. 1514) 70, 187, 276, 280, 281–3, 293, 337
Elward, John, Rector of St Andrews University 339
Epiphany, Feast of the (Uphaliday) 114
Erasmus, Desiderius 283, 285
Erfurt, University of 242,
   Maces 302, 303, 304

390

Ermengarde de Beaumont, Queen of Scots (d. 1234) 145
Essy, Robert, Vicar of Auchterhouse 344
Estergom calvary 329
Eusebius of Caesarea, early Christian historian 9
Evans, Godfrey 325
Exaltation of the Holy Cross, Feast of the (14 September) 112

Fairlie, Reginald 67
Falkland Palace, Fife 73, 74, 191, 219
Fallowside, Widow 129
Fasternis Eve (Shrove Tuesday) 105, 110
Feldew, John, Dean of Canon Law 322
Fiesole, Girolamo da 73
Fife, Earldom of
    Earls of 146, 149, 158, 171
    Sheriff of 205
    Sheriffdom of 123, 206
    Sheriff court 112, 119
Fish, fishing 128–9
    Remains 177
Fish Cross, North Street 129
Flanders 85, 123
Fleming, see also Mainard
    Peter 149, 158–9
    Simon 149, 158–9
    Simon II 149
Flemish settlement in Scotland 12, 164, 167
Flodden, Battle of (1513) 285
Florence, Italy 103
Fogo, John, Abbot of Melrose 339
Folkhyrde, Quentin, author of *Nova Scocie* 342
Fordoun, Angus, Shrine of St Palladius at 90
Fordun, John of, *Chronica Gentis Scottorum* 9, 253
Foreman, Andrew, Archbishop of St Andrews (d. 1521) 210, 219, 287
Forfar, Angus 154
Forsyth, Alexander, of Nydie 210
Fothad, High Bishop to the Scots (d. c. 1093) 22, 53
Fouquet, Jean 301, 303
Fouty, John 91
Fowlis Easter Collegiate Church, Perthshire 65
Fowlis, William, master and archdeacon of St Andrews 245
Franciscan Order of Friars 8, 13, 16, 223
    Friary 14, 15
Fraser, Andrew 213
Fraser, James 27
Fraser, William, Bishop of St Andrews (d. 1296) 213
French, John 74
French, Thomas 74

Gamelin Bishop of St Andrews (d. 1271) 156
Gardiner, Robert, St Andrews master 340, 343
Geddy, John, map of St Andrews, c. 1580 1, 18, 63, 70, 73, 103, 113, 118, 127, 173, 180, 187

German, family of 163–4
Gerson, Jean, theologian 335
Gesta Annalia (text attached to Fordun, *Chronica Gentis Scottorum*), 9–10
Gilla Christ, Abbot of Culdees of St Andrews 32
Gilzam, Henry 134
Giric King of Scots (878–889) 21
Giric, Bishop or Archbishop of St Andrews (d. 1107) 30
Gladney, near Ceres, Fife 155–6, 165, 384–5
Glasgow, 95
    Bishops and Archbishops of 16, 87, 94, 254
    Cathedral 39, 59–60, 91, 92, 259, 320, 322
    University 268, 269, 270, 273, 278–9, 288, 298, 300, 305, 337
    Mace 298, 300, 302, 304, 319
Glastonbury, Abbey of 325
Glendinning, Matthew, Bishop of Glasgow (d. 1408) 94
Goldenes Rössl 329
Golf 127
Gordon of Rothiemay, James 62, 63
Graham, Patrick, Bishop and Archbishop of St Andrews (deposed 1478) 211, 344
Grange, Jean de la, Cardinal 59
Gray, William, notary 124
Great Schism (1378–1419) 241–2, 272, 332–4
Greece 5
Greenlaw, Gilbert, Bishop of Aberdeen (d. 1421) 91
Gregory, cleric of St Andrews (early twelfth century) 30
Greifswald, University of 298
Greigston, Fife 212
Greyfriars (Franciscan Friary) in St Andrews 1, 100, 226, 229
    Archaeological excavation at 180
Guardbridge, Fife, bridge at 88, 121
Gui, Bernard 49

Haakon V, King of Norway (1299–1319) 147
Haddington 150
    Church of St Mary's 63, 90
Hadrian, Roman Emperor (117–38) 43–44
Hadrian I, Pope (772–95) 44
Hague, The, Dominican Church at, Netherlands 72
Hailes Abbey, Gloucestershire, England 84
Haldenstone, James, Prior of St Andrews (d. 1443) 59, 88, 89, 205, 209, 216, 221, 263, 341–4
    Letter book of 209
Halle, University of 298
Hallow Hill, St Andrews 20, 175
Hallum, Robert 338
Hamilton, James, 1st Earl of Arran (d. 1529) 290, 295
Hamilton, James, 2nd Earl of Arran, Duke of Châtellherault (d. 1575) 295

INDEX

Hamilton, John, Archbishop of St Andrews (d. 1571) 18, 73, 75, 79, 105, 113, 294–6
Hamilton, Patrick, Protestant preacher (d. 1528) 290–1, 293, 332
Hammermen, Guild of 114, 118, 124, 125–6, 135, 136, 139
Hammond, Matthew 7, 12 40
Harbour, St Andrews 122, 199
Harding, Robert, English friar 339, 341
Hay, Archibald 291–6
Hay, Gilbert, student 253, 259
Hay, John 291–2, 294
Hay, Nicholas, lord of Errol (d. c. 1306) 157
Hay, Nicholas, of Foodie 210
Hay, William, Lord of Errol (d. 1436) 210
Hay, William, Earl of Errol, Lord Hay (d. 1462) 217
Hay Fleming, David 3
Heidelberg, University of 17, 273, 302, 317
Henry II, King of England (1154–1189) 9
Henry VI, King of England (1422–1461, d. 1471) 85
Henry VIII, King of England (1509–47) 293, 294
Hepburn, Alexander, of Whitsome 220
Hepburn, Elizabeth, wife of William Lundie 220
Hepburn, John, Prior of St Andrews (d. 1526) 53, 75–76, 77, 191, 218–21, 285–7
Hepburn, Patrick, Lord Hailes, Earl of Bothwell (d. 1508) 219
Heresy 16, 331–44
Herewald, Bishop in south-west Wales 25
Hexham Abbey, Northumberland 5, 28
Hides, leather, animal skins and bones 112, 113, 122, 125, 128
Historia Britonum, 30
Holyrood Abbey, Midlothian 90, 250
  Abbot of 142
Holy Trinity, image of 320
Holy Trinity, Parish church of St Andrews, 1, 14, 15, 18, 30, 46, 53, 60–64, 79–80, 99–100, 118, 134, 135, 140, 143, 145, 167, 185, 189–90, 224, 226–7, 232, 233–4
  Altars and chaplainries in the church 232;
    Blessed Virgin Mary, 235; Holy Rood, 137; Holy Trinity, 62; St Andrew, 137; St Eloy, 139; St Fergus, 233; St Katherine, 138; St Ninian, 235; St Mary Magdalene, 134; St Obert, 139
  Cemetery 139, 189
  Parish of 31
Homill, John 265
Horsbruk, Katherine 137
Hospitallers (Order of the Hospital), property in St Andrews 154
  Richard of 154
Hospitals 6, 12
  Pilgrim hospital (St Leonard's) 13, 47, 50, 76, 96, 100, 121, 130, 138, 144, 153, 220, 224, 275

St Nicholas 13, 100, 121–122, 128, 130, 132, 138, 139, 173, 202, 204, 224
Houses in St Andrews 130–2
  Dean's Court 155, 195
  Old Student Union (North Street) 132
  Queen Mary's House 195
  St John's House (67–9 South Street) 131–2, 184
  South Court (South Street) 191
Hugh, Bishop of St Andrews (d. 1188) 144, 147, 154, 160
Hugone, Laurence 135
Hus, Jan, theologian 333, 335, 340
Hussites, Hussitism 331, 334, 338–9, 342–3

Inchbriok 296
Inchcolm Abbey, Fife 92, 93
Inchmurdoch, Fife, Bishops' residence 207
Inglis, Alexander, Archdeacon of St Andrews 284
Innerpeffray Church, Perthshire 65
Inquisition 16
Inverkeithing, Fife 143, 145, 146, 150
Iona 23, 46
Ireland, John 279n

Jackson, John, merchant of St Andrews 124
James I, King of Scots (1406–37) 114, 240, 257, 262, 277, 306, 319, 336
James II, King of Scots (1437–60) 94, 95
James III, King of Scots (1460–88) 96, 217–9, 280
James IV, King of Scots (1488–1513) 71, 93, 94, 96, 121, 138, 220, 284
James V, King of Scots (1513–42) 8, 18, 123, 287, 291
James VII, King of Scots (1685–88) 38
Jedburgh Abbey, Roxburghshire 57, 150
Jerome of Prague, Hussite theologian 333, 338
Jerusalem 46, 102
  Church of the Holy Sepulchre in 39
  Heavenly 303
Joan of Arc (Saint) 66
Joan of England, Queen of Scots (d. 1238) 145
Jocelin, Bishop of Glasgow (d. 1199) 148
Jocelin of Furness 87
John VII, Pope (705–707) 44
John son of Michael the Clerk 156
Johnson, Dr Samuel 1
Josephus, Titus Flavius, historian 9
Justinian, Emperor (527–65) 272

Kalmar, Sweden 17
Kelso Abbey, Roxburghshire 250, 333
Kemback, Fife 32, 278
Kennedy, Alexander, of Urwell, bailie of St Andrews, sheriff of Fife 213–5, 217
Kennedy, Hugh, Provost of St Mary's, archdeacon of St Andrews 67, 214

392

Kennedy, James, Bishop of St Andrews
 (d. 1465) 15, 64, 65, 67–70, 89,
 123, 206, 207, 210, 211, 212, 215, 216,
 218, 221, 228, 261, 276–9, 308, 324–9,
 337
 Foundation of St Salvator's College 277, 324–9
 Tomb of (St Salvator's Chapel) 68
Kennedy, John, Provost of St Mary's, archdeacon of
 St Andrews 214
Kennedy, Thomas, of Kirkoswald 214
Kennedy, Margaret 137
Kerr, Stephen 264
Kilmany, 216, 278
 Hugh of 152
Kilrimund (Cilrígmonaid), Early name for
 St Andrews 5, 6, 21, 29
Kilspindie, Malcolm of 156–8
Kilwhiss, Fife 216
Kinaldy, Fife 32, 216
Kincraig, Fife 220
Kingask, Fife 32
Kinghorn, Fife 143, 145
Kinglassie, Fife 32
Kinnear, Wester, Fife 152
Kinnear family 152
Kinness Burn 20, 173
Kinninmonth, barony, shire of, Fife 146, 156–8,
 205
 Family of 152, 155
 Adam son of Odo 149, 153, 157, 161
 Alexander, Bishop of Aberdeen 60
 Hugh, Steward of the bishop 160
 James of that ilk 205, 210, 211
 Matthew, Bishop of Aberdeen 32
 Odo, Steward of the bishop 32, 156–7
Kirkcaldy, Fife 99, 148
Kirkheugh, Kirkhill St Andrews 20, 33, 143, 177,
 179, 198
Kirkliston, West Lothian, Bishop's manor at 207
Königsberg (Kaliningrad) 123
Knox, John, Protestant reformer 18, 236, 291
Krakow, University of 17, 242, 298, 306
Kravar, Pavel, Hussite 339, 342–3

Ladykirk, Berwickshire 71
Lamberton, Alexander of 152
Lamberton, William, Bishop of S Andrews
 (d. 1326) 207
Lambie, family of 160–1
 Lambin 160–1
 Andrew son of 162
 William son of 158, 161
 Alexander (14th Century) 162
 Duncan 162
Lambie, family of in Angus 162–3
Lambieletham, Fife 32, 161
Lambin Asa 160
Lammas Day (1 August) 112
Lanark 148

Landallis, William, Bishop of St Andrews (d. 1385)
 212
Largo Parish Church 89, 91
Lascelles, Margery 152
Lateran Council, Fourth 108
Lauder, Thomas, Bishop of Dunkeld (d. 1475) 92
Lauder, William, Bishop of Glasgow (d. 1425) 94
Laurence the Archdeacon 33, 252
Learmonth, family of 119, 212
 John 213
 Robert 213
Leipzig, University of 242, 273
Lent 105–107
Leo IV, Pope (847–55) 43
Leoninus, Parisian composer of the twelfth
 century 9
Leprosy 139
Letham, family of 164–7
 Adam son of Adam of 161, 165
Leuchars, Fife 168
Lichton, Henry, Bishop of Aberdeen 335
Liddel, Richard of 148
Life of St Godric of Finchall, Reginald of Durham 25
Lifris of Llanfarcan 24–25
Lincluden Priory, Dumfriesshire 59–60, 69
Lindores Abbey, Fife 152, 158
Lindores, Laurence of, Rector of St Andrews
 University 266, 275, 276, 277, 279, 318,
 331, 336, 340–1, 342–4
Lindsay, Alexander, of Auchtermoonzie 221
Lindsays of the Byres, Struthers, Kirkforthar and
 Letham, family of 211
Lindsay of the Byres, John 64, 211
Lindsay of the Byres, William 62, 211, 226–7
Lindsay, Alexander, Earl of Crawford (d. 1453) 221
Lindsay, David, Earl of Crawford (d. 1446) 221
Lindsay of the Mount, David 95
Linlithgow, West Lothian 14, 150, 234, 291
 Church of St Michael's 63, 90
 Palace 78
Lisbon, University of 273
Litlyngton, Nicholas, 325–6
Livingston, Alexander, of Callendar 265
Livingston, James, Bishop of Dunkeld (d. 1483) 93
Livingston, Thomas, Abbot of Dundrennan 264–5
Lochore, Constantine of 148
Loch Leven
 Priory of St Serf at (Portmoak) 21, 218, 248
 Estates of the Bishops around (Bishopshire) 7,
 206, 210, 211, 215
Logie, Gavin, Principal of St Leonard's College 290
Lollardy 318, 331, 334–9
London 332
 St Paul's Cathedral 55
Louis XI, King of France (1461–83) 67, 328
Louvain (Leuven), University of 69, 216, 228, 242,
 244, 261, 264, 273, 276, 279, 284, 292,
 303, 304, 317
Lundie, John, of that ilk 211, 220

Lundie, Thomas 220
Lundie, William, of that ilk, bailie of St Andrews Priory 220–1
Lundin, Fife 220
Lundin, Thomas 157
Lundy, Andrew, *Primer* 320
Lutheran preaching and texts in St Andrews 290, 332

MacClauchane, Andrew 265
MacDuff's Cross 146
Maces, ceremonial 300–6
Madras College, South Street 187, 188
Maelbrigde, 'Bishop of St Andrews' 90
Mael Dúin, Bishop of St Andrews (d. 1055) 21
Magask, Over, Fife 212
Maiel, Jean, goldsmith 67–8, 322–8
Mainard the Fleming 12, 40, 141–4, 147, 149, 158, 167
Mainard, Robert 160
Mair, John, of Haddington, scholar 271, 288–90, 293, 295
Makerston, Adam, Provost of St Mary's on the Rock 165
Makeson, Alexander 130
Malcolm I (Mael Coluim mac Domnaill) King of Scots (943–54) 22
Malcolm III (Mael Coluim) King of Scots (1058–1093) 25
Malcolm IV (Mael Coluim) King of Scots (1153–65) 142, 143, 151, 154
Malcolm the *abb* 158
Malvoisin, William, Bishop of St Andrews (d. 1238) 9
Mar, Walter, chaplain in Holy Trinity 138
Marburg, University of 290
Margaret, Queen of Scotland and Saint (d. 1093) 6, 24, 47
  Life of 24
Marian cult 14–15, 84, 89, 315, 317
Martin V, Pope (1417–31) 92, 216
Martin son of Uviet 153
Martine, George, Provost of St Andrews (15th Century) 212, 213
Martine, George, secretary of Archbishop Sharpe (d. 1712) 2, 191, 258
Mary, Queen of Scots (1542–67) 293, 295
Mary of Guelders, Queen of Scots (d. 1463) 96
Mary of Guise, Queen of Scots (d. 1560) 121, 230
Matheson, Robert, clerk of works 67
Matthew Archdeacon of St Andrews 153, 154, 156
Mayelle, Jean, goldsmith *see* Maiel, Jean
McRoberts, David 47, 88
Mechelen, Church of St-Rombaut at 60
Meldrum, David, official of St Andrews 138
Melrose Abbey, Roxburghshire 59–60, 250
Merchants 124
Methil, Fife 156
Methven, Alexander 264–5

Michael, M.A. 312
Midcalder Parish Church, West Lothian 7
Mill Port 201
Mills 127–8, 156
Moncur, Margaret 109
Monimail, Fife, Bishop's manor at 207, 294
Monington, Walter, Abbot of Glastonbury (d. 1375) 325
Montpellier, University of 269
Montrose 14, 151
Montrose, Robert de, Prior of St Andrews 59
Montrose, Robert, canon of St Mary's 227, 275, 276
Monymusk, Aberdeenshire 207
Monypenny, Family of 156–7, 210, 218
  Richard 156
  John of Pitmilly 156–7
  Walter, Prior of St Serf's, Lochleven 218
Moray, Bishops of 254
Morrison, Andrew 134
  John 134
  Robert 134
Morrow, John, mason 59–60, 80
Mouren daughter of King Unuist I of the Picts 26, 30
Muckhart, Clackmannanshire 207, 210
Muckhartshire (Bishop's lands) 7, 207, 211
Musselburgh, Shrine at 97
Mylne, Walter, Protestant (d. 1558) 296
Myrton, Thomas, of Cambo 210

Naiton King of the Picts 27
Nantes, University of 17
Napier, Alexander, saddler 126
Nativity of the Blessed Virgin Mary (8 September) 112
Neville, family of 221
Newbattle Abbey, Midlothian 153, 250
Newcastle-upon-Tyne 11
Newton, George, Rector of Bothwell 343–4
New York 318
Nicholas V, Pope (1447–55) 45, 111, 218, 278
Nicholas of Evesham, Bishop of Worcester 21
Nieheim, Dietrich von 335
Ninian's Cave, Galloway 96
Nixon, William, clerk of works 67
Norfolk 122
North Port, site of the 182
Northwold, Norfolk, England 70
Norwich, Cathedral Priory of 100
Nostell Priory, Yorkshire 52, 54
Notaries and scribes 124
Nydie, near St Andrews 148
  Family of 155
  Hugh son of Hugh of, the butler 150, 153, 154, 155, 157, 161

Occam, William of 271
  Followers of 272, 288

INDEX

Ochil Hills 7
Ogilvie, James 336
Ogilvy, Marion 137
Oldcastle, Sir John, Lollard 335
Oliphant, John 77, 79
Onuist son of Vurguist, Pictish King 5, 6
Orabile daughter of Ness son of William, Lady of Leuchars 168
Orléans, University of 241, 261, 269, 280
Örnefot, Jakob Ulfsson, Archbishop of Uppsala 17
Oxford 332
   University of 8, 243, 247, 269, 273, 280
      Balliol College 332
      Arts faculty 304

Paatz, Walter 300
Paisley Abbey, Renfrewshire 59
Paniter, Patrick, secretary of James IV 284, 288
Paris 246, 313, 318
   Maces made in 313, 318, 326, 329
   Notre-Dame Cathedral 8–9
   University 67, 217, 241, 243, 245–7, 262, 269, 271, 273, 274, 280, 290, 292, 301, 307, 322, 327
      Collège de Beauvais 66
      Collège de Cluny 67
      Collège de Montaigu 284–5, 288
      Maces 301, 303
Paschal I, Pope (814–24) 44
Passion, Devotion to 84, 97
Patersoune, Andrew, weaver 126–7
Patrick (Máel Patraic), Master of the Schools of St Andrews 33, 155, 252, 259
Pattenmaker, Arnold, cobbler 125
Paul II, Pope (1464–71) 96, 337
Paul III, Pope (1534–49) 293
Pavia, University of 279
Pay, Stephen, Prior of St Andrews (d. 1386) 59
Peebles 151
   Collegiate Church of 91, 97
Peebles, John de, Bishop of Dunkeld (d. 1390) 92
Peirsoune, Thomas, citizen 138
Pends, gateway 12, 59, 122, 196
Pentecost (Whitsun) 109
Perotinus, Parisian composer of the twelfth century 9
Perth 12, 14, 40–41, 131, 142, 146, 150, 155, 158, 165, 175, 266, 341
   Church council at (1418) 306, 313–4, 339, 341
   Church of St John's 63, 90
Pilgrims, pilgrimage 45–50, 75, 112
Pilgrimage to St Andrews 112, 113, 117, 121–122
   Pre-1100 6, 23–25, 27, 143
   Decline of 14, 84–98
Pilgrim Badges 86
Pilgrim Hospital (St Leonard's) 12, 15, 47, 50, 75
Pinkie, Battle of (1547) 294
Pisa, Council of 241, 245, 247
Pittenweem, Fife 122

Pius II, Pope (1458–64) 50, 96
Pitsporgie, Fife 32
Pitkenny, Fife 32
Pitmilly, near Kingsbarns, Fife 157
Plague 84, 95, 100, 101, 139, 291
Plumber, William, of Tweeddale 125
Pottery, evidence for, in St Andrews 174–5, 189
Prague 334, 335, 341
   Four articles of 323
   University of 17, 342
Premonstratensian Canons 95
Priory Acres (south of St Andrews) 111, 117, 137, 207
Prophecy of Berchan 22, 24
Purrock, family of 171, 384–7

Queensferry, 24, 47
Quincy, family 158
   Robert de, 168
   Saer de, Earl of Winchester and Lord of Leuchars 161, 168

Rabbits 113
Rabelais, François 289
Ramsay family 119, 155
Ramsay, Alexander 133
Ramsay, Duncan 148
Ramsay, Janet 134
Ramsay, John, of Gladney 155, 170–1, 384–7
Ramsay, John, Lord Bothwell 220
Ramsay, William, of Brackmont 210
Ramsay, William, of Clatto 155
Ramsey Abbey, Cambridgeshire, England 309
Rathelpie, near St Andrews 144, 170
Reform, Twelfth-century 3, 6
Reformation, The Protestant 1, 15, 18–19, 84, 96–97, 102, 109, 115, 225, 228, 232, 234, 235–6, 268, 294–7
Registrum Anglie, catalogue of works in religious houses 250–1
Resby, James, Lollard 339–41
Restalrig, Shrine of St Triduana at 89, 97
Richard, Bishop of St Andrews (d. 1178) 144, 147, 149, 153–4, 160, 167, 170
Ripon Minster, Yorkshire 58
Robert I (Bruce), King of Scots (1306–1329) 12, 87, 121, 146, 147
Robert II, King of Scots (1371–1390) 87, 91
Robert III, King of Scots (1390–1406) 123, 333
Robert Bishop of St Andrews, Prior of Scone (d. 1159) 6–8, 10, 11, 22, 25, 31, 36, 39, 52–53, 141, 144, 149, 153, 154, 225, 248, 252
Robert Prior of St Andrews (d. 1160) 22, 144
Robert of Wilton 165
Robin Hood, play 110
Roger, Bishop of St Andrews (d. 1202) 144–5, 147, 151, 160, 169, 170

Roger of Pont-l'Evêque, Archbishop of York
  (d. 1181) 55–58
Rome 13, 28, 37–50, 102, 112, 284
  Castel S. Angelo 45
  Lateran Basilica 38
  St Peter's Church in 37–38, 42
  Vatican Basilica 38
  Vatican Borgo 42–45, 49
Rosemarkie, Ross and Cromarty 99
Ross, Bishops of 91
Rossie, Easter, Fife 212
Rostock, University of 17, 298n, 318
Roxburgh 150, 154, 155
  Walter of 154–5
Rutherford, David 233
Rutherford, Richard, burgess of Aberdeen 91

St Andrew
  Cult of 3, 6, 14, 23–24, 27, 84–98, 315, 317
  Feast day of (30 November) 113
  Relics of 4, 23–24, 27, 28, 29, 84, 88, 103–104, 112, 113, 115
St Andrews
  Archdeaconry of 108
    Court of 119
  Bishops and Archbishops of 4, 6, 87, 119, 123, 156–7, 205–222, 226, 254–6
    Ecclesiastical courts 113, 119, 133
    Efforts to secure archepiscopal status by 16, 22, 27, 28, 39, 49, 118, 144
    Household of 170, 254–6
    Lands and temporal rights 6, 119, 205–222
      Golden Charter (1452) 205–6, 211
    Officials 206, 208
  Burgh (urban settlement) of see Burgh
  Castle 1, 12–13, 18, 110, 114, 121, 124, 126, 192–3, 206, 207–8
    Brewhouse 129
    Chapel of 79
    Siege of (1546–47) 75, 79, 193, 294
  Cathedral 1, 12, 15, 18, 35, 50, 121, 124, 192, 196, 205, 224, 232
    Pre-twelfth-century great church 5, 28, 29, 30, 53, 143
    Construction in the twelfth and thirteenth centuries 36, 37, 54–58, 144
    Shrine of Saint Andrew in 8, 14, 36, 40, 85, 86, 121, 143
    Lady Chapel 15, 89
    Late medieval reconstruction 15, 58–61
  Culdees (céli Dé) ofsee Culdees
  Diocese of 7
  Foundation Accounts 4, 6, 22, 23–24, 26–30, 35
    Account A (FAA) 26–27, 28–30, 33, 35, appendix 2
    Account B (FAB) 26, 28–30, 89, 103, 104, 112, appendix 1
  Nunnery, possible pre–1100 26
  Parish churchsee Holy Trinity

Population estimates for Medieval St Andrews 13, 101, 118
Prior of 16, 149, 218
  Court of 119
  Officials in temporalities 209
Priory of (Augustinians) 4, 7–8, 18, 31, 33, 75, 85, 86, 100, 104, 110, 142, 218, 232–4, 239–41, 247, 250–8, 333
  Fishing rights 106
  Guest Hall 200
  Lands and jurisdiction 206, 211
  Library 8–9
  Mill 128, 201
  Music manuscript owned by 8–9
  Precinct Wall of 12, 118, 192, 201, 219
  Prior's House 205
  Priory acres (property south of St Andrews) 117, 137, 207
  Relations with the burgh 152–3
  School 15, 248–60
  Teinds Yett and barn 201
  Royal hall (pre-1100) 39, 158
  Sarcophagus 5, 20, 26, 197
  University of see University of St Andrews
St Aneglas, Church of 30
St Anne, Chapel of, in St Andrews 46
St Aubert, Feast of (8 December) 114
St Augustine of Canterbury 39
St Augustine of Hippo
  Rule of 7
St Bartholemew, Feast of (24 August) 112
St Brigid,
  Church of at St Andrews (early twelfth century) 30
  Cult of at Abernethy 5
  Feast day of (1 February) 115
Saint Cadoc, Life of 24
St Columba, cult of at Dunkeld 5, 92–3, 97
SS Cosmos and Damien, Feast of (27 September) 112
St Cuthbert, shrine of at Durham 17
St Damian the elder, Church dedicated to (early twelfth century) 30, 46, 115
St Duthac, 90
  Shrine of, at Tain 89, 97
St Eloi, 135
  Feast day of (1 December) 114
St Emeria 30
St Kentigern 39, 87, 95, 97, 320
St James 48
St John, ante Portum Latinum, Feast of (6 May) 109, 308
St John the Baptist 315
  Nativity of (Midsummer) 111
St John the Evangelist 317
St Lawrence's Day (10 August) 112
St Leonard's School 12
St Leonard 317
  Parish of 146

St Margaret of Antioch 315, 318
St Martin, Feast of, Martinmas (11 November) 113
St Mary of the Rock, former Culdee house, college of secular canons (see also Kirkheugh) 7–8, 9, 13, 20, 30–31, 33, 46, 100, 101, 104, 165, 192, 199, 206, 227
St Mary Magdalene, Chapel of 197
St Merinus or Merinachus, Feast Day (28 September) 104, 112
St Michael the Archangel 315, 318
    Church dedicated to (early twelfth century) 30
    Cult of 89
    Feast day of, Michaelmas (29 September) 112, 113, 115
St Nicholas, Feast of (6 December) 110
    Farm, archaeological dig at 175, 176, 179, 202
    Hospital see Hospital
St Ninian 315, 317
    Cult of 97
St Palladius, Cult of 90
St Peter 13, 320
    Chapel of, in St Andrews 46, 194
SS Peter and St Paul, Feast of (29 June) 111
St Potentia 30
St Regulus 4, 5, 27, 28, 103, 115, 197
    Church of (St Rule's) 1, 12, 18, 29, 36, 40, 46, 51–54, 61, 79–80, 143, 192–3
St Salvator, College and chapel of see University
St Stefano, Church of, Bologna 39
St Triduana 30, 89–90, 97
    Feast day of (8 October) 113
Salisbury, James 63
Samuel, Master 29–30
Santiago de Compostella 13, 36, 48–49, 123
Sarum Rite 104
Sawar, Agnes 133
    Walter 133
    William 133
Scheves, John, Official of St Andrews (d. c. 1456) 90n, 215–6
Scheves, John, of Demperston, son of Henry 217
Scheves, Henry, of Kilquhous (Kilwhiss) 134, 216–8
    Steward of the archbishop 208
Scheves, Robert 216
Scheves, William, Archbishop of St Andrews (d. 1497) 89, 134, 209, 216–9, 280
Scissors, John 227
Scissors, Patrick 227
Scone 5, 21, 52, 154, 157
Scotscraig-on-Tay, Fife 207
Scotichronicon, fifteenth-century chronicle 7–8, 21, 207, 237–8
Scot, Bege 109
Scot, Margaret 135
Scott, Alexander 236
Scott, Sir Walter 2

Scrope, Richard, Archbishop of York (d. 1405) 85
Senzie (Synod) Fair at St Andrews 109, 119
Sentences of Peter Lombard 289, 341
Seton Collegiate Church, East Lothian 66
Sharpe, James, Archbishop of St Andrews (d. 1679) 3
Shaw, John, monk of Dunfermline 341
Ships and shipping at St Andrews 122–123
Shore Port 197
Sibbald, Sir Robert 37–38
Sibylla, Queen of Scots 33
Siena. Italy 284
Sixtus IV, Pope (1471–84) 219
Skene W.F. 28
Slezer, James (d. 1717) 37–38, 79, 204
Smith, Robert, metalworker 126
Southwell Minster, Nottinghamshire 57
Spalding, William 341
Spott, East Lothian 207
Spottiswood, John, Archbishop of St Andrews (d. 1639) 314
Steel, John chaplain of the Holy Rood 137
Step Rock, archaeological excavation at 180
Sterecrag, Godric 144
Stewart, Alan, Justiciar and Steward of the Bishop 208
Stewart, Alexander, Earl of Mar (d. 1435) 314
Stewart, Alexander, Archbishop of St Andrews (d. 1513) 75–76, 96, 209, 284, 285, 287
Stewart, David, Duke of Rothesay (d. 1402) 333
Stewart, James, Archbishop of St Andrews, Duke of Ross (d. 1504) 209, 219, 220
Stewart, James, Commendator of St Andrews Priory, Earl of Moray (d. 1570) 8, 18, 291
Stewart, James, son of Robert II 253, 259
Stewart, Margaret, daughter of Robert III, Duchess of Touraine (d. 1450) 69
Stewart, Margaret, daughter of James I, Dauphiness of France (d. 1445) 67
Stewart, Robert, Duke of Albany, Governor of Scotland (d. 1420) 266, 314, 334
Stewart, Thomas, Archdeacon of St Andrews 241
Stirling 13, 14, 148, 150
    Castle 73
    Church of the Holy Rude 63, 90
Stockholm 17
Stow in Wedale, Berwickshire 207
Stralsund 123
Strang, Walter of Pitcorthie 210
Strathkinness, Fife 32
Strathtyrum, Fife 32
Streets of Medieval St Andrews
    Abbey Street (Priors Wynd) 103, 130, 131, 132, 153, 179, 231
    Argyll Street see Argyll
    Baxter's Wynd 128
    Butler Wynd 216

Streets of Medieval St Andrews (*cont.*)
  Castle Street (Castle Gait) 13, 103, 153, 155,
    160, 176, 179, 181, 193–4
  Church Square 190
  City Road (Cowgait) 117, 186
  College Street 184
  Doubledykes (Dunsy Dubs) 117
  Fisher's Vennel 129
  Johnston's Court, excavation at 181
  Market Street (Market Gait) 13, 14, 42, 47,
    100, 127, 128, 129, 131, 133, 137, 144,
    155, 173, 181, 182–4, 187–9, 216, 224,
    229–31
    Archaeological excavations in 177
  Muttoes Lane 125
  North Street (North Gait) 13, 40, 42, 47–48,
    103, 125, 127, 129, 132, 143, 144, 153,
    173, 179, 181, 216, 224, 225, 229–31
  Scores, The (Sea Street) 129
  South Castle Street (Ratton Row) 232
  South Street (South Gait) 13, 14, 40, 42, 47,
    100, 103, 111, 117, 127, 128, 131, 132,
    137, 138, 149, 173, 190–2, 216, 224, 226,
    229–31, 233, 295
    Archaeological excavations in 177
    Known as 'the street of the burgesses' 143,
      147
  Swallowgait 125, 193
Struthers, Fife 209
  Castle of 211
Swanson, R.W. 248
Symmachus, Pope (498–514) 44
Symson, George, merchant 124
Symson, Marion 138

Tannadice, Angus 293, 295
Tanning, tannery 125, 181
Tarvit, Fife 296
Tay, River 106
Templars (Order of the Temple), property in
    St Andrews 154
  Brother Robert of 154
Theatrical entertainment in St Andrews 109,
    110
Thomas, Prior of Galloway 95
Thomson, William, cook for the priory 129
Toledo, Archdiocese of 48
Torphicen Priory, West Lothian 65
Tours Cathedral, France 73
Trade from St Andrews 123–24
Trail, James, of Blebo and Magask 208, 210, 214
Trail, Thomas 213, 214
Trail, Walter, Bishop of St Andrews (d. 1401) 87,
    124, 208, 213, 214, 221, 257
Traquair Bible 338
Trinity College, Edinburgh 223
  Chapel 72
Trinity Sunday 109
Tweed, River 106

Tuathálan abbot of Kinrymont 20
Tübingen, University of 317
Tullibardine Chapel, Perthshire 72
Turgot, Bishop of St Andrews and Prior of Durham
    (d. 1115) 6, 24, 54
Turin, University of 242
Turnbull, William, Bishop of Glasgow
    (d. 1454) 94–95, 276, 277–80, 337
Tynemouth Priory, Northumberland 57
Tyningham, East Lothian 207, 293, 295

Ulster, Annals of 20
University of St Andrews 1, 2, 13, 15, 16, 100, 226,
    237–67, 268–97
  Chancellor 261, 273–4, 276
  Discipline 120, 286
  Faculties
    Arts 110, 113, 275, 279, 298, 305, 306
    Dean of 275, 276
    Canon Law 298, 313
    Theology 305
  Foundation of 15, 100, 105, 118, 237–48, 268,
    335
    Charter (1413) 130, 240, 260
  Hebdomadar 286
  Library Collections 8, 15, 251, 269
  Maces of the University 15, 275, 298–330
    Arts 298, 307, 308, 309–22
    Canon Law 298, 308, 309–22
    St Salvator's College 303, 308
  'Nations' of 274
  Number of masters and students 101, 133
  Parliament Hall 73, 75
  Pedagogy 278, 279, 284–5, 288, 291, 295
  Rector of 119, 120, 215, 274, 306
  St John's College 73, 226, 227, 232, 275, 276
  St Leonard's College 15, 50, 96, 100, 120, 122,
    130, 138, 219, 226, 231, 232, 263, 268,
    285, 290, 295, 296
    Chapel 73, 75–78, 79, 200
    Statutes of 129–30, 286–7
  St Mary's College 100, 191, 226–7, 268, 275,
    292, 293–6
    Chapel 73–75, 81
  St Salvator's College 3, 15, 18, 100, 120, 182,
    226, 230–1, 232, 268, 278, 285, 287,
    289–90, 307, 320
    Chapel 1, 15, 64–70, 75, 78, 79, 81, 182, 291,
      294, 332
    Hebdomadar's Building 183
  Seal matrix of 274
Universities, Medieval 17, 270–73
  Curricula of 270, 283
Unuist I son of Urguist (Hungus or Angus son of
    Fergus) King of the Picts 24, 26, 27, 29,
    103, 104
Uppsala, as ecclesiastical centre 17
  University of 273
Urban II, Pope (1088–99) 48

Urban VI, Pope (1378–89) 333
Urwell, Kinross 215

Vairement, Richard, historian and canon of
    St Mary's of the Rocks '*Veremundus*' 9,
    253
Valladolid, Church of San Gregorio at 328
Vienna, University of 304, 317
Vincennes, Château of, France 59
Vorbrodt, Günter and Ingeburg 300

Wagner, Marcus, German book-collector 8, 50
Walsingham Abbey, Norfolk, England 84
Walsingham, Thomas, English chronicler 95
Walter Prior of St Andrews 163
Wardlaw, Henry, Bishop of St Andrews
    (d. 1440) 15, 60, 88, 121, 130, 207, 213,
    215, 221, 257, 262–3, 265–6, 314–5,
    318, 342
  Foundation of the University 238–44, 246–8,
    273, 275–7
Wardlaw, Henry, of Spott 213
Wardlaw, Thomas, marshal of the bishop 213
Wardlaw, William, of Wilton and Torry 213–4
Watson, James 91
Watt, D.E.R. 247
Wedale, Estates of the Bishop in 7
Wemyss, family of 211
Wemyss, John, of Kilmany, constable of St Andrews
    Castle 210, 213–4, 217
Westminster Abbey 303
West Port, the 117, 186, 229
Wharram-le-Street, Yorkshire 54
White, John, Prior of St Andrews (d.
    1258) 149–50, 153

Whitekirk, East Lothian 50, 66, 97
Whithorn, Galloway 40, 95–6
  Cathedral and shrine of St Ninian 92, 95, 259
  Lady Chapel 95
Wilfrid, Bishop of Hexham 28
William I (the Lion), King of Scots (1165–1214)
    42, 147, 148, 154
William, Bishop of Moray 39
Williamson, Marion 137
Winchester Cathedral 55, 100
Windsor, Berkshire, England 85
Wine, imported 113
Winton, Henry of 152
Wishart, George, Protestant preacher
    (d. 1546) 294
Wishart, William, Bishop of St Andrews
    (d. 1279) 59
Wittenburg, University of 50
Wolfenbüttel, Herzog-August-Bibliothek, former St
    Andrews manuscripts in 8–9, 50, 345–6
Wood, Sir Andrew, of Largo 91
Woodman, Isla 260, 264
Wool and wool fells 112, 113, 122–3, 126
Woolf, Alex 5, 11, 27–28
Wyclif, John, theologian 332, 335–6, 338
Wyntoun, Andrew, Prior of St Serf's, Loch
    Leven 21, 87
Wyrfauk, Roger 152

Yalulok, William 265
Yellowlee, Duncan, vicar of Cramond 137
York 85
  Archbishops of 21, 39, 55, 57, 91
  Minster 55, 144
Ypres, Flanders 85, 102

St Andrew Studies in Scottish History
Previously published

I
Elite Women and Polite Society in Eighteenth-Century Scotland
Katharine Glover

II
Regency in Sixteenth-Century Scotland
Amy Blakeway

III
Scotland, England and France after the Loss of Normandy, 1204–1296
'Auld Amitie'
M.A. Pollock

IV
Children and Youth in Premodern Scotland
edited by Janay Nugent and Elizabeth Ewan

V
Medieval St Andrews: Church, Cult, City
edited by Michael Brown and Katie Stevenson

VI
The Life and Works of Robert Baillie (1602–1662):
Politics, Religion and Record-Keeping in the British Civil Wars
Alexander D. Campbell

VII
The Parish and the Chapel in Medieval Britain and Norway
Sarah E. Thomas

VIII
A Protestant Lord in James VI's Scotland:
George Keith, Fifth Earl Marischal (1554–1623)
Miles Kerr-Peterson

www.ingramcontent.com/pod-product-compliance
Lightning Source LLC
Chambersburg PA
CBHW052132010526
44113CB00035B/1963